W9-BSV-179

A HISTORY

OF

MODERN PHILOSOPHY

A SKETCH OF THE HISTORY OF PHILOSOPHY

FROM THE CLOSE OF THE RENAISSANCE
TO OUR OWN DAY

BY

Dr. HARALD HÖFFDING
PROFESSOR AT THE UNIVERSITY OF COPENHAGEN

TRANSLATED FROM THE GERMAN EDITION

By B. E. MEYER

AUTHORISED TRANSLATION

VOLUME II

DOVER PUBLICATIONS, INC.

This new Dover edition, first published in 1955, is an
unabridged republication of the English translation
originally published by Macmillan and Company. It
is reprinted by special arrangement with St. Martin's Press

Manufactured in the United States of America

CONTENTS

BOOK VI

THE GERMAN ENLIGHTENMENT PHILOSOPHY AND LESSING

BOOK VII

IMMANUEL KANT AND THE CRITICAL PHILOSOPHY

BOOK VIII

THE PHILOSOPHY OF ROMANTICISM

BOOK IX

POSITIVISM

BOOK X

PHILOSOPHY IN GERMANY 1850-1880

BOOK VI

THE GERMAN ENLIGHTENMENT PHILOSOPHY AND LESSING

CHAPTER I

CHARACTERISTICS OF THOUGHT IN THE AGE OF THE ENLIGHTENMENT

By the middle of the eighteenth century the Wolffian philosophy had established its ascendency in Germany. This philosophy supplanted the neo-Aristotelian and scholastic philosophy founded by Melancthon, and acquired a great influence on intellectual development throughout Germany, as, owing to its clearness and sobriety, it readily lent itself to popularisation In this respect, indeed, a notable work had already been done before Wolff's time, by CHRISTIAN THOMASIUS, a jurist, who had been zealous in attempts to break down the lines of demarcation, hitherto so sharply drawn, between learned and lay. Amongst other things he lectured and published philosophical works in the German language, a proceeding which excited no small indignation ; indeed the College of Censors actually sent back one of his books with the message that it was impossible to pronounce judgment on a work treating of philosophical matters in the German tongue. Altogether, Thomasius did much both by word of mouth and by his writings to promote a free and enlightened treatment of social and moral questions in wide circles. Together with the critical and practical trend of his nature went a mystical and religious tendency ; and it is this, and not merely the fact that in the orthodox they had a common enemy, which explains his having been able for some time to work with the pietists. The pietistic tendency, which had developed in Germany since the end of the seventeenth century, was also at work in the service of intellectual liberation, for it turned back from external faith in the letter, determined by authority, to inner experiences within the life of the soul. Traditional dogmatism and external religious ordinances were ranked below the subjective inwardness of the individual. Thus the emancipation of the individual was now being carried on within the religious sphere itself, whereas the State-Churchism of the seventeenth century had compelled the merging of all individuality in common religious forms. Now that personal inwardness was recognised, individual differences also began to attract attention; they excited more interest than differences of creed, and were soon acknowledged to possess value and interest, even where they did not fit in to the scheme of penitential struggle which pietism had laid down from the beginning. The clergy as a body were taught that the rights of the laity must be recognised, since great things may be consummated in the souls of laymen as well as— perhaps even better than—in the orthodox souls of priests, versed in all the rubrics of dogmatism. Pietism broke with the belief in the letter and with dogmatic scholasticism, and in so doing led back to the natural, the practical, and the useful. Thus it was akin to the other tendencies of the age, not excepting the Wolffian philosophy, although for some time it appeared as the bitter enemy of the latter. Wolff and his disciples aimed at popularising philosophy; pietism aimed at popularising religion. The two tendencies united harmoniously enough, however, when once Wolff had victoriously asserted his position. Many of the most prominent men in the Wolffian school were pietists, and worked at one and the same time for the enlightenment of the reason and for the deepening of religion.

But the dawn of the so-called age of Enlightenment saw other influences at work besides those which sprang out of the philosophical and religious movements in Germany itself. English empirical philosophy became the subject of eager study. Christian Thomasius, as may be seen from his conception of the philosophy of rights, was already powerfully influenced by Locke; while among the younger Wolffians Locke's influence struggled with that of Wolff, so that their philosophy finally became a combination of the systematised rationalism taken over from Wolff and the empirical philosophy established by Locke. The secret of this is to be found in the fact that Wolff's rationalism could really lead to nothing but the construction of a system of rubrics; and that the greater the perfection to which this system of rubrics was carried, the greater necessarily became the hunger and thirst after an empirical content wherewith to fill out the same. We find here a contrast-effect similar to that which, within the religious sphere, had set pietism in opposition to orthodoxy. Within the philosophical sphere this contrast-effect showed itself in the great interest taken in empirical psychology. Instead of speculative metaphysics, psychology, grounded in experience, came more and more to be regarded as the fundamental science. The science of the life of the soul, as observation teaches it to us, was the basis from which æsthetic, moral, and religious problems were attacked. This signalised an important turning-point in the history of psychology;—a point at which this science gained in independence and approximated more nearly to natural science. Wolff had still attributed more value to speculative ("rational") than to empirical psychology. This was now changed. Men sought to make experience the basis, and only after this was done did they try, taking this as a starting-point, to see to what further results they could attain. The most prominent representative of the Enlightenment Philosophy, JOHANN NICOLAS TETENS, expresses this very clearly in the preface to his *Philosophischen Versuchen über die menschliche Natur und ihre Entwickelung* (Leipzig, 1777, i. p. xiii.); "metaphysical analysis," he says, "must conclude, not begin, our inquiry as to the nature of the soul. It must be preceded by psychological analysis. Once this has been accomplished, metaphysical analysis is reduced to that of a few fundamental faculties and modes of operation, and is then, in this abridged form, to be carried as far as may be. Where this empirical knowledge of the fundamental faculties is still lacking, however, it is useless to attempt to explain them by means of so obscure an organisation as the soul. Moreover, however far we proceed in metaphysical psychology, the authenticity of its propositions must always be tested by empirical knowledge." Kant had already expressed himself in the same sense (*Nachricht von der Einrichtung seiner Vorlesungen in dem Winterhalbjahre von* 1765-66). He maintained the necessity of proceeding by way of analysis instead of construction in philosophy, and emphasised the importance of securing an empirical foundation. Hence he began his philosophical course with empirical psychology, in which nothing was taught concerning the nature of the soul since, at this stage, it is not even possible to determine whether there be such a thing !

This predominant interest in empirical psychology had no small share in investing the German Enlightenment Philosophy with its peculiar character. Within this general character appear many *nuances*, which we cannot here examine more closely. In the first volume of his *Geschichte der neueren deutschen Psychologie* (Berlin, 1894) MAX DESSOIR has given a detailed and interesting exposition of the manner in which psychological problems were handled by the inquirers of that time. We can only pause to discuss those which are of interest for the history of philosophy in general.[1]

The psychology of the Enlightenment is chiefly based on two notions borrowed from Leibniz ; *i.e.* that the difference between darkness and clearness is the fundamental difference in psychical life, and that ideas are the constituent elements of this life. The deeper-lying motives and presages contained in his psychology were unregarded. This was the hey-day of rationalism. "Enlightenment of the understanding" was the catchword, and everything within the life of the soul which was not immediately transparent was conceived as a chaos of dark ideas. The practical consequence of this intellectualist psychology was an unbounded confidence in the future ; only light, then all would be well ! A turning-point was reached, however, when it was perceived that the life of the soul consists of other elements besides the intellectual. English psychology (since Shaftesbury and Hutcheson) had already perceived this. Rousseau, whose influence on the German Enlightenment was extraordinarily great, had enthusiastically championed the cause of feeling and protested against the over-estimate of the intelligence. Last of all pietism, too, had tended in this direction. Thus the period of rationalism gave place to a period of sentimentality. The word "sentimental" dates from the eighteenth century ; it seems to have been coined by Sterne, the English novelist, and was, on Lessing's suggestion, rendered in German by *empfindsam*. The peculiarity of feeling as an independent side of the life of consciousness was first established in the course of efforts to develop an æsthetic theory. During their investigation of æsthetic feeling the attention of J. G. SULZER (see his treatises in the papers of the Berlin Academy 1751-52) and of MOSES MENDELSSOHN

(*Briefe über die Empfindungen*, 1755) was drawn to the fact that they had here before them an immediate and positive side of psychical life to which justice was not done as long as it was regarded as a chaos of dark ideas, prevented by our imperfection from attaining to perfect clearness. According to the psychology of Leibniz and Wolff, feeling was nothing but a dark and undeveloped idea.   A. C. BAUMGARTEN, a Wolffian (*Aesthetica*, 1750), was the first to use the word "æsthetics" in its modern sense, *i.e.* theory of the beautiful.   True to his system, however, he conceived æsthetics as the doctrine which establishes rules for the darkest ideas, *i.e.* for the inferior part of the faculty of knowledge, while logic lays down rules for clear ideas, *i.e.* for the superior part of the faculty of knowledge.   The great interest in the inner events of psychical life, as well as in poetry and art, which was kindled in the middle of the century in Germany could not fail to create a craving for a new psychology which should assign to the life of feeling a positive and independent position within the life of consciousness. Mendelssohn very rightly points out (*Brief IV. Philos Schriften. Verbesserte Auflage*, Berlin, 1771, i. p. 22) that, if Baumgarten's view were correct, the feeling for the beautiful must vanish with the progress of enlightenment, so that beings of a higher order than ourselves, in possession of greater mental clearness, would have reason to lament " that miserable prerogative which seals up the sources of the pleasure with which lower beings are so richly endowed."   It is a fact of no little significance that the typical representative of the philosophy of the Enlightenment should have been the man to make this reflection.   He demands precisely in the interest of enlightenment that the distinction between darkness and clearness should not be the only one recognised within the life of the soul, and asserts that the obscure has no necessary connection with pleasure or pain. In his opinion the feeling of pleasure is conditioned by the harmony of the manifold which makes itself felt in the soul (or, where it is a question of sensuous pleasure, in the nervous system).   We are here dealing with a positive psychical force, however, not a merely obstructed state.   In a later work (*Morgenstunden*, 1786) Mendelssohn designates feeling the " capacity of approval," thereby aptly indicating the important function exercised by this side of the life of consciousness.[2] Kant, in his work " On the Clearness of the Principles of

Natural Theology and Morals" (*Über die Deutlichkeit der Grundsätze der natürlichen Theologie und Moral* (1762)), lays great weight on the distinction between knowledge and feeling which Sulzer and Mendelssohn had pointed out. "Only in our day," he says, "have men begun to perceive that the faculty of thinking the true is knowledge, while that of intuiting the good is feeling, and that these two must not be confused with one another." Kant is here influenced not only by his German predecessors, but also by Hutcheson and Hume, and, most of all, by Rousseau. The decisive step, however, was taken by TETENS, who established a distinction between "sensation" and "feeling," two words which had hitherto been regarded as synonymous. "Feelings," he says (*Phil. Versuch.* i. p. 168) "as opposed to sensations, are those affections in which we are merely aware of a change in us or an impression on us without reference to the object producing this change or impression. Sensation points to an object which we feel by means of the sensuous impression within us and at the same time find outside us." Yet the two elements are so intimately connected that Tetens proposes — not altogether to the promotion of clearness — to use the word "feeling" as a common designation for both. He protests against Leibniz' and Wolff's practice of terming all the elements of psychical life "ideas," and proposes (in accordance with Hume's usage) that the connotation of this word should be restricted to representations. He calls the faculty of forming and combining ideas "understanding," hence his psychology leads him to the tripartite division of feeling, understanding, and will, the last two faculties denoting the active, the first the passive, side of the life of consciousness. Kant adopted Tetens' tripartite division, but was more consistent in carrying out the distinction between sensation and feeling. There was no clear understanding at that time as to the significance which ought properly to be ascribed to these psychological distinctions. The tendency was to construct a special psychical faculty for every fresh psychological distinction as it was discovered, while it was quite the exception for psychological inquiry to attempt tasks higher than those of mere description and classification. The important foundation for an explanatory psychology already supplied by the association theory of Spinoza and the English inquirers was almost entirely neglected. Nevertheless, the psychology of the Enlightenment was of no little importance ;

it sharpened men's power of introspection, and, in virtue of its recognition of feeling as an independent side of the life of consciousness, it indicates an important and permanent advance.

The strong movement in favour of feeling which took place in the middle of the century became, in France, the hotbed of revolutionary ideas ; while in Germany, where the call to engage in public affairs was far less urgent, it found vent partly in the study of psychology, and partly in artistic production in the direction newly initiated by Herder and Goethe. Intellectual and æsthetic interests occupied the foremost place. Hence it is characteristic of the period that its empirical psychology should attach but little weight to the will, to the active side of the life of consciousness. Enlightenment and feeling were the centres of interest. But the more profound spirits felt that something was wanting here. FRIEDRICH HEINRICH JACOBI,—whose sentimentality bears the stamp of his age, although, as will be shown later in another connection, as a philosopher he was strongly opposed to the men of the Enlightenment—speaks in his first work of the unhappiness of a life of feeling debarred from its natural outlet in action. After intimating that civil life in the modern state offers no external scope for great feelings and characters, we find the following passage in his Dialogue, *Der Kunstgarten* (1779): "Ah ! how little is the soul helped by feeling and thoughts which do not proceed from actions and are not directed towards action. . . . Our finest knowledge only serves us in the end for idle reflexion, our most exalted feeling for solitary, unfruitful delight." It was the age of "beautiful souls" and of "noble hearts"; men believed themselves capable of the highest things ; all was ferment and commotion : *Sturm und Drang* were in the air, the immediate needs of the heart were set over against all reason, all rules and all morality ; the original force and simplicity of Nature, which men believed themselves to have re-discovered, were opposed to the forms of culture and of society ; chaos was regarded as the highest ; the faculty of producing new forms, fashioned from within, was declared to exist within the sphere of poetry alone. This period of fermentation in which ideas were determined by feeling, while the philosophy of the Enlightenment had declared the converse to be the only possible relation, was at the same time an empirical confirmation of the teaching of the new psychology as to the independence of feeling. It was the eruption of Romanticism in the very centre of the rationalist camp. Henceforward and under many successive forms, Romanticism prevailed in literature, effecting the re-birth of human fancy after the long labour of intellect. And, as we shall see, this whole artistic renaissance reacted on the development of philosophy and was destined, at an important point in its history, to determine its direction.

It was the psychological interest of the Enlightenment philosophy which revealed to it its limitations. In the classical age of the Enlightenment and by its typical representatives, however, these limitations were not perceived. Enlightened thinkers thought themselves furnished with reason sufficient at any rate to have led them to take the right road, even though they might not have travelled over its whole length. These thinkers, moreover, although they admitted the possibility that posterity might progress in enlightenment, did not see that this admission logically committed them to the conclusion that in themselves there must still be considerable darkness. That which pertains to happiness—so they argued—that, at any rate, our reason can discern. But to this belongs, before all things, faith in God and immortality ; without this faith we can never feel secure. They adopted and discussed in an enormous number of treatises the "natural religion" which had been taught by English and French authors. But the polemical attitude taken up by natural towards positive religion only appeared in Germany in a few isolated cases. Protestant theology was more elastic than Catholic. Offices in the Church and the theological faculties were, for the most part, occupied by Wolffians who recognised nothing as revelation which did not satisfy the demands of reason, but who, at the same time, were fully convinced that they could show the contents of the Scriptures to be entirely in accordance with reason. Hence this *ecclesiastical Rationalism* laid great weight on a natural explanation of the miraculous content of the Bible, for it assumed as a matter of course that Christianity must be in harmony with the religion of reason—was indeed nothing else than its historical announcement. This rational knowledge—collected from experience and from the thought of preceding ages—was thus spread abroad by the agency of the ecclesiastical organs throughout the whole nation. In this way

an important work of education was carried on. The Church became an organ of the Enlightenment—of its good as well as of its
weak sides. But the reconciliation between natural and positive
religion was not so easily effected in all cases. During this period
of individualism, where so many different motives wrestled
together in consciousness, it followed as a matter of course that
the religious development of individuals took very different directions. A remarkable example of a course of development starting
from orthodoxy, passing through pietism into rationalism, and
from this to a standpoint which reminds us of that afterwards
adopted by Lessing, Herder, and Schleiermacher is described
by JOHANN CHRISTIAN EDELMANN (1698-1767) in his
Autobiography (published by Klose, Berlin, 1849). The worship
of the letter and the externality of orthodoxy drove him to
pietism, where he moved among prophets and sectaries. The
pietists' hatred of reason and love of power, however, excited
his indignation, and in his despair he discovered that the open-
ing words of the Gospel of St. John ought to be rendered, not
by "*the word* was God" but by "*Reason*" (Logos) was God!
If reason is God, religion can contain nothing contrary to
reason ; thus the transition from pietism to rationalism was
effected. On becoming acquainted with Spinoza's assertion
that God is the *immanent* and *inner*, but not the *external,* cause
of things, however, he abandoned rationalism as ordinarily
understood. He now believed God to be the eternal essence
of all things—to be one with the innermost essence of all.
Everything in the world which is true and good is God. The
world is everlasting. Christ was a man who brought men nearer
to God by saving them from false ideas of Him, and by teaching
them that mutual love is the supreme good. The priests condemned him because they thought he wished to overthrow
their rule, although (as afterwards Edelmann and all his true
successors) he always referred the rabble to the priests. The
last day dawns in every man who awakes out of the slumber of
illusion. Edelmann believed it possible, by the help of historical
criticism and symbolical exegesis, to discover true religion
from the biblical writings. The matter appeared otherwise to
HERMANN SAMUEL REIMARUS (1694-1768), one of the
most eager champions of the truths of natural religion
against materialists and other godless men. He was firmly
persuaded that the purposiveness of Nature (especially the

instincts of animals, to which he devoted a special work)
witnesses to the origin of the world in a wise and gracious
God, and that, in a future life, better and more lasting pro-
visions will be made for human blessedness than is possible in
this life. But he was no less firmly convinced that the contents
of the biblical books are contrary to the reasonableness and
morality inculcated by natural religion. This latter conviction,
however, he thought he ought not to divulge. He had tried,
in private, to reduce to clearness his thoughts on biblical
history and on the books of the Bible, and had busied himself in writing a book which he called an " Apology for the
reasonable Worshippers of God," in which he subjected biblical
literature, both from the historical, as well as from the scientific
point of view, to a sharp and disintegrating criticism. He
assigns a touching reason for not publishing this work ; he
fears lest orthodox fanatics should rob him of the love of
wife and children, or stir up a persecution against him which
might extend to them. " Those gentlemen, the clergy, may
be sure," he says, " that an honest man does no little violence
to his conscience when his whole life long he is obliged to
dissemble." No one dreamt of what lay concealed in the desk
of the Hamburg professor who had adduced such beautiful
proofs of God and of immortality. LESSING, to whom, after
the death of the author, the manuscript was shown by the
family, published fragments of it, describing it as a manuscript
found in the library at Wolfenbüttel. DAVID STRAUSS (*H. S.
Reimarus und seine Schutzschrift.* Leipzig, 1862) afterwards
published the whole work in an abridged form. It is
Reimarus' general standpoint which is of interest for us here—
natural religion suffices ; a revelation is therefore superfluous.
Moreover, such a thing is both physically and morally impossible. God cannot interrupt His own work by miracles ;
nor can He favour some men above others by revelations
which are not granted to all, and with which it is not even
possible for all to become acquainted. But of all doctrines
that of eternal punishment is most contrary, Reimarus thinks,
to true ideas of God, and it was this point which first caused
him to stumble. Besides this there were many other details in
the biblical narratives which seemed to him doubtful ; hence
his criticism led him to a purely negative result. The only
explanation of the origin of the narratives which he was able

to suggest was that they were due to the fraud of the Jewish priests and of the apostles.   Thus we see that the conscientious investigation of the German philosopher led him to the same results as had been reached by Voltaire, by means of a more airy process of reasoning.   Revelation or fraud : this is a dilemma, of which, from this time onwards, orthodox and free-thinkers are alike heartily convinced, and on which religious disputes still often turn, as though no new points of view had come to light in the philosophy of religion since Reimarus and Voltaire.

MOSES MENDELSSOHN (1729-86), who has given the most popular exposition of natural religion, conceived the relation between natural and positive religion to be less inimical.   A Jew from Dessau, he had accompanied his teacher of the Talmud to Berlin.   Like Spinoza before him, he was impelled by an inner craving for a higher intellectual culture than that offered by Hebrew literature to make himself acquainted with the literature of Western Europe.   This was all the more difficult as, at that time, Jews were forbidden to learn the German language.   The energy of the youth over-came all obstacles, however ; he learnt German and Latin, and Locke and Wolff became his favourite authors.   He took upon himself the task of expressing in literary German (so far had his zeal brought him !) the subject matter which Wolff and his disciples had set forth in many-volumed works of verbose and pedantic exposition.   He gained an admired position in German literature, enjoyed the friendship of Lessing and Kant, and may be regarded as a type of the popular philosophy of the time.   He never separated himself from his brethren in the faith, but, on the contrary, did his utmost to procure them a better social position.   In his interesting work, *Jerusalem oder Über religiöse Macht und Judenthum* (1783), he attempts to show that right principles as to the ordering of the relations between Church and State must inevitably bring with them greater freedom in civil matters for those of his faith.   According to his view, Judaism contains no dogmas incompatible with the contents of rational religion ; the Jewish religion consists in a law valid for the Jewish people.   And since he also believed that he could adduce proofs of the immortality of the soul (*Phädon*, 1767) and of the existence of a personal God (*Morgenstunden*, 1786) he could see nothing but the most beautiful harmony between religion and philosophy. The grounds of his proof of immortality are—firstly, that since the faculty of thought cannot be explained as a product of material combination, the soul must be immaterial, and, as such, must also be imperishable ; secondly, that a being destined for perfection cannot be arrested in its course. He proves the existence of God partly by the ontological proof taken from Descartes, partly from the purposiveness of Nature. The last-named work (*Morgenstunden*) did not appear until after Kant's " Critique of Pure Reason " had ushered in an entirely new period in the history of Philosophy. Mendelssohn announces in his preface that he is indeed well aware that the school to which he belongs, and which, " in the first half of the century, wished perhaps for too exclusive dominion," is now no longer in such good repute. New tendencies have arisen, but his weak health has prevented him from making nearer acquaintance with them ; nevertheless he allows himself to hope that the " great iconoclast Kant," whose penetration commands his admiration, will " build up in the same spirit that he has pulled down." On a previous occasion, *i.e.* in the postscript to his *Phädon*, he had spoken with still greater candour on behalf of philosophy. " After so many centuries of barbarism," it runs, " in which human reason has had to bow before superstition and tyranny, philosophy at length sees better days. By means of a happy observation of Nature, all branches of human knowledge have made considerable progress. In this way we have even learnt to know our own souls better. Through a more exact obser- vation of their actions and passions several data have been established, and from these it is possible, by means of an approved method, to draw correct conclusions. The leading truths of natural religion have, thanks to this improvement in philosophy, attained to a certainty which eclipses all the knowledge of the ancients." After this utterance we under- stand why he calls Kant, whose " Critique of all Speculative Theology " had already appeared, the " great iconoclast ! "

We have yet to mention a few interesting attempts made by the philosophy of the Enlightenment in the interest of the *problem of knowledge.* The Wolffian philosophy was, it is true, in the ascendency, and its adherents attempted to stamp its fundamental thoughts on the general consciousness. Notwith- standing this, however, greater weight was laid on experience and on the necessity of collecting material, and various attempts were made to combine Locke's philosophy with that of Wolff. Thus there grew up an *eclecticism* not exactly coincident with the popular philosophy, which latter adhered more closely to Wolff. The chief seat of this eclecticism was the University of Göttingen, where FEDER and MEINERS were its leading representatives, while the popular philosophy had its headquarters in Berlin, where Mendelssohn's writings were published, and where NICOLAI'S *Allgemeine deutsche Bibliothek* and BIESTER'S *Berliner Monatschrift* disseminated enlightened ideas among the educated public. Only a few thinkers recognised the problem which had to be faced, if both Locke and Wolff were to be acknowledged as right, and the necessity admitted both of collecting material and of elaborating this material according to the laws proper to its nature. These thinkers are the immediate predecessors of Kant within the sphere of epistemology. C. A. CRUSIUS, a Leipzig professor (*Entwurf der notwendigen Vernunftwahrheiten*, Leipzig, 1745), showed that the distinction between sense and thought does not coincide with that between dark and clear ideas ; sensuous perception may be perfectly clear and plain ! This is analogous to Sulzer's and Mendelssohn's contention that the feeling of pleasure and pain is something other and more than dark ideas. It naturally caused Crusius to attribute greater significance to experience than Wolff could consistently do. Crusius drew a sharp distinction between the grounds which lead us to perceive a thing, and the causes which, as a matter of fact, produce things (grounds of knowledge and real grounds) ; a distinction which Wolff, in common with the whole dogmatic philosophy, had wiped out. At the same time he refuted Wolff's attempt to deduce the principle of causality from the law of contradiction. And since the problem of the relation between thought and reality thus became emphasised, Crusius was also obliged to contest the ontological proof of the existence of God, resting as it did on the assumption that, since God is thinkable, He must also exist. JOHANN HEINRICH LAMBERT, who has won renown as a natural philosopher as well as a mathematician, came still nearer this crucial problem. In his *Neues Organon* (Leipzig, 1764) he emphasises the necessity of beginning with experience and of applying the analytical method. We cannot begin with construction, since the first thing to do is to arrive at a correct determination of the particular concepts with which we operate. We must first, as Locke did, set about an anatomical investigation of concepts. Nor is it sufficient to discover the simple concepts contained in our experience; we must also find out in how many different ways these may be combined with one another. In this way the transition from analysis to construction is effected; from a mere statement of concepts we proceed to the discovery of the fundamental axioms and postulates which may be contained in the same. Lambert saw no difficulty in this transition. If only we begin with the simplest concepts and proceed without omitting any possible combination, we may confidently undertake the work of construction. He knew well enough, however, that by this method we can reach empty forms only, containing no real content; and in a letter to Kant (February 3, 1766), whose thoughts at this time were moving in the same direction as his own, he raises the question, *whether, and if so, how far, knowledge of the form leads to knowledge of the matter of our knowledge.* To this extent, therefore, he is in doubt as to the justification of philosophical construction; he even touches on the crucial point, but he does not enter more closely into the problem itself. Kant held his predecessor in such high esteem that he had intended to dedicate his "Critique of Pure Reason" to Lambert, but the latter died before it appeared. Lambert still adhered to the confident dogmatism of the Enlightenment philosophy, since he did not see—what had dawned very early on Kant—that the transition from the analytical to the constructive method presupposes conditions which involve as a principle the limitation of knowledge (cf. Kant's letter to Lambert, December 31, 1765). JOHANN NICOLAUS TETENS, of South Schleswig, who, after discharging the duties of professor of philosophy and mathematics in Butzow and Kiel, filled a series of high administrative posts in Copenhagen, where he died in 1807, approached still nearer to Kant's fundamental thought; but he had been put on the scent by that work of Kant in which the fundamental thoughts of the critical philosophy first saw the light, *i.e.* the Dissertation of 1770. Tetens' *Versuche über die menschliche Natur*, is, both in respect of psychology as well

as of epistemology, the most important philosophical work
which appeared in Germany in the period immediately preceding Kant's great work. We have already pointed out
its significance in connection with psychology. In his theory
of knowledge Tetens proceeds from a thought the assertion
of which might, perhaps, have served to introduce greater
clearness into Kant's philosophy : *i.e.* that all conscious
perception is the perception of a relation. In every act
of attention we single out that to which we attend from
its surroundings. "The word 'see' expresses at least this
much, that the object which I perceive is a separate thing.
Perception is a distinguishing, an *Auskennen*" (I. p. 273).
The next step is conscious comparison. Here, too, through
the act of thought itself, a relation (of similarity or difference)
between things is established. We have in space and time
a special class of relations ; as Kant had already taught
in his Dissertation they are forms in which our knowledge
arranges the material furnished by the sensations. "As Herr
Kant has reminded us, we cannot abstract the concept of
time from presentations of felt objects ; it is the acts of feeling
which are continually going on within us which have succession
and duration, even when no perceptible object is felt which could
afford material for the abstraction of time" (I. p. 398, cf. 277).
Among the latter class of relations belongs the relation
of dependence (causal relation), and Tetens has here tried, not
very clearly, to mediate between Hume and Wolff. "Without
experience, I should certainly not have supposed," he says
(I. p. 320), "that the occurrence of one phenomenon would
draw after it another given phenomenon ; but "—he goes on
to say—"I express this supposition through a judgment that
my reason is necessarily compelled to pass, and which, therefore, is something other than habit or association of ideas : *i.e.*
a true thought, although preceding experience." This is, of
course, no answer to Hume's problem ; Tetens nowhere proves
that the judgments which our reason passes with logical
necessity can be valid of actual events. When Kant read
Tetens' *Versuche*, which he prized very highly and which (as
Hamann relates in a letter) was always to be found on his
writing-table, he had already hit on the idea which was
requisite, at this point, to carry the theory of knowledge further.

CHAPTER II

GOTTHOLD EPHRAIM LESSING

IT will appear from what we have already said that the so-called period of Enlightenment led out beyond itself at several points. It had, it is true, a certain tendency to consider itself perfect, and to look back with a pharisaical air on the darkness of preceding ages ; but, at the same time, it was an age rich in possibilities, while for Germany it was a time of transition to a magnificent period of poetical and philosophical flower. The feeling that he lived in an age of transition was particularly strong in the leading spirit of this period. Although LESSING was on terms of personal friendship with Mendelssohn and Nicolai—a friendship in which the latter were by no means mere recipients—yet he was not so satisfied with the Enlightenment as they were. He felt himself a stranger to his age. Unsatisfied by the given forms of intellectual life he, like Socrates before him, emphasised the subjective, personal side of the striving after truth. The chase, he says, is better than the prey. In virtue of this accentuation of the personal feeling of striving and endeavouring he is the child of his age ; while this same feeling enabled him to enter into other times and other standpoints more than was possible to the men of the Enlightenment and the Sentimentalists. The difference between different ages and standpoints comes out, of course, most clearly when we consider the results to which they led ; while in the inner strivings, the subjective forces which produce the results greater kinship is to be found. Lessing's historical sense is connected with his favourite idea of the eternal striving. And that his eyes were turned so eagerly towards the future in the hope of what it held in store is still more closely connected with this idea.

This is not the place to discuss Lessing's significance as a poet and æsthetic inquirer, although, no doubt, it would be interesting to trace the fundamental character of this great inquirer in all the different spheres in which he busied himself. Nor can we enter here into the details of his biography, since it contains no data which could help us to understand him as a philosopher of religion. He was born at Kamenz in Lauwitz in 1729, studied at Leipzig, afterwards lived in Breslau, Berlin, and Hamburg, occupied in writing poetry and works on æsthetics until, in 1770, he became librarian at Wolfenbüttel. From his youth up he had been addicted to philosophical studies, and had sketched out philosophical treatises. It was during the Wolfenbüttel period, however, that this side of his interests first became predominant, and, more especially, in the course of the controversy in which he became involved through his publication of the fragments of Reimarus' " Apology " (" The Wolfenbüttel Fragments "). He here carried on a literary war with the narrow-minded orthodoxy of his day, now remembered only on account of the skill in exposition, learning, and fulness of ideas it occasioned Lessing to display. He died in 1781.

Lessing was well aware that his chief power lay in criticism. He lacked the creative faculty. Nevertheless he possessed two valuable qualities which distinguish him from most of his contemporaries. He had an unquenchable thirst after true and fresh spiritual life,—in religion as well as in philosophy and æsthetics. And he possessed the historic sense and a great capacity for appreciating the original intellectual contributions of earlier times.

It is perhaps his historic sense which places him in sharpest contrast to his contemporaries. If neither orthodoxy, pietism, nor rationalism contented him,—and none of these directions appeared to him to be the one in which the religious life of the future could develop,—this was a consequence of the clearness with which he kept before him the historical character of all positive religions. Instead of regarding the Scriptures, over the interpretation of which men can never agree, as the most important form under which Christianity had appeared, Lessing harked back to the national life and to the whole religious development and tradition of which they were the outcome, and which explain to us how they arose. His assertion (in his defence of the publication of the Wolfenbüttel fragments) that Christianity does not stand or fall with the Bible was no mere stroke of diplomacy. He maintains the view that Christianity is older than the Bible, and that its future depends neither on book-learning nor on descriptions of " the spirit and the power," but on the continued life and presence of this " spirit and power " (*Über den Beweis des Geistes und der Kraft*). He here appears as the opponent of the over-estimation of book-learning and of the theological leading-strings which had become general in the Protestant Churches in consequence of Luther's eager appeal to the Bible as the rule of doctrine. He pointed out that if Christianity is to endure it must have other proofs than those to which orthodoxy had hitherto clung. He welcomed the appearance in his own time of the Herrnhüters, since he recognised in this movement a departure from the externality of orthodoxy—an inwardness which places the life higher than the letter. Against Göze, his orthodox opponent, he maintained that Christianity is essentially a matter of the heart, of feeling, and that no criticism of historical and philosophical proofs touches simple believers.

Lessing, however, has stated with sufficient clearness in his letters, as well as in his works, that he himself goes beyond the view here indicated of the Christian religion as the highest truth historically revealed. His *Duplik*, his *Antigöze*, *Nathan der Weise, Erziehung des Menschengeschlechts,* and *Gespräche über die Freimaurer* afforded him an opportunity of developing a complete religio-philosophical theory,—a theory which was not only very remarkable in its own time but which may well, even at the present day, afford food for reflection. It was an idiosyncrasy of Lessing's to provide opponents as well as friends with new arguments. Owing to his great love of truth and his clear insight he was often able to find weapons for his opponents which they themselves could never have discovered. On this account he was sometimes claimed by Christians as a brother in the faith, while, on other occasions, they accused him of dishonesty. So little is the world (even the so-called Christian part of it) accustomed to see a man helping his enemies ! His endeavour to include everything which could serve to throw light on the problem did not, however, prevent Lessing from developing his own ideas to their fullest extent.

The best starting-point for an exposition of these ideas is a famous passage in the *Duplik*. " Not the truth which is at the disposal of every man, but the honest pains he has taken to come behind the truth make the worth of a man. For not through the possession, but through the pursuit of truth, do his powers increase, and in this alone consists his ever-increasing perfection. Possession makes us quiet, indolent, proud. . . . If God with all truth in His right hand, and in His left the single, unceasing, striving after truth, even though coupled with the condition that I should ever and always err, came to me and said, ' Choose!' I would in all humility clasp His left hand and say, ' Father, give me this! is not pure truth for Thee alone?'" These words were aimed at the orthodox as well as the philosophers of the Enlightenment, and both schools stood in need of the reproof. It may indeed appear as though there were something tantalising in this eternal search, especially as Lessing is prepared to accept along with it the condition that he should always err. But we must remember that Lessing was speaking hypothetically. He is *conceiving* a choice between eternal seeking and erring on the one side, and on the other the mere possession of truth. It is clear that he is contemplating a case which can never actually take place. That this is so is evident not only from the form in which it is stated, but also from his assertion that the value of a man consists not in the possession of the truth but in the " honest pains " he takes to acquire it. This value, that is to say, is conditioned by the fact that the powers of men *become extended* by inquiry. But such extension would be impossible if no result other than continual error were to ensue. The consequences would then be disablement and contraction, not extension. In and for itself eternal striving is a self-contradiction. But it is another thing to say that every result to which we attain is only provisional and becomes the starting-point for further endeavours. And it was precisely this which, as will be seen from the sequel, was Lessing's meaning.

Lessing definitely expressed his attitude towards positive religion in his treatise *Über den Beweis des Geistes und der Kraft*, and in his later works he often returns to it. Were the historical foundation of Christianity beyond question yet—as already explained—historical truths could prove nothing here. How can the knowledge of the eternal interconnection of things be founded in special historical facts? How can I be expected to transform all my ideas for the sake of certain events which happened eighteen centuries ago? History is one thing, Philosophy another. "This is the wide and dreadful gulf over which I cannot pass, often and earnestly though I have attempted the leap." Lessing consistently maintains that be the origin of Christianity what it may it has left permanent traces on the course of development. In a fragment entitled *Die Religion Christi* he shows how difficult it is to decide whether Christ was more than man, if, indeed, it be granted that He was man. We ought, therefore, to abide by Christ's religion, to that religion which was Christ's when He was man ; the question as to the Christian religion, as to the truth of the doctrines taught by the Church, may then be left open.

The religion which Lessing supported is based not on a few supernatural events but on the great inner interconnection within nature and history. The various positive religions seem to him to be members of this great interconnected whole, for he regards them as stages in the spiritual development of man. Instead of deriding or growing indignant at positive religions he prefers (as he says in the preface to the *Erziehung des Menschengeschlechts*, "Education of the Human Race") to see in them "the only road by which the human understanding in each instance has been able to develop and along which it will develop still farther." What education is to the individual man, revelation is to the whole human race. By means of revelation the human race is raised from lower to higher stages.[3] The Israelites learnt through the relation of obedience towards their God, whom they regarded as the most powerful of all gods, to accustom themselves to the idea of one God long before a reasonable concept of this one God was possible. And by means of promises and threats they were induced to practise good and avoid evil. Not till later, after they had become acquainted with other and more enlightened nations (Chaldeans, Persians, and Greeks), could they develop a more idealistic conception of religion. The strict discipline which they had to undergo was necessary in order that from among them might spring educators of the whole human race. Christ was the first to inculcate purity of heart in view, not of earthly reward and punishment, but of another life. Both the New and the Old Testaments, however, are no more than the primer of the human race, with which men cannot remain content, although they must not abandon it until they are thoroughly versed in its contents, and although it may be desirable that for the time the scholar should regard his primer as the epitome of all science. But let the more advanced scholar, who impatiently turns the last leaf of his book, beware lest he too soon disturb the tranquillity of his weaker fellows! On the other hand, it may be injurious to keep the pupils over-long at their primer, for this makes them sophistical and superstitious. The truths of revelation must be transformed into truths of reason if the human race is ever really to assimilate them. Lessing tries to show by a symbolical interpretation of the doctrines of the Trinity and of the Atonement the truths which lie concealed under dogmatic formulas. Sooner or later, education must attain its goal. The time must come when men will no longer require the conviction of a future life to supply them with the necessary motives for their actions, but will do good for its own sake. Then, indeed, will the new eternal gospel, the third age of which the dreamers of the Middle Ages spoke, be come! We must await in patience the coming of this future. The course of development proceeds by small steps and with many détours. In the "Conversations for Freemasons" we find: "The Freemasons quietly await the sunrise, letting the candles burn as long as they will and can, —to extinguish the candles and perceive that the ends will have to be re-lit is not the business of Freemasons." For Lessing, the significance of religion was, in the long run, distinctly ethical. It is an education in doing good for the sake of good. For him the most important part of Christianity (as he shows in the beautiful little dialogue, entitled, *Das Testament Johannis*) is the earnest exhortation to love. In the "Conversations for Freemasons" (which is perhaps the work which expresses at once Lessing's religious, ethical and social views most finely and clearly) he conceives the Freemasons, of whom he here gives us an idealised description, as a free community of brethren, whose aim is to throw down the barriers between men which religion, nationality, and the State have hitherto set up.

Shortly after Lessing's death, great interest was excited by JACOBI'S assertion in his letters to Mendelssohn (*Briefe über die Lehre des Spinoza*, 1785), that Lessing had confessed himself an adherent of Spinoza. As Spinoza was regarded

by the spokesmen of the Enlightenment as the essence of godlessness it was small wonder that the assertion excited not
only interest, but, in the breasts of some of Lessing's friends,
especially Mendelssohn, sorrow and indignation also.

Jacobi (to a certain extent a modern Herbert of Cherbury)
had travelled to Wolfenbüttel in order to visit Lessing, and to
get his help in refuting Spinoza ; he took the opportunity to show
him Goethe's " Prometheus," a copy of which he had brought
with him. He handed him the poem with the words " You
who have offended so many people shall now be offended
yourself." After Lessing had read it, he said, " I see nothing here
to offend me ; I had all that long since from the fountain-head.
. . . The point of view from which the poem is written is my
own point of view. . . . The orthodox conceptions of the
Deity are nothing to me. I cannot away with them. Ἑν καὶ
Πᾶν ! (One and all !) I know nothing else. This is the standpoint of the poem, and I must confess it pleases me greatly."
Jacobi : " Then you are pretty well agreed with Spinoza ? "
Lessing : " If I were to call myself a disciple of any one, it would
be of him." In the course of the conversation Jacobi confessed that he could neither refute Spinoza nor prove his own
belief in a personal God, existing apart from the world, but
that he took refuge in a leap, in a *salto mortale* from knowledge
to faith. After a somewhat wordy exposition from Jacobi, in
which he hopes to shine by his (not altogether thorough)
knowledge of Spinoza, Lessing says : " Your *salto mortale* by
no means displeases me, and I understand a man making
a somersault of this kind in order to get away from where he
was. Take me with you when it comes off." Jacobi : " If you
would only step on to the spring-board, it would come of
itself." Lessing : " But a leap is also necessary, which I dare
not exact from my old legs and heavy head."

This is the substance of the famous conversation (July 6,
1780). It contains, however, several utterances of Lessing
on especial points which are of particular interest. Lessing
explains that he cannot believe in a personal God, existing apart
from the world ; that on the contrary he conceives God rather
as the soul of the world. This is in harmony with the thought
which he developed in several philosophical fragments written
in early life, viz., that nothing can exist besides God, since,
if we thus set anything outside Him, God would be limited

and finite. He asserts an inner and immanent relation between God and the world, and refuses to conceive God as analogous with a human personality. He could not reconcile himself to the idea of a personal Deity in unchangeable enjoyment of the highest perfection. As he said to Jacobi, it was associated in his mind with " an idea of such infinite boredom, that the very thought is grief and pain to me." It was but natural that a thinker whose ideal was a state of unceasing striving should be dissatisfied with a God, finished and complete. This is one of the points, moreover, which go to prove that we must not take Lessing's adherence to Spinoza too strictly. Becoming and development were alien to the Spinozistic concept of God. Lessing further expresses himself against " the human prejudice which leads us to regard thought as the first and finest, and to deduce everything from it, whereas everything, including ideas themselves, is dependent on higher principles. Extension, motion, thoughts are all evidently grounded in a higher power, which they are far from exhausting." Lessing is here polemicising against the theology so prevalent during the period of the Enlightenment, which rested its proof of the existence of God on the purposiveness of Nature. The passage is entirely in agreement with Spinoza, who regarded both thought and extension as attributes of substance, which, in addition to these, possesses infinitely many others. In the course of the conversation, however, Lessing refers to Hume's *Dialogues*, in which a similar line of thought appears. Finally Lessing begs for a purely natural explanation of all things. He cannot consent to a leap into the supernatural. On this point, too, Lessing reminds us of Spinoza, of whom he had once said in a letter to Mendelssohn that he was the first thinker who had been led by his own system to conceive the possibility of explaining all the changes of the body through its own mechanical forces. (It would, however, be more correct to say the converse, viz. : that the thought of this possibility had led Spinoza to his system.)

Mendelssohn attempted to explain the whole conversation as a mere intellectual exercise on Lessing's part. But this explanation is untenable, even though Lessing may perhaps have thought that his sentimental friends might profit by such an exercise, and though it be incorrect to credit him with all Spinoza's views. Lessing gave in his adhesion to no definite

system, but we can discern a body of thoughts by which he
was guided—at any rate in the privacy of his chamber. It
was not merely indignation at the fact that Spinoza had for so
long been treated as "a dead dog," which induced Lessing to
defend him. Moreover, a general increase of interest in this
heretical thinker may be traced. Jacobi regarded his as the
most logical form of pure philosophy. Enthusiasts like Edelmann, and pious, orthodox souls like THOMAS WIZENMANN,
Jacobi's young friend, sympathised with Spinoza, in so far as they
could not reconcile their religious feeling with the thought of a
God distinct from the world. GOETHE, with his half artistic, half
naturalistic, and HERDER with his religio - naturalistic faith
enthusiastically welcomed the "one and all" proclaimed by
Lessing.[4]   At various standpoints a pressing need was
beginning to make itself felt for a deeper conception of life than
that which either the Enlightenment or popular philosophy
were able to supply. This need could only be satisfied philosophically when the nature and scope of human knowledge
had been subjected to a thorough examination. Such an
examination was required in the interest both of the problems
of knowledge and of religion. In the year after the conversation between Lessing and Jacobi (so remarkable for the light it
threw on the religious standpoint of the best men of the time),
which was also the year of Lessing's death appeared KANT'S
"Critique of Pure Reason."

BOOK VII

IMMANUEL KANT AND THE CRITICAL PHILOSOPHY

CHAPTER I

CHARACTERISTICS AND BIOGRAPHY

EVERY great intellectual work has its own particular fate. Since each such work gives expression to many different intellectual interests, the aspects and qualities which make it an object of admiration and appropriation may be very different at different times, and that which was for the author of the work the guiding thought or leading *motif* may not be the one to which its permanent significance attaches. During the time which has elapsed since the appearance of the "Critique of Pure Reason" almost every decade has seen a new edition of it, and to this day it is studied in wider circles and with more thoroughness than any other philosophical work. Contemporaries were chiefly impressed by its combination of the overthrow of the proofs on which the conceptions of religion had rested with the energetic assertion of the grandeur of the moral law, and with its demonstration of the intimate connection of this law with the intellectual nature of man ; while a smaller circle regarded its treatment of the problem of knowledge as of the first importance. But here again the emphasis might be laid on different sides. Prominence might be given either to the claim of the faculty of reason to arrive at knowledge without the help of experience, or to the restriction of the validity of this knowledge to the empirical world. The idealistic side of the system might be accentuated, according to which reason determines what reality is ; or the realistic side might be emphasised, according to which the activity of reason only acquires real significance when it receives its material from a source to which it itself is not able to penetrate. Finally, the main interest may turn either on the psychological analysis of the nature and mode of operation of consciousness and knowledge, or on the consequences which may be deduced from these with regard to the conditions and limitation of knowledge. All these different *motifs* have decided the influence of the system on subsequent times ; sometimes one, sometimes the other being predominant. It is the task of historical investigation to trace out the mutual relations of these different *motifs* in Kant's philosophy and in the course of his development. Perhaps we shall then find it possible to reduce them all to a single fundamental one, uniting in itself the practical and theoretical interests, the speculative and empirical tendencies, the psychological and the epistemological problems, and which Kant himself terms *the self-cognition of reason in scientific form* (see *Prolegomena*, § 36).

In Kant's view, thought sets to work *dogmatically*, i.e. with involuntary, frequently naïve, confidence in its own powers and in the validity of its own assumptions. Hence it believes itself able to solve all problems and to penetrate to the innermost nature of the world. This is the age of great systems. Later comes a time in which it appears that these thought-constructions cannot reach the heavens, and that the architects cannot agree as to their plan. This is the age of doubt, of *scepticism*. Men mock at these futile attempts with their inner contradictions, and console themselves, half sadly, half cynically, with what appears to be an absolutely negative result. This is a natural reaction against blind dogmatism. Kant attacks both these tendencies. He found one task which had been neglected by dogmatists and sceptics alike, *i.e.* the inquiry into the nature of our intellect and of our knowledge itself, with a view to discovering what forms and powers we have at our disposal for the comprehension of things, and how far these forms and powers can take us. Kant finds the fundamental form of all our knowledge in the unity which all knowledge seeks to effect. Knowledge at all its stages is a synthetising, a uniting together of what was scattered. The simplest sense-image is formed by the weaving together of many different impressions, and the same character of unity is to be found in the greatest systems to which thought, in its highest flights, can mount. To this extent the dogmatic systems arise out of a real, human need. They try to embrace everything in a form of unity. They are attempts at a realisation of that towards which knowledge, at all its stages, tends.

But Kant goes on to show that knowledge is bound up with experience, and that this search after unity, when it ventures beyond the limits of experience, becomes involved in contradictions ; at any rate it can adduce no proof of the validity of its results. Thought (to use one of Kant's striking images), is like a dove which should think that, because it is so easy to fly in the air, it would be still easier to fly in a vacuum. It is precisely the resistance which bears it aloft, but which also, it is true, imposes limits on its movement. Sceptics are unjust to the dogmatic systems when they only look at them in their completed form ; we must go back to their origin, must examine what human power and what need led to their production, and to what conditions the employment of this power and the satisfaction of this need are subjected. By means of such self-knowledge Kant thinks to deliver the human mind from its own earlier works, which may all too easily become fettering shackles. At the same time he intends, although with clearer insight into its conditions and limitations, to continue to exercise the same power as that which had produced these previous works, and he thus cleared the way for a comprehension of these works such as negative criticism alone could never have supplied. *By so doing Kant laid down the programme for all mental science.* It is true that he himself worked at the solution of special philosophical problems only. Nevertheless, the point of view which he adopted possesses general significance for the study of religion, art, literature, and languages, as well as for the study of institutions and the forms of society. The relations are everywhere analogous, and the problem remains essentially the same—*i.e.* by a study of the powers which produced the work of earlier times to effect the liberation of these powers, so that they may achieve the work of the future with clearer understanding. We have to demonstrate and preserve the continuity while showing how the powers undergo these metamorphoses. This endeavour lay at the heart of Kant's great and profound intellectual work, and it is in virtue of it that he occupies the central position in the history of modern thought, even though many of his own favourite doctrines have had to be entirely abandoned.

Kant's life presents nothing calling for comment, nothing interesting or piquant. It was a quiet, judicious career, dedicated to thought. His life was that of an ordinary citizen, and he was by no means free from a certain pedantry and philistinism. Out of the deep inner subsoil of this unassuming and insignificant outer life, however, there sprung up great thoughts which illuminated human knowledge and human life. And the feeling for the great and sublime—the species of æsthetic feeling which Kant understood and described best—thrives best, perhaps, in narrow circumstances, where only the sky can be seen. Unfortunately, we have no records of Kant's inner personal development. Those of his biographers who were most intimate with him (BOROWSKI, JACHMANN, WASIANSKI), and who, immediately after his death, published accounts of his life and character, confined themselves, for the most part, to external details, and have given us no insight into the inner, spiritual currents, which shaped his development. Those of his letters which have been preserved (of which there is to this day no complete collection) were chiefly written in the later years of his life. We are, therefore, obliged to construct his intellectual development from his writings. Before we attack this problem, however, we must dwell for a little on the main features of his life.

IMMANUEL KANT was born at Königsberg, April 22, 1724. His father was a saddler of Scotch origin ; his name was really Cant, but the philosopher changed the C into a K, to prevent its being pronounced like S. Both his parents had sound and healthy dispositions and met the misfortunes of life with a gentleness taught them by their pietistical religion. Kant was particularly influenced by his mother. Her pietism did not blind her to the beauty and splendour of Nature, to which she sought to direct her son's attention. In later life Kant often spoke with enthusiasm of his parents, and the tendency towards inwardness and the subjective side of life, so characteristic of pietism, left its mark on his subsequent development. Königsberg pietism was particularly gentle and humane. Nevertheless, Kant encountered the dark side of pietism, i.e. its formalism and intellectual constraint, chiefly at school, where fixed hours of prayer and compulsory morality produced hypocrisy and affectation. These experiences also influenced Kant's attitude towards religion in after years. At school classical languages formed his chief study, and Kant was, throughout his life, a skilled Latinist, on whom an appropriate quotation was never lost. From his sixteenth to his twenty-second

year he studied Wolff's philosophy and Newton's physics at the
University of Königsberg. His teacher in these subjects was
MARTEN KNUTZEN, one of the most independent of the
Wolffians. Kant, it is true, entered the University as a theological student, but he attended very few theological lectures.
His means were scanty. He supplemented them by private
teaching, and from his twenty-second year onwards he was house
tutor in several families belonging to the East Prussian nobility.
Although he considered himself to have no particular talent
for teaching, he managed to impress several of his pupils with
his own deep sense of the freedom and dignity of man ; for it
can have been no mere accident that several of the leaders
of the movement for the abolition of serfdom were former
pupils of Kant. Kant himself is said to have remarked at a
later period of his life that his bowels were moved within him
when he thought of the bondage existing in his own country.
The years spent as a tutor in distinguished families taught
Kant a knowledge of the world for which his otherwise retired
life would have offered no opportunity, and gave him the manners
of a polished man of the world, which, according to the testimony of his contemporaries, he could so well assume when he
wished. It was during these years, too, that the foundation of
the wealth of thought and knowledge which he displayed on
his first appearance as an author and a University teacher was
laid. At the age of thirty-one he returned to Königsberg. In
this year (1775) he made his first appearance both as a
University *docent* and as an author, for, previously to this, he
had only published one short treatise on a problem of physics.
While some of his lectures on physical geography and
empirical psychology were intended to be popular, and were
addressed to wider circles, others were strictly philosophical.
Herder, who was one of his hearers in 1762 and the following
years, has given an enthusiastic description of Kant as a
teacher of philosophy in his earlier years (in vol. ii. of *Briefe
zur Beförderung der Humanität*). He himself announced the
principles on which his teaching would be based in a programme of his lectures which he published at this time
(*Nachricht von der Einrichtung meiner Vorlesungen in dem
Winterhalbjahre von* 1765-66). He lays stress firstly on the
need of a firm empirical foundation, that young students may
not begin to speculate too soon ; secondly, on the fact that

he aims, not at instructing his hearers in a ready-made philosophy, since no such philosophy exists, but at teaching them *to philosophise for themselves.* Even in the first period of his development, which may be assigned to the years 1755-69, there is a decided breach with dogmatism.

Characteristic of this period is the independent criticism which he directs against his teachers, Newton and Wolff. In one of his most brilliant works : *Allgemeine Naturgeschichte und Theorie des Himmels* ("General Physiogony and Theory of the Heavens ") (1755), he criticises Newton's assertion that the present order of the solar system cannot be explained by the mechanical laws of nature, and propounds the famous hypothesis that the present system of the heavenly bodies has developed out of a gaseous atmosphere, endowed with primary rotation. In the firm interconnection of all the elements of the universe to which these natural laws witness he saw a proof of the fact that the whole universe has its ultimate ground in an absolute and all-comprehending Being. Thus he here unites his scientific with his religious views, although, even here, he rejects the ordinary proofs of the existence of God. He has worked out this point of view in his *Einzig möglicher Beweisgrund einer Demonstration des Dasein Gottes* ("Only possible Ground of Proof for the Being of God "), (1763). He had lost confidence in Wolff's dogmatic constructions, and had become convinced that philosophy must proceed by way of analysis if it is to attain to certain and clear concepts. He discussed this question in a series of works written in 1762-63. The influence which, according to Kant's own confession, both Hume and Rousseau exercised upon him ought, most probably, to be assigned to this period. As I shall endeavour subsequently to prove, this sharp accentuation of analysis as the philosophical method brought him, by a natural transition, face to face with the problem of causality, as propounded by Hume. For this problem was raised in connection with the question as to how we can justify the assumption of a necessary relation between cause and effect if they are two different things, so that the effect cannot be discovered by means of an analysis of the cause. Rousseau's emphatic assertion of the rights of feeling and of the difference between faith and knowledge also helped to revolutionise Kant's line of thought. Up till now, faithful to the principles of the

Enlightenment, he had sought for the essence and nobility of man in the understanding only ; now he discovered a still deeper foundation, common to learned and lay, in which the simplest peasant might be equal with the profoundest thinker. And Rousseau's appeal to immediate feeling and immediate faith must have seemed all the more significant to Kant, since he was just on the point of undermining the proofs which had hitherto been supposed to support the assumptions on which the doctrine of natural religion was based. Kant, like Rousseau, was brought by a natural advance to attribute to intellectual development in general a more *indirect* significance for spiritual life than he had originally assigned to it. His own critical study had here led him in the same direction as Rousseau, and when the latter's *Émile* appeared, Kant was prepared to appreciate it. No wonder that on the day that he received it, he omitted, to the great astonishment of his neighbours, to take his usual walk at his appointed hour !

In his writings of this period Kant lays great weight on psychology as the foundation of philosophy, especially of ethics, and quotes Shaftesbury, Hutcheson, and Hume as his predecessors in this respect. He maintained a sceptical attitude towards speculative constructions and systems. In the *Träumen eines Geistersehers erläutert durch Träume der Metaphysik* ("Dreams of a Ghost-seer illustrated by the Dreams of Metaphysic") (1766), one of the most brilliant of his works, he shows how easy, in a certain sense, it is to construct far-reaching spiritualistic explanations, but also, how immature and unfounded are the concepts with which such thinkers operate. His conclusion is : " How many things there are which I do not understand—but how many things there are which I do not need ! " Socratic ignorance—" the philosophy of ignorance " or " negative philosophy " was at that time (as may be seen from his notes) his favourite thought. Had he been acquainted with Cusanus' expression : *docta ignorantia*, his preference for Latin catchwords would have led him to adopt it.

Kant remained a *privat-docent* until his forty-sixth year ; the only public office which he held being a miserably paid sub-librarianship. The bad times consequent on the Seven Years' War were partly the cause of his not having been given any permanent appointment at the University.

He declined a chair of poetry which was offered him. In 1770 he was appointed professor of philosophy, and in the same year appeared his Latin treatise, *De mundi sensibilis atque intelligibilis forma et principiis* ("On the Form and Principles of the Sensible and Intelligible World"); in future this work will be alluded to for the sake of brevity, as the Dissertation; in it the fundamental notions of his definitive philosophy first made their appearance. In several passages occurring in his letters and notes he indicates the year 1769 as the one in which his fundamental conception took shape. Thus he says somewhere, "The year '69 afforded me much light." And in his last years he only cared to acknowledge the works written after 1769.[5] The thought which then dawned upon him was that *such forms and presuppositions as are the conditions for anything whatever becoming an object of our knowledge must be valid of all experience.* In the Dissertation he applied this thought to space and time as forms of our sensuous perception. The appearance of this thought, and its application to all scientific knowledge, characterises the second period of Kant's philosophical development. We may judge of the magnitude of the problem, and of Kant's thoroughness in working it out, from the fact that it was eleven years before he saw his way to extending its application from sensuous experience to rational knowledge. In the Dissertation it is only sensuous perception which is bound up with subjective forms and presuppositions. The sensuous world is phenomenon only, but with the help of the understanding we can rise above it to a knowledge of things-in-themselves. The world of thought is real, the world of sense is phenomenal. We may see from letters and notes written in the seventies what pains it cost him to arrive at the conviction that the understanding, no less than sensuous perception, has its forms and presuppositions, and that therefore no scientific knowledge is able to lead us beyond the phenomenal world of experience. When Kant discovered that rational knowledge, like sensuous perception, consists in a synthesis, in a combining, uniting mental activity, the goal was reached. The result of many years of excogitation, Kant tells us, was committed to paper in the greatest haste, in from four to five months! It is clear, therefore, that he could not have attributed much importance

to the form of his exposition.   He probably incorporated earlier
sketches, written at various times, without always examining
carefully whether they agreed with one another.   Hence the
Kritik der reinen Vernunft ("Critique of Pure Reason") (1781),
is a book which is difficult to read, not only on account of
its subject matter, but also because of its mode of exposition.
It seems hardly possible to believe what one of Kant's biographers tells us, *i.e.* that Kant submitted every sentence to
the judgment of his friend Green, a merchant, before he wrote
it down.   Had a practical man directed the exposition it
would, we may be sure, have been clearer.   It contains a
mass of formalisms and not a little scholasticism.   Kant
himself remarks of this book that it must seem the quint-
essence of pedantry to any one glancing through it, and
yet its whole aim is to make an end of pedantry.   Moreover, in addition to contradictions and scholastic pedantries, it
contains redundancies and repetitions, calculated to weary or
confuse the reader.   Nevertheless we have in this book an
immortal masterpiece of philosophy ; a work which stands
as a mile-stone in the long wanderings of human thought.
Through his researches into the innermost nature of knowledge,
Kant succeeded in discovering the conditions on which it rests ;
also the limits beyond which it cannot pass.   He shows us
at once the grandeur and the limitation of thought.   His faith
in reason was not weakened by this limitation ; for the barriers
arise out of the very nature of reason itself, and are known
according to reason's own laws.   Subsequent inquiry has
subjected Kant's determination of these limits to a revision,
and has found them sometimes too narrow, sometimes too
wide ; at any rate it is certain that they are not exactly
where he placed them ; but this in no way derogates from
his greatness as the man who had the keenest eye for the
form and activity of knowledge, and was most aware of the
significance of the problem of knowledge for the whole of
the spiritual life.

Two years after the appearance of his chief work he gave
(in the *Prolegomena*) a shorter and more readable presentation
of the argument contained in it.

After the publication of the "Critique of Pure Reason"
Kant set about developing his views on ethics.   He had
already, in the Dissertation, abandoned the psychological founda-

tion of Ethics, which he had previously, following the English school, adopted. In the moral laws, as these immediately reveal themselves every time that we feel we *ought* to do something, he found reason active in the practical sphere. He has given a fresh and clear exposition of his conception of ethics in his *Grundlegung zur Metaphysik der Sitten* ("Fundamental Principles of the Metaphysics of Ethics") (1785). His chief ethical work, however, is the *Kritik der praktischen Vernunft* ("Critique of Practical Reason") (1788). Kant had one more great work to write in order to complete his critical philosophy, which was to comprehend all sides of life. In the *Kritik der Urtheilskraft* ("Critique of Judgment") (1790), he discusses the problems which are suggested by the beauty and purposiveness of Nature, and attempts to solve them in a way analogous to that in which he had solved the epistemological and ethical problems. This work contains profound suggestions of a possible interconnection between the different spheres which had been so sharply distinguished in his previous critical inquiries.

Kant spent his whole life in East Prussia, but he observed with great interest everything which went on in the physical as well as in the human world. Travels were his favourite reading, and, as already mentioned, physical geography played an important part in his course of teaching. He never lost sight of the development of the natural sciences, and he observed the course of political events with the closest attention. The Revolutions in North America and in France excited his enthusiasm, and he regarded the general interest felt throughout Europe in these events as an indication of moral progress. The most recent event in science or politics was generally the topic of his table-talk. After the publication of his chief work Kant was a famous man. His intellectual labours and his ideal view of life and its duties aroused the enthusiasm of the best minds of his age. Pilgrimages were made to Königsberg from great distances in order to see him, and many turned to him for advice in moral difficulties. He was in great favour with Zedlitz, the all-powerful minister of Frederick the Great. Zedlitz had made himself acquainted with Kant's lectures from notebooks which were sent to him in instalments from Königsberg, and the "Critique of Pure Reason" was dedicated to him. The king himself was no admirer of German literature and philosophy.

In his early years he had been an eager disciple of Wolff's, but he afterwards became an adherent of Voltaire and Bayle. Kant, however, congratulated himself on living in Frederick's time, under a prince who, while he ruled with a firm hand, was not afraid to allow thought free play. Kant used to say he lived not in an enlightened age, but in an age of enlightenment, *i.e.* in an age that was progressing in enlightenment. (See his small treatise, *Was ist Aufklärung?* " What is Enlightenment " ?) (1784).

But a time came when Kant was no longer regarded with favour in high places. Frederick William II., a dissipated man of weak character, given up to spiritualism and mysticism, and terrified by the force of the revolutionary movement in France, established the ascendency of the priests and increased the severity of the censure. Zedlitz was dismissed. Wöllner, bigoted and *borné*, was placed at the head of the departments of education and religion, and a college of censors, consisting of three theologians, was appointed. Special attention was devoted to Kant as the most important representative of free inquiry, and an attempt was actually made to prohibit him from writing. This, however, did not succeed. But the storm broke in 1794 when Kant published his work on the philosophy of religion, *Religion innerhalb der Grenzen der blossen Vernunft* (" Religion within the Boundaries of Pure Reason ") in which he attempted to expound from his standpoint the significance of Christianity as the historical form of an ethical idea, while at the same time he entered several protests against the orthodox view. He had taken the precaution to inquire of the theological faculty in Königsberg whether his work would be submitted to the theological censure, and on receiving an answer in the negative had solicited the permission of the philosophical faculty to publish it.[6] This, however did not prevent the issue of a royal mandate, inspired by Wöllner, in which the royal displeasure at his inquiries was expressed, and further disagreeable measures were threatened if he continued in the same course. The aged thinker (he was now seventy years old) had done nothing to deserve such treatment. He had always spoken reverently of Christianity and its founder, and had only used the right of free inquiry to investigate the relation of Christianity to human nature and to reason. Kant's papers show us how conscientiously he deliberated as to what was the right course to pursue under the circumstances. One of his notes runs as follows—

" Recantation would be abject, but silence, in a case like the present, is the duty of a subject." In his answer he makes a candid attempt to show that he has been guilty of no fault ; but at the same time he declares that—as His Majesty's most faithful subject—he will abstain from writing on the philosophy of religion. There was a reservation here ; he only considered the promise binding as long as he was a subject of *this* king. When, a few years afterwards, Frederick William II. died, and his successor adopted a more liberal - minded policy, Kant resumed his works on religious philosophy, and (in the preface to the *Streite der Fakultäten*, 1798) gave a history of the quarrel.

This history is an appalling example of the way in which narrow fanaticism frequently seeks to fetter free intellectual life. Such life, happily, cannot be checked ; hence we can afford to laugh as well as to be indignant. Those who attacked Kant's venerable figure have their place in history alongside of those who laid violent hands on Galileo, and forced him to declare that the earth stands still. The spirit no more stands still than the earth.

The last years of Kant's life witnessed a slow and sad dissolution of those mental powers which had been so unceasingly active. He lost his memory and power of synthesising ; coercive ideas, chiefly strings of words and melodies of his childhood, forced themselves upon him ; unpleasant dreams at night and ceaseless restlessness by day tormented the aged sufferer. It is supposed that he suffered from some disorder of the brain. During his lucid intervals he sat at his writing-table, writing a last concluding work, of which a few fragments are extant. They show signs of the weakness of old age. Together with a few brilliant thoughts they contain very many repetitions from his earlier works. After a lingering illness, Kant died February 12, 1804.

CHAPTER II

PHILOSOPHICAL DEVELOPMENT

WHEN Kant says somewhere that the first step in philosophy is always dogmatic he is probably not only thinking of the history of philosophy, but is speaking from personal experience of his own development. And yet in no work of his that we possess does Kant appear as a thorough-going dogmatist. From the first he had always entertained a lively conviction that the great systems of speculative philosophy contained much that was immature from a scientific point of view ; and as early as his treatise of 1755 he speaks ironically of "those gentlemen who are wont to reject as chaff every thought which has not been put through the mill of the Wolffian or some other famous system." Characteristic of *the first period of his philosophical authorship* (1755-69) is his dissatisfaction with existing philosophical systems, and his attempt to find means to erect a new and more thorough, even though less imposing, structure. While engaged on this work, it occurred to him that a speculative system must be preceded by an examination of the concepts with which it operates, and that such concepts contain within them very great problems. Thus metaphysic became for Kant a doctrine of the limits of knowledge, and he began to speak of a critique of reason itself. Many years later (in the preface to the *Prolegomena*, 1783) he announced that it was the memory of David Hume which *roused him from his dogmatic slumbers and gave a new direction to his investigations in the field of speculative philosophy*, and this awakening may most probably be assigned to the year 1762-63, although it may be noted as a proof of the independence and continuity of Kant's philosophical thought that it is impossible to find any point in his development where it is absolutely necessary to assume a

strong influence from some other author in order to understand
its subsequent course.

Referring my readers to my article on "The Continuity of
Kant's Philosophical Development" (German translation, "Die
Kontinuität im philosophischen Entwickelungsgange Kant's,"
Archiv für Geschichte der Philosophie, vol. vii.) for the grounds on
which my view of the course of Kant's development presented
in the sequel is based, I shall only pause here to discuss a few
of the most important points.

The positive and permanent value of those of Kant's works
which appeared prior to 1769, in which year, according to his
own account, his philosophy took definite shape, rests principally upon two lines of thought.

(*a*) As I have already intimated, Kant attempts in his
"General Physiogony" to extend Newton's demand that
demonstrable causes (*verae causae*) be assigned to all phenomena
over a far wider range than that great inquirer, to whom Kant
himself looked up, had thought possible.

It was this which led him to his famous hypothesis as to
the origin of the solar system. The attempt here begun was
never afterwards abandoned by Kant. In the "Critique of Pure
Reason" (in the Doctrine of Method) we find him still maintaining that the wildest hypothesis is preferable to an appeal to
the supernatural. This eagerness in extending the series of
natural causes and in excluding any interruption is connected
with the fact that, at the beginning of his first period, Kant's
philosophy of nature and of religion were intimately associated
with one another. It is a false assumption, he thinks, to
suppose that if Nature were left to herself she would produce
nothing but disorder and chaos. Nature produces order and
purposiveness, not by chance, but according to her own
laws. It is this very mechanical order of Nature, embracing
all phenomena, and according to whose laws the particular
elements act and react upon one another, which witnesses to
one common ground of the universe, one infinite power which
stirs in each particular element. The individual atoms (as
Kant shows at length in an interesting treatise of 1756,
Monadologica physica) are points of force, not small extended
particles, and the fact that they act and react upon one
another according to law proves that there is no original and
absolute separation between them. Had every element in the

world its own particular nature it could only be an accident if they fitted together so as to render a connected system of things possible. Their reciprocal action would be impossible if they were not collectively dependent on a common ground. In this common ground both the mechanical order and the purposiveness of nature find their explanation. Instead of trembling because natural science reveals physical causes, we ought rather to rejoice that, by this means, the great original fact—reciprocal action, the interconnection of nature—is more clearly revealed.

It is in causal connection as an ultimate fact, then, that Kant here finds the foundation on which to build his theory of religion. There is a remarkable kinship between his line of thought and that of Spinoza, although he can only have been acquainted with the latter through presentations which are far from doing him justice. On the other hand, Kant already rejects the ordinary proofs of the existence of God, especially the " physico-theological " proof which, from the purposiveness of Nature, deduces the necessity of assuming the intervention of a power existing outside Nature.

(*b*) But while it was in natural causal connection that Kant found the only possible ground of proof for a religious conception of the world, yet at the same time he set about examining the nature of our thought. It consists, he found, in comparing and analysing. Every judgment rests on the comparison of an attribute with a thing ; the attribute is either predicable or non-predicable of the thing. Thus we always operate according to the principles of identity and contradiction, and can only pass over from one concept to another when the identity of the latter with the former can be proved, *i.e.* when I can arrive at the latter concept by means of an analysis of the former. Philosophy cannot, like mathematics, begin with construction, and thus create its own concepts. It must find them by means of an analysis of experience ; but how in that case can it offer any guarantee that the analysis has been exhaustive, so that no other characteristics remain undiscovered ? Kant attributes the imperfection of previous philosophy precisely to the fact that it operated with incomplete concepts, for, assuming that we must be able to construct in philosophy just as we do in mathematics, it had passed on over-hastily from analysis to construction. Kant adduces here very important examples of such incomplete or subreptive concepts. The first is the concept of spirit employed by Descartes, Leibniz, and Wolff in their spiritualistic psychology. We possess no exhaustive concept of the nature of spirit such as could authorise us in attributing to it an independent existence, apart from matter. We have an empirical concept of mental phenomena, but empirical psychology cannot determine whether there is or is not a soul-substance. The " Dreams of a Ghost-seer " affords a humorous proof of the ease with which a complete spiritualistic system may be constructed if the concept of a soul-substance be taken as given. The works of Swedenborg are cited in illustration.

The second example is the concept of cause. If thought is analysis, then only those relations are intelligible of which the second member can be deduced from the first. But can the analysis of one phenomenon discover to us the necessity for the occurrence of a second phenomenon? And yet it is this which is expressed by the causal concept. There is no contradiction in not passing beyond the first phenomenon. But if this be so, how can the causal concept be valid? Kant here, first of all in his remarkable treatise : *Versuch den Begriff der negativen Grössen in die Weltweisheit einzuführen* ("The Attempt to introduce the Idea of Negative Quality into Philosophy ") (1762), arrived by his own route, but very probably also led by the remembrance of Hume, at the problem of causality, which however he set aside for the time as insoluble. There must now have arisen a violent conflict in Kant's mind between these two lines of thought ; for while one asserts, in the interests of natural philosophy as well as of religion, that the causal nexus is the great ultimate fact, the other maintains that this ultimate fact is itself incomprehensible! He also touches on the causal problem in the " General Natural History " and in the " Ground of Proof," where he infers the existence of a common ground of all things, as otherwise the reciprocal action of the elements would be incomprehensible. But the treatise on negative quality is remarkable for the transference of the problem from the *objective or metaphysical form to the subjective or epistemological form.* This transference followed naturally from Kant's increasing conviction that analysis must precede construction.

Since the analysis of a concept so important for exact science as the causal concept presented a problem which

Kant found himself unable to solve, it is no wonder that his general tone of mind towards the end of the fruitful year 1762-63, which produced no less than five important treatises, was distinctly sceptical. He appeals ironically to the rational philosophers whose numbers increase daily, and begs them to solve for him the simple question which had brought him to a halt. From this frame of mind sprang, a few years later, the "Dreams of a Ghost-seer." To no other period of Kant's life does the expression "awakening from dogmatic slumbers" apply so well as to this. He himself afterwards defined dogmatism as "the presumption that we may follow the time-honoured method of constructing a system of pure metaphysic out of principles that rest upon mere conceptions, *without first asking in what way reason has come into possession of them, and by what right it employs them*" ("Critique of Pure Reason," 2nd edition, p. xxxv.). This being Kant's definition of dogmatism, he could not possibly have meant that he was still wrapped in dogmatic slumbers when he wrote the treatise on negative quantity and the "Dreams." If so, he certainly has done himself an injustice. Some eminent students of Kant, however, think that the awakening from dogmatic slumbers ought not to be assigned to so early a date. I have opposed this view in the monograph already quoted, where, in attempting to give an exhaustive discussion of the question, I have shown the lack of unanimity amongst the commentators of Kant on this particular point in the continuity of his philosophical development.

The second period in Kant's development (1769-81), which closes with his chief work, is devoted to an inquiry into the possibility of a transition from analysis to construction. In the year 1769, which he himself has described as a turning-point, ideas suggested themselves to him which he developed in the following year in the Dissertation. A passage from one of Kant's notes tells us clearly in what this turning-point consisted : "*I found that many of the axioms which we have regarded as objective are, as a matter of fact, subjective : that is, they express the conditions under which alone we are able to apprehend or understand the object.*" He has himself compared the discovery here made with that of Copernicus. As it is due to our position on the earth that the heavenly bodies appear to move round us, so it is owing to the nature of

our senses that we perceive things in space and time.
What Newton called absolute space and absolute time are
only schemata or forms which we construct when we take
account of how we perceive things.   The laws of space
and time are the laws of our sensibility.   Hence everything
which experience shows us must be subject to these laws
(for otherwise they could not be perceived by the senses),
and we now understand how it is that applied mathematics
can lay down *a priori* laws of phenomena.   But since we
perceive everything according to the forms of our perceptive faculty, the senses can only show us phenomena,
not things in themselves (*noumena*).

In the Dissertation Kant only applies this Copernican
principle, *i.e.* that the knowledge of things is determined
by the nature and forms of activity of the knowing subject,
to sensuous perception.   As regards the understanding, he
is at present no less confident than he was in the "Only
Possible Ground" that, when sufficiently developed, it can
attain to a knowledge of things - in - themselves.   He does
not, however, enter upon any closer inquiry into the
nature of the understanding.   Nevertheless Kant was right
when he afterwards said that his definitive philosophy first
took shape in the Dissertation ; for in it the principle,
which we will call, for brevity's sake, the Copernican principle,
was established ; and this done, there only remained to make it
good in all spheres.   In and for itself, it was not astonishing
that Kant hesitated to admit the impossibility of any sort of
scientific knowledge of things-in-themselves.   The old opposition, which originated with Plato, between noumena and phenomena, the world as it is in itself and is known by thought
on the one hand, and the world as it presents itself to the
senses on the other, seemed now about to receive a fresh confirmation at his hands.   And the sharp distinction between
perception and understanding seemed also to show that their
spheres must be different.

It appears from Kant's letters, however, that, shortly after
the publication of the Dissertation, he became conscious of the
great difficulties involved in its conclusions.   How can concepts of the understanding, which we form by means of the
activity of our thought, be valid of things which are entirely
independent of us ?   Since these concepts (*e.g.* cause, substance,

possibility, reality, and necessity) are framed by us, they cannot
be mere products of the things ; and in any case, if they are
only the results of experience, they cannot serve to establish
axioms which claim to be valid apart from any foundation in
experience. As may be seen from his letters and notes, Kant's
method of handling this problem was to subject the fundamental
concepts or categories with which we operate in our attempts
to know the world to a strict examination, reducing them to
as small a number as possible ; while, at the same time, he
endeavoured to establish, beyond all question, how many there
are of them. The long time which elapsed between the Dissertation and the "Critique of Pure Reason" was occupied in
this attempt. He tried several combinations and classifications.
His attention was especially directed towards those concepts
which express relation. He became convinced that a relation
can be effected not only by comparison, but also by combination. Thus the concepts of substance, cause, and reciprocity
presuppose different combinations ; the combination of thing
and quality, of cause and effect, and of two causes. And when
it dawned upon him that we operate with concepts which
express our efforts to bind together phenomena in different
ways under different forms, he had gained a point of view from
which it became evident that, in spite of differences, rational
knowledge is nevertheless of like nature with sensuous perception. For when trying to show in the Dissertation that
space and time are forms of our perception, he had founded
his argument on the fact that they are those forms under which
our perceiving faculty *orders and combines* the given. They
are grounded in a "synthetising and ordering power" (*vis animi,
omnes sensationes secundum stabilem et naturae suae insitam
legem co-ordinans*) and are themselves *schemata co-ordinandi*
(Diss. § 15, D.E.) But now the understanding also proves to
be a faculty of uniting and combining ; by means of it we
seek to unite phenomena in certain reciprocal relations (*e.g.* as
cause and effect). Thus the *concept of synthesis*, which in the
Dissertation was only predicated of sensuous perception, is now
found to be predicable of the understanding also. And we
reach a conclusion here similar to that arrived at with regard
to space and time ; when, and only when, phenomena admit
of being united in the ways specified in our categories which
express the forms of our understanding, are we able to

understand. Synthetic unity is the condition of all understanding as well as of all sensuous perception. Hence we
are able by means of the categories to *anticipate* experience.
The Copernican principle has now been applied in all spheres ;
the impossibility of knowing noumena, things-in-themselves, is,
however, the unavoidable conclusion.

The connective principle which had been a stumbling-block
to Hume, seemed to Kant, on the contrary, to be the original
principle of all knowledge—from sensuous apprehension up to
the highest knowledge of the understanding. The applicability
of this principle determines the limit between what we can and
what we cannot understand. But Kant was not content to
have found, by means of an analysis of fundamental concepts,
the general forms or the general type of the activity of the
understanding. He wished to feel sure that *all* the fundamental
concepts had been discovered ; to establish *a priori* a complete
list of categories. This he thought could be accomplished if
the doctrine of judgments were taken as a basis. Every
judgment is a combination of concepts and is, in so far, a
synthesis (so, at least, he now conceives judgment ; in his
treatises of 1762 he had not advanced beyond the view that
the predicate of the judgment must always be discoverable by
means of an analysis of the subject). Hence he concludes
that there must be as many special forms of synthesis, or as
many categories, as there are forms of judgment. He had,
however, to modify the doctrine of judgments established by
the older logic before he could use it. He arranges judgments in four classes, each with three subspecies, and thus gets
twelve categories. Far more important than this attempt at
systematisation, both with regard to epistemology as well as to
psychology, is Kant's idea of synthesis in general as the fundamental form of the activity of consciousness. In this he had
found a concept which led him beyond the atomistic psychology
which underlay empiricism, and the spiritualistic psychology
from which, till now, most of the idealistic systems had started.
In opposition to empiricism, which attempts to explain the
unity of the mind as nothing more than the result of a manifold
of impressions, Kant maintains homogeneous activity to be
the fundamental characteristic of intellectual life, and asserts
that this life cannot be explained by external influences only ;
while, in opposition to spiritualistic psychology, which, it is true,

recognised this fundamental characteristic but dogmatically assigned it to a mystical substance lying behind consciousness, he maintained that our knowledge cannot lead us farther back than the fundamental form and the fundamental law of intellectual life as it appears in experience. At the same time he takes us beyond the psychology of the Enlightenment, which restricted itself to that which is clearly conscious and comprehensible by the understanding. Synthesis is the invariable presupposition of consciousness, but need not itself appear as the object of consciousness. It may work blindly and instinctively, as a hidden art of our innermost nature. Kant's theory of knowledge was now framed, and he proceeded to elaborate it. We will therefore pass on to the statement he has given of it in his chief work.

CHAPTER III

THEORY OF KNOWLEDGE. "CRITIQUE OF PURE REASON"

IN the ensuing sketch of the contents of this work I have not followed the arrangement of the work itself, but have adopted an order in which the main lines of the course of thought out of which it arose are more clearly discernible. By this means a natural system takes the place of the more artificial one followed by Kant.

(a) Subjective Deduction (Psychological Analysis)

Critical philosophy is distinguished from dogmatic by the fact that it examines the faculty of knowledge itself, and, by the light of this inquiry, decides which are the problems this faculty is able to solve, and which are those which lie beyond its reach. But the faculty of knowledge is only known to us through its activity in experience. We must investigate experience, therefore, when we shall discover that it is a complex, composed of elements some of which are due to the faculty of knowledge itself, while others are the result of the way in which this faculty is determined to activity from without. That which is given by the faculty itself, Kant calls *form*, while that which is produced by external influences he calls *matter*. Kant has nowhere systematised the analysis of experience on which he bases this distinction between form and matter which runs through the whole of his theory of knowledge. On a deeper study of the Dissertation and of the "Critique of Pure Reason," however, we find (as shown in detail in my monograph on "The Continuity of Kant's Philosophical Development," *Archiv für Geschichte des Philosophie*, vol. vii. pp. 389-392) that the forms may be discovered by a consideration of the constant and universal element in our knowledge, while the matter is that which may change and vary. Space and time are forms of our perception ; for whatever the nature of sensations, and however much they may change, the spatial and temporal relations in which their content is presented to us remain the same ; a space or a time does not change, whatever be its filling out. When I have abstracted from all sense-qualities something still remains, *i.e.* extension and succession. Further, whatever the given phenomena, we only understand them when we are able to bind them together in certain relations,—principally those which are expressed in the concepts of quantity and cause. By means of a judgment, a combining activity, we say that one phenomenon is greater or smaller than another, or is cause or effect with reference to another. The same form of synthesis (quantity or causality) may be employed however widely the content differs. Common to all these forms, as we saw above, is the fact that they express a synthesis.

Kant, however, is not content with merely showing that our knowledge operates with forms ; he must also determine the number and kind of these forms. He thinks that as we are here dealing with that which lies nearest of all to us, *i.e.* with our own knowledge, we must be able to attain to a perfect and sure understanding of all its forms. But this is obviously a dogmatic assumption. For the analytic method employed by Kant cannot guarantee completeness ; we can never be perfectly certain that all the forms have been discovered. Neither can we feel sure that the forms we have discovered are the most fundamental. The forms are the constant element in experience, and from this constancy Kant argues that it must be the faculty of knowledge which is active. But this is, and will always remain, nothing more than an hypothesis. In the preface to the first edition of the "Critique of Pure Reason," Kant remarks that " the subjective deduction " (*i.e.* the establishing of the forms of knowledge by means of analysis) may seem to be an hypothesis, since its aim is to discover the cause of a given effect (namely, the constant in experience). He is of opinion, however, that this is not the case, and promises to prove it on some other occasion. This promise, however, he never fulfilled. His wish to arrive at a definitive result made a dogmatist of him here. He was not in a position to adopt the only possible way of escape, *i.e.*

to employ the foundation discovered by means of analysis merely as we employ an hypothesis, leaving it to future investigation to discover one which shall be still better. Kant was under the delusion that a " critique of reason " might be undertaken once and for all, and did not see that every attempt at a critical philosophy must start from assumptions that are to a certain extent dogmatic, and the examination of which must be the task of future critiques of reason.

If we turn to Kant's system of forms we find it consists of three groups.

(*a*) *Forms of Perception.*—Space is the form of all perception within the sphere of outer experience, time the form of all perception within the sphere of inner experience. Space and time are forms of *perception* (not of *understanding*), for both in space and time the facts are comprehended within the totality, they form the totality ; moreover we can only represent to ourselves any constituent part of space and time as within the whole of space or the whole of time, and there is only a single space and a single time. Space and time are *forms* because every single experience pre-supposes them. They are the necessary presuppositions to which every experience must conform. As a combining and co-ordinating activity (which Kant calls *synopsis*, combination) the perception of space and time has an active character in comparison with pure sensation, which gives us particular qualities. Kant, however, compares it more particularly with the higher grade of activity displayed in the activity of the understanding, and, in comparison with this, he designates it receptivity. It cannot give real knowledge.

(*β*) *Forms of the Understanding.*—Perception without conception is blind (as conception without perception is empty). In perception a manifold is directly united to a totality. Knowledge only arises when this combination is consciously performed, with an express turning of the attention towards it, so that this act of attention (Kant calls it *apperception*) is the form or unity common to the whole content. The unity of consciousness and its identity with itself are the necessary conditions for the combining of a given content. In order, for example, to cognise a line I must draw it, *i.e.* combine its individual parts in a definite manner by means of an intellectual activity which apprehends the single facts one after another, not forgetting the preceding when passing on to the following, and finally collecting them all into a totality. The unity of this operation is the unity of consciousness, and this it is which constitutes the line an object. Where I perceive the freezing of water, I apprehend two states (fluidity and solidity) in a temporal relation, such indeed that the former is at the same time the condition for the occurrence of the latter. It is only by the application of the causal conception that I apprehend the transition from fluidity to solidity as an objective event. Kant traces syntheses such as the one here exemplified back to the faculty of imagination, which forms the connecting link between perception and understanding. When we have become conscious of the forms according to which the imagination works, we have found the categories, *i.e.* the different species of synthesis, within the sphere of the understanding.

As already mentioned, in establishing his system of categories Kant starts from his fourfold division of judgments. Corresponding to these he finds four groups of categories, to which again four groups of fundamental axioms correspond. The causal concept, for instance, corresponds to hypothetical judgments, for to say that a causal relation exists between two phenomena means that they are related to each other as the conditioning to the conditioned judgment ; *if* the one is given, the other follows of necessity. And the causal axiom asserts that a similar relation exists between every phenomenon and a certain other definite phenomenon.

The twelve categories, which we need not here enumerate, are arranged by Kant in two classes, *i.e.* the mathematical and the dynamical categories. The concepts of quantity and cause, in fact, include all the categories, and are the two leading forms of the synthesis in which all knowledge consists. Such a reduction is all the more necessary since the sharp distinction between the different classes of logical judgments [7] drawn by Kant is altogether untenable, so that, in any case, the doctrine of judgments certainly does not suffice to supply a system of different categories.

(γ) *Ideas of Reason.*—By reason in the wider sense Kant understands the whole of our faculty of knowledge. By *reason in the narrower sense* he understands our faculty of knowledge in its tendency to perform *unconditioned* syntheses. While perception fashions the chaos of sensations into spatial and temporal sense-images, and while the understanding arranges these sense-images in the interconnection given by the concepts of quantity and causality, it is the task of reason, in the narrower sense of the word, to close the series of terms, *i.e.* to form absolute totalities. Reason, that is to say, demands an absolute beginning and absolute limits to space and time, absolute maxima and minima, and an absolute conclusion in a first cause [8] to the causal series. This is the continuation and consummation of the co-ordinating and combining activity which is already exercised in perception and understanding. It is synthesis in its highest form. Concepts which designate an absolute conclusion of this kind are called by Kant *Ideen* (Ideas) while, in the literature of the seventeenth and eighteenth centuries the word *Idee* had gradually become synonymous with *Vorstellung* (presentation). Kant reverts to Plato's use of the word, according to which *Idee* denotes an object of thought which cannot, on account of its absolute character, occur in experience. " Plato perceived very well," he says, " that our reason naturally raises itself to cognitions far too elevated to admit of the possibility of an object given by experience corresponding to them."

As with the forms of perception and the categories, so too, here, Kant tries to show that there are a certain definite number of Ideas. There are, in his opinion, three such Ideas : the Idea of the soul, the Idea of the world, the Idea of God. We seek, that is to say, for a definitive knowledge of inner experience, a definitive knowledge of outer experience, and a definitive knowledge of the origin of all things in existence. Kant attempts to prove that these Ideas are not invented, but proceed from the very nature of reason itself, by showing that they correspond to the three forms of conclusion which are ordinarily distinguished in logic (the categorical, the hypothetical, and the disjunctive forms). But this deduction is very strained, far more so, indeed, than the deduction of the categories from the species of judgment.[9] It does not hold good, if only because, as Kant himself had formerly pointed out (in his treatise on "The false Subtilty of the Four Syllogistic Figures ") the conclusion requires no function of thought other than that used in the judgment. Kant's unfortunate love of systematisation made his work clumsier than was necessary. But, as a matter of fact,

he is right in tracing the Ideas of the soul, the world, and God
to the involuntary craving of consciousness to reach a conclusion, to affix the chain of thought to a fixed and immovable
hook, to form an absolute synthesis in imitation of the
synthesis which is the fundamental form of thought.

By means of the analysis of our knowledge, as it develops
and displays its activity in experience, Kant believed himself to
have discovered all the forms of its activity. But to establish the forms is not to establish the justification of their
application. At first this validity is not called in question.
There is a natural disposition to attribute absolute reality to
the forms of perception as well as to the categories and to
the Ideas. Reason is active first, and tests afterwards. Her
first aim is to erect her structures as quickly as possible, and
not till after this has been accomplished does she begin to
inquire whether the foundation has been laid sufficiently
deeply and firmly. Reason's first step is dogmatic. When
she has learnt wisdom by painful experience, she becomes
sceptical. But the third step, which presupposes matured and
full-grown power of judgment, is the critical testing of the
capacities and scope of Reason. The *subjective* deduction,
consisting in psychological analysis, is only preparatory to this.
It shows what are the forms and laws which our knowledge
naturally follows. The next question—which it is the task
of the *objective* deduction to answer—is : Subject to what conditions and limits may these forms be employed?

As I have already mentioned in my general characterisation
of Kant, it must be reckoned as his greatest merit that he
pointed out a law which might be called *the law of the three
stages ;*—a law which is valid not only for the development of
knowledge, but also, under analogous forms, for the development
of intellectual life in general. Kant here adopted a point of view
destined to acquire great importance at the hands of subsequent
thinkers (Fichte, Hegel, St. Simon, Comte). It indicates that
development does not, after all, proceed along such a straight
line as it had been the fashion to believe during the age of the
Enlightenment.

(b) Objective Deduction

If space and time are the forms under which we perceive
everything, no phenomena can be given in experience which

are not spatial and temporal, and which do not obey the laws of space and time. It is this which gives to applied mathematics its validity ; although it rests on *pure* (i.e. *independent of experience*) *reason*, yet *it is valid for all possible experiences*, because it merely formulates what follows from the general laws of space and time. On the other hand, these laws are *only* valid of things as they are presented to us, of things as *phenomena*. Hence, we have no right to make the conditions of our perception conditions of the essence and nature of the things themselves ; neither are we justified in regarding our forms of perception as the only possible ones. We can only speak of space and time from the standpoint of human beings. Mathematical laws are laws of pure reason, and are valid of all experience possible for men—and our knowledge is restricted to such experience and to the phenomena which can occur in it.

The same holds good of the categories;—since they are the forms of our understanding, everything which we are able to understand must be subject to them, must fulfil the conditions they impose. It is not enough to constitute experience that a something should be perceived (spatially or temporally or both at once), but the different perceived phenomena must be combined in a definite way. Strictly speaking, experience demands not only applied mathematics, but also applied logic. All phenomena, if we are to understand them, must be comprehended within the concepts of quantity and cause. The concept of quantity excludes any hiatus or leap (*non datur hiatus, non datur saltus*) ; every increase or decrease of extension or degree must be continuous. The concept of causality excludes chance and absolute necessity (*non datur casus, non datur fatum*) ; if the causal axiom is valid, every phenomenon must be conditioned by another phenomenon, this latter, again, by a third, and so on. All the different fundamental axioms corresponding to the categories, as Kant has indicated in one single passage [10] (unfortunately without developing this thought at length), may be traced back to a single fundamental axiom, *i.e.* the *axiom of continuity*. The causal axiom is only one form of this general principle which demands continuous interconnection. That the fulfilment of this demand is a condition of experience Kant shows as follows : if there is to be any difference between *experience* and imagination, there must be required for the constituting of experience a definite order of sequence of phenomena according to law, so that I cannot transpose the numbers of the series at will (as in my imaginings, dreams, and fancies), nor can there be any breach of continuity (while in the world of dreams I can take as wide leaps as are anyhow possible). The law of continuity (which includes within it both the law of continuity of space and degree and the law of the causal relations of all phenomena) is valid for all phenomena, because it formulates the general conditions under which we can have real experience (as distinguished from imagination). We formulate the possibility of experience in principles which are then valid *a priori* of all possible experience. While Wolff vainly sought to deduce the axiom of causality from the principle of contradiction, *i.e.* to give it a purely logical proof, Kant here attempts to give an epistemological (or as he calls it, using a barbarous scholasticism, *transcendental*) proof of the same, basing its validity on the fact that it is a necessary condition of experience. But here, as with space and time, confirmation is accompanied by limitation. *Only* as the condition of experience has the law of continuity (including the causal law) validity ; just as geometry would be mere subjective imagining were space not a condition of all outer experience, so the causal law and the law of continuity in general would be purely subjective maxims if they did not state the condition of real experience. Experience is, as Kant expresses it, an empirical synthesis, which invests all other syntheses with reality. We know phenomena only ; not things as they are in themselves but only as they are apprehended by means of the forms of our understanding, which (like the forms of perception) have significance from the human standpoint only.

No objective deduction (no " transcendental " proof) of the Ideas is possible. For since they refer to an unconditioned, while everything in experience is conditioned and limited, we here lack that foundation for demonstration which was afforded by the possibility of experience in the case of the forms of perception and the categories. The Ideas have their subjective origin in the need of Reason for unity, but no object given in experience can correspond with them. Experience cannot exhibit an absolute totality such as, under different forms, the Ideas of reason require. With space, time, the series of degrees and of conditions, we can always proceed farther — but whether an absolute conclusion is possible, can never be shown. On the Ideas, therefore—unlike the forms of perception and the categories—no science can be based.

It is doubtful whether the distinction between the three classes of forms is as sharp as Kant thought. For continuity, causality, time and space—as conceived by Kant—possess an ideal perfection to which there is no corresponding experience. Continuity is an idea to which experience only gives us approximations. What Kant calls forms are, as a matter of fact, abstractions and ideals which, in accordance with the nature of our knowledge, we set up and use as measures and rules for our inquiries. The fundamental axioms, therefore, are hypotheses, not demonstrated truths. Experience in the strict sense of the word, as Kant conceives it in his " transcendental " proof, is itself an ideal and it was the existence of experience in the sense in which Kant used the word that Hume, whose objections against the causal axiom Kant attempted to refute, denied. Kant, therefore, has not solved Hume's problem (which is indeed insoluble) ; but he has the merit of having brought out a side of the problem, or rather a side of our knowledge, which was neglected by Hume ; and by so doing, he has advanced the theory of knowledge very considerably. His enthusiasm for his " Copernican principle " led him to attribute greater demonstrative power to his line of thought than it really possessed. Instead of being content with the significance of forms as types, patterns, and anticipations, he attempted to provide a necessary proof of their applicability to reality—and in this he did not succeed. (Cf. for further details on this point " The Continuity of Kant's Philosophical Development," *loc. cit.* pp. 396-399.)

(c) *Phenomena and Things-in-Themselves*

The result to which Kant's examination of pure reason brought him was, that though our thought commands forms and principles which do not originate in experience, yet these forms and principles can find no valid application beyond the sphere of experience. Their origin is not empirical, but only an empirical use can be made of them. And since we only have experience by means of the application of our forms of

perception and categories, everything that we know is phenomenon only, not thing-in-itself.   But there arises the question :
What is this "thing-in-itself," this "noumenon," this "intelligible," this "transcendental object" (the thing-in-itself is called
all these different names by Kant)?—and, above all, by what
right do we assume the existence of any such thing?

In discussing this question, however, we must observe that
the problem of the thing-in-itself, which occupied such a
prominent place in the earliest discussion of Kant's philosophy,
was not the problem with which Kant himself was chiefly
occupied.   His task was to discover what faculties we possess
besides mere perception for the acquirement of knowledge.
And he found that it follows from the conditions of this
knowledge that it can only deal with phenomena.   His problem
was concerned with the relation of reason to experience—not
with the first origin of the content of knowledge.   But yet it
was natural that this latter problem and the consequences
following from it which seemed inevitable, according to Kant's
philosophy, should attract special attention.

To the question *what* the thing-in-itself is, Kant answers
that he does not know and does not need to know, since it is
never to be found in experience ; all objects of experience are
phenomena.   We do not even know whether the thing-in-
itself is within or without us.   The concept of the noumenon
or thing-in-itself is only a limiting concept, a purely negative
concept to which we are brought by means of the investigation
of the conditions—which are also the limits—of our knowledge.   Shining through the Kantian phraseology, however,
in several passages, we can detect an inclination to conceive
the unknowable under idealistic form, not unlike, perhaps,
Leibniz's world of monads (in connection with which it is
interesting to notice that Leibniz himself sometimes called the
world of monads the intelligible world, in contradistinction to
the sensible world).   Kant, it is true, emphatically denied that
there was any scientific justification for Leibniz' use of
analogy in the construction of his metaphysical idealism ;
nevertheless, in the background of his consciousness this
conception seems to have asserted itself.[11]   And, as we shall
see presently, he practically justifies analogy when he tries to
prove that faith is possible where knowledge is impossible.
It is only so long as he is speaking from a purely theoretical

standpoint that he declares the thing-in-itself to be an entirely negative concept.

Kant never questioned the *existence* of the thing-in-itself. In accordance with the ordinary view, he assumes an absolute reality, and his critique is only concerned with the establishment and limitation of the knowledge which we can have of it. In the course of his inquiry, however, he goes so far (although never more than incidentally) as to *assign grounds for the assumption* that something other and something more than phenomena exists. Kant gives three such grounds. Firstly, it would be an improbable and unauthorised assumption to suppose that our mode of knowledge (in space and time and according to the categories of the understanding) is the only possible one. By so doing we should commit the same mistake—this must be Kant's meaning here—as was committed before Copernicus, when the standpoint of the earth was regarded as the absolute standpoint. The concept of the thing-in-itself, that is to say, denotes that all our knowledge is conditioned by our nature— that this nature of ours is a co-operating element in respect of the way in which the objects of experience present themselves to us. Secondly, knowledge has its ground in our nature in respect of form only ; the matter, the content is given to us (in sensations), and our attitude towards it is receptive. Nevertheless this content must have some cause! In answer to one of his critics, Kant says : " Objects, as things in themselves, *give* the matter of empirical perceptions ; they contain the ground for determining the faculty of imagination, according to its sensibility." [12]   Kant finds the third ground, as we shall see later, in the contradictions in which reason becomes involved when it oversteps the limits of experience ; contradictions which, in his opinion, can only be solved by means of the distinction between phenomena and things-in-themselves.

The difficulty which Kant's earliest critics found in his assumption of a thing-in-itself is connected with the second ground. The first and third were not discussed. In a work entitled, *David Hume über den Glauben, oder Idealismus und Realismus* (" David Hume on Belief; or, Idealism and Realism ") (1787) Jacobi attempted to show that Kant ought in consistency to deny all existence beyond that of our ideas, and must hence only embrace a pure idealism (subjectivism). The assumption of a thing-in-itself as the cause of our sensations is contradictory to Kant's doctrine of the causal concept as the expression of a form of understanding the application of which is only valid *within* the domain of experience. A similar objection was raised some years later by G. E. SCHULZE, in his anonymous book *Aenesidemus* (1792). From Kant's standpoint,[13] this objection admits of no answer. It is based on Kant's own pregnant and fundamental thought, viz., that the limitation and confirmation of our knowledge are closely connected with one another.

Kant would have been consistent had he merely asserted that the matter of knowledge cannot be deduced from its form, nor the varying and special elements from the fixed general scheme. Experience is no longer possible when all sensations cease. But how sensations arise is a question which it is not for the critical philosophy (the theory of knowledge) to discuss. Hume had a clear understanding of this when he pronounced (Treatise, I. 3, 5) the first origin of sensation to be incomprehensible, adding : " Nor is such a question anyway material to our present purpose." Kant's position with regard to this question was identical with Hume's.

A closer scrutiny will show us (see *Kontinuität im philosophischen Entwickelungsgange Kant's*, pp. 399-402) that Kant regarded the thing-in-itself not merely as the cause of the matter of knowledge, but also as the cause of the definite forms under which we apprehend and arrange this matter. But if this is so, it is clear that the question of origin arises with respect to the form as much as with respect to the matter. With regard to our perception of space especially we find in Kant many intimations that the ground why we apprehend things in this particular way (in three dimensions, etc.) must reside in things-in-themselves.[14] Indeed he attributes "the whole connection and extent " of our perceptions in general to the transcendental object (" Critique of Pure Reason," 1st ed. p. 494). Thus not only the matter of knowledge, but also its forms are a product of the thing-in-itself. And since the forms can only hold good so long as the thing-in-itself is unchangeable in its mode of working, it is clear that the knowledge which we can construct on the basis of forms alone can never be more than hypothetical—while, on the other hand, it is more than phenomenal ; since it teaches us how the thing - in - itself operates. Directly this point is brought out clearly and all its conse-

quences unfolded Kant's whole system undergoes a change.
The a priorism as well as the phenomenalism becomes limited,
and the inconsistency vanishes.   For all these three sides of the
Kantian philosophy depend on his absolute distinction between
matter and form ; a distinction open to many objections, too, on
purely pyschological grounds.

Even, however, when the thing-in-itself is regarded as the
cause of the form as well as of the matter of our knowledge,
there is very little that we can know about it—absolutely
nothing definite, says Kant (*Prolegomena,* §§ 32 and 57).   It
remains a great X, which admits of no scientific determination.
And yet this determination is attempted by all religions and
all speculative systems.   Kant has here the great merit of
having *defined the philosophical place of religious and metaphysical
speculation.*   The struggle between positive and natural religion,
between spiritualism and materialism, between monism and
pluralism turns on this X.   The boundary-line between science
and speculation had never before been so clearly marked
out.

(d) Critique of Speculative Philosophy

With respect to the Ideas of Reason an objective deduction
has proved impossible.   And yet attempts have been made to
use the Ideas of the soul, the world, and God as the foundation
of sciences which soar far beyond experience.   Kant found the
result to which he had been led by his general inquiry into
the epistemological value of the Ideas confirmed by a special
critique of these so-called sciences, *i.e.* speculative psychology,
speculative cosmology, and speculative theology :—

a. Critique of Speculative Psychology

The belief that it is possible to establish a doctrine of the
soul as a being existing apart from the body rests on a false
inference.   From the unity which is the general form of the
activity of consciousness the existence of a non-composite
substance behind consciousness is inferred.   From synthesis
we infer substance.   But we have no justification for so doing.
The form of activity alone tells us nothing as to the nature of
the underlying essence.   Consciousness is not simple, not a

particular presentation, but a form common to all presentations. Psychology is a purely empirical science which can teach us nothing about a being or about qualities (*e.g.* unity) which are not themselves given in experience.   There is, therefore, no justification (as Kant shows more particularly in the first edition of the "Critique of Pure Reason") for regarding the distinction between physical and mental phenomena as a distinction between two kinds of substance or essence.   This would be to confound a distinction in our mode of apprehension with a distinction between things.   That which underlies outer phenomena may be the same as that which underlies inner phenomena.   If this were so there would be an end to dualism and also to all the difficulties which have arisen concerning the reciprocal action between soul and body.[15]

β. *Critique of Speculative Cosmology*

The concept of the world or nature as a totality presupposes that the concepts of quantity and causality extend beyond experience, since the latter never shows us anything more than limited parts of space and time and incomplete causal series. This gives rise to a series of contradictions (antinomies), since mutually contradictory propositions can be proved correct, a sign that we have ventured beyond the limits of our knowledge!   Kant gives four such antinomies (corresponding to the four classes of categories and of logical judgments).   They may, however, be reduced to three, of which the first two involve the concept of quantity, applied to space, time, and matter, whilst the third involves the concept of cause.

1. *Thesis.*—The world must have a beginning in time and be enclosed within limits of space, for an infinite series cannot be thought as given.   *Antithesis.*— The world can have no beginning and no limits, for otherwise, antecedent to its beginning, there must have been an empty time, and an empty space outside it, in which case neither beginning nor limits would be conceivable, since in empty time and empty space there can be no distinction between different points in time or places in space.

2. *Thesis.*—Division of matter must lead finally to that which is absolutely simple and indivisible (to atoms or monads). *Anthithesis.*—Everything which we can perceive or imagine is

divisible, and the absolutely simple and indivisible is an idea which can never be confirmed by experience.

3. *Thesis.*—If we go back from effect to cause we must at last arrive at a cause which is not, in turn, an effect ; for otherwise we should not have found the complete cause of a thing. Hence there must have been an absolute cause antecedent to all events in the world, and perhaps also, in the course of the world, other absolute causes (*i.e.* beings with "free" wills). *Antithesis.*— An absolute first cause is inconceivable, since it would be bound by no law to its effect. Yet there must be something which determines the absolute cause to begin to work precisely at this definite moment !

All three questions leave us, according to Kant, with problematical judgments. There is a misfit between our ideas and experience. Are the former too large for the latter, or is the latter too small for the former ? We cannot blame experience, for it is precisely the possibility of experience which enables us to draw the line between category and idea. The blame must therefore rest with the Ideas, or rather perhaps with the way in which we apply them. According to Kant two different interests are represented in the theses and antitheses respectively. The theses, he thinks, express the speculative standpoint of dogmatism while, at the same time, they satisfy the practical interest, which demands a close to the sequences of thought,—and this is also in accordance with the popular view ; the antitheses, on the other hand, appeal to empiricism and the strictly scientific interest, but involve consequences which imperil the practical interest.

Kant does not regard the first two antinomies in the same light as the third. In the former, he thinks, both theses and antitheses are false : the world is neither finite nor infinite, matter neither absolutely divisible nor absolutely indivisible ! The problems cease to exist when we distinguish between our mode of apperception and the thing-in-itself. Our apperception is a successive synthesis, which proceeds from member to member; here continual progression is possible and a conclusion impossible; every limit may be overstepped by thought. But we must not transfer that which is valid for our conception—which is always setting itself fresh tasks—to things-in-themselves. The only significance for us of the Idea of the world as a totality is that it leads our inquiry further and further, preventing us from coming to an over - hasty conclusion. It is not difficult to see that although Kant believes himself to reject the antitheses as well as the theses, he really justifies the antitheses ; as we saw, he explains them as having arisen out of the strictly scientific interest. For the antitheses assert infinity in the sense of a process continued *ad infinitum*,— not a given, completed infinity, which is self-contradictory.[16] As regards the third antinomy, Kant is of opinion that both the thesis as well as the antithesis may be right, the former of the thing-in-itself, the latter of phenomena. In experience the causal series is always, without exception, continuous ; if a phenomenon were not subject to the law of causality, it would be indistinguishable from an illusion ! But this continuous conditionedness does not hold good of the thing-in-itself. Man, as an empirical being, is, in accordance with his phenomenal or empirical character, subject to the law of causality ; but as thing-in-itself, as *homo noumenon*, in accordance with his intelligible character, he must be regarded as free. The intelligible character does not appear as a phenomenon but must be regarded as the cause of the whole series of actions in which the empirical character unfolds itself. Kant does not mean by this to assert the reality of the free will, but only to show that, if we are led to believe in the freedom of the will on practical grounds, such a belief would be compatible with the conformity to law of the empirical character. He did not succeed in proving this, however. For how can the intelligible character be the cause of the empirical, if the temporal relation is not applicable to it ? And if the empirical character is regarded as an effect of the intelligible a purely empirical (phenomenal) explanation of the origin of the former is excluded. Lastly, the intelligible character itself is not " freely " chosen ; hence Kant's remarkable doctrine is not a doctrine of freedom but of fatalism : the intelligible character is unchangeable—and it is this which determines the whole series of human actions !

γ. *Critique of Speculative Theology*

Kant regards the Idea of God as an expression of the need of Reason to come to a perfect close. Such a close would be attained if thought could assign grounds for the assumption of a self-necessary Being, the author of everything which possesses reality. This Idea therefore expresses an ideal of knowledge ; in proof that it lies in the nature of human reason to entertain such an ideal Kant quotes the facts that science is ever striving to reduce all the forces of nature to one single original force, and that a tendency to monotheism continually displays itself in national religions. This ideal of knowledge has great significance. But whether we are justified in erecting it into an objective being (*i.e.* hypostatising and realising it), still more in making it a personal being (*i.e.* personifying it), is quite another question.

1. The proper proof of the existence of God, the validity of which is presupposed by all other attempted proofs, would be the *ontological*, which deduces the existence of God from the concept which we are able to form of Him. But this proof could only lead thought to a perfect close, if it led to a concept the object of which must exist whenever it is thought. We should thus at last reach the thought of something which has its ground in itself. Such a proof, however, according to Kant, is not forthcoming. From the concept of a thing we can never infer its existence. The concept may be quite precise and complete, but the question still remains whether the object thought of under such a concept exists. For existence is not a quality like other qualities ; existence only means that the thing, as we think it according to its concept (with all its qualities), at this moment also really exists. The assumption of existence means the positing of that which was thought under the concept, and adds no new content. A hundred real thalers contain no more, as regards the concept, than a hundred possible ones. There is, therefore, not the smallest contradiction in thinking something under its complete concept, and at the same time thinking its non-existence. We convince ourselves that a thing exists by the fact that it has a place in the connected whole of our experience—that between it and other things a connection according to law exists. But we can adduce no other proof of existence except this empirical interconnection. For the fact that a concept contains no contradiction is not sufficient to warrant us in attributing existence to its object.

2. While the ontological proof starts from thought and attempts to reach existence from it without the assistance

of experience, the other proofs proceed from experience. The *cosmological* proof argues from the fact that something exists (*e.g.* I myself) to an absolutely necessary cause of this something. This proof extends the causal axiom beyond all possible experience, and at the same time places the conclusion of the causal series in an absolutely necessary Being, a Being that has its ground in itself. The causal axiom, in and for itself, only leads on from member to member in an uninterrupted continual relation of conditionedness ; in assuming an absolutely necessary Being the cosmological proof presupposes the validity of the ontological proof, for it presupposes the existence of a Being having its ground in itself, *i.e.* the existence of which can be inferred from its concept. But such a close is impossible for us ; however exalted our conception of the Deity may be, we cannot forbear to ask from whence it came. Human reason, thinks Kant, here finds itself arrested by an impassable chasm—a chasm which we can only by an illusion conceive as filled up.

3. While the cosmological proof starts from the general experience that something exists, the *physico-theological* proof starts from the order and purposiveness exhibited in Nature. But how do we know, asks Kant, that this order and purposiveness is accidental ? that it is not an effect of those very laws of Nature according to which the elements and forces work (cf. Kant's critique of the physico-theological argument which occurs in his early writings) ? And even apart from this, the proof only leads us to the assumption of an overseer or architect who has his matter given to him—not of a creator. If we are to arrive at the assumption of an absolute Being, we must employ the cosmological and the ontological arguments, and these have already been criticised.

Thus we see that neither by way of pure thought nor of experience can a proof of the existence of an absolute Being be adduced, and the result already arrived at, *i.e.* that the Ideas cannot form the basis of any scientific knowledge, has received its confirmation in the case of all three respectively. But this fact does not rob them of their significance. Just as they have their origin in the structure of our minds itself, so too they serve as ideals and principles for our inquiries, even though they cannot themselves be applied to the knowledge of real existence. The Idea of an absolute totality impels us to seek for ever greater unity and ever-increasing interconnection in our knowledge ; it keeps us also from pausing too soon. The thought that everything in the world stands in reciprocal inter-connection according to law, *as though* it had sprung out of a ground of unity, becomes a guiding principle. Analogous to this is the significance of the Ideas of the soul and of the world for our inquiries within the spheres of inner and outer experience respectively. The Ideas have regulative, but not constitutive, significance. They guide and regulate our progress within the sphere of experience—when they pass beyond (transcend) this, however, they lose their signifi-cance, just as do the categories. There may, in Kant's opinion, be a "transcendental" knowledge ; it consists in the knowledge of those presuppositions and principles on which our empirical knowledge is based; but a "transcendent" knowledge, *i.e.* a knowledge which passes beyond the sphere of experience there cannot be (nevertheless Kant sometimes uses the word "transcendental" in the same sense as "trans-cendent"). But if, remarks Kant, we attain to the conviction of the existence of God by another way than that of scientific knowledge, then the idea of an absolute Being becomes of very great importance, since it assists us to keep our thought of a Deity free from all sensuous and anthro-pomorphic ideas.

The result of the whole critique of speculative philosophy, then, is that it seeks to erect a tower which shall reach to the heavens, while the material at its command proves only sufficient for the building of a house. High towers and the metaphysical high-flyers which resemble them, says Kant, about whom there is, generally speaking, a great deal of wind, are not for me : my place is in the fertile valley of experience !

Kant's speculative successors, like Henrik Ibsen's builder Solness, thought it altogether beneath them to build houses for men to live in ; so, like him, they betook themselves to building castles in the air. Kant thought it no ignoble task to labour in the "fertile bathos (valley) of experience" as long as he had a wide horizon stretching before him. It is this which is expressed by his doctrine of Ideas, with its accentuation of the view that the highest life is a never-ending striving,—that one stone is content to fit in with another even though it knows that heaven will always be in the far distance.

Kant's doctrine of the fundamental form, of the mode of activity, and of the limits of the human spirit supplied Lessing's conception of eternal striving as the true duty of man with a firm and deep foundation. But this thought had more than a merely theoretical significance for Kant. It is not till we come to the practical sphere, as our examination of Kant's ethic will show us, that it acquires its complete and proper significance.

(e) Natural Philosophy

If we take a survey of Kant's theory of knowledge we notice that, in the form under which it appears in the "Critique of Pure Reason," it has acquired a more constructive character, or, in other words, a more rationalistic stamp than it possessed during the years in which the awakening probably took place, when it was predominantly analytical and empirical. Kant now believed himself able to bring forward an *a priori* proof of the fundamental principles which condition experience. As already mentioned, he was not successful in this attempt. But he felt so sure of his position relatively to this point that, not content with supplying a deductive proof for the causal axiom, he also attempted to bring forward a similar proof in support of the assumption of certain original forces and laws of Nature. In his *Metaphysischen Anfangsgründen der Naturwissenschaft* ("Metaphysical Basis of Physics") (1786) he first defines matter as the movable in space, and then tries to show that its essence consists of an interplay between a repulsive and an attractive force. By means of the repulsive force space is filled ; it is therefore the first condition for the existence of matter ; but if it alone were in operation *matter would be dispersed over infinite space*. There must therefore be an opposing force which prevents repulsion going on *ad infinitum*, and causes the parts of matter to collect together ; but if this attractive force alone were in operation *all matter would be collected together at a single point*. Thus both forces belong to the essence of matter. Kant here takes a step on which Newton never ventured,—he pronounces attraction to be an original force. And since he believed himself able to explain the essence and nature of matter (the movable, that which we perceive in space) as the result of the interaction of these two original forces he rejects atomism, which he had supported thirty years before in his *Monadologia Physica*. His attempt to deduce matter from forces and his application of the constructive method in natural philosophy prepared the way for the speculative natural philosophy of the romantic movement. He gradually became more and more estranged from the scientific mode of conception which had played such an important part in his philosophical development. Nevertheless Kant himself—in spite of his dynamic constructions—held fast to the strictly scientific mode of explanation for all material phenomena. From the conception of matter as the movable in space he infers that all causes of material change must be external and must be sought for in space, outside the point which changes its state of motion. With this principle physics stand or fall. " Hylozoism " (*i.e.* the assumption that material points have inner forces or an inner life) in any form would be the deathblow of physics. The same objection may be brought against this deduction of the law of persistence as has already been urged with regard to Kant's proof of the causal axiom, viz., that to establish an idea as a regulative ideal for our inquiries is not to prove an objectively valid law. The zeal with which Kant emphasises the law of persistency, however, shows that he has no intention of relaxing the stringency of his demand for a scientific explanation of natural phenomena.

The work with which Kant occupied himself during the last years of his life was intended to form a transition, by means of the constructive method, from the general principles established in the " Metaphysical Basis of Physics " to physics itself. This was an impossible task, and it was more than the senile decay of the thinker which prevented its execution. But the attempt shows how strong the constructive and rationalistic tendency had gradually become in him.

CHAPTER IV

ETHICS (" CRITIQUE OF PRACTICAL REASON ")

KANT'S system of ethics is most widely known under the form it finally assumed—in which form not only did it make a deep impression on his contemporaries, but subsequent thinkers have regarded it as the expression of a typical ethical standpoint. The special characteristics, which are also the merits of the Kantian system, are, firstly, that it finds the law for man's right action in man's own innermost nature, and regards this law as peculiar to man, in whom it finds its practical realisation when once he is able to probe the depths of his own nature and to clearly understand himself. Secondly, that it emancipates ethics from empty theory, from metaphysics, from theology, assigning to it an independent foundation in the practical side of man's nature. And thirdly, that although the moral law is to be found in man's own nature, yet it is austere and grave in character, points beyond the individual limitations of man, causes him to regard himself as a citizen of a great kingdom, and asserts the pre-eminence of duty over every selfish consideration, every sensuous inclination, and every immediate desire after happiness. Kant makes front against theology—for he maintains the independence of ethics over against religion ; against the rational enlightenment—for he declares the practical nature, the will, to be the innermost essence of man ; and against the idylls of the current hedonistic doctrine,—for he sounds the trumpet call of unconditional duties and claims. His ethical thought moves in an atmosphere of lofty freedom.

Before we pass on to expound this system in detail we must supplement the description of the course of Kant's development already given by an examination of the way in which his ethical system originated.

As already indicated in the sketch of his life, very many
elements co-operated thereto. Kant's pietistic upbringing left
its mark in the deep earnestness of his ethics. This was
remarked by his contemporaries. Schiller wrote to Goethe
(December 22, 1795): "There is always something about
Kant, as about Luther, which reminds one of a monk, who has
indeed quitted his cloister, but who can never quite rid himself
of its traces." But too great weight has often been laid on
this point (*e.g.* by Schopenhauer). When we discover how
Kant's development actually proceeded, we shall see that the
matter was by no means so simple. These after-effects of his
childhood are modified in a hundred ways by the operation
of other elements, while, on the other hand, certain sides
of Kant's nature tended to set him in opposition to ethical
rigorism. Previous to the definite taking shape of his system,
we can distinguish two distinct stages in his development as an
ethical thinker (see for a more detailed exposition of this point
my treatise on "The Continuity of Kant's Philosophical Development," chap. iii.).

(*a*) *First Stage* (1762-66)

Rousseau's influence was very marked. It probably operated contemporaneously with that of Hume, *i.e.* in the fertile
year 1762-63. The dogmatists attempted to order everything
in the ethical, as in the theoretical sphere, according to their
"eternal truths." Rousseau, on the contrary, demanded a study
of human nature, and this is only possible where this nature is
allowed to develop itself freely ; hence all theorising and
regulating have a merely indirect and negative significance.
Imaginary needs, spiritual as well as material, must be
cast aside. Not in any mere clearness of the understanding,
but, first and foremost, in feeling, in the fervour and depth of
the heart, consists the true dignity of man. Rousseau taught
Kant a new valuation of man. Formerly—as he has himself
told us—he, in common with his age, had regarded enlightenment as the highest good, and had despised the ignorant
masses ; Rousseau taught him *to honour man* (as such). Kant
owes to Rousseau's influence the idea of the dignity of man
as a personal being,—an idea which Kant never abandoned at
any subsequent stage of his development, and which witnesses

to its continuity. But the study of the English moral philosophers (Shaftesbury, Hutcheson, Hume) was also influencing
Kant at this time. He referred his hearers of that time to
their writings, and hoped to carry on their line of thought. The
distinction between knowledge and feeling which he draws in
psychology as well as in ethics is to be traced to this French
and English influence—perhaps, too, to the efforts of Sulzer
and Mendelssohn, his German predecessors in this respect.

It is characteristic of this stage of Kant's ethics (according
to his notes—which are all we have of this period) that all
ethical judgments are said to be derived from a basis of feeling.
They are dictated by an immediate feeling. And, in his
interesting little work : *Beobachtungen über das Gefühl des
Schönen und Erhabenen*, (" Observations on the Feeling of the
Beautiful and Sublime ") (1764), Kant specially describes the
ethical feeling as that of *the beauty and dignity of human nature*.
Owing to this psychological foundation there is a decided dis-
crepancy between this view of ethics and his definitive theory,
in which he turns his back on psychology. Moreover, he is not
content with immediate psychological perception, but passes on
to a comparative psychology, inquiring how the feeling of the
sublime and beautiful, which includes the ethical feeling, varies
between different races, different temperaments, and the two
sexes. In a fragment written at this time, he says : " In
establishing the primary principles of the metaphysic of morals
we must take into account the differences of human moral
feeling as it varies with difference of sex and age, education
and government, race and climate." And in the announcement of his lectures 1765-66, he announces his intention of
employing, in his ethical lectures, a method which he calls " a
beautiful discovery of our own day," and which consists in first
considering historically and philosophically that which *actually
happens* before passing on to declare what *ought to happen*.
We must discover the constant elements in man's nature in
order to understand the kind of perfection which beseems him
respectively in a state of rude simplicity, in a state of wise simplicity, and when he has passed beyond both these limitations.

Even in this first ethical stage, however, Kant never
thought that immediate feeling was all-sufficing. " True virtue
can only be based on *principles* which are nobler and more
sublime in proportion as they are more general. These

principles are not speculative rules, but the consciousness of a
feeling which dwells in every human breast, *i.e.* the feeling of
the beauty and dignity of human nature" (*Beobachtungen über
das Gefühl des Schönen und Erhabenen*, "Observations on the
Feeling of the Beautiful and Sublime ") (Königsberg 1764, p. 23).
Here then we come upon the trait which characterises Kant's
ethics at all its stages,—the assertion of the superiority of the
guiding ethical principle to the lower nature of man. Kant
remarks that the ethical feeling here described is in certain respects akin to melancholy; for " a solitary soul feels dread when,
inspired by a great purpose, it descries the dangers which have
to be overcome, and prepares itself for the difficult but great
conquest of self-mastery " (" Unfinished Writings," p. 28). The
sanguine temperament is not susceptible to this feeling. The
ethical feeling of the sanguine man bears the stamp of beauty,
not that of sublimity ; is dependent, not on principles, but on
the impression of the moment (p. 34). Kant's assertion of the
necessity of general principles conflicts with his comparative
method, which admits the possibility of very considerable
variations of ethical feeling. Perhaps this contradiction was
one of the motives which carried Kant beyond this first stage.
The last work in which this psychological ethics still predominates is the " Dreams of a Ghost-seer " (1766).

(*b*) *Second Stage* (1769-80)

The turning-point at which Kant's philosophy arrived at
the end of the sixties led, as has already been pointed out, to
a sharp distinction between the senses and understanding and
between matter and form ; also to the emphasis of reason and form
as the basis of the universally valid elements of our knowledge.
It is quite possible that Kant may have introduced this sharp
distinction between the understanding and the sensuous side of
our nature (under which latter, from this time forward, he placed
feeling) into the ethical sphere earlier than into the theoretical.
The transition probably took place as follows. As far back
as the " Observations " Kant had attributed the greatest importance to principles ;—for it is they which denote the
constant and active elements of our nature, in contradistinction
from the changing and passive. But so long as principles
were derived from feeling and were only the consciousness of

feeling they seemed to rest upon an insecure and empirical foundation. The prospect—opened out by the discovery of the Copernican principle—of attaining to a rational knowledge, independent of experience, was naturally accompanied by the attempt to discover for ethics also a rational foundation, independent of experience. In the Dissertation (1770) he expressly breaks with Shaftesbury's school, accusing it of Epicureanism! Moral Philosophy is now to be a purely rational science. Moral conceptions are gained, not from experience, but from pure reason itself. We only know the form which Kant's ethical views assumed in the interval between the Dissertation and the "Critique of Pure Reason" from a few fragments found among the papers he left behind him. A rough sketch, written in the seventies, shows us that he laid chief stress on a "practical idealism," on an "idealism of reason, of wisdom," according to which happiness is to be sought, not without, but within our own selves. This thought is elaborated in a fragment published by R. REICKE (*Lose Blätter aus Kant's Nachlass*, i. p. 9-16) which (as I have attempted to prove in the *Archiv für Gesch. d. Philos.* vii. p. 461) belongs to the period immediately preceding the final redaction of the "Critique of Pure Reason." As the ultimate presupposition of all rational knowledge is the inner activity of thought (apperception), by which alone connected perception and understanding are possible, so too it is self-activity, the capacity of producing our own happiness, which forms the firm foundation of happiness. The matter of happiness is sensuous, but its form is intellectual ; for we only retain our freedom and self-dependence when our will remains in harmony with itself. Morality is freedom under a general law expressed by this harmony with ourselves. Thus it is the cause of happiness although happiness is not its end. Neither morality nor happiness depend on external happenings, on passive feelings, or on the commands of authorities. Thus, according to the standpoint here taken, the highest good consists in that self-activity in virtue of which every man is the architect of his own happiness. This standpoint is differentiated by its individualistic and eudæmonistic character from the preceding as well as the subsequent standpoints. But it indicates an important step in the direction of emphasising the formal side of ethics. Kant had here arrived at one of the leading features of his ethical system, *i.e.* the inner relation between action and law, which, in his opinion, can only take place when the law is a purely formal one,—for only then can the law be really independent of experience. This is the first time that Kant applied within the ethical sphere the distinction between form and matter, reason and experience, which was of such cardinal importance in his philosophy.

(c) *Third Stage* (after 1785)

We can trace three leading *motifs* which effected the transition to the definitive form of the Kantian ethics ; firstly, his conception of psychology and the history of civilisation ; secondly, the conviction reached by means of his " Critique of Pure Reason " that the principles of pure reason are universal, valid for all reasonable beings ; and thirdly, the immediate observation and analysis of the ethical feeling, as it expresses itself in practice.

(a) Kant had early been led to regard history as a process of development. In the famous work of his youth " A General History of Nature " he had brought forward an hypothesis concerning the development of the solar system ; while in later treatises he had discussed the condition of the earth in pre-historic times, and the origin of the human races. His unflagging interest in physical geography and anthropology, on which subjects he gave popular lectures, could not fail to excite in him a lively interest in the natural history of man ; while, at the same time, his thought was searching for the final grounds of our knowledge and our ethical judgments. Two of the leading thoughts contained in the doctrine of evolution are to be found in Kant : the principle of actuality, according to which the past is to be explained through causes which we know from the experience of the present, and the principle of the accumulation of small effects into great and remote results. In the idea of evolution Kant found the solution of *Rousseau's problem* of the relation of civilisation to the happiness of the individual. As we have seen, Kant had felt himself strongly stirred by this problem on the first appearance of Rousseau's pregnant and suggestive works (at the beginning of the sixties), and at the beginning of the eighties, after the publication of his own chief work, he returned once more to Rousseau's problem.

He had become increasingly convinced that the happiness of the
individual affords no test of the value of historical development.
He gradually came to take a gloomy view of human nature, as it
is exhibited to us in experience and history. We meet with this
empirical pessimism [17] in his notes and in an " Anthropology "
which was published later, also all through his writings on ethics
and the philosophy of religion ; the beauty of human nature on
which he had laid such stress in the " Observations " has faded
before him. We are an idle, cowardly, and false race, a race of
which foolishness with an admixture of malice is the sign-manual.
In his " Anthropology," Kant quotes with approval Frederick the
Great's words to Sulzer, the optimist : " My dear Sulzer, you
little know to what an accursed race we belong." It is only with
the greatest distaste that we observe the appearance of man on
the great theatre of the world. Far greater than the suffering
which nature entails on man is that which men bring upon one
another. Kant's solution of the problem is as follows : evolution, unknown to the single individual, works towards a natural
end of the race,—an end which is attained by means of this
very dissension, malice, and unhappiness, and concerning which,
even were they aware of it, individuals would perhaps not
trouble themselves. Kant elaborates this idea in a remarkable
little work, *Idee zu einen allgemeinen Geschichte im weltbürger-
lichen Absicht* (1784), and takes it up again, a few years later,
with especial reference to Rousseau, in his treatise : *Mutmass-
lichen Anfang des Menschen-Geschlechts* (1786). The conditions
of individual life are not coincident with those of the race.
All that part of man's nature which consists of animal instinct
can attain to full development in the individual, but the
characteristics peculiar to man as a rational being can only be
developed in the life of the race. The evolution of reason
requires a long series of generations—for art is long and life
short. What has been acquired by one generation can be used
as a stepping-stone by the next, and thus it is that history
displays an advance. An advance it is true, which—as long
as the goal is unattained—involves greater suffering on individuals than the life of instinct in the state of nature.
Kant lays special weight on the point that the human
race attained to physical maturity long before it reached
rational maturity, and that civilisation increases the inequality
between men. Were the happiness of individuals the end,

man must have remained in the paradise of the life of instinct ; after the breach with instinct—which breach is described in the old story as a fall into sin—and after man had set out upon the path of reason there was nothing for it but to travel over the whole path again, so that the insight thus acquired might take the place of instinct in the regulation of life. Instead of immediate happiness, then, it becomes the end of every individual to make himself worthy of happiness through free self - activity. But the attainment of this goal presupposes that a free civil—indeed, in the last instance a cosmopolitan—society should be formed.[18]   A society in which the freedom of the individual, in virtue of his obedience to the law, is compatible with the freedom of all other men is, how- ever, only developed at the call of dire necessity. Throughout their life together, men carry on a ceaseless conflict with one another.   They are necessary to one another, but their ambi- tion and greed produce eternal dissension — both between individuals and states. This struggle is necessary, for other- wise the race would perish through indolence, and no faculties would be developed. The trees in the forest seek to rob one another of light and air ; on this account, however, they compel each other to seek light and air in higher zones, and thus attain a beautiful, tall, and slender growth. All civilisation and art, all social order is the fruit of anti-social tendencies, the mutual opposition between which forces men to yield to discipline and to develop their natural dispositions so that they may attain the highest degree of skill. The greatest suffering, however, is endured while this perfectioning of nature is in process. The period of transition is painful, and Rousseau was not altogether wrong in preferring the state of nature to that of semi-civilisation.

Kant does not mean that the ideal and distant goal towards which history tends is any merely external harmony of the egoistic interests. The highest culture includes morality ; for all good other than that which is rooted in a morally good disposition is nothing but appearance and glittering squalor. Kant here regards morality as the keystone of human education.

In the year after the publication of the *Idee einen allgemeinen Weltgeschichte* (" Idea of a General History of the World "), we find it stated (in the *Grundlegung zur Metaphysik der Sitten*, 1785, " Fundamental Principles of the Metaphysics of Morals") for the first time that the moral law, as it expresses itself in a clearly conscious conscience, may be summed up as follows : so act that the rule followed by thee may be a universal law, and that every human being is treated as an end and not merely as a means. Thus we see that what Kant, from his definitive ethical standpoint, regards as the content of the moral law or of duty is *an anticipation of the goal of historical development*—just as, in the theoretical sphere, *a priori* principles *anticipate,* by means of the concepts of cause and quantity, the course of experience. The ideal, derived from human experience and the needs of humanity, of a free society of human personalities—an ideal which constantly recurs, under many different forms, in the history of ethics and of religion—denotes at one and the same time for Kant the final goal of history, towards which it advances through egoism, antagonism, need, and distress, and the *content* of the moral law, which declares itself within the breast of individuals. Kant's ethic is the formalisation of an historic ideal, and is not altogether so *a priori* as he himself believed. Experience plays a part here, as in the shaping of all other ideals.[19] The sublime, absolute, and unconditional character which, in Kant's view, marks the moral law, in contradistinction to the sensuous nature and the limited capacity of the individual, finds its natural explanation in the fact that it is the end of the race which makes itself felt in the consciousness of each individual. Herein lies the mystery of the moral law, and, indeed, of all other racial instincts. The great opposition which, in Kant's view, exists throughout history between the end of the individual and that of the race led him to assume a no less sharp distinction between the moral law and all the empirically given elements of human nature. Psychology offered no means of filling up this gulf. Only by a leap can Kant pass from psychology to ethics. While in the " Idea of a General History " he had still regarded morality as the highest stage in the evolution of civilisation, it afterwards (" Critique of Judgment," § 84) seemed to him impossible that any grade of natural development could satisfy the unconditional demands of the moral law. He broke behind him the historical ladder by which he had reached his definitive ethic.

(β) The influence of Kant's epistemological investigations (in the " Critique of Pure Reason ") becomes very apparent in the development of his ethic to its definitive form. In the year immediately following the publication of the " Critique of Pure Reason " Kant was occupied in writing an exposition of the principles of ethics (as appears from a letter from Hamann to Hartknoch, January 11, 1782). In spite of his endeavour to draw a sharp distinction between theory and practice, the two are still intimately connected in his system. In the " Critique of Pure Reason " one of the leading thoughts was that an empirical world, a Nature, could only arise for us on the presupposition of objective and universally valid laws. Kant now conceives the moral law in express analogy with the natural laws : " The validity of the will as a general law for possible actions is analogous with the general interconnection of the existence of things according to general laws, which is the formula of Nature,"—hence the moral law, the unconditional command (the categorical imperative), may be expressed as follows : " Act only according to those maxims which thou canst at the same time wish to be general laws " (" Fundamental Principles of the Metaphysics of Morals," 3rd ed. p. 52, § 1). As the causal axiom opens to us the great world of reality, so, by the moral law, we gain access into an ideal world.

In the former the question is, how far have my *ideas*, in the latter, how far have my *actions*, attained objective validity ? The basis of all objectivity is law. Even in the fragments which show us the second stage of Kant's ethics, inner consistency, harmony with ourselves in all that we will is regarded as the main thing. This way of looking at things receives a still wider extension when all that is purely individualistic is eliminated ; the law of our action is to be the law for a world of spiritual beings. I fall into contradiction with myself when I judge myself differently from other men.

Now, experience can never establish a general law ; on the contrary the possibility of experience rests on the validity of the law. This holds good practically as well as theoretically. Hence human nature given in experience, as we learn to know it from psychology and history, can afford us no foundation for the moral law. The origin of this law is independent of all experience, and admits of no empirical or theoretical explanation whatever. Moreover, the whole of human nature, as given in experience, is subject to the moral law, and is regulated by it ; hence it cannot itself be the source of the law. Experience is always conditioned, while the law is unconditioned. Reason must take up a position outside phenomena if she is to be able to subject all to her unconditional laws. The law, however, does not, on this account, cease to be the law of man's own innermost essence ; but it springs from that element in man which cannot enter into experience; from the intelligible character of man—not from man as phenomenon ; from man as thing-in-itself, as noumenon,—not from man as a sensuous being. As early as in the " Critique of Pure Reason " (1st ed. p. 553) we find it stated that reason itself is not a phenomenon nor subject to sensuous conditions ; and the whole doctrine of the intelligible character shows that the principles which led to the peculiar and important modification which Kant's ethics underwent had already taken definite shape when he wrote his *magnum opus.* In the " Critique of Practical Reason " (§ 5) we find it stated that the pure form of the law has nothing whatever to do with phenomena ; on the contrary, it makes men independent of the whole world of phenomena. Man himself, that is to say, is a citizen of two worlds : as a member of the intelligible world he lays down the law for himself as a member of the phenomenal world ; he is at once lawgiver and subject. He need not go beyond himself—only beyond his sensuous phenomenal nature—to find the unconditioned. A " thou shalt," therefore, exists for man only because he belongs to the sensuous as well as to the intelligible world.

But with this Kant entirely precludes any explanation either of the moral law itself or of the possibility of its application within the empirical world. It is no more possible to explain how " reason can become practical " than to explain how the intelligible world, the thing-in-itself, can be related to the phenomenal world. It is not given to any mortal to perceive how the intelligible world underlies the sensuous world.

We can trace the increasing idealism of Kant's ethics. In his zeal to assert the sublimity of the moral law and of the dignity of personality he raises both above the empirical world, until any connection between the law and the empirical world becomes inexplicable. He sets the foundation of the ethical beyond the limits of knowledge, and thus prepares for it the same fate as that encountered by the debatable limiting concepts in which his theoretical thought found its close. In his increasing and sharpened antagonism to empiricism he

makes advances to mysticism ; [20] he even states expressly that
from the ethical point of view mysticism is less dangerous
than empiricism ("Critique of Practical Reason," i. 1, 2).
Kant's rationalism was almost a transition to mysticism, as the
mysticism of his time had contributed, in the form of pietism,
to the development of rationalism. We find here a decided
inconsistency in Kant's philosophy. Since, according to Kant,
forms are discovered by analysing experience, they cannot be
severed from experience and placed in absolute antithesis to
it. The forms are not intelligible. They are acquired by
means of abstraction and analysis, and must be regarded as
belonging to the world in which they were found, especially
if in this world they are to have the great significance of forming the basis of all objective validity. This must apply to the
formal moral law as well as to the forms of perception and the
categories. Kant's ethical interest led him to assign the moral
law a place in the intelligible world, or at least to regard it as
the portal to this world, while, in spite of the analogy between
them, he is not disposed to attribute a similar dignity to the
causal axiom. As so often happens with ethical idealism, over-
straining had brought it into contradiction with itself. It is
doing no service to ethics to assign to it a basis lying outside
all experience. For it is precisely in the world of experience
that the ethical has to live and work. All that is of significance in Kant's fundamental ethical conception could have held
its ground even if he had not turned his back upon psychology.
The opposition between the ethical ideal and the lower elements
of our nature, which he emphasised so energetically, is, as a
matter of fact, taken from psychological experience, and Kant
only clothes this experience in a mythological form when he
identifies it with the antithesis between the intelligible and the
phenomenal world.

γ. In his ethical works ("Fundamental Principles," 1785,
and "Critique of Practical Reason," 1788) Kant succeeded in
establishing the principle of ethics by means of an *analysis of the
ordinary moral consciousness, as actually given*. He holds it to
be the task of philosophical ethics to discover and think out the
principle which the practical human reason involuntarily employs.
He first exhibits the ethical phenomena or data ; secondly, finds
the law of which these are evidences ; thirdly, discovers the
force which operates according to this law.

(1) Even the ordinary moral consciousness is aware that the ethical value of an action does not depend on its external effects. It depends not on outer effects, but on the inner will; nothing is good except the good will! The good is to be found not without but within the acting personality itself! Accordingly, that action only is good which springs from duty or out of regard for the moral law. Neither use and wont, nor experiences, nor examples of times gone by—even the sublimest —make an action good. Every custom, every example, and every empirically given ideal must first be tested and judged. Even the Holy One of the gospel must be compared with our ideal before we can acknowledge Him. Hence a theological and a psychological basis for ethics are alike impossible. Duty springs neither from authority nor from experience. All feeling is empirical, sensuous, egoistic; even the so-called moral sense and sympathy are in reality nothing but forms of the desire for happiness. The characteristic feature of the ethical is *autonomy* (*i.e.* the property possessed by the will of being a law unto itself). From this follows the inwardness of the law. By subjecting ourselves to the law of our own will we become independent of experience and authority, while at the same time we are not only active but self-active.

Now experience shows us that human nature contains elements which only submit with a struggle to this inner law contained in the practical reason. It is precisely on this account that we call it a law, and that its demands appear as unconditional commandments, as categorical imperatives. We are dealing here with an "ought" which is yet one with our innermost will; but this innermost will encounters opposition within our own selves. We have a tendency not to be autonomous, not to follow the inner law of our own will. It is on this account that the fulfilment of morality assumes the character of *duty*, of a moral compulsion, and that the moral law displays itself as exalted above all the empirically given elements of our being.

All moral consciousness, according to Kant, yields, on analysis these two features,—the inwardness and sublimity of the law and its harmony with the real nature of man combined with a strongly-marked opposition to phenomenal man. These features may be traced, he asserts, even in the greatest reprobates. While in his early work ("Observations," 1764), he had recognised very considerable variations of moral feeling, he now, in the true dogmatic manner, makes human nature more uniform than it really is. He is only able to do this, however, by transcending experience.

Kant lays very great stress on the contradictions contained in human nature. From extreme cases, he thinks, we learn best of all how different are the elements and forces which this nature comprehends. Nearly all the examples on which he bases his analysis contain a moment of conflict. The idiosyncrasy of the ethical comes out all the more clearly the stronger the conflicting forces, and the more the support of non-ethical motives is excluded. Accordingly in the "Methodology of the pure practical Reason" (the concluding section of the "Critique of Practical Reason"), he specially recommends that cases of conflict should be examined, since they correspond in ethical analysis to the method of reaction in chemical analysis.[21] But Kant does more than say that the ethical element *emerges most clearly* in cases of conflict between the moral obligation on the one hand, and sensitive and egoistic interests on the other. He even declares that it is only under such conditions that the good will *is really present :* " The condition in which, in the event of a collision between certain of my ends and the moral law of duty, I am conscious of preferring, the latter is not merely a better but the sole good condition." Schiller has caricatured this rigoristic tendency of Kant's ethics in a well-known epigram, in which he draws the conclusion that we only do our duty when we do it with aversion. But this was not Kant's meaning. He himself breaks out into a hymn to Duty, that sublime power dwelling in the human breast,—and he held that duty must be performed with candour and enthusiasm. His only scruples were concerned with the duties which are so very easy to perform, and he was inclined to look upon this characteristic as a sign that the real duty had not been discovered ; he demanded that in questions of duty men should abstract from all self-interest and from all immediate allurements. The relation of duty does not do away with the independence of the individual ; it limits it only.

(2) But what is the *content* of the law which, according to Kant, declares itself in the consciousness of every man (whether or not he is able to formulate it)? Since, in virtue of its

inwardness and sublimity, the law is independent of all experience, it seems somewhat difficult to find an answer to this
question. Kant decides it quite consistently ; the moral law is
purely formal ; it only states the form which the will must
assume in order to be good ; and the form consists in this,
that the principle which I follow in my action must be such
that it can form the basis of a general legislation ; that is to say,
it must be valid for all rational beings who find themselves in
a similar case to my own. The individual willing must apply
a universal measure to himself, must so regard his action as
though he were on the point of creating by its means a new
nature. By the light of this rule, Kant thinks, it will be easy
to discover our duty in any particular case ; far more easy,
indeed, than to attain to happiness. That I must not retain
goods entrusted to me nor tell lies now becomes self-evident,
for were this a universal right all confidence between men
would be destroyed. Thus, in his estimation of worth, the
individual regards himself as one among many, and he restricts
his volitions in accordance with the conditions demanded by
the common life of many. Kant expressly distinguishes
between his moral principle and the old rule : " What thou wouldst
not that men should do unto thee, do not thou unto them,"—a
rule which admits of a purely egoistical interpretation. His
principle, however, contains something more than an empty
formula, than mere logical consistency ; it contains in addition
the presupposition that there are other interests besides my
own private ones, — that besides myself, there are other
personalities, each of whom is a central point of the world.
Can I—as Kant believes—know this *a priori* by the light
of pure reason ? It is surely only through experience that
I can know I am a member of a society, whose needs are
a law for me. And, as we have seen, Kant's ethics did
actually arise under the influence of his view of the history of
civilisation. He is himself obliged to admit that the moral
law is historically and empirically determined, *i.e.* is not
purely formal, *e.g.* (*Tugendlehre*, § 27) " The legislative
reason includes in its idea of humanity in general the whole
species." But this is an idea which has a history,—and a
very slow and laborious history. Moreover, Kant felt the impossibility of advancing by means of a purely formal principle,
since all action presupposes positive ends and tasks. But if

the categorical imperative, the unconditioned member in the relation of duty, is to remain intact, the ends chosen must be such as possess absolute worth : otherwise it cannot be regarded as a duty to adopt them. The dignity of my personality— to paraphrase Kant's argument—depends on my capacity for following, in my inner man, the universal law ; what end, then, can unconditional duty require of me? One only, runs the answer : *i.e.* to respect the dignity of other personalities, which is likewise founded on *their* capacity for autonomy. While Kant's *first ethical formula* ran as follows : " Act so that the maxim of thy action may serve as a general rule," his *second formula* is : " So act as to treat humanity, whether in thine own person or in that of any other, in every case as an end withal, never as a means only " (*Grundlegung*, 3 ed. p. 66 ; *Kritik der prakt. Vernunft*, i. 1, 3 ; *Tugendlehre, Einleitung*, §§ iii.-iv.). Kant held that the latter formula was deducible from the former, but this is impossible, if the first is to be taken purely formally. Both formulæ presuppose that we actually feel ourselves to be members of a kingdom of personal beings. Moreover, if the law exists for the sake of personal beings and not *vice versa* it is, if anything, the first formula which may be deduced from the second ! In spite of the artificiality of the deduction, Kant has given utterance to a great and significant principle. It is the principle of personality in its noblest form, a thought which will live long after the imperfect and un- natural foundation on which Kant based it has been forgotten ; a thought of great ethical value both as against the principle of authority—when this claims to be anything more than an educative principle—and against the doctrine of happiness and external good, which feeds on husks, and loses sight of the kernel.

Kant himself, however, never lost the conviction that his moral principle was purely formal, an expression of pure reason. But then the question arises : How can this intelligible law determine a will which is active in experience ? How can the law become a *motive ?* In his eagerness to assert the inwardness and sublimity of the law Kant has taken no heed of psychology. He would not base morality on feeling because feeling is a passive condition, dependent on experience. But he cannot deny that action would be impossible without feeling to set it in motion. Accordingly he seeks to show that the thought of the universal moral law itself excites in us a feeling of esteem and veneration. Esteem, he thinks, is a feeling which cannot be explained through experience; it is neither pleasure nor pain, but pure interest excited in our breasts by the sublimity of the law—an influence which the thought of this law exercises on our hearts. Here, then, is a motive which is able to impel our practical will. A motive, indeed, which offers as great a mystery as does the relation between the intelligible and phenomenal world in general ; and,—what is still more important in this connection,—it is a motive the possibility of which contradicts Kant's own view of the validity of the causal axioms for all phenomena, both inner and outer ; for esteem is said to be quite inexplicable by phenomenal causes ! Here, too, Kant's ethical idealism has led him astray ; but here again it is no very difficult task to strip the deeply significant thoughts it contains of the wrapping in which Kant presents them.

(3) From the phenomenon, from the moral consciousness of the practical man, Kant passes to the law, and from the law to force. The law is the expression of a consciousness of freedom. Law and freedom are, to a certain extent, one and the same ; if we attempt to distinguish between them, we reason backwards from the law to freedom (*Krit. der prakt. Vernunft*, § 6). The law proceeds from the will itself (*Grundlegung*, 3rd ed., p. 104 f. ; *Rechtslehre, Einleitung*, § iv.). For the law, we must remember, is the fruit of our own legislation, the expression of our autonomy as reasonable beings. By freedom Kant understands above all *spontaneity*, the capacity of working according to inner principles and forces, independence of what is given and external. But Kant goes beyond this definition of freedom. Freedom also implies for him the *capacity to make an absolute beginning*, to initiate an absolutely new causal series. He regards this capacity as a necessary consequence of originality and independence. But, if this be so, there is no freedom to be found in the world of phenomena, which, as Kant himself pointed out in his " Critique of Pure Reason," shows us no absolute beginnings. If freedom is the capacity to absolutely create the motives [22] which determine the will which is active in experience (as was already implied in the doctrine of esteem), then it is only to be found in the intelligible world (Can it be even begun and practised there, since time has no validity ?). Kant does not inquire whether the union between

independence and the capacity to make an absolute beginning is absolute. New centres might be formed in the world, which, after they were formed, would work according to an inner law, independently of external influence. Kant makes every particular will a god, instead of letting it win its divinity by development and work.

And, in addition to these two definitions of freedom (as independence and as the capacity to make an absolute beginning) we find in one or two passages (*Krit. der prak. Vernunft,* Kehrbach's ed. p. 116 f.—*Religion innerhalb der Grenzen der reinen Vernunft,* passim), a third : *the capacity to do one as easily as the other of two opposite things.* That Kant ever came to frame such a monstrous conception must be explained by his assumption of a sharp antithesis between the ideal (intelligible) nature of man, and man as he appears empirically. He thinks as meanly of the latter as he does highly of the former. There is a great tension between the two poles, and it remains inexplicable how man, whose innermost nature is good (for freedom, in the first sense, is tantamount to good) can entertain such motives as experience reveals to us. Kant explains this—by assuming a still more inexplicable capacity.[23] Here again Kant is more correct in the facts he brings forward than in the theory he deduces from them. Human nature includes within it the greatest contrasts, dispositions to good and dispositions to evil. There is a faculty of forming sublime and pure ideals, and there is also perversity, unwillingness, and filthiness. These opposites must be closely related to one another in human nature ; they must have developed according to definite rules and under definite conditions. Kant, who elsewhere adopts the standpoint of scientific inquiry in regard to human relations, here, by his unfortunate dualism between ethics and psychology, renders it impossible to find any solution.

(d) Applied Ethics

Kant has given us his applied ethics in two works—the *Rechtslehre* (" Doctrine of Rights ") and the *Tugendlehre* (" Doctrine of Virtue "). Both appeared in 1797, and betray the weakness of old age at many points. The imperfection of these expositions is mainly the result of the systematisation which had so gained the upper hand with the aged thinker; while, at the same time, of course, the onesidedness of Kant's ethical conception in general makes itself felt in his treatment of many questions. Above all indications of decay and one-sidedness, however, rises a sequence of noble and virile thoughts, Kant's great bequest to humanity.

The two works stand in a certain opposition to one another, since the *Rechtslehre* does not go farther than legality, the external harmony of my action with the law which secures freedom to other men as well as to me, while the *Tugendlehre* requires, in addition, morality, *i.e.* action must arise from a disposition, an inner will to acknowledge the law. The moral law (the categorical imperative) demands the limitation of my will by such conditions as are imposed by the freedom of others. But the observation of this restriction may be brought about by fear or self-interest, not by purely ethical motives. The evolution towards the ideal condition in which there is no more war may take place under the influence of many different motives, all of which are not, properly speaking, moral. The contrast between legality and morality is not an absolute one ; for the basis of legality and of the claim of the law is the categorical imperative : " *There shall be no war,* neither between me and thee in the condition of nature, nor between us as States—for that is not the way in which every man is to pursue his rights " (*Rechtslehre*, Conclusion). This passage confirms the view taken above, *i.e.* that Kant's moral law is an anticipation of the result of historical development. The ordering of rights — although it demands legality only — is a means postulated by morality. " Reason," says Kant (*Rechtslehre*, § 49), " imposes on us by means of a categorical imperative the duty of striving after the condition of greatest harmony between the constitution [of the State] and principles of right." Kant admits, that is to say, that the realisation of the highest moral aim may be prepared through the influence of other than strictly moral motives. And it is precisely this external assurance of freedom, rendered possible by the order-ing of rights, which is a condition for the development of the inner moral disposition (*Lose Blätter aus Kant's Nachlass*, p. 528). In those works in which he lays the foundation of his ethics (the " Fundamental Principles " and the " Critique of Practical Reason ") Kant assumes a sharper contrast between legality and morality than he is able to maintain in his more detailed investigation.

Kant defines right as the sum-total of the conditions under which the free will of one may be reconciled with the free will of another, according to a general law of freedom. There is only one single inherent right belonging to every human personality, and that is freedom, i.e. *independence of the constraining will of another, in so far as this is compatible with the freedom of all according to a general law.* Thus the right of ownership is justified not merely because I have taken possession of a thing before any one else (*prior occupatio*) but rather because I acknowledge that others have the same right over that of which they have first taken possession. It is clear here, if anywhere, that Kant's ethical principles always presuppose the existence of a State, as historically given. The State itself, however, Kant conceives to have arisen out of a contract, restricting the freedom of individuals by regard to the equally great freedom of others. But he does not conceive this contract as an historical event. He uses the idea of a contract as a guiding idea, a rational principle, in estimating and developing social relations. In this connection, he regards the historical origin of society as a matter of indifference. And in virtue of this standpoint he denotes a great advance in comparison with the mythology of the previous expounders of natural right. But he omits to raise the question as to how the rational principle itself arises in human consciousness; here again Kant appears as a dogmatist.

Peculiar to Kant's theory of rights is the emphatic assertion of the rights of the individual as a human being, which he bases more especially upon a sharp distinction between person (the being who is a law unto and accountable to himself) and thing. A person must never be treated merely as a means. From this principle Kant deduces not only personal freedom, but also freedom of speech and the right to take part in legislation. The legislature must not appoint anything for the nation which it would not appoint for itself,—it must not, *e.g.* introduce any fixed dogmatic system, by means of which the right of progress in enlightenment would be annulled, nor must it establish an hereditary nobility. Kant had welcomed with enthusiasm the North American War of Independence and the French Revolution, and this enthusiasm still lingers in his theory of rights. He regards the republican form of government as the constitution of the future ; he considered the spirit of republicanism, however, to be more important than the external constitution, and he sees no reason why a monarchy should not be conducted in this spirit. He detested patriarchal government. A sovereign has no right to make a man happy against his will. Right has its origin in freedom, not in happiness, and it is freedom, not happiness, that the sovereign has to preserve. Hence punishment must not be inflicted as a means of promoting the good of the community or of the criminal himself, but simply and solely because the criminal willed his action. It would be treating man as a means, as a thing, if punishment were to be regarded as anything other than retaliation. Retaliation is a categorical imperative. Punishment must not be inflicted for the sake of any advantage ; on the contrary, it must be inflicted, however great the disadvantages which may accrue from it. Even if a people be on the point of setting forth to seek new lands it must first execute all murderers ! *Fiat justitia, pereat mundus* means, as translated by Kant, "Let justice prevail, though all the knaves in the world perish !"

In his *Tugendlehre* (personal ethics) Kant lays chief stress on that attitude of character which corresponds to his general conception of the ethical. In his view, virtue consists in strength of soul (*fortitudo moralis*), in the power and dignity which follows from the consciousness of possessing the law of our own action within ourselves and of being united by means of this law into one great whole.

The ends posited in Kant's personal ethics are (1) the perfection of self, (2) the happiness of others. Not our own happiness,—for we strive after this involuntarily and with such eagerness that we hold it to be other men's duty to consider it likewise. Nor the perfection of others,—for only they themselves can effect this ; for perfection consists in nothing else but in making ourselves, according to our own conception of duty, our own end [as if happiness were so easy to attain, and as though, in the struggle towards perfection, we could dispense with the help of others !]

(1) The striving after our own perfection includes the development of all lower and higher faculties—all culture. Man must raise himself above the condition of brutishness : "The characteristic of humanity in contradistinction from

brutishness, is the faculty of choosing an end. Bound together with the end of humanity in our own person is the further duty of making ourselves worthy of humanity by culture," and first and foremost by "moral culture," *i.e.* by the faculty of letting our actions be determined through the inner law. Kant derives everything which can make a man an active and useful member of society from human dignity; to be useless and superfluous is to dishonour humanity in our own person. One very characteristic section is entitled " On toadyism." As a person, man is of inestimable value. Humility before the law within his own breast commands him to hold his own before others, even were he confronted with an archangel. Humility towards others is no duty ; on the contrary, it may become pharisaism or baseness, if by means of it favour or advantage are sought. Never, therefore, be any man's servant. Let not your rights be trampled under foot ; accept no benefits which you can do without. Bear yourselves bravely, and shun unworthy complainings over suffering ! Kneel to no one, for the ideal is within yourselves, and that which appears to you from without may be only an idol ! Low bows and many external demonstrations of politeness only express man's propensity to toadyism. And if we act the worm we must not complain if we are trodden under foot.

2. In connection with the second end which Kant posits in his personal ethics, *i.e.* the happiness of others, he is confronted, although he himself is not clearly conscious of it, with an extremely difficult problem : viz. are we to be guided here by our own or by other men's ideas of happiness ? This is a problem which carries us into the most hidden recesses of personal life, especially if, like Kant, we have a sharply-defined conception of the value of personality, as determined by its own legislation. Kant is very vacillating on this point. Sometimes he says others have no right to demand from me that which, in my opinion, does not promote their happiness; and he speaks of the thankless task of promoting the true good of other men, when they do not recognise it as such ; at other times he says I can benefit no man according to my own conceptions of happiness; to rob another of the freedom to *choose his own* happiness cannot be called a beneficent action. Kant classifies duties towards others as "duties of love" and "duties of esteem," according to whether there is a relation of attraction or of contrast.

The duties of esteem are immediately deducible from the first principle of Kant's ethics. Love offers greater difficulties ; partly on account of the sharply-defined independence which he attributes to every particular personality, partly owing to his pessimistic conception of actual human nature. Love must be limited by the right of the loved one, for the latter foregoes his dignity as a man if he is not master of himself and of his condition. Moreover, love is an immediate feeling and a need which refuses to be regulated by the commandment of reason. And as men actually are, it cannot be required of us to find pleasure in them. It is our duty to wish them well and to benefit them, and this duty does not cease to be binding on us after we have learnt from real experience that, on a nearer acquaintance, our race does not prove particularly lovable. Only benevolent love, therefore, not complacent love (*amor benevolentiae, non complacentiae*) can be required from us as a duty. In the relation of friendship Kant finds a harmony of attraction and contrast, of love and esteem ; true friendship certainly is, like the black swan, a *rara avis ;* nevertheless, black swans do really exist. We will not attempt to argue with such a hardened Benedict as Kant on his very imperfect understanding of the marriage tie. He discusses it not in the *Tugendlehre* but in the *Rechtslehre.* He regarded it merely as a contract according to which, two persons of different sexes engage to enter into sexual relations with one another and with no one else. Kant alludes to the sexual instinct as a strictly isolated need of human nature, regards it from the purely sensual side only, and has no sense at all of its fine gradations, and of its possible connection with some of the most ideal feelings.

CHAPTER V

PHILOSOPHY OF RELIGION (" CRITIQUE OF PRACTICAL REASON " AND " RELIGION WITHIN THE LIMITS OF PURE REASON ")

(a) Morality and Religion

KANT'S ethic is autonomous—is (or believes itself to be) independent of any other premises than those which are contained in the innermost essence of man, in the activity which forms his innermost nature ; hence it is independent of physics and hyperphysics, psychology, and theology. To find a natural transition from morality to religion, therefore, could not fail to present a great difficulty to Kant. For how can dependence be deduced from pure self-dependence and self-activity ? And yet Kant had early (in 1766, see the conclusion to " Dreams of a Ghost-seer ") become convinced that religion can only be based on morality. The explanation is to be found in this— the unconditional duty imposed upon the inner man has to be performed by a finite, limited being. The moral law teaches us our inner freedom, and with this, our independence of the whole empirical world. But it is precisely in the empirical world that it is to be put into effect and to completely permeate our personality. Hence there arises a need of the reason, a moral need, which demands the fulfilment of those conditions without which a complete realisation of ideal claims is impossible. The first condition is continual existence, for only in a progress continued *ad infinitum* can the will be brought into complete agreement with the moral law. Thus personal immortality becomes a postulate of faith. The second condition is the harmony of the moral endeavour with the natural need of happiness. It cannot be proved from experience either that virtue always leads to happiness or happiness to virtue ; when this is the case it is the result of accident. And yet the highest good must include not only virtue (the greatest good) but happiness also. There must be a deep underlying harmony between the world of nature and that of freedom. We must, that is to say, postulate a power which is able to reduce the two worlds to inner harmony, so that morality shall not feel itself an alien in this world. He who is permeated by the moral law is therefore obliged to believe in the existence of a God.

Practical reason thus leads us to entertain convictions concerning something which lies beyond the limits defined by the theoretical reason. The X (thing-in-itself) which the theoretical reason had to leave undetermined becomes accessible to us when we comply with the need excited in us by the practical reason to postulate a perfect realisation of the moral ideal. Kant enumerates three postulates, for the limits of theoretical knowledge were already transcended by the assumption of freedom as an unconditioned capacity ; this, then, is the first postulate.

The need from which this postulate is derived is neither sensuous nor egoistic, but is a consequence of the presence and activity of the moral law in the minds of men ; hence it is a consequence of that in man's nature which is universal and valid for all. It is a need of pure reason. Strongly as Kant emphasises the difference between this need and every other possible wish, he no less strongly emphasises its purely subjective character. The faith (or rather hope) to which it leads is itself not a duty although it is evoked by the law of duty. It cannot, Kant thinks, be a duty to believe in that which cannot be known (*Kritik der praktischen Vernunft*, Kehrbach, pp. 151, 172 f). Kant is of opinion that if man feels the law within him he will also *inevitably* feel the need of accepting the conditions under which this law can be carried out. And, relying on this inevitability, he also, among other things, declares it to be a duty towards ourselves to be religious, since otherwise we cannot assert our moral convictions (*Tugendlehre*, Conclusion—*Lose Blätter*, p. 513). Indeed he even allows himself to say that the well-disposed man may sometimes falter in his faith, but can never renounce it (*Kritik der praktischen Vernunft*, Kehrbach, p. 175).

The question is whether the rational need out of which the

postulate springs is really a universal one—whether it necessarily occurs in all individuals who acknowledge an unconditioned moral law, and who carry within them an infinite ideal. Kant did not see that this question cannot be decided *a priori*, that it can only be answered by the help of psychological experience. He cannot, consistently with his own premises, raise any objection against the man who, without faltering in his moral conviction, but also without any sort of " postulate," is yet able to face the eternal want of harmony between the ideal and reality. Indeed in one isolated passage he actually considers this possibility. This passage is particularly interesting, since it shows us clearly what Kant hoped to reach by means of his postulates : " We may then suppose," says Kant (" Critique of Judgment," § 87), "the case of a righteous man (*e.g.* Spinoza) who holds himself firmly persuaded that there is no God and also no future life ; how is he to judge of his own inner purposive destination by means of the moral law which he reveres in practice? He desires no advantage to himself for following it, either in this or another world ; he wishes, rather, disinterestedly to establish the good to which that holy law directs all his powers. But his effort is bounded, and from Nature, although he may expect here and there a contingent accordance, he can never expect a regular harmony according to constant rules with the purpose that he yet feels himself obliged and impelled to accomplish. Deceit, violence, and envy will always surround him, although he himself be honest, peaceable, and kindly ; and the righteous men with whom he meets will, notwithstanding all their worthiness of happiness, be yet subjected by nature, which regards not this, to all the evils of want, disease, and untimely death, just like the beasts of the earth. So it will be until one wide grave engulfs them together and throws them back—who were able to believe themselves the final purpose of creation—into the abyss of the purposeless chaos of matter from which they were drawn." Kant means to say here that without the religious postulates a man cannot hold fast to the *end* which the moral law obliges him to set before himself. But it was the aim of his ethics to abstract from all ends and to require a will that wills in accordance with the inner law—whatever may be the consequences ! Only at the cost of logical consistency can he erect the concept of the *highest good* (the union of happiness and virtue) as an *ethical* aim ; for the first sentence of his ethics runs (*Grundlegung*, p. 1), " Nothing can possibly be conceived in the world, or even out of it, which can be called good without qualification, except a *good will.*" By his postulates—especially the first and second—Kant virtually cancels the independence of ethics.

The postulates become necessary when the need of thinking the ethical in connection with the whole of our world-conception makes itself felt. This is, to be sure, a need which does not arise in the breast of every man, and which, from the ethical point of view, need not necessarily arise. Nevertheless, the great merit of Kant's philosophy of religion consists precisely in this—that he traces the religious problem back to a personal need, determined by the relation to ethical ideals, more clearly and penetratingly than had ever been done before. The position of the religious problem at different times and with different persons will depend upon whether this need is present, and on the particular manner in which it makes itself felt. There will be here, as experience shows, innumerable individual differences which Kant's dogmatism led him to ignore. But with the same certainty of touch with which, from the theoretical point of view, he determined the philosophical place of the assumptions of religion, he here assigns a corresponding determination of place to the practical and psychological side of these assumptions.

(b) The religious postulates in relation to Kant's epistemology and to " natural religion "

With the postulates we transcend the limits of knowledge. But how is this possible, for the " Critique of Reason " showed once for all that our forms of knowledge must be restricted within these limits? We cannot possibly supply ourselves with other forms of knowledge. Kant now emphasises the point that the categories (everything turns here, as nearly always, on the causal concept) do not originate in experience, but in the faculty of thought itself. Hence he believes it possible to apply them beyond the limits of experience or of phenomena, in order to *think* the content of the postulates, even though we may not be able to *know* it. For knowledge, a co-operation of perception and thought is necessary. Per-

ception, however, is excluded here. The human faculty of
knowledge is characterised by the distinction between perception and thought, and also by the fact that our perception
is always sensitive (spatial or temporal). A supersensitive
perception would be fantastical, and would kindle a "magic-
lantern of phantoms." We conceive God as the cause of the
world, we conceive a continuation of our striving, and we conceive our ideal will as a first beginning, even though these
concepts cannot be supported by intuitive data.

But even such a use as this of the forms of thought is
not in accordance with the "Critique of Reason," according to
which concepts without percepts are empty (as percepts without
concepts are blind). And even if we admit such a use, yet
they are certainly not the ordinary ideas of God, freedom, and
immortality—not the ideas of "natural religion"—that Kant's
pure concepts enable him to express. With perception the temporal relation must also cease to exist : how, then, can we speak
of a *continued* existence (a future life), of a beginning, and of a
creation ? And if all empirical data are to be excluded, we must
purge the idea of God from everything which is derived from
human psychology. We know no understanding except that
which works its way upward to truth by means of successive
and discursive apprehension and reflection, and no will which
does not choose ends and seek for the means by which to attain
them. But such activity cannot be predicated of the unconditioned and infinite Being, and it disappears together with the
temporal relation. And if we ask Kant what there is left of
our psychological concept after we have subjected it to a change
so radical as to make it predicable of God, he answers clearly
and candidly (although this answer is always passed over in
the popular expositions of his doctrine) only the *empty word*
remains. " Is there a single quality of which it cannot be
shown that, when purged of all anthropomorphism, there
remains nothing but the empty word with which not the most
insignificant concept, from which we could hope to gain any
extension of knowledge, could be united ?" Passages to the same
effect are to be found in all Kant's chief works.[24] Spinoza
could not have expressed himself more clearly.

If we ask how Kant can attribute value to the religious
ideas since theoretically they are entirely empty, the answer is
that, in Kant's view, all religious ideas are *symbolical*. When

the scientific use of our concepts ceases, we must help ourselves out with analogies and symbols.   Thus the ideas of a
personal God and of personal immortality are only symbols of
a something which thought cannot express in an adequate form.
It is not a higher *knowledge* which is gained by the transition
from knowing to believing.   " The need of reason," here, in fact,
enlists poetry into her service.   The postulates are projections
into the unknowable of pictures which have taken shape in the
empirical world.   If we examine more closely into what all this
means we discover that there is a great difference between
Kant's religious standpoint and that of natural religion.   Like
Lessing, Kant had an esoteric and an exoteric doctrine,[25]
though he never distinguished quite clearly between them, and
did not realise all the consequences involved in his belief in the
symbolical character of the religious concepts,—for instance,
that symbols cannot be imposed, but must be the object of free,
individual choice, so that *my* need of reason may perhaps find
other symbols more attractive than those chosen by Kant.
Moreover, Kant is inclined to attribute somewhat hastily to the
thing-in-itself everything which he felt the need of believing,
without pausing to find out whether the different postulates
may not mutually contradict one another (*e.g.* God's omnipotence and man's freedom).   " Religion within the Limits of
Pure Reason " (2nd ed. p. 215 f. ; *Lose Blätter*, p. 544).   He
makes the same use of the limits of knowledge that Holberg's
heroine makes of the folding screen in her confinement, he
conceals behind them the different elements which he can spare
from science to give to faith, without reflecting that the quarrel
would break out again—behind the folding screen.   For the
one thing we do require of our symbols is that they should
not be mutually contradictory.

   The symbolic character of the religious ideas is closely
bound up with the source of religious faith in a personal need.
We seek for forms under which we can figure to ourselves
existence as a kingdom in which that which we conceive to be
highest in value comes by its full rights.   On this point, too,
Kant's philosophy of religion—with all its imperfections—
denotes a great advance in comparison with the theology of
orthodoxy and of the Enlightenment.

(c) Positive Religion

The ideas of positive religion must encounter the same fate as those of natural religion.   Kant draws this conclusion in his remarkable work *Religion innerhalb der Grenzen der blossen Vernunft* (" Religion within the Limits of Pure Reason ") (1793). Instead of asking whether the ideas of positive religion could stand before the judgment-seat of natural science and historical criticism, Kant inquires as to their ethical significance for human life, and as to what parts of their content are able to nourish and support life.   And this is, and will indeed always remain, the chief question, for on the answer given to it depends the value which is to be attributed to these ideas (irrespective of the sentence passed by physics and history).   That Kant only occupied himself with Christianity, the positive religion which lay nearest his hand, is but natural.   But it is curious that he should choose for special discussion the dogmas of sin and atonement,—precisely the dogmas to which least attention was paid during the period of the Enlightenment.   Kant sees in them the embodiment of deep ethical truths, since what are described in the Bible as external and historical events may be interpreted to mean inner spiritual relations in the minds of men, to be the expression of the conflicting opposites in the human will.

In the doctrine of sin and the fall Kant finds the expression of a truth which is confirmed by experience, *i.e.* that in opposition to the inner will, whose law is the moral law, there is a tendency to place the claims of the senses higher than those of the reason.   Law stands against law, as in Boehme God against God ; for it is not sense itself which is bad.   Badness is that will which inverts the right relation in which reason rules secure, and erects the converse relation into the rule.   The radically bad in man is this conversion of the relation between motives.   Philosophical ethics accepts this radical badness as a fact, as empirically given.   The Bible describes its origin as an historical event, for it makes man's good nature precede his evil nature in time, and lets the state of innocence be interrupted by a fall into sin.   By the introduction of a tempter, however, it at the same time admits that no absolute explanation can be given.

Side by side with radical badness, however, we find in man a constant disposition towards the good, which can be developed best of all by the study of great examples. The capacity of honouring the good, even when we cannot ourselves practise it, never entirely disappears. This capacity, which develops into the moral consciousness, is the ideal element of our nature; the inner heaven within us as opposed to the radical badness which is the inner hell. We have given us in our nature an incomprehensible archetype, an indwelling ideal, which is described in the Bible as the Son of God, who came down to earth and took upon Himself human form. The God-man is the idea of human nature in its perfection. Here, too, we have described as an historical event what the philosopher regards as an eternal relation—the relation between human nature and the good or ideal as a force within it which is sharply opposed to other of its tendencies. The battle between Satan and Christ is a battle which is waged in the depths of human nature. While it is raging the God in us has to suffer for the deeds of our evil will. The new man who is to arise suffers for the sins of the old man. Answering to this in our experience is repentance, which presupposes a new direction of the will, and which takes upon itself the sufferings involved in getting free from the old will. This is the ethical content of the dogma of the atonement. It is true, indeed, that the arising of the ideal man in us can never be a completed process ; an approximation thereto is all that is possible. From the highest standpoint, however, successive approximation is regarded and estimated as a whole, since the temporal relation is left out of account.

Kant is very well aware that this symbolical interpretation differs entirely from the historical meaning. He leaves the latter to learned investigation. He maintains that it is only in virtue of such ethico-symbolical interpretation that sacred books have any permanent ethical worth ; and, as a matter of fact, this is the method which men adopt (and have always adopted) whenever their aim is to make religion bear practical fruit. And such an interpretation is the more justified since man's moral dispositions have already involuntarily exercised their influence in the development of the religious ideas, and have set their stamp on revelation itself. We could never have learnt to know the ideal and the divine

in any purely external, historical fashion.   The highest archetype is always to be found in our own spirits.   Only by means
of the God within us do we learn to know the God without
us, and the God within us is the only God to whom all bow
the knee (*Lose Blätter*, p. 218).   This God within us is the
expositor of everything which lays claim to be called a revelation.   Had Abraham consulted this ideal he would never have
been ready to turn his hand against his son ; had the inquisi-
tors regarded it they would have condemned no man on
account of the dogmas he held.   The moral law within us is
more sure than any faith (*Religion innerhalb*, etc. p. 289).

In Kant's opinion such wonderful things happen within the
human breast that there is no need to assume external events
in order to explain them—especially since every such explanation is illusory.   He leaves the mysterious side of the events
recounted in the Bible unquestioned, since he honours the
outer shell of a doctrine whose credentials rest on a witness
which is inextinguishable in every soul and which needs no
miracles (*Religion innerhalb*, etc. p. 117).

He makes *one* demand only, viz. that the historical and
dogmatic (*statuarishe*) element of religion should be subordinated more and more to the inner and ethical element.
Historic faith has only provisional and symbolic significance.
The visible church must approximate more and more to the
true, invisible church, in which every individual stands in inner
and immediate relation to the highest truth.   Then, too, the
demoralising distinction between learned and lay will vanish,
for it is conditioned by the necessity of possessing historical
learning in order to understand positive religion.   God's kingdom is not a kingdom of priests.   No unqualified progress
has been made since the Reformation : to forbid the laity to
read the Bible or to say " Read your Bible diligently, but find
at your peril anything in it different from what we have found
there " comes to the same thing.   Indeed, it were better to
tell us at once what you have found, that we may be spared
the trouble of reading (*Lose Blätter*, p. 402).   Still more
burdensome than the external observances demanded by
Catholicism is the dogmatic confession of faith.   If that
constitutes Christianity, says Kant, it has no right to say " My
burden is light."

Kant could not but feel how different was the reading of

Christianity given by the Church.   Nevertheless, he entertained
an honest conviction that religious development would proceed
in the direction he had indicated.   He may still be justified
in this, although religious differences have become even more
sharply accentuated in the course of the century which has
elapsed since the appearance of his work on the philosophy of
religion.   For the philosophy of religion itself this work was
epoch-making.   Its permanent value is assured by its struggle
on behalf of the inner as against the outer, and its assertion
of the significance of the inner happenings of personal life.   It
leaves much to be desired as regards the psychology and
historical conception of religion.   To complete Kant's thought
in these spheres, however, was to be the task of the new century.

CHAPTER VI

SPECULATIVE IDEAS BASED ON ÆSTHETIC AND BIOLOGICAL CONSIDERATIONS ("CRITIQUE OF JUDGMENT")

(a) *The two worlds and their possible unity*

IN his *Kritik der Urtheilskraft* ("Critique of Judgment") (1790) Kant develops thoughts which pass beyond the limits within which his philosophy otherwise restricts itself. Instead of the appeal to a moral belief which rounded off his conceptions in previous works, his thought here attempts a bolder view of a great whole, within which a unity of the opposites hitherto held apart might be possible.

Kant had operated extensively with sharp distinctions. These had been necessary to him in order that he might attain his results. Only by help of the distinction between phenomena and things-in-themselves had he been able to adduce his proof of the real validity of rational knowledge, and he believed that it was only by the distinction between the empirical and the intelligible world that he could unite the originality and autonomy of the will with the determination of the empirical character by nature. The two worlds—on one side the phenomenal (that of nature, of experience) on the other the intelligible (that of freedom, of ends)—confront one another as though they were entirely different and quite strange to one another. This is the result of Kant's epistemology and of his ethics, while his philosophy of religion, with its postulates, supplied only an external remedy. With characteristic critical deliberateness, however, Kant reverts to these results and asks whether we are quite justified in supposing these opposites to be absolute and irreconcilable. Man himself, indeed, is a natural as well as an intelligible being, phenomenon as well as

thing-in-itself.   Here then is a point of union between the two
worlds.   Man lives and acts in nature but must and can follow
the law of freedom; it is by means of human development in the
world of experience that the end posited by the ideal law is
to be attained.   The two worlds, then, cannot fall outside one
another ; there must be a basis common to nature and the moral
world.   And may not Kant's constant use of the distinction
between our perception of things and their real nature suggest
the question whether the assumption of these opposites may
not itself be bound up with the nature of our cognition, for
there is nothing to prove that the opposites which appear to us
as such (with our discursive thought that must distinguish
and analyse in order to know) are also opposites in the innermost nature of things.   Just as Kant had already intimated in
the " Critique of Pure Reason " that that which lies at the base
of the matter of our knowledge may be identical with that
which determines the form under which we arrange the same—
and that that which underlies material phenomena may be the
same as that which underlies spiritual phenomena—so he here
at last discusses the possible identity of the basis of the world
of nature with that of the world of freedom.   Like the architect
who on the completion of the building pulls down the scaffolding, Kant takes back again, now that he is on the point of
completing his work, those distinctions of which he had made
use in the upward movement of his inquiry.   From the distinction between knowledge and the world he deduces the
conclusion that this distinction—which is made by our knowledge itself—cannot be absolute.   In so doing he relies on
certain facts which gave him occasion to bring into prominence
problems which he had not hitherto handled, facts which show
that Nature, working according to her own laws, tends in the
direction of that which our mind, when it knows and estimates,
wishes and requires.   Can we therefore suppose her a stranger
to the ideal ?

(b) Reflections on Æsthetics

An æsthetic judgment is a judgment in which we pronounce a phenomenon to be beautiful or sublime.   We have
now to ask whether such judgments possess any general
validity? whether they can be anything more than the expression of a purely individual satisfaction ?

The beautiful is distinguished from the pleasant and the good by the fact that it does not depend upon the real existence of an object, but only on the picture, perception or idea we have of it. Æsthetic pleasure is disinterested and free. It originates in the free play of the cognitive faculty, which is excited when a picture brings into harmonious co-operation our powers of imagination and our understanding, in such wise that the details of the picture are bound together, easily and naturally, into an immediately comprehensible whole. The subject under consideration here is neither the purely material impression nor the pure concept: mere matter gives no totality, and the pure concept gives an abstract rule which, in regard to matter, appears as a constraint. In the English manner of laying out gardens,[26] in musical compositions, in the plastic arts, the single elements co-operate immediately to produce a total impression which satisfies a very essential spiritual need in us. Kant lays very great weight on the entire immediacy of the æsthetic judgment, and undervalues the more remote ideas which the picture may have excited. He only recognises " free " beauty (determined by what Fechner calls the direct factor) as such ; " secondary " (*anhängende*) beauty (determined by the associative factor) has no right to the name of beauty, since it presupposes certain ideas. A flower, an arabesque, a musical fantasia are examples of free beauty ; the beauty of a human being is secondary, because it presupposes an idea of that which is called a man.

Judgments on beauty (*i.e.* free beauty) are subjective, in so far as they spring from a feeling aroused in us by the picture. But this does not prevent them from having general validity, since the feeling is here determined by something which is common to all men, *i.e.* the relation between the cognitive powers, the need of a harmonious relation between the faculties of perception and the faculty of understanding. Æsthetic judgments (judgments of taste) are not susceptible of proof, but they may be evoked when an opportunity for immediate perception occurs. Their general validity is exemplary, *i.e.* it is gained by means of examples, not rules. Hence æsthetic criticism is an art, not a science.

The sublime also arises in a disinterested feeling of pleasure, but here the relation is more complicated. The

great, the unfathomable, the infinite in extension and power
overwhelms our perceptive faculty and conquers our self-pride.
This feeling leads us to abandon all that is finite and of the
senses ; we feel within us a power which is subject to no limitation whatever, *i.e.* the power to think infinite ideas and to
formulate the unconditional law.   Moreover, after a temporary
check, a higher kind of self-assertion arises in us when we
find ourselves confronted with the power of Nature.   The
really sublime, then, must not be identified with external phenomena ; these only afford the occasion for the great within us
to make itself felt.   Here, too, generally valid judgments may
be passed, since judgments concerning the sublime are founded
on a feeling which must be capable of being aroused in every
sufficiently developed man.

In the phenomena which we call beautiful and sublime,
Nature, working *according to her own laws*, produces in us a
feeling of pleasure which is free from all self-interest.   This
is a significant fact, especially since the æsthetic feeling, in
virtue of its disinterestedness, is akin to the ethical feeling.
Kant does not merely investigate the estimation of beauty.
He also investigates the production of the beautiful in art.
This production, like the estimation, is carried on without the
guidance of abstract rules, and, for the most part, without
deliberate intention, and yet in such wise that that which is
produced is the object of general recognition, and may serve
as a model.   Art is the work of genius.   Genius is "exemplary" originality : a disposition by means of which Nature
gives rules to art.   Genius does not work according to rules or
ideas ; nevertheless rules may be deduced from its works, and
ideas found therein.[27]   The fact of genius, then, like the fact
of the æsthetic judgment, shows that the world of Nature and
the world of freedom are not absolutely separate, but must
have a common foundation.   These facts, Kant thinks, we
ought to consider carefully before we form our definitive
conception of the world.

(c) *Reflections on Biology*

It is not only by the production of beautiful and sublime
phenomena, and by her activity working through genius, that
Nature shows herself in harmony with the laws of our spirit.

She exhibits organisms, *i.e.* beings so constituted that their individual parts are only comprehensible as the means or conditions for the existence of the being as a whole. We find here the same inner union between the parts and the whole as in the works of genius. In the organic world Nature works as genius in a manner which differs from the mechanical production of a whole by means of the co-operation of the parts, and also from the conscious forming of a totality, by means of the combination of the parts according to a definite plan. The organising activity of Nature has, properly speaking, nothing analogous with any causality which is known to us ("Critique of Judgment," § 65). We can only understand it by regarding organisms *as though* they had been produced under the guidance of the thought of an end (whether this be conceived as conscious or unconscious). But this is only a regulative principle ; we cannot exclude the possibility of the different classes and forms of organisms having arisen through a natural process of development according to mechanical laws. The analogy which exists between the different organic forms may indicate a common origin, so that Nature may be supposed to have progressed step by step from the lowest to the highest forms. It is conceivable that aquatic animals adapted themselves to live at first in morasses, after-wards on dry land, by ridding themselves of the forms which were least adapted to the several circumstances in which they found themselves. There can be few even of the most acute natural investigators, says Kant in the "Critique of Judgment," § 80, to whom an hypothesis of this kind — merely as a venturesome flight of reason, of course—has not occurred.

The whole opposition between mechanism and teleology— between an origin in the blind co-operation of parts and an origin in a combination according to a plan—is perhaps only due to the nature of our knowledge. Our understanding proceeds discursively—passes from the parts to the whole and regards the latter as the product of the former ; if it is to think the nature of the parts as determined by the whole, it can only do so by thinking the idea of the whole as the subjective cause of the formation and conjunction of the parts. To us, therefore, mechanism and teleology must always seem strongly opposed to one another. But in the hidden ground of Nature the mechanical and teleological forms of combination may be united in one single principle—a principle, however, which our reason would be unable to formulate.

With this thought—the most profound of all those which we owe to Kant—he takes up once more a line.of thought with which he had been much occupied in his youth, *i.e.* that that which underlies the causal relation between things also underlies the purposiveness and the harmony of nature. "The continuity of Kant's philosophical development" displays itself most clearly at this point. His speculative successors were content to begin where he ended. Kant himself regarded it as a final view, a concluding hypothesis, of great value for inquiry, but not to be dogmatically assumed as a starting-point. His wonderful capacity for never losing sight of the great while occupied with the small does not desert him here. Our presentation of this great thinker's philosophy can find no more appropriate conclusion than the mention of this characteristic feature of his thought.

CHAPTER VII

OPPONENTS OF THE CRITICAL PHILOSOPHY

A WORK such as Kant's could not hope to be understood at
once. It discussed so many problems—and these in such
intimate connection,—it presented by its assertions as well
as by its denials such a peculiar standpoint, that we cannot be astonished that no contemporary criticism shows signs
of having completely entered into the spirit in which it was
written. Many of the judgments passed upon it are of no
interest for the general history of philosophy. The misunderstandings of which the Enlightenment philosophy and the
Wolffian School were guilty only bear witness to the difficulty
experienced by those who are wedded to an older, deep-rooted,
and self-satisfied standpoint in working themselves into a new
line of thought. Not every one was possessed of such self-
knowledge and modesty—and at the same time of such a
beautiful belief in truth—as Mendelssohn exhibited in the preface to his *Morgenstunden*. In contradistinction to the above,
however, we find a very significant opposition offered by a group
of men who all, under different forms, maintained the significance of immediate feeling and of historical tradition ; speaking
broadly, we may say they defended the undivided, concentrated
activity of the spirit in opposition to Kant's analysis and
criticism which led him, at so many points, to make sharp distinctions between elements which, as a matter of fact, are only
given in indissoluble union. These men, for the most part, do
Kant injustice, for they overlook the attempts which he himself made to reunite that which he had only put asunder for
the sake of clearness and the furtherance of investigation.
And to a certain extent their objections are directed not only
against Kant's philosophy but against all philosophy, indeed

against all inquiry in general. Their work, however, affords a valuable counterpoise to Kant's analysis, for they insist on the living concrete interconnection of things. Kant's opponents, moreover, relied chiefly on the thinker whose work Kant had hoped at once to continue and to overcome, the man to whom he owed his own awakening, *i.e.* Hume. In their struggle with the Enlightenment philosophy, to which, in their eyes, Kant still belonged, they took their stand on experience, more particularly on feeling and that which has been historically experienced. They carried Kant's opposition to the Enlightenment so far that they ended by coming into conflict with Kant himself. Finally, they indicated ideas and points of view which were operative in wide circles, far beyond the sphere of philosophy, and were of great importance in arousing a new conception of poetry and history, as well as a deeper comprehension of life in general.

(*a*) Foremost in this group stands JOHANN GEORG HAMANN, Kant's friend, and, like him, a native of Königsberg : " The Magus of the North," as he has been called. His religious experience taught him the power of faith and the great and conflicting forces of life. A religious crisis experienced during his residence in London, where the weak side of his character had been revealed to him, influenced his whole subsequent life. His deep, seething nature had known violent agitations which he characterises himself in a letter to Kant of July 27, 1759, where he alludes to himself as a man " who is taught by the malady of his passions to conceive and feel a strength which a healthy man does not possess." He felt like a man in a deep chasm, who sees at midday the stars which those who live in the daylight are not able to perceive. An inner feeling of the mystery of life, and of the contradictions encountered in existence by the finite understanding as soon as it penetrates beneath the surface of things, is Hamann's chief characteristic. He loves mysterious intimations and paradoxical utterances, and his works are full of allusions to whatever he was reading at the time, so that they are often incomprehensible without a commentary. Quaint conceits alternate with the profound ideas and deep pathos which explain the impression he made on some of the greatest minds of his age. The pious-minded, sighing over the Enlightenment and lack of faith, hailed him as a prophet come to unseal afresh the sources of the old faith ; while to the whole of the younger generation he appeared as a spirit whose lofty flights outstripped the reason of the age, and whose thought, in which imagination and feeling worked together in passionate concentration, arrayed itself with mighty power against the prevailing rationalism and sentimentalism of the day. But, precisely because his burning thirst could be assuaged by nothing less than the collected force of all the currents which make up life, he was the sworn enemy of all analysis. In his very first work (*Socratische Denkwürdigkeiten*, 1759) he pronounced it presumption to attempt to carry out analysis to the final elements —for that is nothing else but to seek to grasp at the invisible essence of the godhead itself! It may be that Nature and history contain mysteries which only a power quite different from our reason can solve. Hence he lauds the Socratic ignorance.

We must *believe* in our own existence as well as in that of things external to us ; there is no other way by which we can posit it. Belief is not the work of reason and cannot therefore be governed by reason. It does not build on reasons any more than do taste and sight. When ignorance halts, the divine genius—which had greater significance for Socrates than the wisdom of all the world—comes to our aid. The ground of religion, he says later (*Zweifel und Einfälle*, 1776), lies in our whole existence, and is more comprehensive than the sphere in which our knowledge moves. Knowledge is the most abstract form of our existence ; only by means of passion do abstractions get hands, feet, or wings. Life must be taken as a whole. Philosophers sunder that which nature has joined together. In order to give appropriate expression to this concentrated fulness of life, Hamann employs Bruno's principle of the coincidence of opposites (*coincidentia oppositorum*) which he pronounced to be of more value than Kant's whole Critique. Reason (he wrote as early as the year 1759 to Kant)—as Hume has set forth—was given to you not in order to make you wise, but to show you your foolishness and ignorance, as the Mosaic law was given to the Jews, not to make them righteous, but to make sin more sinful for them. We obtain everything we can know from experience, tradition, and speech.

Hamann read Kant's works with the greatest interest (" The Little Master's," later "Our Plato's ") and he was, of course,

especially stirred by the " Critique of Pure Reason." Immediately after the appearance of this work he drew up an outline
of a Critique, which, however, he withheld from publication ;
partly because, as he knew, his poor head, when pitted against
Kant's, would fare as clay against iron, — partly that he
might not wound Kant, to whom he was under obligations.
His *Metakritik über den Purismum der reinen Vernunft* was
not printed until after his death (1788). He saw in Kant's
philosophy an unsuccessful attempt to make reason independent of all tradition, all belief, and all experience ; and he
especially polemicises against his severance of matter from
form, of the senses from the understanding. To what end
this violent, ineffectual, and stubborn separation of what
Nature joins together ? A constant circular motion takes
place ! Percepts mounting ever aloft to reason, concepts
sinking into sense ! In a letter which he wrote while he
was reading the proof-sheets of the " Critique of Pure Reason,"
he calls Kant the " Prussian Hume," adding at the same time
that he prefers the English one. " Hume is the man for me,
for he at least honours the principle of belief, and includes it
in his system, while our countryman is always chewing the cud
of his causal whirligig, without a thought for belief. I don't
call that honest " (Letter to Herder, May 10, 1781). And in
a still earlier work (*Des Ritters von Rosencreuz letzte Willens-
meinung über den göttlichen und menschlichen Ursprung der
Sprache*, 1772), he says : " Finally, philosophers, know ye not
that the bond between cause and effect, means and end, is not
physical but spiritual and idealistic, to wit, implicit faith ? "
and here he expressly refers to Hume.

Hamann wrote no large works, and gave no detailed
exposition of his thought, but his oracular sayings inspired
HERDER and JACOBI, who continued his work, for, like him,
and with a similar appeal to Hume, they oppose faith to reason.
They were, however, more the children of their age than
was the " Magus of the North," who was called the most
believing of believers (also, however, the freest, because the
deepest). Hamann was an orthodox Lutheran. Herder and
Jacobi were more in sympathy with the age of Enlightenment,
especially in its sentimental form, although they, like their
master, took up arms against the reason which would analyse
and assign grounds for everything.

(*b*) Hamann (born 1730, died 1788), was a poor Custom-House officer in Königsberg. His view of life had defined itself before Kant had been aroused from his dogmatic slumber. JOHANN GOTTFRIED HERDER (born 1744, died 1803), attended Kant's lectures as a youth, and was markedly influenced by the standpoint adopted by Kant in the sixties. But he fell in with Hamann also at Königsberg, and the latter's influence predominated with him. With a great sense for the original, the national, and all that has a natural development, he set himself the task of infusing into literature a fresher and more vigorous spirit. Goethe relates (in *Aus meinem Leben*) how Herder had taught him that the art of poetry is a gift to the nation, to the whole world, not the private inheritance of a handful of refined and cultured men. Herder championed the rights of the natural and human in the spirit of Rousseau ; but he possessed the historic sense to a far greater degree than Rousseau did, while in his conception of Nature he was influenced by Goethe, with whom, while Superintendent in Weimar, he sustained a lively interchange of ideas, until differing views on art and politics effected a breach between them. In his chief work (*Ideen zur Philosophie der Geschichte der Menschheit*, 1784-91), he came into collision with his sometime teacher, Kant. Herder cannot allow that the end must lie in the race and not in the particular individual. To each particular individual is allotted such happiness and development as is possible at the given stage ; but in order that this end may be reached, there must be reciprocal action between individuals and a transmission of acquired means of culture from generation to generation. It is this interconnection between individuals and generations which produces humanity and a philosophy of history. Even in unconscious Nature ideal forces were at work, forming and organising according to a definite type. Leibniz' doctrine of monads is transformed, with Herder, into a doctrine of organic forces, which, in analogy with the active force in our thought, operate in different degrees and at different stages throughout the whole of Nature. The force which thinks and works in me is, in virtue of its nature, a force as eternal as that which holds the sun and stars together. All existence resembles itself ; it is an indivisible concept (*Ideen*, i. pp. 7, 8). Thus the thought

which expressed Kant's final conjecture is here taken as
a foundation-stone, and by means of the great analogy with
Nature an interconnection of all things in the universe and
in history is asserted,—an interconnection which also teaches
us to find the bond between science and religion. Herder
uses the word " Nature " in his book in order to avoid the
frequent mention of the name of God—" God is everything in
His works."

Man, too, is included in this great whole of giving and
receiving. His reason is by no means free to choose its
own path. The word *Vernunft* (reason) comes from
vernehmen (to learn), and indicates that we have acquired
our thoughts through tradition, speech, and external influences.
Reason is a product ; it is not innate. Religion is the
first form of spiritual culture. Before the first abstract
thought could be formed there was a religious consciousness of
invisible forces in Nature. It is in virtue of this consciousness
that man rises above the brutes. The propensity to humanity
is older than reason. But it only develops by education,
and under the influence of examples. Man cannot develop
everything out of himself. And just because every particular man can only become a man through education,
there is an education of humanity. Every single stage
of this development is not only a means to reach the
next, but is also an end in itself. All the means used
by the Deity are ends, and all these ends are means to reach
higher ends. To sum up : what every man is and can be,
that it is which must be the end of the human race. And
what is this ? Such a measure of humanity and blessedness
as obtains in this place and in this degree, *i.e.* as exhibited by
this particular, definite member of the chain of culture which
stretches through the whole race ! By this line of thought
Herder corrects the violent antithesis between the individual
and the race posited in Kant's philosophy of history, an
antithesis which involved such far-reaching consequences for his
ethics. Herder, however, is content with enthusiastic assertion,
he does not grapple with the great problem which the idea he
had posited is seen to contain when applied in detail.

The fundamental conception of Herder's philosophy, as
far as his lyrical and flowery style permits us to gain a
clear view of it, was based on the thought which had acquired

such great significance, even in Kant's earliest works, viz. : that the interconnection of things according to law presupposes a ground of unity in existence. And this thought, by a natural transition, brought Herder into sympathy with Spinoza. He regarded Spinozá as the most logical of philosophers, and found in repeated study of his work satisfaction for his craving to transcend all dualism between God and Nature, spirit and matter. A God existing outside the world seemed to him to contradict the concept of God, the concept of the world, and the concept of space ; and personality, he thought, could not be a quality of an infinite Being. Hence he could in no way share Jacobi's horror of Spinoza. He appreciated the mystical side of Spinoza, while Jacobi only perceived his abstract rationalism (and both were blind to his realistic side). He even wrote to Jacobi that if he reduced the deepest, highest, and all-comprehensive concept to a mere name he, not Spinoza, was the atheist. Herder's hatred of all abstractions carried him over and beyond the distinction between God and the world. He broke with Jacobi for the same reason that he had broken with Kant, and that had led Hamann (to whom both the negative and positive interest of his friend in Spinoza were incomprehensible) to adopt Bruno's principle of coincidence. In his work entitled *Gott* (Gotha, 1787) Herder defends Spinoza against Jacobi. His knowledge of the details of Spinoza's philosophy was not so thorough as Jacobi's. He misrepresented Spinoza's conception of Nature in particular, introducing into it his own "organic forces," in fact, his modified Leibnizism ; nevertheless his work did much to excite interest in the innermost kernel of the Spinozistic philosophy. He himself was regarded as a renegade by the orthodox group which gathered round Hamann. His religious standpoint had from the first differed from that of the "Magus of the North," whom he so much admired. They were alike in the stress they laid on the historical, the traditionary, the involuntarily developed, in contrast to the preference of the age for the clearly conscious and voluntary. Herder was the first to really shake the popular belief that religious ideas "originate in the arbitrary inventions and frauds of princes and priests." His love of national poetry also taught him to appreciate the spirit of originality and natural power displayed in the books of ancient religions. His longing to develop all faculties at once is here apparent. He was in search of a philosophy for the whole man, and he found it in the religious works which were the outcome of an age in which the mental faculties of man had not yet begun to work apart from one another. His need was poetical rather than philosophical—poetical too, rather than religious. Herder always found it difficult to keep poetry, philosophy and religion apart, and it is this which makes him the most characteristic forerunner of Romanticism. He did a great deal to further the comprehension of religion by his assertion of its immediate and involuntary origin in the human spirit, and by his demand that it should be read and understood in its own spirit. His own exposition—although he himself was not always clearly aware of it—was symbolical and ethical. His standpoint differs from the orthodox as well as the rationalistic (at any rate, the ordinary rationalistic standpoint). To a certain extent it is a continuation and further extension of Lessing's, for since he traces the activity of divine powers throughout the whole of Nature, he does not feel any need of defending revelation in the narrower sense, *i.e.* in sharp antithesis to the general revelation which is displayed in all natural and human life. His ethico-symbolical conception of Christianity is given in the 17th book of the *Ideen* and in his work *Von Religion, Lehrmeinungen und Gebräuchen* ("On Religion, Dogmas, and Customs") (Leipzig, 1798). He looked on the ruling Church as a gigantic Antichrist. Herder regarded Christ as the spiritual saviour of the race. He came to raise up God-men who, whatever the laws under which they lived, would further the good of others according to the purest principles, and who themselves, in all toleration, would rule as kings in the kingdom of goodness and truth. Christ's discourses bear the stamp of the purest humanity, but His words have been construed into speculative dogmas and His symbolic actions turned into magical processes. (So wrote a General Superintendent towards the end of the last century!) Nevertheless, Herder never doubted the ultimate victory of the pure religion of Christ.

In his criticism of Kant's teaching Herder gave an exposition of Hamann's *Metakritik* without adding anything of his own. His significance is connected with the positive fulness which he partly created, partly knew where to find. And by the time the prolix and spun-out works (*Meta-*

kritik, 1799, and *Kalligone*, 1800) in which he criticised Kant's philosophy appeared, the critical philosophy had already received further developments and had been turned into new channels by Kant's successors,—partly, it is true, under the influence of considerations which had from the beginning determined Hamann's and Herder's attitude towards it.

(*c*) FRIEDRICH HEINRICH JACOBI (1743-1819), a brilliant man of the world and a seeker after truth, one of the most characteristic representatives of the period of "genius," contributed largely towards determining the peculiar direction taken by German philosophy subsequent to Kant. As already mentioned, Jacobi had, with great acuteness, laid bare the grave difficulties involved in Kant's doctrine of the thing-in-itself, and had declared that that doctrine must be abandoned if a logical system is to be attained. His criticism is right so far as it goes, but his objections do not touch Kant's main problem. The doctrine of the thing-in-itself was only a consequence of the Kantian philosophy, not its main problem. Instead of going back to Kant's *original* task and investigating his method in order to find where the weak point was concealed, attempts were made—for the most part under the influence of Jacobi's criticism—to remedy the defects of the completed system. Jacobi could not feel satisfied with the Kantian philosophy any more than Hamann and Herder, and for the same reason, viz. because immediate faith was not given its due. And faith alone can grasp the truth. The aim of all science is to construct, to produce its objects by means of an inner action, to dissolve everything into pure activity. For we only understand a thing in so far as we construct it. Everything which we understand we picture to ourselves as a member of a series of a complete interconnected system in which all differences are annulled. The most logical of all systems is subjectivism, which takes our own ego as the first link of the chain and deduces from this the other links. Hence Jacobi hailed the turn given by Fichte to the critical philosophy as the consummation of speculation. His letter to Fichte (*Jacobi an Fichte*, 1799) gives us, perhaps, the best view of his philosophical conception. He had previously asserted that Spinoza was the only logical philosopher ; now he places Fichte still higher, because the ego, consciousness itself, must necessarily form the first member in the chain of knowledge. But all logical philosophies must agree in denying to the original, the unconditioned, that which has its ground and worth in itself, all qualitative differences and idiosyncracies. All philosophy seeks to found and deduce, and to reduce quality to quantity. It cannot, therefore, include the immediate, the free and the original. Hence, thinks Jacobi, it is evident that the more consistent the philosophy, the clearer it will become that philosophy cannot discover truth. On this ground, therefore, he urges and incites to complete consistency, for only then will it become evident that truth cannot be reached in this way. His letters on Spinoza emphasise this as against the Enlightenment philosophy, his dialogues on idealism and realism urge it against Kant, while his letter to Fichte expresses it most clearly and distinctly in opposition to this " Messiah of speculation." He found one other opportunity to bring his old thoughts to bear against a new system, _i.e._ when Schelling believed himself to have founded a new philosophy of religion by way of a philosophy of nature (Jacobi's _Von den göttlichen Dingen_ (" On Divine Things"), 1811). Although Jacobi himself was no logical thinker, yet he had a great sense for the consistency of systems, and was able to bring out with great energy the leading features of a line of thought.

No proof, thinks Jacobi, can ever convince us of the existence of a reality outside consciousness, for every proof exists within consciousness itself. Immediate perception is a miracle which we must accept if we ever hope to grasp truth : things only exist for us through faith. Only through faith does God, the original creator of all things, the source of all the worth of existence, exist for us. God cannot be known, He can only be apprehended by faith. A God who could be known would not be a God at all. Indeed it is even to the interest of science that there should be no God : for God's existence interrupts the series, and makes interconnection impossible ; God reveals Himself immediately within us (the true God cannot reveal Himself in the outer world) as things immediately reveal themselves to our senses. We have an immediate intuition of something better and greater than ourselves : we find God by finding ourselves in God. Finally, freedom, in the sense of the spirit's capacity to intervene in the world of matter, can be believed only, never understood. Freedom, it is true, does not consist in any ridiculous capacity to decide without reasons, but since it is an absolute self-activity it is inaccessible to science.

The opposition between science and faith posited by Jacobi is closely connected with the great movement on behalf of feeling which, since Rousseau, had governed the age. Jacobi himself expressed this tendency in poetical expositions. He defended the rights of feeling against the objective grounds of understanding, which are unshaken by all individual excitement. He also urged the claims of individual feeling within the ethical sphere. "The beautiful soul" which, resting and moving securely in its own moods, unfolds its inner dispositions without regulating itself according to general principles seems to Jacobi the highest, although he does not overlook the dangers to which it is exposed. He defends exceptional cases against the strict, universal law framed by Kant in his categorical imperative, which seems to require the same behaviour from all men in all cases. Kant's moral law takes account of the formal consequence of the action only, not the heart, from which the action must spring. The law exists for the sake of man, not man for the sake of the law. The book of life must be written before the table of the law can be drawn up. A system of morality is nothing but an anticipated code. And yet it claims to regulate life, and, without any regard to individuality and to exceptional cases, to establish rules of universal validity. Jacobi expressed his opposition to this in his letter to Fichte in the oft-quoted words : "Yes, I am that atheist and godless man who will lie as dying Desdemona lied : will lie and deceive as Pylades did when he feigned to be Orestes, will murder as Timoleon did, etc." [28]

Jacobi, in common with Hamann and Herder, has the merit of having maintained the significance of that element in life which cannot be translated into terms of generally valid knowledge. He fought for the rights of immediacy, of reality, and of individuality, and in so doing contributed important corrections to the direction which philosophy was on the point of taking, and along which he himself would fain have enticed her. But he was under the illusory belief that the objects of his faith were given in immediate revelation. In the first place, he takes the word "faith" in two very different meanings : sometimes as the involuntary trust in sensuous perceptions, sometimes as religious faith in that which cannot be

perceived. Secondly, the content of his religious faith is a very
old acquaintance, *i.e.* the Cartesian spiritualism, now declared
by Jacobi, as formerly by Rousseau, to be the object of *faith*,
while the dogmatic school, on the contrary, had pronounced
it susceptible of proof. But do different individuals, different
" beautiful souls " necessarily find the same content of belief
within them ?   No definite content can be deduced from
feeling : nothing but the general necessity to hold fast to the
validity of that which is of highest worth.   By establishing
certain dogmas (even if only the dogmas of "natural" religion)
as the only form which could satisfy this need, Jacobi violated
the inwardness and individualism of feeling which he elsewhere
defends.   And it is this which first brings out the sharp contrast between his faith and his knowledge ; his faith is beset
with all the difficulties involved in the Cartesian spiritualism.
As a matter of fact, his faith and his knowledge constituted
two distinct philosophies ; hence it was no wonder that he
complained that his head and his heart were at variance : he
had taken it into his head that his heart could only beat
artificially, and that to do so was its true nature.

CHAPTER VIII

FURTHER DEVELOPMENT OF THE CRITICAL PHILOSOPHY

THE same need which led Kant's earliest opponents to raise a protest against his work on behalf of feeling, moved his first independent disciples to the attempt to reduce his many ramified inquiries and innumerable distinctions to a few simple principles — if possible, to one single principle. Such an endeavour could not fail to be aroused in thinkers whose enthusiasm for all that was new and great in Kant was coupled with a clear realisation of his defects. Hence it came to pass that a closer discussion of Kant's doctrines brought to light problems which the master himself could not have formulated with perfect clearness, and the treatment of which determined the further direction philosophy was to take after it had passed the great turning-point. In this connection three men deserve special mention—Reinhold and Maimon, in connection with the theoretical problem, and Schiller in connection with æsthetic and ethical problems.

(a) KARL LEONHARD REINHOLD was born at Vienna in 1758, and as quite a young man was a novice in the Order of Jesuits; when this Order—to the great sorrow of Reinhold and his fellow students (as is described in a letter given in the biography published by his son)—was dissolved he entered a Barnabite College. He was induced to take this step by love of study rather than interest in religion. While in this college he taught philosophy. The rationalistic tendency prevalent under Joseph II. acquired great influence over him; the contrast between his opinions and his position as a member of a religious house finally became so sharp that, at the age of twenty-five, he quitted the cloister. He then joined the staff of Wieland's paper, the *Deutscher Merkur*, in which paper he published, *inter alia*, his *Briefe über die Kantische Philosophie* ("Letters on the Kantian Philosophy"), (1786), a popular exposition, which may be said to have first spread the knowledge of Kant's doctrines in wider circles. At the time of Reinhold's appointment to a professorship in Jena (1787) that University was the centre of the philosophical movement. Nearly all the philosophical tendencies which successively developed in the course of the attempts to carry on Kant's inquiry originated at Jena. (Besides Reinhold himself there were Fichte, Schelling, Hegel, Fries, Herbart). Reinhold's chief work is his *Versuch einer neuen Theorie des menschlichen Vorstellungsvermögens* ("Attempt at a New Theory of Human Understanding") (Prague and Jena, 1789), in which he attempts to reduce the philosophy founded by Kant to one single principle. Reinhold did not, however, hold fast to the standpoint which he takes up in this work, and to which his significance in the history of philosophy attaches. His great receptivity of the thoughts of others, and his disinterested love of truth, caused him to change his standpoint repeatedly, for he was always discovering in other philosophical writers of the time (and these not always of the first rank) important advances towards the solution of problems. As early as 1793 he left Jena and went to Kiel, where he was active until his death (1823). He is of interest for Danish literature on account of his friendship with Baggesen, of whom he gave a delightful characterisation in his letters to Erhard.

According to Reinhold, Kant had not gone back to the ultimate presuppositions—or rather the ultimate presupposition. It was Reinhold's conviction that philosophy can only become a true science when it deduces all its doctrines from one principle. Not only had Kant made a sharp distinction between the senses and the understanding, between theoretical knowledge and practical belief, but he had also employed a double method : partly that of analysis of the forms of knowledge (subjective deduction), which is essentially a psychological investigation, partly that of construction out of the presuppositions of experience (the objective deduction). These different methods and these distinctions appeared to Reinhold an imperfection ; he demanded one single starting-point and one single route proceeding from this starting-point. It was this demand which started critical philosophy on a speculative course. It rests on a mistaken identification between the search after unity—of which all inquiry is an expression—and an absolute principle ; the unity sought after always presupposes a given manifold to be systematised which, in and for itself, is not sufficient to express the ideal of knowledge. Nor is this demand even in accordance with the nature of our knowledge, since every conclusion consists in a combination of several premises. The enthusiastic thinkers of this period set before themselves an infinite ideal, and believed themselves in possession of powers sufficient to attain to it. Reinhold called his fundamental principle the *principle of consciousness.* All knowledge consists of ideas (while not all ideas are knowledge) ; the principle of consciousness tells us that every idea is related on the one hand to a subject and on the other to an object, so that it is partly to be distinguished from both of them, partly to be united with them. Consciousness itself consists in such a relating of the idea to the subject and object. Reinhold next seeks to show in detail, by means of a series of investigations, that all the forms and principles established by Kant can, when carried further, be shown to arise from this principle, and are indeed only special ways in which ideas may be related to subject and object. That element of the idea through which it is related to the subject is its form, while that element through which it is related to the object is its matter. And since form cannot produce matter, nor subject object, we are forced to assume a thing-in-itself ; there must be something in the idea which is not produced by consciousness itself but by some cause other than it. But as Reinhold holds that the essence of consciousness consists in a relating activity, the idea of a thing-in-itself must necessarily be self-contradictory, for it is concerned with a something which cannot be related to the subject nor be apprehended and formed by its activity. Reinhold says, moreover, " of the reality of the thing-in-itself nothing but a contradictory idea, an empty mockery, is possible." And he declares that the connection between the activity peculiar to consciousness and the thing-in-itself is " one of those questions which no one will ask who understands its meaning and knows the limits of presentability." (*Versuch.* pp. 456-460). The problem of the thing-in-itself thus becomes restricted to much narrower issues than it was with Kant. Reinhold lays far greater emphasis than Kant did upon the unity and activity of consciousness ; hence the mystery of the eternal limits, the contradiction involved in believing that a something exists which at one and the same time *must* be thought and yet *cannot* be thought, is all the more apparent. G. E. SCHULZE'S *Aenesidemus* is especially directed against this doctrine of Reinhold's. It became more and more evident either that greater admissions must be made to Hume than Kant had allowed, or that the way taken by Reinhold must be continued boldly, and the unity and activity of our consciousness declared absolute, by which means the thing-in-itself would entirely disappear. Reinhold's subsequent uncertainty was due to the fact that he could not decide between these alternatives.

(*b*) SALOMON MAIMON, also a disciple of Kant's, brought very great penetration to bear on the discussion of the questions which his master's teaching had occasioned. He was able to refrain both from the dogmatising which overtook so many Kantians and from the titanic speculations to which the demand for singleness of principle led. The circumstances of his life helped to develop his critical independence. A Lithuanian Jew of poor family (born in 1756), he was destined to become a rabbi, and distinguished himself, while still quite young, by his learning and acumen. But his thirst for knowledge drove him beyond the Talmud and the Jewish theology. He has described in his autobiography— an excessively interesting work from the point of view of psychology and the history of culture—the miserable circumstances out of which he had to struggle up to scientific knowledge. An accidentally discovered Hebrew astronomy revealed to him the existence of other sciences besides the Talmudic. With great difficulty he learnt the elements of German, and in order to share in the knowledge of the West, he ran away from his family (he had married in his twelfth year), and begged his way to Berlin, where he soon attracted the attention and interest of Moses Mendelssohn. He now studied Wolff, Spinoza, and Locke. The very inadequate means of culture he had had at his disposal had forced him to fill up what was lacking by his own acuteness ; hence he had acquired great skill in discovering the essential elements in any line of thought, and in drawing conclusions therefrom ; this enabled him to take up an independent and critical attitude towards all the views with which he came in contact. This was the attitude he adopted towards Kant's works. Out of the annotations which he made during his study of the " Critique of Pure Reason " there grew up a work (*Versuch über die Transcendentalphilosophie*, Berlin, 1790), which evoked from Kant, who had seen it in MS., the pronouncement that not only had none of his opponents understood him so well as Maimon, but that few men possessed the acuteness requisite for such investigations to such a high degree. Maimon elaborated his views on epistemology in a series of works, among which we need only mention here the *Versuch einer neuen Logik oder Theorie des Denkens* (Berlin, 1794). Philosophical thought was everything to him—the highest perfection as well as the highest felicity. In this he resembles the older thinkers of his nation (Maimonides, Spinoza). After having long led a wandering and uncertain life, he spent his last years in Silesia with a landed proprietor who took an interest in him. He died in the year 1800.

We already find in Maimon that criticism of the Kantian philosophy which will probably be accepted as final. Since, he says, we can only discover the forms of knowledge by way of experience, we can demonstrate neither their necessity nor their completeness. We can obtain no guarantee that we have found all possible forms. And the distinction between matter and form can only be a relative one : there can neither be pure matter nor pure form, but only approximations to these. Mere sensation is an " idea " in the Kantian sense of the word: in spite of all possible degrees of approximation to a sensation in which form does not enter this extreme is never reached. There are here two limiting points or ideas : on the one hand, the single element in consciousness, on the other, the perfect synthesis. Our knowledge moves in the interval between these. It is an apprehension, not a comprehension. Every time that we attempt to form an idea of a totality, an all-embracing thought, we find that this idea starts from something limited and finite. In opposition to Reinhold, Maimon asserts the impossibility of establishing a single highest principle. Reinhold's principle of consciousness only expresses that which is common to all principles, and the special principles are not

deducible from it.   Consciousness-in-general is an altogether
indefinite concept.   Maimon joins issue with Kant more
particularly in connection with the fact on which Kant rests
his "objective deduction": *i.e.* that we have *experience* (as
something different from subjective presentation).   Even if
Kant were right in supposing that our thought commands a
system of categories, yet he was wrong in thinking that we
could actually apply these categories to the given.   For the
given exhibits temporal relations only, not *necessary* transitions.
Only within the sphere of pure mathematics have we an
objectively valid rational knowledge, a "real thinking."   In
empirical thought consciousness of the subject precedes consciousness of the predicate : the latter cannot be deduced
from the former.   It is different in mathematics, but in
mathematics only.   Hume was by no means refuted by
Kant ; indeed, he cannot be refuted.   When Hume says the
causal concept is taken from experience, he does not, like
Kant, understand by experience a necessary order in the
sequence of phenomena, but only the invariable perception, by
means of which habit and expectation are begotten in us.   The
causal axiom expresses a postulate, an idea, which we seek to
apply to phenomena, but the applicability of which can only
be approximately shown.   While Maimon thus takes up a
mean position between Hume and Kant in his view of the
axiom of causality, he further develops Kant's interesting
suggestion of a connection between the concepts of causality
and continuity.   He shows that throughout our knowledge
there runs an endeavour to reduce the opposition between
phenomena as far as possible.   To search for the cause
of a phenomenon is the same as to search for its continuous arising or to fill out the lacunæ in our perception.
What do we understand in natural science by the word cause
except the development and dissolution of a phenomenon,
so that its continuity with the preceding (and following)
phenomena can be shown ?   It is only in virtue of this
continuity that perceptions become experience.   The word
experience, then, connotes for Maimon not a necessary relation,
but merely a relation of actual continuity between the perceived phenomena.   The much discussed problem of the
thing-in-itself may, in a certain sense, be said to disappear for
Maimon altogether.   For the thing-in-itself is said to be the

cause of the "matter" of our knowledge; but, according to Maimon, there is no pure matter; we only approach matter— like the determination of $\sqrt{2}$—by means of an infinite series of approximations: that is to say, the point in our chain of thought at which the question concerning the thing-in-itself can arise, lies at an infinite distance! That something is *given* us, or that our capacity of knowledge is affected, only means that something arises in our consciousness which cannot be deduced *a priori* according to the general laws of consciousness and knowledge. The given is that part of a presentation of which we are aware without any consciousness of activity on our part. No one faculty contains the ground of its special application. But a thing, an object, can only exist in and for consciousness. An object which should be an object for no one is an impossible thought and may be likened to an *imaginary* number, while the given, the point at which we are absolutely passive, may be likened to an *irrational* number. And when we inquire as to the cause of the given we find this is a question which admits of no answer. It cannot, for instance, be decided whether the given originates in something different from us or in our own faculty of knowledge; we only know that which appears in our consciousness, and the faculty of knowledge, apart from its functions, is just as much a thing-in-itself as the unknown cause of the matter of knowledge posited by Kant and Reinhold. The concept of an absolute subject, like that of an absolute object, is an idea only, a limiting concept which cannot become part of our knowledge.[29] It is the task of our understanding to *apprehend* phenomena, *i.e.* to understand them through their reciprocal connection, by means of the law of their relation. Our imaginative faculty, excited in its turn by our attempt to reach the highest, continually seeks to extend our presentations beyond the limitations of our experience, and to *comprehend in a single picture* the whole of the manifold which is subject to law. All that Kant calls Ideas, concepts of an unconditioned in various forms, Maimon deduces, not from reason, but from the faculty of imagination. The instinctive desire of our knowledge for totality has its ground in the instinctive desire after the highest perfection; hence the instinct to form ideas expresses itself chiefly within the ethical and religious spheres. But as soon as we conceive these totalities *as objects* we limit them, and in so doing check this desire. For every object must have its place in the continuous interconnection of knowledge. The striving after totality is a perfection ; but the idea of totality as an object is an impossibility. It is not the idea but the striving which is of religious and ethical value.

Maimon calls himself a sceptic not only as regards dogmatic, but also as regards the critical philosophy. It was the dogmatism of the Kantians which led him to adopt this appellation. In reality, however, he suggested an epistemological theory capable of leading beyond the difficulties which had arisen during the discussion of Kant's works. On the relation between thought and experience (Kant's point of difference from Hume) as well as on that between knowledge and faith (Kant's point of difference from Jacobi) he has suggested views which are capable of scientific development. Of all Kant's disciples, Maimon is the one who carried on his work best (even though Maimon's attempt at a continuation pleased the old master no more than that of Reinhold and other "hypercritical friends).[30] The romantic fermentation of the time, however, prevented any continuous development of the critical philosophy in the spirit which had animated Maimon. The romantic craving for unity, the longing to revel in the absolute, to unite thought with artistic conceptions, was far too strong to permit of Maimon's critical and sceptical considerations exciting any permanent interest. Speculative philosophy and its historians consider Maimon's significance to lie in the fact that he formed a middle term between Kant and the pure speculation introduced by Fichte. But he has independent and lasting significance, and represents far more than one of the "overcome standpoints" which speculative philosophy swept past in its triumphant march.

(*c*) There is a certain analogy of circumstance and thought between Reinhold, Maimon, and Schiller. All three were obliged to extricate themselves by flight from the cramping environment in which their youth was spent, in order to be able to attain to that free mental development after which they yearned ; while as thinkers they were occupied with the same task, although under different forms,—taking their stand on the critical philosophy, they sought to introduce unity and harmony in place of the distinctions and oppositions which with Kant had occupied the forefront.

FRIEDRICH SCHILLER (1759-1805), the great poet, whose
biography it is not the task of a *History of Philosophy* to write,
entertained throughout his whole life the deepest interest in
philosophy. As he has himself told us, however, he felt that
art alone afforded full scope for his powers, and he finally
employed his philosophical theory to prove that the artist
alone is the true man, a proof which logically enough denoted
for him the transition from his philosophising period to that
of his magnificent poetic production during the last decade
of his life. The study of Kant was not the first thing to
excite his interest in philosophy. While at the Karlsschule,
Stuttgart, he had taken a scientific interest in medicine and
philosophy, and speeches and treatises of this period show that
even then thoughts which were to exercise great influence on
his later views had already established themselves in his mind.
Of especial interest is the *Versuch über den Zusammenhang der
tierischen Natur des Menschen mit seiner geistigen* ("Essay on
the Connection between the Animal and Spiritual Nature of
Man") (1780), in which he maintains that the pleasure and
pain associated with the organic functions are not only of
significance for self-preservation but also help to excite the
mental powers, either stimulating or checking and exhausting them, while, conversely, mental pleasure and pain react on
the organic condition. The ethical ideas to which Schiller gave
utterance at this time betray the influence of Rousseau and the
English moral philosophers of the eighteenth century. After
his flight from Stuttgart (the Duke, who had taken offence at
"The Robbers," had prohibited Schiller from publishing any but
purely medical works) he devoted himself to the study of the
ancient poetical classics, and from this time onwards he regarded
Greek humanity, expressed in Greek art and life, as the great
ideal which had shown itself during a happy period in history,
but which, during the subsequent development of culture, had
fallen into neglect. This ideal was bound up in a curious manner
with the critical attitude towards civilisation which the study of
Rousseau had led him to adopt. The vague idea of an un-
restricted life according to Nature was now supplanted by that
of a harmonious development of life determined from within. He
now saw in art a vital power which, by means of an involuntary
harmonising of instincts and forces, and without exercising
any compulsion, raises human life above the life of the brutes,

just as it leads by means of its symbols to an apprehension of the truth long before the abstract thinker can attain to it. And art denotes not only the beginning of the higher spiritual life, but also its zenith. Thus we find Schiller addressing artists (in *Die Künstler*) as follows :—

> Mit euch, des Frühlings erster Pflanze,
> Begann die seelenbildende Natur ;
> Mit euch, dem freud'gen Erntekranze,
> Schliesst die vollendende Natur.

He regarded art as the peculiar characteristic of man :—

> Die Kunst, o Mensch, hast du allein.

Schiller was already acquainted with Kant's treatises on the history of philosophy in which such a prominent place is given to the problem of culture when he wrote this poem. But it was not until after he had become Reinhold's colleague at Jena that he made any deep study of Kant's works. The great thoughts contained in them fell on a well-prepared soil. Schiller, who had had to struggle against external hindrances as well as refractory desires and doubting thoughts, was well able to appreciate the master's struggle to search out the ground of truth and to maintain the supremacy of the ideal above the immediate natural instincts. His artistic temperament and his enthusiasm for the Greeks, however, was too strong for him ever to abandon his demand for the harmonious development of human nature. Thus the problem presented itself to him the solution of which was his contribution to the development of philosophy. It is a noteworthy fact that he, from his artistic standpoint, made the same demand as Hamann from his religious standpoint, *i.e.* "not to put asunder what Nature had joined together." "Even in the purest manifestations of the divine part of his nature," we find in the treatise *Über Anmut und Würde*, (" Grace and Dignity ") (1793) "man must not leave the sensuous behind, he must not found the triumph of the one on the suppression of the other. Only when it flows from his entire humanity as the result of the united action of both principles, when it has become second nature to him, is his morality secure." Hence Schiller demands that moral action shall have beauty and grace. He defines grace as " the harmony of involuntary movements which accompany a freely willed action, and which themselves indicate a moral frame of mind."

There must be nothing constrained, fanciful, or rude in an action if it is to be perfect. This demand, it is true, says Schiller, is not in verbal agreement with Kant's ethics. But, he continues, the great thinker was the Draco of his age, because it was not ready for a Solon. Hence he forgot that the children of the house do not deserve that he should care for the valets only. Shall the most disinterested feeling in the noblest breast be regarded with suspicion because impure desires often usurp the name of virtue? and is not perfect humanity to be found in the beautiful soul which, guided by immediate feeling, performs with instinctive ease the most painful duties, and offers the most heroic sacrifices? With a beautiful soul it is not individual actions which are moral, but the whole character. A beautiful soul has no other merit than to be a beautiful soul. Sense and reason, duty and inclination are in harmony with one another, and this harmony finds outer expression in grace. Nevertheless, Schiller is content to demand that only those actions shall be graceful which lie *within* the limits of human nature. Duties may be imposed on man which lead him to the limits of human capacity, where duty and inclination no longer harmonise. Here painful struggle is the only possibility, and here Schiller demands that man shall act with dignity and so express the want of harmony as to let it be seen that victory remains with the nobler power. A certain hesitation in Schiller's course of thought makes itself apparent. He regards harmony as the highest good, and yet he doubts whether harmony is attainable in all cases. Whether grace or dignity is the higher is a question to which he only returns a hesitating answer. This vacillation is connected with the fact that, like Kant, he never subjected the differences existing between different individualities to any ethical investigation. He speaks of the limits of human nature only—not of the limits of particular individualities, and he takes it for granted that these limits are identical for all individualities. He expressly says, "Our moral judgment brings every individual under the measuring-rod of the race, and man is forgiven no other limitations save those which are common to humanity."

Schiller unfolds his ideas in close connection with the

problem of culture in his *Briefen über die ästhetische Erziehung des Menschen* (1795), (" Letters upon the Æsthetic Education of Man "). The fundamental thought of his poem *Die Künstler* is here developed at length. The progress of civilisation has dissolved the Greek harmony between mind and nature, reflection and imagination, universality and individuality. Division of labour is the cause of the evils under which we suffer. The struggle between forces furthers the progress of civilisation, and is, in so far, a gain for the race; single individuals, however, become one-sided and mutilated. State and church, law and morality, labour and consumption have become separated from one another, and each particular man is only the fragment of a man. Perfection of culture alone can bring help here. A purely rational precept cannot decide the matter, for only desire can drive out desire. Moreover it is the sign of an imperfect culture when the moral character can only be maintained at the expense of the sensuous; and when the triumph of unity and coherence involves loss of fulness and the mutilation of the manifold. The problem can only be solved by means of æsthetic education. Take men in their leisure hours, in their distractions; surround them with great spiritual forms, with symbols of the good, and let appearance overcome reality without the use of any force; let art conquer nature! The involuntary fulness of the natural life must be united with the independence and freedom of the moral life, resignation to changing conditions with the unity of personality, the material with the formal instinct. This task is performed in play. Here the powers work according to their natural laws and yet are not bound to material needs; they work from within but without any self-constraint. Production and reception merge into one another. Man feels himself raised above the influence of sensuous nature, and yet sensuous nature works according to its own law. He determines himself freely; he is self-active, he is led by the formal instinct, and yet the senses and matter are not curtailed. The condition is that there be a certain surplus of force which can be used in the free play of functions. When this is reached we get the real beginning of human life. Only in play is man truly man. In the free play of its powers human nature expresses itself on all its sides and as a totality, with the possibility of taking certain directions, which possibility, however, is never realised as long as the æsthetic condition persists. "All other exercises," says Schiller in his twenty-second letter, "give to the mind some particular aptitude, but for that very reason they impose upon it a particular limit ; only the æsthetic leads to the unlimited. Every other condition in which we may find ourselves refers us to a previous condition, and requires for its solution a following condition ; the æsthetic alone is a whole in itself, for it unites in itself all the conditions of its origin and of its continuation. Here alone we feel ourselves snatched out of time and our humanity expresses itself with a purity and integrity, as though it had as yet sustained no injury from the operation of external powers." Thus, the *æsthetic condition* which Schiller describes is one in which all the human powers work freely and harmoniously, without being set in motion by external needs, and without any single one becoming predominant. He regarded this condition as the perfection of culture, and not merely as a means to soften rudeness and mitigate discord.

It is a disputed question whether Schiller occupies the same standpoint in the *Briefen über die ästhetische Erziehung* as in the *Anmut und Würde*, or whether he does not, in the former, regard the æsthetic state as the highest good, while, in the latter, in respect of limiting cases, he retains a place for dignity beside grace. As we have seen, he had already in *Anmut und Würde* pronounced grace to be the highest good ; still more decidedly, however, is it brought out in the *Æsthetische Erziehung* as a fundamental thought that, where there is no harmony and no totality, there the *summum bonum* has not been reached.[31] We catch an echo of the Renaissance as we follow Schiller's course of thought. With the exception of Kant's legal State, grounded on the principle of freedom, no other solution has been offered of Rousseau's problem so important as Schiller's theory of the free and total play of forces as the highest—not only as an end but also as a means which may lead to the perfection of culture. He is however very well aware that we have still a long way to travel before we reach this end, and for himself, at any rate, he was convinced that he could best approach it through art. "Take my advice," he writes to a friend (Letter to Erhard, May 26, 1794), "and let poor, unworthy and immature humanity look after itself for the present. Be content to dwell in the cheerful and serene

region of ideas and leave it to time to introduce them into
practical life!"   At the conclusion of his philosophical period
(1789-95) he sought to clothe his ideas in artistic form.
He had no pleasure in the speculative philosophy which
now began to develop, while to the end of his life he remembered with enthusiasm the great circles of ideas to which
Kant had introduced him.   " Speculative philosophy," he wrote
to Wilhelm von Humboldt (April 2, 1805), "if it ever
attracted me, has disgusted me with its hollow forms ; I found
no living springs and nothing to nourish me on its barren
plain ; but the deep fundamental ideas of the idealistic
philosophy are an abiding treasure, and, if only on their account,
we must count ourselves happy to have lived in this age." We
cannot conceive a more beautiful epilogue to that philosophy
with the building up and fate of which we have here been
occupied.

BOOK VIII

THE PHILOSOPHY OF ROMANTICISM

A. THE PHILOSOPHY OF ROMANTICISM REGARDED AS AN IDEALISTIC DOCTRINE OF DEVELOPMENT

THE spirit in which the philosophy of Kant was carried on in Germany itself was determined at the outset both by the nature of the objections raised against it by its earliest opponents, and of the attempts at emendation made by his first pupils. Totality, the conception of a whole, was felt to be lacking in Kant's doctrine ; the living unity of the spirit seemed violated by his work of analysing and distinguishing ; the need was felt for ideas which should embrace the whole content—if possible all at once—of spiritual life. The men of this period pointed to religious faith on the one hand, and to artistic conception and creation on the other, as methods which, unlike the critical philosophy, did justice to the fulness of life. And even from the strictly scientific point of view, they thought, the critical philosophy was unsatisfactory as long as all principles were not deduced from a single absolute principle. Kant had been deterred from any such formal completion of his philosophy by his assumption that knowledge always presupposes a something outside itself, a something which never lets itself be approached but always escapes us : *i.e*, the thing-in-itself. This assumption, however, leads, in Kant's philosophy, to self-contradiction, and is, moreover, connected with his untenable distinction between the matter and the form of knowledge. Why not, therefore, abandon this assumption ?—then there would be no obstacle to a logical construction of philosophy starting from Kant's own deepest thought of synthesis as the essence of spirit. Kant's ultimate assumption, his fundamental hypothesis, was now taken as a starting-point for a great systematic construction. Young thinkers were filled with enthusiasm at this thought and did not see that they were in reality searching after the philosopher's stone. All externality, isolation, and division would disappear from spiritual life if the unity of things were thus exhibited, if all forms of life could be shown to be degrees and phases of the same infinite life which lives in all of them. In this way not only the conscious life of individual men, but also the historical life of the race and, by the method of analogy, the life of Nature would be shown in a new light. And we should thus obtain an explanation not merely of one side of the spiritual life of man ; if the guiding principle were conceived in all its depth it must lead beyond the existing separation between knowledge, religion, and art, and reconcile all discords of the spirit.

Such an ideal of knowledge may rightly be called Romantic. It stands before us sublime and distant, arouses our longing and enthusiasm, and influences us in virtue of its exaltation rather than by any prospect it affords us of clear and sober realisation. That a whole generation should have been content to clothe its ideal of knowledge in this form is not sufficiently explained by the preceding development of philosophy ; if we are to understand it we must take into account motives which were contained in the spirit, the needs and the tendency of the age as a whole. We find a strictly philosophical motive, it is true, in the conviction aroused by Kant of the originality and activity of spirit. In itself, therefore, it was a justifiable experiment in speculation to try whether this originality and activity were not absolute, without limits and without conditions. But the audacity with which this experiment was made is only comprehensible in the light of other tendencies of the times. The close of the eighteenth century was a period of upheaval. The French revolution had stirred men's minds. It threw down what had previously stood firm, and attempted to reconstruct human society on a new basis. Even where it failed to impose its practical ideals and their corollaries it imparted its feeling for an absolute point of view and its desire to follow up, at all costs, a principle which had once been established. The comparison which has so often been drawn between the speculative movement in Germany and the contemporary revolutionary movement in France [32] is something more than an analogy. We see here a movement of feeling which vented itself in a twofold manner, according to the different circumstances, whether inner or outer, which moulded it. This period was at the same time the golden age of German poetry.

In the poems of Goethe and Schiller art had produced immortal pictures of the longings and aspirations of life. Was the human spirit to be less powerful in the world of thought than in that of art? Could thought not attain, within her own sphere, to a unity and harmony analogous to that which art presented in hers? May we not, indeed, say that poetry and knowledge are, in their deepest nature, one and the same, *i.e.* expressions of one and the same creative force? NOVALIS (Hardenberg), the most characteristic representative of Romantic poetry, attempted to show in an unfinished work called *Heinrich von Ofterdingen* that poetry is the innermost essence of all things. He regretted that poetry had a separate name and that poets formed a class of their own. In his opinion poetry is nothing else than the mode of action peculiar to the human spirit; does not every man "poetise" and aspire at every single moment of his life? The separation between poetry and philosophy is, according to Novalis, superficial and ingenious. Philosophy is only the theory of poetry, it has to show us that poetry is all and everything. We must find "the mystic word" which solves all the riddles of the inner and outer world (Novalis' *Schriften*, 4th ed. i. pp. 201, 286 f.; ii. p. 240 f.) The difference here between the Romantic philosophers and the Romantic poets is that while the poet regards philosophy as the expounder of the poetry of life which is to be found in all things, the philosopher prefers to conceive poetry as a pictorial form, intuitively perceived, of the thought which moves in all things. Religion appears as the third member of the alliance. There was stirring at that time—as the appearance of such men as Hamann, Jacobi, and Herder already showed—the need for a deeper religious experience than that offered by dry and shallow "Rationalism." The sentimental religion of feeling was not more satisfactory. But if it is allowed that the task of thought is to show us the unity of all things, can philosophical endeavour differ in its essence from the religious yearning which likewise seeks to transcend the oppositions and unrest of life? And must we not be able to reconcile religion and knowledge, if only we can attain an adequate conception, thorough and consistent, of the nature of reason?

The philosophy of romanticism proposed to solve the religious problem not by loading reason with fetters but by going back to the innermost spiritual nature which underlies religion as well as knowledge.   Thus SCHLEIERMACHER seeks to demonstrate in his work, *Über die Religion: Reden an die gebildeten unter ihren Verächtern* (1799), the necessity of religion for the depth and harmony of spiritual life.   Owing to the development of natural science towards the end of the century discoveries and ideas came to light which caused greater importance to be attributed to the unity of Nature than had been the case in the immediately preceding period.   The discovery of galvanism, and the founding of modern chemistry (by Lavoisier) and of comparative anatomy could not fail to suggest in manifold ways new views of Nature.   And Goethe, whose poetry exercised so great an influence on all the awakened spirits of his time, had been led by his scientific studies more particularly to the presentiment of the inner unity of all things, a presentiment which his study of Spinoza had nourished, and which had already influenced Herder.   The conception of Nature offered by Goethe and Herder gave Romantic speculation its foundation, and determined its direction.   Finally there was the dominating influence of Spinoza's system, which had only recently emerged from the obscurity of misconception, and was now recognised by friends and foes alike as the ideal philosophy, not only in virtue of its thought but also of its strict unity of form.   Thus there were forces enough at work which might prompt a thinker to hazard the attempt, and build a systematic structure.

The method adopted was, for the most part, deductive and constructive.   The material employed in systematisation had been brought together by the labour of the preceding age. The distinguishing aim of the Romantic philosophy was to throw into systematic form everything which had been revealed in Kant's theory of knowledge and ethics, in the æsthetic teaching of Lessing and Schiller, in Goethe's poems, in Herder's conception of history, and in Hamann's passionate religious consciousness.   Systems as such are not productive, but presuppose productive force.   The great figures of Goethe and Schiller were not thrown in the shade by Romantic poetry; on the contrary they shone out after the Romantic period with undimmed brilliancy.   Just as little did the Romantic *philosophy* succeed in giving such a form to the content which these heroes of the intellect had produced as to reduce the latter to the position of mere forerunners. He who seeks for true nourishment will again and again go back to the original sources which precede the system-makers. Moreover, the speculative period in Germany at the beginning of our century cannot compare in originality and productive force, in closeness of thought and significance for the future treatment of problems with the age of great systems in the seventeenth century. Nevertheless, it cannot be denied that, in virtue of their eager endeavours to throw the content of intellectual life into one interconnected whole, the most prominent men amongst the representatives of the Romantic philosophy shed light on many problems and gave utterance to many significant ideas which will outlive the systems themselves. From a literary point of view the majority of these thinkers have crippled their influence by the use of an academic terminology, a kind of jargon which makes their writings obscure to all who have not learnt to think in this language.

CHAPTER I

JOHANN GOTTLIEB FICHTE

(a) Biography and Characteristics

IT is a leading characteristic of German thought, from the mysticism of the Middle Ages onwards, that it asserts the independence, inwardness, and validity of spiritual life and bases its conception of the world on this assumption. The inner and original element in us is the light in which, consciously or unconsciously, we view everything in heaven and earth. The greatest deed of the German nation, the Reformation, was a struggle on behalf of free inner conviction against ecclesiastical authority. The critical philosophy founded by Kant carried on the work of the Reformation ; it went still farther back to the innermost sources of all knowledge and worth. JOHANN GOTTLIEB FICHTE, Kant's greatest disciple, possessed not only the faculty of entering into the self, the mystical vein which leads into the depths of the inner life, but also the indomitable will and the strong self-confidence without which the conviction of the everlasting right of the inner and of the supremacy of the inner over the outer cannot be asserted and maintained. The son of a Saxon peasant, he was born at Rammenau, in Lusatia, on May 19, 1762. His strong character, the defects of which were obstinacy and pride, was an inheritance from his mother, as so often happens in the case of famous men.

As a child he fed the loom or herded geese. He distinguished himself by the attention with which he listened to sermons, and by the excellence of his memory, which enabled him to reproduce them. It was here that his feeling for spiritual things found its first nourishment, and it was this that brought about the first opportunity for his further education. A landed proprietor of the neighbourhood arrived one Sunday too late for the sermon, and was referred to the goose-herd to learn what the preacher had said. Astonished at the boy's ability, he determined to adopt him and help him to an education. Fichte's last years at school were years of great excitement— it was the time when Lessing was waging his theological battle, and his polemical pamphlets made an unforgettable impression on the young students. From 1780 on, Fichte studied theology, philology, and philosophy at Jena and Leipzig. He was in needy circumstances. His benefactor had died and his parents could do little or nothing for him. He had a hard struggle with his mother who would have made him a preacher at all costs, while he had planned for himself a free development of his faculties in every direction. Want had almost reduced him to despair when, in 1788, he obtained a post as tutor in Zurich. During his stay there his plans matured, at least so far that he became conscious of an urgent desire to influence his contemporaries by thought and word. The direction of this influence and the means by which it was to be effected were still hidden from him. It was characteristic of his personality that the will thus preceded the thought. His whole life through he seemed driven by an inner power to work in the sphere of ideas, yet he was only imperfectly able to translate this inner need into definite thought, although he toiled with unceasing energy until his death at new and more adequate statements of his system. And his philosophy itself rests on the fundamental thought which he did more than any other thinker to emphasise and inculcate, *i.e.* that our innermost essence consists in a willing, a working : and that all our presentations and thoughts are conditioned by this practical faculty, which lies at the root of the ego. It was a great piece of good fortune for him that he made the acquaintance, while in Zurich, of the noble woman who was afterwards his wife, Johanna Rahn, Klopstock's niece. Not only did his aim become clearer but the harshness of his character was softened.

One may see from their correspondence how well she understood all sides of his nature. She stood by him faithfully in good and evil days. He did not long retain his tutorship in Zurich, for, finding that the parents stood in need of education no less than the children, he addressed to them a weekly criticism in which he drew their attention to the educational

errors they had committed in the course of the week! He
resumed his wandering life in order to continue his education
and to find a sphere of activity. While at Leipzig (1790) he
studied Kant's works for the first time. This was a decisive
turning-point in his life. He now found definite problems
with which his thought could occupy itself, and definite principles
whereby he might actually influence the age as he so much
longed to do.

He made the acquaintance of Kant himself in the following
year at Königsberg. In order to ingratiate himself with the
aged Master he wrote a work (*Versuch einer Kritik aller Offenbarung*) which he submitted to his criticism and which consisted
of an application of the Kantian doctrine to the philosphy of
religion, which Kant himself had not at that time treated. The
work not only gained Kant's approval but was even, as it
appeared anonymously (owing to a misunderstanding), believed
by many people to have been written by Kant himself. This
was the crisis in Fichte's life ; the way to literary and scientific
activity was now open to him. He now agreed to the wish of
his betrothed that they should use her money to make a home
for themselves. During the following years he published works
on the French Revolution and the freedom of the press, in
which he defended the struggle for freedom against the reaction
which the terrorism of revolutionary times had begun to
arouse. Fichte occupied himself with practical problems before
becoming absorbed in those of pure speculation. He was led
by the natural course of events to the consideration of the
latter when called to Jena in 1794 to succeed Reinhold as
professor. In this capacity he proved himself a brilliant,
energetic teacher, and developed his own peculiar system, which
was first presented in the *Grundlage der gesammten Wissenschaftslehre* (" Foundation of the Sciences ") (1794), but was afterwards
subjected to many revisions in order to make it more complete
and easier to understand. In neither respect did Fichte ever
satisfy himself.

A later treatise, *Erste Einleitung in die Wissenschaftslehre*
(" Introduction to the Doctrine of Knowledge") (1797), affords
the best opportunity for becoming acquainted with his views ;
and it is in the light of this work that we shall here attempt to
give a provisional account of Fichte's point of view.

According to Fichte there may be two philosophical

systems, each of which taken by itself is logical and consistent. One of these he calls idealism, the other dogmatism. The task of philosophy is to explain experience. Our experience contains ideas of things. Now it is open to us either (with dogmatism) to deduce the idea from the thing, or (with idealism) to deduce the thing from the idea. Which of these two possibilities will be selected depends upon " what kind of man one is." A philosophical system is not so much inanimate baggage to be acquired or transferred at will ; it springs from the depths of the soul. The choice will depend on whether the feeling of self-dependence and activity or of dependence and passivity has the upper hand. A closer scrutiny will show us, however—Fichte declares—that even from the purely theoretical point of view, idealism has the advantage over dogmatism. For from the pure thing, from empty being, we shall never be able to deduce an idea, a consciousness of the thing and of being (Sein). Dogmatism involves the inconsistency that though itself a doctrine, a system of thought, yet it can never explain the possibility of the existence of ideas. Hence dogmatism (which includes materialism, spiritualism, and Spinozism) is an impossible philosophy. Idealism, on the contrary, starts from thought itself as the ultimate datum, and from this it can deduce—not indeed things themselves, for they are never given—but experience, the different ideas we have of things. It is the task of the doctrine of knowledge (*Wissenschaftslehre*) to show that our ideas of things are produced by the activity of thought assigning definite limits in accordance with its nature. The doctrine of knowledge proceeds on the assumption that there can be nothing in the ego which is not a product of the ego's own activity. While Kant had worked back from the manifold given in the content of consciousness to the all-embracing unity, Fichte adopts the converse order, and starting from the original activity of the ego attempts to deduce from it the special forms of the manifold. To succeed in this attempt would involve nothing less than the construction of actual empirical consciousness. That philosophy which is not in agreement with experience he condemns as false. The method employed by Fichte in this inquiry will be described in our discussion of the *Wissenschaftslehre*. Here we have only to indicate the spirit and tendency of Fichte's teaching.

Fichte presented his doctrine of rights and his ethics in his

Naturrecht (" The Science of Rights ") (1796), and his *Sittenlehre*
(" Doctrine of Morals ") (1798), which latter may be considered
the most significant of his works.

It was due to the energy and violence of Fichte's
character, as well as to the circumstances in which he was
placed, that the time of his work in Jena was marked by much
friction and serious discussion which finally culminated in
catastrophe. In addition to disagreements with his philosophical colleagues who were not able to follow him in his reform
of the Kantian philosophy, he also became involved in a
quarrel with the theologians, who were scandalised at his giving
lectures on practical ethics to the students on Sundays, and with
the students, because he attempted to reform the rough student
life which had been allowed to flourish unchecked from time
immemorial. The upshot of the conflict with the latter was
that Fichte was attacked in his own home, and had to leave Jena
for a time. The gravest and most important quarrel, however,
was the atheism-controversy (1799). In order to make this
comprehensible we must first describe Fichte's point of view as a
religious philosopher. This can only be understood by keeping
in mind the opposition between idealism and dogmatism.

It might seem as though there were no place in Fichte's
philosophy for any principle except human thought, the human
ego ; for Fichte proposed to deduce everything from thought,
from the ego. But he had guarded against this frequent misconception in the very first statement of his doctrine of knowledge. It is indeed true that Fichte lays down the proposition
that everything which is to be found in consciousness must be a
product of the ego ; but he shows at the same time that there
is very much in our consciousness which we are not conscious
of having produced. The ego which we know in experience is
always limited, enclosed in a system of limitations, has objects
(non-egos) outside it which it has not itself produced. There
must, therefore, be active in consciousness some principle more
comprehensive than the finite (empirical) ego ; only in this
principle, which Fichte calls the pure or infinite ego, can we
look for the ground of the world of objects or of limitations in
which our finite ego is enclosed. Now the ultimate ground of
the limitation, which gives rise to the finite ego and its limits,
can never be discovered by theorising ; for what can set limits
to an infinite activity ? But if our conscience is right, and

labour and effort is the highest life, we understand why there is a finite world ; for without resistance there is no labour, and without means no end. The actual world is the stuff of our duty. And the certainty that resistance is to be overcome through progress, that we can always do our duty and work towards complete spiritual freedom as our highest aim, rests on the conception of an order of things which makes conscientious action possible and enables it to have free course—an order of things which does not indeed appear in sensuous experience, but of which, nevertheless, I feel myself a member every time that I act from purely ideal motives.

Now the essential element of religion is that man should build on a moral world-order of this kind,—on this, the divine, exalted above all transitoriness ; that every man should recognise his duties as arising out of this order and as contributing to its development. For it is not an order finished once for all, it is found in a continuous development. Neither is it a contingent order, presupposing in its turn the existence outside ourselves of a being to whom the order is due. No harm is done by men in thinking this world-order under the form of a person, so long as they do so only to vivify their own conception of it. But if they conceive God as a tyrant, on whose favour future pleasures depend, they worship an idol, and they ought to be called atheists. For every attempt to think the infinite principle (the pure ego, the moral world-order) under the form of a concept is doomed to failure ; to conceive is to limit. If a thing is conceived it ceases to be God, and every so-called concept of God is necessarily the concept of an idol.

Fichte developed these views in his treatise, *Über den Grund unseres Glaubens an eine göttliche Weltsregierung* (" On the ground of our Belief in a Divine Governance of the World ") (1878), and also—a formal complaint having been lodged against him—still more emphatically in his masterly polemics, *Appellation an das Publikum* (" Appeal to the Public ") and *Gerichtliche Verantwortungschrift* (" A Public Defence ") (1799). The course of the quarrel was as follows :—An anonymous pamphlet having raised an outcry over Fichte's treatise, the Government of Saxony confiscated the latter, and complained to the Government of Weimar that atheistical doctrines were taught at the University of Jena, which was attended by

Saxon subjects. To which Fichte responded with the polemics
above mentioned.   The authorities at Weimar would have
preferred to hush the matter up.   They neither wished to fly
in the face of the Saxon Government nor to interfere with
Fichte's activity.   What they did wish was that Fichte should
remain passive.   But this was contrary to his nature, and
he addressed a defiant letter to a member of the Weimar
Government. All the privy councillors—including Goethe—
were incensed at this letter, and Fichte received a curt dismissal.   This was a flagrant interference with the liberty of
the University, as the Government had taken it upon them in
their letter to pass judgment on Fichte's teaching.   In spite
of repeated protests from the students the Government held
to their decision, and Fichte was obliged to leave Jena.

For the next few years Fichte lived in private in Berlin,
busied with re-writing his system and giving popular lectures.
It has been thought that there is a radical difference of standpoint between the Jena writings and those which were published
afterwards.   A difference there certainly is, but it can only be
called a difference of principle if we regard the *Wissenschaftslehre*
in its first form as an attempt to deduce everything from the
particular, finite, empirical ego.   But we have seen that this
view is incorrect.   Even in his earliest writings Fichte, strictly
speaking, did not teach pure idealism as he defined the term,
for he assumes a something which works within us without our
being aware of it.   In calling this something an ego he employs
an analogy with the working of consciousness.   It is only by
means of this advance from the empirical to the infinite ego,
rendered possible by this analogy, that Fichte can maintain
his idealism and conceive all reality as the appearance or
symbol of thought.   But in his later works he teaches that
this thought (the infinite ego), of which everything is the
appearance, is itself only the appearance of an absolute reality,
an infinite force, a life, a light, of which only broken rays reach
our consciousness.   That is to say, he emphasises more than
he had previously done the mystical (or dogmatic) element
which lies beyond all conscious thought and which had already
appeared in his first presentation of the *Wissenschaftslehre*.
This was followed by a change of feeling, if indeed it is not
rather the change of feeling which led to the change of view.
In his early writings Fichte had laid most stress on restless

striving and working, on continual activity, so that even his religion, consisting in the belief in a moral world-order, is essentially the religion of joyful right-doing ; afterwards he laid greater weight on the life which stirs and wells up within us, but which neither our will nor our reason are able to produce. Characteristic of this point of view is his *Anweisung zum seligen Leben* (1806), while his general philosophical and psychological views, as they took shape in later years, may most easily be gathered from his posthumous work *Die That-sachen des Bewusstseins* (" Facts of Consciousness "). The changes we have mentioned were naturally accompanied by a change of front in Fichte's polemical attitude. Up till now he had attached orthodoxy and dogmatism. Now he turns against the barren " enlightenment " : the empty and negative movement of the understanding which contented itself with its own sapless concepts while it lacked any deeper sense of spiritual things. And this polemic acquires a special interest because it afforded him occasion to present his conception of the historical development of spiritual life. This is given in his remarkable work *Die Grundzüge des gegenwärtigen Zeitalters* (" Characteristics of the Present Age ") (1806). He distinguishes here five periods of development. At first *reasonable instinct* is supreme—a group of individuals (the " normal nation ") arises, among whom life is ordered in noble and perfect forms without the need of science or art. When—in the course of natural events—the normal nation is scattered amongst the savage children of Nature a struggle ensues between culture and barbarism. The second period begins when that to which the rational instinct prompts is set up by the most prominent individuals as the law and norm for others. This is the period of *authority*. Against this authority the impulse after freedom and the thirst to comprehend array themselves. These overthrow authority ; but with it falls the reason which had unconsciously given it its content and worth. Nothing remains in the period of *empty freedom* but the arbitrary powers and sensations of individuals. Men turn their backs in scorn on the darkness of the past, secure in the concepts they have acquired, which they make the measure of all things without having the least idea of what true comprehension means.

The character of this age is *Auf- und Ausklärung* (" clearing up and clearing out "). It is quite evident that Fichte is

here describing his own age.   As the distinguishing mark of
the fourth period he names *reasonable knowledge, i.e.* true and
complete understanding, with a clear consciousness of the
greatness of the task.   But knowledge alone does not suffice ;
the goal is only reached when a *reasonable art* has developed,
an art which aims at ordering all human relations in accordance
with reasonable knowledge.   Fichte himself draws attention to
the fact that the third period stands in distinct opposition to
all the others.   It bears the stamp of negation, while in all
the others positive forces prevail—instinct and authority or
knowledge and art.   It is a period of transition.   Thus Fichte
(like Kant and Schiller) really assumes three stages—a positive,
a negative, and again a positive stage—so that the new positive
forces work their way up through dissolution.   Dissatisfied with
modern times, especially with the critical and rationalistic
tendency of the eighteenth century, he awaits a new age which
possesses a deeper need of and better means for the understanding and conduct of life.

The great events which were taking place at that time
soon gave Fichte an opportunity for addressing still more
searching words to his contemporaries and to his nation.   After
the battle of Jena Berlin was garrisoned by the French, and
Fichte went to Königsberg, where he taught for some time at
the University.   When this town too fell into the hands of the
enemy he went for some months to Copenhagen.   On the
conclusion of peace he returned to Berlin, which continued to
be garrisoned by the French for some years.   The time for
the rebirth of Prussia had now come, and Fichte belongs to
the circle of distinguished men who by thoughts, words, and
deeds laboured for the restoration of the nation.   During the
winter of 1807-8 he delivered at Berlin his famous *Reden an die
deutschen Nation* ("Addresses to the German Nation").   For
the moment the struggle on the field is at an end ; now
ensues a struggle within the sphere of character and ideas.
The nation can no longer control its external life.   But the
education of its youth still remains in its power.   And this
power must be used to produce a generation which shall be
capable of choosing great aims and sacrificing itself for them.
The whole nation—not merely one particular class—must be
aroused ; and above all things it is necessary that scope should
be given for the independent development of character.   The

starting-point must be sought in the original need and impulse which exists in every man, for education can impart nothing to a man which he does not already—at least in germ—possess. Every man stands in need of esteem, at any rate the esteem of other men, if he has not yet felt the need of self-esteem. This feeling at its best produces the power of forming, freely and independently, ideals of action. Only such ideals, formed in freedom and independence, can produce a living emotion ; that which is received from without cannot have the same effect. The German people in particular, on account of their feeling and zeal for spiritual freedom and the inner self-dependence of faith and thought, are susceptible of such an education. Is it not the nation which produced Luther's reformation, Kant's philosophy, and Pestalozzi's system of education ? Pestalozzi's fundamental notions are here carried out by Fichte on a larger scale. He had become acquainted with the great educationalist during his stay in Switzerland.[33]

Fichte became Professor at the University founded in Berlin in 1810. On the outbreak of the War of Liberation (as in 1806) he wished to accompany the army into the field as a preacher. This plan was not carried out. Nevertheless, he fell a victim to the war, for he was attacked by an infectious hospital fever, which his wife had contracted while nursing the wounded, and he died of this illness on January 27, 1814.

(b) *Doctrine of Knowledge* (" Wissenschaftslehre ")

Fichte's most important contribution to philosophical discussion is the *Wissenschaftslehre* in its original form, and it is this which we shall here keep in view.

We have to find the first principle of all knowledge. If I fix my attention on my ordinary consciousness I find that I can think both of myself (the ego), and of something which is not myself (the non-ego). But even when I think of the non-ego I can only do so in virtue of a spiritual activity, an activity of the ego. The non-ego exists only in virtue of an activity of the ego, only because it is posited. We may perhaps feel bound or compelled to imagine certain definite things to which we attribute reality ; but this binding or compulsion presupposes something which is bound or compelled.

Limitation presupposes something which is limited. The

presupposition of all knowledge is the free, infinite, spiritual activity which appears determined or bound in each particular idea, but which is absolutely bound to no single one. Our immediate consciousness does not reveal to us this original activity; we only find there its individual products. We are never immediately aware of our will and of our activity. Limits and results are perceived, but not that which is limited, and which produces the results. The first principle, therefore, is, strictly speaking, concerned not with a fact (*Thatsache*), but with an act (*Thathandlung*), as Descartes intimated by his *Cogito, ergo sum*, and Kant by his synthesis. This primitive activity (the pure ego) can only be discovered by means of reflection and abstraction, by holding fast to the idea of an activity, free from division and limitation, for which the antithesis between subject and object, action and result, does not exist. A kind of higher intuition, an intellectual intuition, is necessary to grasp that which does not reveal itself to immediate apprehension, while yet it cannot be clothed in the form of a concept, since every concept presupposes an opposite. This innermost active essence of our being can only be discovered by means of spiritual energy and self-dependence. Most men would find it easier to conceive themselves a piece of lava on the moon than a purely spiritual activity. Hence the assumption of a separate soul, distinct from the body as a " being " or a " substance " for itself, such as spiritualistic metaphysic assumes, is entirely rejected by the *Wissenschaftslehre*. (Fichte states this very clearly in a later work : " The existence of a soul is absolutely denied, and the whole concept rejected as a bad invention. And this is not an indifferent matter, but an essential criterion for our system. With the belief in such a soul a man cannot abide in the system, nor even enter it." *Die Thatsachen des Bewusstseins*, Stuttgart and Tübingen, 1817, p. 105 f.) [34]

But this first principle of a spiritual activity as the source of all things in consciousness does not explain how it is that something besides the ego is posited in consciousness. A second principle must therefore be laid down, which cannot be deduced from the first. If the first is formulated as follows : *the ego posits itself*, the second must run : *the ego posits a non-ego*. Like the first, this second principle is discovered by reflecting on what is given in consciousness. But now arises the necessity of connecting the two propositions of effecting a synthesis by means of the union of thesis and antithesis, and this is possible if we lay down as a third principle—*The ego posits a limited ego in opposition to a limited non-ego.*   By means of this synthesis we return to our immediate consciousness, which can be explained neither by the assumption that the ego is absolutely posited, nor by the assumption that the non-ego is absolutely posited, but only by the assumption of a mutual limitation—a reciprocal action between the ego and the non-ego.

The method which Fichte employs may be called the antithetical method.   First of all one proposition is asserted which brings out an essential moment of the truth ; then follows a second proposition which expresses an opposite moment (which cannot be deduced from the first) ; finally we attain the union of the two.   The necessity for finding a union between the opposed propositions is contained in the first principle, that everything in consciousness is due to an indivisible spiritual activity, for it follows from this that the relation of opposition cannot be fundamental.   However limited our consciousness (the finite empirical ego), yet the pure ego works within it as the ultimate source not only of all it does, but also of all it suffers.

It is not our business to trace the further use Fichte makes of this method in which each synthesis becomes in turn a thesis, to lead in combination with a new antithesis to a new synthesis.   The method has great value, but in Fichte's detailed application of it it became arbitrary and unfruitful, for such an application demands a more exhaustive analysis of experience, *i.e.* in this case, a psychology richer in content than any he had at his disposal.   His aim was to *deduce* the forms and principles which Kant had set out in a merely schematic fashion.   Fichte finds the principle of identity contained in his first principle : the proposition $A = A$ is true originally of the ego in its pure, self-identical, constant activity.   The form of time arises when different acts of the ego (*e.g.* positing the ego, positing the non-ego) occur in such a manner as to be dependent on each other in a definite order.   The form of space arises when different determinations of the non-ego are posited, each one distinct and yet without a breach of continuity and without the mutual dependence involved in a definite time-order.   The principle of causation is contained in the third principle, which demands mutual limitation, *i.e.* reciprocal action between the ego and the non-ego. When the different determinations of the non-ego are at the same time conceived as mutually dependent on one another (as in natural science), the concept of activity, proper to the ego, is involuntarily transferred to the non-ego. Fichte, however, can only deduce the general forms of empirical consciousness—not its special particular empirical content, and this is all he intended to do.[35] In the picture of the world, as a whole, formed by ordinary consciousness, we have, according to Fichte, the product of an involuntary activity, of which we ourselves are not aware. We project time, space, logical identity, causality, just as we project the sense-qualities. But it does not follow from this that our world-picture is an illusion. The concept "illusion" can only be used in opposition to reality, but there is no such opposition here ; or rather, true reality resides in the activity which, without our knowledge, produces the world-picture in our consciousness, and this activity is a *necessary* activity working *in conformity to law*. Philosophical reflection only, which must be carefully distinguished from our everyday practical consciousness, discovers this deep, hidden power which is at work in every finite ego, and in virtue of this discovery, can understand how it is that every ego forms the same world-picture. This is Fichte's solution of the problem of knowledge.

If we are to understand Fichte's method as well as his result we must always remember that the second principle can never be deduced from the first. This differentiates his antithetical method from the so-called dialectical method of Hegel. And from this follows also a limitation to pure theory on which Fichte himself could never lay too much stress, and which is in the highest degree characteristic of his system. For the question arises : Why does the ego (the pure ego) produce or posit a non-ego within itself? Why is the pure, identical activity interrupted ? Why does the straight line of the original activity become a curve ? Fichte explains that theoretically this question admits of no answer. To explain this resistance or curvature we should have to assume a force outside the absolute force, and this would be a self-contradiction. We can only understand it by the light of our moral consciousness, which holds effort and labour and the struggle for the attainment of great aims to be the highest good. For labour presupposes limits, struggle, resistance. Thus the ethical significance of the fact that we are confronted with a world of non-egos, of objects, is that it makes labour and struggle possible. Nature is the material of our duty. An object means something over against us (*Gegenstand*), and what is over against us means that which opposes us (*Widerstand*). Without a system of limits there would be no moral life. Our highest aim is freedom and self-dependence, and these are won by struggling with all the hindrances our ego encounters. Thus practice holds the key of theory.

Practical, like theoretical, philosophy presupposes the first principle. In establishing this principle the emphasis laid by Fichte on the original activity as the ultimate element of our being is of especial significance for ethics. There is a primal impulse to act for the sake of acting, quite apart from external prompting or duty. This impulse makes itself felt in conscience as well as in the natural instincts. Kant's categorical imperative, for which he himself could find no explanation, becomes comprehensible in the light of this original impulse towards activity at any price. This same impulse explains the unruliness of the sense instincts. The individual things or objects presented in Nature appear to us from the beginning merely as means or limits for the satisfaction of our lower or higher impulses. Our conception of the world is practical from the very first. "The whole system of our ideas," says Fichte in the *Wissenschaftslehre* (2nd ed. p. 288), "depends on our impulses and our will."

(c) Ethics

When the original striving and working is bound to certain definite objects which vary in accordance with the character of each particular individual it appears as natural instinct, and terminates in enjoyment. Through enjoyment we become dependent on objects. It is, however, possible, in virtue of the infinity of that striving and working which expresses my independence in the face of all the given, of all objects, for a consciousness, a reflection, to awaken in me which shows me possibilities other than the immediately given. On this depends my freedom. It is one and the same primitive impulse which asserts itself in natural instinct on the one hand, and on the other in reflection and the desire for freedom, which can deliver us from dependence on the senses. But the natural instinct and the desire for freedom are not necessarily opposed to one another : each natural want may be satisfied in such a way as to become the means to greater freedom and independence. This gives us the ethical law : *every particular action must form part of a series which leads me to complete spiritual freedom.* In this way the infinite ego is realised in the empirical world. The posited limits are transcended. This is an infinite goal, but a continual approximation to it is possible, since each end we attain becomes in turn a new starting-point. When the two forms in which the primal impulse expresses itself (*i.e.* natural instinct and the desire for freedom) are in harmony with one another we have a feeling of self-esteem, a very different kind of pleasurable feeling from the enjoyment afforded by the senses ; indeed it would be better not to call it pleasure at all. In the opposite case we have a feeling of self-contempt. We call the capacity for having such feelings conscience. Only that action is moral which springs from conscience. To act in accordance with authority is unconscientious. The first commandment is : *Act according to thine own conviction of duty.* And this conviction is won by comparing the contemplated action not only with my momentary conception of it, but also with every conception which I can anyway think ; when, that is to say, I consider whether the action is one which I could acknowledge as mine through all eternity. The morally bad is the result of slothfulness—disinclination to reflect, to rise above that which is given at the moment, dislike of passing out of our present condition, a tendency to remain in the given track. Slothfulness leads to cowardice and falsehood, for slavery is preferred to exertion, and appearance is used as a cloak to cover that which we should not be prepared to defend in open war. But how is it possible to excite the desire for freedom when it does not already exist ? A man cannot set free his own power ! The answer is to be found in the doctrine of a reasonable instinct, developed in the *Grundzügen des gegenwärtigen Zeitalters,* but already indicated in the *Sittenlehre.* In some few individuals the original impulse is so strong as to raise them above that which is given through the senses in a manner inexplicable alike to themselves and to others. They have a kind of " genius for virtue." They serve as ideals for other men, they arouse and draw them upwards. It is at this point that Fichte finds the explanation of the origin of positive religions. The individuals endowed with this deep spiritual force, as well as those who are under the influence of their personality, naturally regard this power which has developed in them, and which streams forth from them as a miracle. Certainly the empirical ego can give no explanation. The belief in such a miracle is not without significance when it serves as a means to arouse slumbering energy and attention. Hence it is of great, of paramount importance that a man should live among other men. Only among other men is he man. And, as a matter of fact, the many individuals have all one single aim— the realisation of the idea of the ego. From the ethical point of view my personality is not my highest good. But it is the only means through which I can work for the highest. My aim is also reached when others act morally. If every one followed his own conviction all would work towards the development of the highest and deepest self-dependence, and the realisation of reason in a community of free beings. What in religious parlance is called the " communion of saints " is nothing but the manifestation of the pure ego in the totality of reasonable beings. In comparison with this infinite aim the individual is only a means, a tool, and is but of vanishing significance. The individual, therefore, must annihilate his individuality, not by mystical brooding, but in active work for the eternal aim. In his later writings Fichte expresses himself still more strongly regarding this vanishing importance of particular personality, in curious contrast to the emphasis he elsewhere lays on individuality.[36] Ultimately individuality becomes to him something which ought not to be, a limitation which must be annulled, a negation which must be rescinded. The pure ego crushes the empirical. Fichte is here overtaken by Nemesis. He sought an absolute foundation for his ethical system by closely linking it with his speculation, but in the end this very union made shipwreck of his ethics. On the way, however, and before he fell into this speculative abyss, he had come upon ethical thoughts of lasting value.

In Fichte's applied ethics, his conception of Church and State deserves especial mention. He conceives the Church as a union of individuals for the purpose of arousing and strengthening ethical conviction. The bond of union con-

sists in symbols, figurative forms, under which the highest
thoughts can influence all — learned and unlearned alike.
Only by means of such symbols is general and reciprocal
spiritual influence possible. For as regards the highest
thoughts themselves in their pure, intellectual form, it would
be impossible to hope for general understanding and general
agreement. The symbol appeals to every one on account
of its figurative form, and its interpretation is undetermined. This constitutes its value. Even when the ethical
teacher of a people attributes no literal truth to a symbol, he
will still be able to use it if he is inspired with a living wish
to influence the spiritual life of other men.[37] The spirit of
Protestantism, however, demands that all symbols shall be
developed to clearer and more perfect forms. All symbols,
not only the ideas of positive religions, but also those of a
personal God and a personal immortality, are merely makeshifts. Symbols are valuable in proportion as they make the
thought of a higher ethical world-order clear and living.

Just as the symbols of every church are makeshifts, so
every existing State is merely a makeshift. The State deals
with the external nature of man only ; hence, in Fichte's
opinion, a sharp distinction should be drawn between the
doctrine of rights and ethics. The doctrine of rights is based
on the principle that every man who lives with other men (no
matter for what reason) must limit his own freedom by regard
for the freedom of others. The relation of right is based on
the mutual recognition of this. The sole duty of the State is
the maintenance of this relation, and, when necessary, it must
force individuals to recognise the freedom of others in all that
concerns the body, property, and self-preservation. But Fichte
does not only find the State imperfect when it does not ensure
this external necessity. He maintains (and in doing so it is
obvious that he transcends the concept of the State as a mere
police force or guardian of rights), that the State can only
demand the recognition of the rights of property from all
men when it strives to further a condition in which *all*
men shall possess property. Every man ought to be able to
live by his own labour. Within the State there should be
neither paupers nor idlers. Philanthropy is only a miserable
and questionable expedient. As early as his *Naturrecht* and
his *Sittenlehre* Fichte had thrown out suggestions tending in

the direction of what has since come to be called socialism. In his *Geschlossenen Handelsstaat* (" Complete Industrial State ") (1800), he demands the transference of foreign trade to the State, in order that the internal economic development of every nation may take its natural and independent course. He has no fears that the intercourse between nations will suffer thereby ; science, not trade, promotes this intercourse, in so far as it has any real value. Fichte, as has been truly remarked (see GUSTAV SCHMOLLER'S study of Fichte in the *Jahrbücher für Nationalökonomie und Statistik*, 1865), is Germany's first socialistic author. In spite of his sharp distinction between rights and morality, his doctrine of the State is based on ethical considerations. In the version of his doctrine of rights and of the State which he drew up in his later years, he emphasises the fact that the State—which from constraint and through constraint must educate men for freedom—cannot attain this end unless it strives to procure for every individual property, leisure, and means to higher culture.

CHAPTER II

FRIEDRICH WILHELM JOSEPH SCHELLING

(a) Period of Natural Philosophy

SCHELLING is the typical philosopher of Romanticism. Fichte is still under the influence of the critical philosophy, and distinguishes carefully between consciousness and its content : he may be called a Romanticist, however, in virtue of his striving after the limitless, which with him takes the place of Kant's idea of an infinite progress. But in Schelling we find the true Romantic impulse to revel in a content which is attained by intuition and symbolism, rather than as the result of critical thought. So he runs riot first in nature and art, afterwards in religion. With such tendencies, it was small wonder that, although he began as Fichte's pupil and collaborator, he soon found his ego altogether too arid. The trend of his mind was towards great symbolic intuitions, in which the contradictions contained in things are at once revealed and reconciled. Intuitive vision was for him the highest ; and if, in his speculations, he lays weight on contradictions, he does so in order to fill out and bring into relief the pictures woven by his thought. Fichte, on the other hand, emphasised contradictions because they were the condition of work, struggle, development. His philosophy is ethical through and through : Schelling did not trouble about ethics at all.

Schelling was born on January 27, 1775, at Leonberg in Würtemberg. At sixteen he went to Tübingen as a student. Like all his fellow students, he was deeply stirred by the French Revolution. He was suspected of being the author of a German translation of the Marsellaise, which Duke Charles, the tyrant of Schiller's youth, made the pretext for adopting harsh measures

towards the students. Schelling began with the study of theology;
he also took an interest in mythology and the historical exegesis
of the Bible. But he very soon became absorbed in philosophical
studies, and devoured the works of Kant, Fichte, and Spinoza.
In various treatises of the years 1794 and 1795 he still further
extended Fichte's *Wissenschaftslehre.* A temporary residence
in Leipzig, as tutor to two young noblemen, gave him an opportunity for engaging in the study of natural science, and it was
here that he wrote his first work on natural philosophy : *Ideen
zu einer Philosophie der Natur* (1797). Originally conceived as
a supplement to the *Wissenschaftslehre,* his philosophy of nature
subsequently led him to take up an antagonistic position towards
the latter, which gave rise to a bitter controversy between the
former friends. From 1798 he worked as a professor at Jena, to
which office he had been called through the influence of Goethe,
Schiller, and Fichte. It was in Jena really that the Romantic
School originated. The brothers Schlegel with their gifted wives,
Novalis, Tieck, Steffens and others here came in contact with
Schelling, and this " Republic of Despots " overflowed with
poetical, religious, philosophical, and scientific ideas—sometimes
at variance with one another, sometimes in harmony. Friederich
Schlegel wrote to Schleiermacher : "What with religion and
Holberg, galvanism and poetry, we've a pretty lively time of
it here." And Dorothea Schlegel gives a similar description :
" We live in a fine whirligig of wit and philosophy, conversations on art and on everything under the sun." [38] At this time
Schelling drew his inspiration mainly from nature and art. The
religious enthusiasm of Novalis and Tieck even roused in him,
by way of opposition, an anti-religious enthusiasm which found
poetic expression in the shape of a poem called " The Creed of
an Epicurean " (*Epikurischen Glaubensbekenntnisse*), which was
to have been published in the Schlegels' " Athenæum," but was
withheld on Goethe's advice. Schelling subsequently printed a
portion of it in his " Journal for Speculative Physics." It is
given complete in the work entitled *Aus Schellings Leben*
(Leipzig, 1896), i. p. 282 f. The following lines are illustrative
of Schelling's natural philosophy—like it also, they are better
in verse than in prose :—

> Drum ist eine Religion die rechte,
> Müsst sie im Stein und Moosgeflechte,
> In Blumen, Metallen und allen Dingen

So zu Luft und Licht sich dringen,
In allen Höhen und Tiefen
Sich offenbaren in Hieroglyphen. . . .
Hinauf zu des Gedankens Jugendkraft,
Wodurch Natur verjüngt sich wieder schafft,
Ist Eine Kraft, Ein Pulsschlag nur, Ein Leben,
Ein Wechselspiel von Hemmen und von Streben.[1]

In addition to the *Ideen*, the following works also treat of natural philosophy :—*Erster Entwurf eines Systems der Naturphilosophie* (1799), and *Einleitung zu dem Entwurf eines Systems der Naturphilosophie, oder : Über den Begriff der spekulativen Physik* (1799). In the *System des transcendentalen Idealismus* (1800) he exhibits natural philosophy in its connection with the *Wissenschaftslehre* and proclaims artistic intuition to be the only way by which we can conceive mind and nature, the subject and object, in their inner unity,—the only standpoint from which the oppositions presented in life, especially that between theory and practice, are overcome. In the year 1801 he began an abstract systematic statement of his theory (*Darstellung meines Systems*, in the second volume of the *Zeitschrift für spekulative Physik*), which, however, he never completed. In the *Methode des akademischen Studiums* (1803), however, we possess an encyclopædic presentment of Schelling's philosophic ideas in a freer form, as they took shape towards the end of his first period. After his departure from Jena (1803) his production took a new turn, and soon after suffered a remarkable interruption. But before we proceed to consider the second great religio-philosophical period of his thought, we must give some account of his natural philosophy.

In the first place, Schelling demands, in the name of idealism, a more positive recognition of Nature than was possible in Fichte's system, where Nature was merely a limit or a means. The secrets of the spiritual world, Schelling says, can only be unlocked after we have learnt to understand Nature, and no longer regard it as an alien power. With Fichte, Nature is object only; but the object is only comprehensible if it is of like essence with the subject. Nature can only

---

[1] " If a religion, then, be the right one, it must force its way to air and light in stones and mossy patches, in flowers, metals, and everything, in all heights and depths ; it must reveal itself in hieroglyphs. . . . up to the young strength of thought, where Nature renews herself and wins her youth again, one force, one pulse alone, one life, one interplay of checking and of striving."

be understood if it bears the stamp of spirit. And when we find that the forces operative in spirit already exist in Nature, we understand how spirit has developed out of Nature. Nature is then seen to be an Odyssey of the spirit—it is the striving of the spirit to return once more to itself and its inwardness after passing through the form of outwardness which surrounds it in Nature.

Modern natural science has sought to reduce everything in Nature to motion, to explain everything by the reciprocal action of material particles. If this explanation exhausts the essence of Nature, the ideal must either be entirely abandoned or we must suppose it to have penetrated into Nature from without. But to explain the purposiveness of Nature as the result of a divine understanding is, according to Schelling (*Ideen*, 2nd ed. p. 63), not to philosophise but to indulge in pious reflections. Moreover, it leaves the main philosophical problem untouched, *i.e. how do we perceive* the whole system of causes and effects which forms the world? how does such a system *arise for us?* The scientific inquirer lives in Nature as an immediately given reality, while the philosophy of Nature asks how it can be given to us (cf. *Ideen*, 2nd ed. pp. 4, 27 f.). The problem appears in another form as the question of the origin of sensibility in Nature. How can the organism become its own object? ("First Sketch," p. 174).[39]

No one can deny that we are here dealing with a real problem, and that, from the standpoint either of idealistic philosophy or of exact science, it is clearly stated. If we are to understand the spiritual side of existence, we must be able to discover qualities and forces working in Nature other than those which the mechanical science of Nature knows and has formulated in its laws. Schelling's solution is as follows: the same duality of an infinite and a limiting force which Fichte has shown us in consciousness must pervade the whole of Nature. Since conscious life rests on contradiction (doubleness), the whole of Nature, out of which conscious life develops, must exhibit opposing forces, but at lower powers; or, as Leibniz would say (cf. *System des transcendentalen Idealismus*, p. 190), all the forces of Nature are powers of representation at different degrees. Matter is slumbering spirit, spirit in equilibrium; and spirit is matter in process of becoming. But Schelling goes further than any such general principle or postulate. He believes himself able to trace in detail the stages through which Nature rises to spirit. He starts from the spiritual forces, and conceives these working throughout Nature at lower powers. He has given a clear statement of his method in his treatise : *Über den wahren Begriff der Naturphilosophie* (Collected Works, i. 4. p. 85 f.). " We can only conceive the objective in its first arising by *depotentialising* the object of all philosophic thought, which at its highest power = the ego. Having thus reduced the object to its lowest power, we must start from this and reconstruct from the beginning." That is to say, we must argue from higher to lower grades. Schelling does not inquire how far this is possible (for one and the same object may appear under different forms at its lower and higher stages). His construction is, in fact, a poetical and symbolic exposition, in which the forces and forms of Nature are conceived as forming progressively graduated approximations to conscious life. Like every metaphysical idealism, his depends upon analogy; and his faith in this method is so great that he believes himself able, with it as a foundation, to construct a speculative physics which will not only shed a new light on the results already attained by natural science, but will finally actually supersede it. Nature can only be understood when viewed from within, when regarded as spirit made visible. Boyle and Newton ruined physics, as Bacon philosophy, by introducing a purely external and empirical standpoint. Mathematical astronomy-can never lead us to know the real nature of the planetary motions ! For, according to Schlegel, the innermost essence of natural phenomena cannot be understood so long as we explain one by means of another ; we must exhibit their origin in a common ground ; it is this which constitutes the unity of Nature. The empirical student of Nature looks not at the symbolic significance of natural phenomena, but at the external symbol, and thinks that in explaining this, he explains everything (*Methode des akad. Studiums. Vorlesung XI. Über die Naturwissenschaft im Allgemeinen*).

The romanticism of Schelling's philosophy of Nature lies not in the problem as he originally stated it, but in the boldness with which he attempts to substitute his own symbolic reading of Nature for the laborious attempts of science to explain it by the reciprocal interconnection of individual phenomena. He forgets that the unity of Nature can only be established scientifically by means of this despised interconnection. This point constitutes the decisive difference between Schelling's philosophy of Nature and such speculations as those of Spinoza and Leibniz, which take this real interconnection as their fundamental principle. Schelling does not even think it necessary to appeal to empiricism for the final verification of his system. Speculative construction reveals to us the inner type of all things, which must be the same for all since all have a common origin ; it suffices unto itself, therefore, and is able to penetrate into regions from which experience is shut out by insurmountable barriers.

Let us look a little more closely at Schelling's attempt to exhibit spirit in Nature. The different phenomena and forces have to be exhibited as ascending powers. And it must also be demonstrated that every stage, every power, contains within itself a moment of contradiction (*duplizismus* or polarity), which is a lower degree of the moment of contradiction appearing in consciousness under the form of subject and object (the ego and non-ego). The concepts of *powers* and of *polarity* are the fundamental concepts of Schelling's philosophy of Nature. By means of these concepts he constructs a scheme in which the different natural phenomena are assigned a place. It is interesting to observe that in Schelling's romantic attempt to frame a speculative doctrine of Nature, as in the exact natural sciences, all qualitative differences are reduced to differences of quantity. Schelling has himself drawn attention to this point of similarity between his natural philosophy and the atomistic doctrine, and proposes to call his theory " dynamic atomism." The difference between them is that while mechanical atomism explains everything as a relation between material facts, the philosophy of Nature explains everything as a relation between forces. Schelling, however, is far inferior to the atomists in clearness and logical application of the general thought. The general scheme which he had constructed by means of the concepts of powers and polarity is filled out in the most arbitrary manner, often by a mere play upon words, so that the name " philosophy of Nature " has rightly enough acquired an evil sound in scientific ears. Nevertheless a survey of Schelling's symbolism of Nature is not without historical interest.

The absolute principle (the *original ground*) which underlies all things contains the absolute unity of subject and object.

At no point of existence is this unity annulled ; but either one or the other pole may preponderate : on this quantitatively differing relation between the poles depends the difference between the different powers.   In *nature* the objective, in *spirit* the subjective pole preponderates.   If the absolute is symbolised as $A = B$ (where A stands for the subject and B for the object), nature may be symbolised as $A = {}^+B$, and spirit as ${}^+A = B$ (when the plus sign indicates the preponderating pole).   There are three powers to be distinguished in nature.   The first appears in the elementary attractive and repulsive forces, which hold the world-structure together : *gravity* is the characteristic expression of this first power.   *Light* (as also magnetism, electricity, and the chemical process)—the second power— expresses the uniting of that which is separated by the disjoining forces, and is also an indication of the process of becoming in the spiritual sphere.   In *organic life*—the third power—we have a world in little, a system of processes which are reciprocally end and means ; and in the capacity of the organism for feeling (sensibility) the spirit of nature at last breaks through its barriers.   The powers of *spirit* appear as the three activities of *knowledge, action*, and *art.*   When he wrote the *System des transcendentalen Idealismus* Schelling regarded artistic intuition as the highest form of spiritual life.   Art is the only true and eternal organon and at the same time document of philosophy.   It is ever authenticating that which philosophy cannot exhibit externally, *i.e.* the unconscious in action and production, and its original identity with the conscious.   It is precisely on this account that the philosopher regards art as the highest, for it reveals to him, as it were, the holy of holies, where, in eternal and original union, burns, as it were in one flame, that which is sundered in Nature and history, and which in life and action, as in thought, must eternally flee one another. The view of Nature which the philosopher constructs for him- self artificially is for art the original and natural one (*System*, p. 475).   It is but logical that a philosopher who erects his system by means of poetic symbolism should end by declaring art to be the highest.   To him, as to Novalis, everything is in reality poetry—the process of Nature is an unconscious poetry which bursts into consciousness in and for man.

Schelling did not mean in any literal sense that Nature is the previous development of spirit.   His philosophy of Nature differs from the modern theory of evolution not only by its depreciation of the mechanical interconnection, but also—which, indeed, follows as a corollary of this—by its denial of an *actual* transition from one "power" into another. One stage does not grow out of another, but the creative activity of Nature or the absolute, of which experience can only show us the products, not itself, can only attain complete development by means of a series of forms. Each particular form originates in the infinite process of production itself, not in other forms. In the absolute there is an eternal unity of subject and object, to the development of which the "powers" of Nature and of spirit, which are only its different reflections in the medium of experience, are not necessary. This standpoint of Schelling's, which was virtually the one adopted by Goethe, became paramount with many scientific men who perceived the kinship between natural forms but could not reconcile themselves to the thought of an actual descent   The kinship existed, in their view, in the innermost recesses of Nature, in the creative imagination of the Deity, or however they might express it : not between the actually existing groups of natural beings. Agassiz, Darwin's most famous opponent, supported a theory of this kind; it is represented in Danish literature by I. C. SCHIÖDTE. It was an idealistic, not a realistic, doctrine of evolution.

(b) *The Religio-philosophical Problem*

As already mentioned, Schelling's development was interrupted at a certain period by an inner discord, followed shortly after by an arrest. He had begun writing very young, his first philosophical work having been composed at the age of nineteen. The period of Romanticism exhibits not a few of such early matured and early checked faculties of production. In Schelling's case discord and cessation alike may partly be traced to three causes : (1) the route he had taken could lead him no further, (2) a new problem had presented itself to him, and (3) his purely personal relations.

The problem which now presented itself to him was the religious problem. We have seen that Novalis' religious enthusiasm had excited in Schelling a spirit of opposition. During the Jena period he had been too much absorbed in Nature and art for more practical problems to take any hold

of him. In a letter dating from the early part of 1806, he
writes : " In my retirement at Jena I was concerned very little
with life and very much with Nature, to which my thinking
was almost entirely confined. Since that time I have learned
to see that religion, public faith, civil life, is the point on
which everything turns " (*Aus Schelling's Leben*, ii. p. 78). It
was one of his pupils who first led him to occupy himself with
the religious problem. ESCHENMAYER, in an interesting little
work (*Die Philosophie in ihren Übergange zur Nichtphilosophie*,
Erlangen, 1803), asserts that the sphere of religion is higher
than that of philosophy. For even if philosophy could overcome all antitheses and exhibit the absolute as the highest
unity, the question would still remain, How did the opposites,
the different powers, originate? and only faith in a creating
God can supply the answer. Philosophy is not in a position
to establish the existence of a finite world, split up into
opposites, a world of differences and powers, existing apart
from the absolute unity which speculation recognises as the
highest. Schelling admits that differentiation presents a great
problem, but is convinced that this problem must be solvable
by philosophy. Philosophy must extend its borders ; but
there is no reason for assuming that religion and philosophy
are altogether different. He affirms that it certainly is impossible to deduce difference from identity, plurality from unity ;
it was precisely on this account that he had stated in his
philosophy that antithesis (difference, plurality) is a no less
original principle than unity. A *living* unity is one which
contains the opposites—however great the tension between
them—not without but within itself. In the work entitled
Philosophie und Religion (1804), which he wrote after he had
withdrawn from Jena to Würzburg, he admits that there are
forces active in Nature and history too markedly antagonistic
to be deducible from the idea of the absolute unity—an antagonism which must be harmonised through the different stages of
Nature and history. He had previously called Nature the
Odyssey of the spirit ; he now uses this expression of history
also. The undisciplined and irrational in Nature and history
testify, according to him, to a falling away from the idea, to
a discord which has crept in and which cries out to be reconciled. Against Eschenmayer, as a few years later in his
polemic against Fichte, he asserts, however, that such opposi-

tion and discord is necessary in order that there may be life and harmony. Without opposition no life. This line of thought, especially after he had settled in Munich, was nourished by the study of the old mystics, more particularly Jakob Böhme; indeed there was a general revival of Böhme at that time. St. Martin and Franz Baader revived his line of thought in France and Germany respectively. In the most important and able work of Schelling's religio-philosophical period, the *Philosophischen Untersuchungen über das Wesen der menschlichen Freiheit und die damit zusammenhängenden Gegenstände* (1809), he attempts to show that we are only justified in conceiving God as a personal being if we posit an original antithesis within the absolute, within the essence of the Deity,—a dark irrational ground which becomes purified and harmonised, as he had taught in his philosophy, in the course of the life-development of the Divine Being. He here attributes great religious significance to his philosophy of Nature, with its gradually ascending powers. Personality develops only in contrast with a natural foundation, and, with this as a basis, through conflict with opposing forces. Finite beings have this contrast, this basis, *outside themselves.* If the infinite Being possesses personality it must contain this relation of opposition *within itself:* there must be something in God which in and for itself is not God but which can become God. Theism, says Schelling in a polemic against Jacobi, may be constructed on the soil of naturalism; but from a pure theism, from the rational God of the Enlightenment or from the non-natural God of ordinary theology, it is impossible to establish the existence of Nature. *Given* opposites may be transcended, and it is this which constitutes life; but given opposites can never be explained out of pure unity. In the primitive difference Schlegel, following ever in Böhme's footsteps, sees the beginning of evil. When man obeys the deep-lying impulse to egoism, to self-assertion, he follows a will which leads back to the first ground of things. All evil consists in a striving to return to the chaos out of which the order of Nature has proceeded. Thus it becomes comprehensible that Nature should always show us a residuum which is not transparent to the understanding, and which cannot be reduced to definite laws, *i.e.* the survival of the ancient chaos. But without chaos, without conflict and dissolution, there is no real unity; without dis-

sension love cannot reveal itself. Had God prevented evil
He must have destroyed His own personality ; in order to
prevent the existence of evil God would have had to annul
His own existence !

Schelling's remarkable work—a blending of deep thought
and fancy—owes its philosophical interest to his admission of
an irrational, *i.e.* a something which is impervious to thought as
Schelling knew and exercised it, and to the fact that he hereby,
and to this extent, proves that speculative philosophy cannot
reach its goal, but must allow that critical philosophy is right
in assigning limits to knowledge. To this extent, too, it indicates a reaction against speculation, and has a certain realistic
character. It is interesting, further, because it ushers in a new
discussion of the concept of God, and investigates the conditions under which an absolute infinite Being can be conceived
as having personality. In conformity with Böhme's axiom :
"Without opposites no consciousness," an opposition *within*
the nature of God is now postulated as the necessary condition
for conceiving God as a person. This thought, resting on
ideas contained in Böhme's philosophy and revived by
Schelling, became the basis of the *philosophical theism* subsequently developed by eminent thinkers such as C. H. WEISSE
(1801-1866), in his *Das philosophische Problem der Gegenwart*
(1842), and afterwards in his *Philosophischen Dogmatik* (1855-
62) ; and HERMANN LOTZE. The difficulty for philosophical
theism is that if the antithesis, the overcoming of which is the
necessary condition for the personality of God, is intra-divine,
contained within God's own nature, it cannot be taken very
seriously. The battle then becomes a game, a divine joke.
Personal life as we know it, and as alone we are able to form
a conception of it, must wrestle with *external* (not self-made)
limits ; a personal life the inner forces of which are not being
continually partly nourished, partly checked, by external circumstances is unthinkable. With regard to Schelling more
particularly, he never meant that a *successive* process went on
in the Deity ; struggle does not *precede* peace ; in God there is
no first or last, but eternal circular motion. But this makes
the idea of the whole entirely unthinkable ; every attempt to
think such an eternal circular motion must in the end make
us giddy. Even Arnauld in his criticism of Descartes' doctrine
of God as *causa sui* (see vol. i. p. 225 of the present work),

had shown the contradiction in which this involves us. Weisse saw clearly that we can only find a meaning for this thought by assuming that the being of God has suffered an actual historical development in time. But this is contradictory to the concept of God as the absolute Being, nor does it lessen the difficulty of philosophical theism.[40]

We have seen the turning-point in Schelling's philosophical production. Cessation followed close upon it. At the conclusion of his treatise of 1809 he promises a presentation of the philosophy of spirit based on the foundation he had acquired. In spite of various attempts, and even somewhat noisy announcements, however, this promise remained unfulfilled. His productivity was checked. Perhaps it was owing to the death of his brilliant wife that he now allowed himself to give way to an attack of hypochondria. But Hegel's appearance and victorious progress in the philosophical world certainly helped to determine Schelling to keep in the background. In Erlangen and München his philosophy of religion took shape quietly in the form of lectures, and almost the only things of his which were published were some bitter onslaughts on his victorious rival at Berlin. When, after Hegel's death, the so-called Left of his school, with Strauss and Feuerbach at their head, deduced from his teaching heterodox religious consequences, Schelling obeyed the call of King Friedrich Wilhelm IV., who sympathised with the Romanticists (1861), and appeared as a kind of philosophical redeemer. It was now expected that he would publish the thoughts which had so long occupied him. But his appearance in Berlin was a fiasco. His theory did not appear in print until after his death, which took place in 1854. It consists of a *Philosophie der Mythologie*, and a *Philosophie der Offenbarung*, and is an attempt to show how the Odyssey of spirit, the progressive reconciliation and harmonisation of the restless and opposing forces take place in the course of the development of the religious consciousness. One and the same process extends through the mythologies leading up to Christianity, and through the development of Christianity into free religion. The details of this exposition are not interesting;[41] Schelling treated religio-historical facts no less arbitrarily than he had handled the facts of natural science in his youth, and the ideas of his later years are lacking in the Titanic boldness, and the romantic spirit by which so many of his early writings are distinguished.

CHAPTER III

GEORGE WILLIAM FREDERICK HEGEL

(a) Biography and Characteristics

IN a conversation with Eckermann (February 17, 1831) Goethe described the relation between the two parts of *Faust* as follows : " The first part is almost entirely subjective ; it is the outpouring of an individual imprisoned in his passions. In the second part the subjective element has almost disappeared—we get here a higher, broader, clearer, less passionate world." The development of German philosophy in the various systems which arose after Kant, offers a parallel to the difference which Goethe thus describes between the two parts of his great work. Kant and Fichte began with subjective searching and striving, with a sharp distinction between the ideal and reality, and their efforts were, to a certain degree, carried on by Schelling. In Hegel's system we reach the close ; we become reconciled with reality by plunging into its different spheres, so that what had hitherto hovered before men as a distant ideal to be pursued is now found to be the innermost kernel of things. That which Goethe meant to express in the second part of his *Faust, i.e.* reconciliation with reality won by actual experience and faithful work, was precisely what Hegel intended his system to express, in opposition to the critical philosophy and to Romanticism. There is yet another respect in which the parallel holds good,—the transitions and details of the Hegelian system offer to the understanding difficulties as great as do those contained in the second part of *Faust.*

The reader of Hegel's works is struck from the first, not only by the abstract character of his developments, but still more by the many technical expressions he employs. This is especially deterrent to the modern reader. But he who succeeds in penetrating this outer husk will become aware of another characteristic which presses into the foreground, and which must occupy this foremost place if Hegel's portrait as a thinker is to be drawn with historical accuracy. This characteristic is his great interest in the content of spiritual life under all forms and at all stages. His speculative method and his abstract form of exposition notwithstanding, Hegel's was a realistic nature. He felt an urgent need to lose himself in the objective powers of life. He wanted to re-think the fulness of life, to translate it into the form of thought. In order that this rich content may become the property of thought it must be expressed in a circle of thought, the individual members of which are as intimately bound together as are the individual moments of existence (Dasein), no one of which can be disturbed without a tremor passing through the whole. By means of his dialectical method, Hegel believed himself able to present such a circle of thoughts. But by the irony of fate the very method which he believed would lead him to the goal prevented his thoughts from attaining a form and foundation such as could ensure them the lasting significance which they deserve.

Hegel was born at Stuttgart, August 27, 1770, and studied theology at Tübingen at the same time as Schelling, who was his junior by five years. In addition to theology he studied natural science and philosophy ; he felt particularly attracted by Kant and Rousseau. While quite young, he took a great interest in politics, and his admiration for classical antiquity, which he shared with his friend, the poet Hölderlin, sprang up equally early. During his residence in Berne, in the capacity of tutor in a private family, he continued his studies. Some essays on the philosophy of religion, written at this time, betray a distinctly rationalistic tendency. We may gather that his interest in politics was undiminished from the fact that he studied the system of finance of the Canton of Berne down to its minutest details. The productions of friend Schelling filled him with amazement ; he declared his himself to be still a learner. He grew to his full estate as an independent thinker at Frankfort, where he lived from 1796-1800, still as a private tutor, but under freer and more favourable conditions than formerly. It was here that his philosophy took form. In a letter to Schelling (November 2, 1800) he writes that the *ideal* of his youth must now transform itself into a *system*—an utterance characteristic alike of his personality and his philosophy. What this ideal was may be gathered from his notes of this period, which were published first by Rosenkranz (*Hegel's Leben*, Berlin, 1844), and afterwards by Haym (*Hegel und seine Zeit*, Berlin, 1857). His study of history—more especially the history of politics and of religion—had led him to prize those nations and ages in which men lived wholly and entirely in great thoughts, held in common, which revealed to them the kernel of existence. In Hellenism and Christianity he found forms of culture, both of which exhibited this characteristic. In these the individual did not feel himself a separate member, cut off from the whole, did not confront the whole with subjective criticism, but was inspired by it and absorbed in it.

But these ages of harmony are over. Fervently as Hegel agreed with Hölderlin in his enthusiasm for antiquity (he has expressed this feeling in a poem entitled " Eleusis ") ; and eagerly as he studied mediæval mysticism, yet he never fell under the illusion that these ages could be revived. The ideal for which he looked was the appearance of this spiritual life in a new form. He felt as impatient with the subjective, critical, rationalistic, and revolutionary tendency of the time as Fichte showed himself in the *Grundzügen des gegenwärtigen Zeitalters*, and this impatience really underlies the whole Romantic movement. But in maintaining that the ideal must be translated into a system, Hegel meant that a complete interconnected thought-system must be substituted for the empty search of the critical philosopher and the capricious attitude of Romanticism towards reality.

The dangers and difficulty of such a transition lies in the fact that while the ideal denotes vista, lack of conclusion, an open horizon, system aims at giving an interconnected and completed explanation. In the process of transition we are likely to find that the ideal conforms unduly to reality, or reality is twisted to fit in with the ideal. Hegel's system suffers from both these defects. The reality to which he points as the revelation of an ideal has only too frequently already received at his hands a twist in the interests of idealism. It must, therefore, be acknowledged that his whole system rests on the soil of Romanticism.

In the year 1801 Hegel was appointed to a professorship at Jena. Since the time when Reinhold had come forward as the champion of the Kantian philosophy the University of Jena had been the home of the philosophical movement. It was here that Schiller, Fichte, and Schelling laboured ; here, too, Herbart and Fries studied during the same years.

For some time Hegel and Schelling worked together. Together they published a journal in which Hegel polemicised against the " philosophy of reflection " which could not rise to the idea of the absolute unity of subject and object, nor see everything in the light of this idea. (This criticism referred in particular to Kant, Fichte, and Jacobi.) Their ways soon parted, however, owing to the difference of intellectual disposition between the two men. Schelling's strength lay in intuition, in powerful grasp, in pregnant intimations ; but he was not the man for the quiet execution of detailed work. And the speedy attainment of a new standpoint was followed—throughout his entire youth—by a no less speedy renunciation. Hegel was slow to develop, but from the time when his system was first sketched out in its leading features (1800) it was never changed, and he devoted all the remainder of his life to developing it by means of the method which he held to be the right one. He broke with the " Reflective philosophy " because it taught a dualism between the subject and reality ; he broke with Schelling on account of the formlessness of his thought and the unsteadiness of his method. The breach was announced in the preface to the *Phänomenologie des Geistes* (Phenomenology of Mind) (1807). In Schelling's philosophy, he here says, the Absolute is " the night in which all cows are black," for it is described as the unity or identity of all differences. Schelling, it is true, recognises opposites, for he works with the *schema* of polarity ; but it is nothing more than an empty *schema*, in which real development never comes by its rights. Schelling is like a painter with only two colours on his palette, who believes he can reproduce all things by their means. The important point is to show how the different elements in existence (*Dasein*) pass over into one another with an inner necessity. It is only by means of this inner interconnection between all things in the world that we can understand that the absolute is no dead being (*Sein*), no passive unity, but process, life, spirit. Hegel is here urging the claims of the dialectical method, which really contains within it, as we shall presently show, his whole system. The *Phänomenologie des Geistes* is intended to furnish an introduction to the system. In this work Hegel shows how ordinary consciousness develops into speculative consciousness, rising through different grades or forms to knowledge. That truth is neither dead being (Substance) nor mere subjectivity, but a living unity of the two,—a knowledge, moreover, to which the individual consciousness can attain all the more easily since "the world-spirit has had the patience to pass through these forms in their long series in time and to undertake the huge labour of the world-history in which it shapes out in each one the whole content of which it is capable." (*Phänomenologie : Vorrede*). The course of development described in this unique work is at once that of the individual and of the race ; it gives at the same time a psychology and a history of culture—and in the exposition the two are so interwoven with one another that it is often impossible to tell which of the two is intended.

The battle of Jena, and circumstances resulting therefrom, led Hegel to move to South Germany. He was so absorbed in speculative thought that this catastrophe failed to kindle his patriotism. Indeed, on the very day before the battle he had watched with interest and speculative curiosity the Emperor, "this world-mind on horseback" as he rode out to reconnoitre. He felt himself a spectator only, looking on at a drama in the world's history, whose only concern was to find a quiet corner for himself. He spent some time at Bamberg editing a paper. After that he became Rector of the *Gymnasium* at Nürnberg (1808-16). It was here he published his chief work, the *Wissenschaft der Logik* (Science of Logic) (1812-16), consisting of a presentation of all the fundamental concepts of science, developed according to the dialectical method. It was but natural that he should wish to be once more connected with a university. From 1816-18 he was Professor at Heidelberg, where he published his *Encyklopädie der philosophischen Wissenschaften im Grundrisse* (" Encyclopædia of the Philosophical Sciences "), and during the last years of his life he was active at the Berlin University, where his *Grundlinien der Philosophie des Rechts* (" Sketch of a Philosophy of Law ") appeared (1821). During the Berlin period his influence was at its height, partly on account of the boldness of his system, which seemed to offer a living frame wide enough to embrace the whole spiritual content of the time, and which soon drew a large following round him ; partly on account of the conservatism of his philosophy of rights and of religion which came in the nick of time for those in authority.   It was the age of unfulfilled political promises and of clerical reaction in Germany, and yet Hegel taught the ideal truth of the existing civil order and of the ruling religion !   However unattractive the manner in which this tendency of Hegel expressed itself— especially in his attacks on thinkers who held opposite views which brought them into disfavour with the authorities—there can be no doubt that his conservatism sprang out of his idealism.   He was convinced that the idea is never too weak to penetrate reality either in Nature or in the State : " As to Nature, philosophy, it is admitted, has to understand it as it is. The philosopher's stone must be concealed somewhere *in Nature itself,* we say ; Nature is in itself rational, and knowledge has to apprehend the reason actually present in it.   But the ethical world, or the State which is, in fact, reason potently and permanently actualised in self-consciousness, is not permitted to enjoy the happiness of being reason at all.   On the contrary, the spiritual universe is looked upon as abandoned by God, and given over as a prey to accident and chance."   This conviction explains his indignation against those who believed themselves possessed of more reason than had developed historically in the State.   At this point Hegel is close to the so-called historical school which regards the ordering of rights as the work of history, exalted above all individual reflection and will.

He even goes so far as to say that philosophy must always come too late to teach us how the world ought to be. Thought is the last product of the world - process.   When reflection awakens it is a sign that an historical form of life has drawn to a close : " The owl of Minerva takes its flight only when the shades of night are gathering."   Hegel's conservatism ought, properly speaking, to have led him to attribute far greater weight to the empirical method than he actually did. For if thought always follows after, and cannot anticipate the new, how is it possible to discover truth by way of pure thought, of the dialectical method ?

Hegel died of cholera on November 14, 1831. A few years afterwards his collected works (*Religionsphilosophie, Ästhetik, Geschichte der Philosophie,* etc.) were published by his pupils, partly from his MS. notes for his lectures.

(b) The Dialectical Method

Hegel understands by what he calls dialectic (1) a property of all our thoughts, in virtue of which each particular thought necessarily passes over into another, but also (2) a property of things in virtue of which every particular thing necessarily belongs together with all other things. Hence, in his view, the way in which thought reaches truth is also the immediate expression of the innermost life of existence (*Dasein*); when we think existence, existence thinks in us.

(1) Since every concept is limited, it passes over when logically thought out into its opposite, its negation. To think it out is to annul it. But through the negation there arises a new positive; for what is negated is only the definite, finite content, not all content whatsoever. Negation, then, means that a new concept comes into force. But since this new concept is determined by its relation to the previous one, and by the recollection of the same, it is richer than the latter. The concept which is now formed contains the preceding one taken up into a large whole. Further, negation is only an annulling in the sense that the negated concept is raised to a higher unity. A unity of opposites comes into being which contains both the concept posited and its opposite. " In this way," says Hegel in the introduction to the " Logic," " the system of concepts has to form itself and to complete itself in a ceaseless, pure, progression—free from any accretion from without."

The Hegelian system, accordingly, develops itself in triads in which the concept and its opposite having both been negated, the unity of the opposites, the higher unity which includes both position and negation, is posited—to be subjected in turn to the same process. If we begin with the most abstract of all concepts, that of being (*Sein*), it passes over into the concept of nothing, since pure undifferentiated being, without content and determination, is the same as not-being. By uniting these two concepts we get the concept of becoming, for becoming is both being and not-being, since it is the transition from one condition to another.   The concept of becoming, however, leads in turn to the concept of qualities which arise or are annulled, and so on.

(2) But this forwards-striving dialectic is the expression of the self-development of existence (*Daseins*).   The pulse of existence itself beats in our thinking,—with the same rhythm, moreover, as everywhere else.   Every finite phenomenon points, in virtue of its limitation, beyond itself ; it is but a moment in the one great whole.   In maintaining the objectivity of the dialectic Hegel has two particular experiences in view, as may be seen from his application of it in detail. These are, first, the passing over of opposites into one another, precisely because of their oppositional relation, *e.g.* the psychological effect of contrast, the rhythm of life and death, light and darkness (for too strong a light—no less than absolute darkness—deprives us of the power of seeing), and within the social sphere, the shifting over of strict right into crying wrong (*summum jus, summa injuria*), etc.   At the summit of evolution, dissolution sets in :   this was the law according to which Hegel attempted to construct Nature and history. Secondly, however—and this is the essential point of view— he is mindful of the fact that the results of earlier stages of development determine development in its later stages.   The innocence of the child is annulled by the unrest of doubt, of reflection, and of passion ;   but this purging fire develops a firmer, more harmonious character, in which the immediacy of childhood reappears in a higher form.   The seed-corn must perish if the plant is to come into being, but the plant contains all that was of the essence of the seed-corn.   What Hegel tries to express by his doctrine of the dialectic as a world-process is his conviction of the conservation of the forces and values in existence.   In his mystical parlance, the memory of the world-spirit contains everything ; destruction means the annulling of external existence, not the destruction of what is essential.   Never before had such a magnificent attempt been made to extend the conservation of force and of worth to the spiritual sphere.   The turning-point at which the ideal became transformed into a system with Hegel was the moment when he ceased to doubt the conservation of worth in existence.   As long as a sharp distinction is made between

the ideal and reality it still remains an open question whether
the ideal might not vanish from existence (so that the " happy
ages " could never return), even supposing the elementary forces
were not lost, but persisted under other forms.

Thus significant ideas lie behind the dialectical method.
The most important thing to notice here, however, is that the
speculative philosophy laid down for the first time an independent and peculiar method, in which pure reason could
develop itself according to its own inner laws. Hegel's " Logic "
is the first resolute answer to Kant's " Critique of Pure Reason."
If Hegel were right, the problem which Kant pronounced
insoluble, *i.e.* to establish by way of thought the knowledge
of existence, was solved. But since negation is a purely
logical operation which always remains within our own power,
we should, if Hegel were right, be able to spin the thread of
thought farther by our own unaided effort, since out of any
concept whatever new positive concepts could be conjured.
Unfortunately this is not the case. It is in our own power
certainly to negate, and to negate this negation—but the
negation of negation always leads us back again to the
original position, just as $\div (\div 2) = 2$, but is not a new number.
If by negation of not $- A$ I could arrive not at A again but
at B, then, and only then, could the thread of thought be spun
to infinity purely *a priori*. Hence the systematisation of our
fundamental concepts of knowledge is only apparently, not
really, furthered by Hegel's dialectical method. As a matter
of fact, the triad (position, negation, higher unity) is only a
schema into which he presses the empirical content more or
less arbitrarily.

Hegel's dialectical method is a further development of
Fichte's antithetical method. But Fichte was well aware that
the antithesis (as positive proposition) cannot be deduced from
the thesis. The different opposed propositions were, in his
eyes, only different attempts to express the given ; each
proposition denotes a fresh onslaught on reality on the part
of thought, and the synthesis unites what each proposition
has established. Hence the new position is always reached
through experience. But, according to Hegel, the antithesis
ought always to be deducible from the thesis without the help
of experience. Like Fichte's antithetical method, Schelling's
potentialising or depotentialising method was also a precursor

of the dialectical method.   The Romantic attempt to reach a purely idealistic construction of the world-conception concludes with Hegel.   History dealt out to him the fate prescribed by his own dialectic ; when once it was understood what a thorough-going speculative idealism involved, thought turned away in search of other starting-points and other methods.

(c) The System

Hegel's system falls—in agreement with the fundamental law of the dialectic—into three parts.   The first part consists of the Logic, which is for Hegel not merely a doctrine of the forms of our thought, but also a presentation of the eternal thoughts which underlie existence.   He himself refers to the idea of the *Logos* as the world-creating and world-ordering principle.   The world of Nature, as well as that of spirit, is ruled by general laws and thoughts which the Logic exhibits in their pure abstract form, by showing how one concept develops out of another.   The second part of the system is the Philosophy of Nature, which exhibits the thought-content of existence not in logical abstraction, but in the form of " externality " in space and time.   The transition from the Logic to the Philosophy of Nature must proceed with dialectical necessity.   This is one of the most difficult points of the Hegelian method.   The transition may indeed be said to take place naturally, for the abstraction on which the Logic builds is annulled, and the thinker goes back to the experiences from which he abstracted the concepts with which he operated in the Logic.   The " Philosophy of Nature " has rightly been called the *partie honteuse* of the Hegelian system.   Hegel is even more arbitrary than Schelling in his treatment of the concepts of natural science.   Schelling had already placed Kepler (on account of his *Mysterium cosmographicum*) and Goethe (on account of his doctrine of colours) above Newton.   Hegel goes still farther in the same direction.   We have here a Romantic attempt (in which the decided change which took place in Kepler's views was entirely ignored) to suppress the mechanical conception of Nature.   (See vol. i. of this work, p. 169.)   Hegel, like Schelling, starts by attempting to arrange the concepts of the forces and forms of Nature in such a manner as to show how Nature has worked itself up, stage by stage, from mere externality to the inwardness of spirit. The most important stages are, mechanism, physics, organism. These stages, however, no more indicate a real development than they did with Schelling. Hegel expressly declares (*Encyclopædia*, § 249) : "Nature must be regarded as a system of stages (degrees), in which one necessarily proceeds from the other . . . not, however, in such a way that one is naturally *produced* by the other, but in the inner idea which constitutes the ground of Nature. *Metamorphosis* can only happen to the concept as such, since change in it alone is development. . . . Thinking consideration must banish such nebulous and at bottom senseless ideas as the so-called *proceeding* of plants and animals from water, and the *proceeding* of highly developed animal organisation from lower ones, etc." This passage is characteristic of the *idealistic* doctrine of evolution, which regards the strict mechanical deduction of one natural form out of another as externality and sensuousness, an outrage on the pure self-activity of the idea. The third part of the system is the *Geistesphilosophie* ("Philosophy of Spirit"). The transition is effected by the annulling, in its turn, of the form of externality under which the idea appears in Nature. Inwardness, independence of time and place takes the place of the material divisibility and extension of Nature. Although here, too, there is a hitch in the proof of the dialectical necessity, yet the origin of conscious life presents no difficulty in principle to Hegel since he conceives the idea, the spiritual principle, as the innermost essence, the true existence underlying Nature. Hegel's philosophy is really philosophy of spirit from beginning to end ; it is an attempt to make the science of mind absolute science, just as materialism is an attempt to make the science of matter absolute science. When one of Hegel's pupils (the elder ERDMANN) designates his system "Panlogismus" on account of the attempt which runs all through it to display the whole content of existence under the form of abstract categories, and to conceive the movement of thought as the law of the universe, he lays too great weight on the form of the Hegelian system. Another of his pupils (ROSENKRANZ) was much nearer the truth in calling it "philosophy of spirit." The real object of the dialectical method is to show that all things are as intimately interconnected as are the thoughts of the mind —that like the latter all things form a great totality, and that the true expression of the essence of existence runs :

Everything is spirit, and spirit is everything. Kant's " synthesis " has here become a world-principle. The " Philosophy of Spirit," like the " Philosophy of Nature," falls naturally into three parts. The first part treats of the subjective mind (in the graduated series of soul, consciousness, reason), the spiritual life of the individual subject—the content, that is to say, of what would now be called psychology. Then follows objective mind—spiritual life as it displays itself in the different social forms and institutions of history. Here belong law, morality, and the ethical life of the family, of civil society, of the State (social ethics (*Sittlichkeit*) as distinguished from morality (*Moralität*)). The higher unity of subjective and objective spirit is absolute spirit, the totality of the spiritual life of existence " the spirit in its community" (" *das Geist in seiner Gemeinde*"), where every distinction between the individual and that which fulfils and supports the individual has disappeared. Art, religion, and (speculative) philosophy are mentioned as forms of the absolute mind.

This highest stage itself, the culmination of the dialectical movement, must, however, be the stage on which the *human* spiritual life, the only one known to us, stands. But Hegel treats this point with a certain ambiguity. Although art, religion, and philosophy express human striving, yet he really conceives them as life-forms of the *world-spirit*. But in his Philosophy of Nature (*Encyclopædia*, § 290, cf. 280) he makes a naïve admission that, after all, these life-forms are realised at a definite place in the universe, and indeed, so far as we know, are only realised here when he tries to show that the planets are more perfect heavenly bodies than the sun, and that the earth is the most perfect of the planets! The " most perfect " must mean here that which is most fitted to develop spiritual life. But, in that case, what is the good of the rest of the universe? The grave doubts of old Boehme (vol. i. p. 70 ff) might raise their heads once again! In spite of all his dialectic Hegel was not able to rise above the geocentric and anthropocentric standpoint, which, indeed, we are forced to adopt. No dialectic can teach us to jump off our own shadows.

Two sections of Hegel's Philosophy of Mind are of especial interest for the history of civilisation as well as for philosophy, *i.e.* his doctrine of rights and the State and his doctrine of religion.

(*d*) *Philosophy of Rights*

The ideal of Hegel's youth had been the antique State, conceived as a divine power embracing and absorbing all individuals, in contradistinction to the modern individualistic conception which regards the State as originating in a contract between individual egoisms. So later, in his Philosophy of Rights (which is a further development of what appears in the system under the head of Objective Mind), he contrasts social morality (*Sittlichkeit*) as it exists in family life, civic society, and the State, partly with right, as the expression of the individual will, partly with "morality" (*Moralität*), as the expression of the subjective conscience, which in its isolation from the objective power of society becomes pure caprice, evil ! Only in social life can right and morality flourish ; they are offshoots of the Whole and are not themselves wholes. In a moral social order the good finds lasting existence as in a world animated by itself. The decision here no longer rests with the individual conscience and caprice. There is something in the ethical world which transcends the consciousness of the individual. It was in this sense that Sophocles' *Antigone* declared the laws to be eternal ; no one knows from whence they come. The life of particular individuals is regulated by ethical powers, which, it is true, find in individuals points of attachment, but which, nevertheless, are not dependent on them. Indeed, Hegel even goes so far as to declare (§ 145), "Whether the individual exists or not is a matter of indifference to the objective moral order, which alone is steadfast. It is the power by which the life of individuals is governed." Yet it is only in objective morality that the individual finds his right sphere ; he only becomes free when he lives in it ; the relation between the individual and society then becomes so close that faith and confidence are no longer appropriate terms, since they presuppose a certain relation of difference. The natural will has been replaced by a new and higher nature, morality (*die Sitte*). Where the ethical substance, the spirit of the family, of civic society, of the State, rules, there the particular duties of the individual as such necessarily arise, and are not difficult to discover.

Of the various ethical communities the State is the most

important.   As the higher unity of both it unites in itself the essence of the family and of civic society.   It is the full reality of the moral idea.   Spirit has realised itself much more perfectly here than in Nature, where it still slumbers.   The State is the progression of God in the world, and must be honoured as something half earthly, half divine.   As the duties of each individual spring immediately from his place in society, and there is no need for him to devise them for himself, so too the constitution of the State is the natural outcome of its nature.   It is true that the constitution develops in the course of time, historically ; but it is not " something made." As empirical proof that constitutions are not made Hegel quotes the constitution which the leaders of the French Revolution devised and attempted in vain to establish, also the constitution, reasonable enough in itself, which Napoleon tried to force on Spain.   Hegel's philosophy of rights has the great merit of emphasising the connection between the life of the constitution and the historical character of the State as a whole, which transcends the wishes and thoughts of every particular individual. He approximates here to the historical school and to positivism. AUGUSTE COMTE'S first independent work (*Système de la politique positive*, 1821) was, accordingly, very well received by Hegel (as may be seen from a letter of Comte's to a friend at Berlin) while, on the other hand, Comte's interest was excited by what he heard of Hegel's lectures on philosophy, although, in his opinion, Hegel was "encore trop métaphysique," and "spirit" played all too important a part in his system : " Je n'aime point du tout son *esprit*, auquel il fait jouer un rôle si singulier."   (See Littré, *Auguste Comte et la philosophie positive*, 2nd ed. p. 157.)

It was not Hegel's intention, however, to revive the antique State, to the defects of which he was not blind.   The modern State must be the organisation of freedom.   Civic society, the family, and private individuals must find in the State the satisfaction of their particular interests.   The State must only demand as a duty that which is properly the right of the individual.   The great aim of the State ought not and can- not be reached without the support of the smaller societies and individuals it embraces ("*not without* the private knowledge and will of particularity itself, which must preserve its right," § 260).   Nevertheless, in his detailed exposition, Hegel makes the objective element altogether predominant.   Even that modest "not without" is not respected—for, as we have already heard, the social morality (*Sittlichkeit*) of the objective substance is indifferent to the existence or non-existence of particular individuals. To a thinker who finds the divine-earthly, "substantive reason," in the State, and that not in the idea or ideal of the State, but in the State as it actually exists, the ideals, criticisms, and reasonings of the particular individual naturally appear as subjective opinions and wishes, as a giving one's self airs, a "knowing better," which fails to recognise the deep truth of that which has historical existence. In accordance with the principle, "Those who know, οἱ ἄριστοι, should rule, not the ignorance and vanity of those who know better." Hegel recognises in the bureaucracy the true representatives of the State.

"The government rests with the world of officials." He believed this principle realised in Germany, more especially in Prussia. This was the most satisfactory spectacle which discovered itself to him when he concluded his lectures (1820-30) on the philosophy of history with a survey of the condition of Europe. The progression of God in the world had got so far. The reactionary, speculative thinker did not perceive that the foot of the Deity was already raised to take new and strong steps, which would for the time shatter every system, without, however, blotting out the view into the world of the ideal.

In the preface to his "Philosophy of Rights," Hegel makes an odious attack on FRIES of Jena, a disciple of Kant. Fries had taken part in the German students' festival on the Wartburg (1817)—a festival of which the reactionaries highly disapproved—and had made a speech in which he had said : "When a nation is really inspired by a common spirit, then from below, from the people, will come life sufficient for the discharge of all public business. Living associations, united indissolubly by the sacred bond of friendship, will dedicate themselves to all branches of public service and all schemes for educating the people." So, cries Hegel, the ethical world is to be given up to the contingency of subjective opinions and caprices, and the work on which reason has been engaged for more than a thousand years left to the mercy of personal feeling ! In his zeal to translate the ideal into system Hegel was unjust to those to whom the existing system did not appear ideal. History has proved him wrong. It has shown that the State can only grow strong through the free co-operation of the people. To establish the German kingdom, founded by war, Bismarck at once introduced universal suffrage.

(e) *Philosophy of Religion*

In the sphere of religion also Hegel demands absorption of the individual in that which has developed historically. There must be no subjective reasoning, no individual feeling. But he also promises that, in the work of history, the peculiar work of the world-spirit, thought will find its own essence again! He makes front against rationalism as well as against orthodox theology. Orthodoxy clings to the literal expression of dogmas, and does not perceive that the age of immediate, naïve religion has yielded to increasing culture, reflection, and enlightenment.

Rationalism, on the other hand, makes the concept of God empty and finite, sets God outside the world, the infinite outside the finite, and doubts altogether, perhaps, the knowledge of God. And if (as Schleiermacher did) we hope to get help by appealing to feeling, yet even this does not take us beyond our own subjectivity. Feeling alone cannot justify itself; its worth rests on its content and its object. Feeling cannot decide, for man has it in common with the brutes; and if it were only a question of feeling, the dog would be the better Christian.

The task of the philosophy of religion is to find a way out of this opposition between belief in the letter, on the one hand, and rationalism and subjective feeling, on the other. Philosophy cannot certainly produce a religion, but it can recognise the religion which exists, and can investigate the relation of religion to the other factors of our conception of life. And a closer scrutiny reveals the fact that the more philosophy approximates to a complete development, the more it exhibits the same need, the same interest, and the same content as religion.

Speculative philosophy must recognise the unity of existence which underlies all opposites if it is to understand as an infinite all-containing and embracing spirit understands. But this is precisely what the dogmas of religion express. They, too, in the highest forms of religion, express the truth that all things ultimately spring from one infinite spirit. The difference between religion and philosophy is only that in religion the content is conceived in the form of imagination, so that what are for the philosopher ultimate relations, expressions of an eternal truth valid for all times, are regarded as historical events, and are conceived in figurate form. This external, pictorial, historical form drops off when philosophy translates the content of religion into the form of thought. The distinction between religion and philosophy consists in this difference of form alone.

Hegel attempts to show that the different religions admit of being arranged in a graduated series, which leads dialectically from the most elementary forms to the highest religion, to that in which the concept of religion has attained to full development, since in it the conception of the deity as spirit is taken seriously. This religion is Christianity. Humanity, says Hegel, had not to wait for philosophy to become aware of truth. Religion contains truth—under the form of imagination.

Philosophy does not wish to overthrow religion, but only to translate the truth which it contains into the form of thought. How Hegel conceives this to take place may be gathered from some of his examples. In the dogma of the creation God and the world are posited as opposites ; the latter is regarded as a product of the former. Thought, on the contrary, cannot allow that this opposition is valid ; for if the infinite had the finite outside itself it would be limited by it and would no longer be infinite. The truth which the dogma of creation contains is that the infinite does not exist in self-dependence and isolation, but always points beyond itself ; the essence of the finite is its limitation, but precisely because of this limitation, of this negation, it hangs together with the whole content of existence, and is taken up into the infinite and determined by it. In the dogma of the atonement this relation between the infinite and the finite finds still more striking expression. God Himself is dead, as an old hymn puts it ; without detriment to His infinity God betakes Himself to the finite world, negates Himself (by becoming man) and annuls this negation again (through suffering, death, and resurrection). Thus the great images of dogma teach us that finitude and suffering, so far from interrupting the union with the highest are, on the contrary, themselves moments of the divine. With this the explanation of existence is given us ; that which constitutes the pain and anguish of finite existence is precisely that which witnesses that it is a member of an infinite whole.

In his speculative zeal Hegel overlooked the fact that to the believer in revelation the whole point is that dogma is more than a figure. Every positive religion must assume that, at certain points, the difference between symbol and reality disappears—only under this condition can the concept of revelation possess validity. In the concluding words of his *Vorlesungen über die Philosophie der Religion,* moreover, Hegel says that, for the philosopher, too, the discord between faith and reflection falls away when he absorbs himself in the essence of religions to find here again the highest ideas of thought ; but philosophers form only a small part of humanity, and he is obliged to conclude with the following words :—" How the temporal, empirical present finds its way out of its disruption, what form it takes must be left to it. It is not the immediately practical affair and concern of philosophy."

Further, Hegel disregards the fact that a change of form may very possibly denote an opposition in principle. He explains the dogmas of creation and of the atonement as symbolic expressions of the interconnection between the elements of existence, as expressions of the infinite life life-process which interpenetrates all things and from which we are never separated, even when we feel most bitterly the limitation and pain of finitude. Hegel's own powerful and manly way of looking at life here comes to light. But even if this exegesis were right —even if it were really the case that such an experience of life had found in these dogmas symbolic expression, yet if the creation denote a supernatural act, and the atonement an historical happening in which a supernatural God suffered and died as man, we get a very different conception of life from Hegel's. The change of form which Hegel represents as quite harmless, effects, as a matter of fact, a transition from a dualistic to a naturalistic or monistic conception of the world. This soon became evident in the religio-philosophical debate which arose within the Hegelian school. On this as on other points, Hegel himself appears as a Romanticist who searches out the old forms of spiritual life, although he transforms them to meet his own requirements. And the permanent truth contained

in the Hegelian philosophy of religion is this ; the religious
ideas of bygone times can only retain their value if we are able
to discover that in one way or another they express our own
experiences and our own thought.   This leads, of course, to no
historical interpretation ; for the nutritive value of ideas may
depend on many changes in point of view, but when such a
rediscovery is in no way possible, the ideas of the past are
mere curiosities of learning.   Hegel had caught sight of a great
ideal when he attempted to show that no values are ever lost
in history—but it was an ideal which his own system could not
realise.   His psychology, which reduces thought to a few
elements of consciousness, was particularly unsuited to serve as
a basis for this attempt.   In this respect his rival, whom we
shall now pass on to describe, had a great advantage over him.

CHAPTER IV

FRIEDRICH ERNST DANIEL SCHLEIERMACHER

(a) Characteristics and Biography

THE charge which Reinhold had laid upon his age of deducing philosophy from a single principle was complied with most fully by Hegel, and the Jena school (as the whole series of thinkers, Reinhold, Fichte, Schelling, and Hegel, may be called, since it was at the University of Jena that their thoughts were first developed) might be exhibited as a dialectical process producing in the course of its progress, with inner (perhaps even with world-historical) necessity, one system after another. To trace out this process of development was a task of which the Hegelians never wearied ; for in so doing were they not historically deducing the ideas of their master ? in accordance, too, with his own method. We have already seen that other forces were at work here besides that of the inner dialectic. Be that as it may, the Hegelians were not a little embarrassed by the presence, at a time when their master's sun was at its zenith, of a man endowed with no less a measure of spiritual power than he, and who had long been influencing by the weight of his peculiar personality the thinkers and seekers among his contemporaries, to whom, nevertheless, no place could be assigned in their graduated series, since he was distinctly opposed to the whole movement. Schleiermacher's attitude in the history of philosophy is characterised by the fact that he kept alive the spirit of critical philosophy within the sphere of Romantic philosophy—a union which his Socratic personality rendered possible, possessing as it did, in an unusual degree, the capacity of uniting complete and inward surrender with clear reflection.

He had in his personality what Hegel believed he had in his system, *i.e.* the reconciliation of opposites in a living unity.

FRIEDRICH SCHLEIERMACHER was born of a race of preachers on Nov. 21, 1768. His grandfather had been so strongly stirred by that radical form of pietism in which subjective feeling led to revolt against the ruling church that he had staked his own and his family's existence on the game. His father's was a practical nature, the rationalistic tendencies of which were repressed by the need of exercising a practical influence on men. Filled with enthusiasm for the religious life of the Herrnhüters he placed his fifteen-year-old son in their school at Niesky, and afterwards in their seminary at Barby. Schleiermacher himself, throughout his whole life, considered that the years spent among the Herrnhüters in his youth had been of the greatest importance for his spiritual life. His own nature had indeed expressed itself still earlier ; in a work (1801) in which he defends his views he says : " My way of thinking has indeed no other foundation than my own peculiar character, my inborn mysticism, my education as it has been determined from within." One of his most prominent traits was that he stamped everything which he adopted from without with his own personal mark. The Herrnhüter religiosity, however, with its intense life of feeling, its retirement, its attempt to let each individual soul live through the content of religion in its innermost life, while at the same time intercourse with kindred souls was zealously fostered, stamped him with a character which he never afterwards lost. Later in life he felt himself a Herrnhüter of a higher order. Higher—for Herrnhütism soon became too narrow for him. He longed for a life in common with other men, and with a richer content than any monastic retirement could afford ; above all things he was impelled by an intellectual need and a spirit of doubt which soon led him beyond the timid theology of his Herrnhüter teachers. After a violent struggle his father granted him the fulfilment of his wish to study at Halle. He here became acquainted with the theology and the philosophy of the Enlightenment, and soon afterwards with Kant's works also. If we are to understand Schleiermacher's development, it is of the first importance to remember (as DILTHEY shows in his excellent but, unfortunately, incomplete *Leben Schleiermachers* (1870), based on youthful notes of Schleiermacher's) that he

arrived at his decisive standpoint before he fell under the influence of the Romanticists, and before he had studied Spinoza.
At the University of Halle, and later, during his residence in a
nobleman's family in the country and when a preacher in a
little country town, he was led by solitary study and medita-
tion to his own peculiar religious standpoint, a standpoint which
enabled him to harmonise his critical intelligence with his lively
feeling. This standpoint was the resultant of the struggle
between the Herrnhüter religiosity and the critical philosophy.
He never abandoned the conviction that the innermost life of
men must be lived in feeling, and that this, and this alone,
can bring man into immediate relation with the Highest. But
he learnt from the critical philosophy to recognise the definite
conditions and limits to which human knowledge is subject.
He asserted, even more emphatically than Kant himself, that
all ideas which transcend experience possess symbolic value
only. Hence not only the ideas of Christian theology but
also the favourite dogmas of the Enlightenment theology, *i.e.*
those of a personal God and a personal immortality acquired,
in his eyes, a new sense. Schleiermacher's idiosyncracy—which
makes him one of the most significant figures in the history
of the philosophy of religion—was his view that that which
cannot stand before criticism, by which it is allowed no
objective validity, need not lose its religious value if it
can be exhibited as the symbolic expression of an experience
made by man in his innermost life of feeling. And these
experiences of feeling, these inner frames of mind, which can
never find complete expression in words, were what Schleiermacher regarded as real religion. He let the purging fire of
the critical philosophy consume all that was finite and external
in his faith while he retained the kernel only, which was all
the more valuable in his eyes now that he had tested it. But
he did not adopt Kant's philosophy as he found it. On the
contrary, he assumed a critical attitude towards it, so critical
indeed that he was accused of doing an injustice to the great
master, whose disciple he really always remained. His criticism
was directed against the external manner in which Kant united
ethics and religion. Schleiermacher shows (as may be seen
in the *Denkmalen des inneren Entwickelung Schleiermachers*, first
published by Dilthey in the appendix to the biography) that
purely ethical motives cannot lead us to infer a something

which lies beyond knowledge. He thus performs what Kant
had attempted, *i.e.* the freeing of ethics from dogmatic opinions,
by overthrowing Kant's own moral theology. Not until after
he had formed his own views by means of his own criticism
did he study Jacobi and Spinoza and conclude an alliance
with the Romantic School. He found here a definite world-
conception and an endeavour to gather up the whole fulness
of life in one homogeneous form, which transcended every
external limit. In the face of these new influences, however,
he retained his wonderful faculty for uniting surrender with
criticism, a faculty which is naturally connected with the
impulse to spiritual self-preservation which demands the
acceptance of all that affords nourishment, as well as the
rejection of the opposite. Schleiermacher was always alive
to this impulse. The assertion of the importance of each
particular individual appears in his youthful papers, and
remained a leading thought with him throughout his whole
life. This accentuation of individuality made him critical
towards Spinoza's and Schelling's systems, deeply though he
sympathised with their striving after a monistic conception.
Moreover, he considered that these systems overstepped the
limits of knowledge, and that they did not recognise the
importance of immediate feeling. On the other hand, the
great Romantic movement of thought and imagination procured him fulness and breadth of view, and opened to him
worlds to which hitherto his eyes had been sealed. His
friendship with FRIEDRICH SCHLEGEL marked a turning-point
for him in this respect. In him he encountered, in its most
marked form,[42] the curious blending of individualism and mysticism which the Romantic movement contained. Different as
the two friends were, yet their intercourse was fruitful, owing
to Schleiermacher's great faculty for understanding a strange
individuality and for translating into the forms of his own life
all that was to be learnt from it. Schlegel, too, throughout
all his restless vacillation, felt antagonistic towards the attempt
to confine philosophy within a system ; only with him it was
caprice, while with Schleiermacher, in addition to his individuality, it was his critical sense which determined his attitude.
Schleiermacher found in Schlegel his own tendencies, but in a
chaotic and restless form. Through Schlegel he came in
contact with the other members of the Romantic circle ; an

acquaintance which afforded him a rich opportunity for the exercise of his talent of separating the kernel from the husk, and, at the same time, of taking note of the union between them. The "Fragments" published in the Schlegel brothers' *Athenäum* was the product of the collaboration between the two friends.

The first work in which Schleiermacher fully expressed himself was his *Über die Religion : Reden an die Gebildeten unter ihren Verächten* (1799). He draws a sharp distinction here— in a manner which we shall discuss presently—between religion on the one side and knowledge and ethics on the other, and declares immediate intuition and immediate feeling to be the organs of the former ; while, on the other hand, he attempts to show that intellectual, moral, and æsthetic culture can only attain completion when it leads back to living in the immediate feeling of the infinite (of the universe or the world-spirit) as that which embraces and supports all individualities and all finite existence. Spinoza is praised because he was penetrated with this sublime world-spirit, so that the infinite was for him beginning and end, and the universe was his only and eternal love. In a later edition an enthusiastic eulogy of Novalis is added, who strove within the sphere of art in the same direction as Spinoza in that of thought. While these addresses describe the religious feeling as that by which man, in his complete individuality, may feel one with the eternal and the infinite, his next work— *Monologen* (1800)—takes up the matter from the point of view of individuality itself, since it asserts the significance of personal self-dependence and idiosyncracy. As we have already pointed out, Schleiermacher had early in life become convinced of the positive significance of individuality. It is this which places him in an attitude of opposition, not only towards Spinoza and Schelling but also towards Kant and Fichte, who assumed a general moral law, valid for all. For him it was a matter of positive conviction that every man must express humanity in *his own* way, and with a unique blending of its elements, in order that it may reveal itself under all possible forms, and that all differences contained in its womb may develop in the fulness of space and time. Humanity is not a homogeneous mass (see especially the second Monologue). In these two works Schleiermacher gave utterance in a more indefinite and rhetorical form to the fundamental thoughts, the carrying out and maintaining of which in theory and practice was the task of his life. His was an eminently practical nature. When he lays weight on individual development it is not with a view to encouraging self-culture in isolation and retirement. According to his conception the energetic assertion of one's own personality, self-statement, is the only way in which one can influence others. For no man is able to directly intervene in the life of other men. Regarded from this side, then, individualism became for him a means. Like Socrates, he did not allow the urgent impulse towards self-knowledge to deter him from influencing others. His activity as a preacher arose from the need of uniting the two impulses. It took the form with him of a striving to induce individuals to reflect on themselves and on the innermost basis of their lives, to quicken the immediate life in the eternal and infinite, and to emancipate from everything finite and sensuous. He regarded dogmas merely as symbols which may be used as auxiliary ideas in this process of deepening and liberating. Such a conception of the preacher's office was only possible in an age which, partly in the form of rationalism, partly in that of Romanticism, adopted a free attitude towards orthodox dogmas; and even then it caused much offence and even indignation that Schleiermacher moved in circles which were anything but orthodox. He never seems to have felt at home in company with preachers, and in another age he would perhaps hardly have elected the office of a preacher. In a letter written in the year 1802, he says preaching is now the only means by which personal influence can be brought to bear on the thought of the average man. Later, during Prussia's unhappy period, and during the reaction after the War of Liberation, he evinced his strength and courage by supporting national independence and personal freedom both as a preacher and editor and in ecclesiastical disputes.

During the years he spent in Berlin as a preacher (1796-1802) Schleiermacher became acquainted with life in larger and variously coloured circles, breathed for the first time the atmosphere of the Romantic School, and published his first work. After that, having passed the two following years in Stolpe, also as a preacher, he went in 1804 to Halle, as professor of theology, where he exercised great influence by his philosophical as well as his theological lectures. His study of Greek philosophy, more particularly of Plato (whose dialogues he translated), had widened his horizon and strengthened him in his own point of view. He welcomed Schelling's philosophy with joy. He believed that if once idealism acknowledged the particularity of the life of nature, it would also be obliged to acknowledge religious life as something other than the life of mere thought and will, so that a higher realism might arise. He regarded Schelling's system as mere formalism, since, for him, the unity of the subject and object of thought and being was only an abstraction ; only living feeling can take us beyond these antitheses. Moreover, he considered that it did not sufficiently emphasise individual existence. In Halle, however, he had as his colleague HEIN-RICH STEFFENS, and in the latter's modification of Schelling's doctrines Schleiermacher found his own views expressed. In Steffens's works on natural philosophy, which are based, to a far greater extent than those of Schelling, on independent, scientific study, it is a fundamental thought that throughout Nature, from the lowest grades up to the highest, and through the progressive development of the earth and of organic life, a radically *individualising tendency* may be traced, so that the more individualised a natural form, the more it leaves the stamp of infinity ; *i.e.* the richer the content and the sharper the antithesis it embraces. A sentence such as the following : " The stage which most embraces the infinity of nature is the most individual " (Steffens, *Beiträge zur inneren Naturgeschichte der Erde* (Freiberg, 1801), p. 173), could not fail to attract the author of the *Monologen* and the *Reden über die Religion*.[43] A later work in which Steffens develops this thought in con-nection with his general ideas concerning knowledge (*Grund-züge der philosophischen Naturwissenschaft*, Berlin, 1806) is said to have been the presentation of philosophy of which Schleier-macher most approved, and on which (according to a passage in Steffens, p. 22), perhaps, he himself may have had some influence.[44] The battle of Jena put an end to Schleiermacher's activities at Halle. He now went to Berlin, where he did his best by preaching and in other ways to inculcate courage and stimulate national feeling. In the group of men to whom Germany owes her national re-birth, he occupies a prominent place. On the founding of the University of Berlin he was appointed professor of theology, but he also lectured on philo-sophy and the history of philosophy. In addition to this, he influenced still larger circles by his preaching. His political independence brought him into disfavour during the reactionary period. Indeed for some time things went so far that he could not send his letters through the post lest they should be opened. His participation in ecclesiastical matters was also displeasing to the government. Schleiermacher, who himself belonged to the reformed church, though his whole way of looking at things led him to attach very little importance to differences of creed, supported the king's scheme of bringing about a union between the two Protestant sects, but he was very much opposed to the suggestion of effecting this union by force.

It was inevitable that, as Schleiermacher became more and more occupied with theological and ecclesiastical affairs, the positive content of religion should play an increasingly greater part in his expositions. This comes out very clearly in the later edition of the *Reden,* and in his chief work : *Der christliche Glaube* (1821-22). And yet it is not possible to put one's finger on any change of principle between the standpoint of the first edition of the *Reden* and that of the work which may truly be described as the greatest which Protestant theology has produced since the time of the Reformation. He himself believed it to be the same. After he had sketched out the plan of his treatise on theology, he wrote to a friend of his youth (1818) : " A treatise on positive theology, which I have at last prevailed on my self to write, will show you that I have not changed since the ' Addresses on Religion ' ;" and, a few years later (1882), he repeats this expression before the appearance of the third edition of his *Reden.* He found himself in very sharp opposition to Pietism, and to the belief in the latter which had grown up round about him. This was not the fulfilment he had conceived of his youthful dream of a revival of the religious life. He had at first intended to procure recognition for religion as an essential and sustaining side of spiritual life. Afterwards, his idea was to revive Protestanism. He rejoiced at the founding of the Berlin University because he hoped that here he would be able to found a theological school, capable of reanimating and remodelling Protestantism to meet modern needs. (Letter to Brinckmann, December 17, 1809.) The fundamental thoughts on which this school was to be based were, as a matter of fact, those to which he had given utterance in the *Reden über die Religion.* That he himself believed he had retained his views unchanged is of course no proof that it was so ; on a closer scrutiny, however, it will be evident that the relation between his early work and his concluding theological work is as follows. What was at first indicated in its leading features only and in rhetorical form subsequently received a more definite development after Schleiermacher had worked out his theory of knowledge and ethics (as may be seen from his posthumous works : *Dialektik*, and *Philosophische Sittenlehre*), and had acquired, by means of a more penetrating study of theology, a more thorough knowledge of the historical forms under which religious feeling had procured expression for itself in Christendom. He never abandoned the conception that all dogmas have arisen through reflection on the immediate experiences of feeling. On the other hand, he was still uncertain, even when he came to working out his dogmatics in detail, where the line should be drawn between that which is properly religious (which he calls in a letter "immanent dogma," by which he probably means those ideas which are inseparable from feeling when at its height), and the mythological (which he calls transcendent or mythical dogma). (Letter to Blanc, March 23, 1881.)

Schleiermacher's philosophy of religion owes its great and lasting interest to the clearness with which he conceives the relation between feeling and idea within the sphere of religion. The logical consequences of this conception would, it is true, carry him much farther from the orthodox view than he believed himself to be. He did, indeed, clearly perceive that he felt himself one with others more than they felt one with him ; a letter written towards the end of his life (to Reichel, April 3, 1832), after touching on the opposition and misconstruction from the extremists of both sides to which he was exposed, contains the following passage : "For my part, I learn, in all quietness, to feel myself one with many who think themselves very far from me, and this is a source of peculiar and life-refreshing power." The Romantic element in Schleiermacher showed itself in his neglect of the great difference that exists between regarding dogmas as symbols of human feeling, and as authentic announcements of eternal truths. He had advanced a great step towards the deeper understanding of religious phenomena ; but, at the same time, he had assigned to religion quite another place and another signification than that which is assigned to it by orthodox tradition. It required the whole weight of his Socratic personality to be able to labour in the service of the Church while holding such a conception. While still a young man he had had to defend himself against the accusation of dishonesty and unseemly accommodation. He then pointed out with pride that his capacities would easily procure him another sphere of efficiency were it not that it was his own particular pleasure and vocation to employ them in the office of preaching ; while with regard to the relation between his religion and his philosophy, he says : " I am persuaded that I really possess the religion which it is my duty to promulgate, even if my philosophy is quite different from that of most of my hearers. Nor is there in me any unworthy prudence or *reservatio mentalis*. I attribute to words precisely that meaning which is assigned to them by every man *engaged in religious contemplation*, nothing more and nothing else" (*Life of Schleiermacher*, iii. p. 284). This is a characteristic utterance, for it transfers the distinction between religious ideas to the philosophical, *i.e.* the theoretical sphere, and asserts that religious ideas do actually receive another meaning when feeling is at its height than in quieter moments.[45] Feeling at its zenith creates its own forms or takes possession of the traditional ones : it here reveals itself as the dogma-creating power, and this, which is properly speaking the birth-hour of religion, Schleiermacher regarded as religion itself ; at this point the lines converge ; here, too, he found a point of contact between his own and many other lines, which, in their further course, seemed actually to run in an opposite direction.

Schleiermacher's life in Berlin, in which he had to encounter opposition both from without and from above, found its most beautiful ornament in a very happy family life. After a short illness, in which he retained perfect mental clearness and freedom till the last moment, he died on February 12, 1834.

b. Dialectic and Ethics

We shall be better able to form an idea of the harmony which exists, according to Schleiermacher, between religious feeling and scientific thought if we consider (1) how far he aimed

by way of thought at reaching results which allow free scope to
religious feeling, and (2) how far he aimed through religious
feeling at reaching results which allow free scope to thought.

In his epistemology he seeks to mediate between Kant
and Schelling. He saw clearly that Schelling transcends the
limits of knowledge and in his *Dialektik* he attempts a fresh
determination of these limits. By dialectic he understands the
doctrine of the principles of the art of philosophising. It forms
the prolegomena to philosophy as systematic knowledge. It is
the task of philosophy to discover the interconnection between
all knowledges, and dialectic discusses the conditions of an art of
knowledge. These are of two kinds, for it is necessary to knowledge that each particular thought should be bound up with
other thoughts, and that there should be a real being (*Sein*) corresponding to each particular thought. These two conditions are
inseparable. If knowledge is to be valid, there must be lower
and higher kinds of being (*Sein*) corresponding to our lower and
higher concepts, so that just as the higher concepts contain the
ground of the lower, so the higher being (*Sein*) must contain the
ground or force which reveals itself in the lower being as a
plurality of phenomena. Similarly, the union of concepts expressed in judgments must correspond to a real interconnection
between existing things, to a causal relation. This assertion of
a harmony between knowledge and being is characteristic of the
difference between Kant and Schleiermacher, for the latter was
carried lightly over the critical difficulties of the former by the
Romanticist impulse to absorb himself in existence (*Dasein*).
On the other hand, he reminds us of Kant in his determination
of limits. It is true that for him the identity between
thought and being is the presupposition of all knowledge : it is
a presupposition however, which cannot itself become knowledge—although the other Romanticists regarded it as the
highest knowledge of all. In Schleiermacher's opinion Schelling's attempt to lay down a doctrine of absolute identity had
only resulted in the establishment of more or less successful
schemas. Schleiermacher here takes up again Kant's doctrine
of Ideas, defining the Idea (*Idee*) as a problematical concept, as
a concept indicating the limits of thought, a limit which it never
reaches, far less transcends. In all our knowing there are
two elements ; one, that of the organic function, is derived from
the senses and from experience ; a second, that of the intellectual

function, to the faculty of construction and speculation. Neither of these two elements can be altogether dispensed with ; empiricism is right in maintaining that the being (*Sein*) of particular things is never exhausted in the concept ; but it is wrong when it asserts that the being of particular things is the whole of being. Speculation is right in holding that all particulars must have their ultimate ground in the source of all being and knowing; but it hovers between knowledge and fiction when it believes itself able, by the method of construction, to deduce things from this ultimate source. The idea of God as the unity of thinking and being is the presupposition which, consciously or unconsciously, underlies all knowing ; but from this idea we can only construct a formal *schema*. Bound up with it is the idea of the world as the totality of the manifold of all existing things. As the idea of the Deity is the formal starting-point (*terminus a quo*), the idea of the world is the real conclusion (*terminus ad quem*) towards which our knowledge is continually moving, although it can never reach it. For the terminal point cannot be translated into real knowledge any more than the starting-point. Just as every knowledge which we possess contains construction and empiricism, in varying reciprocal relation, so every knowledge that we possess lies at a certain point between the starting and the terminal points. In so far all our knowledge is provisional. It is the task of scientific criticism to compare our actual knowledge with the ideal of knowledge ; this latter is in the theoretical sphere what conscience is in the practical. An absolute systematic conclusion is impossible ; moreover it follows from the above-mentioned relation between speculation and empiricism that philosophical systems set themselves an impossible task when they attempt to deduce the finite from the infinite, and to determine the inner physics of the infinite being. It is only in religious feeling that the unity of opposites is experienced ; science is not able to grasp this, either in the sense of a principle or in that of a totality. The figures, however, under which this feeling expresses itself are subject to scientific criticism. Only such figures are permissible as express the difference between the idea of God and the idea of the world as well as the inseparability of these two ideas. They are correlatives : no God without the world and no world without God. The art of philosophising can admit all figures that do not transgress this rule. But just as this art asserted of speculative philosophy that it would get no further than the establishment of *schemas* so also it asserts that the religious idea (*Vorstellung*) cannot get beyond the establishment of figures. The word, person, *e.g.* when used of God, can only be used figuratively ; so, too, will the term " force " and any other which might be used. Atheism is, for the most part, nothing but the denial of the validity of figures and of anthropomorphisms.

Just as the unity of thinking and being is the presupposition of all knowing, so the unity of willing and being is the presupposition of all action. For as knowing would be impossible if there were no point of junction between thinking and being, so action would be impossible if the will were absolutely strange and isolated in the world. The external world must be susceptible to our intervention, and must be able to receive the ideal impression of our will. Underlying all conscience is the idea of the unity of the will and of being, an idea which cannot be different from the idea of the unity of thinking and being, but which, no more than the latter, can be moulded into a scientific concept.

This consideration leads dialectic on to ethics, whose place in the whole system Schleiermacher assigns as follows. The presupposition and final aim of all knowing (or acting) is the unity of thinking (or willing) and being. At every stage of existence known to us one of these two elements has the upper hand. The science of that part of existence in which being has the upper hand over thinking and willing, Nature over reason, is called physics, which is further subdivided into natural history (empirical physics) and natural science (rational physics). The science of that part of existence in which thinking and willing have the upper hand (or are on the way to have it) over being, Reason over Nature, is called ethics, which also is divided into two parts, history (empirical ethics), and morality (rational ethics). All these antitheses, however, are only relative. Without Reason and Will no Nature ! Nature is a lesser ethics ; she shows us the will in a series of stages—*i.e.* in inorganic form in the life of plants and animals, and in its highest development in man. Without this unity between Nature and Reason ethics proper would be impossible. It is the further and higher development of a something which already makes itself felt in nature (cf. *Dialectic*, §§ 213, 214). At this point Schleiermacher found a very necessary supplement to his doctrine in Steffen's natural philosophy. He could not, as Kant and Fichte had done, exhibit ethics in sharp antithesis to Nature. He demands (as early as the *Kritik der bisherigen Sittenlehre*, 1803) that ethics should be brought into connection with the whole of science, and on this point he quotes Spinoza and Plato as models. Hence he asserts with great emphasis that no absolute beginning of ethical development can be posited (*Philos. Sitten-lehre*, §§ 103, 124, 325). A foundation, a relative harmony, is always given which can serve both as a starting-point and as a point of attachment. In this way ethics enters into relation not only with Nature but also with history, since every ethical development begins at a certain point in the development of the species. The individual man possesses in the organs with which he was endowed at birth the results of exercise in pre-ceding generations (*Philos. Sittenlehre*, §§ 147-148). Although Schleiermacher's doctrine of development was built up mainly by way of construction and bears the stamp of idealism, yet he here hints at a point of view which has been frequently discussed in modern biology. But he is of opinion that we can only suppose such an organisation of the nature of species to have taken place in the case of man; animal species remain stationary. A process of development goes on in Nature, then, but not in the sense of a real transition from one form to another.

The relation in which ethical development stands to Nature is that of reciprocal action. The ethical process consists partly in an organising, shaping, and forming, partly in a symbolising, expressing, and defining activity. To the first kind of activity belongs man's endeavour to make himself master of Nature. The single individual seizes upon a bit of Nature which he culti-vates and thus makes into his own property, while together men form a confederacy of rights which secures intercourse. To the symbolising activity belong all the ways in which man gives expression and form to his spiritual life, and in so doing puts something into the world which is of value solely as a mark of the inner life. In the individual this endeavour expresses itself as the impulse of religion to procure for itself poetic forms of feeling, since the latter in itself is not transfer-able. Art is the medium in which alone individual particularity can find expression ; hence it makes spiritual intercourse with others possible. Art is for religion what speech is for science.[46]

In a certain sense, therefore, every individual must be an artist. The universal form of symbolisation is the science which expresses that which is common, identical, and consequently transferable, in the life of consciousness. Thus the whole development of culture is a part of ethical development, and the latter is radically freed from the subjective and formal way of looking at things which played so important a part with Kant and Fichte. In his *Monologues* Schleiermacher was still impatient at material culture (which he afterwards called the work of organisation) playing so large a part in life, and was inclined only to recognise the ethical in the effort to express one's own personality (by means of symbolisation). In his later conception, however, he attempted to unite the two. An endeavour to symbolise which does not recognise the significance of natural starting - points he now (*Philos. Sittenlehre*, § 209) calls *cynical* one-sidedness, while a work of organisation, in which symbols are ignored, he calls *economic* onesidedness.

We look in vain in Schleiermacher's ethics for any deeper study of subjective antitheses and conflicts. He describes the ethical process without dwelling on crises. And yet one of the chief merits of his ethics is that it so clearly sets forth the importance of individuality. It is true that he admits to Kant and Fichte that reason is one and the same in all men, but he adds that the nature of the individual is not exhausted in what is thus common to all. If the race actually splits up into a manifold of individuals, each particular individual can only acquire moral value if he expresses in an altogether distinct and peculiar manner this common human nature. With regard to ethics therefore, there is something in the action of the individual which cannot be transferred to the action of others nor be valid for the latter. If he has not been present in his action with his complete and full personality his action is imperfect, he has not been entirely active. On account of this individualisation of conduct there are points on which every man must be his own judge. But because he is his own judge it does not follow that he is his own teacher.[47] The concept of personality implies not only that the individual is separate from others, but also that he has others alongside of him. As early as the *Monologen* Schleiermacher had laid down the principle : "Without love, no culture." The clearer the individual's sense of his

own idiosyncracy the keener must be his sense of the idiosyncracy of others. Here imagination is the organ. Commonly,
however, man only becomes conscious of his own idiosyncracy
as a member of the race. Afterwards Schleiermacher also laid
weight on division of labour, which assigns to each individual a
particular calling suited to his nature. This fact contains a
warning not to regard one's individuality as complete so long
as it has developed in isolation or in narrow circles only.
Schleiermacher's personal experience had taught him the value
of individuality. He was a virtuoso in discovering and handling
different personalities. As he wrote in a letter to Henriette
Herz, December 17, 1803, he found no man insignificant who
possessed any idiosyncracy and represented any side whatever
of human nature. And his ethics commands as a duty that
every man shall be idiosyncratic and shall act in his own
peculiar manner. In this way, too, the individualising tendency
of Nature is carried still further.

In a series of academic treatises (which were all that
Schleiermacher published on ethics, in addition to his *Kritik der
bisherigen Sittenlehre*) he discussed the fundamental ethical
concepts of duty, virtue, and the good, and showed that they
do not denote different parts of the content of ethics, but
different sides from which one and the same content may be
regarded. The concept of the good—which was for Schleiermacher exactly the same as the concept of the complete
realisation of spirit or of reason in nature (by means of organising and symbolising)—must form the basis, for duty and
virtue find in it alone their real foundation.

(c) Faith and Knowledge

Dialectic and ethics show us how far thought and will can
attain when they develop in accordance with their own laws.
As a third leading form of man's spiritual life Schleiermacher
takes religion, which has its source and seat in feeling, and he
endeavours to show that it is able to develop according to its
own laws, independently of the other forms, and without intervening in their independent development;—and yet it is only
in religious feeling that full harmony and reconciliation are
reached.

In his *Reden über die Religion an die Gebildeten unter ihren*

Verächtern Schleiermacher attacks two religious standpoints in particular—(1) that according to which religion is conceived as a doctrine (either revealed or grounded in reason only), and (2) that which regards religion merely as a means towards morality. Religion, in his view, consists in the *immediate* consciousness that everything finite exists in and through the infinite, everything temporal in and through the eternal. While knowledge passes from thought to thought, from phenomenon to phenomenon, and while the will is directed to definite tasks, feeling rests immediately in itself, and is raised above all opposition! Knowledge and action depend on particular talents ; in both man works onesidedly, and on objects different from himself. But feeling contains the delicate, infinite movement in which the full individuality of each can unfold itself, while at the same time this individuality is interpenetrated by the infinite. In describing religious feeling we must be careful to seize the moment in which the inner life moves as a whole and undivided, before it exhibits itself as thought and figure, or will and action. At this point the universal and the individual coincide, the distinction between subject and object not yet having come into force. In this immediate feeling the individual appears as dependent not on any finite against which a reaction would be possible, but absolutely dependent. And this absolute feeling of dependence becomes the consciousness of God as soon as reflection awakes and seeks an expression of that on which our entire being, passive as well as active, is dependent, for " the true God denotes the *whence* of our sensible and self - active existence " (*Der Christliche Glaube*, § 4, 4).

Some have thought to discover a radical change of view between the *Reden* and the *Glaubenslehre ;* for in the former, religion is described as an immediate feeling of unity rather than a feeling of dependence, which latter expression occurs for the first time in the *Glaubenslehre*. Moreover, especially in the first edition of the *Reden*, religion is described as conditioned by the intuition of the universe or world-whole, while the *Glaubenslehre* makes a definite distinction between God and the world. The standpoint of the former work has even been described as monistic, and that of the latter as dualistic.[48] But the religious relation is already described as a relation of dependence in the *Reden* in so far as we go back to the point where

consciousness first arises in single moments, and where no
difference as yet makes itself felt. Here, at the root of
consciousness, the universal coincides with the individual, but
the individual which is first conceived in process of becoming
must evidently be dependent. And if ordinary expressions,
such as *universum* or world-whole, occur in the *Reden* (especially in the 1st edition), Schleiermacher himself has repeatedly
explained that precisely what constitutes the world a whole is
God (*Philos. Sittenlehre*, § 287, and note to the second address
in the 3rd edition). When he distinguishes in the *Dialektik*
and the *Glaubenslehre* between God and the world, he understands by world the totality and by God the unity ; and, as we
saw, he shows that there is a very close interconnection between
these two concepts. His ideas have undergone a process of
development, but his feeling of not having changed did not
deceive him.

Both in the *Reden* and in the *Glaubenslehre* it is distinctly
asserted that there are no concepts or axioms belonging to the
essential nature of religion, but that they are all deduced from
and have their origin in reflection on states of immediate feeling. As we have already seen, the word " God " denotes the
" whence " of the peculiar feeling of dependence. The impulse
after expression and communication causes us to seek for
words and images to express the feeling which in itself is
inexpressible. When these figures are taken for literal truth
we get mythology.

The problem of the *Glaubenslehre* is to translate the
figurative expressions of feeling into true expressions, or at
least to set definite limits to these figurative expressions. No
proposition contained in the *Glaubenslehre* must be deduced
from any other ; each one must be immediately deduced from
religious experience, and only after this has been done can it be
synthesised with the rest. The only proof of which such propositions are susceptible, then, is that other men have similar
experiences to those of the propounder. Hence Schleiermacher
rejects all symbols which cannot thus be traced back to
immediate experiences of feeling, or, at any rate, he declares
them to be symbols only, and not necessary expressions of
religion. Such are *e.g.* the ideas of the personality of God, of
the Creation, of the first man, of the origin of sin, etc. He
denies that religious experience leads to the belief in a breach

in the interconnection of nature.   In that case, certainly, there would be a relation of opposition between the consciousness of God and the consciousness of the interconnection of Nature, but the religious interest, Schleiermacher asserts, can never require us to conceive a fact in such wise that its conditionedness by the interconnection of Nature should be annulled by its dependence on God, for these two relations coincide. Hence miracle is only the religious name for an event or a matter which has excited religious attention, and to which, therefore, especial value attaches.   Revelation does not denote a doctrine but a fact having religious significance, which cannot be explained by the historical connection of events.

Such a revelation Christians believe themselves to have received in Christ, because only by regarding Him as a historically-revealed sinless prototype are they able to explain the consciousness of their redemption, *i.e.* the experience that that which checked their consciousness of God and thus caused them to suffer has now been cleared away.   The religious feeling is, in and for itself, a feeling of blessedness, but since it always occurs in consciousness together with other feelings, which are determined by the nature of man as a finite and sensuous being, and since these feelings may partly harmonise with the religious feeling and partly check it, the contrast between religious pleasure and religious pain arises.   And it is precisely this annulling of religious pain that the Christian can only explain to himself if in Christ a prototype has appeared, whose pure God-consciousness transmits its redeeming and reconciling power through the community to individuals who are confronted with the picture of His personality.   The same relation holds between the consciousness of redemption and belief in Christ as the pure ideal as between the feeling of dependence and the God-idea.   In both cases there is an inference from effect to cause.

The great question, then, is whether we can point to any justification for such a conclusion.   From a state of pure feeling we cannot conclude to the exciting cause without the help of other experiences, and Schleiermacher is bound in consistency not to appeal to such other experiences.   That feeling (as Hume once so excellently described) leads, through its desire for extension and intensification, to the forming of ideas of an ideal being is a psychological fact, but this process can only, as

Schleiermacher himself elsewhere acknowledges, lead to symbols. Schleiermacher confuses the impulse of feeling towards symbolisation with its significance as a fact pointing to the existence of a definite cause. As a philosopher he held firmly to symbolisation; he could only be an ecclesiastical theologian because he confounded symbolisation with a causal explanation. This confusion, moreover, brought him into conflict with his own philosophy. His theory of knowledge declares the concept of an absolute being to be untenable, while his theology obliges him to posit such a concept. His natural philosophy declares an absolute beginning to be unthinkable; his Christology, however, obliges him to make an absolute beginning with Christ's appearance, since with Christ something occurred in history which cannot be explained by the previous course of historical development.

Schleiermacher's philosophy of religion, like Hegel's, is an attempt at restoration. It is in this respect characteristic that while he defends religion, pointing out its significance for spiritual life as the power which deepens, harmonises, and infinitises, he does not, conversely, judge spiritual life according to its relation to religion as its highest norm. He starts, that is to say, with a measuring-rod which is not that of religion. Schleiermacher concludes his exposition of Christian dogma with a passage which calls to mind the concluding words of Spinoza's Ethics : not a single sentence in his book, he declares, would lose its significance even though there were no continued existence of personality after death (§ 158). The life which we know and live in the world of experience, therefore, must be deepened and developed, and it is its needs which supply the highest standard of measurement. And while positive religions claim not only to bring peace and harmony to men's minds, but also to defend knowledge and morality, according to Schleiermacher religion has no business whatever within these spheres.

That the concept of religion had undergone an essential change at his hands he was well aware. Neither Protestantism nor Christianity in general had, in his view, reached their final form. A continuous development has to take place within the religious sphere also, and it is the task of free theology to guide this development. Neither the dogmas of faith nor Christian ethics were, in Schleiermacher's view, given once and for all :

the New Testament sets forth the conception held by the first generation only. It is especially true of ethics that it must undergo continuous change and development, both as regards motives and results. There is no exposition of morality which can be the same for all ages of the Christian Church ; each one has full value for a certain period only (*Christliche Sitte*, p. 69, cf. p. 94 f.). The Church has not adopted this fine conception. Had Schleiermacher lived in our own day he would have found it still more difficult " to feel one with many who believe themselves to be very far apart from him."

Schleiermacher's philosophy of religion is distinguished from that of Hegel by its more correct psychology. It is a leading point with Schleiermacher that religion is related to feeling, not to pure thought. Even when dogmas are reduced to symbolism there remains something over, viz. the experiences of feeling which led to the production and acceptance of the dogmas. The problem is : do these feelings disappear or do they continue to exist, or are they converted into other forms when the objective truth of dogmas is rejected ? Schleiermacher himself assumed a continued existence, neither a disappearance nor a transformation. In this he is wrong. But his standpoint was rounded off and harmonious. He knew an ebb and flow between feeling and knowledge, but could not understand Jacobi's lament that with the heart he was a Christian, but with the head a heathen. In virtue of his fine understanding of Nature and of the conditions of personal life he takes his place as one of the leading spirits in the Romanticist circle.

B. THE PHILOSOPHY OF ROMANTICISM AS A PESSIMISTIC CONCEPTION OF LIFE

ARTHUR SCHOPENHAUER

(a) *Biography and Characteristics*

SPRINGING out of the same spiritual soil as the idealistic doctrine of development, and yet in sharp antithesis to it, is Schopenhauer's philosophy. The spiritual kinship between them shows itself in the latter's bold attempt to provide a purely subjective solution of the problem of existence ; the antithesis consists partly in the critical view of knowledge taken by Schopenhauer, partly in his sharp emphasis of the want of harmony and of the irrational element in existence. Like Schleiermacher, Schopenhauer is a critical philosopher. He places the problem of knowledge before the problem of existence, and he lays far greater weight on experience and immediate intuition than did Fichte, Schelling, or Hegel. Like Schleiermacher, too, it was while trying to assimilate Kant's ideas and to carry them farther that his own philosophy took shape. He regarded himself as Kant's true heir, and denied that anything of importance had taken place in philosophy between Kant's time and his own. But there is no doubt that he owes a great deal more to Fichte and Schelling than he is willing to admit. While Schleiermacher supports an idealistic optimism and believes with Hegel in the development of reason through Nature and history, Schopenhauer occupies a unique place in the whole of European thought, for he breaks with the fundamental presupposition of a harmony of existence on which western theology and philosophy had hitherto, more or less decidedly, always been based, and—appealing to the experience of the sorrow of life—he lays down the principle that the innermost kernel of existence is a blind, undisciplined, never resting and never satisfied want. Not only the problem of knowledge, then, but also the problem of the estimation of worth is here stated in quite another way, and answered in quite a different direction than it was by the previous group of thinkers, whom Schopenhauer therefore regarded as the antipodes to himself. In his solution of the problem of worth, not less than in his solution of the problem of existence, however, Schopenhauer distinctly stands on the soil of Romanticism. He carries on its opposition against rationalism and the " Enlightenment " ; his philosophy is a systematised doctrine of the limitation and impotence of reason. He sympathises with Romanticism in its rediscovery of the Oriental spirit, which, in contradistinction to western optimism, is pessimistic. Nor is his sympathy restricted to Romanticism ; he also extends it to Christianity, for the greatest significance of Christianity, in his eyes, lay in its pessimism. He accounted for the optimistic elements of Christianity as due to the after-effects of Judaism. In a remarkable fragment (*Neue Parali-pomena*, § 446, written at the earliest in 1852), he expresses his sympathy for Romanticism and orthodoxy as against humanism and materialism. Since his philosophy is thus closely bound up with his experience and conception of life, his presentations of it—apart from his epistemological investigations—gain a personal and living character, a force and brilliancy which invest them with a literary value in which the works of his speculative opponents are almost entirely lacking. The faculty of discussing philosophical questions in a clear and comprehensible form which distinguishes the French and English schools was possessed by Schopenhauer—whose education was for the most part English and French—in a very high degree, and is combined in him with one of the most unique personalities known to modern literature.

ARTHUR SCHOPENHAUER was born on February 22, 1788, in what was at that time the free imperial city of Dantzig. His father, a rich merchant and an eager champion of the freedom of his city, after Dantzig had become Prussian refused many brilliant offers, and withdrew with his family and business to Hamburg. The son was to be educated as a man of the world. " My son," said the father, " shall learn to read the great book of the world." Arthur was accordingly educated in France and England, and spent a part of his early youth in travelling with his parents in Europe. He was next placed in a business house in Hamburg, since his father would not accede to his wish to devote himself to study. Here, in Hamburg, he has told us, the foundation of his pessimistic conception of life was laid. " In my seventeenth year, without any but the most elementary school education, I was as possessed by the sorrow of the world as was Buddha in his youth at the sight of illness, old age, pain, and death. The truth which the world cried loud and clear to me soon mastered the Jewish dogmas which I had been taught " (*Neue Paralipomena*, § 656). In this case certainly (as probably also with Buddha or the founder of the Buddhistic legend) it was not only what he saw around him that determined the result he arrived at. His temperament, his whole personality are expressed in it. It must be noted that Schopenhauer was " burdened " from his youth up. There was mental weakness both in his father's and his mother's families. His father was of an energetic but rough and irritable nature, and he suffered from groundless attacks of anxiety. He is said to have been out of his mind at the end of his life. Arthur Schopenhauer inherited his father's temperament. He was tormented by melancholy, anxiety, and suspicion. While quite a boy he brooded over the misery of man. When he was not entertaining suspicions of others or was not overcome by his hasty anger and his unbridled self-assertion, his susceptibility to suffering moved him to sympathise with others. On a journey through the south of France, he was unable to share his mother's delight at the beautiful landscape, because he could not refrain from thinking of the miserable lives which must be spent in the ruinous hovels which they passed. As early as this he dwelt on the thought which he afterwards brings forward in his chief work in answer to the optimistic appeal to the beauty of nature. " These things are certainly beautiful to *look at*, but *to be* is quite a different matter." But there were other elements in him also which prevented him from taking a cheerful view of life. His was a nature with strong, sensual instincts, which granted him no rest, and which he was never able to master ; on the contrary, again and again, they dragged him down " from heaven's height to the dust of this earth." In some youthful poems, dating from the time at Hamburg, he describes the inner struggle between his endeavour to lead a life of contemplation on great and high things and the continual attractions and entanglements of a life of pleasure. When, in his philosophy of life, he finds the solution of the problem of the world in the belief that there stirs at the heart of all things an untameable, never-satisfied need, he is building on his own experience. His frequent choleric moods, resulting in bitterness and anger, his strong self-love and ambition, embittered by lack of recognition, and his sensuality, left him no lack of first-hand material. And this need which he felt so strongly tantalised him not only on account of its undisciplinedness, but also, and more particularly, on account of its opposition to the other need which was alive in him, — to wit, that of leading a quiet, contemplative life. His was a contemplative nature ; in this respect he had inherited the temperament and talents of his mother, Johanna Schopenhauer, a once well-known novelist.

All the three parts of which, according to Plato, the human soul consists—thought, self-esteem and the sense of honour, and the sensuous impulse—were here present in their extreme form, and in inevitable conflict with one another. When, in his solution of the problem of existence, he proposes to conceive the world in analogy with his own microcosmus, it is evident that this method would lead to no harmonious result. In a fragment of the year 1814 he declares himself opposed to the assumption of an essential unity in man,—inner discord is his essence as long as he lives. And such inner discord, accordingly, he found in the whole of existence.

After his father's death his mother removed to Weimar, where she soon gained entrance into Goethe's and Wieland's circles. After much opposition, her son succeeded in being allowed to study. He threw himself eagerly and with brilliant success into the study of classical literature, natural science, and philosophy. He was now firmly resolved to dedicate his life to thought. He said to Wieland that life was a precarious affair ; he had resolved to spend his in meditating upon it. His stay at Weimar with his mother became of great significance for him through his acquaintance with Goethe. The young pessimist and the great optimist were brought together by their interest in the theory of colour. They worked for some time together ; to Goethe's great displeasure, however, Schopenhauer—who in other respects, with the rest of the

Romantic philosophers, supported Goethe against Newton—broke with him, for while Goethe believed himself to have found a physical explanation of colour qualities, Schopenhauer gave a psychological explanation. Notwithstanding this, however, Goethe took a great interest in Schopenhauer's activities as an author, and was particularly drawn towards him by the weight which he laid on immediate intuition in comparison with speculation and reflection.

The self-conscious youth, already full of bitter complaint against the world and man, received the following advice, written in his album, from the old master :

> Willst du dich deines Wertes freuen,
> So musst der Welt du Wert verleih'n.

Schopenhauer's academic studies were pursued at Göttingen and Berlin. At the former, G. E. Schulze (the author of *Änesidemus*), at the latter Fichte, was his instructor in philosophy. But his real teachers were Plato and Kant. His critical sense caused him to take an interest in Kant's epistemological inquiries, the significance of which, in his opinion, had been misunderstood by Kant's successors. But what more particularly lent importance to Plato and Kant in his eyes, was the circumstance that in Plato's antithesis between the clear world of ideas and the dark world of sense, and in Kant's antithesis between the law-abiding world of phenomena, and the " thing-in-itself " lying beyond all concepts and laws, he found expressions of the dualism between thought and will, contemplation and lust, which his personal experience had impressed upon him. In addition to Plato and Kant, the study of the sacred writings of the Hindus (*i.e.* the Latin translation of Anquetil du Perron) contributed to the development of his views. The Hindus had long ago halted at the problem which Schopenhauer regarded as the main problem of philosophy, *i.e.* the problem of moral and physical evil. He ranked Buddhism and primitive Christianity so highly because these religions consist in faith in a redeemer rather than in a creator. The wonder which, according to Plato, is the beginning of philosophy, is characterised by perplexity and distress. And the problem is so pressing because evil—although this is said not to be so—has its roots in the heart of the world, since it certainly could not have arisen out of nothing. Herein lies the *punctum pruriens* of metaphysics, which stings men to an unrest which neither scepticism nor criticism can deaden.

His first concern, however, was the epistemological foundation of his system. True to his fundamental principle of maintaining the attitude of a thoughtful spectator towards life, he retired, in 1813—when the youth of Germany were rallying round their standards to free the fatherland, while all around him was enthusiasm for the conflict, and the din of arms—to remote Rudolstadt, and in that idyllic spot wrote his graduation treatise, *Über die vierfache Wurzel des Satzes vom zureichenden Grunde* (1813). He here attempts to show that all our ideas are inter-related according to certain laws which appear under four forms: (1) as the relation between ground and consequent; (2) as the relation between cause and effect; (3) as the spatial and temporal relation; (4) as the relation between motive and action. Emphasising anew the important distinction between ground and cause, he proceeds to show that the causal principle works immediately and involuntarily in every sensation, since, by means of an unconscious construction, we regard the causes of our sensible feelings as external objects in space. Schopenhauer means by this to correct Kant's sharp distinction between perception and understanding. He is here influenced, more than he is inclined to allow, by Fichte's *Wissenschaftslehre*.

As regards the limits of knowledge, Schopenhauer arrives at the same result as Kant. Since, from the nature of our mind we interconnect all our ideas in conformity to the principle of sufficient ground, and since we know nothing which eludes this great law of interconnection and of relativity, we cannot know the absolute nature of things, the thing-in-itself. But he differs from Kant in asserting that there remains one way by which we can pierce to the heart of existence, although this can never be done by means of rational knowledge. We can make our way into the fortress by a subterranean passage. For Kant has overlooked (or has at most, in his doctrine of practical reason and the intelligible character, indicated), that the core of existence must be in us, within our own breasts. We bear the "thing-in-itself" within us. The desire and striving which expresses itself in our pleasure and pain, our fear and hope, in all feelings and in all willing, is a revelation of the kernel of existence, and gives us the key to the understanding of all Nature. If we remain at the standpoint of rational knowledge, the world is only phenomenon, only idea. But if we apply the analogy of our own impulses and will, we discover that the essence of the world is will—in many forms and grades. These are the fundamental thoughts of Schopenhauer's chief work, *Die Welt als Wille und Vorstellung* (1819).

This work took shape in his mind during a residence of several years in Dresden. In character it is to a certain extent akin to Spinoza's ethics, inasmuch as it embraces within one frame a whole series of different problems in reciprocal combination. It gives, as a continuous development, the theory of knowledge, cosmology, æsthetics, and ethics. And the different ideas it contains have, according to an utterance of the year 1813 (*Neue Paralipomena*, § 630) become imperceptibly interwoven with one another, so that he was not able to say which of the different parts of his system took shape first. It grew within him as the child grows in the womb of its mother. Philosophy as the intuition of the whole, as cosmology, was in his view an art rather than a science. In virtue of the principle of sufficient reason science moves from principle to principle, from phenomenon to phenomenon, from one point in space and time to another. The art of philosophy, on the contrary, forms an intuition of the whole which no more affords an answer to a "wherefore" than it makes a new "wherefore" possible, but which answers the last decisive question : *What* is the world? The intuition of the whole is formed by the philosopher at those moments in which he is able to take a purely objective view of things, and to seize the great typical features of life. This intuition must next be translated into concepts, and it is in the endeavour to do this that philosophy differs from the fine arts, which do not advance beyond intuition, and hence give fragments and examples, but no rule or totality. This conception of philosophy [49] is developed by Schopenhauer in notes, dating from the years 1811-18, and which have been collected together in §§ 1-29 in the *Neue Paralipomena*, recently published by GRIESEBACH (cf. also *Die Welt als Wille und Vorstellung*, Part ii. Chaps. 7, 34, and 36). We shall meet Schopenhauer's thought if we compare philosophy as an art with the writing of history, which also lies on the borderland between science and art. And this comparison may be carried still farther, since, according to Schopenhauer, philosophy as art presupposes critical philosophy, just as the writing of history presupposes historical criticism.   If Schopenhauer thought that he was the first philosopher to hold this view he was mistaken.   Metaphysical idealism under all its forms—especially with Leibniz, Herder, and Schelling—is based on a conception of the whole which illuminates the deepest depths of the world by means of the analogy with that which lies in the depths of man himself.   It is on such a conclusion from analogy that Schopenhauer's artistic intuition of existence is based. Neither is Schopenhauer's answer to the question *What? i.e.* the innermost essence of the world is will, new.   Kant, Fichte, and Schelling had already looked in this direction for the solution of the riddle of the world, although Schopenhauer may have expressed the thought with greater energy.

Schopenhauer's work may be compared to a drama in four acts (as Spinoza's " Ethic " was a drama in five acts).   Book i. treats of the world as appearance, subject to the principle of sufficient ground.   It contains Schopenhauer's theory of knowledge, of which the foundations had already been laid in the " Fourfold Root."   From the world as mere idea he goes back to the will as the innermost essence of the world ; here lies the solution of the riddle of the world.   Book ii. gives a more detailed description of the different stages and forms of will in Nature, and describes the will to live as the blind impulse towards existence which, working up from stage to stage, pressing knowledge into its service, and finally awaking to the full consciousness of its misery, is present in all things.   The question then arises whether any deliverance from this unhappy, restless striving is possible.   Book iii. points to art ; in the æsthetic contemplation of nature and of life it seems as though the wheel of life stood still, and the will was at rest.   But the rest so brought about only lasts for a few moments.   If the goal is ever to be reached—as Book iv. shows—it can only be by the will to live losing itself in sympathy or asceticism. Existence is a tragedy.   Schopenhauer's drama contains no such cheerful, reconciling conclusion as Spinoza's.

On the completion of this work Schopenhauer travelled in Italy, where, principally in Venice, he stayed for some little time.   He here turned from pondering on the riddle of existence to throw himself once more into a gay life.   While walking with his inamorata he met Byron, who was also at this time

residing in Venice.   Both the philosophical and poetical pessimist knew how to enjoy the good things of this evil world.   From
everything which might have claimed him in Italy, however,
Schopenhauer tore himself loose, and returned to Germany to
give lectures on philosophy.   He established himself at Berlin,
on which occasion he came into collision with Hegel.   He had
no success as a lecturer.   It was not his vocation to further
philosophy in this way.   Moreover, he chose, out of spite, the
very hours in which Hegel gave his most popular lectures.
After another journey, he selected Frankfort (1831) as a place
of residence.   He displayed great business ability in saving his
fortune from a bankruptcy with which it was threatened, and
from this time on he led a solitary, quiet life, entirely dedicated
to study and the labours of authorship.   His pessimism was
intensified by the small success with which his works met.   In
his indignation he could only explain this to himself as the
result of a conspiracy of envious philosophical professors.   At
that time nearly all the professorial chairs in Germany were
occupied by pupils of Schelling and Hegel, and Schopenhauer,
who regarded Fichte, Schelling, and Hegel as nothing more than
"three great wind-bags," must have felt still greater contempt
for their descendants.   He was rightly indignant at the intermixture of theology and philosophy which flourished at that
time.   On the other hand, he had very few words of recognition for the stream of critical activity within the spheres of
the philosophy and the history of religion which emanated
from the schools of Schleiermacher and Hegel.   In the natural
sciences Schopenhauer believed he had found a fresh empirical
confirmation of his doctrine of the will to live ; he collated
them in his work, *Der Wille in der Natur* (1836), which he
himself regarded as the clearest and most thorough exposition
of his cosmology.   It discusses the subject treated in Book ii.
of his chief work.   He developed his ethical views in his *Die
beiden Grundprobleme der Ethik* (1841).   Since the forties,
but more especially since the beginning of the fifties, his works
began to excite greater attention.   Several authors attached
themselves to him, and busied themselves in furthering the
knowledge of his writings.   In 1844 a new edition of his chief
work appeared, with the addition of a second part, in which, in
sections corresponding to those of the first part, he discusses at
greater lengths the subjects treated in the book itself.   Still

later (1851), he published *Parerga und Paralipomena*, two volumes of smaller, more popular treatises, which throw light on several of his ideas.

After the disappointment of the hopes of 1848 a reaction set in in all spheres, and the pessimism which was in the air opened the way for Schopenhauer's conception of life. Then came the split in the Hegelian school which stimulated afresh the sense for critical philosophy and the urgent desire for it, which was such an essential part of Schopenhauer's system ; now, too, he met with greater support in his admiration for Kant, although Kant had been regarded by many as representing a long " overcome " standpoint. The brilliancy of Schopenhauer's exposition, now that he began to be known, soon procured him a large circle of readers. He eagerly accepted the incense offered him, and charged his pupils strictly to send him every eulogistic critique which appeared. He was determined not to lose a single drop of his tardy fame. Old age was a happy time for him, and, in spite of his pessimism, he wished for a long life. He himself always preferred to follow the directions given in the third book of his chief work for obtaining deliverance from the tyranny of the will rather than those contained in the fourth. He was never an ascetic, although he admired ascetics, and the characters of St. Francis and Rancé profoundly impressed him because they had gained the mastery over the world within them. Old age at last, to his great consolation, delivered him from the torment of the sensual instincts. GWINNER, his friend and biographer, relates that on this theme the old man overflowed with high thoughts and deeply-moving feelings. (*Schopenhauer's Leben*, Leipzig, 1878, p. 526 f.) A lung attack brought his life to a sudden close, September 21, 1860.

(b) The World of Knowledge regarded as Appearance

In 'our exposition of Schopenhauer's philosophy we shall follow the order of the four books of his *magnum opus ;* our first point, then, will be : the world as idea or as appearance. Sensation is all that is immediately given, and this only corresponds to changes of our body. A conception of the world as something external arises as follows : the understanding, which cannot be separated from the senses, immediately refers sensation to an external cause, which is conceived as acting in time, and as spatially distinct from our bodies. This act of the understanding, however, does not enter our consciousness, but goes on involuntarily and unconsciously with *one* blow. Space, time, and causality, forms which lie pre-formed in our faculty of knowledge, are liberated. Only by means of causality, in immediate connection with time and space, is external perception possible. Schopenhauer brings forward this theory against the Kantian theory, according to which the causal category does not come into operation until sensuous images have been formed by the help of the forms of space and time. But he agrees with Kant that the causal axiom cannot be grounded in experience, since it is precisely by means of the involuntary application of it that sensuous perception is possible. And from the causal axiom the law of inertia and the law of the conservation of matter follow as necessary consequences. There is no doubt that Schopenhauer developed this theory of the causal principle as active in sensuous intuition itself under the influence of Fichte, whose lectures on " The Facts of Consciousness " he attended at Berlin. A comparison between Fichte's and Schopenhauer's doctrine on this point shows such complete agreement that had Schopenhauer found his ideas applied in this way by another author he would most certainly have complained of gross plagiarism, and would have found in it a new proof of the worthlessness of man. This theory has not been without significance for the modern physiology of the senses, for HELMHOLTZ has taken it as the basis of his work on sensations of tone.[50]

It is, however, not definitive ; for the question arises whether this faculty of projecting and localising is not subject to development, and whether experience and association do not exert an influence on this development. Schopenhauer denies this. Physiologically, he says (" Fourfold Root," § 21), the intellect [*i.e.* the faculty of knowledge, the forms of which are time, space, and causality] is a function of the brain which is no more taught by experience to function than the stomach is to digest or the liver to secrete bile.

But if the whole manner in which the world exists for us is due to the forms of our faculty of knowledge, the whole world is and remains for us idea only, or rather a series of ideas

held together by the principle of sufficient ground. This does
not imply that it is a deception or a semblance : its empirical
reality is not shaken, for it is precisely through the use of these
forms that our experience arises. On the contrary, it seems
to lead to materialistic consequences, since every phenomenon,
in obedience to the laws of inertia and of the conservation
of matter, which, according to Schopenhauer, follow immediately
from the causal axiom, finds its explanation in another phenomenon. Moreover, Schopenhauer is of opinion that the aim and
ideal of natural science must be a more complete materialism.
He even explains knowledge itself as a product of the brain,
and repeats (in the MSS. of his lectures) a forcible passage
from the French author CABANIS : " As the stomach digests,
the liver secretes bile, the kidneys urine, etc., so the brain
secretes ideas." Materialism, however, according to Schopenhauer, only holds good so long as we are speaking of the world
as appearance or idea. It founders not only on the fact that
the series of causes extends into infinity, and that it cannot
explain the different forces of nature, but also,—and this is the
main thing—because the whole materialistic world-scheme is
only our idea, not a thing-in-itself. Thus the centre of
gravity of existence falls back into the subject, whose states
are immediately given. All matter exists only for a knowing
being and in his idea.

We seem to be moving in a circle here : matter produces
an idea, and matter is itself only the object of the idea. This
difficulty vanishes, however, if we remember that time, space,
and causality—the principle of ground in its different forms—
are not valid of the thing-in-itself. The world as idea (to
which matter itself also belongs) is only the external side of
existence. Directly we ask *what* that is which presents itself
to us in the infinite series of phenomena, ordered according to
the principle of ground, the principle itself can, of course, no
longer help us. If we were merely beings who could know
and have ideas the question could never be answered. It is
only by combining inner with outer experience that a solution
becomes possible. The will, which is the essence of man,
must also be the essence of the world. The world can only
be understood through man. Our essence must be rooted
in that which is not appearance, but the thing-in-itself. We
may say of the will, as Faust said of Mephistopheles : " Das

also was des Pudels Kern." If this view be not accepted, Nature, as exhibited in the causal series, remains incomprehensible, but the veil is rent if we accept the doctrine that that which is active within us as will is identical with that which acts at the different stages of natural causality. (This is set forth most clearly in *Über den Willen in der Natur* ("Will in Nature") at the end of the section on physical astronomy.) Schopenhauer did not consider that he had overstepped the limits of knowledge in giving this explanation. It is true that it is open to the objection that our life of will (*Willensleben*) unfolds itself under the form of time, and that every individual act of will is subject to the law of motivation (the fourth of the forms under which the principle of sufficient ground appears). How, then, can the will, which is itself phenomenon, and which we only know by the help of ideas, be identical with the thing-in-itself? This difficulty (as KUNO FISCHER : *Arthur Schopenhauer*, Heidelberg, 1893, p. 239, remarks) seems only to have occurred to Schopenhauer when he was writing the second volume of his chief work, which was not published till twenty-five years after the first. He is obliged to admit that possibly the will itself is only phenomenon ; but, he goes on to say, the will is that phenomenon which is identical with our own subject, which stands in the innermost and closest relation to us, in which, in fact, we have the thing-in-itself most immediately presented to us, with the most transparent covering. It is the *Urphänomen* (original phenomenon), (a term borrowed by Schopenhauer from Goethe's theory of colours,) by means of which we explain to ourselves all other phenomena. If the further question is raised as to what the will-in-itself is no answer can be given (*Welt als Wille und Vorstellung*, II. chaps. 18, 26, and 41). It is evident that in setting this limitation to his solution of the problem, Schopenhauer virtually confesses that he has not solved it. For an *Urphänomen* is still a phenomenon, even if it be that which lies nearest to ourselves. Schopenhauer never examined his fundamental assumption that precisely that which lies nearest to us is the essence of existence. On investigation it will be seen that the whole problem of knowledge arises over again.[51] This point is of no small importance for Schopenhauer's philosophy ; for only if the will is absolutely identical with the thing-in-itself has Schopenhauer the right to regard it as groundless, as

exalted above the law of ground ; if it be phenomenon—
even though *Urphänomen*—it must in this respect share the
fate of all other phenomena.

Even if the will is regarded as phenomenon Schopenhauer
has overlooked one question, the question which both Hume
and Fichte, each from his own point of view, raised, *i.e.* how far
are we able immediately to perceive ourselves as willing ?
Schopenhauer proclaims an immediate perception of the will,
just as he proclaims that this immediate perception reveals to
us the innermost nerve of existence.   His psychology, like his
cosmology, is Romantic.   And the psychological difficulty becomes all the greater here, since, according to his view, knowledge and will are absolutely (*toto genere*) different.   The will-
in-itself is groundless, while knowledge operates everywhere
according to the principle of ground ; the former is eternal and
unchangeable, whereas all that we know, as well as knowledge
itself, has a genesis, develops and changes.   Moreover, the will
governs knowledge.   It guides the course of our ideas without our perceiving it.   And knowledge is from the beginning
only a means for the will.   In order to satisfy the will to live
the individual must know what are the relations in which he
stands to other things ; the whole of our knowledge, indeed, is
nothing but the sum of such relations.   No wonder that knowledge can never give us access to the absolute !   The mystics
of all ages, especially the Christians, have been perfectly right
in asserting the limitation of the natural light !   In his view of
knowledge as the tool of the will, Schopenhauer anticipated
the modern doctrine of evolution, of which his expression—the
will to live—also reminds us.   Schopenhauer's psychological
conception of the will is, however, very elementary.   By will
he understands impulse, striving (the Greek θέλημα) not the
capacity to deliberate and determine (the Greek βούλησις) ; he
expressly says (*Neue Paralipomena*) that the concept should
include only that which is common to man and beast.   But
while he limits the concept on one side, he extends it on the
other, for he calls all feelings and strivings of the heart expressions of the will ; hence he rejects the view that feeling is to
be regarded as a separate side of conscious life.   Not only
striving and wishing, but also pleasure and pain, hope and fear,
love and hate are expressions of the will.   These are but different
forms of the never-ceasing, blind impulse to self-preservation,

the will to live which either stimulates or checks the development of knowledge, and which invests consciousness with unity
and interconnection ; it is on the identity of the will, not on that
of consciousness, that personal identity depends.   Schopenhauer's personal experiences here led him to emphasise differences which the Romantic philosophy—especially the Hegelian
system—was inclined to wipe out.   His own inner life had
taught him how sharp a contrast exists between thought and
impulse ; his intellectual and æsthetic gifts drew him in one
direction, while sense, terror, and irritability frequently led
him in another, and in these elementary forces he sees the workings of the obscure power which urges ourselves and all things
forwards.   Hence his philosophy is important as an attack on
intellectualism, although it conceives an unnatural cleavage to
be the normal state of things.   This cleavage between knowledge and will is necessary for Schopenhauer's pessimism, for
it is the blind, irrational will which explains to him that the
world is—as it is.

(c) *The World as Will*

That which, as above described, reveals itself to our self-
consciousness, to our inner experience, as will, presents itself to
our outer experience, according to Schopenhauer, as our material body.   He assumes this to be self-evident.   There exists
no causal relation between the will and the body, that which is
given to our knowledge as body and to our self-consciousness as
will is one and the same.   The distinction arises from the different
method in which we conceive the inner and the outer.   Thus
the activity of the muscles is not the effect, but the sensuous
appearance of the will.   The will, that is to say, is not only
identical with the brain, but also with the whole body,—as
in like manner it is identical not only with the force which
moves the muscles, but also with that which forms the muscles
out of the blood.   The different organs and functions correspond to the different impulses.

In so saying, Schopenhauer gives a new extension to the
concept of will, beyond the sphere of conscious life.   It becomes for him identical with what is called natural force.
The different natural forces are only particular forms of a will
which works throughout the whole of Nature.   Matter is the

visible form of will. The difference between blind natural force and deliberate action is only a difference of degree, and applies to phenomena only, not to the being which reveals itself through them. In thus reducing the concept of force to the concept of will instead—as is usually done—of adopting the converse procedure, Schopenhauer is in strict agreement with his fundamental axiom, *i.e.* that the mediately known must be reduced to the immediately known. All natural force is conceived in analogy with that which we know in ourselves as will. What it is that takes place in impact, in attraction, in the oscillation of the magnetic needle, in chemical process, in organic growth can only become clear to us when we regard them all as different forms and degrees of will. Schopenhauer attempts to give a detailed proof of this in his work entitled *Über den Willen in der Natur.*

As happens so often with Schopenhauer, he adopts the identity hypothesis without attempting to establish it. It is not impossible that on this point—as on his whole doctrine of will —he had borrowed his *motifs* from Fichte, who, in his lectures on " The Facts of Consciousness " which Schopenhauer attended, had developed the theory that body is the external material form which the ego must assume in order to be able to struggle against material limitation, for matter can only be driven out of its place by other matter. Fichte, then, attempts a proof ; Schopenhauer only gives a proclamation. Moreover, Schopenhauer is guilty of a very great inconsistency in assuming, as a matter of course, that the brain produces ideas. On this point, that is to say, he expresses himself as though he were a thorough-going materialist, and he does this without scruple, although, generally speaking, he is full of scorn for the materialists. His standpoint is as follows : The idea of the world is a product of matter (in the brain) ; matter itself (including the brain), however, is nothing but an appearance in (the shape of a sensuous idea) of the will which is the absolute reality. The unpsychological dualism between idea and will appears here in its boldest form. The romantico-artistic view of existence which Schopenhauer has himself told us led him to his system, carried him with a light heart over the most obvious contradictions. Schopenhauer's natural philosophy reminds us of Schelling's. The latter attempted to exhibit an ascending series of potencies in Nature, by means

of which matter raises itself to spirit ; and Schopenhauer also
exhibits a series of stages through which the will passes on
its ascent from the purely elementary to the clearly conscious
form.   Lowest of all comes purely mechanical interaction
when cause and effect have the same nature, and where the
relation in which they stand to one another is immediately
perceptible.   In the more specialised forces of nature (heat,
electricity, etc.) the relation is less transparent on account of
the dissimilarity between cause and effect.   And still more
mysterious does the causal relation become within the organic
sphere, when the cause appears under the form of the exciting
stimulus, and the effect contains far more than the cause
does.   Finally, in conscious beings cause becomes motive—
but in this case self-observation unveils to us the inner nature
of the causal relation, when we discover that it is a will.   The
will strives after the highest possible objectivation, *i.e.* to
appear as phenomenon, as object.   This striving is identical
with the impulse towards existence.   Hence nature's infinite
wealth of forms and stages !   Each stage is a limit the overcoming of which is attempted.   The unity and inner kinship
of nature become comprehensible in the light of the principle
that one and the same will moves in all things ; its variety
and manifoldness by the fact that the infinite impulse towards
existence is never checked at any stage, or comprehended in
any form.   And one form comes in the way of another ;
hence the struggle which goes on throughout nature, more
especially within the spheres of vegetable and animal life.   The
restlessness of the will expresses itself, too, in the movement of
the heavenly bodies in space, which is without rest or aim.   But
it is in the world of living beings that this conflict which is
essential to the will appears most plainly.   (" The World as
Will and Idea," § 27.)   Everything presses forward to existence ; when possible, to organic existence, and then again to
any possible higher form of life, and in the course of this striving, conflict and mutual destruction ensue.   Men and animals
devour one another and also plants which, in their turn,
devour air, water, and other material.   Everywhere is *Gedränge
und Gewirre,* and hence the chase, sorrow, and suffering.
Schopenhauer was able to illustrate this in detail by pictures
from the life of nature with which his extensive reading had
made him acquainted.

In the course of this struggle for existence appears, *inter alia*, consciousness. This is at first merely a means of self-preservation, for it brings with it the advantage that movements can be performed before the occurrence of the stimulus, which can be anticipated by motives.

Thus, at one blow, arises the world as idea. By means of ideas, however, which are its products, the will to live continues in operation. When we imagine life to be a good and in consequence strive to preserve and develop it, this is entirely due to the influence of the world-will on our ideas, although we ourselves are not conscious of it. It dangles goods before us and is constantly exciting new expectations, merely to procure for itself new means of clinging to existence. We ourselves are one with this will ; hence we are obliged to live, and because we are obliged to live we believe life to be good. We are goaded on from behind, while all the time we believe ourselves to be making for own freely-chosen ends. This holds good not only of the self-preservation of the individual but also of the preservation of the race by propagation. It is in connection with this that the individual experiences the strongest impulse, and its satisfaction procures him his most intense pleasure : and yet he is here only a means to the striving of the will after persistent existence in the race. Even in choosing his partner in the sexual relation, the individual is attracted, without his knowledge, to that individual who, in conjunction with himself, can leave to the world the best possible posterity. Underlying all things is the blind universal impulse to existence.

While the optimist in his blindness allows himself to be befooled by this dark deceiver, the pessimistic thinker sees through the illusion and discovers that life is a business which does not pay. In proof of this, Schopenhauer appeals to experience, which shows us the suffering and nothingness of life. An empirical proof, however, can never be adequate. Hence (see " The World as Will and Idea," i. §§ 58, 59, and ii. chaps. 28 and 46), *a priori* considerations based on the nature of feeling or the will must decide the question. The only positive feelings are those of pain ; it is in them that the unceasing desire and the unceasing lust which preserve and carry on life make themselves felt. Each time that this inner fire is for the moment quenched by the satisfaction of desire a feeling of pleasure arises, but the nature of this feeling is essentially negative since it only supplies a want. We are the dupes of an illusion when it appears to us a positive condition.[52] Moreover, feelings of pain are far stronger than feelings of pleasure. We remark pain but not freedom from pain, care but not freedom from anxiety, fear but not security. Well-being is an entirely negative condition. Health, youth, freedom—the greatest goods—all escape our notice until we have lost them. And while habit damps enjoyment it creates the possibility of new suffering when that to which we have become accustomed ceases. The misery which thus underlies all things is unnoticed by the great majority. Men of genius discover it more easily because in them the spiritual forces are most active, and their wishes most keen, hence opposition and disappointment are felt the more strongly. The whole result here reached is quite in accordance with the assumption previously made, viz. that the principle of ground does not hold good for the world-will. This will is both practically and theoretically a problem, an irrational principle, a something which cannot be understood either now or at any other time.

It will be seen that Schopenhauer's natural philosophy leads him to a conclusion very different from Schelling's. Through all the different stages of Nature the opposition gets more and more tense until it finally bursts into the light of consciousness, where it assumes its most aggravated form. His conception of Nature is more realistic than Schelling's.[53] This appears, too, in the distinction he draws between *Naturätiologie*, *i.e.* the demonstration of efficient forces and causes, and " natural philosophy," *i.e.* the interpretation of the absolute being which expresses itself in these forces. If only he had held to this distinction ! It did not, however, deter him from attacking the mechanical conception of Nature, while in consistency with his own teaching he ought to have allowed this view to attain its full development, and only then have attempted to give it a metaphysical interpretation. In this connection we must remember that, like the other Romantic philosophers, he assumed no real progressive development of Nature in time. It is true he alludes to the influence of want and custom on organic development, yet he considers Lamarck to have been mistaken in believing in an historical development from lower to higher species. Schopenhauer regards

the different forms and stages of Nature as expressions of the
world-will which radiate from it without, however, standing in
any real connection with one another. Nevertheless, in virtue
of his will to live and of the great significance which he
attributes to the strife and struggle of Nature, he must be
regarded as a herald of the evolutionary theory in the form
in which it was afterwards promulgated by Darwin. He was
not blind to the efficient causes on which Darwin takes his
stand, but he would not admit that these causes were able to
produce the different natural species. Such differences of
kind seemed to him like Plato's ideas, eternal forms of the
expression of the untameable will, without origin.

His opposition to Schelling comes out in his pessimistic
interpretation of life even more strongly than in his realistic
tendency. His personal view of life unmistakably imparts its
colouring to his cosmology, and his keen powers of observation
and deep indignation invest his expositions—as long as they
move within the sphere of human life—with a strongly-marked
character of their own. And it was through his philosophy of
life principally that he gained his extensive influence.

(d) *Salvation through æsthetic contemplation*

The knot is now tied—the question is whether it can be
untied ? We notice that it is always to the individual that
Schopenhauer looks for a solution. History is for him a mere
play of accidents, like the ice-crystals on the window pane, or
the figures of a kaleidiscope ; he has no belief in a progressive
development of the race in the course of which evil is eliminated. The will remains the same at all stages, however
different knowledge may be ! How this is possible is a great
psychological riddle. Knowledge is called into being to serve
the will ; but good servant though it may be, it in its turn
exercises no influence on the will. On the other hand, it is
possible in certain cases for knowledge to escape from the
bondage of the will, at which times the individuality of man
is cancelled and he becomes entirely absorbed in disinterested
contemplation. This happens, for instance, when we " lose "
ourselves in the contemplation of a work of art. This revolution and emancipation, in which the will disappears and pure
perception has the upper hand, can only be explained as a

sudden breaking forth of the faculty of intuition.   Our attitude towards the world is then purely contemplative, which is only possible so long as we forget that we belong to it.   With the will suffering also disappears ; only art can effect this.   Knowledge is ever passing onwards from ground to ground, and the will striving restlessly forwards.   But art is everywhere at the goal ; she shows us things in their eternal rest, *sub specie aeternitatis.*   Schopenhauer has a special word of praise for Dutch art on account of the quiet, resigned spirit which breathes through it and which is necessary to the attainment of this objective contemplation.   The highest art, however, in Schopenhauer's view, is music, which exhibits the will, the world-will, in its rising and falling, in its elementary and its complicated forms, and reveals to us its recent history, its rebuffs, its struggles, and its torments.   In reality it is we ourselves who are the stretched, torn, and quivering strings !

It requires a very great effort, however, to maintain the artistic attitude towards existence, and few there are who possess the requisite amount of energy.   The will with its never-resting urgent misery strives unceasingly forwards.   Men of genius are endowed in a high degree with the faculty of enjoying artistic representations of that which, in its naked reality, they flee.

The opposition between art and life posited by Kant and Schiller was ridden to death by Schopenhauer.   He forgets the sympathetic absorption in the object, which indeed presupposes that we attribute worth to the object.   The value of art would ultimately disappear if there were really no value in life.   Adapting Goethe's epigram we might say—

> Willst du des Werts der Kunst dich freu'n,
> Musst du dem Leben Wert verleih'n.

Moreover, it is clear that in the deliverance by art from "the will," Schopenhauer is forced to posit a will; for—as he rightly says—it requires an effort to persevere in artistic contemplation.   He can find no name for the energy which selects ideal ends, since he denies the possibility of the elementary will-to-live will to live undergoing a metamorphosis.   Hence he is here again driven to one of those rash leaps which occur so frequently in his system.

(e) Practical Deliverance

Even in the case of a man of genius, the deliverance from life afforded by art is but momentary, never entire. Art can never bring us perfect rest, absolute contentment; she offers passing consolation only.

The world-will which is as active in each one of us as though each one were the whole, drives us on to attack one another. It is true that the fear of the State deters men from commiting acts of injustice. But egoism is never really conquered until we bethink ourselves that one and the same life is astir within each one of us, so that the sinner is in his innermost nature one with the sinned against, although in his madness he believes himself to be quite distinct from his victim. True remorse and true virtue arise with the dawning conviction that individuality is an illusion. Human love, in particular, implies knowledge of the oneness of all men. Since, according to Schopenhauer's psychology, every joy presupposes the removal of a grief, love can only aim at alleviation, hence it appears under the form of sympathy. Schopenhauer finds in sympathy the " ground-phenomenon of ethics," and in his view it is altogether inexplicable if we do not assume as our ultimate ground the unity of all men.

Absolute quiescence, however, is only attained by those who through complete resignation entirely negate their will to live. Only great ascetics and saints attain so far that the will-to-live is no longer active in them. Asceticism, therefore, is not mortification—undergone for the purpose of gaining blessedness in a future life ; it is a consequence which follows involuntarily when the impulse towards self-preservation, the impulse to carry on the existence of the individual and the race, has died out. We may find examples of it in Buddhism and in primitive Christianity. He who has seen through the torment of existence and the illusion of individuality desires nothing more except quiescence. At this point man passes into Nirvana, a condition which seems to those whose highest reality is this sensuous world as a state of nothingness.

The philosopher knows this involuntary dying to be the highest form of deliverance. But just as it is not necessary that the saint should be a philosopher, so it is not necessary for the philosopher to be a saint. The philosopher has only to clothe his conception of the world in clear ideas when he finds in the ecstacy of the ascetic his highest ideal, before which he reverently bows the knee, although, perhaps, he himself has taken another path.

Here again—as with the deliverance effected by Art— Schopenhauer omits to explain the source of the energy of the will which is able to deliver us from "the will-to-live." For a will is necessary thereto, even if it be only a negative, inhibiting will ; and this is even more evident in the case of the ascetic than in that of the man of genius. Moreover, this breach with the will cannot take place without a breach with the forms in which the will expresses itself, although these are said to be subject to the law of causality. Schopenhauer had already sinned against his own theory of knowledge in declaring sympathy to be an inexplicable phenomenon for psychology. At several points (in addition to those already named, in his explanation of spiritualistic phenomena, with which he was much occupied in his last years) he makes, contrary to the spirit of the critical philosophy, the thing-in-itself interrupt the phenomenal series. Quite apart from this, however, Schopenhauer has to face the great difficulty which besets every attempt to deduce all things from a single principle. He has to explain how this opposition and conflict (this duality which is essential to the will) can arise within the one world-will, and how it is possible to deduce the differences of the phenomenal world from the single principle which moves in all things. This was the problem with which Böhme, in his religious speculations, was constantly occupied, this the problem with which Tschirnhausen confronted Spinoza and Eschenmayer Schelling. FRAUENSTÄDT, one of Schopenhauer's pupils, brought a similar reproach against his master. Schopenhauer's reply (in letters of the autumn of 1853) only amounts to saying that the differences must have their ground in the thing-in-itself, but he does not say how this is possible.[54]

Schopenhauer's thoroughgoing pessimism is a phenomenon of no little interest for the history of civilisation. The manner in which he attempted to establish it is of no particular consequence. Neither his empirical proof nor his attempt at a psychological deduction afford a valid foundation for absolute pessimism. On the other hand, however, we are not justified in regarding the whole thing merely as the outcome of his particular temperament. Every important individuality is a point of view for the human race from which men catch sight of possibilities and aspects of existence which would otherwise have escaped them. And the energy and impartiality with which Schopenhauer laid bare the discords and seamy sides of nature and civilisation have caused the problem of the estimation of worth to pass into a new phase. A concealment of facts and the blunting of the problem at this point are more difficult now than before. This is of great theoretical and practical significance. And this gain suffers no diminution from Schopenhauer's truly Romantic attempt to make his own experience of life the measure for all existence. The constant endeavour of those Romanticists who, while holding a theory of evolution, were diametrically opposed to Schopenhauer, was to keep their own personality in the background that the content of thought might develop according to its own laws. Schopenhauer's philosophy, on the contrary, is, as we have seen, individualistic. This trait is also apparent in the arbitrary leaps his thought takes when a transition is wanted between ideas, each of which forms an integral part of his personal philosophy of life, but the interdependence between which, based on rational principles, he is unable to exhibit. Fortunately he himself has supplied corrections in his theory of knowledge which carries on Kant's inquiry. Like Schleiermacher, he affords an interesting example of the combination of the critical philosophy with a sharply-marked individualistic conception of life. The personality of these two thinkers sheds light on the relation between thought and life, even though the solution they offer cannot be considered definitive.

C. UNDERCURRENT OF CRITICAL PHILOSOPHY
DURING THE ROMANTIC PERIOD

SCHLEIERMACHER and Schopenhauer are prominent witnesses
to the fact that Kant's thought had not received its due in
Fichte's, Schlegel's, and Hegel's systems. Kant's was no
" overcome standpoint," and if we do not confound the history
of real philosophical thought with the history of superficial
streams of thought we shall see that in the midst of the
apparently undisputed sway of Romantic speculation there
was a group of faithful and understanding successors who
remained true to him. This constant undercurrent, it is
true, was not strong enough to stem the speculative surface
current until it was reinforced by natural science and
historical criticism. Nevertheless, it is of importance in the
history of philosophy, partly on account of the results it
contributed to philosophical investigation itself, partly as a
witness that the continuity of the history of thought was
not interrupted by the experiments in thought of the
speculative philosophers. It is especially important to notice
here a whole series of men, who made no pretensions to
being professional philosophers, but whose conception of life
was shaped by Kant's philosophy, and who remained true to
this conception while leading an active life in larger or smaller
spheres. In various parts of Germany groups of men, varying
widely both in age and position, banded themselves together for
the purpose of a common study of Kant ; and there were many
individuals, some of whom were among the most conspicuous
men of their time, who were able to hold fast to the kernel of
the master's thought while they discarded the inessential forms
in which he had clothed it. It is of especial interest to note
that not a few of the men to whom, after the reverses at the

beginning of the nineteenth century, Germany owned its spiritual
and political re-birth were pupils of Kant's. We may mention,
in addition to Schleiermacher and Fichte, WILHELM VON HUM-
BOLDT who organised the Prussian Department of Education,
and THEODOR VON SCHÖN who effected the abolition of
serfdom. In Denmark there was A. S. ÖRSTED, the great
jurist who, a zealous Kantian in his youth, was able
in his old age to declare that the influence which Kant's
ethics had exercised on his thoughts and feelings had
never diminished. The following passage occurs in Örsted :
" A statesman who had played his part in the re - birth of
Prussia and who had always remained faithful to the spirit
in which it was conceived (v. Schön, the Minister of State),
received, on the anniversary of his coming into office, an
eloquent and warm tribute of esteem from his fellow-citizens.
In responding he declared that if he had done anything of
service to his country he owed it entirely to the mode of
thought into which his great master Kant had inducted him, and
he therefore felt bound to pass on the thanks brought to him to
their true source, of which he was only a small tributary. Without being able to institute a comparison in any other respect
I am seized by a similar feeling when I reflect upon what Kant
has been to me and to many others of my countrymen." It was
not only Kant's ethical influence, however, which maintained
itself in the face of the Romantic movement. His stringent
demand for proofs, and the critical understanding of the limits
of knowledge to which he had won, caused very many of his
disciples to regard with indignation and contempt the speculative turn which philosophy had received at the hands of his
most prominent successors. This comes out in an extremely clear
and interesting manner in the case of a zealous Kantian,
JOHANN BENJAMIN ERHARD by name, a physician, whose
autobiography and correspondence have been published by
VARHAGEN VON ENSE. In a letter, dated May 19, 1794,
he writes (*a propos* of Fichte) : " The philosophy which *proceeds*
from a *single* fundamental principle, and pretends to deduce
everything from it, is and will always remain a piece of artificial
sophistry ; that philosophy only which *ascends* to the
highest principle and exhibits everything else in perfect
harmony with it is the true one. . . . Kant's philosophy has
not yet prevailed with his disciples, for they seek to make

reason *constitutive*. . . .   I have already written to Reinhold on
the subject and demonstrated to him that we cannot have a theory
but only an analysis of the faculty of imagination." Erhard
goes on to show that all our judgments are formed by means
of analysis.   This holds good not only in the empirical sciences
but also in philosophy, " for there we attain all our knowledge by
*means of a dismemberment of the concept which we have formed
unreflectingly*; if we lose sight of this we construct for ourselves a
system of original concepts, instead of learning to know the real."
The scruples which Erhard here expresses were shared by
several of his friends, and also, as already mentioned, by
Schiller.   ANSELM FEUERBACH, the famous jurist, expresses
himself in the same sense in a letter in which he says that he
who has been nourished by the spirit of Kant, and knows that
the play with empty concepts is no philosophy, cannot share
the enthusiasm with which the new philosophy is received
by most people (*Biographischer Nachlass*, 2nd ed. i. p. 51).
At the time when Hegel stood at the zenith of his fame,
Wilhelm von Humboldt felt impelled to write an appreciation of Kant, penetrated with the deepest admiration.   He
mentions three special reasons for his praise of Kant : (1)
because by means of his critical work he had provided philosophical analysiš with its true foundation, (2) because he had
united a perhaps unsurpassed dialectic with a sense for the
truth which no dialectic can reach, (3) because he had taught
philosophising rather than philosophy, had incited men to seek
rather than imparted to them the results of search (*Über
Schiller und den Gang seiner Geistesentwickelung.*—Einleitung
zum Briefwechsel zwischen Schiller und W. von Humboldt,
Stuttgart and Tübingen, 1836, pp. 45-49).

While Erhard was expressing his scruples at the constructive turn taken by philosophy, two of Fichte's hearers in
Jena were working at criticisms of the *Wissenschaftslehre*,
which proved to be but the first step in a long labour of
thought.   FRIES and HERBART both took upon themselves the
task of carrying on Kant's work in his own spirit, for they
could not allow the manner in which Fichte proposed to
continue the Kantian philosophy to be the right one.   Each
in his way sought to further determine the psychological foundation on which, as a matter of fact, Kant's philosophy rested,
although he himself would have been unwilling to admit this.

Hence they are of great significance in the history of psychology. They maintained the rights and the importance of
empirical psychology in opposition to the constructions of the
speculative philosophers. Their absence of bias and their
thorough knowledge of the physical sciences entitles them in
many respects to rank as representatives of a line of thought
which it is not customary to date back to the period of
Romanticism. They were afterwards joined by BENEKE,
whose chief merit also lies within the sphere of psychology.
That these three thinkers were only able to maintain and carry
on an undercurrent of thought which was unable to stem the
surface-flow must be attributed to their retiring and diffident
natures. They were at home in the sphere of empiricism and
criticism, not in the world of dazzling ideas and brilliant
theories. Their quiet work, however, was not without its
fruit.

(a) Jakob Friedrich Fries

Like Schleiermacher, Fries was originally a member of the
Moravian brotherhood. The influence of this connection on his
spiritual life may be traced partly in the great importance he attributes to feeling as the foundation of faith and intuition, and
partly through a natural association by contrast, in his criticism
of the part played by feeling in dogmatising knowledge and
paralysing the will. And like Schleiermacher, too, he thought for
himself, and worked his way out of the limitations of the creed
taught at the Moravian Academy at Niesky, which he entered in
1792 at the age of nineteen. He has told us himself (in some
notes which are incorporated by Henke in his *Jakob Friedrich
Fries: aus seinem handschriftlichen Nachtlasse dargestellt*, Leipzig,
1867) how he was weaned from any positive faith by his
personal experience and his study of psychology. In vain had
he striven and struggled to force himself into that meditative
frame of mind which was required in the many " quiet hours "
of the Moravian Academy. He now saw clearly that he had
been trying to force his natural feeling and imagination to an
artificial height. Moreover, the doctrine of the Atonement
excited ethical scruples in his breast. But this did not
deprive the religious life of its significance in his eyes. Like
Schleiermacher he believed in the symbolical value of religious
ideas, and in spite of all negation of dogma he still felt spiritu-

ally akin to the fraternity and kept up a warm and life-long
friendship with several of its members.   His philosophical
development was determined by his initiation into the Kantian
philosophy while still at the Moravian college, where it was
expounded to the students in the form in which Reinhold had
thrown it.   Only in secret could Fries read Kant's own works,
and he was particularly interested to learn from them how
Kant had arrived at his results.   The psychological analysis
which played so large a part in Kant's early works, appearing
as the " subjective deduction " in the *Kritik der reinen Vernunft*,
but which was afterwards more and more neglected, was regarded
by Fries as of cardinal importance.   But even as early as
this, Fries missed in Kant a thoroughgoing discussion of the
psychological foundation of the theory of knowledge, and he
made it the task of his life to fill out this omission.   After he
had left the Moravian college he studied first in Leipzig, where
PLATTNER, the psychologist, exercised a great and lasting
influence on his views, and, afterwards in Jena, at the time when
Fichte was at the height of his power and fame.   Fichte's
Wissenschaftslehre by no means satisfied him.   The attempt
to establish a single highest principle, and to deduce everything
else from it failed, in his view, to meet the very first requirements of scientific method.   First, psychological description,
then analysis and abstraction, and only after this has been
done, and where possible, construction (which, however, can never
be more than hypothetical),—these were the principles which
Fries had been led to adopt, partly by his own thought and
partly by his eager study of mathematics and natural science,
begun at Niesky and continued at Jena.   Before going to Jena
he had already written a series of treatises setting forth the
importance of empirical psychology for philosophical problems.
He noted down the objections to which, in his opinion, the
speculative philosophy was open as they were suggested to him
by Fichte's lectures ; and these notes afterwards served as the
foundation for his polemic, *Reinhold, Fichte, und Schelling* (1803,
published in 1824 under the title *Polemische Schriften*, i.).   It
was this book which first made his name known, and it retains
its interest to this day in virtue of the characterisation of right
philosophic method which it contains.   He spent some years
as private tutor in Switzerland, where he continued his philosophical and scientific studies.   Afterwards he became a *docent*

in Jena, opposing on the very hearth of Romanticism the prevailing speculative philosophy. When Professor in Heidelberg he published *Wissen, Glaube und Ahndung* (1805), a popular exposition of his views on epistemology and philosophy of religion, and soon after his chief work, *Neue Kritik der Vernunft* (1806-7), in which he returns to Kant's line of thought, and attempts to correct and continue it. He was influenced also by Jacobi, whose emphasis of the claims of immediate consciousness and feeling chimed in with his own conviction of the fundamental importance of psychological experience. While, however, according to Fries, Kant attempts to prove too much, and thereby betrays us into a new dogmatism, Jacobi seeks to prove too little, and hence, strictly speaking, remains outside the pale of philosophy. In a polemic (against Schelling)— *Von deutscher Philosophie, Art und Kunst* (1812)—Fries has explained in more detail his relation to Kant, Jacobi, and the Romantic philosophy. During the whole of the latter part of his life (1816-43) Fries held a professorship at Jena. His political views, which he expounded in novels and pamphlets, tended towards Radicalism : hence he was particularly glad to find himself back again in the dukedom of Karl August, for that petty state was the only one in which the royal promises of the introduction of a constitutional government had been kept. A true disciple of Kant, Fries lays great weight in his Ethics on the feeling of personal dignity, and insists that a powerful personality can only develop in a public life permeated by the ideas of honour and justice. In his *Ethik*, published 1818 (p. 377), he says : " To thus indulge the private ends of individuals or of individual classes is the shame of nations—and that in the State public ends should alone be considered is the true demand of civil freedom." He exerted himself to promote this spirit among the students, who now, the war being over, were returning once more to their studies ; while at the same time he endeavoured to modify the roughness which had hitherto been so conspicuous a feature in student life. He was untiring in his warnings against secret societies, but he sympathised with the forming of a general German *Studentenbund*, whereby the bonds formed in the common struggle against Napoleon, " the world-conqueror," could be sustained. The part which he took in the festival of the Wartburg (1817), where speeches to this effect were made, and where, in imitation of

Luther's burning of the papal bull, several (real or supposed) reactionary books were burned, raised a storm against him, from which Karl August, who was favourably disposed towards him, sought in vain to protect him. His dismissal was demanded by Prussia and Austria alike, and when Sand, a pupil of Fries, murdered Kotzebue (who was regarded as the symbol of reaction and of foreign influence) the pressure was too great to be resisted, and Fries gave up his professorship of philosophy, only, however, to be appointed instead to a professorship in physics. When in Heidelberg he had lectured on physics as well as on philosophy—a proof of the thoroughness of his scientific education. He published a Mathematical Philosophy of Nature, a work on Physics and a popular Astronomy, works which Gauss and Alexander von Humboldt stamped with their approval. This side of Fries' activity is important in virtue of his reassertion of the strictly mechanical conception of nature which the Romantic natural philosophy had ventured to put on one side as a mere contingency. In his *Geschichte der Philosophie, dargestellt nach den Fortschritten ihrer wissenschaftlichen Entwickelung* (1837-40), one of the most remarkable works of its time, Fries expresses his firm conviction that it is only in virtue of the strictly mechanical conception of the phenomena of outer and inner experience that the philosophical problems of modern times become real and living. On this side he sympathised with Spinoza, whose identity hypothesis he supported, although he opposed him as a constructive philosopher. His *Psychischen Anthropologie* (1820-21) is based on introspection and physiology, and contains valuable contributions to the theories of sensation and the association of ideas (the pyschical mechanism), as well as to the doctrine of the unity and activity of mental life at all its stages. In spite of its many defects, this book is a precursor of the psychology of modern times.

Fries always considered himself a Kantian. Only two years before his death he wrote to his friend and pupil, DE WETTE, the theologian : " As regards my faith in Kant's victory in the future, I believe that if ever again philosophy should demand clear and well-grounded knowledge, it will be admitted that we are right. But when that time will come I cannot tell " (Henke, p. 268). He did not mean, however, that he approved of Kant's philosophy as it stood. He looked in vain for any psychological foundation for the self-knowledge in which,

according to Kant, critical philosophy consists. Self-observation
must show us what are the forms which our knowledge (reason
in the widest sense, as active in sensation as well as in thought)
involuntarily employs. This done, we may pass on, by means
of abstraction (not induction) from psychological experience, to
deduce those fundamental concepts which express these forms.
The result, however, to which we may thus attain can never be
more than probable ; there is no absolute guarantee that we
have succeeded in finding the true fundamental principles.
An apodeictic knowledge can only be a knowledge which is
based on the forms of the self-activity of the knowing mind ;
this self-activity, however, is never unconditioned ; it must
always be excited by stimuli which it does not itself produce.
And even when (as in logic and mathematics) we have found,
by means of abstraction, pure forms of thought, the knowledge
which can be based upon these forms is purely formal. Nevertheless, Fries was of opinion that it was possible to exhibit
a complete system of fundamental concepts (categories and
ideas) which would enable us to survey the entire field of the
natural sciences. He considered that Kant had succeeded in
giving such a complete enumeration of fundamental concepts,
for which reason he follows Kant's system ·in his own exposition. But a problem arises here which Fries never faced. He
admits that all psychological experience is "*Stückwerk*"
(fragmentary) ; only by means of reflection, of re-cognition, of
attention directed towards our own involuntary mental activity,
do we discover those forms which we use immediately and
involuntarily, and this reflection takes place successively and
occasionally, and is never complete. Nevertheless, according
to Fries, it enables us to discover the *constant* and *invariable*
manner in which our reason works (see more particularly *Neue
Kritik*, i. pp. 198-200). Fries is right in saying that the whole
secret of philosophy lies concealed here. But he did not shed
as much light on this secret as he thought. Kant's systematising and Jacobi's faith had too strong an influence with him ;
they led him to stop half-way in his analysis.

A second leading objection which Fries raises against Kant
is that the latter was under the delusion that he could adduce
a proof of the objective validity of experience. Fries agrees
with Maimon that Kant only showed that as a matter of fact
we possess and make use of certain categories (*quaestio facti*),

but not that we are justified in using them (*quaestio juris*).
The objective validity of our knowledge can never be proved.
We cannot compare knowledge with existence ; we can only
compare mediate reflected knowledge with immediate knowledge.   Truth does not mean the agreement of knowledge
with its object, but the agreement of mediate with immediate
knowledge ; in the long run, therefore, every proof must be
subjective (*Neue Kritik*, vol. i. pp. 288-295 ; *Polem. Schr.* pp.
124, 351-354).   Kant intimated this but did not work it out,
hence his speculative successors have been betrayed into confusing the relation between the subject of knowledge and its
object (a relation which does not lie outside knowledge itself)
with a causal relation, and to riot in mystical ideas of the
identity of thought and being.

Against the speculative philosophers Fries asserts not only
that we cannot lay down any final *constitutive* principles, but
also that our principles are merely regulative.   He further
maintains that in any case the proper work of philosophy consists
in employing the regressive, analytical method which, starting
from the given, leads to the discovery of the fundamental concepts
conditioning the understanding.   Speculation easily deteriorates
into intellectual indolence ; it is only the critical philosophy
which constrains to industry.   Idealism and dogmatism are
not, as Fichte thought, the great antitheses.   Idealism can be
just as dogmatic as materialism when it forgets to examine its
own assumptions.   They are only opposed to one another in
results, not in method.   But the most important opposition is
that of method, the peculiar art of philosophy, and here the
critical philosophy on one side is opposed to all dogmatism,—
whether this appear under the form of idealism or materialism,
—on the other (*Polem. Schr.* p. 257).

A system is not so important as a method.   A system is
of significance because it brings order and clearness into our
knowledge, but he who hopes by its help to reach something
more, he who thinks to extend his knowledge by means of a
system is self-deceived (*Neue Kritik*, § 70).

Fries holds that the limit of our knowledge is indicated by
the fact that we can form no finished series in knowledge, can
attain no completed whole.   All things in material nature are
subject to the laws of physics, all things in mental nature to
the laws of psychology, and, by way of analogy, we can

imagine that the relation between a material outer and a spiritual inner exists everywhere. But, in so doing, we do not transcend the finite ; knowledge, indeed, knows no way from the finite to the infinite and eternal. Faith alone can grasp the eternal. Faith arises by conceiving the limits to which our knowledge is always subjected transcended, — through a negation. Every phenomenon, every object of knowledge is limited, hence faith in the existence of an eternal Being behind the world of phenomena can only be generated by negation. We can form no positive concepts of the eternal. Every positive idea of it (as in the ordinary idea of God and immortality) is figurative, and when regarded as knowledge becomes mythology. It is equally impossible to deduce the finite (phenomena) from the eternal ; speculative attempts of this kind only lead to philosophical romances, varying according to the fancy of the writer. There is only *one* truth ; hence it is one and the same reality which science reveals to us as the finite world of phenomena and faith as borne by one eternal principle—just as it is one and the same phenomenal world which we study in physics from the outer and in psychology from the inner side. Fries adopts Kant's distinction between the " Ideas " of an absolute totality, and " concepts," the objects of which are always relative and limited, but neither Kant nor the Romanticists would agree with his assertion that the Ideas arise through negation. Something more than a mere negation of limits is requisite to faith ; faith is a conviction based on interest, on the feeling of value. And even if the content of faith only admits of symbolic representation yet there are certain phenomena which may be interpreted as revelations of the Eternal, inaccessible though it be to thought. The intuitive belief that the Eternal is the true essence of all things is based on the beauty and grandeur of Nature, and the highest beauty and grandeur of all may be presented in a human personality. Fries' philosophy of religion, although arrived at independently, reminds us very much of Schleiermacher's, but he differs from him in conceiving the relationship between religious and æsthetic feeling to be a very intimate one. Fries' theoretic philosophy is developed more definitively and in further detail than Schleiermacher's, hence he guards himself more carefully than the latter from any real or apparent accommodation to the doctrines of the

Church. His symbolism is far freer and less dogmatic. His criticism of Christianity is chiefly directed against its encouragement of the passive and humble feelings and the doctrine of Atonement, which he regarded as repugnant to morality. In Kant's conception of the personal dignity of man he found the clear and full development of a notion for which neither Greek nor Christian teaching had hitherto been able to find room ; a notion which can only attain its realisation in public life in the State, for there only is the personal education of a man completed. The inner development of the individual is bound up through his calling in life with the community, hence we are justified in regarding ethics, as Aristotle did, as included in politics, although the fundamental ideas of ethics are higher than all politics.

Scorned by Hegel, and still scoffed at by those who entertain a romantic admiration for Romantic philosophy,[55] this sober inquirer has nevertheless in his theory of knowledge, as well as in his psychology and ethics, developed thoughts which have always maintained their validity and their value, while the speculative systems have long ceased to possess any but historical interest.

(b) *Johann Friedrich Herbart*

This thinker, the most prominent figure of the group we are now considering, used to describe himself as "a Kantian of the year 1828."[56] By which he meant that though his philosophy rested on the Kantian foundation he claimed to have carried thought a step farther. His admiration for Kant did not exclude a still more piercing criticism of his teaching than that given by Fries. In common with Fries he adopts what the latter called the regressive or analytic method. He had already made up his mind when attending Fichte's lectures at Jena that it is impossible to deduce everything from a single principle. An all-embracing principle may be the conclusion, but can never be the beginning of thinking. For how can we start our process of deduction from a single principle? How can one thought pass over into another? We notice already here that obstinate adherence to the principle of identity, to the axiom that everything is what it is, which is so characteristic of Herbart's thought. All becoming and all change contain a contradiction, for in them identity is continually being annulled. Hence, in Herbart's eyes, the romantic systems with their evolutions from one absolute principle were an uninterrupted series of contradictions, continual trangressions against the fundamental law of thought. Herbart laid these objections before his teacher, Fichte, who could not but recognise the acuteness of his young critic, although it was directed against his own favourite concept of the *ego*. Herbart considered this concept altogether self-contradictory since the ego was said to be at once unity and plurality, to become and to develop.

Only after great opposition on the part of his friends was Herbart (born at Oldenburg, May 4, 1776) allowed to indulge his inclination for philosophical thought, which went hand in hand with an interest in theoretical and practical pedagogics. After he had completed his studies at Jena he, like so many other German philosophers, spent some years in Switzerland as tutor in a nobleman's family, and it was here that he laid the real foundation of his philosophy. He agreed with Kant that experience only shows us phenomena. But while Kant held fast to the antithesis between phenomenon and thing-in-itself, Herbart (in the sketch of a *Wissenslehre* drawn up at Berne) propounded the view that every representation (*Vorstellung*) must, in the long run, point to something which is represented, and which is not in its turn the representative of something else, but is different from all representations. These " Reals," as Herbart generally calls them, must be so conceived as to do away with the contradictions contained in the concepts of experience (more especially in the concept of the ego, from which Herbart started). This was the programme with which, in the year 1802, Herbart began his career as a teacher in Göttingen. The course of his development, which is of no small philosophical interest, is described in a treatise by ROBERT ZIMMERMANN : *Perioden in Herbarts philosophischen Geistesgang* (Sitzungsberichte der philos.-hist. Klasse der kaiserl. Akademie der Wissenschaften, Band 83, Wien 1876). Herbart's later life presents no very striking features. Quiet and conservative in his tastes, he expended all his energies in his studies, lectures, and exertions on behalf of education. After several years of work at Göttingen, he filled Kant's professorial chair at Königsberg for a long term of years, but he returned to spend his last years at Göttingen, where he died in 1841. Herbart had already (1808) expressed his views in two important works (*Hauptpunkte der Metaphysik* and *Allgemeine praktische Philosophie*). His inquiries are concerned partly with metaphysics (under which he includes the theory of knowledge and also the discussion of the problem of existence, cosmology), partly with psychology and ethics. In his *Einleitung in die Philosophie* (1813) he has provided an excellent propædeutics of lasting value for all who wish to learn how to philosophise without at the same time swearing allegiance to any particular system. Although, of course, the fundamental ideas of Herbart's own philosophy make their appearance at several points, the book as a whole is penetrated by the spirit of the critical philosophy, which may be called the spirit of seeking and toiling thought. The *Lehrbuch zur Psychologie* (1816) elaborates what had already been indicated in the *Hauptpunkte der Metaphysik* (§ 13) as the elements of a future psychology. Previous to the publication of this text-book Herbart had written his great psychological work (*Psychologie als Wissenschaft neugegründet auf Erfahrung, Metaphysik und Mathematik*), although it did not appear till 1824-25. Finally, in the *Allgemeinen Metaphysik nebst den Anfängen der philosophischen Naturlehre* (1828-29) he discusses the problems of knowledge and of existence.

(*a*) We start and must start from experience. But, says Herbart, experience gives us no immediate knowledge. It itself is not knowledge, but only becomes so after it has been elaborated. The compelling power of experience is the inevitable starting-point, behind which we cannot go. But though we cannot go backwards we can go forwards. And we must go forwards, since the sensations which we experience are not presented as an unformed aggregate, but arrange themselves in forms and series which set tasks to thought. Until these tasks are performed thought finds no rest. It may perhaps require much patience to combine empirical data with the requirements of strict logic. But so long as we build on experience and indulge in no castles in the air we are on firm ground. The age has been wonderfully spoilt by those people who laid down, once and for all, a single principle and a single method ; this has been the ruin of the sciences, and has made many fight shy of philosophy. This shyness can only be overcome by regular investigation.

In every sensation a definite something is given which we must take as it is. An *absolute position* is given. This does not mean that sensations are copies of things or that they afford us immediate knowledge of them. We can never know things-in-themselves ; this is a proposition which no dogmatism can confute. We know, however, that they exist ; they are posited in sensation. And even if we call that which is contained in our sensation "appearance" (*Schein*), this appearance is still unthinkable unless we assume a being (*Sein*). We must therefore lay down the following proposition : all appearance implies being (*Hauptpunkte*, p. 20). Every particular sensation points to a particular being, a particular position. It is a leading principle of all metaphysic first established by the Eleatics, says Herbart, that being is absolutely simple (*Hauptpunkte*, p. 20). As soon as it is conceived with inner contradictions thought is confronted with a problem—for identity is annulled. This does not exclude the possibility of several beings, since each particular being is the object of an absolute position. The relation between the different beings is a question for thought only, which compares and combines, not for the beings themselves.

When experience shows us becoming and change we have an appearance which we cannot accept as it is. Our task is to find the underlying Real. This problem presented itself to Herbart first in connection with Fichte's ego, which is conceived in unceasing self-activity. Afterwards he realised that the same problem is contained in all change, hence he compared Fichte with the ancient Heraclitus ; the former's assertion "The ego posits itself," and the latter's "Everything is in flux" are both based on experience, the former on inner, the latter on outer experience, but Herbart cannot regard either position as final. He brings forward a third problem, the so-called problem of inherence which is involved in the assumption that one and the same thing can have several qualities. The concept of the ego comes under this head also, in so far as the ego is supposed to embrace an inner plurality.

The necessity for assuming a *manifold* of existing things (Reals) arises when we try to explain our experiences of change and of things possessing several qualities ; to explain means, with Herbart, to remove contradictions. Everything is what it is. Hence when a thing is presented in experience with a new quality which it did not possess before, we must, if we are to explain this, go beyond the thing itself and assume the existence of one or more other Reals with which our perception relates it. The difference between the first and second appearances of the Real A is to be explained as the result of my now thinking it together with B. A has not changed, but I have brought it into connection with B (in itself equally unchangeable). Thus A preserves its immutability, although experience shows us a modified A. According to Herbart the causal axiom must be interpreted to mean that a thing does not change because it works ; the causal relation, then, is a timeless relation ! Activity (which is change) only seems to occur in experience because we relate one thing to another thing. And when one thing seems to have several qualities this again is the result of our relating it to other things. Combined with B, A looks different from what it does when combined with C, D, or E (one and the same thing is different in the dark and in the light, presents itself differently to the eye and to the ear, etc.) The method which Herbart applied to the resolution of the contradictions existing between the concepts of experience has been named by him the *method of relations.* The ground of that which experience shows us lies not in the particular Real itself but in the relation in which we place it with regard to other Reals. This relation, however, is for the Real itself inessential, contingent. It is a matter of indifference to A whether we compare it with B or not ; our relating and comparing is only a *contingent view.*

Although Herbart maintained, in opposition to Kant, the necessity of arguing from phenomena to things-in-themselves (from appearance (*Schein*) to being (*Sein*)), yet he himself really arrives at the result that between phenomena and Reals there is a very great antithesis. In his *Psychologie als Wissenschaft* (§ 149, note 2) Herbart consistently asserts that appearance is not an essential quality of being, but that every true explanation of the sensuous world must exhibit appearance as entirely contingent to being. Being and appearance, then, are quite different in essence. The true reality does not become, does not change, is neither increased nor decreased ; it is subject to the strict law of identity. It is what it is and requires no

development.   There are a manifold of Reals, hence it is comprehensible that we, who cannot refrain from combining and
comparing, experience changes and composite qualities.   Each
particular Real (or absolute position), however, is independent
of all others.   Two propositions sum up the result of Herbart's
attempt to correct the concepts of experience : (1) In the kingdom of being there are no events (*Allg. Metaphysik*, § 235) ;
(2) Every continuum is excluded from reality (*Allg. Metaphysik*, § 209).

It is obvious that Herbart only resolves the supposed contradictions between the Reals by transferring them to our ideas
and thoughts.   If nothing is to happen in the world of Reals
all the more must go on in the world of our ideas and thoughts,
where, amongst other things, the said contradictions arise, are
dealt with and resolved.   Herbart has himself experienced and
described that inner unrest which is felt as long as problems
are unsolved.   These great inner events, however, are nothing
but appearance !   As Herbart founded his psychology not
only on experience but also on metaphysics, this conclusion is
inevitable.   Nevertheless it would be a mistake to regard
Herbart as an extreme realist.   According to him, indeed, we
can know nothing at all of the proper nature of the Reals,
hence we cannot know if they are material or spiritual.   It
cannot be denied that the materialistic idea of absolute unchangeable atoms accords better with Herbart's Reals than
with the idea of spiritual being.   Moreover, Herbart himself
maintained (in opposition to metaphysical idealism) that inner
experiences possess no prerogative above outer in determining
our ideas of the nature of the Reals.   Nevertheless he cannot
refrain from employing analogies with mental phenomena.   For
instance, he speaks of the conservation of the self-identity of the
Reals in spite of their relation to other Reals as their *self-preservation*.   The idea of self-preservation is only justifiable where
there is a real obstacle to be overcome in preserving the identity,
and where a task has to be performed ; but these are events.
Self-preservation (and to that extent change) is activity, not
merely being.   The self-preservation of the Reals appears
more particularly in those beings to which we attribute force
and life, and which attain to consciousness in our inner experience as sensations.   And Herbart admits that the only
example of self-preservation accessible to us is that of our

sensations (*Allg. Metaphysik*, § 329). So that it is clear, and was admitted by his most acute pupil and interpreter, (DROBISCH, *Über die Festbildung der Philosophie durch Herbart*, 1876, p. 20) that Herbart, in his way—like the metaphysical idealists in theirs— conceives the Reals in analogy with our own inner states. The following contradictions, however, are retained in his system : (1) We must infer from appearance to being, and appearance is contingent for being ; (2) The Real is unchangeable—the Real strives to maintain itself.

(β) Herbart leaves on one side the contradiction which emerges here between his metaphysics and his psychology on the ground that metaphysics which is to test all the concepts of experience must also form the foundation of psychology. Psychology has to build on metaphysics as well as on experience, and, as we have already seen, the problem of the ego is only a special form of the problems of inherence and change and is solved with them. The soul is a Real like other Reals ; its sensations and ideas are expressions of its self-preservation. A sensation arises in the soul when it has to maintain itself against another soul. And since Herbart assumes that the Real underlying psychical phenomena is other than that which underlies material phenomena he ends in a spiritualism which differs from the ordinary (*i.e.* Cartesian) form in its assertion that those beings between which reciprocal action takes place are not different in kind.[57]

The necessity for assuming a psychical Real is occasioned by the fact that our ideas are always reciprocally connected, and act and react on one another. Sometimes they blend (by means of assimilation), viz. when they are nearly related ; sometimes they bind themselves together in groups (complexes), viz. when they are heterogenous (*e.g.* colours and tones) ; sometimes they check one another, viz., when they are homogeneous, and yet are not able to blend. The fact that they cannot remain either undisturbed by one another or disunited and unbound proves them to be expressions of the self-preservation of one and the same representing being. They have a constant tendency to form one single activity, in so far as they do not inhibit one another. By assimilation and complication there arises a total force which expresses what we call our ego (which is therefore a resultant and not a principle), and which determines what we shall assimilate in the future. Only that which can blend with the prevailing group of ideas (or in Herbart's language, can be " apperceived " by it) can attain to psychical existence. The apperceiving group of ideas forms the character of the personality.

The great significance of Herbart's psychology lies in the fact that he starts from single elements (sensations and ideas) as the foundation of all psychical phenomena. In so doing he adopts the path first taken by Hume and Hartley, and which, a few years after the appearance of Herbart's great psychology, was struck out again by James Mill in England. Herbart is one of the most prominent representatives of that psychological tendency which regards the manifold of elements as the foundation of psychical life, and the unity of consciousness as merely the product of the reciprocal action between these elements. What the English call "association" is called by Herbart " assimilation " (association by means of similarity) and " complication " (association by means of contiguity). We owe him lasting thanks for his substitution of simple elements in place of the psychical faculties still retained by Kant, and for his demand that psychical phenomena should be explained according to the definite laws of their reciprocal action. Psychology has been much advanced by his works, and those of the many excellent psychologists of his school (DROBISCH, WAITZ, ZIMMERMANN, VOLKMANN, NAHLOWSKY, STEINTHAL, LAZARUS). The spiritualistic assumption of a soul-substance, however, stands in curious contradiction to this accentuation of the manifold as the fundamental aspect of psychical life. If, instead of founding his psychology on metaphysics, Herbart had based it exclusively on experience, he must have learnt to see in the fact that there is no unconnected manifold in consciousness an essential characteristic of conscious life. He would then have felt constrained to show in detail how this characteristic (consciousness as combining activity) reveals itself in the psychological laws. As it is, he ends in a psychological atomism, and runs counter to experience in attributing to every particular idea the tendency to persist eternally.[58] And the elements, through the interaction of which he proposes to explain everything in consciousness, are only cognitive elements. Feeling and will are supposed to be merely the products of the relations between ideas. Feeling arises when one idea is cramped by other ideas, so that it cannot move freely ; desire, when an idea works itself up in the face of hindrances, and in so doing determines other ideas more and more in accordance with itself, partly by rousing, partly by suppressing them. Psychological observation affords no confirmation of this doctrine of Herbart's that feeling and will, in contradistinction to knowledge, are always derived.

Herbart was evidently influenced by his desire to reduce psychology to an exact science when taking the manifold as the basis of consciousness. He pronounced the unity of consciousness to be nothing more than a product, and feeling and will resultants of the conflicts between ideas. As the title of his chief work on psychology shows, he attempted to base psychology not only on experience and metaphysics, but also on mathematics. He finds this possible in virtue of the fact that ideas increase and decrease in clearness, or, as he expresses it, rise and sink, and that this rising and sinking is conditioned by their reciprocal relation. Here it is their reciprocal inhibition which decides the matter. Herbart's mathematical psychology seeks to find definite laws for the reciprocal inhibition of ideas. The only difficulty which he encounters here is the fact that the forces with which each idea seeks to maintain itself in consciousness cannot, like physical forces, be measured by a movement in space ; it is, in fact, only a figurative expression when we speak of rising and falling.

There is no standard of measurement in the psychical mechanism. In default of such a standard, Herbart proceeds from the fundamental axiom that the sum of inhibition in consciousness at any moment is the smallest possible, since all ideas strive to maintain themselves. It must then be determined mathematically how this least possible inhibition (darkening) is to be distributed among the different simultaneous or struggling ideas. In spite of the interest of this line of thought Herbart did not succeed in harmonising the results at which his mathematical method enabled him to arrive with those obtained by introspection. Nor can the fundamental axiom on which he builds be pronounced valid. Its validity rests on the assumption that ideas are independent forces. But if the nature of conscious life consists in a combining activity, the particular element can have no independent energy. Whether it can maintain itself in consciousness against the other elements will depend not on itself alone, but on the total energy which consciousness is able to devote to its combining activity. The more energetic the synthesis the greater the number of conflicting ideas which can be embraced within it without mutual inhibition. This is partly due to the fact that ideas are not the only elements. An idea may, owing to a state of feeling, suffer a less degree of inhibition than would be the case if this were determined solely by its relation to other ideas. Accordingly, Herbart's school have practically dropped his mathematical psychology, or, at any rate, have not carried it any farther. But even if Herbart's attempt was a mistake, yet the attempt itself witnesses to the energy with which he sought for the truth, and to the firmness of his conviction that conformity to law characterises the world of spiritual nature, no less than that of material nature.[59]

(γ) According to Herbart there is no principle of knowledge which can unite in itself the explanation of reality and the proof of worth. The science of the estimation of worth (which Herbart calls " æsthetic " in the widest sense) must therefore be kept entirely apart from the science of the reality of things. In this separation between theory and practice Herbart again reminds us of Kant. Here, too, he attacks the Romantic philosophy, whose principle of unity claimed to be at once the explanation of reality and the measure for the estimation of worth. The distinction between the two was all the more necessary for him since, in his view, theoretical science ends with the assumption of Reals existing out of all relations, while judgments of worth, on the other hand, are concerned not with realities but with the relation between realities. When we call a thing beautiful or ugly, praiseworthy or shameful, we are considering relations between the qualities of things, or between the different inclinations of a particular man, or between the wills of different men. Ethical judgments proper are distinguished from æsthetic judgments in general by the fact that they are passed on something which is not merely possessed as a thing of worth but which constitutes the unconditional worth of the person himself.

Important as it is to subject the concepts of experience to a searching criticism, it is no less important to test the concepts of the estimation of worth, especially of ethical worth. We often pass judgments on worth without remarking that we do so; hence false associations may very easily creep in; other than purely ethical motives may come into play, mixing with the latter. We must, therefore, bring to light the simple fundamental relations involved in the estimation of worth if we are to discover what are the practical ideas by which we are guided. A practical idea is a pattern which hovers before us whenever we pass a clear judgment on the harmonious or inharmonious relation between a man's convictions and acts, or between the endeavours of several men who stand in relation to one another. There may be a want of harmony between that which a man considers to be right and the direction his will actually takes ; such a relation we condemn as contrary to *the idea of inner freedom.* Or the energy with which he strives to follow his convictions may be insufficient and the conviction itself too faint ; such a relation we condemn in the light of the *idea of perfection.* Similarly, the *ideas of right, of equity and of benevolence* appear in our judgments on the relations between the wills of different individuals. These judgments, however, are only certain and of universal validity when the relations are pure and clear, and when all conflicting interests are excluded. There must be an individual as well as a social development before men reach the point where the estimation of worth is determined by practical ideas. If these ideas are to become a power in the soul they must be bound up with (apperceived by) sufficiently strong groups of ideas. Kant's formulation of the categorical imperative is a witness to the preceding development. But he was wrong in supposing that the practical ideas always reveal themselves in the shape of powerful constraint. He who is able to form these ideas and to keep them alive in his soul will learn how gentle their rule can be.

In ethical matters Herbart was influenced by the English thinkers of the eighteenth century, especially, perhaps, Adam Smith, whose "impartial observer" instituted precisely such estimations of worth as Herbart desired. He thinks, however, that any nearer psychological explanation of ethical judgments should be excluded, as also he would exclude any practical end or basis from the estimation of worth. He wishes the relations between human wills to be estimated exactly as we estimate musical compositions. His ethics is æsthetic in character, and we look in vain for any recognition of the fact that ethical judgments when they are genuine and primary, spring from a will and are grounded in the thought of a practical end which has to be striven after.   Nevertheless, Herbart's ethics retains its interest in virtue of the clear description and analysis which it contains of the most important relations into which the will enters, and of its endeavours to defend the independence of ethics over against theology.   The latter point is of all the greater interest as Herbart was a conservative in politics and in religion.   In matters of faith he held fast to the Protestant church.   In spite of his theologising philosophy of religion, however, he emphatically asserts that the concept of God is always thought by means of psychological and ethical determinations borrowed from men.   Hence in order that we may arrive at a right conception of God it is important that the ethical ideas should be developed in their purity and self-dependence.   Herbart's theoretical philosophy offers no points of contact with theology,[60] hence his philosophy of religion holds together somewhat loosely with the rest of his views. But we may trace the effects of his psychological views in his insistence on the importance of the religious ideas having such form and content as should enable them to fill the minds of men and form large and predominating (apperceptive) groups of ideas.

(c) Friedrich Eduard Beneke

In a letter to Herbart dated May 22, 1824, Beneke writes : " Independently of one another we have both arrived at the conviction that if psychology is to solve the problems which have been raised, it must undergo a thorough reform." The two thinkers, however, were not quite agreed as to the special task of psychology.   Both allow that it has to explain what Kant—and after him Fries—called " forms " as the results of psychical processes and not as ready-made forms of activity existing from the beginning.   Beneke was even more energetic than Herbart in conceiving them to be mental products whose origin is to be explained by a process of evolution determined in accordance with psychological laws.   But while Herbart proposed to found psychology not only on experience but also on " metaphysics," which means here on an investigation of the nature of existence prior to any psychological investigation, Beneke asserts that psychology is the fundamental science of philosophy, since the concepts of all other philosophical sciences are psychical products. Psychology itself he treats as an empirical science. It is no doubt the task of philosophy to construct a world-conception. But its immediate object is the life of consciousness, for it is this which interests us most and this is the side of existence which we immediately know, the material side being only known to us through consciousness. Moreover, before we proceed to discuss the highest problems we must critically examine the powers of the human mind. In making empirical psychology the foundation of all philosophy Beneke resembles the English school ; indeed, he admits that he is a disciple of Locke's. Only in Germany, he says, are we unaware that psychology, and with it the whole of philosophy, is based on experience. Hence it is that in comparison with other nations who have been willing to learn from Bacon, Locke, and Hume, we stand so far behind in philosophy. Even Kant does not hold fast to the empirical method, but abandons it directly he passes from criticism to positive construction. His speculative successors, in spite of all their talent, have only injured philosophy. They met with great support because the enthusiasm which Kant had aroused came to their aid. But the entire speculative period must only be regarded as a phenomenon in the history of civilisation ; these bold systems require not a refutation but an historical explanation.

When Beneke thus expressed himself on the subject of philosophy, especially the philosophy of his day (in his work *Die Philosophie in ihrem Verhältnisse zur Erfahrung, zur Spekulation und zum Leben*, 1833), he had fought his first battles and published his most important works.

During his student years he had been mainly influenced by Fries (through his friend and pupil De Wette) and Schleiermacher. Jacobi, too, counted for something in the forming of his views, owing to his insistence on the significance of immediate observation, but his fear of analysis and of proof repelled him. At the age of twenty-two he conceived a plan of working a reform in philosophy, which, in his view, suffered under intricate speculations, and in the same year (1820) he entered himself at the Berlin University. In a few smaller treatises he set forth his views on the task and method of psychology, and as a *privat-docent* he gave lectures which were well attended. After the publication of his *Physik der Sitten* (1820), a companion to Kant's *Metaphysik der Sitten*, however, his name was struck off the list of teachers, and he never, in spite of repeated attempts, succeeded in extorting any explanation of this proceeding. He was only told by the Chancellor, a patron of Hegel's, that a philosophy which did not deduce everything from the Absolute was not worthy to be called philosophy! Beneke himself believed Hegel, to whom a pupil of Fries and Schleiermacher was unwelcome at the University, to have been at the bottom of it. Perhaps the title of his book had suggested that Beneke taught materialism ; although by the term " Physik " he only meant the attempt to find a natural empirical foundation. The book itself is of no small interest for the history of ethics, for it supports the view that ethics must rest on a psychological foundation, and attempts to show that ethical judgments are the result of reflection on the manner in which feeling is set in motion by human action, either that of the self or of others. Beneke treats ethical judgments exactly as Schleiermacher treated the dogmas of faith ; indeed, there can be no doubt that he was influenced here by Schleiermacher's lectures. Moreover following Jacobi, but in opposition to Kant's absolute and universal moral law, Beneke maintains the importance of individualistic assumptions in deciding what, in particular cases, is right and duty. And while his German post - Kantian predecessors would exalt the ethical estimation of worth above all consideration of the effects of actions, thus giving to ethics a predominantly subjective character, Beneke stoutly maintains that the manner in which actions affect the weal and woe of living beings determines the estimation of their ethical value, which may differ from the legal estimation, since it is primarily concerned with the frame of mind which prompted the action.[61] Although Beneke published an excellent defence, he was prohibited from teaching in Berlin. For the next few years he laboured at Göttingen, and here he published, under the modest title of *Psychologische Skizzen*, his most important work (1825-27). A place was now again found for him in the Berlin University, and in needy circumstances, debarred by the ruling Hegelianism from holding a regular professorship, he developed a fertile activity, teaching and writing on psychology, theory of education, and ethics. His educational writings in particular found their way to wide circles of readers. He was drowned

on the 1st of March 1854; probably, overcome by long
illness and sadness, he put an end to his life while out of his
mind.

While Herbart tried to explain conscious life in its different
forms and at its different stages as the mechanical product of
a manifold of particular elements (through their blendings, complications, and mutual inhibitions), Beneke's psychological theory
is more biological in character. He conceives the development
of conscious life as the growth of given germs or dispositions
which he calls the "prime faculties" (*Urvermögen*) (*i.e.* the
faculties of sensation and movement). Herbart, on the contrary, regards the soul as a *tabula rasa* until other Reals,
by coming into relation with it, excite its impulse to self-
preservation. The prime faculties are associated with impulse
and striving. They involuntarily seek out external stimuli,
which are able to further their development. And under the
influence of outer experiences new faculties are always being
formed, for the earlier stimuli do not entirely disappear but
leave behind them traces and dispositions which co-operate
with later stimuli. Hence reciprocal action between the conscious and the unconscious is continually going on. By the
concept "faculty" Beneke means to express nothing more than
the unconscious inner conditions which exist from the very
beginning, and afterwards co-operate, at every stage, with outer
experiences. We are not able, it is true, to distinguish clearly
between that which comes from outer experience and that
which is due to inner conditions ; but there can be no question
that the inner and outer unceasingly co-operate. The relation
in general between the conscious and the unconscious is made
by Beneke the subject of an interesting investigation. Among
the many psychological phenomena which are discussed in
his chief work (the more important part of which afterwards
appeared in a shortened form in his *Lehrbuch der Psychologie
als Naturwissenschaft* (1833)) may be mentioned the significance for feeling of the relation of contrast and the tendency
of psychical elements to diffuse their character over the whole
psychical state (Beneke calls this process "equalisation" (*Ausglei-
chung*) ; it would perhaps be more fittingly termed " expansion ").
Since the development of the life of consciousness is determined
by so many elements and laws it is no wonder that the higher
stages may differ so widely from the lower as to seem altogether

inexplicable by the latter. But as we cannot see in the germ of a cherry tree any indication of the cherries, which only appear as the fruits of the fully developed tree, so we must not expect to find the higher forms of psychical life preformed in the lower. These higher forms are neither innate nor introduced into the soul from without ; they arise in the course of the soul's development according to its own particular laws. Beneke's psychology would form a worthy subject for a monograph which should investigate its relation to the older psychology (especially that of Hume and Tetens) as well as to that of the most recent times.

Beneke, however, did not always keep clearly before him the biological character of his psychology, nor did he always abide by it. His great zeal in defending psychological investigation against the speculative philosophy led him to extol inner experience not only at the expense of abstract thought but also at that of outer experience. He pronounces inner experience to be far clearer and more exact than outer, maintaining that in inner experience we are able to trace the individual elements in their interaction. But this seems to assume that we are able to see in psychical products the elements out of which they are composed : an assumption which is contradictory to the qualitative differences between elements and products which Beneke elsewhere so rightly emphasises. "We must not forget," he says (*Skizzen*, ii. p. 329), "that complication, too, is something and that the product, even though it contain nothing more in itself than the sum of its factors, yet as their sum and as an organic interrelated whole is different not only from each one of these factors but also from a mere juxtaposition of them." In every such organic complex (*e.g.* when a new faculty originates) there must always be something which does not reveal itself to introspection ; indeed, throughout the whole of nature the origin of new qualities presents the greatest problems. And within the sphere of external nature we can point out much more clearly than in that of inner nature those conditions under which new qualities arise.

That Beneke has thus erroneously overestimated the completeness of psychology as a science (or rather its prospect of completeness) is due, we may be sure, to the great importance which he assigns to it as the fundamental science for philosophy. Starting from psychological observation, we find a clue to existence. The principles of natural philosophy are taken from psychology; since in our inner experience we have the opportunity of becoming acquainted with a part of existence as *it is in itself* we naturally conceive that part of nature which we know only as external, objective being (material nature), *in analogy with ourselves.* Accordingly, employing the method of analogy, we transfer the forms and laws of the psychical world to material nature. Natural philosophy, as taught by Beneke, is distinguished from that of Schelling by the fact that it is conscious of its hypothetical character, and assumes an analogy only, not, as Schelling would have, an identity between the psychical and corporeal. And while Schelling thought it was possible to substitute this idealistic interpretation, based on analogy, for the mechanical conception of nature, which he regarded as erroneous, Beneke insists on the justification and necessity of a thoroughgoing materialistic explanation of all material natural phenomena. Hence he recognises the attempts to give a purely physiologico-anatomical explanation of phenomena in the case of mental diseases, although he lays much stress on the significance of the psychical symptoms. In this connection he supports Spinoza's view (see especially his work entitled *Das Verhältnis von Seele und Leib,* 1826, pp. 219 f., 243 f.), although there are other passages which seem rather to point to a view akin to Herbart's, for they proceed on the assumption that the difficulties of conceiving a reciprocal action taking place between two heterogeneous elements disappears if we conceive it as taking place between the soul and the being analogous to the soul which underlies the material elements. Beneke never arrived at any clear decision between the two alternatives.[62] As the conclusion from analogy leads us in natural philosophy to conceive all material beings as members of a descending series, our own standpoint in existence being taken as the starting-point, so in the philosophy of religion it causes us to frame ideas of higher beings similar to ourselves. All religion and all science of religion, however refined and spiritualised the latter may be, is nothing more than anthropomorphism. And since the distance between God and man is probably far greater than that between man and worm— since, moreover, in the philosophy of religion we have no real points of attachment such as the philosophy of nature possesses in the mechanical natural sciences—the religious ideas are the object of faith, and it becomes the essential task of the philosophy of religion to investigate the psychological development of the ideas used by religion as well as the spiritual need itself which seeks to find satisfaction in religion. In the following passage Beneke's conception of the philosophy of religion as applied psychology comes out clearly and interestingly : " The philosophy of religion will no longer pare down religious dogmas, historically conceived, to meet the requirements of a preconceived and narrowly limited norm. It undertakes to reconstruct, deduce from the depths of self-knowledge, and to interpret all the forms in which the supersensuous reveals and has revealed itself to the human spirit. Hence, recognising all such forms, but at the same time subjecting them to a keen critical scrutiny, it displays them as members of the organic whole, which, from the very beginning of human culture up to our own time, they have gradually been building up. Here again, then, it is psychology which must disentangle and illuminate the manifold which seems at first sight so bewildering and shrouded in darkness (*Die Philosophie*, etc., p. 27).

In the sphere of psychology and natural philosophy (cosmology), ethics and philosophy of religion,[68] this once neglected thinker appears as the precursor of thoughts which were to find in the next generation a more fruitful soil than had been afforded them by the Romantico-speculative age in Germany.

D. TRANSITION FROM ROMANTIC SPECULATION TO POSITIVISM OR POSITIVE FAITH

(a) Criticism of the Hegelian Philosophy and Dissolution of the Hegelian School

THE philosophical situation in Germany at Hegel's death (1831) was as follows : A speculative school, founded by eminent thinkers, had unmistakably won the mastery, while the opposition offered by critical philosophy and specialised investigation was only represented by smaller groups of thinkers. It was an event of no little significance, therefore, when a rebellion arose within the camp of speculative philosophy itself against the conclusion which Romantic thought had reached in Hegel's system. Then came thinkers who, while they had no intention of giving up speculation, could not recognise Hegel's system as final. The task they set themselves was to retain Hegel's fundamental thoughts, but, at the same time, to lift him and his whole system into a higher unity —to treat him, in fact, as he had treated his philosophical predecessors. And the necessary supplement to the Hegelian system was taken partly from the sphere of experience, partly from that of positive faith. Thus we find SCHELLING, who had kept himself in the background as long as Hegel lived, announcing a new philosophy which was to harmonise speculation with empiricism and with religion, and being summoned to Berlin by Friedrich Wilhelm IV., for the express purpose of refuting Hegelianism. Schelling gave a series of lectures in which he maintained that, by purely rational methods, we can only arrive at a knowledge of general possibilities and general laws ; while knowledge of reality, which is always simple and individual, requires an act of the will springing from that personal need which neither possibilities nor general laws can satisfy. Schelling called the transition from the former rationalistic philosophy to this knowledge, grounded in faith and will, a transition from negative to positive philosophy. Only positive philosophy can maintain the personality of God—the chief problem with which Schelling had occupied himself since 1809, and the problem around which interest centred during the first decade after Hegel's death. In his philosophy of religion Hegel believed himself to have effected a reconciliation between thought and faith. Soon after his death, however, it became a debateable question as to how far it could be said that Hegel's philosophy led to the acceptance of a personal God and a personal immortality.[64] Schelling, and the thinkers who stood nearest to him, especially C. H. WEISSE and the YOUNGER FICHTE, maintained that Hegel's system was pantheism. They attempted, however, to construct, by way of thought, a theism which, instead of denying pantheism, should include it, and so raise it to a higher power. They sought to show that all fundamental thoughts ultimately centre in the idea of personality, and that this idea must be regarded as the expression of the highest reality ; and also (by a further development of the ideas contained in Schelling's treatise on Freedom (1809)), to exhibit the possibility of attributing personality to an infinite being. As a matter of fact, however, they were all obliged to confess that theism cannot be based on knowledge. Schelling's transition from negative to positive theology was really a transition from thought to faith. The younger Fichte, in whom tendency was stronger than intellectual interest, turns back to the ready-made God of popular theology ; Weisse, at once the most acute and most profound of these thinkers, goes back to Schleiermacher, whose philosophy of religion he carries on in a very interesting manner, maintaining the close connection between religious feeling and moral ends and duties. In his daring thoughts on religion he does not shrink from the logical consequence that a God of whom personality can be predicated must also be subject to development in time, and he emphasises the real causal connection of all the ideal content of existence. But with him, too, the programme of speculative theism, which professes to provide a scientific basis for the assumption of a personal God, has practically to give place to an appeal to personal feeling as the only force which can here carry us to the goal.

Tending in the same direction as speculative theism were the religio-philosophical views developed by KARL CHRISTIAN FRIEDRICH KRAUSE (1781-1832), and which, together with his ideas on the philosophy of right, have been published in their most accessible form in *Urbild der Menschheit* (Dresden, 1811). Krause, however, has no liking for the term "personality," and does not predicate it of God. He names his view *Panentheismus*, because it asserts that as the Absolute Being God has the world within Himself, without, however, being exhausted in the world. Krause's philosophy is characterised by the unclearness of mysticism as well as by its noble qualities. It became of especial significance for the philosophy of rights owing to the prominence it gives to the conception of humanity as forming an organic whole made in the image of the divine and primal Being, and to the view that right is the form in which the life of this whole develops itself. This point of view led to a conception at once idealistic and reformatory ; a conception which presented a characteristic contrast to Hegel's conservative doctrine of right, and which has been of no small importance for the development of freer and more humane ideas. Thanks to the labours of his pupils, especially to those of HEINRICH AHRENS (1808-1874), Krause's views gained an influence in extended circles, not only in Germany, but also in Spain and Belgium. But the further development of the philosophy of religion was determined by the ideas of Schelling and Hegel, and by corollaries from these ideas.

In Hegel's own school this accentuation of the religio-philosophical problem occasioned a split. Some Hegelians maintained that, rightly understood, the philosophy of their master accords with ordinary faith and the teachings of the Church. Others declared that when logically carried out it is found to stand in irreconcilable antagonism to the latter. Strauss, who himself belonged to the latter group, compared this opposition with that between the Right and Left of a parliamentary assembly, and it soon became general to speak of the Hegelian Right and Left. The adherents of the latter were also frequently called "young Hegelians." The chief representatives of the Right were GÖSCHEL, ROSENKRANZ, and J. E. ERDMANN. The Left, which was of far greater importance for the development of thought, was represented within the sphere of the philosophy of religion by DAVID FRIEDRICH

STRAUSS and LUDWIG FEUERBACH, and in the sphere of the philosophy of rights and sociology by ARNOLD RUGE and afterwards by KARL MARX and FERDINAND LASSALLE.

Feuerbach occupies the first place among these thinkers. The transition from Romanticism to Positivism, from speculative thought to a conception of life and of the world based on scientific experience, is characteristically illustrated in the development of this energetic thinker. This development contains a criticism of the whole Romantic philosophy, while at the same time it may be taken as the type of many a personal life-development from the faith of childhood to the conviction of the mature man based on reflection and experience. Strauss, in his *Leben Jesu* (1835), raised the religious problem anew in its sharpest form, but Feuerbach's contribution to the elucidation of this problem is one of the most important offered in the course of the following decade.

Philosophic thought, however, was not exclusively occupied with the religious problem during the thirties and forties. An epistemological discussion of great value in its time, not least on account of its criticism of the speculative method, was supplied by ADOLPH TRENDELENBURG in his *Logischen Untersuchungen* (1840). Trendelenburg insisted that philosophical problems spring out of the soil of experience. Reflection upon that which is given in empirical knowledge leads, according to him, to philosophy. He attempted to solve the problem of knowledge by showing that motion is a determination common alike to thought and being ; the movement of thought in perception and construction has its parallel in the motion to which all material phenomena may be reduced. And if the movement of the will is determined by the thought of an end, Trendelenburg finds something analogous to this also in material nature, for he considers it impossible to understand organic phenomena if the concept of end is to have no validity in the natural sciences. Far as he is from the speculative philosophy of Nature, he has a lively conviction of the inadequacy of a purely mechanical conception of Nature. He lays stress on the finitude and limitation of our knowledge, and, with Kant, he holds it to be impossible to give our fundamental concepts an extension sufficiently wide to render them applicable to the absolute. Our faculty of thinking consists in apprehending rays of light clouded and broken into a play of colour ; but we

need not, on that account, deny the existence of the pure light
from which the rays emanate. In addition to his work on
epistemology, Trendelenburg published one on the Philosophy of
Rights which is of great value (*Naturrecht auf dem Grunde der
Ethik*, 1860).[65] Lastly, he was one of the most distinguished
of the inquirers who occupied themselves with the history of
philosophy. In this endeavour he joined forces with the
disciples of Hegel, to whom we owe a series of works—some of
them monumental—on different periods of the history of philosophy. EDUARD ZELLER and J. E. ERDMANN, and in more
recent times KUNO FISCHER, are worthy of special mention.
During the strife of systems it was only natural that the need
for historical and comparative information should make itself felt.
The history of philosophy, as a separate discipline, really arose
during this period.

(b) David Friedrich Strauss and the Religious Problem

While still a young student, Strauss (who was born at
Ludwigsburg in 1808 and studied theology and philosophy at
Tübingen) had raised the question whether the historical elements of the Bible, especially the Gospels, formed a part of what
Hegel regarded as the eternal thought-content of religon, or if
they must only be regarded as the form of imagination under
which this content presents itself to the popular consciousness.
Afterwards, in his *Leben Jesu* (1835), he attempted to show
that we have in the story of the Gospels neither history nor
conscious fiction (the dilemma brought forward by orthodox
theologians) but myth, *i.e.* unconscious poetry, the *motifs* of
which are supplied partly by the religious ideas which inspired
the age and nation (particularly the Messianic idea), partly by
the tremendous impression which the Founder of Christianity
had made on His disciples. What the Gospels give us, therefore, is, as Strauss afterwards expressed it, not the Jesus of
history, but "the Christ of faith." As a strictly historical
person Jesus is really quite unknown to us ; the Christ of faith
alone is a being with definite features. In a section at the
conclusion of the *Leben Jesu* it is argued that the idea of the
God-man cannot be applicable to any one individual ; on the
contrary, it is only the whole human race, consisting of an
infinite number of individuals, which is able in its continual

suffering, striving, and labour to realise the divine. The teachings of the Church concerning Christ retain their validity if they are transferred to humanity. In a later work (*Die christliche Glaubenslehre, in ihrer geschichtlichen Entwickelung und im Kampfe mit der modernen Wissenschaft dargestellt* (1840-41)). Strauss showed that the reconciliation of Christianity with philosophy which Hegel believed himself to have effected is only possible when Christianity is conceived as a monism; as a matter of fact, it is distinctly dualistic. According to Christianity, the unity of the divine and human was achieved in the case of one single individual only—all other individuals remain outside this unity! And the unity of God and man is only possible in each single individual under the form of suffering and by the intervention of supernatural powers! On several sides, therefore, within Christianity itself the opposition between the two worlds, the divine and human, emerges. Primitive Christianity, indeed, gave up the idea of the divine world permeating the human, and lived in the expectation that, in the near future, the former would destroy the latter by supernatural means. Strauss concludes with a sharp antithesis between believers and non-believers, and an energetic protest against all attempts at reconciliation.

Strauss's particular merit in connection with the religious problem consists in his having opposed the concept of myth or unconscious fiction to the usual dilemma : history or intentional invention. This concept expresses unambiguously that which Kant, Herder, and their successors, in a more accommodating spirit, designated symbol. It possesses a further advantage, for it suggests the question : " Why did these particular pictures arise ? " it has a more historical sound than " symbol." Strauss did not enter any further into the question as to what psychical forces and impulses produced the great images and symbols which, thanks to national religions, have become the possession of the race—what set the whole process of constructing ideals in motion. He afterwards acknowledged that Feuerbach had found the conclusive answer to this question.

Strauss had intended to found a free critical theology. His heretical views, however, prevented his appointment to any theological professorship. Hence he lived as a private individual, occupied throughout many years with literary and biographical studies.   He wrote interesting works on Ulrich v. Hutten, Voltaire, and others.   Towards the end of his life he occupied himself once more with the philosophy of religion. In *Der alte und der neue Glaube* (1872) he attempted to show that the religious problem arises not only when, as in his earlier works, the logical consequences of speculative philosophy are considered, but also when we draw conclusions from modern natural science.   He had set himself a task beyond his strength.   He was a scholar rather than a thinker, and an artist rather than a scholar.   The book is written in a brilliantly lucid style, but his conception of religion lacked depth and inwardness, and was lacking in logical consistency with the standpoint which he attempted to defend against materialism. In æsthetic contemplation of life, especially in music, he found a substitute for religious worship, a proof of how far he was from having thought out the religious problem on all sides. After a severe and painful illness, borne with great meekness and resolution, he died in the year 1784.

(c) *Ludwig Feuerbach's Psychology of Religion and Ethics*

In this energetic and richly endowed thinker we have a fine example of the way in which the core of a personality which undergoes many transformations may yet remain essentially unchanged.   One and the same interest prompted him to occupy all his many changing points of view.   From his earliest youth up he had yearned for a real and positive human life, for satisfaction of soul ; he had longed to occupy himself with those questions on the answers to which depends the value of life for man, and the answering of which, therefore, becomes a matter of conscience.   It was this longing—as he explained later in a description of himself—which drove him first to theology and afterwards to philosophy, and—within philosophy itself—from the speculative philosophy to a standpoint, almost identical with the one already established by the French philosopher, Auguste Comte, under the name of Positivism.   Thought, with him, was always subservient to life. He regarded himself as a Positive thinker, and his criticism and polemic (which, in the eyes of his generation, was his most conspicuous feature) merely as an instrument for threshing out the corn from the chaff in matters of religion.   He wanted to pierce to the living human needs which lie behind the ideas of religion ; hence it was that he directed a sharp criticism against the latter. Far from holding that thought exhausts the nature of man, he says of himself (when pressed to write his autobiography) : " I find it impossible to express that which moves me most deeply ; how much more, then, to set down in black and white for the benefit of an indiscreet public my inner life." And in another passage he says that the thoughts by which we seek to become conscious of our nature are very inferior to this nature itself. This incommensurability between thought and personality must be kept well in mind if we are to understand this ever-seething, ever-seeking and ever-unsatisfied spirit.[66]

LUDWIG FEUERBACH was born at Landshut in 1804, of a highly talented family. His father was the famous jurist Anselm v. Feuerbach, and several of his brothers won a name for themselves in the worlds of art and science. He studied theology in Heidelberg, but soon gave it up in favour of philosophy, which he pursued under Hegel in Berlin. Hegel's philosophy put an end to the inner conflict which theology had had no power to assuage, and he regarded Hegel, who had made him a philosopher, as his second father. Feuerbach worked for some years as *docent* at Erlangen, but then retired, partly, it seems, on account of a lack of skill in verbal exposition, partly owing to attacks from the theological party, from whom it could not be concealed that he was the author of a heterodox work entitled *Gedanken über Tod und Unsterblichkeit* (1830). He now withdrew into the country and settled in Bruckberg, the seat of a manufactory, some shares in which formed part of his wife's dowry, and here he developed great fertility in authorship. He devoted a series of excellent works to a discussion of subjects taken from the history of modern philosophy. Of chief note among these is his *Pierre Bayle*, in which he laid great stress on the opposition between theology and philosophy, and maintained the independence of ethics over against the former. A definitive religio-philosophic standpoint is distinctly discernible even here, although it was not clearly and decidedly set forth till the publication of his chief work : *Wesen des Christentums* (1841). While Strauss, like Hegel, was mainly occupied with the *content* of dogma, Feuerbach sought to discover the *source* of dogmas in human feelings and impulses, fears and hopes,

longings and wishes.   His task is not the impossible one of
formulating the content of dogmas in terms of concepts of knowledge, but of understanding their psychological origin.   From
the official documents of religion he goes back to the spiritual
and inner life which there found expression, and he is no less
sympathetic towards the source in which dogmas rise than he is
critical towards dogmas themselves.   This constitutes the great
difference between his attitude towards religion and that of
Voltaire.   Feuerbach goes much farther in criticism and negation than the French freethinkers, but he has far more understanding and sympathy with the inner motive of religion than
Voltaire with his dilemma : folly or knavery !   The studies
and experiences of the time which had elapsed since Voltaire's
day had not been in vain.   There is a great and characteristic
difference between the freethinkers of the eighteenth and of
the nineteenth centuries (if we consider only those freethinkers
who really thought).   Feuerbach's efforts in the sphere of the
philosophy of religion (like those of Lyell in geology at almost
the same time) are directed towards explaining the forms of
past times in the light of the forces which are now in operation.   The so-called principle of actuality underlies his famous
saying that " all theology is psychology."   In greatness of plan,
in depth and in energy, no other of Feuerbach's works can
compare with the *Wesen des Christentums,* although he, as well
as his friends, placed the *Theogonie* (1857) higher.

The breach with speculative philosophy to which Feuerbach had been led in connection with the conception of religion
was of great consequence for his philosophical views as a
whole.   In his *Grundsätzen der Philosophie der Zukunft* (1843)
he sketches the programme of a new philosophy, in which,—
in remarkable agreement with expressions in Schelling's
Positive Philosophy,—it is asserted that only the particular is
real, and that this real is inexpressible, impenetrable by thought,
and hence only to be grasped by passion.   Reality is no
merely theoretical matter ; it is " a question of life and death."
The subject of modern philosophy is not that which transcends
experience, but man himself, with Nature as his foundation.
Later, in his *Gott, Freiheit und Unsterblichkeit* (1866), he
developed his views on the spiritual and material ; this work
occupies a similar place among his productions to *Der
alte und der neue Glaube* among Strauss' works.   During his

last years, troubled by illness and pecuniary anxieties, Feuerbach occupied himself in constructing an ethical system ; interesting fragments of this work were published after his death (1872) by Grün.

As early as *Pierre Bayle* Feuerbach had demanded an " analytico-genetic " philosophy, and in the *Grundsätzen* he had sketched out a somewhat more detailed programme. But he never, either here or in his later works, got beyond a vague demand for such a philosophy. He nowhere enters into any epistemological questions, and even when he assumes the rôle of an arch-realist, his thought is not free from some dogmatic and mystical elements. Nor had he the least idea that the demand which he urged had been already complied with in the works of Comte and Mill. By the time he arrived at Positivism it had long been established in the French and English schools. The same may be said of his ethics. There is something tragic about Feuerbach's position within the philosophical development of our century. He lived in a period of transition, and had to suffer accordingly. He had spent so much force in working himself beyond the speculative standpoint that he had afterwards neither energy, desire, nor leisure for the positive and scientific working-out of his new point of view. On the other hand, he comes before us as one of the most strongly-marked characters, one of the most truth-loving men of our century. And he is one of the most important champions of a humanistic conception of life. Humanism was the name which he himself considered most appropriate for his tendency of thought. We will now examine in turn, first, his philosophy of religion, then his general scientific standpoint, and lastly his system of ethics.

a. Schleiermacher had defined the religious feeling as a feeling of dependence, but had left it undecided from whence this feeling derives its object. Feuerbach now tried to show that the feeling itself *produces* its object, so that the latter not only expresses the feeling, but has actually arisen out of it. He replaces the bare feeling of dependence by the trust and living wish of the heart, and in his eyes the peculiar property of faith is that it frees the wishes of men from the bonds of reason and of Nature. That which is the object of the innermost aspirations and longings of man is revealed by faith as an objective reality, as the Absolute. The opposition between

wish and reality is annulled. Schleiermacher had attempted
to show that every conflict between faith and knowledge arises
either in a misunderstanding, or because neither faith nor
knowledge have attained perfection. Feuerbach, on the
contrary, maintains that the phenomena peculiar to religion
are due to the impulse to satisfy the wishes of the heart
bursting through the limits imposed by reason ; thus, at their
highest point, religious phenomena take on an anti-rational
character.

Feuerbach made an energetic and thoughtful attempt to
trace wishes, needs and hopes back to the psychological foundation of religion. The wish, he says (in the *Theogonie*) is the
fundamental phenomenon of religion, the theogonic principle.
This assertion is established in the *Wesen des Christentums* by
a line of argument which is of general philosophic interest.

Man can never get beyond his own nature : all his conceptions and thoughts bear his own stamp. Hence we may learn
to know his nature from the objects to which he relates himself,
for they are but occasions for the unfolding of his nature. It
is only in virtue of a man's own nature than an object can
gain any power over him. At the very beginning man has no
reason to mark out limits to his nature. He quietly surrenders
himself to all ideas, and attributes to them unlimited validity.
It is especially characteristic of the nature of feeling that it
is inclined to infinitise its object, to regard it as real. Doubt,
then, can only arise when man learns to know his limits, and
when understanding begins to distinguish between the subjective
and objective, a distinction which is unknown from the standpoint of faith. For faith is nothing else than belief in the
absolute reality of subjectivity.[67] Not everything subjective,
of course, becomes an object of religious faith. Religion arises
in a separation, an estimation of worth ; man does not regard
as divine that to which he is indifferent, but only that to which
he attributes the greatest value. Every man who has a highest
aim has a god. That which a man praises and treasures is his
god ; that which he blames and rejects is the godless. God is the
book in which man has inscribed his highest feelings and thoughts.

Man's heaven is an anthology of flowers formed by selection
from the flora of this world. This is as true of the heaven of
the civilised man as of the heaven of the savage ; only that the
former's, owing to his education, is less crude than the latter's.

In man's God and heaven, then, we may discover man's own longings and aspirations. In the divine qualities we have the qualities which man, at that particular stage, estimates most highly. That God is personality means that personal life is the highest; that God is love means that there is nothing more excellent than a loving disposition. In the Christian religion God suffers ; this means, to suffer for others is divine. If we are to understand religion, we must everywhere take as subject what it takes as predicate and *vice versâ*. Christianity exhibits the religious principle in all its depth and fulness. In it the heart, the life of feeling acquires an inwardness and strength, and at the same time a freedom from limits, which paganism never knew ; suffering is felt more deeply, love is, therefore, all the more fervent. The levity of the Olympian gods shipwrecked on the needs of the human heart, but the Christian's God is a tear of love shed in deepest secrecy over the misery of man. In religion man regards the world of wishes and ideals as an independent, distant world, as the real world, in sharp contrast to the world here below, the world of finitude, of suffering, and of struggle.

But, it may be urged, how can we deduce religion from the heart's illimitableness, from the omnipotence of feeling, when it is precisely in religion that man feels himself finite, imperfect, and sinful ? Feuerbach explains this feeling as a kind of contrast - effect : man, who has unconsciously bestowed everything upon his God, feels in comparison thereto poor and miserable. He sees his own nature in God and must, therefore, feel empty and poverty-stricken in comparison with God. But in God his own nature is preserved. In God man can enjoy his nature in far richer fulness than when he dwells on his own limited, real nature. Another objection runs : Theology has long recognised the distinction between God's essence and those qualities which we attribute to Him, and Schleiermacher in particular has worked out this distinction. To which Feuerbach answers, that in doing away with the divine qualities we also do away with the divine essence. The said distinction is the fruit of scepticism and unbelief. True faith knows it not. For what is left when all qualities are taken away ? The history of religion shows that as long as man wishes to know anything about God, he knows it. The classical age of religion knew no such distinction. Feuerbach's one aim is to exhibit to consciousness the peculiar, primitive and involuntary character of religious phenomena. He is concerned with religion in its original form only, not with religiosity modified by criticism and more or less scientific culture. Hence, he emphasises the difference within Christianity itself between primitive and modern Christianity. Christianity, too, has had its classical age, and it is this age alone in which Feuerbach is interested ; not in the "dissolute, characterless, comfortable, bellelettristic, coquettish, epicurean Christianity of the modern world." But not even the theologians nowadays, he thinks, know what Christianity is. They have dulled the edge of the great antithesis of primitive Christianity between this and the future world. Protestantism, in fact, denotes a new conception of life, differing from that of primitive Christianity. Its morality is purely human ; only its faith leads back to primitive Christianity. It assigns miracles to the past, and sets the last day in an indefinite future—and yet the belief in the near-approaching destruction of this world forms part of the essence of Christian faith and cannot be separated from the remaining content of faith ; for this world must pass away in order that the world of infinite wishes may come. The key to modern Christianity, according to Feuerbach, consists in the fact that the theogonic wish, the prime phenomenon, is no longer present.

This is Feuerbach's theory of the philosophy of religion. If we ask what value he attributed to religion we find, as already intimated, that he is by no means antagonistic to it where it is original and genuine. Religion—in its classical period—is the only means by which man can become conscious of his own nature and of the tasks it imposes upon him—the only way to the understanding and deepening of self. Moreover, it gives man a widened horizon ; it extends his sensuous consciousness by showing him his own nature as something distant, exalted and infinite. On the other hand, in some respects religion exercises an injurious influence. When the believer finds his all in his God, and supernatural forces are regarded by him as the true reality, he cannot feel the need of family affection of science, of art, of civil life. The impulse after culture cannot arise in him. Religion and culture have the same end, and the more a man hopes to gain by following one of these roads the less he will seek to get by the other ; an inverse relation will exist between them. Moreover, the projection which takes place whenever man regards his ideals as qualities of an absolute Being whom he believes to be different from himself is by no means harmless. The more the distinction between God and man is emphasised, the more it will cause qualities (goodness, justice, etc.) to be taken in a different sense when they are applied to God from when they are applied to man. Man must therefore put shackles on his own conscience and his own reason that he may be able to obey the divine will, even when it commands something contrary to that which, in respect of men, is called goodness and justice. Here lies the source of all fanaticism, the source of all those dismal phenomena which the history of religion exhibits. Feuerbach finds the two aspects of the religion of the estimation of worth clearly expressed in the Christian doctrines of faith and love. Love removes all barriers ; it makes all things one in spite of everything which might otherwise sunder them ; but faith replaces the barriers between them, and awakens bigotry and lovelessness. Love is only one predicate of God, and the divine subject has other claims to enforce than those of love ; we cannot conclude from what love demands to what God demands. Hence, for Feuerbach, the necessity of abandoning the standpoint of religion. He protests, however, against the supposition that his own standpoint is purely negative. He recognises the value of the divine qualities, but precisely on this account he will not have them attributed to a Divine Being as to a separate subject. The true atheist is he to whom these qualities are nothing, not he to whom their subject is nothing. The qualities only get their due when they are separated from the supposititious subject. This is especially true of love, the sentiment in which the unity of the human race expresses itself. It existed before Christianity. Christ was the figure under which the unity of the race exhibited itself to a national consciousness. And even when faith in Christ has disappeared, Christ's true essence remains in existence wherever love reigns. In Feuerbach's opinion, therefore, nothing of real value is lost by the abandonment of religious faith. We merely cease to project. We no longer cross the stream to fetch water because we have discovered that the water which we fetched comes out of the stream itself.

Without being able to enter on an exhaustive criticism of

Feuerbach's philosophy of religion, we may pause to point out that in his doctrine of feeling or desire (the theogonic wish) as the productive force he does not sufficiently consider the reciprocal relation between feeling and the other sides of conscious life. In and for itself feeling can produce nothing and yet "out of itself and only out of itself" (*Theogonie*, p. 57), the theogonic wish is said to produce the idea of God. Feeling can only work on already existing ideas, acquired either by tradition or from personal experience, choosing, strengthening, and idealising them. This conception of the givenness of ideas helps us to understand how it is that an element of resignation enters into religion, and the object of faith appears to men to be imposed by authority. As regards Feuerbach's estimation of the value of religion, he is perhaps a little too optimistic in assuming that nothing would be lost by the abandonment of religion. Even if religion contains, and can contain, nothing more than the nature of man, it is conceivable that this content might operate much more powerfully in the form given to it by religion than it could in any other way. At any rate, there might be natures who could never be very strongly influenced except by religion. This great problem is still unsolved. Lastly, Feuerbach overlooks the fact that it is impossible to adduce any strict proof of the proposition that "all theology is psychology." Religious philosophy can only point out the possibility of explaining all religious ideas as psychological products ; but that they really are not, nor ever can be, anything more can never be proved. The mere fact that the matter of faith is in harmony with human wishes is not conclusive one way or another. Perhaps some one may be found to accept Feuerbach's method while rejecting his result, in which, with passionate conviction, he asserts the reality of that after which the heart, in its infinite longings, aspires.

This is, at any rate, one form under which the religious controversy might be carried on now that we have Feuerbach's contribution to it ; we shall perhaps discover others in the course of our study.

β. If all theology is psychology, all philosophy must, of course, be psychology also ; thus the philosophy of religion brought Feuerbach to the standpoint which Fries and Beneke had long since adopted. In his *Grundsätzen der Philosophie der Zukunft* he proclaims man — including Nature, on which humanity rests—to be the only subject of philosophy ; anthropology, that is to say, — including physiology, — is the universal science. This brilliant little work is full of striking sayings, but there is something oracular about its style which derogates from the value it might have possessed had the thoughts contained in it been fully elaborated. It champions the rights of individual facts and of sensation ; but it does not enter on the problems which arise in connection with the relation between experience and knowledge, sensation and thought, psychology and theory of knowledge.

Feuerbach's attitude towards materialism in his later works displays a similar want of clearness. He was an eager student of physiology, and wrote an enthusiastic review of MOLESCHOTT'S *Lehre der Nahrungsmittel* (1850) in which the following passage occurs : " The doctrine of foods is of great ethical and political significance. Food becomes blood, blood becomes heart and brain, thoughts and mind-stuff. Human fare is the foundation of human culture and thought. Would you improve a nation ? Give it, instead of declamations against sin, better food. Man is what he eats." And he adds that if the people had better nourishment (peas instead of potatoes) a future revolution would have a better chance of success. This passage (printed in *Nachlass*, ii. p. 90) was often quoted by the theological party to show how low Feuerbach had sunk. It illustrates his capacity for emphasising in powerful and paradoxical fashion whatever lay next his heart—and at the same time his want of clearness on decisive points, especially in regard to the relation between " man " and his " basis." Nearly as Feuerbach seems to approach materialism in these and later utterances, he himself considered this term altogether unfit to express his way of looking at things (see *Nachlass*, ii. p. 307).

In his opinion man is not to be regarded as a mere product of matter. We must make man our starting-point—instead, as materialism does, of regarding him merely as a result. For, says Feuerbach, life, sensation, thought is something absolutely original, *genial*, inimitable, irreplaceable, unlosable. Hence we have to find an Archimedian point between materialism and spiritualism, from which man can be regarded as a material and as a spiritual being (*Werke*, x. p. 162 f.). Feuerbach is deterred from drawing the conclusions to which his materialistic sounding utterances might lead by the same principle—it might be called the principle of subjectivity—with which he operates in his philosophy of religion ; *i.e.* the principle that the final ground of knowledge is to be found not outside but within man. He employs this principle first against theology and speculation, and then against materialism, but with much more clearness in the first case than in the second.

γ. Feuerbach's ethical views underwent several modifications. At first he maintained the independence of ethics over against religion and theology, appealing principally to the ethical systems of Kant and Fichte (*e.g.* in *Pierre Bayle*). In his *Wesen des Christentums*, as already mentioned, he speaks of human love as the feeling in which the unity of the race takes shape in individuals, and exhibits itself to them. Later still he lays such stress on the impulse towards happiness as the foundation of ethics that on a former occasion I described his ethics as "the morality of egoism." It seems, however, from the fragments on moral philosophy published by Karl Grün (*Nachlass*, i.) that I had misunderstood him on this point. For Feuerbach, the happiness of the individual is not the end but the presupposition of morality. For only he who knows from his own experience what it is to suffer need and wrong can sympathise with others. Sympathy and human love presuppose that the person feeling them has himself experienced the need of happiness. Feuerbach urges this against Schopenhauer in particular, who, though rejecting the need of happiness, makes sympathy the basis of morality. Sympathy consists in making other men's impulse after happiness one's own. Ethics can recognise no isolated impulse towards happiness, no distinction between " my own " and another's happiness. As to the physical birth of a man, so also, to the birth of morality, two human beings are necessary. In the relation of the sexes Nature has solved the problem of the transition from the egoistic striving after happiness to the recognition of duties towards others. The sexual relation forms the foundation of morality, since it substitutes for the isolated striving after happiness a two- or more-sided striving. Since the existence of every individual is bound up with that of other men, the feeling of confederacy and companionship arises ; the individual's striving after happiness is limited, and now duties towards ourselves are only spoken of in the sense of indirect duties to others. According to Feuerbach, conscience is not a special faculty, implanted once and for all within us, from which a complete ethic can be deduced *a priori.* It is only another name for the mind, the heart, sympathy, humanity. It arises first in the form of an evil conscience after the deed is done. Evil conscience is sympathy associated with the sting of knowing ourselves to have caused the unhappiness of the sufferer. It presupposes that I am able to feel another's impulse towards happiness, so that I feel in my breast the wounding of this impulse and carry in my soul the accusing figure of the sufferer.

Although Feuerbach has expressed his ethical views in sketches and fragments only, they possess no small interest ; partly because they show the direction in which the thoughts of this sharp critic and untiringly active spirit tended on these important questions, partly on account of their agreement with views which had already been developed by Auguste Comte, the real founder of modern positivism. In the history of German philosophy Feuerbach appears as the most energetic of the thinkers who effected the transition from Romantic speculation to critical self-comprehension, and returned afresh to the investigation of the first presuppositions of all our knowledge and all our estimation of worth.

(*d*) *Philosophy in the North*

It is only in connection with a very few points that the general history of philosophy has occasion to linger with Scandinavian thinkers, and this section will perhaps, in the eyes of many, find its explanation and justification only in the nationality of the writer. The philosophical movement in the North consisted for the most part in the more or less independent appropriation of philosophical ideas which had been developed in larger countries ; an appropriation which was certainly of great importance for the course of mental development in the North itself, but which brought about no results of any moment for that of thought in general. Thus the critical and still more the Romantic philosophy found disciples there. If we look for any distinctive trait in its adoption of the Romantic philosophy we shall find it in the predominance of the practical, personal interest ; of interest in the ethical significance of ideas. And in this respect development in Sweden presented a characteristic difference from that in Denmark.

In Sweden, as early as the beginning of the nineteenth century, we find in the works of THORILD the idea which Swedish philosophy, at its zenith accepted as the expression of absolute reality, *i.e.* that of existence as a living, harmonious whole. Under the influence of such men as Kant, Fichte and Schelling this idea received further development from a series of thinkers, among whom the energetic BENJAMIN HÖIJER deserves especial mention, until CHRISTOPHER JACOB BOSTRÖM (born 1797 in Piteå, died 1866 in Upsala) brought "rational idealism" to a systematic close.

The world which sensation and experience show us cannot, according to Boström, be the true one, because it exhibits external oppositions in space, and develops itself in time. Hence the attempt of German speculation to exhibit the nature of the Absolute as consisting in a continual development was, in Boström's eyes, a sign that they had not risen sufficiently above experience. Even Hegel is an empiric, for he makes the idea unfold itself by means of the positing and annulling of opposites. Only in the notion of an eternal personality, whose ideas again are (finite) personalities existing in a state of mutual harmony can thought, according to Boström and to the national Swedish school founded by him, find its close. In his zeal to preserve reality in its pure, absolute perfection, Boström polemicises not only against the idealistic evolutionary doctrine of German philosophy, but also against the doctrines of the creation and atonement of Christian theology. It was a fundamental principle with him that the higher explains the lower, the perfect the imperfect. Rational idealism is an ethical idealism, since for us the highest is a harmonious society of independent personalities. This idea of a harmonious society furnishes an answer to the question as to what the thing-in-itself, which underlies the sensuous world of phenomena, really is. Boström's philosophy is a modified Platonism in which the ideas are conceived not as abstractions but as concrete personalities. Idealism is here transformed into a speculative philosophy of personality.[68]

While Swedish thought maintained the principle of personality in the ideal world, Danish thought was more concerned to maintain this principle in the world of experience.

Both TRESCHOW and F. C. SIBBERN met German speculation with a healthily realistic world-conception and a sense for psychological experience which precluded all wild speculation. When Hegel's philosophy found its way into Denmark, where it gained many adherents, chiefly among students of æsthetics and theologians, Sibbern published an excellent and trenchant criticism of it (1838). "The object of all my philosophy," said Sibbern once, "is the study of life and reality." He could see no value in abstract and speculative construction. Philosophy must start from a given basis, and its business is to analyse this. General ideas and laws alone cannot make existence comprehensible to us ; we must also know the actually given starting-points from which the evolutionary process of existence proceeds. One of the leading thoughts of Sibbern's world-conception (brought out especially in his *Speculativen Kosmologie* 1846) is that all development starts sporadically from different, often seemingly contradictory, starting-points. Hence his conception of development was far from being as idealistic as Hegel's. While Boström found Hegel altogether too empirical because he believed in a development, Sibbern's objection to Hegel was that he assumed no *real historical* development. And he gives an extremely interesting application of his doctrine of sporadic development in his theory of knowledge and in his philosophy of religion. Since the knower himself is only one of the many sporadic elements of existence he can never get a full view of it in its totality : on the other hand, no one but himself can experience how the universal life lives at his particular point. Hence Sibbern has to defend the limitations of knowledge against the speculative philosophy (*Om Filosofiens Begreb* (" On the Concept of Philosophy ") 1843, § 21), and the significance of individual subjectivity against ecclesiastical dogmatism (Programme of the Copenhagen University, 1846-47). His writings, especially his doctrine of the feelings, have rendered contributions of lasting value to psychology. A work which was of great significance for his time—*Om Fosholdet mellem Själ og Legeme* (" On the Relation between Soul and Body")(1849)—shows how he attempted to harmonise his psychological theories with physiological experiences. He declares against the dualistic view ; it is one and the same life which appears as the life of consciousness and as material life.[69]

SÖREN KIERKEGAARD had more radical objections to urge

against Romantic speculation and its claim of having reconciled the contradictions in life and existence. His leading idea was that the different possible conceptions of life are so sharply opposed to one another that we must make a choice between them, hence his catchword *either — or;* moreover, it must be a choice which each particular person must make for himself, hence his second catchword, *the individual.* He himself designated his thought " qualitative dialectic," by which he meant to bring out its opposition to the doctrine taught by Romantic speculation of continuous development by means of necessary inner transitions. Kierkegaard regarded this doctrine as pure fantasticalness—a fantasticalness, to be sure, to which he himself had felt attracted. Remarkably gifted as a poet and thinker, he had a wonderful skill in drawing out all that was involved in a thought ; and he clothed the possibilities of thought with an intuitive power and a richness of feeling unequalled in Danish literature. He was assisted in so doing by his mastery of language, which enabled him to choose his words so as to display all the little waves in the great sea of feeling, and to give every shade of thought its due. He often, as we may say, played with language as the warrior plays with his weapons. But passionately as he loved the life of thought and feeling and cultivated the art of language, he felt a still stronger need which lifted him out of and above the world of possibilities to a life of reality and deep earnestness. An infinite melancholy caused him to feel the inadequacy of the intellectual and æsthetic life, while, on the other hand, this melancholy—by its need of distraction—impelled him to write the many works on æsthetics and philosophy which mark his first great period as a writer (1843-46). In talents and disposition he was a Romanticist ; it was owing to this fact that he learnt from personal experience how steep may be the path leading from the world of reflection and imagination through the narrow portal of decision (either—or) to the strivings of the individual in the world of reality.

The " qualitative dialectic " appears in Kierkegaard's theory of knowledge in the sharp antithesis he draws between thought and reality. Even if thought should attain coherency it does not therefore follow that this coherency can be preserved in the practice of life. So long as we live we are imprisoned in becoming ; hence we stand ever before the unknown, for there is no guarantee that the future will resemble the past. To decide on purely objective grounds is impossible. Accordingly, a system of thought which should embrace reality is an impossibility. All that is possible is an abstract, strictly logical system ; such a system may perhaps contain in brief the leading features of the experience of the past, but life presses forwards, and is always leading to new possibilities and new choices. Moreover, such great differences and oppositions exist side by side that there is no thought which can embrace them all in a " higher unity." And in any case, individual existences could never come by their rights in such a system. That religious truth could only appear to Kierkegaard under the form of a paradox is a natural consequence of his theory of knowledge ; for this paradox has to express the relation between an existing spirit and the eternal truth. He expressly asserts that it is no concession on his part when he says the object of faith is the paradox that the Highest, the Eternal, is only to be won by subjective choice, based on no objective foundation,—even, indeed, in conflict with such assumptions as objective reasoning would lead us to adopt. There is no criterion of truth other than subjective belief ; subjectivity is the truth.

In Kierkegaard's ethics the qualitative dialectic appears partly in his conception of choice, of the decision of the will, partly in his doctrine of stages. He emphatically denies that there is any analogy between spiritual and organic development. No gradual development takes place within the spiritual sphere, such as might explain the transition from deliberation to decision, or from one conception of life (or " stadium ") to another. Continuity would be broken in every such transition. As regards the choice, psychology is only able to point out possibilities and approximations, motives and preparations. The choice itself comes with a jerk, with a leap, in which something quite new (a new quality) is posited. Only in the world of possibilities is there continuity ; in the world of reality decision always comes through a breach of continuity. But, it might be asked, cannot this jerk or this leap itself be made an object of psychological observation ? Kierkegaard's answer is not clear. He explains that the leap takes place between two moments, between two states, one of which is the last state in the world of possibilities, the other the first state in the world of reality. It would almost seem to follow from this that the leap itself cannot be observed. But then it would also follow that it takes place unconsciously—and the possibility of an unconscious continuity underlying the conscious antithesis is not excluded. Hence to pronounce this concept of a leap valid is purely arbitrary. In his doctrine of the different life-conceptions (or, to quote the less suitable term he sometimes gives them, " stadia "), therefore, Kierkegaard is only able to defend the necessity of this leap because he thinks the different life-conceptions (of which the three leading forms are the æsthetic, the ethical, and the religious) only in their clearly defined, complete, even extreme forms. In his description of the æsthetic stadium more especially he adduces forms which can only be described as " congealed." Small wonder then, that the possibilities demonstrable by psychology are too few. For experience shows that wherever there is development there is still a certain indefiniteness of form ; development from one perfected form to another is generally impossible. Nor can the law of contrast - effects help us ; it could only be applied in cases where there is a certain amount of elasticity left, where life is not dried up. By thus accentuating the leap which takes place in every decision, Kierkegaard himself deprives his ethic of any real content, of the power of dealing with any real, definite problems. The decision is not supposed to depend on the value which the content may have for the man, nor on what power the content may gain in virtue of this value ; for in that case the explanation would be found in the fact that man is able to recognise value. And Kierkegaard's ethics becomes still more formal as he gradually develops the conclusions which follow from the " concept of the individual." The more the individual is isolated from the race, the less he is able to choose definite and real ends, and to perform definite and real tasks. Kierkegaard finally does away with the ethical stadium altogether, and there remain only the two alternatives ; the æsthetic or the religious life. All that does not fall under one or other of these two possibilities he regards as Philistinism. The choice is : either pleasure or suffering ; either the giving up of any earnest living, or out into the tension and pain which the relation to eternal truth necessarily entails on a temporal being ! Kierkegaard came more and more to regard the capability of embracing great contrasts and of enduring the suffering which this involves as the criterion of the sublimity and value of a conception of life. But this is a standard of measurement altogether opposed to natural needs and natural tendencies, and Kierkegaard here expresses a tendency downright inimical to life. In his later years he read Schopenhauer's works with the greatest interest.

Under the influence of this line of thought he became aware of the great problem (already urged by Schopenhauer and Feuerbach) presented by the relation between primitive and modern Christianity, with regard not to dogma, but to ethics. The extremely violent polemic against the existing Church which he wrote in his last years followed as a natural consequence on the whole course of his development. In the Christianity of the New Testament he found his criterion of the highest conception of life (the highest stadium) satisfied. The claim of the modern Church to be a lineal descendant of apostolic Christianity seemed to Kierkegaard a piece of insolent presumption. In his *Öjeblikke* (Moments), he maintains with great pathos and biting scorn the following thesis :—the Christianity of the New Testament is no more! Thus the harmony which Romanticism believed itself to have revealed between knowledge and faith, culture and religion, was at an end ! This was a work for which Kierkegaard's whole nature thoroughly fitted him. He was not a man to help in the solution of problems, either by exhibiting them under new forms or by extending our mental horizon by way of experience. But he passionately reasserted the qualitative distinctions and determinations which speculative philosophy had been inclined to obliterate, and in so doing he laboured on behalf of the force and fulness of life, and has enriched not only those whose standpoint and conception of life resemble his own, but many others also.[70]

BOOK IX

POSITIVISM

A. COMTE AND FRENCH PHILOSOPHY

Two tendencies of thought characterise the intellectual life of the nineteenth century,—Romanticism and Positivism. The former is the outcome of the demands of the heart and of the idealising tendency of thought; the latter takes as its basis the empirically given, for by the word *positive* is meant primarily that which we understand by *real.* The two tendencies, therefore, seem to present the greatest possible contrast. They spring from mutually opposing starting-points. And yet there is an inner relationship between them. Both are supported by the same interest, and rest on the same presupposition. Both are inspired by the desire to gain a rich spiritual content and to become absorbed in great realities.

Romanticism, no less than positivism, aims at grasping reality; but while romanticism seeks to lay hold of this reality by subjective methods, positivism builds on objective facts. Their common assumption is that any ideal which stands altogether outside reality is necessarily false. Hence, thinkers of both schools turned away from the eighteenth-century criticism of the understanding, and gave themselves with enthusiasm to the study of the great process of evolution in Nature and history. The concept of development is no less predominant in romanticism than in positivism. Both were concerned to trace out the continuous interconnection of history which had been so rudely interrupted by the Enlightenment and the revolutionary period. A thorough understanding of past times and of the conditions of the development of intellectual life are an essential element of these two schools, which have played so important a part in the history of thought. Even if we are compelled to admit that differences of view with regard to matters of faith and to conceptions of life have become increasingly accentuated and sharpened in the course of our century, we nevertheless owe to these two lines of thought one great advance : they have taught us to think ourselves into standpoints which are essentially different from those we naturally adopt. By the help of the historic sense, which is a kind of universalised human sympathy, oppositions which logical discussion could never overcome are reconciled with one another. And this betokens a turning-point in the history of human thought. We have acquired a new organon. Romanticism and positivism both attempted in their different ways to carry out the programme of mental philosophy which had been laid down by Immanuel Kant, *i.e.* to discover the moving forces which have produced the work of past ages, to investigate their laws and scope and, by so doing, to set them free to perform the work of the future. Hence it would be incorrect to conceive positivism merely as a reaction against the philosophy of romanticism. That would even be incorrect from a chronological point of view, for the birth of positivism preceded the complete development of romanticism. It was not satiety of one tendency which led to the other, although it is true that the conditions for the spread of positivism in wider circles were more favourable after the decline of romanticism had set in.

There is, however, one essential point on which, from the very beginning, these two lines of thought differed from one another. In its enthusiasm for the unity of thought, romanticism overlooked the manifoldness of reality, while in its firm conviction of the truth of the ideal it neglected the strict mechanical interconnection according to law to which everything which has any lasting existence in the world of reality must submit. Positivism, since it takes as its starting-point the actually given, is alive to the differences and oppositions presented in reality, and strives to discover the laws according to which the phenomena of the real world arise and develop. Hence its difficulties and problems spring up in connection with other points than those which give pause to romanticism. Starting from the actually given, positivism seeks to arrive at the unity of thought and the validity of the ideal, while romanticism travels in the opposite direction. The great thinkers of positivism, therefore, proceeded on the confident conviction that it must be possible to ascend from below ;

while the Romanticists no less confidently assumed the possibility of descending from above. Comparative study must decide which is the better way.

While Germany is the home of romantic philosophy, positivism is a native of France and England. National differences are here characteristically displayed. The English school of thought which had, to a certain extent, come to a conclusion with Hume, now revived, appearing under new forms which, true to the old traditions, retained the realistic stamp by which English philosophy from the Middle Ages onwards had been characterised. Only if we give a very wide interpretation to the term "positivism," however, can it be said to include the main tendency of English philosophy in the nineteenth century. The most important representatives of the latter, indeed, have protested against being called positivists, but they are thinking of positivism in its narrower sense only, according to which it denotes the philosophy of Auguste Comte. It by no means derogates from the importance of the modern English school to represent it as forming the completion and extension of that way of looking at things of which Auguste Comte—who ranks with Descartes and Rousseau as one of the most eminent philosophers of France—had traced the main outline. Such a connection is rendered the more natural by the fact that Comte himself was greatly indebted to the older English school.

It is true that both France and England have in our own century rendered valuable contributions to the development of philosophic thought which cannot be reckoned under the head of positivism, even when this term is taken in its widest sense. But in a general history of philosophy chief weight must be laid on the predominant tendency ; hence I have given the title of Positivism to this section of my book, which deals with the French and English philosophy of the nineteenth century.

CHAPTER I

PHILOSOPHY IN FRANCE DURING THE FIRST DECADE OF THE CENTURY

(a) Revival of the Principle of Authority

THE French Revolution had tried to snap off all connection with the past. The age of the Church and of the old faith was said to form a part of this past. It became evident, however, that the Church had still to be reckoned with as a spiritual power. Leading authors eulogised religion for the services it had rendered to humanity and the poetry which it shed over life ; while in the midst of the violent revolutions which were taking place there were many who sought in the general upheaval for an absolutely fixed point. When the Revolution made visible shipwreck, the ideas of the eighteenth century, as formulated by the French philosophers and their English predecessors, seemed to have played their part. They had not been able—this seemed to have been attested by history —to introduce any fixed order of society ; while the Church, in spite of " syllogism, scaffold and epigram,"—to quote a saying of JOSEPH DE MAISTRE, the most important supporter of the principle of authority (in *Le Pape*, 14th edition, p. 477), —had maintained and renewed itself. In defiance of all that the eighteenth century had thought out and struggled for, a theological school now sought to trace back all order in human life and all understanding of existence to supernatural principles. This school is of more interest for the history of literature than for that of philosophy, and I shall content myself here with indicating a few characteristic features of

de Maistre's chief works, referring my readers for an account of
the whole movement, to GEORG BRANDES' work *Die Reaktion
in Frankreich.*

While modern philosophy, as has been shown in the
preceding sections of this work, based itself on natural
science, making fresh applications of its results, or discussing
its assumptions, de Maistre sought to deprive it of this
support. He denied the possibility of purely physical causal
explanations. That which is material cannot be a cause.
A physical cause is a contradiction in terms.[71] All material
movement is derived from impulses which can only originate
in spiritual beings. In the consciousness of the influence of
our own will we possess a proof that movement originates in
a will. Scientific explanations, *e.g.* the formation of water by
the combination of oxygen and hydrogen, the arising of the
tides through the influence of sun and moon, the influence of
chemical processes on the formation of geological strata, are
declared by de Maistre to be "dogmas" which we do well
to call in question. He is quite willing, however, to allow
scientists the pleasure of occupying themselves within the
sphere of natural science; only let them beware of applying
the conclusions drawn within this sphere to social and religious
relations. It is faith, not science, which must rule men.
God imparts His vital truths not through learned academies, but
through the authorities of Church and State. Prelates, noblemen and high state officials must teach the nations to discern
between true and false within the moral and spiritual spheres.
History has now given us a practical demonstration of the
impotence of human reason to guide men. How few are able
to think aright! And not one is able to think rightly on all
subjects! Hence we must start with authority. Freedom of
discussion should never have been allowed; it has been the
source of all the mischief. It began with the Reformation—
one of the greatest crimes which man has committed against
God! And it was continued in the philosophy of the eighteenth
century—one of the most shameful episodes in the history of
the human mind! The philosophers of the eighteenth century
preached error as religion. And this, not from conviction, but
because they had entered into a conspiracy (*la cabale*) against
the Holiest. Voltaire—that sacrilegious buffoon—posed as a
defender of innocence (although Calas' innocence was never

proved), but in erecting a monument to Locke he displayed at one stroke his fanaticism and his want of patriotism. The only remedy for the present state of things is the recognition of the absolute infallibility of the Pope. Without this it is impossible either to assert the universality of the Church and maintain social peace, or to enforce the sovereignty of the princely power. This is, no doubt, an appeal to a mysterious power, but everything in the social and physical world is mystery. Reason condemns war—yet war prevails throughout Nature, and is a mysterious means to the preservation of life. The hangman is the terror of society—and yet a power which supports society ; take away this incomprehensible social factor and order would give place to chaos. Tradition and authority alone, not human reason, can guide us through the labyrinth of this world's fearful secrets. Nothing more ridiculous, therefore, than the assumption that man has raised himself, step by step, from a state of savagery to one of knowledge and civilisation.

These ideas, which de Maistre expounded chiefly in his *Soirées de St. Pétersbourg,* a series of dialogues which were said to have been written in 1809, but which did not appear till 1821, after his death, are a complete reversal of all that thought, since the days of the Renaissance, had been struggling to build up. Here, as so often, contraries meet. The eighteenth-century philosophers brought neither historic sense nor understanding to the study of the Church and the Middle Ages ; and with the same absence of historic sense and understanding did de Maistre, and those who thought with him, confront the philosophy of the eighteenth century ; the only difference being that wicked philosophers, instead of wicked priests, were now regarded as the source of all evil. The philosophy of the eighteenth century was looked upon as a deliberate conspiracy against authority, as a purely arbitrary process. Hence we need not be surprised to find authority itself conceived as purely arbitrary, imposed from without or from above. This gave rise to a new similarity with the philosophy of the eighteenth century, for if all knowledge is to rest on authority, the independence of the former must be crushed and the free development of its inner possibilities checked. Hence de Maistre, no less than Condillac, is logically committed to the view that man is perfectly passive. Small wonder, therefore, that the theory that man has attained to civilisation by means of a process of natural development seemed to him altogether absurd!

(*b*) *The Psychological School*

The significance of the school we have just been studying lies in its passionate assertion of the value of historical forces in opposition to the psychology of the Enlightenment and of the Revolution, which regarded the heart and reason of each individual as an independent power. But, as now conceived, the principle of authority was an external, blind principle; its inner connection with the life of the soul was not investigated—could not indeed be investigated from this point of view, since all independent value attributed to the inner life of the individual would involve a limitation of the absolute authority. In philosophical matters, therefore (apart from some mystical tendencies, from which it itself shrank back), as already remarked, this school occupied Condillac's standpoint. All the more interesting is it to watch the development out of Condillac's own school, by means of psychological observation and reflection, of a deeper psychology, decidedly opposed both to the philosophy of the French Enlightenment and to the new school which supported authority.

At the outbreak of the Revolution Condillac was victorious. His philosophy became the official philosophy, and his adherents dominated the philosophic section of the National Institute, founded by the Convention. At this philosophic Academy, in the winter of 1797-98 PIERRE JEAN GEORGES CABANIS, a physician, read a series of papers on the relation between body and soul, which were afterwards printed among the Acadamy papers, and later still (1802) were published, with additions in book form, under the title of *Rapports du physique et du moral de l'homme.* Cabanis quotes Condillac with great respect, but he modifies his doctrine on several essential points. Condillac lays stress exclusively on the external senses; from the external world, according to him, man passively receives the whole content and all the forms of his consciousness. Cabanis reproaches him with having overlooked that element in consciousness which corresponds to the organism's own inner condition.

A stream of impressions is constantly being transmitted from the different internal organs to the brain ; moreover, the peculiar state of the brain and nerves themselves must be taken into account.   There is an obscure feeling or sensation, independent of outer sense-impression, which is immediately bound up with the maintenance of life.   This feeling must have been present before the individual was brought, by birth, into relation with the great outer world, from the impressions of which Condillac deduces everything in consciousness.   Cabanis introduced the *vital feeling* into modern psychology, and, in so doing, he at once set a limit to man's passivity in relation to the outer world ; for in the vital feeling the individual possesses an original capital which influences and lends colour and character to all which he afterwards assimilates.   And Cabanis brings instinct into close connection with the vital feeling.   In instinctive actions, too, he finds facts which are incompatible with Condillac's theory.   Instinct presupposes a store of original power which is released through impressions received by way of the inner vital functions, as is shown especially in the instincts of propagation and parental love.   Cabanis attributes such great importance to the concept of instinct that he even hints at the notion that there may be a universal instinct operative in all the processes of Nature ; a notion which has rightly been regarded as a forerunner of Schopenhauer's natural philosophy.   Cabanis, however, had no intention of establishing a philosophical system.   He is concerned with psychology and physiology, not with finding an answer to ultimate questions.   Although one very materialistic passage occurs in his writings (where he says that the brain excretes thoughts as the liver excretes bile), it would be a mistake to regard his work as a contribution to the literature of materialism. His standpoint is indicated in the following passage ; (*Rapports*, xi. 8th édition Peisse, p. 597): "It took a long time before man arrived at recognising that there is only one force in Nature ; perhaps it will take still longer before we adequately realise that since we can compare this force with no other we are not able to form any true idea of its qualities."   In a subsequent work (*Lettres sur les causes premières*) he has given a more precise exposition of his thoughts, which diverges still more widely from materialism than does his *magnum opus.*

Napoleon regarded Condillac's school with little favour. For far from contenting itself with the investigation of sensations and ideas, it busied itself with *ideology* (the name given by DESTUTT DE TRACY, a zealous adherent of Condillac's, to the doctrine of the origin of ideas), and also passed on to discuss, in the spirit of the eighteenth century, theories of morals and of law. Napoleon ascribed all the mischief in France to the ideologists ; he would, no doubt, have preferred to think for France as he had already acted for her. He suppressed the *Académie des sciences morales et politiques*, founded by the Convention ; and works treating freely of philosophical matters were no longer allowed to be published in France. Destutt de Tracy was obliged to have his commentary on Montesquieu published anonymously in America, in an English translation. The ideologists withdrew into small groups. A circle of young men interested in philosophical studies gathered round Cabanis and Destutt de Tracy at Auteuil. MAINE DE BIRAN (born 1766, died 1824), the most important psychologist of this century in France, proceeded from this group.

Biran occupied administrative posts during the Revolution, the Empire, and the Restoration, and was a member of the Legislative Assembly. But his mind was not occupied with the great external events of his time. He was a good patriot, but he had neither the tastes nor the abilities requisite for a public career. The effect on him of the great historical drama was but to heighten his natural emotions — emotions which he early began to observe with the interest of a theorist, coupled with a deep longing after inner peace and harmony. His organisation was of such a nature that the relation between the passive and active, the involuntary and the voluntary, or as he himself has strikingly put it, between temperament and character, presented to him throughout his whole life a theoretical and practical problem. This is evidenced by his *Journal Intime*, the most remarkable of his posthumous works (published by E. NAVILLE in his work, *Maine de Biran. Sa vie et ses pensées*, 1857), which contains notes, written at the beginning and middle as well as at the end of his life. How early and how emphatically his peculiar problem presented itself to him may be gathered from a passage written while he was still a disciple of Condillac (May 27, 1894). "What is, strictly speaking, this so-called "psychical activity"? In my experience the state of the soul is always determined by this

or that state of the body. . . . If I could ever write a
continuous work, I should like to inquire in what degree the
soul is active, and to what extent it is able to modify external
impressions, to increase or diminish their strength according to
the amount of attention bestowed on them—in short, to prove
how far this attention is supreme. . . . It is much to be desired
that some man, well-skilled in introspection, should analyse the
will, as Condillac has analysed the understanding." He com-
plains at the same time of the unceasing changes and flux
of his inner states (*cette révolution perpétuelle, cette roue toujours
mobile de l'existence*) which prevent any one frame of mind
becoming permanent, and produce doubt and disquiet even
with regard to that which with all honesty of purpose he seeks
to hold fast.

In his earlier works Biran followed Condillac's and Cabanis'
teaching ; gradually, however, he laid increasing weight on the
activity of which, in his view, we are immediately conscious
when we exert our wills. "The ego makes itself known, by
means of the inner sense, through the exertion or movement
of the will, which the soul within itself apperceives as a
product of its activity, as an effect produced by its will
(*Rapports du physique et du moral de l'homme. Œuvres philos.*
1841, iv. p. 75). Biran here discovers an original fact which
destroys Condillac's theory of passivity. But he does not
lose sight—that is prevented by constantly repeated inner
experiences—of the sensations and moods which arise involuntarily. He finds fault with the moralists who occupy themselves with the problem of happiness for relying entirely on
general reflections and postulates, and believing that we can
immediately govern our feelings and inclinations. There exists
within us, altogether independent of our conscious will, a host
of changing phenomena which the ego encounters when it
becomes conscious of itself ; these phenomena must proceed
from some inner cause other than the ego. Outside the ego or
consciousness, then, and out of all relation to the outer world
is a series of inner phenomena, which may be discovered by
self-observation, but which exists independently of it (*Journal
Intime*, October 24, 1814). This theory of sensations existing
outside the ego excited great attention and a good deal of
opposition in the little philosophical company which Biran had
gathered round himself in Paris, in whose discussions such

men as the physicist Ampère, the historian Guizot, and the philosopher Royer Collard took part. Ampère was the only one who decidedly adopted Biran's views. Both men regarded the immediate consciousness (*apperception immédiate*) of the energy of the will as the central fact of psychology. But all around the centre the soul fades away into the unconscious, and when an act of self-consciousness takes place the ego finds a whole series of given elements, or at any rate it hears their echo. So it is in awakening from deep sleep, or on reflection on customary conditions. In a hitherto unprinted *Mémoire sur les perceptions obscures* (1807) which was unearthed by ALEXIS BERTRAND (*La psychologie de l'effort et les doctrines contemporaines*, chap. ii.), Biran attempts a physiological explanation of this contrast between the passive and the active sides of the psychical life by bringing forward an hypothesis of different co-operating nerve-centres. He also uses the phenomena of somnambulism to illustrate the duality we find within us. In virtue of his zealous insistence on the necessity of accurate self-observation and of supplementing self-observation by other sources of psychological knowledge, Biran ranks as a forerunner of modern psychology. With such a psychological standpoint he could not but be distinctly opposed to those who supported the principle of authority, and who attributed no importance to the free self-activity of man. Only by deep study of the nature and the laws of psychical life, Biran maintained, can we discover the points at which moral and religious relations have their origin. The advocates of authority, who entirely ignored the individual nature of the soul and appealed to authority, appearing *ex abrupto*, as the foundation of all knowledge, were deficient in love of truth, and let themselves be led astray by practical needs and the desire to influence men. By regarding the soul as purely passive, and supposing its whole direction to be determined by authority, they gave themselves over to scepticism and materialism (*Journal Intime*, 25 juillet 1823)!

In the immediate consciousness of self-activity Biran finds the primitive and fundamental principle of all our knowledge. Through it not only does our own ego testify of itself, but, since this self-activity encounters resistance, we become conscious of the existence of the material world. For the self-activity of which we are conscious is for the most part the working of the soul on the organism, where there is always a certain resistance to be overcome. Thus Biran gives a spiritualistic interpretation of the consciousness of our self-activity and the obstacles it has to encounter, and in so doing he also arrives at an explanation of the antithesis between our own will and the involuntary element in our inner states. He does not, however, adopt the Cartesian doctrine of the soul as substance; we know the ego only as a power which works; there can be no immediate consciousness of substance. The force or activity which we thus feel within ourselves serves as a type to which we refer all external phenomena. It is from self-consciousness that we learn to know the concepts force, cause, unity, identity; and it is only because we are able to deduce these concepts—which are very different from concepts of quality— from this primary, inner *factum* that we are able to apply them to the phenomena of experience. Neither external perception nor authority but the immediate consciousness of our self-activity is the foundation of all our knowledge. As regards the reality of this foundation Biran entertained no doubt, but modern psychologists will hardly admit that he has met Hume's objections to the possibility of an immediate perception of causality.[72]

Biran's most important works were not published until long after his death. He was engaged for some time on a large work which was to sum up all his psychological studies (*Essai sur les fondements de la psychologie*); political affairs, however, prevented him from getting it ready for press, and he afterwards laid the sketch he had drawn up aside to work at a new volume of essays (*Nouveaux Essais d'Anthropologie*). Both works were published in 1859 by NAVILLE (*Œuvres inédites de M. de Biran*). The reason why Biran threw aside his original sketch in his later years was that he had come upon a still deeper mental stratum than any which his previous introspective studies had revealed to him. Up till now he had limited himself to descriptions of the currents which, starting in feeling, overspread the whole inner life, and, in contrast to them, the consciousness of the energy with which the ego seeks to raise itself above the passive and involuntary. In this consciousness of energy he had, after the fashion of the Stoics, found a refuge alike from outer and inner disturbances. In the end, however, this refuge did not avail him. It offered him no adequate

protection from the unrest of the inner and outer worlds. It
aroused in him the need of gaining an absolutely fixed point of
support, of surrendering to something higher and greater than
the moods created by the vital feeling, to something which,
while independent of the soul's own imperfect activity, should
yet proceed from within, not from without. He uses Kant's
distinction between noümena and phenomena, and seeks to
find his fixed standpoint in relation to a something which lies
beyond all phenomena. At this juncture he took refuge in
the fundamental thoughts of religious mysticism, which
he had discovered for himself from his own experience ;
he began to study the Gospel of St. John, the *De Imitatione*,
and the works of Fénelon, instead of Descartes and Leibniz, with
whom, alternately with Condillac and Cabanis, he had previously occupied his time. Biran's religion never shaped itself in
accordance with any definite creed. He was unwavering in his
conviction that religious feeling cannot be produced from without;
it must arise involuntarily; and equally involuntarily arise, under
its influences, those images in which the soul finds expressed
the ideas of the eternal and infinite. Religion is feeling rather
than faith : faith is subordinate to feeling. The task set to our
spiritual activity here is that of preparing a sensibility for the
higher life, for the real spiritual life, *la vie de l'esprit*, in antithesis to the active life in will and in reason, *la vie humaine*,
which in its turn is opposed to the streams of vital feeling, *la
vie animale*. Biran also calls this higher life " the mystical
life of enthusiasm," " the highest stadium which the human soul
can reach, since in it, as far as it is in her power, she makes
herself one with her highest object, and in so doing returns to
the source in which she had her origin " (*Œuvres inédites*, iii.
pp. 541, 571).

It is evident, however, from Biran's diary that his passion
for psychological observation and reflection was not diminished
by his transition to mysticism. Again and again he discusses
the question as to how far the causal explanations of psychology
can account for our innermost and highest states. Sometimes
he says that those who seek to explain everything through natural
causes must sometimes find themselves face to face with the
question : may it not be possible to explain the highest state of
blessed rest and contemplation itself, when the soul is in a state
of ecstasy and is immediately conscious of divine influences, as

a result of the activity of the organic dispositions?—in which case this heavenly blessedness must give place to unrest and tumult as soon as the organic condition changes. Sometimes he talks as if it were certainly known that the idea or feeling which the soul has of the perfect, great, beautiful and eternal cannot originate with itself; moral and religious truths have a source other than that of psychological truths (*Journal Intime*, August 26, 1818, and September 19, 1818). On the last pages of the diary we find, once again, a detailed investigation of the question as to how our own psychical activities of thinking and of concentrating the feelings can, by means of the continual interaction between the active and passive within us, prepare the way for that higher surrender ; and he then goes on to ask how it is possible to distinguish between that which, as a result of such concentration, springs up out of the soul's own soil, and that which is due to the influence of Divine powers. Biran never gets beyond a *soit—soit*, strongly as he feels the necessity of holding fast to the belief that if we seek to pierce to the heart of truth, truth will also seek to pierce our hearts (*Journal Intime*, October 1823).

Previous to the publication (for the most part long after his death) of his writings, Maine de Biran's works were known to few. Among these few the foremost is ANDRÉ-MARIE AMPÈRE, the famous physicist (born 1775, died 1836). Ampère kept up a lively intercourse with Biran both by word of mouth and in writing; he agreed with him in regarding the immediate consciousness of the energy of the ego as the starting-point of philosophy. Ampère acknowledged his friend's priority on this point; but while Biran never ceased to circle round it throughout his whole life, Ampère attempted to supply a complete psychological and epistemological theory. He was much occupied with philosophical studies, and gave lectures on philosophy as well as on natural science and mathematics. Örsted's discovery of electro-magnetism incited him to undertake that brilliant series of investigations which have made his name famous ; but he never forsook his old love, and in his later years occupied himself with studies connected with the encyclopædia and the classification of the sciences, as a result of which appeared his *Essai sur la philosophie des sciences* (vol. i. 1834, vol. ii. with introduction by Ste. Beuve and Littré, 1543), a work which contains several of his most interesting reflections on psychology and philosophy. His correspondence with Biran and some fragments of a treatise, with an introduction by his son, were afterwards published under the title : *Philosophie des deux Ampère*, by BARTHÉLEMY ST. HILAIRE (Paris, 1866). (There is very little of the son's philosophy in the book, however.)

Ampère's relation, quâ philosopher, to Biran was very much the same as his relation, quâ physicist, to Örsted. He surmised Örsted's discovery to be a single example of a general law, and he succeeded in developing this law mathematically, and proving it experimentally. Electro-magnetism was extended by him to a theory of electro-dynamics. The influence of the electric current on the magnetic needle occasioned his discovery of the reciprocal influence of electric streams on one another, and of the influence of the earth on electric currents. Biran's study of the relation between the active and passive sides of consciousness led Ampère to undertake two lines of investigation ; on the one hand he investigated how our sensations and ideas are involuntarily associated before and independently of any conscious activity, and on the other, he inquired how the scientific knowledge of the world, based on the conscious use of its faculties by the mind, is possible. The former investigation resulted in valuable contributions to the psychological doctrine of the association of ideas, the latter in contributions to the theory of knowledge.

Ampère adopts, as his psychological method, that of the English associationists. Unlike Biran and most of the other French psychologists, he is not content with mere description, but endeavours to *explain* the origin of complex conscious phenomena through the blending and association of simpler elements. A blending (*concrétion*) takes place, *e.g.* between a sensation of colour and a sensation of resistance, and these become so intimately associated that we are inclined to mistake such composite associations for simple and primitive sensations. It is only by means of analysis that we discover that a blending has taken place, and that our own involuntary activity and the obstacles it encounters have played an essential part in it. We have another example of *concrétion* in recognition, where the present perception of an object is blended with the reproduction of a previous perception. Through the same process Ampère also explains the fact that if, during the production of an opera, a spectator has the text before him, he can actually *hear* the words, while if he has not the text, he cannot hear them. The words read and sounds heard blend immediately together.[78] It is such explanations as these, as Ste. Beuve testified, which made Ampère's psychological lectures so attractive.

Within the immediate consciousness of the activity of the self, which Ampère and Biran agree in regarding as the fundamental fact, Ampère makes a distinction which would never have been recognised by Biran. He distinguishes between self-consciousness (*autopsie*, later, *émesthèse*) and muscular sensation, pointing out that we can experience the latter when another person moves our leg or arm. In our own movement self-consciousness is the phenomenon which contains the cause, muscular sensation the phenomenon in which the effect appears. Just because muscular sensation can be produced by another I discover that in certain cases I myself am the cause of it. In this experience the causal relation becomes clear to me. I only get it immediately given in my own activity, and I therefore conceive all other activity in analogy with this. In co-operation with immediate consciousness (beyond which Biran did not go), there works, according to Ampère, the faculty of apprehending relations, the faculty of knowledge proper. By means of this faculty we apprehend the relation between cause and effect, between positions in space and time, etc. It is only by means of this faculty that we are able to know more than mere phenomena. Firmly convinced as Ampère is that everything which appears to us is phenomenon only, yet he is equally convinced that the relations (*rapports, relations*) which hold between phenomena and which are not dependent on the qualitative nature of phenomena possess absolute (noümenal) validity. Concepts of mere quality, gained by means of comparison and abstraction, possess no higher validity than that of the sense-qualities which form their content. Those concepts, however, which express pure relations and kinds of co-ordination, such as causality, number, time and space are absolutely valid, and form the bridge by means of which our knowledge passes from the world of phenomena to that of noümena. On this point Ampère declares himself decidedly opposed to Kant, whom he otherwise greatly admires. Nor is he less decidedly opposed to Reid, who assumes an immediate perception of external reality, and in so doing, according to Ampère, confuses a "concretion" with an elementary sensation. We can discover noümenal reality (matter-in-itself as cause of sense-impressions, the soul-in-itself as cause of our own actions, God as cause of all things) by way of inference only, and under the form of hypothesis. We can only apprehend phenomena immediately ; but the non-qualitative relations we discern between phenomena are valid of noümena also. By "relations" Ampère means very much the same as that which Boyle and Locke called "primary qualities."

Biran had at first been inclined to endorse Reid's view on this point. When his philosophic friend besought him to study Kant, he became more of a Kantian than Ampère had bargained for. Against Ampère's theory of relations he asserted (in a conversation quoted in the *Journal Intime*, October 30, 1816) that there were great difficulties involved in effecting the transition from the consciousness of our own activity (the fundamental fact for both Biran and Ampère) to the existence of external causes. In Biran's opinion, we here come upon a gulf which no analysis nor induction can bridge over. From the fact that I am not the cause of the passive states of my ego it cannot be inferred that there is necessarily a cause which produces everything which I do not produce myself. We ourselves are causes, hence it comes quite natural to us to conceive other things as causes ; but this is no proof. When Ampère implies that the absolute validity of relations is proved by the fact that all the conclusions which we draw from our theory of relations are confirmed by experience, Biran answers (in a letter hitherto unpublished, but quoted by A. Bertrand : *La psychol. de l'effort*, p. 188) : "What experience can teach us whether the forms in which phenomena are co-ordinated are absolute, *i.e.* in the things, or whether they are only in the mind which apprehends them ? Can external experience ever shed any light on this question which reflection must raise ? Do not both possibilities fit in equally well with phenomena ? " Ampère's theory of relations would hardly have provided him with any satisfactory answer here.[74]

In his world-conception Ampère is a Cartesian. He divides the sciences into cosmological and noological, the first of which includes the material, the latter the mental, sciences. The noological sciences must not be studied till after the cosmological, for the latter show us the use of the human faculties in acquiring a

knowledge of the world, and in so doing, shed a light on the nature
of the faculties themselves ; they also give us a knowledge of
the world, especially of the physical nature of man, which is of
importance for the understanding of his intellectual and moral
faculties. Ampère's classification of the sciences, when worked
out in detail, becomes very involved, and cannot be compared
for simplicity and clearness with that of Auguste Comte, which
appeared almost at the same time. But his *Essai sur la philosophie des sciences* contains many interesting observations, and
had he been able to carry out his wish and give not only a
classification but also a presentation of the most important
truths, methods, problems, and hypotheses occurring in the
different spheres of thought there can be no doubt that so
eminent a thinker and investigator would have given us both
an able work and an interesting counterpoise to the system of
Comte. Almost contemporaneously with Ampère and Comte,
SOPHIE GERMAIN (born 1776, died 1831), a mathematician,
was engaged in studying the course of development followed
by the sciences in connection with the criterion of truth given
in the nature of human knowledge. Kant's influence is very
obvious. She points out that the nature of our consciousness causes us to feel a need of unity, order, and interconnection ; a need which guides us not only in scientific
investigations, but also in the moral and æsthetic spheres.
Her philosophical work : *Considérations générales sur l'état des
sciences et des lettres aux différentes époques de leur culture*
(published 1833, and again in 1879 by H. Stupuy in his
Œuvres philosophiques de Sophie Germain) is an attempt to show
that one and the same type guides us alike in science, in
morality, and in art. "There is only a single type of the true.
Alike in morals, science, literature and art we seek for unity,
order and proportion between the parts of one and the same
totality." The causal principle is only a special form of this
general principle. We apply the causal principle when we
do not see the object under investigation in its totality. It
appears to us as a fragment, and we ask, what unity embraces
it ? We see it as a part, and seek the whole to which it
belongs. This need of unity and wholeness has led to bold
systems, to the arbitrary use of analysis, and to the assumption
of mystical causes. But it has also led to many happy ideas,
and the sciences progress in proportion to the keenness with

which it is felt. On it depends the unity of the history of science. Gradually, however, man learns to substitute methods for systems, and to ask *how*, and *how much*, in place of *why*. Instead of constructing the world according to the caprices of his imagination, he learns to discern the interconnection which actually obtains within it, and when, in this way, he gradually arrives at finding one great unity running through all things his imagination will regain, in a more secure form, all that it lost when its daring pictures were crowded out by critical investigation.

While the studies of Biran and Ampère were forging a chain of philosophical thought which was destined to lead out beyond the prevailing Condillacism, the latter was deposed from the place it had occupied in philosophical education by Royer Collard and Cousin. ROYER COLLARD'S lectures at the Sorbonne (1811-14) introduced Reid as a philosophical classic in France. Collard laid great stress on psychological inquiry in the direction followed by the Scotch school, and brought into prominence the importance of instinctive perception and immediate moral conviction in opposition to the narrow views and abstract analysis of the ideologists. This new departure was not favourable to a clear-cut statement of problems ; an appeal to common sense only too often took the place of argument. A new direction of thought, however, was thus initiated, and men's eyes were opened to a side of mental life which had been left in the background by the hitherto reigning school. Royer Collard's striking personality lent special weight to his appearance as a philosopher. His successor, COUSIN (born 1792, died 1867), was an enthusiastic orator with a great talent for exciting the interest of the young. Still a youth himself, he shared the expectation of youth that with a free constitution, and after the fall of the military despotism, France would see the dawn of a brilliant intellectual age. His teaching was distinctly historical in character. He introduced the study of the history of philosophy into the French academic course. He had acquired his own philosophical ideas partly from the Scotch school and Royer Collard, partly from Biran and Ampère, in whose philosophical conferences he used to take part. Biran was aware, of course, that Cousin " poached on his preserves," but he expected to gain his share of the spoil, since Cousin's teaching would prepare a good reception for his own great psychological work when it appeared (which unfortunately did not take place till thirty-one years after Biran's death). Cousin combines Reid's theory of the immediate apprehension of absolute reality with Biran's doctrine of the consciousness of our own self-activity and with Ampère's doctrine of absolute relations; to these he subsequently added Schelling's and Hegel's doctrine of absolute reason. He had become acquainted with German speculative philosophy while travelling in Germany, after having gathered a general impression of the post-Kantian philosophy from MADAME DE STAËL'S *De l'Allemagne*. Cousin's philosophy was an eclecticism which borrowed from the different systems all that it supposed to be of lasting value ; each system in itself is imperfect, but none of them are entirely false. In making a choice from among them Cousin's criterion, in the first instance, while under the influence of Reid and Biran, was " psychological perception " ; afterwards it was the " universal reason " of Schelling and Hegel ; later still, during the latter part of his career—when, after the revolution of 1830, he had become the official leader of all philosophical instruction in France—it was the leading doctrines of natural religion and of the Cartesian spiritualism. The boldness and enthusiasm which characterised him on his first appearance [75] as a teacher of philosophy were damped by his historical studies and his official position. Renan, who long after Cousin's death expressed his indebtedness to him in the warmest terms, nevertheless quotes him as a striking illustration of the fact that it is not advantageous to philosophy to win too complete a victory. It must be added, however, that the victory was only an external one. Napoleon had welcomed Royer Collard with joy ; the July monarchy overthrew Cousin.

Cousin's most important work is : *Du vrai, du beau, du bien*, lectures delivered in 1818, and which were published twenty years later in their original form by Garnier, but were " bowdlerised " in subsequent editions by Cousin himself, to whom the unorthodoxies of his youth had become inconvenient. This was the work which had so great an effect on Renan. Cousin's ideas may also be gathered from the prefaces to the five volumes of the *Fragments philosophiques* in which he treats subjects taken from the history of philosophy. In the

preface to the first volume (1826) he states his characteristic
doctrine of the impersonal reason, in which he combines the
teaching of Reid, Ampère and Schelling. By the help of the
psychological method and by means of a more profound introspection he believed himself to have reached a point to which
even Kant had not penetrated ; a point at which the seeming
subjectivity and relativity of necessary principles disappear
and an involuntary apprehension of the truth as the foundation of all logical reflection and all positing of necessary
concepts is revealed. It is only when reason is made an
object of reflection that it becomes subjective ; in itself it is a
light which, independently of all personal differences, burns—
a universal revelation—in the breast of every man.

Cousin professed to build on psychological observation,
but he soon soared beyond it, borne aloft on the wings of
rhetoric and fancy. Not so THÉODORE JOUFFROY (1796-
1842), whose interest in psychological investigation was
stronger and more constant. It is true he over-estimated
the claims of introspection, neglecting other sources of psychological knowledge and distinguishing in strictly spiritualistic
fashion between psychology and physiology as two distinct
branches of inquiry having nothing to do with one another.
It was, however, his serious intention—this is proved by a
whole series of investigations—to come to a clear understanding
as to the relation between self-observation on the one hand and
natural science and philosophical speculation on the other.
He did not display any of Cousin's romantic virtuosity in
building bridges over chasms. His philosophy sprang out of
his strictly personal need for clearness of knowledge for, after
a hard struggle, he had realised that theological ideas had no
longer any value for him. But although his thought betrays
strong personal interest, this interest did not cheat him
into reducing his claims, or accepting solutions which did not
fully satisfy him intellectually. He preferred to pause at
the knowledge that the solution of a problem was unattainable. " There are two ways " he says in one of his lectures
(*Mélanges philosophiques*, 3rd ed. p. 350, f.) in which the
thinking man can win peace for his soul and rest for his
spirit ; the one is to possess or to believe he possesses the
truth respecting the questions which interest humanity, the
other is to perceive clearly that this truth is unattainable, and

to know why it is so. . . . Since the facts which we are able to observe are limited, the conclusions which we can draw from them must also be limited. Science, then, has its horizon, beyond which it cannot see ; its task is gradually to determine this horizon. At this extreme limit of its kingdom it must bid adieu to poetry, who must fare further alone. It owes this parting as a duty to mankind, towards whom it is under the obligation of discovering the truth. Mankind has only too often suffered from hoping and seeking for the truth where it is inaccessible and must always remain so.—Jouffroy appears as a beautiful and attractive figure in the history of French philosophy in virtue of the manliness with which he addressed himself to problems rather than to his treatment of them in detail. In so far as he indicates any definite results they are in the direction of the eclecticism founded by Cousin. In a treatise written at the age of twenty-nine he expresses great hopes for the future of French philosophy. Now that it has ceased to swear by Condillac, it seeks for truth on all sides and is engrossed in the study of human nature which is the philosophical reality. Why should it not succeed in working quietly towards a treaty of peace between all systems?—a treaty which may perhaps be concluded in Paris ! Truth has habitations, however, of which eclecticism knows nothing, and human nature is too comprehensive to be enclosed in any eclectic scheme, even in one so honestly worked out as Théodore Jouffroy's. It will be long before we arrive at a treaty of peace in philosophy.

(c) *The Socialistic School*

DAMIRON, a pupil of Cousin's, published in 1828 a work on French philosophy in the nineteenth century, in which he represented eclecticism as the higher unity or the right mean between Condillac's school on the one hand and the theological school on the other. Biran's and Ampère's valuable and original contributions to thought had not yet seen the light. In his second edition (which appeared in the same year), however, Damiron found himself obliged to notice the ideas which had been brought forward by Saint - Simon and Auguste Comte, although he confesses that he cannot clearly understand their significance. At that time Comte's early writings only had appeared. On the other hand, Saint-Simon had run his course. The seed was sown from which modern socialism and positivism were to spring.

SAINT-SIMON (whose full name was Claude Henri de Rouvroy, Comte de Saint-Simon) was a journalist and social reformer, rather than a philosopher. He is of importance for the history of philosophy, however, because he entertained a lively conviction that a new order of society would only be possible when a new world - conception had won general acceptance. And this new world-conception, he is no less convinced, can only be constructed on the basis of positive science. Saint-Simon, himself, had not received a scientific education. As a young man (he was born in 1768) he took part with conspicuous bravery in the North American War of Independence : afterwards he threw himself into industrial undertakings ; deprived during the Revolution of his rank as a nobleman he began to speculate in national estates and appeared as a " grand seigneur sansculotte." During the Terror he was put in prison, from which the fall of Robespierre brought him release. He used his riches (so long as he had them) not only to live in great state, but also to prepare the scientific and social reform of which he already dreamed. He surrounded himself with scientific men from the Polytechnic and the medical school in order to fit himself for writing an encyclopædia of the sciences. When overtaken by poverty he never for a moment relinquished his schemes ; on the contrary he laboured at them with increase of zeal. He possessed a remarkable gift for drawing eminent men around him, and for inducing them to work with and for him. Augustin Thierry and Auguste Comte were both for a time his secretaries and co-workers, and were proud to call themselves his pupils until their ways parted. While in his earlier period Saint-Simon had regarded the creation of a new encyclopædia as of the foremost importance, because without such a foundation a new catechism could not be drawn up, after the revolutions of 1814-15, he believed it possible to pass directly to a new organisation of human society. The chief feature of this new organisation was the prominence to be given to industrial and economic relations : the system of government proper was to be subordinated to these. Instead of noblemen and lawyers, the heads of large businesses and scientific men were to take the lead in society. The ultimate aim was to be the raising, intellectually and economically, of the working class, the class which suffered most. While after the Restoration in France men lost sight of everything else in constitutional and parliamentary struggles, Saint-Simon maintained the pressing need of a social regeneration. The external form of government is a matter of indifference, in any case a government is only a necessary evil. The guiding principle on which the new order was to be based was first conceived by Saint-Simon as the insight into the harmony of interests, very much as this was conceived by Helvétius, and after him by Bentham. But in his last years he appealed to philanthropy, and wanted to found a new Christianity, in which the law of love should reign supreme, but which should differ from the old Christianity by allowing full scope to this present life, instead of merely regarding it as a means to a supersensuous existence. The right of individual property, in his view, finds its only ground in the advantages which this institution offers to the community at large, not in the claims of the individual as such. The time has now come to form an alliance for the purpose of exploiting the earth. " Things, not men, must be governed," as his pupils afterwards expressed it ; instead of mutually exploiting one another, men must exploit the globe. The State must unite human forces for great works such as canal- and road-making, drainage, and cultivation of the soil. Saint-Simon died in 1825, surrounded by a little band of disciples.

As in his political programme Saint-Simon was opposed to both the conflicting parties of his time, to the Liberals as well as to the Legitimists, so too within the world of ideas he was opposed both to the theological school and to the philosophy of the eighteenth century. His conception and estimate of the Middle Ages, as far back as in his works of 1807 and 1813, are of significance in this respect. He regarded the Middle Ages as a great period of organisation ; the civilised world was held together by brotherliness and common faith. The priests were not charlatans, as Voltaire thought, but the most advanced section of the nation. Since the mediæval system fell a victim to criticism and to the Revolution, we have lived in a spiritual and social chaos ; negation and egoism flourish. A second period of organisation must now be at hand, and the spiritual power which alone is able to inaugurate such a period is positive science.   Hence the necessity for systematising the sciences.   Saint-Simon's friend, the physician BURDIN, in a conversation with the former, expressed ideas on the development of the sciences which were adopted by Saint-Simon, and which are interesting as anticipations of positivism.   All the sciences, Saint-Simon maintains, rested in their infancy on a small number of experiences ; hence during their first period they bear the character of conjectures, often of fantastical conjectures.   Astronomy began as astrology, chemistry as alchemy.   With a gradually progressive experience the sciences pass from a conjectural to a positive form.   Mathematics, astronomy, physics and chemistry have already reached this positive form : physiology and psychology are near it.   Lastly, philosophy too will become a positive science ; it is owing to the imperfect state of the particular sciences that the distance is still so great between the universal science and the special sciences.   It was on this conception of the history of the sciences that Saint-Simon built his hopes of a new world-conception resting on a purely scientific basis.   He was the first to use the expression *positive philosophy*.   Further than this general idea, however, Saint-Simon never progressed.   He was not the sort of man to produce a long consecutive work.   Nevertheless, he represents a decided turning-point.   By his recognition of the Middle Ages as an especial period of culture he betrayed an historic sense which up till the time of his appearance was rare.   And it was this which enabled him to conceive history as a continuous process of development.   While the Enlightenment had regarded the Middle Ages as an arbitrary interruption of development, it was now recognised as having been a period of spiritual and social organisation following on a period of dissolution.   The tables were turned, and now it was the age following on the Middle Ages which was regarded as a period of dissolution.   Criticism and liberalism are, in Saint-Simon's eyes, only means for getting rid of a worn-out system ; they are not themselves a new system.   A new system had now to be developed, and in Saint-Simon's opinion it could only be erected on the basis of empirical science.   A time must come when men will ground their faith and their morality on experience and science. In this way only can a new conception of existence-as-a-whole arise, around which all can gather and life be once more carried on with united forces.

This doctrine of Saint-Simon's was generalised by his school, who distinguished between critical and organic periods throughout the history of the world.   In Kant and Fichte, even indeed in Rousseau, a similar antithesis is to be found. It was only natural that such a conception should prevail in an age which had seen an old order both of faith and of society overthrown by a criticism which had the power neither to produce a new order nor to wipe out the need for such an order.   However much of a charlatan Saint-Simon may have been, it is certain that he possessed true historical insight on certain points, and that he was keenly aware of the spiritual and social needs of his time.   Hence we need not be surprised at his having numbered a great historian and a great philosopher among his disciples.

In Saint-Simon we find the germ of socialism only.   This germ was developed by his disciples,[76] who transformed his doctrine to such a degree that he himself would not have recognised it.   They wished to limit the right of inheritance, and to transfer to the State the task of dividing the produce of labour according to every man's capacity and labour.   The school acquired a more and more visionary and utopian character ; a new hierarchy was instituted with "Father" ENFANTIN at its head ; the school broke up, however, when Enfantin was tried and imprisoned for his directions to the faithful with regard to sexual relations.   From these latter extravagances the representatives of the more reflective and critical elements had recoiled.   The enthusiasm which had bound the Saint-Simonists together—enthusiasm for the end, *i.e.* the acquisition of complete mastery over Nature through the co-operation of human powers—was not without fruit however. A great part of the railways, canals, factories and banks in France owe their origin to *ci-devant* Saint-Simonists.   The intersection of the isthmuses of Suez and Panama was a Saint-Simonistic idea.   The pupils of the Polytechnic school were especially enthusiastic in their reception of the new doctrine. This school, founded by the Convention, was the home of those sciences which, according to Burdin and Saint-Simon, had already become positive, and whose vocation it was to form the foundation of the future faith.   Positive philosophy became the philosophy of the Polytechnic school, while eclecticism was predominant at the *École normale* (where teachers of the higher educational establishments were trained). The real founder of positivism, Auguste Comte, himself a student at the Polytechnic, alludes in a letter *(Lettres à Valat,* p. 339) to the secret but inevitable struggle between the *Normaliens* and the *Polytechniciens,* which he regarded as a special form of the struggle between the metaphysical and positivist schools. The most important contribution rendered by France to the history of philosophy in the nineteenth century was to come from the *Polytechniciens.*

CHAPTER II

AUGUSTE COMTE

(a) *Biography and Characteristics*

THE origin of modern positivism is conditioned by the development of the empirical sciences during the last century, and, more especially, by the enormous progress within the spheres of chemistry and physiology ushered in by the French scientists at the close of the last and beginning of this century. All spheres of Nature were being gradually brought under the scientific principles and methods which Kepler, Galilei and Newton had established. The work which the founders of modern natural science had performed within the spheres of astronomy and physics was extended by LAVOISIER and BICHAT to the spheres of chemistry and physiology. The question for us is : What is the significance of the whole development for our conception of life and of the world ? The answer given by Positivism runs : Is it only scientific specialists and industrial entrepreneurs that are to profit by the progress of science ? Must not, on the contrary, a modification of the whole spiritual life of man, of human faith and conduct, result from this subjugation of all spheres of Nature to empirical science ? There lies in the human mind an involuntary need to apply the same methods and the same theory everywhere. Since we have now gained a comprehension of Nature by explaining its phenomena according to the laws discovered in experience, are we not in a position to base our faith and manner of life and conduct on an entirely new foundation ? As a matter of fact, we find that the empirical sciences always do exercise a determining influence on men's religious and speculative ideas, however strongly it may be asserted that these latter have an entirely different

source.   A certain degree of positivism is found in every
world-conception.   But now that all spheres of Nature have been
brought under the sway of *positive science*, *i.e.* that knowledge
which rests on facts and on the laws of these facts as discovered
by experience, the moment seems to have arrived when its
influence must no longer be concealed and suppressed.   The
time has come for men to select with conscious and deliberate
choice such ideas only as positive science can acknowledge
and confirm when constructing their conceptions of life and of
the world.   It is true that there is as yet no positive science
of the inner life of man ; it remains for positivism to found
such a science.   If it succeed in this, what obstacle is there to
carrying out the programme of positivism ?—The task which
Auguste Comte took upon himself was a double one: firstly,
to make mental science a positive science ; secondly, to give a
systematic presentation of the main facts, laws and methods of
all the positive sciences.   The basis of the world-conception
of the future would thus be laid.   The age of theology and of
speculation is gone by ; positive philosophy is the only salva-
tion.   Men will gradually leave off asking questions to which
positive science can furnish no answer.

There remains a distinction, however, between positive
science and positive *philosophy*.   For particular, isolated facts
are no more able to determine a world-conception than are
special laws.   The human mind, as Comte expressly asserts,
demands unity of method and of doctrine.   Hence positive
philosophy can only arise when the particular, positive sciences
are elaborated into one whole.   It is thus a question of
uniting positivity with generality or totality.   Positivism cannot
use the immediately given as it lies before it, but must subject
it to an elaboration, and form it into a whole.   Here positivism
encounters a difficulty, for such an elaboration cannot be
effected except by the help of hypotheses and assumptions,—but
on what grounds can we establish our right to make use of these?

Auguste Comte's philosophical ancestry may be traced back
to the eighteenth century.   He makes special mention of Diderot,
Hume, Kant and the Scotch School.   But he also admires de
Maistre, and regards the Middle Ages as the last *organic* period
we have had.   He is convinced that only by the consistent
application of positivism within the spheres of faith and conduct
can we hope to regain that unity and harmony of spiritual

and social life which modern criticism and the revolution have destroyed. Enthusiasm for positive thought is accompanied, in Comte, by a fervent, we may say mystical, love of humanity ;—an emotional need which made such energetic demands for satisfaction that it several times threatened to destroy his sanity. The founder of positivism felt himself spiritually akin to the mystics of the Middle Ages. At the end of his life he even wanted to found a new religion, which was to be positive in another sense than that which is generally understood by " positive religion."

The life of AUGUSTE COMTE shows us how the different *motifs* which appear in his work developed in his mind. He was born at Montpellier, on January 19, 1798, of a strict Catholic family. He tells us (*Cours de philosophie positive*, Tome vi. Préface personelle) that he was scarcely fourteen years old when he " went through all the necessary stages of the revolutionary tendency, and felt the necessity of a general political and religious re-birth." Perhaps it was owing to this precocious development, which carried him too rapidly beyond the ideas natural to childhood, that in his later years, after he had spent all his best strength in his philosophical work, he felt so keenly the necessity of having sharply-defined dogmas and definite symbols. The period of seeking was a short one with him, and the experience he gathered was not sufficient to show him the value that such a period may have for the freedom, depth and fulness of personal life. Like most of his contemporaries, he conceived a dislike towards the *critical* period. When quite a boy he had resisted all compulsion and governance, but he was full of veneration for intellectual and moral superiority (cf. the characterisation which he gave of himself as a youth in a letter printed by Littré in his *Auguste Comte et la philosophie positive*). In the year 1814 he entered the Polytechnic School at Paris. In later life he spoke of this school of exact sciences (see a letter of July 22, 1842, to Stuart Mill) as the first beginning of a true scientific corporation. Instruction was given in all those sciences which had distinctly reached the *positive* stage ; hence Comte regarded it as the foundation on which all higher education should be based. Moreover, among the pupils there prevailed a republican tone and a feeling of brotherliness which united them in a common enthusiasm for the influence that their studies could not fail to exert on

the development of civilisation.   It was owing to this spirit
that Saint-Simon's ideas met with so much support from the
school.   The idea of positivity grew up together with that
of humanity.   The reactionary government took occasion
of a demonstration raised against one of the teachers (1816)
to close the school, and send the scholars home.   But
Auguste Comte found it impossible to live so far from the
centre of the movement.   In defiance of his parents' commands he returned to Paris the same year to carry on his
education.   He studied biology and history in order to complete his polytechnic education, and acquired a very solid
encyclopædic grounding.   He procured a livelihood by teaching
mathematics.   Of still greater importance for his subsequent
development was his intimacy with Saint-Simon.   On this
point he writes in a letter of this period (1818): "By co-
operation and friendship with one of those men who see
farthest in the domain of philosophical politics, I have learnt a
multitude of things which I should have sought in vain in books;
and in the half year during which I have been associated with
him, my mind has made greater progress than it would in three
years had I been alone.   The work of these six months has
developed my conception of the political sciences, and has
also, indirectly, raised my ideas of the other sciences, so that
I remark that there is more philosophy in my head than
formerly, and that I have gained a more correct and elevated
view of things" (*Lettres à Valat*, p. 37).   It was from Saint-
Simon that Comte learnt to see the necessity of re-placing the
mediæval hierarchy, which both regarded as an admirable
institution *in its day*, by a new spiritual power.   It was Saint-
Simon, too, who first inspired him with an interest in social
questions, and it is this interest which explains the prominence
he gives to the opposition between militarism and industrialism.
In a treatise of 1820 (*Sommaire appréciative de l'ensemble du
passé moderne*) Comte dates the dissolution of the old social
system as far back as the twelfth century, for he recognised
the first signs of this dissolution in the freeing of the towns
and the introduction of positive sciences in Europe through
the Arabians.   The consequence of all this has been that the
industrial system based on labour has gradually replaced the
territorial system based on conquest, while positive science has
replaced theology.   Although Comte arrived at similar ideas

by his own route, there is no doubt that his intercourse with Saint-Simon hastened his development; it was most unjust of him, therefore, to speak (as he afterwards did) of this acquaintance as having been detrimental to him.[77] The two men were too antithetical in nature and mode of thought, however, to be able to work together permanently. The breach took place when Comte began to feel himself independent of Saint-Simon. They disagreed radically as to the position which science should occupy in relation to labour, and as to the "priesthood" planned by Saint-Simon in his later days. As we have seen, during the latter part of his life Saint-Simon put aside his plans of theoretical reformation in order to devote himself to practical measures. It was here that Comte disagreed with him. The last work in which Comte still spoke of himself as Saint-Simon's pupil occasioned the breach. Saint-Simon protested against the book, and Comte afterwards published it in his own name only. This work, which was entitled *Plan des travaux scientifiques nécessaires pour réorganiser la société* (1822) (and which was republished in 1824 under the title *Politique Positive*), represents Comte's first appearance as an independent thinker. The most important hindrance to the development of civilisation, in his opinion, is the continued ascendency of the revolutionary tendency, as shown more particularly in the principles of freedom of conscience and the sovereignty of the people: these are critical, not organic, principles. Men lack the capacity of thinking themselves into a coherent circle of ideas, and of acknowledging a power grounded in reason. A new social system cannot be constructed at one blow, but must be gradually developed. This is sufficiently proved by the many unsuccessful constitutions which have figured in the recent history of France. The fundamental condition of co-operation for a common end is a common mode of thought and sentiment. The old order of society possessed such a common ground in theology. The new social order can never be firmly established until a comprehensive scheme of thought has been drawn up, which shall be regarded as no less authoritative than the results of the particular sciences in their proper spheres. It is of the first importance that politics should become a positive science.

While within the spheres of mathematics, physics and biology all phenomena are recognised as subject to definite laws, men still think that in the social sphere they can proceed according as seemeth them good ; for example, that they can at their pleasure introduce a social system of their own devising. This belief will vanish when once the fact that human relations are also subject to law is generally recognised. Comte quotes as evidence of this subjection to law of human relations the close connection to be found at every point of history between the social organisation and the whole state of civilisation, *i.e.* between the social order and intellectual development as it appears in science, art, and industry. Civilisation, again, has its source in the instinctive pressing towards perfection which is a characteristic of man.[78] Comte reduces the different stages which civilisation passes through to three— the theological, the metaphysical, and the positive—and then tries to show that there are definite degrees of social development corresponding to each. This *law of the three stages* forms a leading feature of Comte's philosophy, hence we will postpone our exposition of it to the chapter on his philosophy.

This work of Comte's excited great attention among politicians, historians, and men of science generally. Guizot, the mathematician Poinsot, Alexander von Humboldt, and the Duke de Brogli were among those who expressed their recognition of it. Striking at the root of the matter, it led beyond the points round which the various contending parties had hitherto gathered ; while at the same time it acknowledged everything of value by whomsoever contributed. But the plan which lay nearest Comte's heart was still unexecuted. He now passed on to perform the main task of his life, *i.e.* to write an encyclopædia of the matter and methods of positive science. In 1824 he writes to his friend Valat : " I shall devote my whole life and all my powers to the founding of positive philosophy." And almost at the same time he writes to another friend (Gustave d'Eichthal) that his proper task was " an encyclopædic transformation of all our positive knowledge, which indeed must be conceived as forming one single whole." A few years later he presented his " positive philosophy" to a small but select audience (which included A. v. Humboldt ; Poinsot ; Fourier, another mathematician; Dunoyer, the political economist ; the physicians Broussais and Esquirol ; and the engineer Hippolyte Carnot).

Comte supported himself by writing and giving lessons in

mathematics.   He had married a young and gifted Parisian. The relation between them seems to have been an unhappy one from the first, partly because Comte's parents were against the union (which, as a civil marriage, was an abomination in their eyes), partly also because Comte, as appears in a characteristic letter to Valat (November 16, 1825), failed to find in his wife those qualities which he most valued in a woman : " devotion of heart and gentleness of character, combined with that subjection which the feeling of her husband's intellectual superiority must produce in her."   It is very obvious, from the manner in which Comte expresses his hope that these qualities adorn his friend's bride, that he did not find them in his own wife.   She was too independent for him.   Nevertheless, she showed great fidelity and energy during an attack of mental illness which overtook Comte, and which was probably brought on by overwork.   He was placed in an asylum, and his parents, acting on Lamennais' advice, sought to take this opportunity to get him under their influence and place him in a monastery. Madame Comte, whose civil marriage the parents had wished to conceal, claimed her rights, and demanded that her husband should be sent back to his own home ; it was mainly owing to her that he recovered his sanity, and was able once more to pursue his interrupted labours.   (Comte's parents, however, while his mind was still disordered, managed to have him ecclesiastically married, and so disburdened their consciences of the deadly sin of having agreed to his civil marriage.)

Now followed a series of vigorous and happy years for Comte, during which he wrote and published his chief work, *Cours de philosophie positive* (in 6 vols., 1830-42).   He thought out the contents of each volume in the course of solitary walks.   For materials he could rely on his excellent memory. Once his meditations were concluded he wrote down the results at which he had arrived in a comparatively short time. In so doing he laid no particular stress on the form of exposition.   His style is heavy, shows little literary taste, and suffers from repetitions and the frequent use of technical terms ; but it is distinguished by its clearness, thoroughness and impressiveness, and bears the stamp of energy and seriousness.   Often (especially in the last three volumes of the work, which treat of the social sciences) the stream of thought flows so strongly that it carries the reader along with it.   Comte sought to popularise positive philosophy by means of public lectures. Ever since the twenties, former pupils of the Polytechnic had delivered popular lectures on science throughout the country, and in the year 1830, Comte and some of his comrades founded the "Association Polytechnique," for the express purpose of spreading a knowledge of positive science. Throughout a long series of years (till the *coup d'état* of 1851 brought about a change) Comte delivered free popular lectures, at first on astronomy, afterwards (from 1848) on positive philosophy in general. In a little work entitled *Discours sur l'esprit positif* (1844), he has set down the general considerations with which he introduced his astronomical course ; this book forms the best introduction to his philosophy.

Comte never attained any fixed official position. After 1830 he hoped for a professorship in the history of positive science, for which he was eminently qualified. An appeal to the then all-powerful Guizot, however, was of no effect. Guizot describes the incident in his *Mémoires* with extraordinary forgetfulness of the past ; he writes as though he had never seen this man with whom during the twenties — the years when he was in opposition — he had had so many conversations, and enjoyed so much community of thought. A professorship of mathematics at the Polytechnic School was also refused to Comte although, when holding this office provisionally for a year, his excellence had been universally recognised. He had to content himself with the more modest post of coach and examiner for the entrance examination, in which capacity he made yearly itineraries in the provinces. But he lost this post too, which was subject to annual re-election by the teaching staff of the Polytechnic School, because, in the preface to the last volume of his *Cours*, he had made a sharp attack on mathematical specialists and their pride. The time had come, in his opinion, for biologists and sociologists to occupy the first rank in the intellectual world ; the supremacy of the mathematicians is over now that the more concrete spheres are to be subjected to positive scientific treatment. These opinions, and the defiant manner in which they were expressed, were the cause of his not being re-elected to the examinership, and he was once more obliged to earn his bread by private teaching. English and French admirers and friends (amongst the English were John Stuart Mill and the historian Grote ; among the French, the learned Littré) gave him pecuniary help in the shape of a pension. His domestic affairs came to a crisis also ; his wife and he, after a long and steadily-increasing estrangement, parted. His wife, however, continued to take a generous interest both in his ideas and in his personal affairs.

After all these quarrels, with their attendant emotions, and after the heavy expenditure of strength involved in his twelve years' labour at his chief work, Comte fell a victim, for the second time, to a nervous crisis. Though not as violent as his former attack, yet, as he said in a letter to Stuart Mill, his sanity was in danger.[79] There were other circumstances besides those already mentioned which helped to bring about this crisis and invested it with a peculiar character. He had made the acquaintance of a woman who became to him what Beatrice was to Dante. In her, at last, he found some one to whom he could pour out his heart, and in so doing satisfy those emotional needs which had been craving expression all his life. He experienced, for the first time, true depth of feeling and devotion ; and this young woman, Clotilde de Vaux by name, became for him, after her death at the end of a year, the representative of humanity (as Dante saw in Beatrice the representative of theology), to whom he daily directed his thoughts and the *solennelle effusion des sentiments généreux* which he called his prayer. She was the genius who inspired him to his second great work, which was to systematise feeling, as the first had systematised ideas. This work appeared under the title, *Politique positive ou traité de sociologie, instituant la religion de l'humanité* (4 vols. 1851-54). In a letter to Stuart Mill (July 14, 1845), Comte informs him that the new work, the plan of which he had conceived earlier, acquired its distinctive character during this crisis and the *méditation exceptionnelle* to which it led. He now sees that the second period of his philosophical activity must differ from the first by assigning as high a place to feeling as the latter had given to the understanding. The purely theoretical work having been completed the next step is its social realisation, and this consists primarily in a systematisation of human feelings ; for this follows as a necessary corollary to the systematisation of ideas, and is indispensable as a basis for the systematisation of institutions. Had the new work aimed at nothing more than this it would have formed no decided contrast to the first, but would rather have been its continuation, extension, or deepening. As a matter of fact, however, as its title showed, it went much further. It was to found a new religion. While the earlier work started from the world, or Nature, and hoped, on the basis of the knowledge of Nature, to arrive at the understanding of man, this objective method now gives place to a subjective method, which starts from man, and, regarding the whole of Nature from the human point of view, sees in humanity itself the highest being (*le grand être*). The new religion, of which Comte soon grew to feel himself the high priest, was to consist in contemplative absorption in the idea of humanity and in surrender of the heart to it. Not that Comte meant to abandon positive philosophy ; on the contrary, the principles of this philosophy were to provide the dogmas of the new religion, the religion of humanity, with their content ; but he superadds worship and practice. His *Catéchisme positiviste ou sommaire exposition de la religion universelle* (1852) contains a briefer exposition of the subject-matter set forth in the *Politique Positive* with tedious verbosity.

He prepared himself for this last essay of thought by what he called "cerebral hygiene"; by which he meant that he abstained entirely from all reading, and gave himself completely up to thinking out his book. By this means he hoped to exclude all disturbing elements, and to ensure unity of plan. The extensive studies of his earlier days and his faithful memory enabled him to make use of materials already collected. This holding aloof from everything new in science and literature,— the effect of which was to put an end to all real discussion and critical testing of his own ideas,—was accompanied by an absorption in music, in Italian and Spanish poetry and in reading the *De Imitatione Christi*. Comte requires of every positivist that he shall read some poetic masterpiece, were it only a canto of Dante, daily. He regarded the *De Imitatione* as a great poem on human nature ; in reading it he always put " humanity " for " God," and in this way turned the old mystical book into an aid to the contemplative worship of humanity. According to the description of an eyewitness, Comte's whole nature in the last years of his life was permeated with gentleness and goodness. But he had to suffer the disappointment of seeing Littré, his most famous scholar, and one or two others withdraw from him when he ceased to be a philosopher and became the high priest of the religion of humanity—just as he himself had withdrawn from Saint-Simon when he made similar claims. After Comte's long and arduous intellectual labours the mythological tendency of his childhood, favoured by the *hygiène cérébrale*, came once more to the surface, and in this last stage of his career he found few followers.[80] The new religion, however, has its congregations and places of worship scattered about through France, England, Sweden and America. This religion without theology is a characteristic mark of the age. For Comte himself it was a resting-place where his thought lingered over all that was greatest and best in human knowledge and action, and from whence he looked hopefully towards the future which awaits the continually-progressing human race. Love, the principle ; order, the basis ; progress, the aim ;—this was the motto of the religion of humanity. Auguste Comte died September 5, 1857.

(b) The Law of the Three Stages

According to Comte, our knowledge passes through *three stages of development*, which can be traced in the case of each particular science. The more involved and complex the matter of a science the longer time it will require to pass through this graduated scale. The abstract sciences reach the definitive stage first, and after them the concrete. In Comte's view the time had come when the most concrete of all the sciences, *i.e.* sociology, was entering upon this third stage. The circle is closed, therefore, and a retrospect is possible.

First comes the *theological* stage. Here there are only a very limited number of observations to serve as a foundation, hence imagination plays the leading part. The explanation of natural phenomena, the uniting bond between given facts, which the nature of man's mind forces him to seek, is found at this stage in the intervention of personal beings. Only through the medium of ideas of gods and spirits can man at first make the world comprehensible to himself. Hence the great assistance which these ideas have rendered to the development of human knowledge. Had they not presented themselves, and had the wish to discover the activity of these beings in all events of Nature not made itself felt, the activity of knowledge would never have been set in motion, the primitive inertia would have remained undisturbed. The understanding sought for at this stage is an absolute understanding, for thought does not pierce beyond these divine beings, and as long as a natural phenomenon can be explained by their intervention nothing more is demanded. Hence, too, at the beginning, no doubts are entertained as to the possibility of acquiring absolute knowledge. Nor has the influence of the theological ideas been less important on the practical side of life. They have provided a firm foundation common both to moral and social life. This stage of development is the age of authority. Men live in a common confidence in immutable powers. Corresponding to this stage in politics is monarchy.

The theological stage contains within itself a series of grades. In fetichism a spiritual life, similar to man's, is attributed to natural objects. In polytheism, the most characteristic grade of the theological stage, material objects are deprived of their immediate life, and the source of their motions and changes is sought in other beings, who are for the most part invisible and who form a higher world. In monotheism the distance and the antithesis between the principle from which the explanation is derived and the phenomena to be explained is still greater. Hence it is vague, and brings about less spiritual communion than polytheism. It forms the transition to the second great stage, *i.e.*, the *metaphysical*. Here explanation is found, not in personal beings, but in abstract ideas, principles, or forces. It is governed by the endeavour— an endeavour which had already appeared in the theological stage, and had led from fetichism to polytheism, and from polytheism to monotheism—to trace back different phenomena to one single principle. The metaphysical stage carries on this endeavour, assuming as many forces as there are separate groups of phenomena, *i.e.* a chemical force, a vital force, etc. Finally, an attempt is made to reduce all these different forces to one primal force, one single primal being, *i.e.* Nature, a unity corresponding to that of monotheism which closed the theological stage. Common to both these stages is the tendency to seek for absolute solutions of problems. Metaphysics, no less than theology, seek to explain the innermost nature of things, the source and the destiny of all things, and the manner in which all things are produced. The only difference is that the abstract is put in the place of the concrete, argumentation in the place of imagination. Argumentation preponderates over observation here much as imagination had done in the first stage.

According to Comte's conception, the metaphysical stage is essentially a transformation stage or process of dissolution. Argumentation penetrates into the theological circle of ideas, exhibits the contradictions it contains, puts constant ideas or forces in the place of incalculable wills, and, in so doing, weakens the lively impressions and the authoritative influence of those powers which were supposed to rule over Nature and human life. Nothing new can be constructed ; no real equivalents can be given. In the practical sphere the dissolution shows itself in the general prevalence of doubt and egoism. The bonds which bind the individual in a living union with society are torn asunder, and the understanding is cultivated at the expense of feeling. In his later years Comte even speaks of the long revolt of the understanding against the heart. In politics it is the age of the people, as the first stage was the age of kings ; the leading men are jurists, society is supposed to have originated in a contract, and the State to be based on the principle of the sovereignty of the people.

In the *positive* stage, both imagination and argumentation are subordinated to observation. Every proposition enunciated concerns a fact, either a particular or a universal fact. Agreement with facts is the only criterion. This is, indeed, not to be taken to mean that we proceed no farther than isolated facts. Positivism is as far from empiricism as it is from mysticism ; it neither falls apart into disconnected observations on the one hand, nor departs from facts, in order to lose itself in supernatural beings or abstract principles on the other. Instead of seeking out absolute *causes*, and striving to trace out their workings, it seeks for the *laws* of phenomena, *i.e.* the constant relations which exist between observed phenomena. Whether we are trying to understand thoughts and feelings or stress and weight, our knowledge can only show us the relations in which they occur. Science rests on the immutability of natural laws, which immutability was clearly recognised by thought for the first time when the Greeks founded mathematical astronomy ; while in more recent times, it has been discovered to hold good in one sphere after another.

Bacon, Galilei, and Descartes, all formulated this principle ; hence they are to be regarded as the founders of positive philosophy. Even if the laws governing certain cases have still to be discovered, an irresistible analogy now leads us to apply the great philosophical principle of the immutability of natural laws to all phenomena and events.

While the first two stages exhibit the effort to reduce everything in the world to a single, absolute principle, conceived either in theological or in metaphysical form—as God or as Nature—it follows from the character of positive philosophy that an absolute or objective conclusion of that kind is impossible for it. The strict demand for confirmation by experience makes it impossible to reduce everything to a single principle ; experience never shows us more than a limited interconnection, and there will always be many phenomena and events which it will be impossible for us to bring into conjunction with others. There are groups of phenomena (at least as many as there are different sciences) which are irreducible. The many laws cannot be reduced to a single one. Our knowledge can reach a subjective unity only, not an objective one. Subjective unity consists in employing the same method everywhere ; this produces homogeneity and convergence of different theories. Subjectively considered, then, we have only a single science. But this science can be common to all human beings. The positive method produces unity not only within the consciousness of individuals but also between different individuals ; thus positive philosophy becomes the intellectual foundation of the brotherhood of man. Even now we may notice that men are agreed only upon such subjects as have already been reduced to positive science ; on all other subjects widely divergent views are held. As long as it met with no intellectual rivalry from scientific thought Catholicism provided a spiritual brotherhood which may be regarded as a type of that which positive philosophy will one day supply. Positive philosophy finds in the subjective homogeneity which is contained in the concept of humanity the only possible equivalent to the concept of God in theological philosophy, and of Nature in metaphysical philosophy.

The union of theory and practice is much closer in this stage than in either of the preceding stages. For the knowledge of the laws of phenomena makes it possible for us to

determine the future development of phenomena ; and the wish
to be in a position to do this is a co-operating motive in the
transition from the first two stages to the third. To see in
order to foresee (*voir pour prévoir*) is the motto of positive
science. This third stage, therefore, corresponds to industry
in the sense of the exploiting of Nature by man. But we must
not restrict our consideration here to external nature. If the
laws of the states and actions of man can be discovered,
individual and social, no less than purely physical, development
will be determinable by knowledge.

Comte calls attention to the fact (see especially *Discours
sur l'esprit positif*, pp. 41-44) that all the different significa-
tions in which the word *positive* can be used applies to the
philosophy which he calls positive. Positive may mean the
same as *real*, and positive philosophy seeks above all things to
build upon facts. It also means *useful* in opposition to idle,
and positive philosophy aims at the amelioration of our
individual and social existence ; it is something more than a
mere satisfaction of curiosity. By positive again we understand
that which is *certain* and *indubitable*, and it is the task of positive philosophy to lead us beyond the continual doubtings and
debatings of earlier philosophers. Positive may also denote
the precisely determined and positive philosophy puts laws,
constant and definite relations, in the place of the indefinite and
changing ideas of the earlier stages. Finally, positive is also
used as the *opposite to negative*, and this is appropriate to the
third stage with its task of organising, while the second stage
implies essentially a process of dissolution. It is true that
positive philosophy cannot use the explanations which satisfied
theological philosophy, but it has no immediate quarrel with
the latter. Indeed, it admits that it is just as impossible to
adduce a proof for the rejection of those beings in whom
theological philosophy believes as it is to supply a proof for
their acceptance. No one has ever adduced a proof of the
non-existence of Apollo or Minerva ; the belief in them
vanished when it no longer harmonised with general intellectual conditions. Positive philosophy does more than refrain
from attacking theological philosophy ; it strives to give it its
due by an historical investigation of the conditions of its origin
and an estimation of its influence on human development.
Such an understanding was not possible at earlier stages, when

one absolute theory confronted the other, and each particular system regarded it as its duty to destroy the other.

Only one single characteristic of the positive stage is not in and for itself contained in the word positive, and this is that it everywhere puts *relative* in the place of absolute. But this relative character is, according to Comte, a necessary consequence of the other marks of positive philosophy. In putting law in the place of cause it comes to a standstill at bare relation. It asks *how?* but not *why?* It seeks neither for inner production nor for first grounds. Moreover, particular laws cannot be reduced to one single law, and in any case, there remains the relativity involved in the fact that we always regard the world from the human point of view. All knowledge presupposes an opposition between the individual and the outer world. Hence Kant has rightly distinguished between subjective and objective, and deserves everlasting admiration for having, through this distinction, put an end to absolute philosophy, although his thought was not sufficiently positive to prevent his followers from returning to it again.[81] Although knowledge of the world presupposes man, yet the world itself can exist without man. And although man is dependent on the world he is not a result of it (*L'homme dépend du monde, mais il n'en résulte pas. Catéchisme positiviste*, 2nd edition, p. 146). Materialism has in vain endeavoured to do away with the independence and spontaneity of organic life, and has exaggerated the importance of the inorganic outer world. The duality remains.

Comte deduces the law of three stages from the history of the sciences, *i.e.* by way of experience. But after he has established it, he attempts to show that it may be deduced from what we know of the nature of the human mind ; the induction is confirmed by deduction. The human mind can never be without views and concepts by which individual facts are united together. Before the union between phenomena can be discovered by means of the examination of the phenomena themselves, as in the positive stage, it is provided by the mythological notions which grow up involuntarily, or the metaphysical ideas which are so framed as to invest these notions with a more abstract and permanent character. Moreover, it is a tendency of the human mind to conceive everything in analogy with itself, to attribute to things its own inner feelings. An easy method of arriving at an explanation! But if men had not been confident that an explanation would be easily found, they would never have started on the path of investigation.

It would be interesting to compare Comte's law of the three stages with similar theories propounded by Kant, Fichte, Hegel, Saint-Simon, and even by Rousseau and Lessing. Along with characteristic divergences we should discover similarity in one point at least, viz. that after the period in which authority reigns supreme, both in practice and theory, the spiritual life of man passes through a period during which criticism, reflection, and doubt are busied on a work of disintegration. Such a period having been passed through, the task of the present is to acquire a standpoint which offers a positive and common foundation of belief and conduct. This is the great historical experience which has been formulated by the above-named thinkers as the law of the three stages. As for Comte, he only assigns definite characteristics to the first and third stages. It is difficult to resist the impression that he assigns to the metaphysical stage all those movements of thought and life for which he felt an antipathy. He sympathised with the old Catholic system, which he regarded as one of the most wonderful productions of the human mind, and he sympathised with the system of the future, which was to introduce a new spiritual brotherhood based on empirical science. But the intervening critical and revolutionary period he regarded with dislike, although he was obliged to admit that it had performed an indispensable work. The different marks of the metaphysical stage which he brings forward stand in no necessary connection with one another. It would, for instance, be impossible to find any connection between the tendency to explain phenomena through the assumption of specific forces or faculties and the over-estimation of the intelligence or the predominance of egoism. The said tendency appears at a certain point in the history of every particular science, and cannot be taken as a characteristic of human development in general ; in any case it may be combined with the recognition of the central importance of the life of feeling and the reality of the sympathetic feelings. We are, perhaps, more likely to find an over-estimate of intelligence among those who devote themselves to some special science than among speculative philosophers. At the conclusion of his great work Comte realised that his position was strongly antagonistic to all scientific specialism, and he expressed this antagonism so forcibly as to draw upon himself unpleasant consequences. But he found no place in his doctrine of the three stages for the antithesis between positive philosophy and positive special investigation. And yet it is an essential characteristic of modern times that the division of labour within the sphere of science has been carried so far that an intellectual unity, a common world-conception, becomes more and more difficult to arrive at. Herein, we may be sure, lies a far greater problem for the history of civilisation than in any of the evils which Comte finds in the metaphysical stage. Comte's enthusiasm and sanguine temperament blinded him to this. The problem of the relation between positivity and generality—of the possibility of erecting on a positive basis a general world-conception—never defined itself with sufficient clearness in his mind. This omission, as we shall see later, is closely connected with the defects of his theory of knowledge. The positive stage itself, therefore, is not clearly defined at many points. Thus, for example, it is not clear how closely positive philosophy binds us to the facts before us. How far may we travel from them by way of hypothesis? What authorisation has an hypothesis which is the logical consequence of given experiences, but which does not admit of verification ? What authorisation has a faith which cannot indeed be deduced from experience, but which does not conflict with it ? Questions such as these, which are of the first importance in determining the relation between science and the conception of life, were ignored by Comte.

Comte does not draw any absolute line of demarcation between the different stages, but he does not sufficiently bring out the homogeneity of human thought in all stages. He did not, however, mean that there was no positivism in the theological stage. The influence of experience always made itself felt, but so long as the circle of experiences was small, this influence could not be erected into a principle. Nevertheless, it is the stimulating power of experience which expresses itself in the metaphysical principles. For these, as a matter of fact, represent groups of experience which it was found necessary to withdraw from the sphere of mythological caprice. Metaphysic, as Comte says (*Discours sur l'esprit positif*, p. 36), systematises the opposition of dawning science to the old theology. The positive factor was already at work as a co-operating factor in the transition from fetichism to polytheism, and from polytheism to monotheism. In the early stages of its development the positive spirit was unable to formulate its own tendencies, hence it used metaphysic as an organ. Knowledge progresses by continual transitions. Comte by no means expected the complete victory and general predominance of the *esprit positif* in his own life. He writes to Valat, March 30, 1825: "Although I hope for some results from my endeavours, yet I do not conceal from myself that they cannot produce any remarkable result in my lifetime, even if they succeed in giving an impetus to all minds which are able to take an effective part in the great work, and this the future alone can show." Later, when under the influence of his cerebral hygiene and in mystical absorption in his own ideas he had lost all understanding of what was going on around him in scientific and political circles, he became more and more sanguine on this point.

Whether Comte laid greater weight on the negative character of the second stage or on its significance as a necessary connecting link, he was at all times convinced that the decisive battle in the spiritual world would be fought between Catholicism and Positivism. In his letters to Stuart Mill he repeatedly expressed a wish that there might be a hand-to-hand struggle between these two tendencies, without the intervention of Protestantism, Deism, or any other inconsequent intermediary. He regarded it as a very significant sign of the times that Catholicism was demanding freedom of teaching, while the "metaphysical" school (Cousin, Guizot, Thiers, Villemain) supported a State monopoly. Both schools in so doing denied their own principles, the former the principle of authority, the latter the principle of freedom. Comte's hope was that if freedom of speech and of teaching were granted, the fears of the metaphysical school would be justified, while Catholicism would find itself confronted with a hitherto unknown opponent. He only regretted that the representatives of Catholicism since de Maistre's time had been men of such little weight. It seemed to him natural that the opposition should become more clearly defined, and that Catholic orthodoxy should grow increasingly stricter and more systematic, now that the revolutionary movement had betrayed its tendency to base spiritual and social development on a foundation very different from authority. It was against this radical tendency that de Maistre had put forward Ultramontanism as the only consistent system of religion. Gallicanism has already gone to pieces, and a like fate awaits other intermediate standpoints. Comte rejoiced that his friend Valat, after having passed through a religious crisis, went straight back to Catholicism instead of stopping half-way at some intermediate standpoint, although in the beautiful letter which he wrote to Valat on the subject (August 25, 1843) he did not conceal his doubts whether the Catholicism of the present day has the power to confer on those possessed of the highest intellectual and moral culture of the age the peace and harmony which it was able to bestow in its classical period. He cites, in illustration, the difficulties connected with the dogma of the eternal punishment of those who, though rejecting every article of faith, live a life of the highest morality,—and yet this dogma is indispensable to the whole Catholic organism.

(c) Classification of the Sciences

By philosophy Comte understands the whole system of human concepts. This systematisation may, as we have seen, proceed in one of three ways. Up till now the theological and metaphysical methods have prevailed. Comte believed himself to be the first to undertake a systematisation according to the positive method, *i.e.* according to the same method as that by which the concepts or laws of the particular sciences have been acquired. Positive philosophy has to collect and arrange the laws which have been deduced from facts. Since it thus unites what appears as scattered in the different sciences, it seeks to remedy the evils brought about by the division of labour in the sphere of knowledge. Comte regarded the respective attempts of theological and metaphysical philosophy to reduce all special laws to one general law as foredoomed to failure. Were such a reduction possible, positive philosophy would certainly become more perfect, but experience, which exhibits irreducible differences, is against it. The unification effected by positive philosophy, therefore, consists not in bringing all special laws under a single principle, but in employing the same method in all spheres. This method proves to be everywhere applicable, a fact which indicates that, in spite of irreducible differences, there is a certain homogeneity between the different classes of phenomena. Each of these classes corresponds to a particular science, hence the classification of the sciences is one of the most important tasks of positive philosophy.

Comte's classification of the sciences arranges them *according to the historical order in which each one passed over into the positive stage*. Mathematics comes first, then astronomy, physics, chemistry, biology and sociology. This sequence shows us at the same time a progressive transition from *simplicity* to *complexity* of observed phenomena. The more simple the content of any science the more quickly will it pass through the different stages; the more complicated the phenomena under observation the longer will it take to get through the maladies of childhood. Hence biology and sociology come last. The simpler the relations with which a science is concerned the more *universal its validity*, for the simpler relations reappear in the more complicated ones. The laws of mathematics hold good for all phenomena, while the most concrete sciences, biology and sociology, have the *narrowest range*. (Comte might have discovered this relation between *généralité décroissante* and *complication croissante* from the logical doctrine of the inverse relation between the intension and extension of concepts.) Finally, the methods of the different sciences exhibit a corresponding sequence. The more simple and universal the foundation of a science the greater the preponderance of the *deductive* over the *inductive* method. Thus mathematics is the most and sociology the least deductive of the sciences. In sociology the demonstration of the historical course of development is of most importance; after this has been exhibited by means of the inductive method, the next thing to be done is to deduce it from the facts of human nature, as Comte himself attempted to do in his law of the three stages. The inductive foundation of mathematics is so simple that it is often overlooked, and mathematics is regarded as a purely rational science. But there is no such thing as a purely rational science. Even mathematics is a natural science; its concepts, like those of all other sciences, originate in experience. But the facts dealt with in mathematics are so simple that they may be studied in imagination, in abstraction from the physical and chemical qualities of bodies, as easily as in reality. Number, extension, and motion are qualities which we can just as well represent to ourselves in an indefinite medium, conceived as comprehending all bodies in the universe, as in real bodies. Herein lies the explanation of the seeming independence of mathematics of experience. Thanks to these imagined spaces and numbers, the deductions of mathematics are able to unfold themselves independently of experience. Had mathematics no empirical foundation it would be altogether impossible to understand how it is that mathematical deductions are applicable in the study of real Nature. Between the almost purely deductive method of mathematics and the almost purely inductive method of sociology lie the other chief methods, each corresponding to its chief science. Through astronomy, which employs hypotheses established deductively and confirmed by observation, we pass to the experimental method of physics, to the method of rational partition of chemistry, and to the comparative method of biology ; this last forms the transition to the historical method of sociology.

Comte regards these six groups of concepts or laws, which he gives in his *Cours de philosophie positive*, as irreducible. The passage from one sphere to the next is effected by means of a leap ; a new principle comes into force which cannot be deduced from the preceding one. He calls the wish to deduce the higher (*i.e.* the more complex, limited, and inductive) sciences from the lower, materialism. Equally impossible is it to make any one of the said groups all-embracing. And the discontinuity, which prevails between the six groups of fundamental concepts, is also, according to Comte, found within each one. Thus he maintains that the different branches of physics must always remain separate. The same thing is true of organic species as of physical forces. The concept of species would entirely lose its scientific significance if it were admitted that, under the influence of transformation brought about by external conditions of life, one species could pass over into another. Comte expressly asserts that between the plant and animal worlds there is "a real and deep discontinuity, which it is absolutely impossible for any transition to obliterate."

We have here an instructive example of the way in which a tendency of thought may pass over into its opposite. The difference between positive and metaphysical philosophy had been explained as consisting in the substitution of laws for ideas or forces, and of relative for absolute explanations. But with his irreducible groups of concepts Comte himself sets up a Platonic world of ideas. He conceives discontinuity dogmatically, instead of taking it as a mere fact,—as a fact which perhaps proceeds from the imperfection of science. The prominence he gives to the discontinuity of the world places his Positivism in sharp contrast to German Romanticism, which attempts to reduce all differences to ideal continuity. It is, as Comte himself admits, the unceasing task of science to reduce the differences, the interruptions in the continuity of phenomena, to the smallest possible number. No discontinuity, therefore, need be more than a temporary barrier. And the later development of science—precisely during the period which began with the conclusion of Comte's great work (*circa* 1840)—has made it possible to demonstrate or surmise continuity where Comte had declared it to be impossible. Thus the law of the conservation of energy, especially the doctrine of heat as a form of motion, and the proof of the identity of light and electricity have enabled us to form a conception of the unity of Nature such as could find no place in Comte's system. Within the organic sphere, the evolutionary hypothesis has led to the now well-established view that species only denote stages or branches of a connected process ; we may notice in particular that it has become increasingly difficult to draw any sharply dividing lines between animal and plant life. Comte declared himself against the evolutionary hypothesis as it appeared in his day (*i.e.* in the form given to it by Lamarck), and his pupils (Charles Robin, Littré) were afterwards its most zealous opponents. Without anticipating the subject here, we may say that the relation between continuity and discontinuity has proved to be far more complicated than Comte's philosophy supposes.

The connection between the different sciences depends, according to Comte, on the fact that the preceding science, being simpler and more universal, underlies (even though the latter cannot be deduced from the former) the one which succeeds it, and which is more complex and special. Mathematics is the most abstract and universal science, and within mathematics, again, arithmetic is much simpler and more universal than geometry and mechanics ; arithmetic, therefore, is the rational basis of the whole system of our positive know-

ledge.   Comte has here overlooked the fact that there are
fundamental concepts of our knowledge still simpler and more
universal than the concept of number, *i.e.* the concepts of identity
and difference as these are conceived in logic, that is to say,
not only as identity and difference of *magnitudes*, but as identity
and difference of *qualities*.   Hence the first member is wanting
in Comte's series of sciences.   In addition to this, a difficulty
presents itself in connection with his assertion that geometry
and mechanics—which in abstraction and universality follow
immediately upon arithmetic—are valid of all phenomena,
the former of phenomena in equilibrium (from the statical
point of view), the latter, of phenomena in motion (from the
dynamical point of view).   Extension and motion are forms
of material phenomena only ; they are not forms of mental
phenomena.   Now Comte himself rejects materialism because
it introduces the point of view of the lower sciences into the
higher, and attempts to *deduce* man from the world, instead of
merely exhibiting his dependence on the world.   The science
of mental phenomena, therefore, can find no place in Comte's
series of sciences, in which each preceding science is to be
valid of the following one, although the latter is the more
concrete.   Logic and arithmetic are as immediately valid of
the science of mental phenomena as of the science of
material phenomena ; but we cannot say this of geometry and
the science of mechanics, unless we are prepared to follow the
example of materialism, which is at any rate logical, and say at
once that the phenomena of consciousness are spatially extended.   The classification of the sciences is not so simple an
affair as Comte supposed.   His system here presents a difficulty
similar to that which we have already pointed out in Hobbes
(see vol. i. of this work, pp. 256, 257).   Comte himself would not
admit this.   He did not regard psychology as a special science,
hence he allots to it no independent place in the series.   He
denies the possibility of introspection.   We observe all phenomena with our minds (*esprit*), he says ;[82] how then can we
observe the mind itself?   A man cannot divide his mind
into two parts, of which one works while the other investigates
how it does it!   He admits, however, that feelings can be more
easily observed than thought, because they have a different
organ.   Our intellectual activities must be studied in their
productions and results, or by means of the organs with which

they are associated. Instead of treating psychology as an independent science, Comte divides psychological investigations between biology and sociology. Biology alone would not do justice to the fact that the mental life of the individual is determined by the influence of history and society. Comte would have consciousness studied purely objectively. He did good service in strongly emphasising the objective method in opposition to Cousin's and Jeffroy's purely subjective and spiritualistic psychology. But he did not see that, as a matter of fact, the subjective method always underlies the objective ; speaking broadly, we may say that he never sufficiently emphasises the peculiar nature of conscious phenomena. While elsewhere he lays too great weight on discontinuity, he here emphasises it too little. As already indicated, his classificatory system breaks down when the essential quality of conscious phenomena is insisted upon ; such phenomena interrupt the sequence, for even if in themselves they are simple and elementary, yet they always appear in connection with the most complicated material phenomena. Ought they to be placed first or last ? Comte was opposed both to spiritualism and to Condillacism. His chief quarrel with the latter is that it conceives the particular individual in entire isolation, and that it takes note of outer influences only, neglecting inner conditions. The particular individual is a scholastic abstraction ; only the race is a reality. Comte considered the most important work done in biology to be Gall's *Physiology of the Brain*, (apart from his unsuccessful theory of localisation). The number of mental faculties posited by Gall must, it is true, be reduced ; less than ten, however, cannot be posited ; Comte himself would prefer ten or fifteen (*Lettres à Stuart Mill*, pp. 51-55). Gall was the first to bring the study of the intellectual and moral functions into the positive stage, and to assert the significance of inner dispositions. Comte's admiration of Gall is inconsistent with his conception of the relation between the metaphysical and the positive stages ; for Gall's theory of mental faculties exhibits all the signs of " metaphysic." If we ask how Comte reconciles the assumption of ten to fifteen separate faculties with the unity of consciousness, the answer is that this unity, in his view, is not original, but derived ; it is based on the harmony between the different tendencies and powers of man (*Cours*, iii. p. 545). The problem of the relation between discontinuity and continuity recurs in the domain of consciousness, and in a form which calls for special investigation. Comte never arrived at making this investigation, for, as we have seen, he split up psychology into a biological and a sociological part, and left no room for the emergence of any central psychological questions. On this point Comte's work is supplemented by the most recent English school, who attribute especial importance to psychology.

(d) Sociology and Ethics

More than half of Comte's chief work (the three last and longest volumes) is devoted to the science of society—" sociology," as he calls it, a self-coined word which, in defiance of all the canons of philology, has succeeded in establishing itself. It includes an essential part of psychology, the whole of political economy and ethics, and the philosophy of history. Just as Comte had protested against treating the psychology of the individual apart from the mental development of the race, so too he protests against the isolation of politics and ethics from the general theory of society ; and the subsequent development of these sciences has proved him to have been right.[83]   Moreover, neither psychology nor political economy nor ethics can be treated out of relation to the course of human development which history reveals.   Comte works out the relation between statics and dynamics in all the different scientific spheres.   The world is considered statically in geometry, dynamically in mechanics. In physics and chemistry forces are considered partly in equilibrium, partly in activity.   In the organic sphere, statics is represented by anatomy, which investigates organisms ; dynamics by physiology, which investigates functions.   Sociology includes both a social static, which studies the constant conditions of society, and a social dynamic, which inquires into the laws of the progressive development of society ; the fundamental idea of the former is order, of the latter, progress. Statics and dynamics are closely related to one another, for order and progress reciprocally condition one another—a fact which both the reactionary and the revolutionary school failed to grasp.

(a) *Social Statics.*—Society forms a totality the elements of which stand in the closest reciprocal relation, so that no one of them can suffer change without the others suffering, more or less, a corresponding change. Thus, for example, the political and the social constitution are closely connected with the whole state of civilisation. There is a close bond of union between ideas, customs and institutions; and no authority—be it revolutionary or reactionary—can impose changes in social institutions unless they are congruent with the prevalent ideas and customs of the community. Institutions, of course, react on ideas and customs, but such reaction implies a long undisturbed existence, and is most visible in the childhood of the human race. Ideas and customs also act and react on one another. The task of political institutions is to regulate the social life which has grown up spontaneously with the intellectual, moral and physical progress of man. Those elements which have been of the greatest significance during this development will finally become the ruling elements of the society. Authority rests on voluntary co-operation, but the converse does not hold good.

In social statics, *ethics*, regarded from one essential side, finds its place. The ethical laws express the solidarity of all human life. This solidarity reveals itself whenever men follow their social instincts. To explain the origin of social life as arising in a calculation on the part of individuals of the advantage it would be to them to live together involves a contradiction. The advantages can only be seen when the alliance has existed for some time; it cannot, therefore, have been the original motive of any established social life. Comte is here opposing the explanation so often brought forward in the eighteenth century, in which the shrewd calculation of isolated individuals was taken as a basis. In his view, an instinctive impulse to social life, independent of any personal calculation, makes itself felt; here, as everywhere else, feeling precedes knowledge. On this point Comte acknowledges he has taken his views partly from Hume and Adam Smith,[84] who carried him beyond the ordinary theory of egoism, partly from Gall, who believed the social instinct had a definite organ in the brain. Comte finds the first beginning of sociability at that stage of the animal world at which the sexes become differentiated and care for offspring first appears. But even with men the egoistic have at first the upper hand over the social tendencies; in order to indicate their de-

cided antithesis to egoism Comte calls the latter altruism
(from *alter*, neighbour). The personal interest, however, must
not be altogether rooted up. Altruism would be a vague and
unfruitful love if it did not recognise the impulse towards
personal satisfaction in others as well as in the self. But the
egoistic instinct must be brought into subordination, and this
is done by the successive development of intelligence and sympathy. Sympathy frees intelligence from its exclusive activity
in the service of egoism, and intelligence sharpens the sense of
social solidarity. The sympathetic feelings are fostered by
the social state. By extending his feelings till they embrace
the whole race, the individual finds in this social expansion
satisfaction of his need to perpetuate himself, for he regards
the continued life of the race as a continuation of his own life.

Isolated and single, the individual is only an abstraction.
The social unit is the family, in which the first trace of the
propensities which characterise the social organism appear.
The individual here learns to transcend himself, to live in
others, while, at the same time, he obeys his most energetic
instincts. It is the closest form of society—a *union*, not an
association. Co-operation, it is true, plays a part in the family
also, but not the chief part, as it does in larger societies, based
on common work and the supplementation necessitated by the
division of labour. The execution of any definite task by an
individual or a family is a social work. The power which is
to guide this work must proceed from society itself, and must
be based on the confidence which it inspires and the free adherence it meets with. Every society must have a government.
While in individual life the personal instincts, and in the family,
sympathy, are predominant, in larger societies the intellectual
faculties are essentially the governing ones. A certain intellectual solidarity is necessary to a society ; coincidence of
interests and immediate sympathy are not sufficient. Positive
science is of the greatest importance for ethics, for its business
is to determine as exactly as possible the real influence, direct
or indirect, which every action, every tendency and every feeling
exercises on human existence, both of single individuals and
of society as a whole.

According to Comte, the great merit of Catholicism is that
it emancipated morality from the subjugation to politics, under
which it had suffered in the polytheistic period. This emancipa-

tion found its expression in the doctrine of the dual powers and
of the independence of the spiritual from the temporal power.
But Catholicism proved incapable of satisfying the growing
intellectual needs of men, and metaphysical criticism began its
work of destruction. Moreover, Catholicism fostered egoism,
for it caused every individual to be occupied exclusively with
his own blessedness ; and in so doing, though it gave the
Church a powerful motive to work on, it hindered the free
and pure development of the sympathetic and magnanimous
feelings. The positive tendency of thought alone immediately fosters the development of these feelings, for positivism
teaches that our whole development takes place *within* society,
and that it is the individual, not society, which is the abstraction. In social life the egoistical tendencies must be checked
in various ways ; the social impulse alone must be allowed to
develop freely ; and the enhanced activity, which the wide
horizon thus revealed produces, contains in itself a source of
blessedness, of inner satisfaction, which is independent of all
external rewards. The concept of duty has its root in the *esprit
d'ensemble* which positive philosophy brings into play ; in the
light of this principle the single individual is viewed as a
member of the whole race, so that the rules of his action must
proceed from a universal order of things, not from purely
individual interests. The highest idea within the ethical sphere
is that of humanity as such, and the development of humanity
is effected by the co-operation of all individual and social
organs. Comte inveighs against the sharp separation between
private and public functions. This distinction, he declares, is
purely empirical, and appears in periods of transition only,
when a new civilisation is in process of arising and it is difficult
for the new elements to find their right places. It did not
exist among the Greeks and Romans, nor in the theocracy of
the Middle Ages ; it appeared first towards the end of the
Middle Ages, and is especially characteristic of the period of
prosperity which set in after the abolition of serfdom. The
masses of the proletariat have not yet actually become incorporated in the social system. Such an incorporation will be
accompanied by that true self-esteem which consists in feeling
oneself to be a co-worker in a great whole. The day will come
when such a feeling will ennoble even the lowliest occupation ;
when, that is to say, by means of a *positive* education, the

consciousness has been aroused that every individual endeavour is significant for society as a whole.

Comte was firmly convinced that political rest, the avoidance of great political disturbances, was all that was necessary in his time to bring about, by a natural transition, that modification of ideas, feelings and customs which should usher in the positive stage. The most important social difficulties, in his eyes, were not political but moral, and these can only be overcome through the influence of ideas and customs. The concept of duty, with him, is decidedly predominant over the concept of right. No definite theory of law and the State can be gathered from his philosophy. But he believes that, once ideas and customs are changed, institutions will have no difficulty in developing. We notice here already, in his first and, properly speaking, his chief work, the utopian tendency which typified his reaction against the marked emphasis laid on individual rights during the preceding period, and also against the many constitutional struggles with which his own time was occupied. He thought a comparatively short and progressive dictatorship would suffice to bring these ideas and feelings to maturity quietly,—a necessary condition if the West is to attain to permanent social institutions, and the great Revolution to find a positive counterpart.

(β) *Social Dynamics.*—We already know one important law belonging to social dynamics, viz. the law of three stages. As Comte points out, progress can most easily be traced in the intellectual sphere. Corresponding to the different stages of intellectual development, however, as was intimated in the account of the three stages, are different stages of social and political development. *Militarism* corresponds to the theological stage. Properly understood, the value of militarism consists in its inculcation and fostering of law-abidingness and discipline, which are necessary conditions for political organisation. There is a co-operation of forces for the attainment of common ends of urgent necessity. Just as it is obvious that the first spiritual authority must be theological, so too it is obvious that the first governments must be military. At this stage external force alone can effect concentration and interconnection. Moreover, war is a necessary condition of the earliest stages of social development. War reintroduces slavery; in order that the warriors may be free to use their strength all industrial work must be carried on by slaves. Corresponding to the transition period, which is described from its intellectual side as metaphysical, we have a social and political period which may be called *juristic*. A defensive military organisation takes the place of the earlier offensive military organisation. The warlike spirit gradually yields to the productive spirit. The middle classes press forward and demand political rights. The jurists, who are now supreme, have to weigh the different claims against one another. This stage, the social phase in which we now find ourselves, is a vague and unquiet transitional stage. Corresponding to the positive stage is the *industrial* phase, in which the productive forces determine the ordering of institutions and the distribution of power. Social questions now take the place of political. The proletarians gradually discover that the great social problems which press most heavily on them, as a class, cannot be solved by political revolutions. They will naturally sympathise with the endeavour of positive philosophy to place duties higher than rights, in the hope that general attention will be directed towards the solution of the problem which is the social problem *par excellence*, *i.e.* how to procure for all opportunity for mental development and the right to work. Thus there will be a natural understanding between the proletarians and positive philosophy.

This demonstration of the solidarity of human development has an important bearing on ethics, which comes under the head of social dynamics as well as of social statics. Not only is the social feeling strengthened by this proof of the solidarity of development, but an essential part of the content of ethics can only be determined on a dynamic basis. For it is the task of ethics to contribute towards the development of the distinctively human—in contradistinction to the animal and vegetative—qualities. The premises from which ethics draws its conclusions are derived not only from the sphere of social dynamics (*i.e.* the law of the three stages), but also from the results of comparative biology, which show that the higher we ascend in the animal series, the greater the predominance of the animal over the vegetative functions. In men, again, the specifically human qualities, *i.e.* intelligence and sociability, develop in connection with the animal qualities, in proof of which Comte, following Gall's phrenology, quotes the fact that the frontal region of the brain is more strongly developed than that portion which lies near the spinal cord. Within the human race itself, Comte holds, there is a continually progressive development of intelligence and sympathy (altruism), the condition under which the single individual can make himself one with the race. Although an opponent of the Lamarckian theory of evolution, Comte acknowledges that faculties and qualities can be greatly modified by steady and incessant exercise. The nobler tendencies of our nature become more and more developed through social life ; the worse instincts are gradually weakened, partly by self-mastery, partly by want of practice, or else they are gradually forced into the service of the social order.—Comte never succeeded in throwing his ideas on this point into any more definite form, partly because he did not adopt the theory on which Spinoza and Hartley based their doctrine of psychological development (see vol. i. of this work, pp. 324 and 448) and which English psychology afterwards developed still further ; partly too, because he could not appeal to the close union which the evolutionists assume to exist between the development of the individual and that of the race.

At the conclusion of his ethics, Comte says that in comparing the morality of positive philosophy with religious morality, we must not forget that while the former is hardly yet thought out and is not able to work through any regular institutions, the latter, on the contrary, has attained, through the spiritual work of centuries, its full development, and has for a long time found its support in a great social apparatus. During the last years of Comte's life—after the curious nervous crisis in the middle of the forties—he became more sanguine, and no longer held fast to the conviction that we are still in an early stage of development.

(e) Theory of Knowledge

Although Comte never made the theory of knowledge the subject of any special investigation and exposition, yet it is clear enough that the whole of his positive philosophy rests on certain definite epistemological presuppositions, and in single passages (especially in the last volume of the *Cours*, and afterwards in the *Discours sur l'esprit positif*) he expresses himself more explicitly on the subject. An attempt to determine

Comte's epistemological standpoint can hardly fail to be of interest.

Positive philosophy, according to Comte's express and repeated explanations, is not empiricism. As early as 1825, in a treatise entitled *Considérations philosophiques sur les sciences et les savants*, he had set forth the impossibility of absolute empiricism. Science does not consist in a mere accumulation of facts. Its real task is the combining of facts ; it consists of laws, not of facts only. No isolated fact is incorporated in science ; it only becomes so when its isolation is annulled, and it is brought, perhaps by means of an hypothesis, into connection with another fact. Comte even goes so far as to say (*Cours*, ii. p. 300) that no isolated and purely empirical observation can be certain. We have already seen that, according to Comte, it is only in the light of the need of combining phenomena that we can understand why human knowledge has to pass through the theological and metaphysical stages before it reaches the positive stage. In the positive stage the laws of phenomena, *i.e.* their real connection, are sought for. This connection may be exhibited in a twofold way. Phenomena occur either simultaneously or successively ; if the former, we explain them by showing that the relations and laws valid for different groups of phenomena are homogeneous : if the latter, we seek to exhibit their continuous interconnection. In the first case we have a static, in the latter a dynamic, explanation. We may explain *par similitude* or *par filiation*, so long as we bind together phenomena in such a manner that we are able to foresee their occurrence. And in both cases we satisfy the need of the human mind for unity, and discover the constant among all variations (*Discours sur l'esprit positif*, pp. 20, 21).

Beyond these intimations, interesting enough in themselves, Comte's theory of knowledge throws no further light on this point. He devotes no special investigation to the uniting activity of the mind, although he regards it as fundamental ; *tout se réduit toujours à lier*. A closer scrutiny would have carried him farther into subjective psychology than he either desired or considered possible. Nor did he enter upon the question as to the nature of the validity we are to attribute to the above-mentioned laws of homogeneity and succession. He expresses himself on this point with some uncertainty. Sometimes he says science has nothing to do with first principles ; such principles arise involuntarily in the human mind, and are not debatable. He here approximates to the epistemology, based on "common sense," of Reid. Sometimes, on the other hand, he maintains that the principle of the immutability of natural law, on which positive science is based, cannot be established *a priori*, but is always found to rest on simple observation and induction (cf. *Discours sur l'esprit positif*, p. 46, with p. 17, and with *Cours*, vi. p. 618). This latter view, if followed out to its logical developments, would, it is evident, drive him straight on the rocks of pure empiricism and the difficulties which occur in connection with the principle of causation ;—difficulties which were first clearly brought to light in Stuart Mill's resumption and thorough-going discussion of Hume's problem. It is evident that the two positions taken up by Comte are mutually contradictory ; for a principle which is beyond discussion cannot be grounded in facts, since to do this would necessarily involve discussion. Comte's expectation that the principle of the immutability of natural law would gradually penetrate into all spheres was based, as already remarked, on his belief that an irresistible analogy forces it upon us. As he says in one of his earlier treatises, it is impossible for the human mind to think positively in one sphere and metaphysically or theologically in others. The mind strives after unity of method and theory. Here, then, as Hume had already shown, the power of custom makes itself felt. But this can only explain the psychological power of the principle over the mind, not its real validity. Comte never felt the true sting of the problem of knowledge. He attempted to systematise positive knowledge, but he never set himself the task of discovering the ultimate foundation of this knowledge.

There is, however, another side from which Comte approaches the problem of knowledge, *i.e.* from the prominence he gives to the relativity of knowledge. As we have seen, he regarded it as one of the essential characteristics of positive philosophy that it everywhere puts the relative in place of the absolute for which earlier forms of philosophy had sought. He establishes the relativity of knowledge in a twofold manner. Firstly, positive science can only show us the relations of homogeneity and succession between things, not the absolute causes of things, nor the innermost nature of those things between which the relations exist. The relations themselves also appear as bare

facts, which must be taken as given, and cannot be grounded
on any more ultimate principle. Secondly, all our knowledge
is determined by the relation between our organism and its
environment. Comte even speaks of " the great elementary
dualism between understanding and its medium ;" explaining that
while it is true that the environment influences and determines
the understanding, and gives it its material, yet the elaboration
of this—just as in the processes of nutrition—take place
according to the laws of our own organisation, and under its
forms. In all our knowledge, therefore, a relation, on the one
hand to the subject, on the other to the object, enters. In
virtue of this biological theory of knowledge,[85] Comte regarded
himself as a successor of Aristotle, Leibniz and Kant (*Cours*,
vi. pp. 620 f; *Catéchisme positiviste*, pp. 150 f.) It showed him
that our knowledge can only attain to an approximation to
reality, but his practical standpoint prevented him from ever
discussing the question as to how far our knowledge can rightly
be called a reflection of reality. It was enough for him that
the knowledge we possess can be practically used for our
orientation. On the other hand, he lays great weight on the
point that the subject to which knowledge is related itself
undergoes change and development. All knowledge is determined by the stage of development which the individual and
the race have reached. Hence all knowledge has an historical
character. Sociology, no less than biology, leads, as the doctrine of the three stages showed, to the accentuation of the
relativity of knowledge. As long as biology and sociology had
not yet been developed in a positive form, relativity might
escape observation, and such was the case during the whole
period in which mathematics was the leading science. But
now the sceptre has passed to sociology. It is for her to
indicate the final scientific points of view.

The emphasis which Comte here lays on the importance of
regarding knowledge from the biological and sociological points
of view, or, in other words, his assertion that knowledge is
determined by the nature, the needs, and the grade of development of man, introduced an important modification into his
philosophical standpoint. At first he had laid chief stress
on " the necessary and rational subordination of the concept of
man to the concept of the world " (*Cours*, iii. p. 188): but now he
lays increasing stress on the subjective side of knowledge.

Knowledge appears to him as essentially a satisfaction of a subjective need, and he regards every means to attain such a satisfaction as justifiable. The need of knowledge becomes for him an artistic need. He maintains the justification of following the simplest hypotheses, and he overlooks the necessity of a confirmation by experience. He makes no inquiry as to the relation between the satisfaction of the impulse towards unity and simplicity of world-conception on the one hand and positive reality on the other, and he becomes more and more absorbed in the mystical world which had revealed itself to him since his nervous crisis, and in the " méditation exceptionnelle " which this revelation had evoked. He now formed a plan for supplementing the objective system expounded in his *Cours* by a subjective system. Hitherto he had explained man through the world ; he now proceeded to explain the world through man.

(f) *Comte as a Mystic*

Comte's great work as a thinker ended with his exposition of positive philosophy. Afterwards, however, he came to regard this exposition merely as the introduction to higher mysteries. We have already indicated the psychological causes of this change in his views. We will now briefly notice the ideas with which he was occupied in his last years. If they have no significance as scientific thoughts, yet, as symptoms, they are not without interest.

In his positive philosophy Comte had passed from the world to man : he had proceeded from abstract and universal to more complicated relations—and man is the being whose life exhibits the most complicated relations of all. Now he goes from man to the world, consciously adopting the subjective standpoint which, in the childhood of the race, had unconsciously been taken as fundamental. The world is now regarded as the basis which supports human life. From the most complicated—that is to say, the highest—standpoint of existence we must glance back over the lower stages. In the exposition of positive philosophy it was stated that intelligence must necessarily occupy the first place in man's nature. It is through intelligence that we know the laws of existence, and the influence of intelligence on feeling brings about new customs and institutions. Feeling, however, is now placed in the first

rank, and the intelligence is said to require enlightenment from
the heart. Synthesis—unity of conception—now takes the place
of analysis and specialisation. But only a subjective unity of
knowledge is possible. As positive philosophy has shown, the
forces of the world cannot be reduced to an absolute unity. Unity
of conception can be gained, however, if we regard the whole
world (so far as we know it) in its relation to man. Here,
however, Comte feels bound to modify his earlier classification
of the sciences, so as to separate ethics from sociology, and
make it a seventh fundamental science. For if humanity is to
be the point of unity round which all thought is to centre, and
from which it must proceed, we must penetrate into the whole
problem of human nature. But in sociology, thought and
action alone have real significance ; feelings only play a part as
motives, and since the different motives in the long run balance
one another, there is no particular reason, from a strictly
sociological point of view, to attribute any great importance to
feelings. Ethics, therefore, is now seen to be the most complicated of all the sciences, for it gives prominence to an
element which filled a subordinate place in sociology. The
appearance of ethics as an independent member in the system
of sciences takes place, then, in harmony with the law of
progress from the more abstract to the more concrete.[86] All
sciences must now be regarded as forming a part of ethics ;
they must be pursued from this point of view so that each one
may be treated as the preparation for the next and more
complicated one, until with ethics, the concluding science, the
goal is reached. We must take care that analysis does not
again get the upper hand, and all studies which do not further
our knowledge of the order of Nature and our capacity to adapt
ourselves to it, or which can be of no service in guiding our
activity, must be abandoned. New and authoritative scientific
works must be written in which the fundamental sciences shall
be compressed within the necessary limits. Comte now (in his
Politique positive and in the *Catéchisme positif*) characteristically
terms the leading doctrines of the positive philosophy " positive
dogma." His thought sought rest, and every inquiry which
set his goal, *i.e.* the losing of himself in the religion of
humanity farther off rendered him impatient. He regards
feeling as exalted high above knowledge and action, which only
possess value on account of their results ; they are dependent,

moreover, on outer relations, while feeling grants direct and inner satisfaction. The pre-eminence of art over science follows as a corollary from this. The spring of art is feeling. Art leads the abstract consideration of the theorist gently back to reality, while it infuses in the minds of practical men a noble enthusiasm for great ideas. Physiologically, it originates in the involuntary motions which are bound up with feeling, and which at once express and react upon our innermost states. It creates ideal types through the continual contemplation of which our thoughts and instincts are perfected. The priests of the religion of humanity must exemplify in themselves the blending together of philosophy and poetry.

The religion of humanity, of which Comte regarded himself as the founder, is a worship of humanity as *le grand être* in whom all participate ; as the sum-total of all dead, living or future beings who, in smaller or larger circles, have voluntarily laboured for the progress and blessedness of man. This is an ideal concept ; for only those will be perpetuated in the remembrance of the race who have spent themselves in working for it. Comte drew up a positivist calendar in which each month and each day of the month is called after one or other of the heroes who have furthered the development of humanity. This was the first step towards the establishment of a public cult which was to consist in an enthusiastic and grateful commemoration, at regularly recurring intervals, of the benefactors of the race. In private worship persons who have been more closely connected with the individual will represent for him the ideal of the race. Those who have obstructed this progress, as, *e.g.*, the Emperor Julian and Napoleon, " ces deux principaux rétrogradeurs que nous offre l'ensemble de l'histoire," are only called to mind in the positivistic cult, that they may suffer their " well-deserved periodic flagellation." The dignity of the individual is based on the fact that as a member of smaller or larger circles (family, fatherland, etc.), he becomes incorporated in the *grand être*. All thoughts and actions should be directed towards the preservation and perfecting of this being. Altruism (*vivre pour autrui*) is at once the highest duty and the highest blessedness.

The conduct of the cult as well as that of education ought, according to Comte, to be made over to a caste of priests, who have received an encyclopædic education in philosophy, and who are also poets and physicians. Their authority will be voluntarily recognised by all ; hence they will be able to influence public opinion. Throughout his whole scheme of positivist religion, Comte endeavours, wherever possible, to introduce analogies with " everything great and deep which the Catholic system of the Middle Ages effected or even projected." *Sociocracy, i.e.* the order of society as conceived by Comte, is far more akin to theocracy than to the intervening individualistic period with its " endless agitations." Indeed Comte goes still farther back. Just because positivism has completely emancipated itself from old prejudices, it will not hesitate to adopt once more the fetich-istic view of Nature, and attribute life and soul to all things in Nature. This way of looking at things lends power to speech and fosters artistic imagination ; moreover, it vivifies the feeling for everything which can further the preservation and develop-ment of the "great being." Every animal kind is regarded as a human species whose growth has been stunted (*un grand être plus ou moins avorté*). Once again, after the long critical period, comes an age of construction. The new religion regards the world-space as "the great medium" in which the earth, " the great fetich," has shaped itself. The great fetich, again, has abstained from exerting its colossal and elementary forces, and has sacrificed itself in its longing that " the great being " in which the highest perfection appears in the most concen-trated form, may develop. (The highest beings, as Comte had already taught in the *Cours*, are also the most dependent.) The " great medium," the " great fetich," and the " great being," form the positivist trinity.

Comte even gives a sketch of the constitution of the future sociocracy. The idea of right must altogether disappear. No one possesses any other right than that of doing his duty. Individuals are not regarded as separate beings, but as so many organs of the great being. The ruling power in external affairs resides with the captains of industry (bankers, manu-facturers and landlords). These *patricians* will be too rich to entertain any covetous feelings, and they will be able to en-noble labour, for they will undertake it from free choice, moved by the highest personal feelings. Their duty is to conduct industrial affairs in such a manner that all men may participate in family life, which is the basis of human blessedness. It is to the interest of the proletarians that capital should be concentrated in the hands of some few patricians; in this way a centralised and intelligent guidance will be secured. The age of the middle classes is over. The patricians correspond to the organs of nourishment in an organism. In contradistinction to these are the organs of the brain, of reason (*philosophers*), the organs of deep and innermost feeling (*women*), and the organs of energy (*proletarians*). While the patricians represent the existing order, the proletarians are the representatives of progress. It is incumbent on the philosophers (or the priests) to discover what would promote the welfare of "the great being"; it is incumbent on women to arouse the right feeling to carry on the work. Philosophers and women will sympathise with the proletarians, and find in them a support against any possible encroachments on the part of the patricians; while the proletarians have in public opinion and in the power of refusal to co-operate the means of checking any misuse of power on the part of the spiritual or temporal authorities.

Comte's Utopia has the interest which attaches to such schemes when they proceed from powerful minds, open to all the tendencies of their times. Just as many features of Greek life have been recognised in Plato's *Republic*, so too we can detect the historical background in Comte's work. His sketch of the religion of the future has significance, partly as the testimony of a serious and deep-feeling man that the criticism and negation of conceptions-of-life undertaken by the preceding age was not the last word to be said on the subject; partly because he takes as his central point the idea of humanity and love. But Comte could never see that if this idea ever becomes predominant, religious ideas will be able to develop with individual freedom and rich variety in all those who feel the need of them. Few people will be found to sympathise with Comte's taste, as exhibited in his arrangement of a future cult, with the exception of a few brilliant thoughts, *e.g.* that of a new calendar containing the names of historical personalities instead of those of unknown saints. Many will think that the religious problem proper only begins where Comte's religion ends, viz. at the question as to how the development of the world is related to that of the human race and of the human ideal. To this question Comte's new trinity supplies no answer.

Just as, as we have seen, Comte allowed no free play of individuality in relation to religion, so too he allows none in political matters, indeed he goes so far as to exclude altogether any concept of an order of rights or a representative government. Public opinion and labour strikes, however, would hardly afford adequate correctives, in the absence of any fixed forms of public and private life to which those in authority are bound. Most characteristic of all is the prohibition of free inquiry with regard to the "positive dogmas," which are laid down once and for all. The excuse for this must be found in the so-called "cerebral hygiene," which, worn out by his energetic intellectual labours, Comte had felt obliged to impose upon himself. To enforce this prohibition, however, would be to run counter to the spirit of his own best work.

B. JOHN STUART MILL AND THE REVIVAL OF ENGLISH PHILOSOPHY IN THE NINETEENTH CENTURY

THE conflict between eighteenth and nineteenth century thought was less violent in England than in France and Germany. Neither revolution nor Romanticism appeared at first hand in England, although both revolutionary and romantic ideas were at work, stimulating and fertilising in manifold ways. The wonderful power possessed by the English nation of introducing radical transformations without interrupting the continuity of its development is very conspicuous in the sphere of philosophy. After Hume and Adam Smith there was an ebb in English philosophy (cf. vol. i. p. 452 of this work). Hume had drawn such sweeping consequences from the empirical philosophy which preceded him in England, within the domain of epistemology that, for the time, there was scarcely anything more to be done from that point of view. Moreover, practical political and religious interests held the field. Hence we find the men to whom philosophic interest attaches at the beginning of the new century, *i.e.* Jeremy Bentham and James Mill, prompted by essentially practical interests. The ethics and psychology of the older English school were pressed into the service of the new ideas. It is especially curious to notice the different results which an almost identical circle of ideas effected in France and England respectively. Bentham and James Mill are no heaven-stormers such as were the philosophers of the French Enlightenment; we find in them, however, a concentration of thought on definite aims and a sense for the practical application of general principles which form an agreeable contrast to the figures of speech and declamations of the revolutionary French. The English do not care to shoot into the air ; they prefer to hit the mark, even should the roar of their artillery be less imposing. In virtue of their practical sense and the firmness with which they stood by the principles of the older English school, the two men already named are important figures in the history of thought, for they transplanted into modern times all that was soundest in the thought of the eighteenth century. They taught a younger generation to assimilate modern thought without making light of the gains won by the intellectual labour of the preceding age. Stuart Mill's personality as a thinker occupies a central position in the history of English philosophy, for he had the power of understanding and assimilating in all their fulness both the new and the old ideas, and the development which they received at his hands led to a complete revival of English philosophy. He took up Hume's problem again on a broader basis, with greater consistency as well as with greater versatility. With conscientious tenacity he adhered, as long as it was possible for him to do so, to the point of view of the older school, although he never concealed the difficulties it involved, nor failed to appreciate the importance of recent experiences. With regard both to theoretical and practical problems he performed a work of measuring and discounting which was of the greatest importance for the spiritual and social develop- ment of our century, and between 1840-60 he was unquestion- ably the greatest philosophical thinker of the day. But then came the evolutionary theory, and with it new points of view.

Critical philosophy and romantic speculation, however, also found an entrance into the intellectual life of England, and gave it a mighty impulse. By their means a deepening and extension of view was effected which would hardly have taken place had the older English school been left to itself. The tendency called by Schiller " Idealphilosophie " maintained in the face of the prevailing empiricism that there are spiritual values which empirical philosophy cannot explain. This tendency is represented in England chiefly by Coleridge and Carlyle. In the latter, Goethe's humanism and Fichte's doctrine of personality became transformed into a unique historical conception of life, which played an important part in the intellectual development of many individual thinkers, and lent valuable aid to the preservation of the innermost kernel of personal life during the struggle with the problems of the age, and in the midst of the sharp antitheses of the century. There was one question, however, which Carlyle persistently put on one side, when he did not answer it by cutting the knot. This was the question as to how this assertion of the value of personal life is related to the attempt to discover—within the mental sphere as well as in the rest of existence—a universal conformity to law. We come here on the epistemological problem which was discussed in the spirit of the critical philosophy by thinkers such as Whewell and Hamilton, and afterwards, from the point of view of absolute empiricism, by Stuart Mill.

CHAPTER I

PHILOSOPHY IN ENGLAND PRIOR TO 1840

(a) *The Philosophy of Reform*

JEREMY BENTHAM (born February 15, 1748, in London, died June 8, 1832) has his place in the history of the theory of rights and of philanthropy, rather than in the history of philosophy proper. But he exercised no little influence on the development of philosophical ethics, owing to the energy with which he laid down and applied the principle that every institution and every action must be judged according to its tendency to promote happiness or arrest pain. He would have all ethics and all theory of rights based exclusively on the fundamental principle that pleasure is preferable to pain. It is only prejudice, he thinks, principally religious prejudice and love of power, that hinders the public recognition of this principle ; indeed we see that men follow it in all cases in which they use their reason freely, undeterred by any external or internal hindrances. The principle of the greatest possible happiness of the greatest number or, as it is also called, the principle of *utility* (by utility is meant the tendency to produce happiness) is, according to Bentham, a self-evident principle : it is the basis of a practical valuation, but does not itself require a ground. This, at least, is how he expounds the matter in his first work, which appeared the year Hume died (*Fragment on Government*, 1776, chap. i. § 48).

Bentham, however, was not the original discoverer of this principle. It had been formulated in the same words by Hutcheson, and by several others after him. Bentham himself says he had it from Hume. In an interesting passage on his own development he tells us (*Fragment on Government*, chap. i.

§ 36), that on reading Part III. of Hume's treatise the scales had fallen from his eyes. He had been brought up in an orthodox Tory family with strictly conservative views. He regarded Charles I. as a martyr, and revolution in his eyes spelt godlessness. His legal studies introduced him to that theory of natural right which assumes an original contract, and argues from this that if a prince does not fulfil his obligations to his subjects, his subjects are no longer under obligation to render him obedience. This doctrine did not satisfy him either, however ; partly because of the impossibility of adducing any historical proof that such a contract was ever concluded ; partly because, even if we allow the existence of an original contract, there remains the further question as to *why* men are bound to fulfil contracts or promises in general. The only possible answer to this question in his opinion, is as follows : it is to the advantage of society that contracts should be observed, hence every individual man must keep his promises ; if he fail to do so he must be punished, for the suffering which the punishment will cause him will be outweighed by the good which the keeping of promises procures to society as a whole (*Fragment*, chap. i. § 42). Thus the theory of natural right is replaced by the theory of utility, the original contract by the principle of utility. The great significance of this change, as Bentham himself points out, is that with it we pass from the world of fictions to the world of facts. For experience alone can prove whether an action or an institution is or is not useful. The true aim of discussion from this time forwards, therefore, will be the establishment of facts. Hence, the right of freely criticising actions and institutions is of the greatest importance. Bentham saw no danger in such freedom of speech. For every really useful institution will be defended by those who reap its advantages ; it will, therefore, never be left unprotected.

Bentham had to make front against two sides in support of his principle of utility. He adopted a severely critical attitude towards the traditional institutions, and more especially the chaotic legislation of his country. His forte, strictly speaking, is criticism of the existing order of rights and of society (censorial jurisprudence). He mentions the Italian jurist, BECCARIA, as his most important predecessor in this sphere. Beccaria had already laid down the principle of the

greatest possible happiness of the greatest possible number
as determining the aim of legislation, and had applied this
principle in his criticism of penal justice. Bentham gave it
a still wider application. In so doing he came into sharp
antagonism with the conservatives ; but, on the other hand, he
protests strongly against the French revolutionaries' appeal
to natural right, and against their acknowledgment of the
universal rights of man. In Bentham's view, the individual
only possesses rights in so far as it conduces to the advantage
of society as a whole that he should have them. And he
thinks the proclamation of the rights of man tends to foster
egoism, which is strong enough without any encouragement,
while the really important point to arrive at is the reconciliation of the individual to any sacrifice which may be required
of him for the good of the majority.

In his chief philosophical work, *Principles of Morals and
Legislation,* he enters on a detailed application of the principle
of utility. He inquires which feelings of happiness are to be
preferred before others, and points out that consideration must
also be paid to the certainty of the pleasure, to its strength, its
duration, its nearness and " purity," as well as its " fecundity."
He further asks, What are the rewards and punishments by
which men can be induced to perform actions productive of
happiness ? And in close connection with this, What are the
different motives which, generally speaking, determine the actions
of men, and what moral worth do they possess ? His power of
drawing distinctions, of defining and classifying, is conspicuous
throughout the work ; he is a scholastic in a new sphere.
His inquiry into motives is of especial interest, for he was by
no means disposed to underrate their importance. On the
contrary, the principle of utility affords him a standard of
measurement for the estimation of the inner springs of action.
Those motives are to be called good which can be shown to
lead to a harmony between the individual's own interests and
the interests of others, while those are bad which conduce to
the separation of interests. The motive which is most certain
to lead in the direction of the furtherance of the principle of
utility is goodwill or benevolence :—" The dictates of utility
are neither more nor less than the dictates of the most extensive and enlightened benevolence." Next to benevolence come
the need cf other men's esteem, the wish to gain the love of others,

religion, and, lastly, the instinct towards self-preservation and the wish for pleasure, privilege and power (*Principles of Morals and Legislation*, chap. x. §§ 29-42).

Bentham devoted himself chiefly to the reform of legislation in accordance with humane principles, the codification of laws (the word "codification" was coined by him)—so that every one might know and understand them, and thus expenses and abuses might be avoided—the improvement of the prison system, and the development of the constitution into a democracy by means of the introduction of universal suffrage. In his struggle for reforms he took the principle of utility as his starting-point. And since he always took this principle for granted, he came to regard it as a dogmatic principle, as established, once and for all ; hence he did not feel the need of inquiring what reason can be assigned for its recognition. He does not see that a question may be addressed to him similar to the one which he himself addressed to the supporters of natural right. Just as he asked why men ought to keep their promises, so too, we may ask him why we ought to work for the happiness of the majority. It is not logically self-evident. If we turn to Bentham's works in search of an answer to this question we shall arrive at no definite conclusion. We have already noticed his assertion that the claims of the principle of utility are identical with those of the principle of comprehensive and enlightened benevolence. So far we might suppose that, in Bentham's view, the recognition of the principle of utility as a criterion has its spring in the sympathetic feelings. This was certainly the case with Bentham himself. He was a man easily moved to compassion and sympathy, and, in his own person, was very sensitive to pain. But he was lacking in the capacity for thinking himself into the moods and states of other men ; moreover, the many prejudices and hindrances arising from egoism which he had encountered on his way through life left him with no very great opinion of the power of disinterested sympathy in the world. If his own sympathy induced him not only to labour throughout his life, both practically and theoretically, for the furtherance of human happiness,—a labour which brought him neither profit nor worldly honours,—and if, in addition to this, he entertained great hopes that the principle of utility would succeed in enforcing its claims, he depended chiefly,

both in his efforts and in his hopes, on the belief that if only
every individual laboured with prudence and energy to promote
his own happiness, the egoistic interests themselves would form
a harmony resulting in general happiness. In reality, that is to
say, he depends upon the harmony of well-understood interests.
In his *Deontology*, a work published from a pupil's notes after
his death, this point of view is especially prominent. He
adopts a standpoint here which reminds us of that of the
French Helvetius, an author whom he held in high esteem.
Although other pupils of Bentham have protested against
attributing the views expounded in this work, as they stand, to
Bentham, yet it seems probable that we have here a true statement of some portion of his views, and that he himself was not
clear as to the relation in which they stood to other of his
tenets. All virtue is here reduced to the individual sagacity
which prompts a man to help other men in order that he may
receive help from them again ; while hope in the future is
grounded in the belief that public opinion will become increasingly powerful, and that the judgments formed by public opinion
will be more and more determined by insight into the harmony
of enlightened self-interests. The idea of this great harmony
inspired Bentham, as Adam Smith had been inspired by the
harmony of economic interests. That which, with Adam Smith,
is political economy, becomes extended under Bentham's treatment until it practically includes the whole of ethics. He starts
from the conception that the race consists of isolated individuals,
every one of whom is eagerly striving to get the greatest possible
number of goods at the least possible cost. Even such a great
admirer of Bentham as Stuart Mill has admitted that the
former only knew "the business part of human affairs." [87]   But
we must remember that, at any rate, Bentham stood in no
"business" relation to his own views and efforts.[88]

Bentham's ideas soon gained an influence over men who
were active in public life. But nothing that can be called a
school or definite party gathered round him. He lived a very
retired life, and only influenced people through his writings.
Towards the end of his life his tendency of thought was
represented by an organ of its own (*The Westminster Review*)
which took up a sharply antagonistic attitude towards the
old party journals (the *Quarterly* and *Edinburgh Reviews*).
His most active co-workers were his friend James Mill, and

the latter's son, John Stuart Mill. The supporters of Bentham's principle of utility were generally called " Utilitarians," a term which Stuart Mill believed himself to have introduced, but Bentham himself had already used it. Like the name " Positivism," " Utilitarianism " covers various and divergent theories; for an ethical system is not exhaustively characterised by the criterion it employs for the ascertainment of worth. The ethical problem embraces other questions besides this. We may mention, in particular, that a " Utilitarian " (in the widest sense) need not necessarily take the same view as to the psychological foundation of ethics as that held by Bentham.

Among Bentham's co-workers JAMES MILL occupies the first place. His philosophical importance consists mainly in the fact that he attempted to supply the psychological basis which was lacking in Bentham's ethics. His education at the University of Edinburgh, where he had attended lectures by Dugald Stewart, a pupil of Reid's, was a fitting preparation for such a task. He was born on April 6, 1773, in the south of Scotland, and grew up in needy circumstances. His father was a village shoemaker. His mother came of people in a better position, and it was owing to her spirit and ambition that her son's excellent abilities were adequately developed. James Mill afterwards received help from Sir John Stuart, a landed proprietor in whose family he was tutor. He studied theology in Edinburgh, but seems early to have abandoned the idea of becoming a clergyman, although it was not till much later (even later than his son has described in the biography) that his views became distinctly anti-theological. At the age of thirty he went to London, where he gained his living by literary work. An anxious time followed, for he married and had a large family of children whom he supported by his pen. During this hard struggle for existence, however, he never gave up the struggle for humane ends, nor did he sacrifice any of his gradually developed radical views. His chief work at this time was his *History of British India*, which contains a severe criticism, based on thorough knowledge, of the government of the East India Company. It is characteristic of the way in which affairs are conducted in England that notwithstanding this attack, Mill, when seeking a post, was offered one in the service of the Company, which used his knowledge without fearing his criticism. He soon raised himself to a high position, and acquired great influence in the administration of Indian affairs. Of great importance for him was his acquaintance with Bentham, which developed into a faithful friendship, in spite of the passing misunderstandings and collisions which were almost inevitable between men of such sharply-defined and self-confident characters. Mill worked hard to promote the practical application of the principle of utility in many departments of philanthropy and politics. It is even now interesting and instructive to follow his efforts in this direction. ALEXANDER BAIN gives in his *James Mill, a Biography* (London, 1882) a detailed account of Mill's labours from year to year. Mill exerted his influence not only through his writings, but also, and perhaps still more, in conversations with a group of younger men who gathered round him, with members of the Radical party in politics, and with colleagues on the *Westminster Review*. He is the intellectual father of the first parliamentary reform. He attacked the aristocracy and clergy with a zeal and severity which appeared to many, including Bentham, who was by no means inclined to be too soft spoken, altogether too strong. From his study chair he led the great struggle between the classes, which resulted in giving a new aspect to English politics. He showed himself more practical than Bentham in politics, for he did not advocate the immediate adoption of universal suffrage, but restricted his programme to the emancipation of the middle classes. He was persuaded that before the suffrage could safely be extended to larger circles the way must be prepared by the gradual spread of enlightenment and education. He held that the race was capable of unlimited progress if a policy could be initiated, which should be based on general enlightenment of the nation and universal suffrage, and governed by the principle of utility. Like Bentham he thought the most important thing was that men should have an enlightened sense of their own interests, and that they should be free to follow the dictates of reason. His procedure, also like that of Bentham's, was mainly deductive. He too regarded the principle of utility as an eternal verity from which we have only to draw the consequences. Neither he nor Bentham had any sense for the manifold *nuances* of concrete circumstances, among which the general principles of ethics and the philosophy of law are to find their application. Legislation was not, in Bentham's eyes, at all so difficult a matter as Montesquieu had supposed. It is true that Bentham devoted a treatise to "the influence of time and place on legislation," but still he was of opinion that there was a tendency, fostered by prejudices and zeal in the defence of traditional abuses, to exaggerate the significance of historical circumstances. James Mill's advance on Bentham consists in his endeavour to give a more definite basis to the general principle of the estimation of worth, from which all ethical and political *axiomata media* were to be derived. He was led to do this by his psychological studies which he pursued unceasingly throughout his official labours and his philanthropiçal and political endeavours ; they closed with his famous work *Analysis of the Human Mind* (1829).

This work occupies a place of great importance in the history of psychology, for it is the most systematic attempt that has been made to explain all mental phenomena by the association of ideas. It is a renewal of the attempt made by Hartley in his day (see vol. i. pp. 446 f.). James Mill's exposition is characterised by far greater clearness and fulness than Hartley's. Not only does he explain all phenomena of consciousness as having arisen through association, but he also —in a somewhat artificial fashion—reduces all associations to the association of such ideas as have frequently occurred together (which has since been called association by contiguity). In so doing, James Mill attempts to apply the principle of simplicity. He lays down the rule that the number of original facts recognised must be as small as possible. As Bentham had attempted to base the whole of ethics on the single principle that pleasure is preferable to pain, so James Mill attempts to construct the whole of psychology on the single principle that that which has once been experienced can be recalled when experiences which occurred with it, either in space or time, are repeated. If this principle is sufficient to support a complete psychology it must be admitted that psychological theory acquires extraordinary simplicity. Moreover, a prospect of the logical extension of empirical philosophy into all spheres, such as the older English school never dreamt of, is opened up. For not only each particular idea in itself, but also all connections of ideas are entirely determined by whatever has been presented to consciousness from without. Here, then, we have an unlimited prospect of influencing the intellectual life of man and determining the direction it shall

take ; for legislation, education and the ordering of external circumstances in general determines the connections of ideas by
which men are governed. Thus the associative psychology
not only confers the possibility of *understanding* men's ideas,
and how they have united and shaped themselves, but also of
determining which ideas and which associations of ideas shall
prevail in the future. It thus provides a basis for criticism and
for fresh construction, supplies a powerful weapon against
prejudices by exhibiting their origin, and is a means of progress
since it replaces prejudices by new and right associations of
ideas. In addition to Hartley's influence we can detect here
that of Helvetius. The *De l'Esprit* was a favourite work in
Mill's circle, as was also the *Observations on Man.*

The associative psychology, under the form in which it
here appears, we must remember, is to serve as a basis for the
recognition of the principle of utility ; hence James Mill, following Hartley, lays great weight on the point that not only can
association cause one idea to recall another or excite a feeling
of pleasure or pain, but also that several ideas and feelings may
enter into so intimate a union with one another as to become
inseparable, while the new totality, thus formed, possesses
qualities which are not possessed by any of the parts. The
new totality formed by association can itself, as James Mill
expresses it in the clearest exposition which he has given of the
matter (Appendix B to his polemical *Fragment on Mackintosh*),
become " a substantive principle of human nature." From the
nature and value of a feeling, therefore, we cannot conclude to
its origin. Many disputes and misunderstandings have been
occasioned by the confounding of these two things—value and
origin. It has been thought that a psychical faculty must
either be absolutely original, or else that the factors which
make up its existence must be of the same kind as itself.
Psychical events have been compared with mechanical conjunctions, while in the great majority of cases they should be
conceived in analogy with chemical events. The result of this
mistake has been that either—as in the " selfish system "—all
feelings, for the sake of clearness and simplicity, have been
traced back to egoism, or else various feelings, differing in kind
from the beginning (some interested, others disinterested) have
been assumed. But the associative psychology shows reasons
in support of the view that the disinterested feelings, like the

egoistic feelings, have developed out of more elementary
feelings. As Butler has already shown (see vol. i. p. 398),
egoism, in the strict sense of the word, cannot be original, since
it presupposes a conscious reckoning ; disinterested benevolence,
however, is no more original ; it arises as follows :—Pleasure
and pain are very early transferred from the nearest and most
elementary causes to more remote ones, which are connected
with the former as conditions and means of their operation.
Secondary feelings arise dependent on what was at first a
means, but afterwards appears as an end. Thus motives, which
at first only possessed value as conditions for actions, come to
acquire independent value, and it is thus that we can explain
the unconditional value which we attribute to the moral feeling
or conscience. The wellbeing of other men which, at first,
was only a means to the wellbeing of the individual, may
become secondary to this aim. And such secondary feelings
may be just as constant and immediate as the primary feelings.
The analytic examination of the origin of such feelings in
association will, Mill asserts, by no means weaken the value
they may have for us :—" Gratitude remains gratitude, resentment remains resentment, generosity generosity, in the
mind of him who feels them after analysis, the same as
before. The man who can trace them to their elements does
not cease to feel them as much as the man who never thought
about the matter. . . . They are constituent parts of
human nature. How we are actuated when we feel them is
matter of experience which every one knows within himself.
Their action is what it is, whether they are simple or compound. Does a complex motive cease to be a motive whenever it is discovered to be complex ? " (*Fragment on Mackintosh*,
p. 51). Mill here answers an objection which both then and
later has frequently been raised against the psychological
explanation of the moral feeling—both in the form under
which it appears in the older associative psychology, and in
that which it assumes in the theory of evolution.

But the passage quoted above from Mill itself implies that
the deductive application of the associative psychology has very
definite difficulties and limits. Concrete states must first be
studied in their *historical* becoming before their elements can be
discovered. The appeal to immediate experience is a confession
that the matter is by no means so simple as might appear

from the principles of the associative psychology. The new qualities of the product cannot be deduced from the factors. And the historical element in the conscious life of the particular individual which appears—at any rate provisionally—as a hindrance to analysis must offer in the social and political sphere, where it bulks much larger, a still more serious barrier to the deductive application of the principle of utility.

Now this irreducible element, yielding to no analysis, was precisely the point on which emphasis was laid by the philosophy of Romanticism. England's most famous representative of the Romantic school passionately defended that element in life which cannot be understood by means of any mechanical explanation, that original and unique element which is exhibited in every case of personal and historical development.

(b) *The Romantic Personality-Philosophy*

Bentham and James Mill may be compared to two great rocks towering aloft in the new century, against which the waves of Romanticism dashed and broke. It was of the greatest possible significance for intellectual life in England that the new tendencies had such superior and consistent representatives of the older line of thought to deal with. The action and reaction between the old and the new thus became fertile in a degree which is seldom seen. The struggle between the two tendencies was a severe one, and left ineradicable traces on the personal development of many, but it created new forms of life-conceptions and promoted fresh intellectual endeavours which were of epoch-making significance for the whole intellectual life of Europe.

It was through SAMUEL TAYLOR COLERIDGE (1772-1834) that modern German literature and Romantic philosophy gained an influence in England. During his youth, as he tells us in his *Biographia Literaria*, he had been a disciple of Hume and of Hartley. But he was repelled by the attempt, which is so characteristic of the eighteenth century, to reduce all mental phenomena, by means of analysis, to elementary functions, and to discover mechanical laws for the life of consciousness ; to succeed in this, in Coleridge's opinion, would be to destroy the unity and activity of mind. The study of German philosophy carried him far from the English school. A true Romanticist, he revelled in ideas of the absolute, in which the differences and oppositions of the finite world blended together and disappeared. In opposition to the fragmentariness of empiricism he set the totality discerned by intuition ; in place of analysis he put synthesis. He believed himself to have anticipated some of Schelling's ideas ; he had so lived himself into the speculative course of thought that he was able to carry it on on his own account in the direction initiated by its original founders. In preparing his works for the press he occasionally confused fragments which he had translated from Schelling with his own writing, an error which exposed him to accusations of plagiarism. This poetical and easily excitable mind, which was that of a poet and preacher rather than of a thinker, had some trouble in distinguishing between its own productions and that which it had gathered from others. Coleridge's chief loan from the German philosophy was Kant's distinction between reason (in the narrower sense) as the faculty of forming ideas of the unconditioned, and understanding as the faculty of forming categories, which can only afford us a limited knowledge (see above, pp. 53 ff., 57, 67). He brought this distinction into play chiefly in his search for a reconciliation between thought and religion. All the objections which had been regarded by the preceding age as final were now not exactly rejected, but credited to the " understanding," and discounted by an appeal to the deeper insight of " reason." Behind this appeal was concealed a growing sense of those elements in history and in life which resist or have hitherto resisted any scientific explanation. It was a protest against the sufficiency of science as hitherto developed, a protest which was offered (and accepted) as a new solution—a new basis. Coleridge never got beyond intuition and prophecy. He exercised his influence chiefly through conversations (or rather by monologues addressed to his hearers). His great work which was to reconcile philosophy with Christianity—in which he refers all difficult points to the sagacity of his hearers—did not succeed in its attempt. He was opposed alike to the philosophy of the eighteenth century (Hume and Voltaire), and to the ecclesiastical theology, congealed into outward forms and formulas. Like the German systematisers of Romanticism, he too attempted to discover a higher unity in which reflection and dogmatic faith are reconciled. His leading thoughts remind us of the so-called "Right" of the Hegelian school. The Trinity, for example, is to be explained, according to Coleridge, by the application of the scheme—thesis, antithesis, and synthesis—which had played so great a part in German speculation since Fichte. (Under the very obvious influence of Schelling's later teaching, however, Coleridge comes dangerously near to deducing a quaternity, for he regards God as "the absolute will or absolute identity," *i.e.* the prothesis as the basis of the interplay between thesis and antithesis, which become harmonised in the synthesis ! See *Table Talk*, July 8, 1827.) Consecutive thought, however, was never Coleridge's *forte*. He has been appropriately called a religious Epicurean. He revels in religious thoughts and feelings, and in figures in which they can find symbolical expression. His was, however, a weak character. He was master neither of his conduct in life nor of his train of thought. He took refuge from life, as Carlyle says (see his *Life of Sterling*, chap. viii., for an interesting characterisation of Coleridge) in theosophical dreams. All he had to give was transcendental moonshine, which shed a new light on old things for many a young doubter and seeker, but which contained no new life. A man who was himself strongly influenced by Coleridge for some time, viz. John Sterling, the friend of Carlyle and of Stuart Mill, has said of him : " His misfortune was to appear at a time where there was a man's work to do—and he did it not. He was lacking in firmness of character ; he acknowledged doctrines in which he no longer believed in order to avoid the discomfort of a quarrel." It is not quite clear what was the occasion of this accusation, which Sterling repeats in a letter to Carlyle. But when speculation and imagination are made the chief organs of religious thought, it may easily happen that more doctrines are acknowledged than have been realised as personal possessions.

Be that as it may, Coleridge awoke a new sense and new views in many of the younger generation. Has not even a thinker like Stuart Mill, not favourably disposed generally towards German speculative philosophy, placed him next to Bentham, and spoken of them as the two great seminal minds of their time ! Mill's own great and honest endeavours to learn from both of them we will discuss later. Most of those whom Coleridge temporarily influenced would have nothing to say to Bentham, but were willing to be led through the " moonshine " to orthodoxy—to a more pronounced orthodoxy, indeed, than that which had formerly obtained. Perhaps Carlyle is right in saying there would have been no Anglo-Catholic movement (no "Puseyism") if there had been no Coleridge. It is certainly the case that several of the men who joined this movement were interested in poetic and speculative ideas before they were carried away by the positive ecclesiastical movement.[89] That the antitheses contained in the various conceptions of life have become more and more accentuated in our century—at any rate as regards their external formulæ —is attested by the intellectual life of all countries.

THOMAS CARLYLE (1795-1881) found nourishment for his soul in a very different side of German philosophy. His study of German poetry and German thought gave him not a higher speculative knowledge, but a more vivid realisation of the value of personality, a new faith. From the German poets he was led to the German thinkers,—from Schiller and Goethe to Kant and Fichte. Widely different as was his brooding Scotch nature—where even on the most sunny days the clouds never quite disperse—to Goethe's genial humanism, yet he looked up to Goethe as a great example, and his creed was the creed of Faust. From Kant his principal loan was the distinction between the thing-in-itself and phenomena. Everything which Nature shows us is, according to Carlyle, phenomenal only. The "philosophy of clothes" which he expounds in his profound and humorous *Sartor Resartus* (1833) starts from the thought that just as an acquaintance with their clothes does not teach us to know the men who wear them, so an acquaintance with phenomena does not teach us to know the real ground of existence. Existence is, and must remain, an inscrutable and awe-inspiring mystery. The world is the garment of God. Natural science only shows us the external mechanism ; it does not touch the kernel of existence. Nature is a great symbol, a revelation of ideas which can be grasped by no scientific method. The world is not the dead machine science would have us believe. Even the purely external interconnection—the clothes—viewed from our little corner of existence is inexhaustible and incalculable. Moreover, however far our experience and our thoughts may reach, we can never get beyond the forms of space and time, and what are they but forms of knowledge ? They, too, form a part of the vesture of the Deity which is ever being woven anew. The wonder of existence conceals itself from us because, blinded by custom, we take forms for realities and accept as first principles what are often only traditional tenets, to which we have grown so accustomed that we are no longer in a position to question them. What is philosophy, however, but a continual struggle against custom? It is "transcendental" just because it transcends the sphere of blind custom. Hence it is the part of philosophy to reawaken the sense of the mystery of existence, when that sense has become dulled by the mechanical way of looking at things. " The man who cannot wonder, who does not habitually wonder (and worship), were he President of innumerable Royal Societies and carried the whole *Mécanique Céleste* and *Hegel's Philosophy* and the epitome of all Laboratories and Observatories with their results in his single head, is but a Pair of Spectacles behind which there is no Eye. Let those who have Eyes look through him, then he may be useful " (*Sartor Resartus*, i. 10).

It is very obvious that Carlyle applies the distinction between the thing-in-itself and phenomena not in the Kantian spirit but in the spirit of Romanticism. Kant considered it was the task of science to discover the interconnection of phenomena according to law, and that the concept of the thing-in-itself indicates the limit to this attempt. Romanticism, on the other hand, despises and rejects the scientific endeavour to range phenomenon by phenomenon according to definite laws. It is a never-ending task, and brings us no nearer to the heart of things. Carlyle himself, like the hero in *Sartor Resartus* (bk. ii. chap. 3), had gone through a period in his youth when the world appeared to him as a dead machine. The study of Hume, Gibbon and d'Alembert had robbed him of the religious faith of his childhood. For some time he occupied himself exclusively with mathematical studies, and his first literary work was a translation of Legendre's geometry.[90] But his attention was then directed, through Madame de Staël, to German literature, and the great world of Goethe revealed itself to him. " Four years ago," he wrote in 1824 to Goethe, "when I read your *Faust* among the mountains of my native Scotland I could not but fancy I might one day see you, and pour out before you as before a father the woes and wanderings of a heart whose mysteries you seemed so thoroughly to understand and could so beautifully represent."

Like Faust, Carlyle had no patience with science. What is the use of being able to dig a few feet deeper when an infinity remains behind? or, as he said in a conversation with Charles Darwin, How absurd it is after all to trouble whether a glacier moves a little quicker or slower, or indeed whether it moves at all! As a good Romanticist he accepted Goethe's theory of optics, and denied the right of the physicists to criticise it. His hints at a conception of nature remind us of Schelling's, especially of the eleventh lecture on the " Method of Academical Study," where it is stated, *inter alia*, that ideas *symbolise themselves* in things, and that empiricism conceives reality quite apart from its real significance, since it is the nature of symbols to have a life of their own. Natural science, then, takes symbols for absolute reality.

But it is not external nature which attracts Carlyle's interest. Man is for him the real revelation, the true schechina, the highest symbol. No analysis is able to exhaust his essence. Locke and his followers tried to analyse and mechanise the spirit out of existence. And a great endeavour has been made to make the whole of conduct mechanical, to reduce it to the mechanism of feelings of pleasure and pain, to make the principle of utility the rule, and to exclude every original, spontaneous and independent action. Bentham and Utilitarianism were the object of sharp criticism and bitter mockery on Carlyle's part. The only significance he could attribute to the principle of utility was negative and disintegrating. It might be useful in criticising the old order of things, but it could never produce a new one. It sets a dead mechanism of interests in place of the living personal morality which springs from the heart's striving to fulfil its inner ideal. Zealously as Carlyle inveighed against what he called the " cause and effect philosophy," he inveighed no less zealously against an ethic based on " virtue by profit and loss," and he sees in Bentham's theory a solution of the problem : " Given a world of knaves to educe an Honesty from their united action."

Among Carlyle's objections to analytic psychology and to Utilitarianism not the least considerable is that they lay too great weight on conscious reflection. Everything great arises and grows in silence ! Only he who can be silent becomes a great man, and a great act which is undertaken with full consciousness of its greatness is, when viewed aright, seen to be a little

act. The poets do well to hymn the night. Full, clear consciousness belittles and mechanises everything. The highest
truth can only exist for man in the form of a symbol ; the symbol
speaks and is silent, discovers and conceals at the same time.

Carlyle is no more favourably disposed towards theological
dogma than towards natural science and empirical philosophy.
Only under symbolic form can men possess the truth. But
symbols, like clothes, grow old and wear out, and new ones
must be formed to take the place of the old ones. Philosophy,
which is a struggle against custom, has especially to struggle
against religious ideas which have become mechanical from
habit. Carlyle describes his standpoint as *natural* super-
naturalism. The divine powers work within and without us.
But they work within us in a natural manner. As in external
nature the living garment of God is ever being woven anew,
so the inner sense is ever weaving new forms of spiritual life.
Every man must find his own symbol and his own religion,
and every man must commit his work to the ever-flowing
stream of time. " By *Religion*," says Carlyle (*On Heroes and
Hero-worship*, Lect. i.) " I do not mean here the church-
creed which a man professes, the articles of faith which he
will sign. . . . But the thing a man does practically believe
(and this is often enough *without* asserting it even to himself
—much less to others)—the thing a man does practically lay
to heart and know for certain concerning his vital relations to
this mysterious Universe." To speculate further as to the
nature of God is idle. Each one of us has enough to do
in performing the work which lies within our power. Carlyle's
view of religion, however, is the same as that of Goethe and
Fichte in his later works (*Fundamental Features of the Present
Age*, and the *Nature of a Scholar*) ; indeed he explicitly refers
to the latter. Of all the German philosophers, Fichte exercised
the strongest influence on Carlyle. The God-idea penetrates
everything—the spiritual and the physical world ; every spiritual
being is a spark of the same. Whether his concept of God is
theistic or pantheistic he will not decide. In a letter criticising
Sartor Resartus, John Sterling raises, *inter alia*, the objection that the God spoken of in the book was not a personal
God ; Carlyle declares this to be an abstract question which
he neither can nor will discuss (*Life of Sterling*, part ii. chap. ii.).

Carlyle's protests against empirical and critical science as

well as against theology placed him in an isolated position.
He felt a stranger in his age.   It was a decadent age,
undone through scepticism and analysis, the age of mechanism.   It was lacking in spirituality, it was lacking in faith.
Faith is the expression of the truth of life, mysterious and
indescribable like all vital activities.   Since the fall of the
Roman world no age has been so sceptical, so untrue, and so
depraved as the eighteenth century, the effects of which persist
into our own century.   It was an age in which no ideals
could grow and flourish (*On Heroes*, Lect. v., *History of the
French Revol.* vol. i. chap. ii.).   The law of the three stages
comes out clearly enough in Carlyle, who probably had it from
Fichte and the Saint-Simonians.   Carlyle, however, expresses
himself more forcibly than any other author who makes use
of this law concerning the miserableness of his own time.
Both in speaking and writing he deplored the fact of having
been born in such a miserable age.   His powerful imagination, his fervent and easily excitable disposition and his deep
melancholy, which was increased by constant bodily illness
(dyspepsia) caused him to dwell by preference on the dark
side of his age, which he exaggerated in comparison with that
of earlier periods.   He found it difficult to imagine that this
century might be a time of transition to a better, positive age ;
as indeed, according to the law of the three stages, it is said to
be.   Not that he really believed that there could be a breach
in development ; " it is a misunderstanding," he says, " to think
that the phœnix is completely destroyed by fire and there
lies, a heap of ashes, until a new bird miraculously arises ; no,
destruction and creation go hand in hand, and the new
garment is woven while the dissolution of the old is proceeding
(*Sartor Resartus*, iii. chap. vii.).   But Carlyle himself could not
find the new threads, though he is convinced that none of the
spiritual values of preceding ages can be lost : " In spite of
beaver sciences and temporal spiritual hebetude and cecity,
man and his universe are eternally divine, and no past nobleness or revelation of the divine can or will ever be lost to
him " (*Life of Sterling*, part i. chap. viii.).

He does not, like Coleridge and Hegel, attempt to establish
this conviction of the conservation of values by any symbolic
explanation of dogmas and ceremonies.   But he would have
the reverence, the wonder, the passionate renunciation and

labour which the faith of past times partly attested, partly
conditioned, preserved to the life of the future. This endeavour
explains his standpoint—his opposition at once to scientific
criticism and to theological faith. He seeks for the basis of
the conservation of values far deeper than analysis or tradition
could reach, *i.e.* in the core of personality. The living garment
of the never-dying divine force must be woven from within.
But is it possible to evoke once more these inner forces, after
the period of dissolution which we have reached? Carlyle
hovers between faith in the preservation of values or of inner
forces and the gloomy picture which his age presented. This
picture, it seems, appeared to him in darker and darker
colours. In his youth he took offence at Bentham's philanthropy, in his old age to Gladstone's zeal for the political and
material development of England. He declared, one day, in
conversation (March 1867, see the *Diaries* of CAROLINE FOX):
" The country is going to perdition at a fearful rate,—I give
it about fifty years to accomplish its fall." A weeping
Jeremiah, his voice rises in the old song of lamentation, which
he had begun to sing forty years ago ; now, as then, he can
find no light amid the darkness.

The cause which made Carlyle view his own times in such
sombre colours must not be sought in his own melancholy and
hyper-sensitiveness alone. It is contained also in the unrest and
doubt of the age, in the increasingly sharp opposition between
the opposing forces within the sphere of spiritual life, in the
continued balancing of accounts between the old and the
new in which debit and credit are so hard to disentangle. We
have seen a series of thinkers, from Rousseau, Lessing, and
Kant onwards, confronted each in turn with this problem.
But few were predestined to feel its sting by their whole
nature as was the Scotch peasant's son, brought up in the
strict Presbyterian faith, and living through and experiencing
in his own life the spiritual forces and conflicts of his age. It
is a problem which will accompany the human race upon its
way until it reaches—if it ever does—" the third kingdom."
That Carlyle saw darkness only all around him is due to the
high claims he made on the solution of the problem. His own
in-dwelling ideality, his inner light made the darkness round
him so black. He says somewhere that the world must seem
bad to every young and ardent spirit who comes into it with

great aims, and who sees life clearly as it is, for how else can
his force and heroism come into play? Were the world good,
he would be quite useless! Human force and ideality, then,
make the world seem evil ; evil is the shadow of ourselves, a
shadow which does not remain outside our ego, but which
extends to our own hearts. The unhappiness of man arises
from his greatness, from the infinite which stirs within him,
and which can find no breathing space in the forms of finitude
(*Sartor Resartus*, ii. 9 ; *Life of Sterling*, i. 5).

But the cause also lay in Carlyle's incorrigible Romanticism.
He is conspicuous, even among Romanticists, in inability to
discover ideality in that indefatigable faithful work which
ranges member by member and leads through the small to
the great. He has nothing but derision for science, and for
all endeavours connected therewith in the domain of practice.
And yet he who had spoken such noble—even if loud-
sounding—words on the significance of silence and of quiet
preparation would naturally, one would think, have learnt
that from stones which, taken individually, are insignificant
enough, proud and noble edifices can be reared. This was
the faith of Bentham, this the faith of Gladstone. And this
is the faith which underlies all the detailed investigations of
science. Charles Darwin was right when he said of Carlyle
that he was a narrow-minded man. His idealism was timid
because he lacked understanding for the significance of
intellectual and practical work. His faith in personal life was
not firm enough for him to rely on its permanent existence, no
matter to how much analysis and criticism it might be subjected.
But the core of life can surely pass through the fire unscathed !
Carlyle was right in saying that one cannot live on criticism,
but he did not see what ideal forces may lie behind the work
of criticism. At this point the Romanticist became a Philistine.

For the basis of spiritual and social life of the future
Carlyle looks to that which, in his conviction, has been
the support of the past, *i.e.* hero-worship, the cult of great
men. The infinite force which works and symbolises itself
in all things appears in a higher degree in men, and highest
of all in great men. As with Fichte, his belief in the appearance and significance of elect spirits is closely connected
with his faith in the activity of the deity in all finite beings
(see above, p. 150). By heroes or great men Carlyle under-

stands those who lead others and are taken as examples by them; the creators of all that the ordinary run of men try to carry out and attain. All the works which we see accomplished around us in the human world germinated in the hearts of great men. There invisible forces play upon them and, after the period of quiet receptivity is accomplished, bring them to birth in the visible world. Hence the history of great men is the soul of the history of the world. The hero may appear as prophet, poet, or statesman, but under all forms he represents the great concentrated force of life in contrast to all externality, dispersion, and limitation. Confronted with him, there stirs in all men the deep need of reverence, the divine spark. (On this point too, Carlyle reminds us of Fichte, especially of his *Reden an die deutsche Nation*, see above, p. 152.) It is the hero who discovers the hidden thoughts of existence and of the age, and announcing these by word and action to other men advances the human race. Never more than at the present day has there been need of such heroes, of an enlightened aristocracy, able to lead. The great social gulf which makes itself felt throughout the history of the world becomes broader and broader in our times. Carlyle had already indicated this in his *Sartor Resartus* (in his chapter on "Helotage" iii. 4), before his distinctively social works appeared, in which he bewails the bodily and spiritual hunger of the masses. National education and emigration on a large scale are the remedies which he suggests. He looks round in vain, however, for new prophets and new men like Hengist and Horsa to initiate the new measures. But to go deeper into the social question was not Carlyle's intention; he had all too great a scorn for philanthropists, political economists, and politicians. Instead of that he turned to history to find great figures and types, whose example might haply arouse and unite an exhausted and divided race. Carlyle influenced large circles, chiefly by his historical writings. By means of these writings his thoughts at the present day are gaining influence with increasing numbers. To many he himself was one of the heroes whom he described, one of those who possess the faculty of feeling, seeing and expressing the needs and the thoughts of their time. It is not our business to discuss his merits as an historian: that is a question which comes before another tribunal. But we notice, once again, his prevailing Romanticism in the great stress he lays on the original, spontaneous and inexplicable element in great personalities. He makes no definite attempt to explain the relation in which great men stand to the race—although one mark of great men is their conspicuous faculty for owing something to others, because their spiritual sense and needs are higher than those of ordinary men. Carlyle's explanation of a hero is mystical only ; he regards him as an incarnation of the infinite force which works in all things. Here, too, we note the Romanticist's horror of analysis and of the " cause and effect philosophy."

Carlyle, however, does not go so far as a later view, which regards great men as the "aim of history." He looks upon them rather as great causes and, hence, as great servants. He proclaims the cult of the heroic—but he sees clearly that it is no deed of heroism either to be worshipped by or to rule a stupid crowd. " Hero-worship if you will (*Past and Present*, i. 6) ; yes, friends : but, first of all, by being ourselves of heroic mind. A whole world of Heroes ; a world not of Flunkies where no Hero-King can reign : that is what we aim at ! "

(c) *Critical Philosophy*

The year 1829 is notable for the appearance of James Mill's *Analysis*, in which the work of the English school of empirical philosophy was energetically resumed, and the publication, in the *Edinburgh Review*, of WILLIAM HAMILTON'S treatise on *The Philosophy of the Unconditioned*, which sowed the seeds of critical philosophy on English soil. Hamilton was born at Glasgow in 1788, and studied there and at Oxford. When his epoch-making treatise appeared he was Professor of History at the University of Edinburgh, after having spent many years at the Bar. His point of departure in philosophy was the position taken by the Scotch school ; this school was founded by Reid, and gave expression to the reaction against Hume's sceptical and negative conclusions. Reid and his disciples hoped to correct these conclusions by the help of more exact psychological observation, but their zeal misled them into assuming the existence in the mind of a number of original faculties and instincts. They too often rejected results reached by means of analysis and criticism, appealing instead to " common sense " ; an appeal which evoked from Kant the trenchant remark

that a man shows his common sense by using it not by appealing to it, and that Hume's common sense may have been just
as good as Reid's.　Kant is here (in the introduction to the
Prolegomena) taking up the cudgels for Hume, to whom he
owed so much.　But Kant, too, in his own way, attempted to
refute him ; hence Kant too, with Reid and his disciples, must be
reckoned among his opponents.　William Hamilton endeavoured
to unite Reid's doctrine with that of Kant.　He developed his
own particular views in the treatise above-mentioned and in
a series of subsequent ones as well as in the essays published
in the *Edinburgh Review*, amongst which the *Philosophy of
Perception* (1830) deserves especial mention.　They are of
great interest from the point of view of epistemology as well as
of the philosophy of religion.　His collected essays were afterwards published under the title of *Discussions on Philosophy*.
In 1836 he was appointed professor of philosophy in Edinburgh, and here until his death (1856) he delivered lectures to
large audiences on psychology and logic.　These lectures played
an important part in shaping philosophical development in
Scotland.　They were subsequently published under the title
Lectures on Metaphysics (2 vols.) and *Lectures on Logic* (2 vols.).
Hamilton was an acute thinker, an eager searcher after truth,
and, despite his Scotch nature, spiritually akin to Lessing ;
he was a man of comprehensive learning, too, within the sphere
of the history of philosophy.

In his treatise on the *Philosophy of the Unconditioned*,
which is a criticism of Schelling and Comte and, to a certain
extent, of Kant also, Hamilton attempts to show that only
the conditioned and limited can be the object of knowledge,
and that the attempt to set up a philosophy of the unconditioned is doomed to failure.　But he is not content with
destructive criticism ; he gives in outline a complete theory of
knowledge, isolated points of which were still further elaborated in his later works.　His main thesis is : *to think is to
condition.*　He means by this that we determine everything
we are able to conceive and comprehend by its relation to
something else by which it is conditioned and limited.　We
cannot conceive an absolute whole ; every whole is only a
part of a larger whole for us.　Neither can we conceive an
absolute part ; every part can be conceived as, in its turn,
divided into parts and therefore as a whole.　Nor, again, can

we conceive an infinite whole ; for it would take infinite time to review all its parts. Thus, neither the absolutely limited nor the absolutely unlimited can be an object of knowledge. Our knowledge deals with the conditionally limited. The philosophy of the unconditioned, which claims to be able to construct a scientific concept of the unconditioned, which is said to be at once absolute totality and absolute infinity, sins against the nature of our knowledge. In a later appendix to the treatise (*Discussions*, p. 577 and f. ; *Conditions of the Thinkable*) Hamilton argues that since all knowledge consists of a judgment uniting two members, the relativity of thought is demonstrated. Moreover, all knowledge depends on a relation between subject and object ; we can never get beyond this opposition unless we are prepared to follow Schelling and become absorbed in the absolute unity, abandoning knowledge for mysticism.

A second relation which plays an essential part in our knowledge is that between thing and quality, and thing and quality are certainly only known in their reciprocal relation. On a nearer determination of things we determine them temporally (*protensively*), spatially (*extensively*), or with regard to the degree of their qualities (*intensively*) ; all these determinations, however, are relative, for temporal, spatial or quantitative determination presupposes each of the others. The concept of cause, also, is subordinated by Hamilton to a law which might be called the law of epistemological relation (law of relativity). He regards it as a limitation of our knowledge that we can only understand things when we have discovered their causes. We cannot think an unconditioned beginning. The beginning of a phenomenon can be nothing more than an apparent beginning. Neither can we think an unconditioned end. The disappearance of a phenomenon can only be apparent. To discover the conditions of a phenomenon means to unite it with other phenomena, to regard it as a member of a relation, for we are unable to conceive the unconditioned. Every existence appears in our knowledge as relative ; it is united to a preceding existence. Wherever there is a real addition to something already existing—not a mere transformation of this into a new form, and wherever there is a real loss — not a recurrence under another form, we find ourselves face to face with the incomprehensible. There is thus an absolute tautology between an effect and its causes, and the one may be rediscovered in the other. The causal concept, then, is not, as Reid and Kant, each in his own way, assumed, an independent, isolated concept. It is but a special form of the general mode of working of our consciousness, a special example of the fundamental law that our knowledge is by its very nature confined to the conditioned and limited.

Through this epistemological law of relativity Hamilton has shed light on an essential side of our knowledge. Instead of Reid's appeal to the instinct of common sense, and of Kant's scholastic table of categories, Hamilton gives us an analysis of the fundamental forms of cognitive consciousness, and points out a characteristic common to them all. He holds psychology to be the fundamental science for philosophy. Consciousness is to the philosopher what the Bible is to the theologian, and the original pronouncements of consciousness must be accepted as true, since they underlie all our knowledge. On this point Hamilton sometimes expresses himself in the same way as Reid. "The root of our nature cannot be a lie"—hence the assumption of an opposition between consciousness and its object, to which, according to Hamilton, immediate consciousness witnesses, must be accepted as true. This is Hamilton's simple solution of the problem of the existence of a world independent of consciousness. The problem, indeed, is hardly allowed to show itself. In Hamilton's opinion "natural realism" has the right on its side.

On the individual psychological and logical questions which Hamilton has treated with great acuteness and learning we must not enter here.[91] But we will pause for a moment to note the consequences which he deduces from the limitation of knowledge. The value of philosophy cannot, of course, in his opinion, consist in the revelation of absolute truth. Its value depends not on any finished results but on the continual stimulus it supplies to our intellectual activity. Speculation is a gymnastic for the mind. Lessing is right in placing the search after truth higher than the possession of the truth. A waking error is better than a slumbering truth. Philosophy loses nothing of its value because it concludes with the recognition, founded on an insight into the conditions of our knowledge, of our ignorance (with the *docta ignorantia*, as Hamilton, following Cusanus, calls it). In arriving at this its proper conclusion it has developed and exercised our noblest intellectual powers.

This uncertainty with regard to the absolute nature of existence arises because our thought concludes with a dilemma, both horns of which are incomprehensible. If we are to know the unconditioned it must present itself to us either as an unconditioned limited, an absolute totality, or else as an unconditioned unlimited, an infinite in time, place, and quality ; but we can comprehend neither the one nor the other, since both contradict the law of relativity. Hamilton does not believe, however, that we either must or can remain in this dilemma. For, in virtue of the logical principle of excluded middle between two conflicting possibilities, one of the two alternatives *must* be true. Thus there is not merely *room* for belief here, but the *necessity* for faith arises. We have learnt that our knowledge is no measure of existence, and we have learnt that a choice must be made. The idea of an unconditioned is not, as Kant thought, a positive idea, which has its natural root in the nature of our knowledge ; on the contrary, it denotes the negation of all knowledge. While Coleridge accepted Kant's doctrine of ideas, it was precisely on this point that Hamilton differed from him. He considers both the possibility and necessity of faith to be demonstrated ; for in the idea of the unconditioned we have two equally incomprehensible alternatives presented to us, between which, nevertheless, logical necessity obliges us to choose.

The choice, according to Hamilton, is determined by practical ethical considerations. We need an unconditioned Being, on whom our spirits can depend for protection and preservation. And we construct an idea of this Being by means of an analogy with our own nature. Hamilton cannot agree with Kant's criticism of the spiritualistic psychology. Consciousness is certainly, he says (*Lectures on Metaphysics*, i. p. 158), the condition of all our inner phenomena ; but it is itself only a phenomenon ; behind it there must lie something of which it is the property, and this must be something which is different from that which lies behind material phenomena. We now extend, by means of an analogy, the relation which holds between our mind and our body, and conceive it as holding between the unconditioned spiritual Being in whom we believe and the world of relativities which knowledge discovers to us. By means of this analogy,

Hamilton makes the transition from philosophy to theology. The end of philosophy is the beginning of theology. But, he goes on to say that no difficulty presents itself in theology which has not already made its appearance in philosophy. And this is proved by his own doctrine ; for the existence of that unconditioned Being, which must be the object of faith, is proved by an inference from analogy ; it is supposed to be *related* to the world as the soul is to the body ; but in that case it is still conditioned, relative ! Hamilton has nowhere shown how the transition to faith delivers us from the epistemological difficulties which he himself had so forcibly asserted. He holds with Fichte that a God who could be comprehended would be a limited being ; but a God who could be brought into relation with a world, even if He remained incomprehensible, would be a conditioned being, and if we still maintain that His nature is unconditioned our concept of Him contains a contradiction. As regards the content of faith, it is evident from Hamilton—and might be confirmed from a host of thinkers, from Liebniz onwards—that every attempt to construct a speculative or religious conception of the world is based, consciously or unconsciously, on a conclusion from analogy. Hamilton's whole standpoint, which is characterised by his psychological starting-point, his critical analysis of the conditions and -limits of knowledge in which he follows where he does not correct Kant's line of thought, and finally his philosophy of religion based on analogy, reminds us of such German thinkers as Fries and Beneke.

Two years after Hamilton's death, his pupil, HENRY MANSEL, delivered a series of lectures which were published under the title of *Limits of Religious Thought.* He here draws from Hamilton's teaching the conclusion that a scientifically grounded theology is impossible, because our knowledge cannot attain to the unconditioned. At the same time, however, he asserts that science cannot throw stones at theology : only if we possessed an absolute knowledge, a philosophy of the unconditioned, could revelation be refuted. And in agreement with Joseph Butler's *Analogy* (see vol. i. p. 399)—a work which has largely influenced religious discussion in England during the present century—he maintains that the difficulties and contradictions which appear in theological opinions would emerge in any attempt at a complete world-conception, even were the latter grounded on Nature and reason.   From which he concludes that the difficulties arise not from revelation, but from the limitation of reason.   What we are not able to understand, then, we must believe.   It is our duty to believe in the personality of God, although it may seem to us self-contradictory that an unconditioned Being should have personality, since personality presupposes opposition and limitation.   We must believe in the dogmas of atonement and eternal punishment, even though these dogmas conflict with our ideas of love and justice.   What appears to us love and justice may perhaps appear something different to God.   We see a part only, not the whole.   With an extended horizon we should see everything in a different light.   Just as Hamilton had already taught that it is owing to the imperfection of our nature that we conceive things as causes and effects, so Mansel teaches that human ethics are a corollary from the limitations of human nature ; hence we cannot argue from human to divine morality. For instance, it is man's duty to forgive, because his selfishness requires curbing, but this reason for the necessity of forgiveness cannot hold good of God !!   Thus both human conscience and human thought are deprived of all influence in the estimation of religious ideas.   Without rudder, and without compass, man, according to Mansel, must navigate on the ocean of religion.   Whether the theological voyage is more likely to prosper in this way is perhaps open to question—at any rate, until the superhuman thought and superhuman conscience which are exalted above all logical and ethical difficulties stand revealed.   Mansel's philosophy of religion was at first welcomed as a useful weapon against rationalism and speculation.   But the first enthusiasm has somewhat abated,[92] for it has been discovered that this weapon is only too apt to wound those who use it.   It is of course clear that however much the necessity and possibility of a leap from thought and conscience to faith be emphasised, man can never jump off his own shadow, not even by means of the boldest *salto mortale.*

In addition to Hamilton and his disciples there was yet another thinker through whom Kant's theory of knowledge became fruitful in England ; this was WILLIAM WHEWELL (1795-1866), of the University of Cambridge, who devoted himself first to natural science (mineralogy) and afterwards to philosophy.   In the year 1837 he published a work entitled *History of the Inductive Sciences*, which was followed, some years later (1840) by the *Philosophy of the Inductive Sciences founded upon their History*.   In these works he attempts to supply an historical proof of the correctness of Kant's fundamental conceptions, which, however, he did not himself always grasp with sufficient distinctness and clearness.   Whewell stands on the soil of the English school, for he maintains that all knowledge develops on the basis of experience.   Mental science and natural science, therefore, in his opinion, are alike inductive sciences.   Induction, however, does not merely mean the collection and comparison of facts ; it also means the grouping of facts under an appropriate conception, the reduction of them to a general law.   And the history of the inductive sciences shows us that such colligation and reduction is only possible when there are *already present* to the minds of inquirers ideas and points of view such as enable them to discover the law which combines the facts.   The facts must be combined by a psychical act, the possibility of which lies in the nature of the mind.   Every inquirer, therefore, proceeds from premises which cannot be deduced from particular facts.   A closer scrutiny of the manner in which great discoverers, *e.g.* Kepler and Newton, arrived at their results, affords an opportunity of discussing this conception of the method of induction at greater length.   Kepler was already familiar with the conception of an ellipse, and Newton with that of attraction, and it was only in virtue of this familiarity that they were able to make their discoveries.   Whewell does not mean that such conceptions must be already perfect to the mind in their complete form, but that no discovery can be made without the co-operation of an activity working according to its own laws.   Even when special ideas (*e.g.* those of the ellipse and of attraction) have developed under the influence of experience, we come back ultimately to fundamental concepts which express nothing but the laws of the faculty of knowledge itself, and these laws come into play in all experience, from the most simple sensuous perception to the widest induction. If we scrutinise the mode in which our knowledge is active, we discover a number of forms or fundamental concepts—the concepts of time and space as the foundation of mathematics, the causal concept as the foundation of the mechanical sciences, the concept of end as the foundation of the organic sciences, and the concept of duty as the foundation of ethics—concepts which can neither be reduced to simple forms, nor deduced from perception. Whewell contents himself with tabulating these concepts without subjecting them to any closer examination, hence his view acquires a certain similarity to that of Reid's; while Hamilton, as we know, made an interesting attempt to exhibit the different fundamental concepts as different expressions of the epistemological law of relativity. Nor did Whewell display in his conception of the relation between philosophy and theology the critical acuteness which characterises Hamilton. His work is important as a preparation for a theory of induction. It threw great light on the method of induction regarded as a method of *discovery*, but as Stuart Mill, his great opponent urged, it overlooked the importance of induction as a *method of proof*. But an inquirer who occupied himself chiefly with the history of the inductive sciences would naturally place in the foreground that particular point of view which Whewell asserted with so much energy.

CHAPTER II

JOHN STUART MILL

(a) Biography and Characterisation

JOHN STUART MILL, the son of James Mill, was born in London, May 20, 1806. He is an example of early intellectual development. This development, however, was effected at high intellectual pressure, such as a less powerful or original nature could scarcely have borne; even in Mill's case it left traces affecting both his spiritual and bodily health which were only very gradually effaced. His father was his tutor. At the age of three years he began to learn Greek and, soon afterwards, arithmetic; at the same time, of course, he learnt the English language and grammar. Latin was added when he was eight years old. He was given exhaustive works on universal history to study by himself, and was expected to give his father an account of what he had read during their walks. After he had gone through a great part of Greek and Roman literature he attacked logic, which he also read by himself and afterwards, by way of supplementation, went through and discussed with his father while walking. Then followed reading on economics, and a careful study of Demosthenes and Plato, especial attention being paid to argumentation and method. While still a very young boy he had to teach his younger brothers and sisters, which gave him practice in mastering and applying what he had learnt. But there was no sort of "cramming." His father took care that understanding should keep pace with acquirements, or better still, should precede it: "Anything which could be found out by thinking," says J. S. Mill in his *Autobiography* (p. 31), "I never was told, until I had exhausted my efforts to find it out

for myself." Mill holds up the way in which he himself
was educated as a model for others. He thinks that every boy
or girl of average capacities and good health could do as
much as a sense of filial duty had led him to accomplish.
Even if the demands made be beyond the capacities of the
child, Mill thinks it is pedagogically correct to make such
demands : "A pupil from whom nothing is ever demanded
which he cannot do, never does all he can " (*Ib.* p. 32).
He would never for one moment admit that this education
which, as he used to say, had "given him the advantage of a
quarter of a century over his contemporaries " [93] had exercised
any prejudicial effects on his development and his health. But
there can be no doubt that a nervous crisis which came upon
him later, as well as a weakness of the nerves from which he
suffered from his thirtieth year to the end of his life, were
to a great extent the results of the one-sided and forced
development of his childish years. This, at any rate, is the
opinion of his friends (see A. BAIN : *John Stuart Mill, a
Criticism*, London, 1882). Nor will Mill ever allow that work
can be injurious. Although a zealous empiricist he was
spiritualist enough to refuse to admit that physiological dispositions and states exert any essential influence. Hence he
not only believed that mental development can be hastened
forward without any injury to health, but he also acknowledged
no original differences between individuals. The foundation
of the hopes which he entertained for the future of humanity
was his firm belief that all qualities of character are the results
of education and of external social relations, so that human
characters can be changed by means of educational and social
reforms to an indefinite degree in the same direction. In this
connection he constantly enforces the teaching of Helvetius,
who had found in James Mill and Bentham zealous adherents.
But apart from its physical consequences, such an unnaturally
forced education suffers from the defect of developing the
understanding only, at the cost of feeling and imagination.
All the involuntary unfolding of mood and imagination was
checked while this strictly rationalistic education was proceeding. When an old man (when writing his *Autobiography*)
he held up the way in which he had been educated as a model,
but in his younger days he realised its deficiencies. In a conversation in the year 1840, recorded by Caroline Fox in her

diaries, he expressly says that he would hesitate to recommend that all children should be incited, when quite young, to great intellectual exertion, for it is apt to quench the liveliness of childhood and to favour reflection at the expense of activity. " I never was a boy," he says, " never played at cricket ; it is better to let Nature have her own way."

A second point on which Mill's *Autobiography* must be corrected by other accounts of his development is with regard to what he tells us about his ideas on religion when a child. He says in the *Autobiography* that he had received no sort of religious education, as his father had long given up all religious beliefs. Bain (in his *Biography of James Mill*), relying on the recollections of several members of the family, points out that Stuart Mill's memory played him false with regard to his father's change of view on religion. In Stuart Mill's childhood James Mill still went to church, accompanied by his son, and the rest of the family continued to attend afterwards. Certain boyish sayings of Stuart Mill's are recorded which show that he read the Bible with delight. But his father very soon began to discuss religious questions with him. He taught him never to break off any line of thought from a feeling of religious veneration, and never to abandon a problem until he had tried by experience whether it could be solved or not. He pressed upon the boy's attention a difficulty which he regarded as insuperable, and which blocked the way for him not only to orthodoxy but also to the belief in a good and all-powerful creator, this was the impossibility of reconciling any such belief with the physical and moral evil which experience shows us in the world. Butler's *Analogy* led James Mill to the purely negative standpoint which he adopted in his riper years on religious matters. This is not the first or only case in which an apology has produced an effect exactly the reverse to what was intended ; in this case, however, it did so in virtue of its depth and logical consistency. The train of thought on which Stuart Mill was started so early determined his subsequent attitude towards the religious problem, even though, after a spiritual crisis, he adopted a more positive standpoint. In his posthumous treatises on the philosophy of religion we can still trace the after-effects of the father's conversations with his little son.

John Stuart Mill spent one year of his early youth (1820-21) in the South of France, with a brother of Bentham, who possessed an estate there. He considered that the time spent there was not without influence on his subsequent development, and cites in particular the love to France and the interest in French literature and politics which it aroused in him, and to which he remained true throughout his life. Later, during an important period of his development, he was much influenced by French historians, and he found amongst the French a capacity for enthusiasm and self-renewal which he often looked for in vain from his own countrymen. On his return home he took up legal studies and became absorbed in Bentham's works. In these works he came upon an idea capable of unifying his opinions and efforts. He felt himself a different being when he had thoroughly assimilated Bentham's principle of utility. He says on this point in his *Autobiography*: "This principle gave unity to my conceptions of things. I now had opinions, a creed, a doctrine, a philosophy, in one among the best senses of the word a religion ; the inculcation and diffusion of which could be made the principal outward purpose of a life. And I had a grand conception laid before me of changes to be effected in the condition of mankind through that doctrine. The vista of improvement which Bentham opened was sufficiently large and brilliant to light up my life as well as to give a definite shape to my aspirations" (pp. 66 and 67).

Mill joined with enthusiasm the group of young men who were endeavouring to further Bentham's and James Mill's philosophical and political principles. Hartley's psychology, the political economy of Malthus, and Bentham's moral philosophy formed the basis on which they worked : the *Westminster Review*, in which the earliest of Stuart Mill's larger treatises were published, was their organ, and freedom of speech and extension of the suffrage were the chief objects they struggled to promote. They hoped that when once enlightenment and information were made accessible to every one, all social problems would be solved. They looked for a time when, by a wise self-control, the labouring classes would be able to prevent an undue increase of population, which they regarded as one of the main factors in determining the depression of wages. Extension of the suffrage would be the death-stroke of the power of the classes. Men's ideas would change, and with their ideas—

according to Hartley's doctrine of inseparable association—
their characters. Notwithstanding the eagerness with which he
proclaimed these ideals and prospects for the future, however,
Mill says that the reproach so often unjustly levied at Bentham's
disciples, *i.e.* of being " mere thinking machines," was to a
certain extent true of himself during that period of his life.
He looked, for the regeneration of mankind, not to disinterested
love of justice but to " the effect of educated intellect en-
lightening the selfish feelings ;" so too, in his own case, it was
his intellect alone which spoke. " My zeal," he says in his
Autobiography (p. 109), " was as yet little else at that period of
my life, than zeal for speculative opinions. It had not its
root in genuine benevolence or sympathy with mankind ;
though these qualities held their due place in my ethical
standard. Nor was it connected with any high enthusiasm for
ideal nobleness. Yet of this feeling I was imaginatively very
susceptible ; but there was at that time an intermission of
its natural aliment, poetical culture, while there was a super-
abundance of the discipline antagonistic to it, that of mere
logic and analysis. Add to this that my father's teachings
tended to the undervaluing of feeling." Thus the rationalism
of the eighteenth century—thanks to Stuart Mill's education—
worked its way deep into the new century, nourished and
stimulated by a continual struggle against prejudice and
sentimental declamations.

At the age of twenty Mill passed through an intellectual
crisis, from which he emerged with his theory of life modified
on several essential points. The foundation on which his
whole intellectual life had been built up suddenly gave way.
He fell into a state of depression in which he asked himself
the question : Supposing everything expected from intellectual
and political progress were to be realised, would it be a real
joy and happiness to me ?—and he found himself constrained
to answer in the negative. Life now became burdensome and
desolate. He performed his daily occupations purely mechanic-
ally ; the fountains of spiritual life seemed sealed within him.
The habit of analysis had taken the bloom off everything for
him. The psychology in whose tenets he had been brought up
had, it is true, recognised the fact that feelings are influenced
and changed by the development of ideas, but it had failed to
see that deep and strong feelings can only be produced and

preserved by this means when they can find in involuntary experiences and in a constant stream of fresh and immediate influences the nourishment which is indispensable to them. As it was he found himself left stranded at the commencement of his voyage with a well-equipped ship and a rudder, but no sail ! It was only natural that a reaction should follow on the overexertion of his childish years, and all the more since his intellect had received such a one-sided development. But we must remember that it was also a reaction against the whole trend of thought of the eighteenth century—almost inevitable in a young man who, brought up among the ideas of an older generation found himself confronted with those of the new, even though he himself had not yet taken the plunge. Mill worked his way through this crisis by the help of new experiences, new ideas and a new human relation. He was deeply moved by a touching passage in a biography, and thus discovered that the source of feeling was not dried up within him : " I was no longer hopeless ; I was not a stock nor a stone." This gave him fresh courage. He became absorbed in the poets, amongst whom Wordsworth's influence was especially marked. He discovered how indispensable is the spiritual nourishment which poetry affords : hitherto he had been inclined to fear, with Bentham, that it would teach men false ideas. He learnt to give the unconscious and involuntary elements in life their due, and he found out how important it is not to regard one's own happiness as the ultimate goal but to set a higher aim before one : happiness will come while aiming at the realisation of this end : " Those only are happy who have their minds fixed on some object other than their own happiness. . . . Ask yourself whether you are happy and you cease to be so ! " Added to this came new studies, principally of the French historians (Guizot, Michelet, Tocqueville). He learnt from these writers that institutions and laws develop according to natural laws, that there is a natural correspondence between them and the stage of development which society and opinions have reached, and that their perfection is to be judged with reference to this stage ; also that the direction in which progress moves can only be modified by purposive intervention to a very limited extent. The writers who influenced him most were Comte and the St. Simonians. He learnt to recognise the difference between critical and organic periods ; Carlyle's writings, too, appealed to him as the poetry of a great personality.   He now saw that human relations could not, as he had hitherto held with his father and Bentham, be adequately treated by means of a purely deductive method, and that paramount importance must not be assigned to external influences.   He was now prepared to do full justice to experience,—which, indeed, for an empirical philosopher was the most consistent course to pursue.   His religious views, too, were affected by this crisis and its resolution ; on this point, however, he says nothing more in the *Autobiography* than that he had now learnt the importance of the interior development of the individual.   The foundation of the religious opinions which he developed in his posthumous treatises was laid, as we shall subsequently show, during these years.   The Benthamites regarded him as a deserter, while in other circles he was received as a man who had broken with sectarian principles in order to find the truth.   In a conversation recorded by Caroline Fox, John Sterling, Mill's friend, said of him that he had given up the undisputed leadership of a strong party to serve in the ranks of the army of truth. Sterling hoped that Mill's books would help to secure for the feeling of veneration the place which so many had denied it.   But the renewal of Mill's inner life, which emotion and self-forgetfulness had begun, and an extended historical outlook and sense of religion developed, was consummated in his acquaintance with the woman who afterwards became his wife, and to whom he attributed the paramount influence on his mental development, for he looked up to her as to a being of a superior order. His extravagant encomiums of this lady were and remain a riddle to his friends and to the readers of his *Autobiography*, for he seems to attribute to her everything which he had himself contributed.   The secret here, as so often, is that Eros was the great teacher who opened his eyes to ideals and awoke his sense for intimate personal qualities, and the feeling thus set in motion was not restricted to the object which originally excited it.   We need not be surprised, therefore, that Mill's family and friends were not able to perceive anything extraordinary in the person whom he regarded as a genius of the highest rank. One of his brothers, who knew her well, used to say that she was an able and excellent woman, " but not what John takes her to be."   When enumerating in detail his obligations to her

Mill allows that his purely scientific works (the *Logic* and the theoretical portion of the *Political Economy*) owed nothing to her influence. He describes her, however, as a woman who dared to hope much from the future, and whose glance was fearlessly directed towards lofty ideals, although, at the same time, she had a keen sense for concrete actualities, and a remarkable power of making them real both to herself and others. She was also, he tells us, capable of grasping various points of view, and of perceiving their relation to one another.[94] We understand that Mill found in her what had been lacking in his life till now, and to which, owing to his education, he was not very susceptible until he encountered it in an actual personality. He found his Beatrice as Comte had found his.

Mill's entrance into practical life took place very early ; for at the age of seventeen he obtained an appointment in the service of the East India Company, in which he gradually rose to the highest post, which his father had occupied before him. He was for some time chief of the Education Department ; afterwards he conducted the correspondence of the Indian Government with the Indian princes and foreign states until, at last, as Chief Examiner of the Indian Correspondence, he became General Superintendent of the whole administration. The way in which he performed the duties of these various offices did not escape the recognition of competent authorities and, on the dissolution of the East India Company, he was offered a seat on the new council; this, however, he refused from considerations of health. His leisure hours were devoted to his studies. As a younger man he had been an eager member of a debating society in which violent discussions were carried on between the Benthamites and various young men belonging to other schools, some of them Tory lawyers, others followers of Coleridge. His activities as an author were at first restricted to journals and newspapers. His most important papers are published in a series of volumes entitled *Dissertations and Discussions*. By the year 1830 his definitive opinions on philosophical questions were established. Amongst the influences of later years Comte and Carlyle are the most noteworthy. These essays display the extraordinary equilibrium and the astonishing all-sidedness which characterise Mill's thought. When his early education in clear and accurate thinking had been supplemented by richer experiences he found himself able to take an interest in many things and to shed light on many questions.

The reaction against the thought of the eighteenth century, especially against the opinions which originated with Bentham and James Mill, had more effect on Mill's social, literary and religious views than on his general philosophical (*i.e.* epistemological and ethico-philosophical) standpoint. The diaries of Caroline Fox describe him as forming one of the circle of eminent men who were frequent visitors at the home of the gifted Quaker family at Falmouth.[95] Mill had gone to Cornwall to nurse a consumptive brother. His expressions and conversations, as recorded in the diaries, bear the stamp of deep personal feeling, and witness to the seriousness with which he regarded life and its duties. He expressed himself very much in the spirit of Carlyle; and those with whom he came in contact at that time found it difficult to realise that they were in the society of one of the greatest radicals of the century. When his book, entitled *On Liberty* appeared, Caroline Fox, who had listened to his conversation with such pleasure, found it extremely distasteful (as was also the case with Carlyle's *Life of Sterling*). Mill saw no contradiction between the philosophy of personality, which he had been led to adopt, and the strictly rational view of knowledge and of life to which he adhered in his own investigations. One of the most important services Mill rendered was to free the philosophy of personality from the Romanticism and dread of intellectualism with which Carlyle had invested it.

In Mill's opinion, deepness of inner life and enthusiasm were not incompatible with the indefatigable search after grounds of proof and causal explanation. After the crisis we have alluded to, he had learnt that a man may have a great conception of life without necessarily fearing or despising thought. Carlyle could never understand this. " Ah, poor fellow," he said once of Mill, " he has had to get himself out of Benthamism ; and all the emotions and sufferings he has endured have helped him to thoughts that never entered Bentham's head. However, he is still too fond of demonstrating everything. If John Mill were to get up to heaven he would hardly be content till he had made out how it all was. For my part, I don't trouble myself about the machinery of the place ; whether there is an operative set of angels or an industrial class, I'm willing to leave all that" (*Memories of old Friends from the Journals of Caroline Fox*, vol. i. p. 309). Carlyle here, in his humorous fashion, gives a striking description of the difference between himself and Stuart Mill. We ought, perhaps, to add that, unless heaven be specially reserved for Romanticists, an insight into the mechanism of life and a practical application of it is necessary to prepare the way thither. Moreover, it may be presumed that the intellectual powers no less than all other personal impulses will find satisfaction there. Carlyle's objection against Mill is equally valid against Socrates, who expected to spend his time in the future world as he did on earth, *i.e.* in testing and inquiring.

Stuart Mill attributed great practical importance to the theoretical discussions between empiricism and speculation, which were so characteristic of that time. All false views and tendencies within the ethical, religious and social spheres are invincible so long as the assertion is allowed to pass unchallenged that truths can be gained by immediate intuition, by way of pure thought, independently of experience and observation. Such an assertion, indeed, constitutes an opinion its own proof. Never was a better means devised for the preservation of all deeply-rooted prejudices! In opposition to this, Mill asserts that all knowledge is derived from experience, and that the explanation of all intellectual and moral qualities must be looked for in the laws of the association of ideas. Here we shall find no lack of problems, while the intuitive philosophy, which represents the reaction of the nineteenth against the eighteenth century, fosters sloth and offers a shelter to all sorts of Tory prejudices. This line of thought runs through both Mill's chief philosophical works, *i.e. System of Logic* (1843) and *Examination of Sir William Hamilton's Philosophy* (1865). As a logician, he was the first to supply a *theory of induction* and a systematisation of empirical methods, as Aristotle was the first to systematise the methods employed in deductive reasoning. Aristotle's intellectual ancestors were the Greek philosophers and sophists, and he took for his foundation the eager discussions which were so common at Athens, especially in the Socratic schools. Stuart Mill based his theory on the history of modern natural science during the last three centuries, and on an analysis of the forms which had been employed in its creation. His work contains the most thorough-going exposition of empiricism as a theory of knowledge which has ever been written—just as his father's *Analysis* contains the most thoroughgoing application of empiricism within the sphere of psychology. Underlying the whole of Mill's logic we may discern the unfortunate influence of his father's psychological theory. This theory he afterwards abandoned (partly in his notes to a new edition of the *Analysis*, partly in his criticism of Hamilton's philosophy), without seeming to recognise the effect of this abandonment on his theory of knowledge. His great love of truth, as shown by the indefatigable zeal with which he examined every objection raised against him and gave to each its full weight, opened his eyes to truths which he could not have grasped at the beginning of his career. In 1830 he began to write his *Logic*, and in the last edition of his work on Hamilton's philosophy, towards the end of his life, we find him still employed in indicating modifications of his views, which had been brought about in the course of his ceaseless occupation with the subject. While he starts from Hume's and James Mill's view that consciousness consists of a series or heap of independent elements, brought into connection with one another, according to the laws of association, in a purely external and practically inexplicable manner, he ends by recognising the unity and interconnection of consciousness as the fundamental fact of psychology. " The uniting principle" which Hume would have put on one side is acknowledged by Mill as the corner-stone. This indicates a breach with the older English school, the full bearings of which Mill himself did not realise.

In addition to his strictly philosophical works (to which must be added an interesting work on August Comte) Mill has left a number of important works dealing with ethical, social and political questions. Among these is his *Principles of Political Economy* (1848) in which he treats economics as a part of sociology, and draws a distinction between the laws of production and those of distribution ; a distinction which afforded him an opportunity of recognising all that was valid in the socialistic systems. Hitherto, treading in his father's and Bentham's footprints, he had fought in defence of personal liberty against the rule of the classes. He now saw that behind the question of political emancipation lies a far graver one, *i.e.* the social question.   The St. Simonians had opened his eyes to the urgency of this problem.   That he never lost his sense of the importance of personal liberty may be seen from his *Essay on Liberty* (1859).   In his treatise on *Utilitarianism*, he defends utility as an ethical principle against its opponents, and in his *Considerations on Representative Government* (1860) he gives us his theory of politics.

From 1865-68 Mill was a member of the House of Commons, where he gained a reputation for clearness and knowledge of affairs, although he generally spoke on behalf of the most unpopular measures.   Gladstone (in a letter of December 19, 1888, quoted by GOMPERZ : *John Stuart Mill, Ein Nachruf,* Wien, 1889, p. 46) has given the following description of Mill's Parliamentary career :—"We all knew Mr. Mill's intellectual eminence before he entered Parliament. What his conduct there principally disclosed, at least to me, was his singular moral elevation.   I remember now that at the time . . . I used familiarly to call him the Saint of Rationalism . . . Of all the motives, stings and stimulants that reach men through their egoism in Parliament, no part could move or even touch him.   His conduct and his language were, in this respect, a sermon.   Again, though he was a philosopher, he was not, I think, a man of crotchets.   He had, I think, the good sense and practical tact of politics, together with the high independent thought of a recluse.   I need not tell you that, for the sake of the House of Commons at large, I rejoiced in his advent and deplored his disappearance.   He did us all good.   In whatever party, whatever form of opinion, I sorrowfully confess that such men are rare."

The reason why Mill was not re-elected was partly owing to his religious views, of which his opponents made capital, partly because his politics were too ultra-radical for the class of electors who had previously elected him.

J. Stuart Mill died, while staying at Avignon, on May 5, 1873.   With him disappeared one of the greatest, most honest and most noble spirits of our century—a man whom we may place side by side with the great men of past times.   His life, as he has himself described it to us, is a source of instruction to every inquirer, and his works shed a new light on some of the most important subjects of human thought.[96]

(*b*) *Inductive Logic*

Mill's forte as a thinker consists chiefly in his indefatigable power of discussion, in the indefatigable energy with which he returns again and again to a problem, looking at it from every point of view in order to discover the presuppositions on which it ultimately rests. In the later editions of his *System of Logic*, in which the objections which had been brought against his theories are answered, his exposition acquires the character of a dialogue. As the writer of any dialogue that is worthy of the name does his best to exhibit the different standpoints taken up in the clearest and most characteristic forms possible, so too, Mill's great endeavour is to let the opinions and objections of his opponents exercise their full weight ; indeed, he may be said to have looked upon the latter as co-workers rather than opponents. That his comprehension of other standpoints had its limits goes without saying ; these limits are imposed on all his inquiries by his personality and his historical starting-point as a thinker. This limitation appears all the more clearly on a critical investigation, since the psychological foundation of his whole theory of knowledge had shifted without his ever seeming to have become aware of the fact. Whoever sets out to criticise Mill must remember that he is, before all things, a great seeker. His philosophical merit does not stand or fall with the answer to the question whether he succeeded in throwing empiricism into a form more absolute than even Hume had conceived.

Mill regards empirical logic partly as the antithesis to, partly as the extension of, the logic of pure thought. Pure thought cannot extend our knowledge ; it can never do more than show us if we are consistent in our thinking. New truths can only be acquired by observation and experience. The question then arises : What proof can we offer of these new truths which have been acquired by observation ? Mill lays the chief weight on proof, not on discovery. He is chiefly intent on securing the subjection of all judgments to a cleansing fire before they are allowed to pass into the heaven of truth. He is less interested in the way in which judgments originally arise ; logic is concerned with *evidence*. The significance and practical value of philosophy for Mill, as for Carlyle, consists in its struggle with custom : traditionally accepted opinions and those formed by means of the involuntary working of the association of ideas must be sifted and tested in order that those prejudices which are inimical to progress may be excluded. Mill's great hopes in the progress of the human race were largely based on the possibility of bringing all opinions to the test of experience.

Apart from the cases in which a general proposition is established by authority, *e.g.* theological and legal propositions, every general proposition is, according to Mill, nothing more than the sum of a series of particular observations. Deductive logic, therefore, which starts from general propositions, presupposes an inductive logic which shows how we pass from particular observations to these general propositions. Pure thought always presupposes experience. If, *e.g.* I argue as follows :—

All men are mortal,

The Duke of Wellington [who was alive when Mill wrote his *Logic*], is a man ;

therefore,

The Duke of Wellington is mortal—

it is evident that if I am justified in asserting as my major premiss the mortality of *all* men, I must be certain that the Duke of Wellington will also die. In reality, says Mill, I do not conclude from the death of *all* men to the death of Wellington, but I conclude from a great number of experiences of the death of particular men to the death of this particular man, *i.e.* Wellington. Did I really know that *all* men are mortal it would be unnecessary for me to draw any conclusion, since the mortality of Wellington would be included in the general mortality. My argument, therefore, is in reality as follows :—John is mortal, Thomas is mortal, etc. etc., therefore Wellington must also be mortal. Every syllogism, of which the major premiss is not established by authority, is in reality based on *an inference from particulars to particulars.* This is the form of reasoning on which both induction and deduction are based ; first induction and afterwards deduction. The starting-point of the whole process of knowledge consists in the fact that two phenomena (*e.g.* man and death) have been simultaneously presented to me. The next time that the former recurs it will be accompanied in me by the expectation of the latter.   If this expectation be fulfilled I throw all these experiences into a *general* proposition, *i.e.* a proposition which gives me an abridgment of *all my experiences.*   It cannot give me more unless I make an unwarrantable generalisation.   All inference, then, is from particulars to particulars.   Such inferences are made by children.   When a child who has already burnt his fingers sees a candle and draws his hand back, he does so not because he has thought of any general maxim, but because the sight of the flame has immediately recalled the idea of his pain.   Brutes can also reason in this manner, for not only the burnt child, but also the burnt dog dreads the fire (*Logic,* bk. ii. chap. iii. § 3).

Mill is, of course, well aware that this immediate transition from a perception to an idea or an expectation is only an association, the justification of which must be put to the test. This association is an association of the kind to which James Mill sought to reduce all associations, *i.e.* association "by contiguity."   We have often seen A and B together, hence, on the recurrence of A, we expect B.   But how can the validity of such an expectation be *proved?*   For logic is not concerned with what we *do* recognise as valid, but what we *ought* to recognise as such.   "Evidence is not that which the mind does or must yield to, but that which it ought to yield to," (*Logic,* bk. iii. chap. xxi. § 1).   With what right, then, do we conclude from the occurrence of one phenomenon (A) to the occurrence of another and different phenomenon (B)?

Taking as his foundation the history of empirical science, in the adoption of which Mill acknowledges himself to have been preceded by Comte, Whewell, and John Herschel (*On the Study of Natural Science,* London, 1830), Mill expounds four chief methods, by means of which we may distinguish between valid and invalid associations of ideas. The detailed exposition of these methods (the main features of which had been somewhat vaguely described by Herschel) forms one of the most important parts of Mill's work.   We must only pause here to mention one important point, *i.e.* the weight which Mill lays on *negative cases,* those instances in which a phenomenon does *not* occur, although with this exception, the circumstances are the same as in the cases in which it does occur.   In such cases as these the *method of difference,* the chief inductive method, can be applied.   It was mentioned by Bacon as one of the most important *instantiae solitariae* (see vol. i. of this work, p. 199). The one circumstance by which an instance including the phenomenon under investigation differs from the instance in which the phenomenon does not occur, we must regard as standing in causal connection with the phenomenon (either as cause or as effect, or so that both instances are effects of the same cause). We are only justified, therefore, in expecting B to follow A, when it has been shown that the non-appearance of A involves the non-appearance of B. When that can be done, only two instances, one positive and one negative, are necessary in order to establish the law of the relation between A and B.

Only in very simple cases, however, is the inference as simple as this. In complicated relations, where many different elements co-operate, we must first break up the phenomenon into its constituent elements ; secondly, by means of simple inductions, investigate how each of these elements works ; thirdly, by means of deduction, try to find what result will be effected by their united operation, and finally, by the help of observation, show that our conclusions or computations do actually agree with experience. The whole process of knowledge, then, consists of three members,—induction, deduction, and verification. Far from overlooking the importance of the deductive method, Mill, on the contrary, sees in the part which deduction plays in a science an indication of the measure of perfection attained by this science. But he emphatically asserts that all deduction is based on induction, and must be confirmed by the agreement of its results with experience. He rejects pure thought only when it begins without any empirical foundation and ends without any empirical verification.

The method of difference on which the whole edifice of knowledge rests is, as Mill is well aware, only able to afford proof if we assume that the interconnection of Nature is such, that what has once occurred will, in the event of the same circumstances arising, occur again. We assume the uniformity of Nature or the law of causation, then, in every case of inference concerning real phenomena. In his inquiries as to the possibility of finding a proof for the causal axiom itself, Mill takes up once more the great problem of Hume and Kant. He answered it in Hume's spirit, but he aims at throwing light upon it from the *logical* side while Hume had declared it to be incapable of any logical solution, so that the only way out of the difficulty for him lay in a *psychological* explanation.

Mill denies that the causal axiom is grounded on immediate belief, intuition or instinct. In the first place, faith and instinct are not proof. A strong and permanent association of ideas may produce a conviction too strong to be shaken by any evidence to the contrary ; but its strength, in and for itself, is no proof. On the contrary, Mill thinks, the belief in causality might be overthrown and the "instinct" conquered. No one accustomed to abstraction and analysis, and whose imagination can work freely, will find it impossible to conceive an absolute chaos where events may succeed one another at random without any fixed law. Moreover, it is not true that mankind have always believed in the causal law ; they have recognised "chance," and have attributed reality to "free-will." In order to justify the validity of empirical science, therefore, we need not assume that the causal law holds good for all phenomena, as long as we assume it to be valid within those spheres in which our investigation moves ; the motion of the planets, for instance, may be subjected to definite laws even if wind and weather are not. And we have no right to extend the validity of the causal axiom beyond the portion of the universe with which we are acquainted. Experiences can only be based on experiences ; the real foundation of empirical science, therefore, must be established by way of experience. Experience itself must tell us how far we may trust experience. We must *make experience its own test* (*Logic*, iii. 4).

Thus the causal axiom itself must be grounded in experience and proved by induction. Our conviction that an event will not occur unless a certain other event precede it is based on the fact that we have witnessed a similar connection of events countless times. Our conviction of the validity of the causal axiom in any particular case rests upon the same evidence as our conviction that the Duke of Wellington will die. In both cases there is an inference from particular to particular. Mill is of opinion, however, that the causal law is based on so many experiences that we are justified in calling it the widest generalisation we possess. If we can connect our narrower inductions with this widest generalisation they gain in certainty.

But the justification for connecting two future events (A and B) on the ground that they previously occurred together is precisely what inductive logic undertakes to demonstrate ; the " inference " from particular to particular is nothing more than an association. In reality we are not advanced towards the desired demonstration by learning that this connection is based on the causal axiom, for it appears that this axiom itself depends on the " inference " from particular to particular —and this is, as we have seen, nothing more than an association, although strengthened in this case by innumerable repetitions. (In Mill's discussion of the causal axiom A stands for " the occurrence of an event " ; B " the occurrence of a certain other event.") Mill moves in a circle [97] or rather, he never gets beyond the spot where he started. His appeal to the causal axiom as the ultimate basis of particular inductions only enables him to show that the associations which it is most difficult to sever are able to confirm the looser and more uncertain ones ; a new habit may be strengthened by an old habit of like nature. But this is no proof.

Mill goes too far in his zeal for rooting out all *a priori* principles. He confounds, as do so many of his opponents, the explanation of the origin of a principle from the nature of consciousness with the proof of its real validity. He is right in saying that, however much a principle may be grounded in the nature of our consciousness, its real validity is not thereby proved. But it is not impossible that there may be hypotheses which we are compelled to assume by the nature of our consciousness, and the testing of which in detail may be the work of empirical science. The task of scientific knowledge in that case would be the nearer determination and verification of involuntarily assumed premises. Mill's suspicions were always aroused if any one asserted that involuntary assumptions might be of significance for knowledge ; he regarded such an assertion as a pretext for smuggling in dogmas. A continual marking time without advance was the Nemesis which this suspicion brought upon his theory of knowledge.

As a matter of fact, there is no such thing as an inference from particular to particular, if by inference we understand a process which *necessarily* leads from one assumption to another, and if we persist in maintaining a distinction between an inference and a mere association of ideas. If the transition from the one particular (A) to the other (B) is to be justified, it can only be by means of the similarity between the former and some previous particular ; it is because B_1 corresponded with A_1 that I infer that B_2 will correspond with A_2. The transition is mediated here by an analogy, and our judgment as to the justification of the transition must rest on an examination of the validity of analogy. Mill is obliged to admit the importance of the relation of similarity in all inference (*Logic*, vol. ii. ch. iii. 3, and vol. iii. ch. iii. 1), but he does not see that this admission is incompatible with the possibility of inferring from particulars to particulars, as he describes the process, and that it is the principle of identity which is the ultimate premise of all inference, whether this takes place in an inductive or deductive form. A blind coupling together of ideas is not sufficient to give logical connection, and it is only where the relation of identity can be shown to exist that the conjunction is no longer blind.[98]

Mill's empiricism led him to suppose that the fundamental axioms of logic are themselves grounded in experience. I learn very early in life that light and darkness, movement and rest, past and future are different and incompatible predicates. I learn that it is impossible to me to believe and to disbelieve the same thing at the same time. Belief and non-belief are incompatible mental states. Generalising these experiences I pass on to the statement that that which contradicts itself cannot be true. This axiom, however, is invested with no necessity beyond that which is derived from the teaching of experience. Even though we pause at certain assumptions which we cannot reject without a feeling of self-contradiction, this feeling does not entitle us to infer that they really are impossible. There may be associations of ideas so firmly fixed that we are not able to dissolve them. Nevertheless the history of science affords us no lack of instances where what was once regarded as inconceivable has afterwards been found to be true. When we see that incomprehensible things may, in the course of time, become comprehensible, the incomprehensibility of the contradictory of an assumption cannot be a proof of the correctness of the assumption. Only by way of experience, not by means of subjective criticism, can we learn what is possible and actual. Of the two questions, (1) whether there are self-contradictions which are anything more than actual indissoluble associations of ideas ; (2) whether we are justified in assuming that the self-contradictory cannot exist. Mill is obviously much more interested in the latter.   In his later writings (*Examination of Sir William Hamilton's Philosophy*, 2nd ed. p. 67), he even expresses himself hesitatingly on the question as to whether the incompatibility of two mutually contradictory assumptions is grounded in the ultimate nature of consciousness or springs from experience ; but he remains convinced that a subjective necessity can never establish an objective reality.   But Mill overlooks here the stimulating, impelling power of contradiction.   It is precisely because some of those axioms which we deduce from nature are mutually contradictory that we are confronted with problems and incited to endeavours to overcome the contradiction.   Did we not persistently use contradiction as a criterion our thought would soon nod.   As the causal principle provides us with hypotheses, so the principle of contradiction provides us with problems.   Here again, Mill's suspicion led him to overshoot the mark.

Like the fundamental axioms of logic, the fundamental axioms of mathematics are generalisations from experience. Mathematics is, it is true, a rational science, which leads, by way of thought, to necessary results : it rests, however, on principles which can only be derived from experience.   Thus the definitions of geometry contain elements gathered from experience, even when these empirical elements are conceived as possessed of greater perfection and exactitude than they have in experience.   The definition of the circle, for example, assumes that all radii are exactly equal, which is never the case with the radii of any actual circle.   All actual circles, however, more or less resemble the ideal circle with reference to which geometry demonstrates its axioms, and the closer the resemblance the more valid the application of these axioms to reality.   We make a leap from approximate equalities to absolute equalities, because by so doing we are enabled to draw conclusions, and when we come to apply these conclusions we allow for the degree of resemblance.   Thus geometry rests on hypotheses, or if you will, on fictions.   Geometry can only be supposed to possess real validity on the assumption that the nature of space is congruent with the observations we employ in forming our ideal hypotheses or fictions. But whether space is really so constituted throughout the universe we can never know *a priori*. Had Mill realised more thoroughly the nature of the idealisation which leads to the establishment of the hypotheses of geometry, his theory of knowledge would, perhaps, have taken on another complexion. He might then, perhaps, have seen that it is quite possible to recognise an *a priori* element in our knowledge without necessarily thinking that in the absence of further investigation we are justified in basing assumptions upon it as to the nature of existence.

Mill's attempt to construct a purely empirical theory, in which the mind is regarded as a *tabula rasa*, cannot be said to have succeeded. Nevertheless it is not without its value ; for, owing to the acuteness and wide-spreading ramifications of his inquiries, he has shed much light on the nature of our knowledge. The attempt itself may be regarded as a counterpoise to the dialectical method of Hegel : while Hegel hoped to reveal the truth by the self-development of pure thought, Mill sought to discover it by the piecing together of independent ideas received from without.

One peculiarity of Mill's theory of knowledge is its dependence on his psychological assumptions. Mill's logic is based on his father's psychology. Association by contiguity as the fundamental form of all association of ideas, and inseparable association as the explanation of all phenomena incomprehensible to us are the instruments with which he operates. *Psychology* is, with him, the fundamental science on which all other sciences rest. The laws of association are the fundamental laws of all our knowledge.

Mill himself has written no word on psychology, but his treatment of its methods in his *Logic* and of different psychological questions in other works (*Examination*, etc., 1865, and in his notes to James Mill's *Analysis*, 1869) is of great interest. The exposition of psychology to which in his later years he professed most adherence is that given by ALEXANDER BAIN, his friend and pupil, in his two chief works, *The Senses and the Intellect* (1856) and *The Emotions and the Will* (1859). In these works, however, associative psychology proper, as taught by James Mill, is abandoned, and under William Hamilton's influence the relation of similarity is acknowledged to be the basis of all association of ideas, including association by

contiguity. Mill concurs with this view in his notes on the
Analysis. Consistently with this opinion, then, the relation of
similarity ought to exercise greater influence on the theory
of knowledge than Mill had allowed it to do in his *Logic,*
in which, as we saw, he grounds all inference on association
by contiguity. It is true that even in the *Logic* (i. iii. 11 ; v. 6)
he recognises the relation of similarity and difference as a
peculiar, irreducible relation, but he makes no further inquiries
into the *rôle* which this relation plays in all association of
ideas and in all thought.

In his later work Mill still adheres to Hume's and James
Mill's conception of consciousness as a series of states, only he
adds,—of actual or *possible* states. He encounters a difficulty,
however, which had not troubled his predecessors. Both
memory and expectation presuppose that *I myself and no one
else* have had or will have at another time such a state of consciousness as I now have the idea of. In consciousness, then,
there must be something more than the members which form
the series. How can a series know itself as such ? How can
it know that it has past members and will have future ones ?
It is evident that there must be some bond between the individual members of consciousness, *i.e.* the individual feelings
and ideas ; some bond which is just as real as the individual
members themselves, and which is no mere product of thought.
If we are to give this original bond in our consciousness a name,
we must call it " I," or the self. (*Examination,* chap. xii. The
most characteristic and decided expressions occur in the later
edition). In his notes to the *Analysis* (ii. p. 175) Mill expresses himself as follows :—" There is a bond of some sort
among all the parts of the series, which makes me say that
they were feelings of a person who was the same person
throughout, and this bond, to me, constitutes my ego." We can
at present, adds Mill, proceed no further by way of psychological analysis. Here then the associative psychology is
definitely abandoned. As has been strikingly said, Mill opens
a trap-door in the middle of his own philosophy. Consistency
obliged Hume to regard the " uniting principle " as a riddle, for
he proceeded on the assumption that particular sensations and
ideas are the only reality (see vol. i. of this work, p. 432).
But when Mill recognises the uniting bond as equally real with
the particular elements he corrects the entire conception of

consciousness from which Hume, and, following him, James Mill, had started. The laws of association are now seen to be nothing more than special forms of "the uniting principle." The indefatigable analysis of the English inquirers led them to the correction of their own principle.[99] His admission that the relation of similarity and the uniting bond are realities involved Mill in self-contradiction, for he had based his logic on purely external and accidental association. That he should by these means have reached results which led beyond his original premises witnesses to the honesty and acuteness of his inquiry.

There is one more especial application of the laws of association made by Mill which we must notice. He attempts to show that they are sufficient to explain the belief in an eternal world. What I know of the world I know through my sensations. But does there really exist a world, in the sense of something different from my sensations? What is actually given at any moment is the sensation which I have at that moment. But in addition to this I have the memory and expectation of ideas of possible sensations, ideas which by repetition and association are able to form firm and coherent groups. And these groups always appear in consciousness with the same disposition of elements, whether they are given as sensations or not. Hence we get the idea of a something which is permanent, whether we perceive it or not. What is the so-called "eternal" object but the possibility, determined by certain laws, that certain sensations will recur in the same order as that in which I have already experienced them? My belief in the existence of something independent of my consciousness is strengthened when I learn from experience that other sensuous beings have an order of sensations determined, like mine, according to laws. What I understand by matter, then, is in reality nothing more than a permanent possibility of sensation. Fixed associations of ideas, common to all men, cause us to posit the existence of matter. And since we find that the causal axiom is valid within the series of our sensations and ideas we involuntarily apply it to the series as a whole, to the whole content of our sensations and ideas, of which we say matter is the cause. Practical belief, the strong propensity to assume the existence of an outer world, is for Mill no proof. In the light of the principle of firm association such an assumption, he thinks, is unnecessary. We need assume the existence of nothing beyond our own consciousness——only in addition to the actual data of consciousness we must also assume the *possibility* of new states of consciousness. It is evident that in this " possibility " Kant's " thing-in-itself " lies concealed. When Mill says (*Examination*, 2nd ed. p. 189): " The non-ego altogether may be but a mode in which the mind represents to itself the possible modifications of the ego," the question arises whether the ego itself is able to actualise these possibilities so that the changes of its states can be explained through itself. If this be affirmed, the ego appears as creating its inner world out of nothing ; if it be denied we must either deny the causal axiom or assume a reality lying outside the ego. Mill does not discuss this question more closely ; indeed, he never enters on any adequate discussion of the connection between the problem of the reality of an outer world and the problem of causality.

(c) Ethical Principles

The peculiar position occupied by Mill in the history of thought comes out nowhere more distinctly than in his ethics. Brought up in the atmosphere of the eighteenth century, he sought with honest intention to make the modern points of view his own; but since his premises are borrowed from the old school, while the goal at which he aims and the point of view he adopts are due to the influence of the moderns, there arises at certain points in his argument a duality which he himself did not always remark. In his ethical thought this duality is apparent in the fact that, while he never abandons the principle of utility to which Benthamism had introduced him, he attempts to supplement it by bringing it into harmony with the personality philosophy, and its more subjective ethic. He recognised this work of reconciliation to be the most important problem of the ethics of the future, though he himself never succeeded in finding a theoretical solution. The mental crisis which he passed through at a certain point in his development was occasioned by this very problem. That in practice, in the art of life, in his great and productive activity regard for the inner development of the personal life is united in a rare degree with regard for the external effects of individual actions may be seen from his *Autobiography*. But he was never able to reduce this art to theory.

The reason why he never succeeded in so doing must unquestionably be sought in the filial piety he evinced both towards his father and towards Bentham. There was a time, —during the violently agitated subjective period which followed the crisis—when he used to express himself strongly against utilitarianism, accusing it of taking a purely external, business point of view. But now, thinking he had worked through the reaction against the view in which he had been brought up, he appears as its champion ; and he never realised how much he himself had modified the theory he sought to advocate. He never sufficiently guarded himself against the older utilitarianism, and at single points his theory is more influenced by it than was consistent with his real position. Hence his *Utilitarianism* is one of the least clear of his works.

We possess a clear and natural standard for the ethical estimation of worth—and on this point Mill never wavers— only when we restrict ourselves to the *effects* of an action. If we ask *why* an action is good, our decision will ultimately depend upon whether at any point and in any sphere it has produced a feeling of pleasure. Human nature is so constituted that it desires nothing which is not either the whole of happiness or a part of happiness or a means to happiness. Every action is judged—and must be judged—according to the degree in which it promotes what is thus always the ultimate object of human desire. In such judgments we apply the principle of utility.

To the question, *Whose* happiness is to be the standard of measurement? Stuart Mill answers: Not the greatest happiness of the agent, but the greatest total sum of happiness. And he does not, like Bentham in the *Deontology*, establish this assertion by pointing to the harmony of enlightened interests, but by giving a psychological explanation of the origin of the moral feeling. The moral feeling causes us to strive to produce happiness even when this happiness is not our own.

Stuart Mill does not believe the moral feeling to be innate ; he regards it as a highly complex product. The most important of its constituent elements are sympathy, fear, religious feelings of different kinds, experiences of the effects of action, self-esteem, and the desire to enjoy the esteem of others. In this extremely complex product we must seek for the cause of the mystical character which marks the feeling of moral obligation. A great mass of feeling must be extirpated before a man can act contrary to what he knows to be right. Moreover, the association between the different elements is so strong that the feeling as a whole presents an indissoluble unity. And since the laws of association are laws of nature, the moral feeling, although it has a history of development, is a natural feeling. It comes natural indeed to man to speak, to draw inferences, to till the ground, and to build cities, and yet the art of doing these things is not innate but acquired. If there be any one element of the moral feeling which is innate it is sympathy. But the most important point to notice is that social life accustoms individuals to have interests in common, to work with united forces, to consider one another. A kind of instinct is formed which produces a solidarity of feeling and action between individuals. And the higher the development reached by social life and the more the barriers between the different classes disappear, the more this solidarity increases. If persistently fostered by education and the ordering of institutions, and encouraged by public opinion, this feeling of unity may rise to a religion. By means of social life egoism itself is educated, so that regard for others, even if at the beginning it was only a means, finally becomes an aim. While Bentham—at any rate in practice—starts from the egoistic interest as the universal motive, Stuart Mill was convinced of the reality of disinterested feelings. Hence in his interesting treatise on Plato, when he is discussing the teaching of the *Gorgias*, he says it is better to suffer wrong than to do wrong : " The step marked by the *Gorgias* is one of the greatest ever made in moral culture,—the cultivation of a disinterested preference of duty for its own sake, as a higher state than that of sacrificing selfish preferences to a more distant self-interest " (*Diss. and Disc.* iii. p. 340).

Stuart Mill, then, like Spinoza, Hartley and James Mill, believes in a theory of individual development. The principle of inseparable association serves him—as it had served his predecessors—as the foundation and explanation of the inner basis of ethics, while the principle of utility affords a basis for the judgment of particular actions. In clearness and simplicity of exposition, however, Stuart Mill cannot compare with Spinoza or James Mill. There is always a certain hesitation as to what is original and what acquired ; moreover, he involves himself in a difficulty which did not exist for his predecessors by recognising qualitative differences between feelings. A feeling of pleasure may not only be stronger, purer, more lasting, more fruitful in felicific results, common to a greater number of men than any other feeling of pleasure, but it may also be of a qualitatively higher kind, as may be proved by the fact that he who has once experienced it seeks to experience it again even when it is only attainable at the cost of great pain, and prefers it to the greatest possible quantity of any other pleasurable feeling. It is a question whether the "qualitative difference" here affirmed by Mill does not find its explanation in the very fact that certain feelings of pleasure are sanctioned and fostered by the moral feeling, the origin of which Stuart Mill had himself attempted to explain. At any rate the question whether these are qualitative differences of feeling is altogether too complicated to be met by the simple proof which Mill brings forward.

While in his forcible assertion of the subjective foundation of ethics and his recognition of a qualitative difference between feelings Stuart Mill makes a considerable advance on Bentham, yet he is still too zealous a Benthamite ; for he retains the distinction between the value of an action and the value of the agent, and opines that ethics is concerned with the former only. But it is precisely from a utilitarian standpoint that this distinction is untenable. For since every motive contains the possibility of a far greater number of actions than the particular one which is judged at any given moment, our estimation of worth must take cognisance of the motive. Even if the particular action in question were to produce no effects contradictory to the principle of happiness, yet from this same motive actions might arise which we should have to condemn ; hence the motive itself is at any rate ethically questionable. It is only reasonable that our estimation of value should go back to the source. In the *Essay on Liberty* this distinction between action and agent, as we shall see, also plays a great part.

(d) *Social Ethics*

Of the many ethical and economical questions which Mill has discussed in his various books and treatises, we must only pause to discuss those which shed light on his ethical standpoint.

a. The individual and society (*On Liberty*, 1859).—Mill championed the cause of freedom and self-development. He found, however, that political freedom cannot confer real spiritual freedom and self-dependence. Public opinion, a moral police, may only too easily take the place of physical force, as the latter gradually disappears. And this tyranny is more dangerous than political tyranny, since it leaves fewer ways of escape open, penetrates into daily life, and enslaves the mind itself. Men follow the stream even when it is only a question as to how they shall enjoy themselves, instead of following their own instinct and sentiment. The yoke of public opinion is particularly heavy in England, Mill thinks, while the yoke of the law is lighter there than in other countries. Hence a great danger threatens, viz. the ascendancy of the masses, collective mediocrity. The masses must, indeed, always be guided by individuals—but they prefer to take their opinions from men who are not very much above themselves. And yet the impulse to everything noble, everything wise, comes from a few choice spirits. The few men of originality are the salt of the earth! Mill does not, however, desiderate a worship of great men. All that they can claim is perfect liberty to express new ideas. Power to coerce others would finally ruin the great men themselves. The danger involved in the tyranny of public opinion, and in the lowering of the level which is brought about by the ascendancy of the masses may be averted by *liberty ;* this is the only lasting and never sealed fountain of progress, for it creates as many independent centres of reforms as there are persons.

With regard to the interference of others in the affairs of the individual, Mill lays down as a general principle the axiom that the individual must only be limited in the freedom of his action when such interference is necessary in order to prevent his behaviour being injurious to others. The only part of his conduct for which the individual is accountable to society is that part which involves other men. By interference Mill understands partly physical force, partly the moral coercion exercised by the judgment of other men. With regard to the latter, he distinguishes between " moral disapproval or condemnation," and the " expression of displeasure or withdrawal of esteem." But this is a very fine distinction ; for I inflict pain on an individual by withdrawing my esteem precisely in so far as he desires to command it, and, when he does not do this, my displeasure will hardly cause him any pain. This distinction is as difficult to draw as that between actions of which the effects are restricted to ourselves, and those which affect other people also. He who does not develop his personality, or who shows a lack of sagacity and personal dignity, may by so doing deprive others of a power to which they have a just claim. Even if we assert with Mill that it is all-important to secure as many independent starting-points as possible, it is impossible to mark out a sphere of which the significance is entirely contained within the limits of the individual. The distinction between that which concerns the individual and that which concerns other men is just as untenable as the distinction already mentioned between the value of the agent and the value of the action. And yet on both points Mill believes that, thanks to the principle of utility, he has advanced to a more correct view.

Mill emphasises the importance of the greatest possible freedom with reference to opinions as well as to actions. If an opinion be true, what harm can there be in discussing it freely ? If it be but a part of the truth, free discussion is the only way in which it can be decided how large a part of the truth it embodies. And it is only by being kept alive in discussion that it gains influence on characters and actions. Finally, if an opinion can be useful without being true, its utility needs discovering just as much as its truth. In the present day, Mill thinks, the utility of opinions plays perhaps a greater part than their truth. Actions, of course, cannot be accorded so much liberty as opinions. Mill, however, asserts that the value of different ways of life must be tested in experience, and this can only take place if as free play is allowed to differences of character as is possible without injury to other men. It is a condition of individual happiness as well as of individual and social progress that a man's mode of action should be determined by his own character and not by tradition and custom. Strong impulses and wishes are good ; they are the stuff out of which heroes are made ; and men act wrongly not because their wishes are strong but because their conscience is weak.

The line between the individual and society is perhaps not so easy to draw as Mill believes, but his exposition of the matter (which, in the main, is a restatement of the leading thoughts of Kant's *Rechtslehre*) is valuable as showing that the burden of proof must always lie with those who demand a limitation of freedom, and as emphasising the fact that every moral judgment is accompanied with responsibility.

β. *The woman question* (*Subjection of Women*, 1869).—The question of the rights of women is, in Mill's eyes, only one aspect of the greater question of liberty. It is essentially a struggle against the misuse of power, an endeavour to remove the causes which check the free development of personality, to do away with the right of the stronger, to abolish all external authority where this is not necessary for protection and education. Moreover, in discussing this question, he is able to apply his favourite theory of inseparable association in explanation of all those opinions which check development. The current ideas as to the nature of women rest on custom and tradition, not on actual experience. What we call " the nature of woman " is an artificial production. We shall only be in a position to discover her real nature when the barriers which, till now, have precluded her from development and the use of her faculties are overthrown. This is a repetition of the argument Mill brought forward in his treatise on liberty ; constraint must be removed in order that people may learn by experience. We have here a practical application of the method of difference. But Mill writes as if he knew the result beforehand ; he maintains that the mental faculties of women are equal to those of men—an assumption which is not, of course, necessarily involved in the demand for equal rights.

γ. *Parliamentary Representation* (*Considerations on Representative Government*, 1861).—In his discussion of this question too, we find Mill still occupied with the same idea : how can liberty be protected, not only against the despotism of individual men and of classes, but also against the despotism of the majority ? He discusses the dangers and advantages of democracy. At the present day two forms of constitution only have survived and are fighting for the mastery, *i.e.* democracy and bureaucracy. The only possible solution is that democracy should take bureaucracy into its employ, reserving for itself the right of oversight and control. Parliament ought only to give utterance to the will of the State ; it is not competent to draw up laws ; this is a work which should be handed over to a committee of experts. In order that the rights of the minority may be secured Mill recommends, *inter alia*, election by quota. Mill was not blind to the evils of democracy, as may be seen from his *Essay on Liberty* ; but at the same time he sees clearly how short-sighted are they who sigh after a despotism which shall enable them to carry out their plans of reform ; they forget that the development of the people is the most important condition of lasting progress, and do not see that a good despotism, in a country already possessing a certain amount of civilisation, is even more injurious than a bad one, since it is more likely to weaken the spirit and power of the people.

δ. *The social question* (*Principles of Political Economy*, 1848).—As Mill advanced along the path of intellectual development he became increasingly convinced that the social question must take precedence of the political. He never abandoned his belief in democracy ; but not only did he, as we have seen, keep an open mind for its evils, but he gradually formed an ideal for the future which carried him far beyond the programme of democracy. Without great social changes individual and political liberty can never really be enjoyed by all.

In a letter written as early as 1842 (to Robert Barclay Fox, published in Caroline Fox's *Diaries*, ii. p. 272) Mill writes as follows concerning the importance of the social question : " I do believe that ever since the changes in the constitution made by Catholic Emancipation and the Reform Act, a considerable portion of the ruling class in this country, especially of the younger men, have been having their minds gradually opened, and the progress of Chartism is, I think, creating an impression that rulers are bound both in duty and in prudence to take more charge than they have lately been wont to do, of the interests, both temporal and spiritual, of the poor." He adds, however, " But as to the means of curing or even alleviating great social evils people are as much at sea as they were before." Nor did Mill himself ever arrive at a solution. He openly confesses that he finds himself face to face with two fundamental principles, both of which he is constrained to support, although their consequences are, or, at any rate, appear to be, mutually contradictory. The principles to which Mill here refers, and which he pronounces to be diametrically opposed to one another, are

those of individualism and of socialism.   He admits that he
himself cannot see how they are to be reconciled; that he
must leave to the future.   But he is convinced that hitherto
we have seen neither the one nor the other in its best possible
form ; we neither know what free self-activity in its highest
degree and form could effect, nor what possibilities for good
are contained in a thoroughgoing socialistic ordering of
external circumstances.   Perhaps at no other point do Mill's
great qualities as a thinker appear so clearly as here.   While
he entertains great hope for the future,—indeed, we may even
say he takes this hope as his foundation,—yet he enters on a
critical examination of all the different possibilities presented
in experience.   He is not overawed by tradition and custom ;
he quietly investigates the conditions under which they exist,
and inquires whether these conditions might not be replaced
by others.

In his investigation of the socialistic systems he takes up
a far less prejudiced standpoint than was customary among
the economists of his day.   This was in accordance with the
spirit of his philosophy.   He did not, like the ordinary
opponents of socialism, see in the rights of inheritance and
private property dogmas which required no proof.   The
distribution of the national dividend is determined by industrial organisation, custom, and the human will to such a degree
that political economists are under a great misconception in
supposing, as they do, that the mode of distribution which at
present prevails is grounded in the eternal necessity of Nature.
Private property, as an institution, did not owe its origin to
any of those considerations for which it is now retained.   In
the first instance it was for the preservation of peace that
society secured to the individual the possession of that over
which he had already acquired power.   Whether this institution
will be preserved in the future, or supplanted by some other
institution such as has been devised by the various socialistic
schemes, is at present an open question—a question, moreover,
which affords matter for discussion in all classes in civilised
countries.   Mill considers a general reconsideration of all first
principles, coupled with the fact that those who suffer most
under existing institutions have a voice in the discussion as
to their value and authorisation, to be a distinguishing characteristic of our age.   What will be the upshot of it all ?

Mill makes answer (*Princ. of Pol. Econ.* II. i. 3) "If a conjecture may be hazarded, the decision will probably depend
mainly on one consideration, viz. which of the two systems is
consistent with the greatest amount of human liberty and
spontaneity. After the means of subsistence are assured, the
next in strength of the personal wants of human beings is
liberty ; and it increases instead of diminishing in intensity as
the intelligence and the moral faculties are more developed. . . .
An education which taught or the social institutions which
required men to exchange the control of their own actions for
any amount of comfort and affluence, or to renounce liberty for
the sake of equality, would deprive them of one of the most
elevated characteristics of human nature." Mill thinks, to be
sure, that this objection to socialism is often exaggerated, and
he maintains that the restraints involved in such a system
would be freedom in comparison with the present condition of the majority of the human race. But he sees no
reason for abandoning the system of private property if only
the law would do as much towards mitigating its inequalities as it now does to increase them. The present order
fosters egoism more than is necessary even with a system of
private property. But the socialists are wrong in laying
the blame for all social evils on competition. They forget
that wherever competition is not, monopoly is ; and that
monopoly in all its forms is the taxation of the industrious for
the support of indolence. Competition among labourers does,
it is true, depress wages ; all other competition, however, is
for the benefit of the labourers, since it cheapens the necess-
aries of life. The root of economic evils is not competition,
but the subjection of labour to capital (IV. vii. 7).

The remedy, in Mill's opinion, lies in the raising of the
whole level of the working classes, *i.e.* their standard of comfort and of life. This can only be done by means of energetic
intervention on the part of the State. We must endeavour,
by peaceful measures, to attain the progress which the working
classes in France gained by the Revolution. By improved
education, by the parcelling out of land, and by emigration on
a large scale the working classes will be enabled to reach a
social position, and to experience ideal and material wants such
that, rather than reduce their scale of living and depress wages,
they will evince the necessary self-control and avoid the

thoughtless increase of population, even when the effect of this self-denial will only be reaped by a later generation, brought up under more favourable conditions (II. ii. 3). But Mill also expects much from free associations (trades unions and more especially productive co-operation) and he watched their development in France and England with the greatest interest. He considered their chief importance to lie in the encouragement they afford to the virtues of independence, justice, and self-control. In such comparatively small circles experiments in socialism might be made, which would be of great value for the future investigation of social questions.

(*e*) *The Religious Problem*

In the works which Mill published himself he only incidentally alludes to religious questions,—at greatest length in his work on Hamilton's philosophy. He here combats two views. One (which Hamilton had also combated from his point of view) was that brought forward by Schelling and Hegel, *i.e.* that it is possible, by way of pure thought, to arrive at a scientific concept of God, at a concept of an absolute, infinite Being, who is the author and end of all things. Mill maintains that in religion, as in all else, we must start from experience, and that if we are to arrive at the assumption of the existence of God we must be led to it by the observation of Nature. He seems to be of opinion that the grounds for such an assumption may possibly be discovered, for he maintains (in his book on *Comte and Positivism*) that even if we accept Comte's form of the law of the three stages, certain questions will still remain open in the positive stage; hence it would be quite possible to retain theological assumptions provided they are formulated so as not to clash with what we have learnt from experience. The other view opposed by Mill is the one embraced by Hamilton and still more emphatically by Mansel, *i.e.* that even if the scientific investigation of the concept of God as the absolute, infinite, all-powerful, all-good Being, leads to self-contradiction and to consequences which are contrary to that which the human conscience is constrained to affirm, yet we must believe in such a Being, since neither human logic nor human ethics are applicable to the Deity. Mill expresses the greatest indignation against this doctrine. " If," he says

(*Exam.* 2nd ed. p. 103), "instead of the glad tidings that there existed a Being in whom all the excellences which the highest human mind can conceive, exist in a degree inconceivable to us, I am informed that the world is ruled by a being whose attributes are infinite, but what they are we cannot learn, nor what are the principles of his government, except that 'the highest human morality which we are capable of conceiving' does not sanction them; convince me of it, and I will bear my fate as I may. But when I am told that I must believe this, and at the same time call this being by the names which express and affirm the highest human morality, I say in plain terms that I will not. Whatever power such a being may have over me, there is one thing which he shall not do; he shall not compel me to worship him. I will call no being good who is not what I mean when I apply that epithet to my fellow creatures; and if such a being can sentence me to hell for not so calling him, to hell I will go."

This strong language excited great attention and anger, and was used against Mill by his political opponents. It shows us that Mill regarded as the kernel of the religious problem, the moral impossibility of recognising a higher than human standard of moral worth. Bentham (*Deontology*, part i. chap. viii.) had already sharply protested against calling a quality love in the Deity which, in man, would be the opposite of love; that would be to call a stab from a dagger a kiss! And, as Stuart Mill relates in his *Auto-biography*, it was the impossibility of reconciling the evil in the world with the belief in an all-powerful and all-good Creator which led James Mill to reject all religious assumptions, and aroused in him a certain sympathy with the Manichæan doctrine of a good and an evil principle struggling for the lordship of the world. Stuart Mill never gave any decided expression to his own views in any of the works which were published during his lifetime. It was certainly not fear of men which induced him to keep back his opinions. What he did say was sufficient to stamp him as a man whose views on religion were widely divergent from those commonly held. His utterances were used against him by agitators, and when he died an ecclesiastical organ wrote :—" His death is a loss to no one, for he was a crass infidel, however harmless he may have seemed, and a very dangerous person. The sooner those 'luminaries of thought' who hold the same views as his go where he is gone, the better it will be for the Church and the State." What Mill's views were it would have taxed the ecclesiastical organ, which was so well informed as to Mill's fate after death, somewhat severely to say.   The truth is, Mill himself did not regard his views on the religious problem as completely developed : the question was for him really an open one, and he did not wish to speak about it publicly before he had satisfied his own standard of clearness and thoroughness.   Not even his friends knew more about his religious standpoint than what has been already stated until the appearance of his *Essays on Religion* some time after his death.   Of the three treatises contained in this work, two (on the *Utility of Religion* and *On Theism*) were incomplete ; he himself only considered the third (*On Nature*) worth publishing.   Another reason, perhaps, which determined his attitude of reserve was that he did not wish to discuss several problems together, but to investigate each one on its own merits.   He did not feel any necessity to fire his shot in all directions at once.   The secret of the great influence which, in spite of his radicalism, he exercised upon his age is partly to be traced to the fact that he always restricted his investigations to one point at a time. As he himself expressed it to a friend, " I spare no prejudice, but I take care to attack one at a time."

The leading thought of his treatise *On Nature* is that we can no more set Nature, unmodified by human intervention, before men as a pattern than we can conclude from Nature to an all-wise, all-powerful, and all-gracious Creator.   Nature may awe us by her power and force, but her dealings bear the stamp of terrorism and injustice ; she gives to those who possess and is unmerciful to those who possess not.   The only possible way in which the belief in God can be reconciled with our experience of the actual world is by assuming that the Deity is good but not all-powerful.   Omnipotence must be sacrificed to goodness.   This thesis is developed in the essay on *Theism*. The author of the world-order was compelled to submit to conditions which were independent of His will.   The matter and force in the world are uncreated, their properties and laws are independent of the will of the world-organiser. Small wonder, then, that there are so many imperfections : everything which seeks to thwart the tendency observable in

Nature to produce the purposive and the good must be laid
to the account of the material hindrances against which the
Deity has to contend.   The characteristic of the religion of
the future will be the inspiring feeling of being a fellow-worker
with God, a feeling which cannot be combined with the belief
in an all-powerful God without inner contradiction.   We can
only discover what the will of God is by observing everything
in Nature which makes for the general good and the higher
development of life.   To contribute something, however little,
towards the victory of the good is a thought more vitalising
and strengthening than any other by which men can be inspired.
It will be one of the leading thoughts of the religion of the
future.   In a letter of 1841 (to Robert Barclay Fox, see
Caroline Fox's *Diaries*, vol. ii. p. 206) Mill had already brought
it forward in connection with the St. Simonian doctrine of a
continuation of the work of creation.

     There is a point in Mill's polemic against Hamilton which
cannot be rightly understood unless we remember that the
former conceives the Deity as a limited Being.   He cannot
understand why Hamilton should find so many theoretical
difficulties in the concept of God, and, more particularly, why
the law of relativity should present a stumbling-block when
we try to hold fast in thought to this concept.   God is
conceived in relation to the world—but where is the contradiction here ?   Mill asks.   It is evident that he must be arguing
here from his own concept of a limited God ; for the contradiction, of course, only exists so long as the Deity is conceived
as an absolute and infinite Being—and yet in relation to a
something which is not itself, and by which it is determined
and limited ; to which it is therefore relative !   Ethical,
rather than logical grounds, led Mill to adopt this standpoint
in the philosophy of religion ; it is not unlike that taken up
by Voltaire and Rousseau (vol. i. of this work, pp. 460-463,
492-496).

     Mill's argument is based on the tendency to purposiveness
and to a heightened life which may be traced in the world,
side by side with tendencies inimical to the existence of a God ;
his conclusion, therefore, would be wrecked should it be found
possible to give a purely scientific explanation of the purposiveness and the development of life.   Mill himself rejects the
dogma of creation on the ground that every phenomenon must

be explained by another phenomenon ; and perhaps the purposiveness and development of life may also prove to have their definite causes in Nature. This is precisely what the evolutionary hypothesis attempts to prove. Mill recognised this to be the case, for he said that if the evolutionary hypothesis were accepted it could not indeed show that the assumption of a divine intervention is impossible, but it would weaken the ground of such an assumption very considerably. " Let us leave this remarkable speculation to whatever fate the progress of discovery may have in store for it."

Even if the truth of religion can never be proved, Mill thinks, it will not disappear as long as it is useful to man. Mill devotes an essay entitled *The Utility of Religion* to the discussion of the advantages of religion. In common with poetry, religion has its spring in the desire for finer and more beautiful pictures than any which the prose of life can show us. In spite of all progress, human life must always remain so miserable and narrow that man will ever long for a wider and nobler existence. Imagination must be freed from the limitations of positive experience. Even though religion is essentially differentiated from poetry by the great importance it attaches to the real significance of the ideal, yet it is of the essence of all religion that feeling and aspiration should be directed with energy and earnestness towards an ideal object. Comte's religion of humanity satisfies this condition better than any of those religions which entertain a belief in God as the author of the world. The feeling of unity with humanity, of deep sympathy with its welfare and progress, is a disinterested feeling, which contains nothing questionable either from a logical or ethical point of view. There is only one form of belief in the supernatural which is neither immoral nor illogical, *i.e.* that described above in which Nature is regarded as the product of a struggle between a good and wise Being on the one hand and, on the other, either (as Plato thinks) Matter, or (as the Manichæans believed) an evil principle. He who holds this faith can be sure that the evil in this world is not the work of the Being whom he worships. Should this faith be incapable of proof, should it be a hope rather than a faith, nevertheless a true wisdom bids us hold fast to it with all our strength. It enables us to take life cheerfully and joyfully, without excluding reason or criticism. If we fix our gaze

unnecessarily and one-sidedly on all that life has to show that
is sombre, limited and miserable, we only paralyse our power
of action. The hope that beyond the limits imposed by our
experience there exist good powers and an immortal life has its
essential significance in the great extension it gives to the
scale of feeling. Faith in immortality has, according to Mill,
a special influence on the sympathetic feelings; there were
times when the whole significance of religion seemed to him to
be concentrated at this point; he writes to a friend who had
sustained a great loss, " To my mind the only permanent value
of religion is in lightening the feeling of total separation
which is so dreadful in a real grief." In his work on the
philosophy of religion, however, Mill also dwells on the
influence which Christianity has exercised and still exercises
by the great example it has given to the human race. The
work of Christianity has been done not by the idea of God but
by the figure of Christ. And the influence of this example
will in no way diminish, even if we conceive Christ Himself to
have been a purely human and historical person.

Mill's religion has this in common with Kant's—that it is
a hope rather than a faith. He is convinced that all depends
on the answer given to the following question: " Is it unreasonable to let oneself be determined by the imagination to
a hope for the realisation of which it will perhaps never be
possible to assign any probable ground? Ought we to combat
this hope as a deviation from the principle of reason, which
bids us regulate our feelings as well as opinions according to
strict proof?" Mill thinks that this point will long occasion
dispute between thinkers, for each one will answer it according
to his own temperament. But he also thinks that the question
has never yet been taken up as seriously as its great importance requires.

Mill's own solution leaves one aspect of the problem out of
account. If the good principle struggles against the material
chaos, there must be a world-order which, by including them
both, makes the struggle possible. Struggle is reciprocal
action, and reciprocal action presupposes an order of things
which makes it possible for the different operative forces to
come into collision. Thus the old problem crops up again
behind Mill's solution. Mill's religio-philosophical critics in
England,[100] who were armed, for the most part, with weapons

forged in Hegelian workshops were sharp enough in discovering this weak place in his armour, while they did not feel the ethical sting of the problem as keenly as Mill did.   On the psychological side, Mill passed over a factor which plays a great part in religion, *i.e.* the need of absolute absorption by and rest in a Being which does not itself take part in the struggle of life.   This need stands in sharp contrast to another religious need, *i.e.* that of having in the Deity an example of how to live and strive.   The religious problem becomes accentuated when both these spiritual needs demand satisfaction at once.

Mill's greatness, however, does not lie in the results he arrived at.   He no more succeeded in establishing and applying a theory of pure empiricism than Plato succeeded in conceiving and applying a theory of pure idealism.   This juxtaposition of names is the more appropriate since, all through his life, Mill was a great admirer of Plato's.   We might apply to him what he said about Plato : " I have always felt that the title of Platonist belongs by far better right to those who have been nourished on and have endeavoured to practise Plato's•mode of investigation, than to those who are distinguished only by the adoption of certain dogmatical conclusions."

So, too, Mill's significance in the history of philosophy consists in his method of investigation, in the manner in which he brought experience and critical thought to bear on a great number of theoretical and practical questions.   He evoked a spirit of philosophising, of far greater importance than any result.   And here we must leave this thinker who was at once definitive and yet continually striving, logically clear and easily excited by feeling, who not only reflected in his development the problems of his time, but also rendered valuable services to thought by the manner in which he handled them.

C. THE PHILOSOPHY OF EVOLUTION

THE fundamental thought on which positive philosophy in general builds is that our conceptions must be based on perceptions. In explaining empirically given phenomena, therefore, we must proceed from causes which are themselves given in experience. Positivism is in reality nothing but the carrying out of Kepler's and Newton's injunction to seek for *veræ causæ*. As Auguste Comte shows, the difference between the various leading forms of philosophy is determined by the difference in the nature of the causes they assume. But even when the positive principle is accepted, there is still room for significant divergencies. Comte and Mill ended by conceiving the causal relation as a relation between two different phenomena, which appear to us in experience to be bound together. They lay no stress on that side of the causal relation which shows us that the deeper and more transparent it becomes, the clearer are we able to perceive the continuous interconnection of phenomena. Hence, too, the close connection between the causal concept and the concept of development escaped their notice. They do indeed emphasise this latter concept within the social sphere, but it plays no part in determining their conception of Nature as a whole. They laid far too much weight on the differences which experience reveals to us, and did not see that the aim of all knowledge is to reduce these differences as far as possible. They stopped short at the problem of the origin of new forms. In their opinion development takes place in the individual and, by means of the influence of tradition and institutions, in the race also. But that the concept of evolution could become the dominant note in a world-conception never dawned upon them, and the limitations of their thought were, to a great extent, imposed by this fact.

The change in the conception of Nature which was brought about by CHARLES DARWIN'S discoveries and hypotheses may be compared with the changes which we owe to Copernicus and Bruno, Galilei and Newton. Copernicanism extended and infinitised the world. This earth and human life no longer appeared as the central point round which everything else turned. Newton showed that the entire universe is dominated by law, and that even the most distant heavenly bodies are subject to the same laws which hold good on this earth. Darwin's conception of Nature betokened a similar extension of view on the side of organic life. Up till now no great interconnection, no general law of origin and development had been discovered in the sphere of biology. CASPER FRIEDRICH WOLFF and KARL ERNST VON BAER had already proved that the single organism develops through a series of stages from an embryo which bears no resemblance to the perfectly developed individual. Spinoza, Hartley and James Mill had pointed out that a psychological development may proceed within the individual in the course of which, and in accordance with the laws of association, psychical forms arise which resemble the original foundation no more than the forms of the fully-grown organism resemble the embryo. And the historical school founded by Montesquieu, which flourished more especially in France and Germany after the Revolution, employed the concept of development in explaining the origin of social and political forms. In the Romantic philosophy this same concept had been equally prominent. The Romanticists asserted the inner connection of each single thing with the whole, and existence was conceived by them as a series of stages, each one of which exhibited the content of the world under progressively higher forms. The application here made of the concept of development was, however, purely ideal. Development was not conceived as a process in time by means of which one phenomenal form developed out of another ; continuity was conceived as belonging to the ideal kernel of existence only, not to particular phenomena. And no one asked what were the efficient causes which could lead from one stage to another. On the other hand, significant examples of how new forms and states may be formed according to laws of

constant validity were afforded by Kant's and Laplace's hypothesis of the development of the solar system from a gaseous
vapour, under the workings of definite physical and chemical
laws, and by Lyell's theory of the origin of the present state
of the earth's surface in the incessant operation of the same
physical and chemical causes as are in operation to-day.
Darwin's explanation of the origin of organic species is that
the perpetual struggle for the preservation of life in the midst
of the various favourable and unfavourable conditions of the
environment or of other living beings has, little by little,
produced far-reaching modifications of bodily structure and of
habits of life.   He has extended our conception of Nature,
and has revealed to us a process of development reaching far
beyond our calculation, of which the different species at
present existing are the outcome.   While, on the other hand,
he has sharpened our sight for little things by teaching us to
recognise in the frequently insignificant causes which are active
round about us, those forces through whose quiet but uninterrupted activity living races have acquired the form under
which they now appear to us.

The original element in Darwin's teaching was not the
general notion that the different organic species and forms
have been produced by natural causes.   This thought had
already appeared under many forms before his day.   The
importance of Darwin rests on the fact that he *established* this
opinion by pointing out definite efficient causes, working in the
direction of such new forms.   The concept of evolution itself
is, as we have already intimated, so closely connected with the
causal concept and the concept of continuity that it might
have taken its place as a fundamental notion even before
Darwin, by his investigations, gave it such a powerful empirical
corroboration.   Thus, several years before the appearance of
Darwin's epoch-making work, HERBERT SPENCER had adopted
the evolutionary hypothesis, and had pointed out more particularly (in the 1st edition of his *Psychology*) the significance
of this hypothesis in view of the possibility that qualities and
faculties which seem inexplicable so long as we confine ourselves to the experience of the individual may no longer
remain so if we extend our consideration to that of the whole
race.   This extension of empirical philosophy enabled it to
allow full weight to views which had hitherto only been

recognised by speculative and critical philosophy.   Spencer afterwards attempted, in a more detailed systematic exposition, to prove that the concept of development is one of those fundamental concepts to which our experience and our thought leads back from all sides.

CHAPTER I

CHARLES DARWIN

(a) Biography and Course of Development

THE justification for the appropriation of this great inquirer into Nature by the History of Philosophy lies mainly in the fact—as is also the case with Copernicus, Galilei and Newton—that the significance of his method and results extends far beyond his special department; they form a turning-point in scientific inquiry, and still more in our mode of conceiving Nature. Shortly after the idea of his hypothesis had occurred to him (1837), twenty years before the appearance of his famous work, he wrote in his note-book: "My theory will lead to a complete philosophy." But Darwin is of importance for philosophy not merely on account of his consistency, or because he raised the question as to how the new theory must affect our whole world-conception; he also discussed psychological and ethical questions, and has expressed opinions on the limits of human knowledge. As we learn to know him from his *Autobiography* and his letters, he stands out before us, a Socratic figure, unique amid the inquirers of modern times; to be honoured alike for his energy, his love of truth and his feeling for humanity.

CHARLES DARWIN was born at Shrewsbury, February 12, 1809. After having studied medicine in Edinburgh and theology in Cambridge, without feeling attracted by either, his interest in natural science, which dated from his childhood, led him to join the *Beagle* in its voyage round the world (1831-36). The observations made during this voyage formed the first foundation of his theory. He compared the present-day fauna of South America with pre-existing forms, and was struck at once by the similarity and differences (especially in magnitude) of structure which they presented. He compared the animal life of the northern portion of South America with that of the southern, and here again he found the same remarkable combination of similarity and difference. He was especially astonished to find, on the Galapagos Islands, situated nearly 1100 kilometres from South America, a fauna and flora which, while presenting striking resemblance to that of South America, were composed of species to be found nowhere else on the globe : the *species* occurred on these islands only, but they belonged to *genera* which were to be found on the nearest continent. It was as if one and the same fundamental form had suffered such transformation as to fit it to live either on the continent or on the islands. Moreover, each island had its own peculiar species which were not to be found on the other islands. Now how was, on the one hand this relationship, on the other this differentiation, to be explained? Darwin brought this problem back from his eventful journey, and dedicated his whole life to answering it. He lived in the country, near London, under very happy circumstances, unceasingly occupied in collecting facts which might throw light on his problem. The question to be answered was: "How are precisely such forms and qualities preserved and developed as are useful to animals and plants in their environment?"

It was the variation of forms and qualities in correspondence with the environment which struck Darwin as so remarkable. He assumed, as a matter of course, that such variations must have a natural cause—but what was this cause? The reading of Malthus's work on population (1838) started him on his line of thought. Malthus showed that living beings tend to increase beyond the means of subsistence. In that case, Darwin argued, living beings must mutually co-operate, must struggle or contend with one another in order to procure the necessities of life. Life is and must be a struggle for existence, and that individual or group of individuals which, from one reason or another, possesses a faculty or an organ which the rest lack, and which corresponds to the environment, is more likely than others to succeed in the struggle. The propagation of the race will be carried on chiefly by them, and such forms as are wanting in this faculty or this organ will gradually die out. And when a group of living beings have to live within a limited space they can do so the more easily the greater the differences which exist between the forms comprising this group, for in that case their different requirements can be more easily satisfied. If they all require the same food it is clear that not so many can find sustenance as when they feed on different things. In the struggle for existence, then, it is an advantage to any species to possess the faculty of variation.

As early as the forties Darwin began to work at a treatise setting forth his theory, but he laid it aside to make further investigations. In the middle of the fifties he began the final preparation of his work for the press, and it appeared in 1859 under the title *Origin of Species*. This was followed by a long series of other works, amongst which the most important, in relation to philosophy and psychology are: *Variation of Animals and Plants under Domestication* (1868), *Descent of Man* (1871), and *Expression of the Emotions in Men and in Animals* (1872). Darwin's long and faithful labour in the service of science only ended with his death on April 19, 1882.[101] Three years previously he had written in his *Autobiography :* "As for myself I believe that I have acted rightly in steadily following and devoting my life to science. I feel no remorse for having committed any great sin, but have often and often regretted that I have not done more direct good to my fellow-creatures."

(b) *Theory and Method*

The result of Darwin's inquiry was a victory for the principle of natural causation, and a confirmation of the axiom *natura non facit saltum*. He disclosed the presence of continuity in a sphere where hitherto men had believed in supernatural interventions and interruptions, or had stopped short at original and inexplicable differences or, at the most, had appealed to an inner impulse towards development, which might be supposed to lead from one stage to another. Through his explanation of the origin of species in the struggle for existence, Darwin shed light on the conditions not only of physical but also of psychical life which was of no less value than the solution of the particular problem to which he had addressed himself. Without knowing it, he took up again a thought which had been current in the old English school. For his "struggle for existence" reminds us of Hobbes' "war of all against all." The English have always possessed a keen insight into the conditions of life, and have felt the necessity of making a great effort to master them.   This explains the peculiar intermixture of empiricism and idealism which has so often been regarded as a contradiction.   Their sense of practical relations actually given does not, however, deaden their conviction of the value of inner forces, even when they do not express this in the mystical or speculative manner into which continental thinkers so often fall.

The explanation given by Darwin of the origin of species is conceived wholly in the spirit of positivism, hence it was illogical of Comte's disciples to turn, as they did, a cold shoulder to the new hypothesis.   The cause to which Darwin appeals is an actually given, *positive* cause.   He says in a letter that to say that species were created in such and such a manner is no scientific explanation, but only a pious way of saying things are as they are.   And from other utterances of his we may gather that when, at the conclusion of the *Origin of Species*, he speaks of the first forms of life being created, he only means by this to say that we are ignorant as to the origin of life : afterwards he expressly regrets having used the word created, on account of the associations it carries with it.

The expression "struggle for existence" is used figuratively ; it includes dependence of one being on another and on the environment, and has reference not only to the life of the individual but also to that of its progeny.   The plants which grow on the edge of the desert must struggle for their existence, that is to say, their preservation depends upon how little moisture they can manage to live upon.   In the organic world, however, the relation to other living creatures is even more important than the relation to physical conditions.   The mistletoe-berries on the same branch struggle with one another for space and nourishment, but they also struggle with other fruit-bearing plants ; for their increase depends on whether birds prefer the seeds of mistletoe to that of other plants, so that they devour and disseminate them in great numbers.   While the term "struggle for existence" denotes the adaptation of the organism to the living or lifeless environment, Darwin expresses the other side of this relation by the term *natural selection*, by which he means the manner in which the environment favours certain qualities, "the principle according to

which any variation, however small, which is useful to the
individual, is preserved." Struggle is the universal law of
Nature. Existence. or non-existence are the alternatives.
Every being persists in virtue of a victory which it has won at
some time in its life. And the struggle for existence again is
a result of the great increase of organic beings. The whole
economy of Nature becomes incomprehensible to us "if we
forget for a· moment that every individual species tries to
increase as far as possible, and that there is always some
hindrance which checks propagation, even if we are not always
able to perceive it. Owing to this collision between multipli-
cation on the one side and unfavourable conditions on the
other, selection becomes necessary. Those individuals who
exhibit purposive variations are preserved, the others die out ;
in this way differences are fostered, until at last the different
species are evolved which so many people regard as different
in kind." We have here the key to the problem of how different
forms can be related to one another, for we see that they have
developed out of a common ground-form, under increasing
divergence of character. What C. T. Wolff had shown to be
true of the different organs of the same individual, *i.e.* that in
spite of their dissimilarity they have developed out of certain
simple elementary forms, Darwin showed to be true of the
different species in the organic world in general.

Darwin's method is an interesting example of inductive
inquiry. The course followed by him in his investigations
shows with unusual clearness the three chief stages which a
truth which is based on experience has to pass through. The
first foundation of his theory was, as we saw, the observations
made during his journey. These suggested the idea of his
provisional hypothesis, and, — after his study of Malthus's
work—of an explanation by means of deduction from the
strong impulse to propagation taken in relation to the environment. The third branch of his work was verification,
empirical confirmation. This consisted in four groups of facts.
Breeders in England had for many years past produced new
species by "artificial selection." They remarked small variations suitable for their purpose in different individuals, and then
produced new forms by taking care that only such individuals
as exhibited the said variations should propagate the race.
What is here done purposely and methodically takes place

unconsciously and more irregularly in natural selection. The
second class of facts confirming the theory are those which
exhibit the kinship between extinct species and those now
existing. As a rule the former may be shown to be members
of existing groups, but lower forms of them. The third class of
facts is concerned with the geographical distribution of species,
which can be most easily explained on the hypothesis that
the different forms and properties of related organisms have
arisen through the dissemination of the original stock over
widely diversified tracts of land. That the lowest forms of
life are the most widely disseminated is explained by the fact
that their seeds and eggs are small and well suited to be
carried far away by streams and currents. Finally the correspondence which is found to exist in the fœtus stage between
animals, which, when fully developed, are quite different from
one another, witnesses to a still further relationship, and rudi-
mentary organs (which are to be found more particularly in the
embryo stage) are only comprehensible on the assumption of
such a relationship.

Darwin's character is reflected in a most remarkable
manner in the direction and method of his inquiry. As an
inquirer he was distinguished by his open and childlike mind,
to which nothing appeared mean or insignificant. He guessed
at an all-pervading interconnection. Nature was, in his eyes,
no lifeless collection of objects to which natural history has to
assign names and numbers, but a living reality in which the
preservation and growth of one being depends on that of
another. The insect and the flower, the bird and the plant,
the field and the earth-worm, the life, the structure, and the
ornamental appendages of animals, their loves and their
struggles—all these appeared to him as standing in the most
intimate relation to one another, and only separable by
artificial means. He turned the word " Natural History " into a
reality. But together with this childlike receptivity towards
Nature there went a wide understanding which realised that
definite and constant laws prevail throughout Nature, and that
the highest which Nature can show us is not exalted above
these laws, but, on the contrary, proves its sublimity by the
fact that it has developed by means of them. He frequently
said that no one could be a good observer who could not
speculate. It was impossible for him to perceive anything

new in Nature without at once forming some hypothesis as to how it had arisen.   On the other hand, he possessed a remarkable capacity for grasping an objection and keeping it in sight. He observed the rule which he himself has called the golden rule of noting down as they occurred to him every fact and thought which seemed contradictory to results he had already reached.   Hence very few objections were raised against his views which he had not himself already noticed and tried to answer.   In this respect he was more critical than several of his adherents, who sometimes thought that he attributed too much importance to the objections brought against his theory.   He was perfectly well aware that his hypothesis did not admit of any *direct* proof.   He writes of one of his critics in a letter : " He is one of the very few who see that the variation of species does not admit of direct proof, and that my theory will stand or fall according to whether it is, or is not, able to group together and explain phenomena.   It is curious how few judge it according to this, the only correct criterion."

He himself regarded the proof of his theory to lie in the fact that, by an intelligible thread of reasoning it connected together a vast number of facts.   He did not regard his theory as a dogma, but as an instrument which threw light on Nature and which would throw still more light in the future.   The significance of scientific hypothesis consists not least in the fact that they cause further inquiries to be set on foot.   We try whether it is possible to bind *all* our experiences together in the same way as we have succeeded in joining *some* of them ; we discover what sort of questions we must ask of Nature. In this respect, Darwin's doctrine of the origin of species by natural selection has been most fruitful.   It teaches us that throughout the whole sphere of natural science we must seek to trace the importance of a quality, a faculty or a form in the struggle for existence.   It takes for granted that nothing can exist or develop without some definite significance for the whole economy of life.

(c) Limits of the Theory

Darwin acknowledged one limit to his inquiry in the question as to *the first origin* of the individual differences between

which both natural and artificial selection takes place.   A
choice presupposes something that can be chosen, differences
and variations.   Darwin considered it proved that such variations occur, and that they occur the more frequently in proportion as the conditions of life are favourable and the degree of
development to which the species has already attained is high.
He confesses that " with respect to the causes of variability we
are very ignorant at all points " and for some time the origin of
original variations seemed to him all the more mysterious
owing to his tendency to allow very little direct influence
to external environment.   In a letter to Huxley, shortly
after the appearance of the *Origin of Species*, he writes (November 25, 1859) :—" You have most cleverly hit on one point
which has greatly troubled me ; if, as I must think, external
conditions produce little *direct* effect, what the devil determines
each particular variation ? "   (See also the letter he had written
to Hooker, November 23, 1856.)   Afterwards he was led to
ascribe to the environment a more direct influence on variation.
(See his letter of May 4, 1869, to Carus, of October 13,
1876, to Wagner, and of March 9, 1877, to Neumayr).   In
his work on the *Variation of Animals and Plants under
Domestication* (chaps. xxii.-xxvi.), Darwin discusses the question
further, and not only emphasises the direct effect of environment,
but also the effect produced by the use or disuse of organs and
faculties (see also the *Descent of Man*, chap. iv.).   It is all the
more important to keep this point in view in our study of
Darwin, since his critics have so frequently confused the origin
of variations with the natural selection of qualities which are
produced by such variation.   " Natural selection," Darwin says
on this point (*Variation of Animals and Plants*, London,
1868, vol. ii. p. 272), " depends on the survival, under various
and complex circumstances, of the best-fitted individuals, but
has no relation whatever to the primary cause of any modification of structure."   Darwin's hypothesis is mainly concerned
with the *effects* of natural selection between variations, not with
the *origin* of variations.   He believes, of course, that this, too,
has natural causes, but he is not chiefly concerned with their
discovery.   Every hypothesis must rest on a certain foundation
which cannot be included in the proof.   Hence, there is
no contradiction in Darwin's acceptance of variations as
actually given.   Amongst the many objections brought against

him not the least strange was that he depended on " accident " :
Darwin, it is true, makes use on one single occasion of the
expression "chance variations," *i.e.* in the letter to Hooker already
quoted, but he understands by this expression, variations the
causes of which are unknown to us, and he himself pronounced
the term to be inexact.   Just as he regarded the first origin
of variations as in several respects mysterious, so too he
declared the origin of life altogether to be an insoluble riddle.

On the other hand, Darwin found no reason for supposing
that in the development of the human race out of lower forms
special forces were set in motion.   As soon as he became
firmly convinced that the different species had arisen by
natural development he saw at once that the human race
could form no exception to the rule.   In the *Origin of Species*,
however, he contents himself with intimating that the new
theory would throw light on man and his history.   He
had no space there for a special investigation of one single
genus of living beings.   Afterwards, when he addressed himself specially to this point (in his *Descent of Man*), he did so,
as he says in a letter, partly because he had been accused of
not having the courage to make known his views on this
subject.   On this point he stood even more alone than on the
general question as to the origin of species.   Even such men
as Lyell and Wallace, who were otherwise in agreement with him,
hesitated here.   Darwin himself was conscious of no contradiction
between feeling and intellectual curiosity.   The real value and
the real greatness of man suffered, in his opinion, no diminution because man has developed out of lower forms.   He
opposed to the theological and romantic view, which regarded
men as fallen angels, the realistic view of man as an animal
which has developed into a spiritual being.   Neither psychi-
cally nor physically would he allow any but quantitative differences between man and beast.   There is a far greater gulf, he
maintains, between the mental capacities of one of the lowest
vertebrate animals (the eel or river-lamprey) and those of the
highest ape, than between the intellectual endowment of the
ape and of man.   And he points out how difficult it is to draw
a line between mere instinct and reason proper.   The fact that
animals can learn by experience suffices to show that we cannot
altogether deny them reason.   And the same may be said of
memory, of the sense of beauty, and of the sympathetic instincts.

It has sometimes been inferred from Darwin's teaching that there ought to be an uninterrupted progress in perfection in all living beings : hence, it has been urged as a great objection to his doctrine that the lowest organic forms remain the same. Here, again, Darwin had foreseen and answered the objection. Natural selection does not necessarily imply a progress. What use would it be to an entozoon or an earthworm to possess more perfect organs than its present ones? An organ that affords no help in the struggle for existence takes up space and power without being of any use. Where, from any reason, circumstances are such as to exclude any great rivalry, it is perfectly comprehensible that a living form should remain as it is through countless ages (*Origin of Species*, chap. iv. cf. chap. x.). Natural selection is only able to make every organic being as perfect as it needs to be in order to compete with other organic beings in the struggle for existence ; according to Darwin, the marvel is that experience shows us so few cases in which a perfection of this kind is not present. Perfection, however, must always be understood in relation to the conditions of life (" The natural selection of each species implies improvement in that species *in relation to its conditions of life.*"—Letter to Lyell, October 25, 1859). Hence natural selection sometimes effects a return to simpler and more elementary forms of life, especially when the conditions of life are simplified from any reason, so that certain organs become, if not actually detrimental, at any rate superfluous. There is no immanent or necessary tendency in organic beings to ascend the ladder of organisation (*Variations*, etc. chap. i. p. 8).

(*d*) *Ethical and Religious Consequences*

Apart from the objections raised against Darwin's theory on account of its supposed contradiction or lack of agreement with experience, objections of an ethical and religious nature were also brought against it. These did not come exclusively from the theological party. Even such a radical thinker as Eugen Dühring regarded it as objectionable on ethical grounds, and expressed himself violently against it. The very idea of a struggle for existence seemed to many people incompatible with an ethical view of life ; how could benevolence and conscience be united with such an idea?

Darwin was far from overlooking the ethical objection ; on the contrary, he had expressly discussed the connection between the ethical problem and his theory. As a moral philosopher he adopts a standpoint similar to that which Shaftesbury and Hutcheson had founded, and Comte and Spencer, in our century, had developed still further ; but Darwin's scientific views and his doctrine of natural selection gave the whole standpoint a broader basis.

Darwin finds in the fact that man is the only being who can with certainty be described as a moral being, the greatest difference between man and beast. It does not, however, follow from this that the moral feeling has not had a natural development, nor does this admission in any way contradict the theory of the struggle for existence, and "natural selection." Only we must always remember that those qualities and faculties which further natural selection are not only such as benefit single individuals, but such as benefit the whole group or species. Among the animals who are benefited by living in close community, those individuals to whom the society of others is most agreeable will most easily escape danger ; and since the continued existence of the race depends on the preservation of frequently very helpless offspring, it is easy to see that the love of parents to their offspring may be developed by natural selection. Experience shows that animals sometimes expose themselves to danger in order to save others. A race or a group of animals or men in which mutual sympathy and the need of mutual assistance prevails, will be especially favourably placed in the struggle for existence ; more favourably, certainly, than other groups where each man only cares for himself, and where there is no concentration of forces for a common end. Hence we see that in obedience to the law of natural selection, qualities may be preserved and developed in individuals which are conducive to the pre- servation of society, rather than to that of the particular individual. Not only the self-regarding but also the extra- regarding feelings have their natural history. However great the difference may be between that which stirs in animals when they exhibit mutual love and self-sacrifice, and that which is exhibited in the highest human morality, there are, between the two, countless grades, and we have no justification for supposing that natural development is interrupted at any point.

In the human world, too, there are very great moral differences. There are states and forms of human life indeed, which stand far below anything which animal life can show us. Darwin declares that he would rather be descended from an ape that risks its life to save its keeper than from a savage who rejoices in the torture of his enemy, kills his children without any remorse, treats his wives as slaves and is himself a thrall to the most abominable superstitions.[102]

The moral feeling, according to Darwin, presupposes not only sociability and the capacity for sympathy, but also the faculty of memory and comparison. If these exist, past action can be recalled and judged (in the moment of remembrance, if not at all moments) in accordance with the demands of the predominant feeling. If the capacity for speech be developed, mutual praise and blame will influence individuals. A public opinion will be formed. Moreover, constant habit and practice in working for common interest will establish and strengthen social motives and instincts. Perhaps, too, dispositions in this direction may be handed down from parent to offspring. Darwin finds an empirical confirmation of his theory of moral philosophy in the investigation of those qualities which have been regarded as virtues at different times and by different nations, and of the difference of range in the circle of individuals whose weal and woe the moral feeling has at different times taken into consideration.

It is precisely by means of the theory of natural selection that we learn that not every adaptation, not every selection, not every form of the struggle for existence is permitted. We are led from lower to higher forms of this struggle, until at last we come to a stage in which an estimation of the worth of the different forms of the struggle is possible.[103]

It has been thought, however, that Darwinism is not only an immoral but even a materialistic and godless doctrine.

Darwin has nowhere expressed his opinion on the relation between the spiritual and the material. He abides by the fact that the psychical life of men and of animals is bound up with the activity of material organs, and in so far can be studied scientifically like other organic phenomena. Accordingly he investigates the development of psychical life from lower to higher stages in the struggle for existence, and seeks for the definite laws of this development. But there is nothing materialistic in this. As he declares the origin of life to be an insoluble problem so he would certainly have declared the origin of conscious life to be indemonstrable; perhaps he regarded the two problems as identical. Darwin investigated several interesting psychological points besides the moral feeling, *i.e.* sexual feelings and instincts, instinct in general, the expression of the emotions, the development of the child during its first year. Scattered through his works, often where they are least suspected (*e.g.* in his little work on the *Formation of Vegetable Mould by the Action of Worms*), interesting psychological features are to be found. The discussion of psychological principles, however, lay beyond his sphere.

If by materialism we understand merely the reduction of phenomena to definite natural laws, exclusive of all supernatural intervention, Darwin is certainly a materialist. His theory is that organic forms did not exist in the imagination of the Creator as perfectly formed ideas which were then transformed into material reality; but that they are the results of a long process of development from the most insignificant beginnings, under the continual influence of the environment. Darwin extended the sphere of natural interconnection; he introduced the habit, first among scientific men and afterwards in wider circles, of thinking *positively* and of dispensing with theological causes. In a certain sense it is true that he did not hereby introduce a new *principle*, for the principle of assigning natural causes had been established long ago, but the history of science contains few such brilliant verifications as we have here. Several English theologians have recently embraced Darwin's theory, justifying themselves by saying that they restrict the creative act to the beginning of life, when the primitive form or forms arose; and that natural selection is for them the means established by God for the originating of particular species. Darwin himself, however, could not adopt this way out of the difficulty. No less than Stuart Mill he found it impossible to unite the sufferings and discords of the world with the governing providence of an omnipotent Being. He was not a pessimist; he entertained a conviction — which, it is true, he found very difficult to prove—that the happiness of the world distinctly outweighs the unhappiness. But he could never bring himself to regard natural selection, which involves suffering and injury, and produces hatred and cruelty no less than love and gentleness, as a means in the hand of Providence. Was the saw-fly really created to devour living larvæ, the cat to play with the mouse? He had already expressed himself in this sense in his writings (especially in *Variations*, etc., ii. p. 432), but he does so still more strongly in his letters and Autobiography. He always came back to the fact of the existence of evil whenever he was challenged to express his opinions on religion. When he returned from his famous journey he was still a believer in revelation, and when his great work, the *Origin of Species*, came out he was still a Theist ; gradually, however, and without any painful breach his views changed and finally (in a part of his *Autobiography*, written in 1876) he declares himself an *Agnostic*, *i.e.* one who is conscious that our knowledge is not adequate to solve the problem. (This term was first used (1859) by Huxley, Darwin's friend and pupil.) Just as he could never reconcile himself to the thought that the world, as it is, could be the result of design, so he could not believe it to be the result of chance or brute force. "The safest conclusion," he writes to a young man, who had asked his opinion on the subject, "seems to me to be that the whole subject is beyond the scope of man's intellect ; but man can do his duty."

The real significance of agnosticism is that what appears to us as a dilemma need not really be such, since there may be other alternatives beside design and chance, which seem to us the only ones. Darwin concludes with the same result as Kant in his "Critique of Judgment" (see above, p. 108), where he declares that the distinction between mechanism and teleology may perhaps be one of those oppositions which our knowledge forces us to set up, but the validity of which for existence itself we have no right to assume.

CHAPTER II

HERBERT SPENCER

(a) *Biography and Characteristics*

IN the year in which Darwin's famous work appeared, Herbert Spencer was drawing up a sketch of a systematic exposition, which aimed at exhibiting the significance of the concept of development in all the different spheres of knowledge. His earlier studies had led him to regard this concept as one of the leading concepts of human knowledge, and he now wished to dedicate his life to the exposition and inculcation of this view. As his means were small he solicited a grant from Government to enable him to carry out his plan. Men who were acquainted with his earlier works—such as the philosophers, Stuart Mill and Fraser (Hamilton's successor at Edinburgh) ; the historian, Grote ; the physiologist, Huxley ; the botanist, Hooker ; and the physicist, Tyndall—gave him their warmest support. It was at first calculated that the work would require seven, afterwards ten volumes ; when actually carried out it ran to nine volumes. Government refused the grant ; but Spencer, nothing daunted, set to work with great perseverance, in spite of frequently failing powers. The first part of his work (*First Principles*) began to appear in the autumn of 1860, and the last part (the conclusion of the *Principles of Ethics*) in the spring of 1893. The intermediate parts treat of biology, psychology and sociology. It will be interesting to note how the plan of this comprehensive work arose and matured.[104]

HERBERT SPENCER was born on April 27, 1820, at Derby. His father, a prominent educationalist, was firmly convinced that a healthy intellectual development could only be attained by self-education. Accordingly his great effort was to teach his pupils to think and observe for themselves. Spencer very early evinced an interest in natural science and history. He took pleasure in observing the development of insects ; he made himself acquainted with various subjects from books in his father's library ; and he and his brothers eagerly discussed scientific, political and religious questions. His parents were Methodists ; his father, however, became increasingly dissatisfied with the clerical organisation of this sect and joined the Quakers, without, however, adopting their special doctrines. What attracted him was their unsacerdotal system. Hence his son Herbert went to the Quakers' meeting on Sunday morning with his father, and to chapel in the evening with his mother. The consequence was that Bible reading became intolerable to him. Afterwards Spencer went to an uncle, a clergyman (with Broad Church leanings) and a man of eminent qualities, who took part eagerly in the agitation for the repeal of the Corn Laws, and who had done good service in the organisation of Poor Law relief.

Spencer's critical attitude towards any ambitious attempt to order social relations by means of State interference, and his great belief in free development, were established and nourished by the religious and political views which he came across in his earliest youth. It was intended that he should be a schoolmaster like his father ; he worked for some years, however, as a civil engineer. Mathematical studies and mechanical inventions, together with political agitations, took up the greater part of his time. The first works of any note by him are some articles on the true province of government, and a treatise on the nature of sympathy, in which he set forth a theory similar to Adam Smith's. Still earlier his studies in natural history had led him to embrace the theory of the natural development of species. He has himself stated that it was through his study of Lyell's *Geology* (which, in the older editions, disputed Lamarck's theory) that he was led (in 1839) to perceive the correctness of the theory of natural development. This was not without its effect on his religious views. They underwent a change, although it is not possible to point out any decided change at any definite time. In his first important work, *Social Statics* (1850), he conceives social development in analogy with organic ; and this conception plays a great part in his later works also. The perfect development of life seems to him here a divine idea which awaits realisation, and of which there are indications and approximations in Nature. Spencer has told us himself that in writing this work he was influenced by Coleridge, and through him by Schelling. He afterwards abandoned this teleological view, contenting himself with a purely empirical proof of development under its different forms. But even as early as this, Spencer tells us, his theory of evolution was mainly determined by "the law which, darkly hinted at in Harvey's embryological inquiries and afterwards more clearly conceived by Wolff [the anatomist], was finally definitively formulated by von Baer, *i.e.* the law that all organic development consists in a change from a state of homogeneity to a state of heterogeneity." This law was already known to hold good of individual organisms; Spencer extended it to development in all spheres, and he was now convinced that there is no sphere in which development does not take place. In a short treatise of the year 1852 on the evolutionary hypothesis he institutes a comparison between the evolution and the creation theories, and after giving due consideration to the variation of domestic animals and cultivated plants, to the difficulty of distinguishing between species and variety, and to the similarity between the embryos of different forms he comes to the conclusion that species have arrived at their present forms by development under the influence of external circumstances. The working out of his *Principles of Psychology* (1st ed. 1855) permanently influenced his general point of view. The significance of this work lies in the fact that, although based on empirical philosophy, it emphasises the impossibility of explaining individual consciousness by the experiences of the individual himself. All previous empiricism had taken it for granted that it was only necessary to discover the experiences of the particular individual in order to understand his conscious life. This conviction had practical as well as theoretical significance. For if the conscious life of man is determined by the individual's own experience only, it must be possible by means of a purposely designed plan of education and order of society to produce any desired character. Stuart Mill and Comte built their hopes on the future development of the human race to a great extent on this conviction, although it was curiously opposed to the profound comprehension of historical development which both these writers possessed. Spencer now became convinced that development in the mental as well as in the material sphere takes place very slowly, by means of many intermediate forms and stages, not one of which can be dispensed with. Constant modification by the environment causes life to assume new forms, amongst others those forms under which it is now exhibited. We cannot, therefore, hope to explain the conscious life of the individual from his own experiences alone ; we must go back to the experience of the race. And here we find many factors in operation besides tradition ; in the innermost structure of the mind, in the manner in which ideas are associated, and in the direction in which feelings and instincts unfold, hereditary tendencies are active ; these are only comprehensible on the assumption of an after-effect of the experience of preceding generations. Heredity had hitherto been regarded as little more than a curiosity, and significance was attached to it only in a few isolated exceptional cases ; from henceforward it was to be regarded as an ever-present co-operative factor in the determination of the very highest forms of life. This extension of the horizon in the psychological sphere induced Spencer to inquire into the general laws of development, and to ask whether it might not be possible to deduce these laws from the fundamental laws of our knowledge. The idea of a philosophy of evolution was now given. The first sketch appeared in a treatise entitled *Progress : its Laws and Cause* (1857). Spencer here expounds the view that all development is a transition from homogeneity to heterogeneity, and attempts to show that this follows from the law of the conservation of energy. In the first edition of the *First Principles* he only gave the law of evolution in this one form ; afterwards he supplemented it by two others : evolution is a transition from diffusion to integration, and from incoherence to coherence. And now the publication of his great work went quickly forward.

There were other preparatory works, however, besides those already mentioned. In a series of essays, written before he had started on his great work, and published in various journals, Spencer had already discussed subjects of a philosophical, scientific, sociological and ethical nature. His systematic works are only further and broader (often too broad) elaborations of the contents of these short, clear essays, many of them models of form, which are collected in four volumes entitled *Essays*, and which will, perhaps, outlive all his other works.

Spencer overworked himself in preparing the first edition of his *Psychology*, and suffered from a weakness of the nerves from which he never completely recovered. He was a victim to chronic sleeplessness. The evil increased to such an extent that he was obliged to give up almost all work. In the last few years, however (since 1890), he has, in spite of his great age, not only been able to complete his work, but he has also taken a lively and vigorous share in the most recent discussions (evoked by Weissman's hypothesis) within the sphere of biological evolutionary theory.

In judging Spencer's theory our criterion must be : How far does he succeed, by his extension of empiricism and positivism through the concept of evolution, in effecting the reconciliation at which he aims between conflicting views? Even if he cannot be said to have achieved this, however,—even if old problems reappear in new forms after they have passed through the purging fire of the evolutionary philosophy—his extension of the psychological horizon and the proof which he adduces that the concept of evolution is the leading concept in all specialised investigations does not lose its significance. In judging his work we must remember that his original contribution consists in this extension and this proof, and not in the construction of any definite epistemological and psychological theory. We must further remember that it is inevitable that in the composition of a work which extended over a period of more than thirty years inequalities and inconsistencies of treatment should appear, especially since, in the course of writing it, its author had changed his views on several points.

Spencer's works give us a rare opportunity of studying his inner life. The impression which he leaves upon us is that his is not such subjective a nature as—in spite of all their Positivism—were those of Mill and Comte. He did not feel with Mill the need of directly influencing men. The evolutionary theory opened his eyes to the hard struggle which every living being has to pass through, and to the especial difficulties which wait upon the mental and social life of man. It taught him that ideals which even the preceding generation

had expected to be realised in the immediate future presuppose a long series of intermediate stages which have all to
be passed through : these ideals, then, are but the far-distant
goal of the wanderings of the human race. Hence, resignation plays an important part in the conception of life
which arises on the basis of Spencer's teaching. Not that
he meant that the present was altogether to pale before or be
sacrificed to this distant goal. But he would have the present
understood not only in its connection with the past out of
what it has developed, but also as forming the transition to a
higher state of development. Spencer himself, we may be
sure, is among those to whom he alludes in the concluding
words of his great work (*Principles of Ethics*, ii. p. 433):
" The highest ambition of the beneficent will be to have a share
—even though an utterly inappreciable and unknown share—
in 'the making of Man.' Experience occasionally shows us
that there may arise extreme interest in pursuing entirely unselfish ends and, as time goes on, there will be more and more
of those whose unselfish end will be the further evolution
of Humanity. While contemplating from the heights of
thought that far-off life of the race never to be enjoyed by
them, but only by a remote posterity, they will feel a calm
pleasure in the consciousness of having aided the advance
towards it."

One year after Spencer had conceived the idea of an
evolutionary philosophy, Darwin's book on the *Origin of Species*
appeared, giving a new and firm basis to the theory of evolution. In the preface Darwin mentions Spencer among his
predecessors, and later on (in a letter to Ray Lankester, March
15, 1870) he describes him as " the greatest living philosopher
in England." Darwin's whole theory was admirably adapted
to Spencer's system, only that Spencer—though fully recognising
the importance of natural selection—attributed more importance
to direct development through the use of faculties under the
influence of the environment than Darwin did in his earlier
years. It is of no small interest to notice that John Stuart
Mill, who at first demurred at Spencer's evolutionary psychology,
afterwards declared himself convinced that mental development
takes place not only in the individual but also in the race,
by means of inherited dispositions. He expressed this modification of his view a year before his death in a letter to

Carpenter, the physiologist (quoted in the latter's *Mental Physiology*, p. 486).

(*b*) *Religion and Science*

Spencer began his systematic exposition (*System of Synthetic Philosophy*) with a section on the unknowable,[105] in which he expounds his doctrines of the limits of knowledge and of the relation between religion and science.   The object of this preliminary section is to determine the nature of the validity which is to be attributed to the scientific conception of the world which the remaining portions of the system seek to construct. There is a defect here in the order of exposition which Spencer never realised.   Neither the theory of knowledge nor the philosophy of religion can attain to perfect clearness unless they are based on psychology—but psychology is not given a place until much later in the system.

The argument of the first section is as follows :—Religion and science confront one another in modern days as antagonists. The reason of this is that religion tries to solve problems which only science is able to master, and that science seeks to penetrate into the domain proper to religion.   Hitherto every religion has attempted to give a theoretical explanation of existence, for all have offered themselves as a solution of the riddle of the universe.   However different in other respects, all religions are agreed in claiming to be a revelation of a something with which we should otherwise be unacquainted.   The difference between higher and lower religions is that the latter —whether fetichism or polytheism—think it very easy to form an idea of that which works in the world.   Belief in ancestral ghosts may be said to form the basis of primitive theology. Even in aboriginal creeds, however, there is a vague perception that the world, in its innermost essence, is a riddle ; but this perception is very weak and the riddle is regarded as easily solvable.   The higher religions lay more and more stress on the mysterious element until at last they say that every figure, every thought, is insufficient to express the innermost essence of all things ; finally, they go so far as to say that " to think that God is, *as we can think Him to be*, is blasphemy." Religion will have attained to its full development when it admits that the mystery is greater than religions have hitherto believed it to be. Every religion, till now, has believed in a relative mystery, in a mystery which will sooner or later be unriddled. This mystery is absolute, however, if no figure or thought is adequate to it. The contradictions to which religious ideas always lead is due to the belief in an absolute cause. Whether we hold that the world has produced itself, or that it is produced by an external cause we always end with the contradiction that something can be the cause of itself : in the first case the world must be the cause of itself ; in the latter, the being who has produced the world must be self-caused. The special contradictions of the religious ideas —between omnipotence on one side and goodness and justice on the other, between justice and grace, etc.—are, as Mansel has already pointed out, only special consequences of this fundamental contradiction.

Spencer now proceeds to show that the fundamental scientific concepts are not more successful than the religious ideas in their attempt to express the innermost nature of the world. Such concepts as time and space, motion and force, consciousness and personality are clear and applicable so long as we do not go beyond the limited and relative world of experience, but they lead to contradictions as soon as we attempt to employ them to express the nature of an absolute being. Our scientific knowledge moves—both with regard to the outer and the inner world—in the midst of a manifold of continual changes, of which we can discern neither the beginning nor the end, neither the first cause nor the ultimate goal. Moreover, as Hamilton and Mansel have already pointed out, it follows from the nature of our knowledge itself that we can only comprehend the finite and limited. All knowledge presupposes a distinction ; but the Absolute cannot be distinguished from any other, since there can be no other. Spencer adds that all knowledge likewise presupposes the apprehension of similarity, the assimilation of that which is to be known to something resembling it ; but the Absolute can resemble nothing since nothing exists outside itself.

Spencer is not prepared, however, to say with Hamilton and Mansel that the Absolute is a purely negative concept. Knowledge must assume that there is something more and other than it is able to comprehend. Its activity consists in distinguishing, in perceiving similarity, in defining and limiting;

but there must be something which is defined and limited,
something that is formed and which can exist independently
of the particular form which it receives in our consciousness.
We conceive this constant,—although to us it appears indefinite,
—basis of the content of all our knowledge in analogy with that
which, by means of the exertion of the muscles, we feel in
ourselves as *power*. Without power there would be no raw
material for consciousness. This power not only produces the
individual modification which we distinguish and apprehend,
but it is also the basis in us of that which remains constant
throughout all changes. We can form no conception of this
power ; we can only approximate thereto by thinking away,
one after another, the limitations under which, unknowable in
itself, this power occurs in every case in our experience. It is
this primary feeling of power then, which supplies our knowledge with its content, both the constant changes as well as
that which remains " constant under all modes."

Religion and science will ultimately reach the common
conviction that the innermost essence of the world is unknowable and incomprehensible to us, but that we may acquire a
scientific knowledge of the manner in which this nature reveals
itself in the world of experience. Our consciousness of Nature,
regarded from one side, is religion ; regarded from the other,
science. The dissension between religion and science will
cease when the limits of knowledge are determined in the right
manner ; then religion will not seek to bring anything comprehensible under her sway and science will not want to
appropriate anything that is incomprehensible. There can be
no strife between our intellectual and moral faculties ; hence, it
cannot be our duty to believe in anything which involves a
contradiction. It cannot be our duty, as Mansel thinks, to
conceive God as both personal and infinite, when personality
and infinity are mutually exclusive. Our duty can only be to
submit to the limitations of our knowledge, and to acknowledge
the existence of the mysterious actuality which underlies all
things. If the concept of personality cannot serve to express
the Absolute this is not because it is too high, but because it
is too narrow, a concept. We shall never be able to write a
divine psychology; and the quarrel between religion and science
will last as long as the adherents of religion credit themselves with familiar knowledge of that which is an eternal

mystery and accordingly frame concepts which are open to criticism.

Spencer is very well aware that his attempt to mediate between religion and science will itself meet with opposition. Men need more living and concrete ideas ; they are only satisfied when they can believe that there is a community of nature between themselves and the object of their worship ; and only when such a belief finds expression in their creed is that creed in a position to influence their actions. So long as no *organic morality* has developed, which will enable men to act morally from their own inner need of so doing, so long it is of importance that religious opinions should not lose their influence. Every religious faith stands in a definite relation to the stage of development at which men have arrived ; an over-hasty rejection of such a faith, therefore, will only cause the defects of their nature to come out more strongly than they would have done had the creed been retained. We may be sure that any alteration in so deep and vital a conception as that with which we are here dealing cannot take place without pain. He who is impatient at the slowness with which a transition is effected must remember that every religion, even the lowest, contains " a soul of truth " ; that even the lowest religions bestow upon their followers something which could not be obtained in any other way ; and that all forms of faith are members of an evolutionary process which is still far from being completed. Mindful of this, he will be able more easily to reconcile himself to the sophistical reasonings with which traditional opinions are defended, to the unworthy flattery with which men worship their gods, to the arrogance of nescience which far exceeds the arrogance of science, and to the condemnation of actions which spring from unselfish sympathy and pure love of the good.

There is one objection to this doctrine of the relation between religion and science on which Spencer does not touch, *i.e.* that it makes far too external a distinction between absolute and relative.[106] By this relation of contrast the Absolute itself becomes relative. The antithesis between absolute and relative cannot, consistently with Spencer's own view, be such an external one, as may be gathered from his statement that a complete concept of the Absolute can only be attained by the removal of *all* limits and relations. Such a removal, however, is an infinite process, and, as a matter of fact, we cannot contrast the absolute and relative as two *finished* concepts. When, besides this, Spencer says in several places that the Absolute, which he regarded as identical with the unknowable, permeates all phenomena, outer as well as inner (see *First Principles*, §§ 34, 46, and 93) it is evident that this Being must reveal itself in the forms and laws under which phenomena occur ; it cannot really be entirely unknowable ; and Spencer is wrong in pronouncing the leading concept of experience, *i.e.* the concept of evolution, to have no validity when applied to " the Absolute." It would be a contradiction if the laws and forms revealed in all experience were entirely meaningless in relation to that which lies behind or on the other side of experience. It can never be proved that evolution holds good of the husk but not of the kernel of the world. There is a dualism here which Spencer overlooked.

(c) *Philosophy as Unified Knowledge*

The problem of the relation between religion and science not only recurs every time a special science incorporates a new phenomenon, but also whenever an attempt is made to unite the different truths discovered by special sciences with universal truths. According to Spencer, it is the task of philosophy, as it is that of each of the special sciences within its own sphere, to trace out the unity which underlies the manifold of phenomena by discovering the laws which hold good in all the different spheres of experience. Philosophy consists in the discovery of some ultimate truths from which the axioms of mechanics, physical and psychological principles and social laws can be deduced. Hence philosophy may be defined as completely unified knowledge.

Philosophy begins with the provisional acceptance of the validity of those fundamental assumptions on which all thought is based. This provisional acceptance is afterwards justified by showing that the consequences to which it leads are confirmed by experience. The validity of an assumption can only be exhibited by its agreement with all other assumptions. Truth can only consist for us in the perfect agreement of our representations of things with our presentations of things. If our expectations do not agree with our presentations, the assumption

from which we started must be invalid. The complete exhibi-
tion of the validity of an assumption by its proved congruity
with all other assumptions leads us finally to that unification of
all knowledge in which philosophy consists, but the proof of
the validity of any one assumption presupposes the validity of
the activity of thought by means of which we discover that
things differ from or resemble one another. This activity
of thought underlies all knowledge perception as well as
inference, whatever be the subject-matter. Every proof presupposes this *primordial act;* hence the validity of the latter can
never be refuted, for refutation is itself a proof.

We always think in relations. Next in importance to
the relations of similarity and difference come those of
sequence and co-existence. The relation of co-existence
is deduced from that of sequence ; relations of which the
terms can occur in any order are recognised as co-
existences. The fundamental experience which underlies
all conceptions, whether of similarity or of difference, of
succession or of co-existence, as we have already seen, is the
experience of *force ;* of a something which offers resistance or
produces change, and which we conceive in analogy with our
own feeling of exertion. Matter and motion are nothing but
manifestations of force, and time and space are the forms of
the manifestations of force. In the sphere of inner as well as
of outer experience the concept of force is the ultimate concept
to which we are always brought back. We rightly distinguish
between the ego and the non-ego ; these, however, are only different ways in which the concept of force reveals itself. The matter
and the content of our thought are different kinds of force.

The concept of force, then, is a symbolic concept. It is
the ultimate symbol. It points back to our subjective experience. It refers us to our subjective experience in analogy with
which we conceive all else. Spencer's argument here reminds
us of the metaphysical idealism which employs this analogy to
solve the problem of existence. He confesses that were we
free to choose whether we would reduce the spiritual elements
to the material, or the material to the spiritual, we should choose
the latter alternative. It is absurd to reduce the known to the
unknown ; hence a comprehensible hypothesis can only be
reached by reducing the unknown to the known, that is to say,
by considering the objective material elements as in their essence

of like nature with the subjective elements of our consciousness. Such a reduction, however, Spencer believes to be impossible, since we are compelled to explain the spiritual elements to ourselves by the help of forms and relations borrowed from external nature. We only get a clear conception of the nature of consciousness when we use symbols taken from the material world. Hence we cannot get beyond the distinction between psychical and material phenomena, and must be content with showing that both kinds of expressions of force are subjected to the same empirical laws.

A fundamental premiss of all science, according to Spencer, is that there can be neither diminution nor increase of the force existing in the world. All thought consists in relating something to something else. If then, force perished, or if it arose out of nothing—which would be shown in outer experience by matter arising or disappearing, or by motion ceasing or beginning—we should have a relation of a something to a nothing, or of a nothing to a something. But a relation of which one member disappeared from consciousness, or had not arisen in it, would be a contradiction. The force which we are thus obliged to regard as constant is not a relative phenomenal form of force, but the absolute force which underlies all things, so that we come back here once more to that ultimate truth common to religion and science, *i.e.* that underlying all empirical phenomena is the Absolute. It is the task of empirical science to point out the special forms of the transformation of force. The principle of the conservation of energy, however, cannot itself be experimentally proved since, on further reflection, it is evident that every experiment presupposes its validity. All weighing and measuring takes for granted that the unit employed remains unchanged during the process of weighing and measuring. If the force with which a weight tends to the earth varies while the chemist is attempting to determine the weight of the atoms composing it, his conclusion is invalid. Hence the conservation of force is a principle or postulate on which all investigation of the real world is based.

Thus Spencer, with Spinoza, Kant and William Hamilton, regards the principle of the conservation of energy as co-extensive with the principle of causality. We shall find that several of the scientific men who established the principle of the conservation of energy on an experimental basis assumed that it is in reality an axiom of reason, and that what they had to do was to show how it reveals itself in experience. Such for example are Robert Mayer, Joule and Colding. But a distinction ought certainly to be made here. For even if force arose and perished, it would still be possible for law to prevail in Nature, as long as this arising and perishing were bound up with definite conditions. It is conceivable that whenever the condition A were present, B should always occur, although, quantitatively, $B = A + x$; and that where the condition C occurred D always occurred, although $D = C \div y$. In such a case the principle of causation would be valid, although the principle of the conservation of energy would no longer be so. This proves that the latter is a less general principle than that of causation, when this, *i.e.* the principle of causation, is taken to express nothing more than the law of the occurrence of phenomena. The regularity of Nature would not entirely disappear even if the law of the conservation of force were invalid. But this does not hold good if we are prepared to go so far as to say that, just as a logical conclusion contains nothing that was not already in the premises, so in a case of real causation there is nothing in the effect which was not already included in the cause. This interpretation of the principle of causation brings it into very close relation with the principle of ground. And even if we disallow this perfect analogy with logical ground, the causal relation might still hold good. Hence Spencer's deduction is insufficient; although he is right in maintaining that every attempt to prove the conservation of force by way of experiment in a certain sense presupposes it.

From the principle of the conservation of energy Spencer infers that motion follows the direction of greatest attraction or least resistance—that all motion is rhythmical—and that all phenomena undergo a process of development and dissolution. In this way he is led from the consideration of philosophy as unified knowledge to the consideration of philosophy as the doctrine of evolution. Before we follow him into this branch of inquiry, however, we must first ask what inferences he draws from the law of the conservation of force with regard to the relation between psychical and material phenomena. It was not Spencer's intention to devote a special discussion to this question, and we find in his works, as they stand at present, a certain vacillation on this point ; this is probably due to the fact that during the time which elapsed between the different editions of his work he changed his views on the subject, and did not take care that this change of view was indicated wherever necessary in the later editions.   Hence contradictory passages might be gathered from his works.[107]   At first (in the first edition of the *Principles of Psychology* and of the *First Principles*) he conceives the relation between the psychical and the material similarly to that between the different natural forces, and he believes a transformation takes place from the material to the psychical similar to that from motion to heat.   Hence the origin of sensations is explained by the law of the conservation of energy.   Spencer would have any critic who regarded this view as materialistic,—and some of them did so,—to remember that in his eyes matter and motion are nothing more than symbolic expressions of the unknowable force which underlies all things.   Later, however, he became aware that the origin of conscious phenomena cannot be deduced from the principle of the conservation of physical energy.   He saw, for instance, that the hypothesis that sensation originates in movement, and represents an equivalent to it, is inconsistent with the doctrine of the continuity of motion.   Accordingly, in subsequent editions, he conceives the relation between the psychical and the material in accordance with the identity hypothesis, *i.e.* that they are two phenomenal and mutually irreducible forms of the unknowable force.   With regard to the doctrine of evolution (which is always the first consideration with Spencer), it does not matter which hypothesis we accept.   For whether we assume a relation of reciprocal action or of identity between the psychical and the material, development in both spheres may exhibit the working of the same fundamental laws.   This is the important point for evolutionary philosophy.   It is true that, according to the identity hypothesis, psychical development cannot be explained by deduction from the conservation of physical force, but the obverse holds good, *i.e.* the material process corresponding to psychical life does admit of such an explanation.[108]   In working out his theory of evolution, Spencer explains all development by the laws of matter and motion, and yet he illustrates the forms of development by examples from psychology and sociology, as well as from astronomy and physiology. His procedure is justified, however, by the fact that, no matter which hypothesis we adopt, we must admit that there is an interconnection, determined by law, between mental and material phenomena.

(d) *Philosophy as a Theory of Evolution*

The proof that all inquiry is based on one and the same assumption, is not sufficient, in Spencer's opinion, to effect the unification of knowledge at which philosophy aims ; it must be accompanied by the further proof of the existence of a law to which all the phenomena presented in experience are subject. Spencer systematises positivism, partly by reducing all positive knowledge (knowledge of facts) to one common presupposition, and partly by establishing one common law or one common form of everything positive, *i.e.* of all phenomena. Every phenomenon has a history; it appears and disappears. Each science describes the history of *its own* phenomena ; hence what we now have to do is to inquire whether these different historical processes exhibit common features ; for if they do, we shall be able to formulate a *general law of evolution.* All development, it seems, exhibits with more or less clearness three different characteristics, which, taken together, constitute the complete concept of evolution. As we have already noticed, Spencer originally assigned one distinguishing mark only to development, viz. the transition from homogeneity to heterogeneity. Afterwards he was led to see firstly, that in some exceedingly simple forms of development, this characteristic is altogether subordinate, and secondly, that in order to be able to draw a sharp distinction between processes of evolution and of dissolution, we need yet a third distinguishing mark.

(1) *Evolution as concentration* (or integration).—At the birth of a phenomenon there takes place a collecting, combining and concentrating of elements which were previously scattered. If a cloud forms in the sky, or a sand heap on the shore, a development of the simplest kind has taken place, in which the process consists almost exclusively of a dissipation and an aggregation. Such a process of concentration took place, if we accept the hypothesis of Kant and Laplace, when our solar system passed out of its primary nebular state, in

which its component parts were widely diffused and incoherent. All organic growth takes place by means of the absorption into the organic tissue of elements which were previously scattered about in surrounding plants and animals. We get a psychological example of the same process in generalisation, and the framing of general concepts and laws ; by their means we concentrate in one thought a number of different presentations and representations. Social evolution consists essentially in the progressive integration of individuals or groups of individuals who were formerly bound together by no close ties.

(2) *Development as differentiation.* — Only in the very simplest cases can development be described merely as a process of concentration. Not only is there a segregation of the whole mass from the environment, but also, within the mass thus separated off, special concentrations take place, so that the development becomes compound. And, in the course of development, these special concentrations become more and more prominent, so that when we compare the earlier with the later stages we find a transition from homogeneity to heterogeneity. In the course of development of the solar system a segregation of different heavenly bodies takes place, each one of which has its own idiosyncracy. Organic development proceeds from the homogeneous germ to the organism provided with different kinds of tissue, and with differently constructed and differently functioning organs. The whole of organic life was, according to Lamarck's and Darwin's hypothesis, homogeneous at earlier stages, for the existing differences of species are due to development from common parent forms. The senses develop, as we may see if we compare earlier with later stages, from less clear and less exact perceptive faculties to increasing clearness and exactitude, so that more and more differences can be apprehended. Mental life in general is estimated not only according to its concentration, but also according to its richness. In the course of social evolution the different estates and classes are formed through division of labour.

(3) *Evolution as determination.*—But the process of dissolution is also characterised by differences appearing in what has hitherto been a homogeneous mass. In order to distinguish between development and dissolution, therefore, we must add the further characteristic that in evolution there is

an advance from confusion to order — from undetermined arrangement to determined arrangement. Development is a passage from a chaos, of which the parts are scattered and homogeneous, to a united whole, the parts of which are heterogeneous, and at the same time stand in definite reciprocal connection with one another. Thus the solar system, the organism, consciousness and human society are more or less ordered wholes. This third point of view really consists of a union of the two former; an ordered whole is one in which differentiation of the parts and integration of the whole go hand in hand. Everywhere in the world—in great things as well as in small, in the mental as in the material world— evolutionary processes as above described are going on. On the basis of a comparative examination of these processes, evolutionary philosophy formulates the fundamental features of the general history of every phenomenon. But what has thus been inductively discovered must now be deductively confirmed ; it can be exhibited as an inference from the law of the conservation of force.

In the first place, a concentration of homogeneous parts will take place whenever these parts are subjected to the same force working in the same way. This happens when, under the influence of the wind, heaps of dry leaves or sandhills or clouds are formed. Natural selection works in this way, for it demands perfectly definite variations on the part of those living beings which are able to exist under definite conditions ; by this means they are separated off as new species from those which are not able to maintain their existence. Secondly, after a homogeneous whole has been formed, differences arise directly the homogeneous parts are subjected to the influence of heterogeneous forces. And when a differentiation between the parts has been produced by this means, homogeneous forces affect them differently. An organic species will vary under differing physical conditions, and even when different varieties are subjected to the same influences the latter will not have the same effect on each one of them. This follows from the conservation of energy, which would be annulled if like causes could produce different effects on homogeneous objects, or if heterogeneous causes could produce similar effects on similar objects, or like causes similar effects on heterogeneous objects.

In order to get a right understanding of Spencer we must

remember that his theory of evolution did not claim to hold good of the world as a whole, for of this, owing to the relativity of knowledge we are not able to form an idea. It claims to be valid only of particular wholes which exist within the circle of our experiences. It has sometimes been objected that his " evolution " is incomprehensible, for if it is to start from absolute homogeneity, from whence—it is asked—are the differences to come? Spencer himself expressly declares (*First Principles*, §§ 116, 149, 155) that he is speaking of finite phenomena only, and that he assumes only a relative homogeneity and heterogeneity. Moreover, the concepts concentration and differentiation, simplicity and complexity are to be taken in a relative sense. If we could conceive the whole universe in a condition of perfect equilibrium, in which perfectly similar centres of force were distributed with absolute equality through the whole of space, everything would remain in equilibrium through all eternity. Such a thought, however, is excluded at the outset by the fact that we can assign no limit to space. It is true of all the homogeneous masses *known to us* that they necessarily become more or less differentiated.

Evolution must (on the supposition, of course, that it will not be interrupted from without) necessarily lead to a state of equilibrium, in which concentration as well as differentiation will have reached its zenith. In the development of man, this state is identical with the highest perfection and blessedness, and consists in the greatest possible harmony between man and Nature, and between man and man. But since external influences are unceasingly operating, this state of equilibrium must in course of time come to an end. Evolution is succeeded by dissolution when there is no longer sufficient energy to maintain, in the face of persistent disturbances, a harmony between concentration and differentiation. Passing through the different stages of dissolution we finally arrive at a new chaos. Just as, within the circle of our experience, processes of evolution are unceasingly going forward, so there are unceasing processes of dissolution of larger and smaller wholes. Even if our solar system—and all other solar systems—carry within themselves, as some authorities believe, the seeds of dissolution, the possibility of the formation of new systems is not excluded, for there will always be external forces to start

the process of evolution again.   All motion is rhythmical ;
hence development and dissolution will alternate with one
another *ad infinitum.*

While Hegel's idealistic theory of development (see above,
pp. 180-183) guarantees eternal progress, since his " higher
unities" (which correspond to Spencer's harmony between
concentration and differentiation) always become the point of
departure for new developments, Spencer, as a consistent
positivist and in accordance with the doctrine of the relativity
of knowledge, cannot venture to decide whether development
or dissolution is the stronger world-process.   On account of
his dualistic conception of the relation between absolute and
relative he does not attribute absolute significance to evolution
(not even to the entire rhythm of evolution and dissolution).
As already pointed out his view involves a contradiction at this
point, for he admits that there is a connection between phenomena and the unknowable order of things which underlies
them ("the phenomenal order and the ontological order ").
But he is sure of this—that we can no more assign a limit to
the forces operative within the world of phenomena than we
can assign limits to time and space.   He solved his own
particular problem by determining the characteristics of the
history which every phenomenon passes through.

(e) *The Concept of Evolution within the Sphere of Biology and Psychology*

Spencer is most at home within the spheres of biology and
sociology.   It was, as we saw, a biological idea which gave rise
to his whole system, and this idea (development as differentiation) is immediately conjoined with a sociological idea (*i.e.* the
division of labour).   He regarded social as well as conscious
and ethical life as forms of life obeying general vital laws.
Accordingly biology is the predominant concrete science in his
system.   He aims at investigating the development of life at
all stages and under all forms.

Life consists of a continual adaptation of inner relations to
outer.   In a living body an external impression produces not
only a direct but also an indirect effect, for it induces a state
which enables the living being to meet subsequent changes in
the external world.   An inner activity is set going which is or

can be of use on a subsequent occasion. Organic tissue possesses two apparently contradictory qualities, which, when combined, make adaptation possible. These qualities are (1) plasticity, by which external influences reverberate through the whole organic mass or a greater portion of it ; and (2) polarity, by which the ultimate organic particles are aggregated into a particular form. These particles are called by Spencer "physiological units." He regards them as far simpler than cells, but more complex than chemical molecules. A further effect of polarity is that the influence of impressions on the organic mass is mainly determined by the latter's own nature. The origin of the formation of the organic mass is a mystery. Spencer rejects the view of the origin of organic *forms* in inorganic matter. He inclines to the opposite view that at a certain point of time in the process of the cooling of the earth's surface, an organic mass, *entirely devoid of structure*, was formed. Since this original organic mass was without definite structure, this assumption is not identical with that of a first organism. There was organic life without organisation (see especially the Appendix to vol. i. of the *Principles of Biology*). Organic forms have successively arisen under the influence of outer or inner relations. Following the general law of development we must suppose that some constant external influence produces first of all differences in the mass, then a difference between the outer surface and the interior, and that finally, owing to the different ways in which the different parts react on those influences, they themselves gradually acquire a different nature. Spencer even lays down the principle that function precedes structure, and that continuous functioning in a definite manner produces the definite structure which particular organs possess. This direct influence of the environment on the organic tissue is really presupposed in the doctrine of natural selection ; for selection takes place between the growing structures evolved by means of this direct influence, and between the different variations which the organic mass passes through when subject to outer influences. Even where the variations arose out of other, unknown causes, natural selection is only able to sustain them when these spontaneous variations (*Princ. of Biol.* § 61) are such as to facilitate vital activities. The change of structure effected by means of a certain permanent method of functioning may be transmitted if it has produced a change of organic polarity, *i.e.* a change in the manner peculiar to this particular organism in which its physiological units are disposed.

Darwin's doctrine of natural selection (which Spencer would prefer to call the "survival of the fittest") is fully acknowledged by Spencer, and with the greatest admiration. But he, no more than Darwin himself, believes natural selection able to explain everything. In the absence of a belief in the transmittedness of acquired qualities the origin of species seems to him incomprehensible. Hence within the last few years, he has headed an able and energetic protest against "those scientists who are more Darwinian than Darwin himself." He has especially attacked Weissman's hypothesis, which denies that inherited functions can exercise any influence on the cells which contain the germ of posterity, and is accordingly bound to deduce all development from natural selection. With regard to higher organic beings, in particular, who possess a developed nervous and muscular system, Spencer is of opinion that the influence exerted on the organism by the exercise of power is of the greatest significance. He considers this question to be of importance not only for biology, but also for ethics and sociology. " If a nation is modified *en masse*," he writes in his Preface to his *Factors of Organic Evolution* (1886), "by transmission of the effects produced on the natures of its members by those modes of daily activity which its institutions and circumstances involve ; then we must infer that such institutions and circumstances mould its members far more rapidly and comprehensively than they can do if the sole cause of adaptation to them is the more frequent survival of individuals who happen to have varied in favourable ways."

Ethical and social responsibility, then, becomes greater if we believe in the transmittence of acquired characteristics than if everything depends on natural selection. It is this consideration which invests the problem with such interest in Spencer's eyes, and he closes his series of polemical writings with a pressing exhortation to biologists to shed more light on the subject (*Weismannism Once More*, 1894, p. 23). " I have felt more and more that since all the higher sciences are dependent on the science of life and must have their conclusions vitiated if a fundamental datum given to them by the teachers of this science is erroneous it behoves these teachers not to let an erroneous datum pass current ; they are called on to settle this vexed question one way or other." Consciousness, too, is an activity which arises in the course of the living being's adaptation to its environment. When stimuli increase in number, adaptation to them can only be exact if they are arranged in a series, as they are in consciousness. Psychology is so far a part of biology. Spencer distinguishes here between objective and subjective psychology. Properly speaking, only objective psychology, which studies conscious life in the material functions with which it is bound up, has a place in the ranks of the concrete sciences. Subjective psychology, which is based on immediate self-observation, and arrives at its results by analysing this, stands in the same relation to all other sciences as does the subject everywhere to the object ; it is the science of subjective existence as all other sciences together are the science of objective existence. Hence subjective psychology is a science *sui generis* (*Princ. of Psychology*, § 56 ; *Classification of the Sciences*, 3rd ed. p. 26).

Like Stuart Mill, Spencer asserts the independence of psychology which Comte had overlooked. But at the same time he dissociates himself from the older English school, asserting that we cannot regard consciousness as a mere series of impressions and ideas, since there is always something which unites the members of the series together and preserves the unity of the circle of ideas, in spite of all attempts to interrupt it. There must be some underlying substance in contrast to all the changing forms ; but this substance we can never know, since it never appears altogether in any one state, although every state is a particular form of it.

In spite of all the peculiarities which characterise conscious life as it appears in subjective experience, yet it presents the same fundamental traits as life and evolution everywhere else. Its development consists in progressive concentration, differentiation and determination. All transitions take place by degrees, hence qualitative differences have been ascribed—wrongly— to psychical faculties. From reflex movement, through instinct and memory up to reason, from the simplest distinctions and recognition to the highest scientific thought, there is a continuous sequence of stages. The qualitative and quantitative richness of consciousness corresponds to the richness of the relation between the living being and its environment. There is always a correspondence between the life of consciousness and the external circumstances with which the individual has to deal. There is a continuous sequence of stages from the entozoon in an organic tissue up to a Newton or a Shakespeare, whose thought embraces the world.

With regard to the question of the origin of knowledge Spencer makes front on the one hand against Leibniz and Kant, on the other against Locke and Mill. He quarrels with empiricism for two reasons :—firstly, because it does not see that the matter of experience is always taken up and elaborated in a definite manner, which is determined by the original nature of the individual ; secondly, because it is lacking in a criterion of truth. We must assume an original organisation if we are to understand the influence exercised by stimuli on different individuals, and the criterion by means of which alone a proposition can be established is the fact that its opposite would contain a contradiction. In the inborn nature of the individual then, and in the logical principle on which we depend every time we make an inference, we have an *a priori* element ; something which cannot be deduced from experience. To this extent Spencer upholds Leibniz and Kant against Locke and Mill ; but he does so only as long as he is restricting his considerations to the experience of the individual. What is *a priori* for the individual is not so for the race. For those conditions and forms of knowledge and of feeling which are original in the individual, and hence cannot be derived from his experience, have been transmitted by earlier generations. The forms of thought correspond to the collective and inherited modifications of structure which are latent in every new-born individual, and are gradually developed through his experiences. Their first origin, then, is empirical : the fixed and universal relation of things to one another must, in the course of development, form fixed and universal conjunctions in the organism ; by perpetual repetition of absolutely external uniformities there arise in the race necessary forms of knowledge, indissoluble thought associations which express the net results of the experience of perhaps several millions of generations down to the present. The individual cannot sunder a conjunction thus deeply rooted in the organisation of the race ; hence, he is born into the world with those psychical connections which form the substrata of " necessary truths" (see *Principles of Psychology*, §§ 208, 216 ; cf. *First Principles*, § 53. "Absolute uniformities of experience generate absolute uniformities of thought "). Although Spencer is of opinion that the inductive school went too far when they attempted to arrive at everything by way of induction (for, if we adopt this method, induction itself is left hanging in the air), yet, if he had to choose between Locke and Kant, he would avow himself a disciple of the former ; for, *in the long run*, Spencer too thinks that all knowledge and all forms of thought spring from experience. His admission that there is something in our mind which is not the product of our own *a posteriori* experience led Max Müller to call him a " thoroughgoing Kantian," to which Spencer replied : " The Evolution-view is completely experiential. It differs from the original view of the experimentalists by containing a great extension of that view.—But the view of Kant is avowedly and utterly un-experiential."

Spencer, however, is open to his own objection to empiricism when he assumes that the race at any stage of its development could be subject to external influences in the absence of any existing organisation to receive these influences and determine their results. His *Psychology* presents some obscurity on this point, as was already perceptible in his *Biology*. For his axiom that " function determines structure " seems only to admit of the interpretation that organic tissue in the lowest stages must be absolutely passive in relation to all influences which evoke its activity. Such a state of absolute passivity, however, is excluded by his own definition of life as adaptation. It does not exist, even in the case of inorganic beings exposed to external influences ; the stone, *e.g.* exhibits the effects of heat differently from wax. Moreover, Spencer has forgotten that the *validity* of our knowledge is not absolutely guaranteed by the fact that its fundamental assumptions are the result of the experience of countless generations. This can, at most, show us that these assumptions have hitherto proved of practical use in the struggle for existence. It does not afford a proof of their absolute truth.[109]

According to Spencer, the feelings of the individual—even more than his knowledge—presuppose a basis acquired by the race. Continual action and reaction on the outer world, continual struggle with conditions of life produce a disposition to feelings for which it is not always possible to find clear representative expressions. This is the case with the sympathetic feelings—*e.g.* the pleasure of a little child in a smiling face and its distress at a sad or threatening one. The feeling of justice, immediate indignation at encroachments, may arise in the absence of any clear concept of the limits of the individual freedom of action. Spencer reproaches the older utilitarians with having made conscious insight into their beneficial effects precede the origin of the actions and motives judged. In order to learn whether sympathy is useful we must first show sympathy spontaneously. Feeling then enables us to discover utility, but the discovery of utility did not originally produce the feeling. Spencer hopes for continual modifications and progress in human feelings from the education to which man is subjected in his relations with the environment, rather than from that which consists in the mere imparting of already established knowledge. He opposes the principle from which Comte (especially in his earlier works) starts, viz. that ideas rule the world. Feeling and character are the motive powers, and which ideas shall be predominant will depend on the character of the nation, this character in its turn being determined by the substratum inherited from earlier generations.

(*f*) *The Concept of Development in Sociology and Ethics*

The relation between the individual and the race which Spencer brings forward in his *Biology* and *Psychology* becomes of paramount importance in his *Sociology*. If every individual has an original substratum in his character which is traceable to the earlier history of the race, the development of social life cannot suddenly be turned in a new direction by means of educational and constitutional reforms.

Spencer entertains no such immediate hopes for the future as did Bentham, Mill and Comte. Development proceeds slowly precisely because the underlying nature of the individuals, and not merely their thoughts and knowledge, has to be changed. In a conversation during his stay in America, Spencer strongly censured the evils existing in the public life of the United States. He attributed them to the fact that the Constitution, good enough in itself, had been *acquired ready-*

made by a stroke of luck ; it did not grow up spontaneously ; hence, we need not be astonished that the results which flow from it are not such as were anticipated. On an American friend asking if the remedy did not lie in education and the extension of political knowledge ; Spencer's reply was : " No, it is a question essentially depending on character, and only in a subordinate sense on knowledge. It is a frequent delusion that education is a universal remedy for political evils."

Modifications of character, according to Spencer, are only brought about by action and reaction between the race and its environment throughout many generations. Only by practical adaptation, by development and exercise of the powers service-able in the struggle for existence can steadfast characters and healthy feeling be formed. Hence, in his book on *Education*, Spencer emphasises the necessity of letting a child make his own experiences ; he should be allowed to become acquainted with actual circumstances, and must learn to realise the effects of his own actions. Screens should be used as little as possible since they cause double work ; first of all, adaptation to the screen and afterwards to that which is behind the screen—*i.e.* real life. If the child does not burn himself he will not have a salutary dread of fire. And what is true of the character of the individual is also true of the character of the whole race. In his great and boldly-sketched work, *Principles of Sociology*, Spencer attempts to elucidate this point by means of copious illustrations from the most primitive races. With the help of various co-operators and under the title of *Descriptive Sociology*, he has published, arranged in a tabulated series and with references to sources, accounts of the history of civilisation of different races. In his *Study of Sociology*, a most suggestive work, he has discussed the difficulties which a strictly scientific sociology has to encounter.

It is a favourite axiom of Spencer that societies and constitutions grow and are not made. He develops the analogy between a society and an organism. The single individuals correspond to the cells, or rather to the physiological units. In society as well as in the organism the common life is to a certain extent independent of the fate of each unit. There is, however, one great and significant distinction between the society and the organism ; while in the latter consciousness (where it exists) is united with the central organ, in comparison with which the other organs and units are only of subordinate significance ; in a society, on the contrary, the units possess consciousness, while the central organisation as such has no special consciousness. In the organism the parts exist for the sake of the whole, while in society the whole exists for the sake of the parts. Spencer thinks that this difference between a society and an organism is no less important than the similarities they present (cf. *Princ. of Sociology*, § 322, taken in connection with *Princ. of Ethics*, ii. §§ 102, 137). A very important principle, which is verified by the history of societies, can be deduced from this difference, *i.e.* that in a society the central organisation can never be more than a necessary means, while in the individual, in whom alone human life is manifested, it is the supreme arbiter. In social life as in individual education there must be as few artificial shelters and as little guardianship as possible, since they always complicate and retard development, entailing as they do a double adaptation, first to the artificial and then to the natural environment. Experience shows that wherever deeply-rooted natural claims are enforced by external authorities, obedience to authorities increases at the cost of the power of practical adaptation to the realities of Nature. We may also learn from the same source that artificially instituted authorities are never so vigorous and effective as free individual forces. The social machinery consumes too much force in attaining its end—and is only too apt to arrive at ends other than those aimed at ! Private individuals feel much more keenly than state officials can do the direct connection between labour and its reward. Although in theory Spencer adheres to the doctrine (which he had previously expounded in his *Social Statics*) that the earth's surface is the property of the whole nation, yet his dislike to officialism leads him to oppose the Nationalists' proposal that the State ought to undertake the cultivation of the soil. Altogether apart from the financial difficulties which such an undertaking would involve,—difficulties which, according to Spencer, are sufficient in themselves to render the carrying out of the proposal impossible,—the notorious inferiority of public to private administration furnishes, in his opinion, a sufficient ground for rejecting the scheme. (See *Princ. of Ethics*, Part iv. Appendix B.)

Experience shows us human societies at widely different

stages of development ; the degree of development is here, as everywhere, determined by concentration, differentiation and determination. There is *one* opposition, however, which is of the first importance in sociology—and also in ethics, *i.e.* that between *militancy* and *industrialism*. Here we have two types of society, of which the first prevails chiefly at the lower stages and gradually, though slowly and with much hesitation, gives place to the second. A militant society springs out of the necessity of uniting all forces, in order to defend the social group against external enemies ; often, too, from the impulse to gain subsistence and power at the cost of other groups. Characteristic of this type is the absolute subjection of individuals to the community. They are means not ends. Obedience is the highest duty. Peaceful work, the procuring of the means of subsistence, is left to women and slaves. In an industrial society, on the contrary, such work occupies the first rank. The main thing here is free personal intercourse between individuals, and their co-operation in the promotion of common interests. While the militant type of society favours an intermixture of wildness and subjection, the industrial type allows individuals to confront one another freely, and to learn in daily intercourse how they may attain their ends while recognising the right of others to do the same. The education thus received gradually modifies characters, customs and constitution. While under the militant system the regulating apparatus was all-important, its office has been gradually limited to the duty of administering peace and justice among the members of the society. For the fulfilling of those functions which were previously discharged by the State, as by a kind of Providence, voluntary associations are formed, when the spontaneous co-operation of individuals is insufficient. While formerly it was the society which stamped the individual, it is now far oftener individuals which order society according to their own requirements. The struggle between militancy and industrialism is not yet at an end. After many years of peace, militancy received a fresh impetus on the continent, when " that greatest of all modern curses, the Bonaparte family " intervened for a second time in the course of affairs ; and now it flourishes more or less in all countries, and introduces its spirit and type into other spheres beside its own. Coercive regulations now, in many departments of life, take the place of free self-

development.   In the ideal of social democracy, *i.e.* an army
of labourers, each one with his prescribed trade and his
prescribed wage, this same type expresses itself; hence we
need not be astonished to see socialism and militarism
flourishing in the same country, viz. Germany (*Princ. of Ethics*,
ii. § 26, 72).   At present the prospect of improvement is not
encouraging.   "As long as the nations of Europe continue to
divide those parts of the earth which are inhabited by less
civilised races with cynical indifference towards the rights of
these people, it is foolish to expect that in each one of these
nations any very tender regard on the part of government will
be shown towards the rights of individuals (*ib.* § 119).   Spencer,
however, admits the possibility of a third type, which is as superior
to industrialism as industrialism is to militancy.   The industrial
type is prone to fall into the mistake of supposing that all
labour must be for the means of subsistence.   The third and
highest type of human life will be one in which free surrender
to activities which afford satisfaction in their exercise, and not
merely as means to existence, will occupy a far larger place
than is at present the case.   Under the existing social order
we have in the special efforts and institutions for the promotion of intellectual and æsthetic aims indications of the third
type.[110]

The nearer determination of this highest type of human
life is the task of ethics, not of sociology.   For, in
Spencer's opinion, this future type is the goal towards
which all ethical striving is directed.   Until this goal is
reached no stringent ethic is possible ; the realisation of
absolute ethics presupposes a perfect human life in a perfect
society.   In the imperfect stages, relations are so complicated
that only approximations to absolute right and compromises
between absolute right and that which is necessary to the
preservation of life under actually existing circumstances are
possible.   Relative ethics, however, must always be controlled
and regulated by constant comparison with the principles of
absolute ethics.   It is the duty of ethical science to present
a picture of the conditions which will determine the perfect
life, even though, at present, it has to adapt itself to less perfect
conditions.   If we compare different stages of ethical development we shall find that they all exhibit the general characteristics
of development.   Ethical action exhibits greater concentration,

greater coherence, than unethical action ; compare, *e.g.* self-control with heedlessness, love of truth with falsehood ! At the same time it offers a greater wealth of differences, greater differentiation ; for he who pursues his own interests only obtains a narrower outlook and sphere of influence than he who also takes thought for others. The faculties and potentialities of a man cannot all be developed so long as he works exclusively for selfish ends, and the highest grade of development can only be attained where the activity of the individual furthers the welfare of others. Finally, more perfect ethical conduct bears the stamp of greater definiteness than less perfect conduct ; it makes definite allowances and definitely limits the impulses of the individual himself and those of other men, which in and for themselves might extend indefinitely ; conscientiousness, justice, and moderation are examples of this greater definiteness.

In the perfect type of life the development of the individual will only be limited by the equal right of other men to develop ; but, in this state, the individual, moved by his own inner impulses, will spontaneously avoid all encroachments on the normal development of others ; indeed, he will exert all his efforts to promote this development, until at last the work undertaken for the furtherance of distant ends will in itself no longer be distasteful.

The construction of the conditions of the perfect type of life must be based on the principle of benevolence. It is true that Spencer criticises the utilitarianism of Bentham and Mill, but only because it was too empirical, and hence prone to dwell on the immediate effects of actions without noticing those which are more remote, and which can only be known by way of deduction. Here, as in his theory of knowledge, Spencer attempts to show that the empirical and *a priori* theories are reconciled in evolutionary philosophy. He considers the importance of the *a priori* (" intuitive ") ethic to lie partly in its assertion of the importance of deduction and its establishment of ideal principles, which are not immediately based on experience ; partly in the fact that it provides a deeper psychological foundation than that which the individual's own experience is able to supply. In constructing his theory of right he comes to the same conclusion as Kant ;—the fundamental right is the freedom of the individual, in so far as this involves no encroachment on the

right of others to equal freedom ; this is indeed, as we have
already seen, the first characteristic of the perfect type of life.
This agreement between Kant and Spencer, at which Spencer
himself expresses astonishment (see Appendix A, *Princ. of
Ethics*, Part IV.) need not surprise us, for we have seen that
Kant's ethic and doctrine of right are based on a theory of
evolution (see above, pp. 76-79). The great significance of
a priori or intuitive ethic is that it does not limit itself to the
immediate effects of actions ; it is mistaken, however, if it
believes that *in the long run* ethical principles are determined
by anything but the consideration whether actions produce
happiness or unhappiness. And although ethical feeling has
an *a priori* foundation which is independent of individual
experiences of happiness, yet even this foundation must be
explained as the result of the doing and suffering of earlier
generations. In his more detailed exposition of the ethical
feeling Spencer differs from Kant in his assumption that the
sentiment of duty only belongs to a certain stage of development. The sentiment of duty consists in the inner control of
one feeling by another, but at a more advanced stage of development such a control will not be necessary ; by that time an
" organic morality " will have formed itself, which will make the
performance of actions demanded by the ethical principles as
spontaneous and as immediately satisfying as are the mother's
care for her child and the artist's devotion to his work at
present. Man will then be perfectly adapted to the social
environment, and the social environment to man.

Until this perfect stage of development is reached, we must
make shift with compromises. An exact science of ethics is
only possible at the highest stage of life. Spencer's argument
really comes to this : there can be no ethic until it is superfluous. Paradoxical as this may seem, it shows a right appreciation of the difficulties which, under the complicated circumstances in which we have to live, every attempt to construct a
scientific ethic must encounter. Perhaps we ought to go even
farther than Spencer, with his great confidence in the victorious
march of evolution, thought necessary ; he certainly pays too
little regard to individual differences and to their influence on
ethical determinations.[111]—We will now give some examples in
illustration of what Spencer means by the difference between
" absolute " and " relative " ethics.

Our study of sociology showed us that the present stage of human development is characterised by the struggle between militancy and industrialism. While this struggle is going on the freedom of the individual is in many ways more narrowly restricted than absolute ethics would permit. Slavery is an institution belonging to militancy. With the development of industrialism, personal liberty is extended to increasingly larger circles. On account of the dependence of labourers on their employer, however, the relation of dependence in which the slave stands to his master is to a certain extent retained, although this relation now depends on a contract, on mutual agreement and obligation. Whether this state of things will ever entirely disappear we cannot tell; but it is the task of relative ethics to press home the necessity of approximating to the ideal relation of equality as far as is possible under existing conditions. While slavery existed, the poor often enjoyed the paternal protection of their lord. The abolition of slavery was accompanied by the abolition of protection, and with this came the suffering involved in the struggle for existence. The State attempted to relieve this suffering by means of a compulsory Poor Law, since it was evident that the principle of the preservation of the fittest could not be allowed full play. The interference of the State, however, caused greater evils than those which it proposed to remedy; it protected the weak and incapable, and enabled them to bring children into the world and to maintain them at the expense of the capable and diligent! Men attempted to mitigate the pain caused by the sight of the suffering of human beings by a system which, as a closer scrutiny showed, only increased the evil. The present system of State aid is a kind of social opiophagy.

Those sufferings which are involved in the process of evolution cannot be evaded. And we shall not evade them by letting feelings which have their right sphere in purely personal relations and in the family, influence the ordering of political and social relations. Family ethic and social ethic must not be confused; the former is concerned with the education of helpless posterity, the latter with the ordering of the reciprocal relations of adults. When man's estate is reached no system of State aid ought to interfere with the free action of the environment. It is different with private benevolence; for the latter employs its own means, while the

State obtains its means *by coercion*. But benevolence can do no more than prevent unnecessary, and mitigate necessary suffering; if it go any farther it weakens the vital power of the race. Spencer is bound to admit, however, that just as there are many transitional forms between the child and the adult, so room can be found for many compromises between family and social ethics. These systems present no such difference in principle as might be supposed from many of Spencer's utterances. But Spencer is right in his main idea that sympathy with suffering ought not to be allowed to exclude the education gained by interaction with the real conditions of life and which is necessary for the healthy development both of the individual and of the race.

In its rudest form the struggle for existence fosters egoism. Altruism, however, which is rooted in sympathy, gradually, if slowly, comes to the front; at first, under the form of care for the helpless, afterwards, under other and higher forms. There is no absolute antithesis between the two: evolution will modify human nature until the individual will find his highest blessedness in sacrifice, although not so as to hinder the independent development of others; while on the other hand, no one is so egoistic, even now, as to wish to accept the entire self-sacrifice of another. What is now a characteristic of exceptionally elevated characters will, one day, we may hope, be a general characteristic; for what is possible to the best human nature lies within reach of the whole of human nature, and development is incomplete as long as there is still a possibility of life becoming richer and of more value by the unfolding of capabilities which bring immediate satisfaction to the individual himself and at the same time are the cause of benefits to other men. Free activity and a development of life which shall be something more than the means to a future goal, are, as we saw, characteristics of the higher type of life which Spencer had in his mind. There are already, we remember, actions and endeavours which bear this stamp; so that the third kingdom, to which Spencer, like so many other thinkers of our century looks forward, does not lie solely in the future.

POSTSCRIPT

In addition to the writings of Mill, Spencer and Comte, works of considerable importance have been produced both in France and England during the latter half of the century. We must not pause to describe them here, however; for though they have played no small part in determining the course of intellectual development in the countries in question, they have brought no new principle to bear on the discussion of problems. For this same reason we have omitted any account of the peculiar philosophical development which has taken place in Italy.

In English literature, however, there are several works, treating of special subjects, which are of importance to philosophical thought in general. These are the logical works of Boole and Jevons, and Sidgwick's works on ethics.

Stuart Mill's work on inductive logic, bringing out as it did the limits within which alone the purely inductive method is capable of furnishing proof, was followed by a new exposition of deductive logic by GEORGE BOOLE, entitled *An Investigation of the Laws of Thought* (London, 1854), according to which deduction consists in finding all the logically possible combinations of certain concepts, a particular combination of them being given. That is to say, it is the task of deduction to give exhaustive information as to the logical value of a given judgment. Boole's method is ingenious, but somewhat artificial in form. His leading thought was carried out in a much simpler form by STANLEY JEVONS in a series of works beginning with *Pure Logic, or the Logic of Quality apart from Quantity* (1864) and ending with the *Principles of Science* (1874). Jevons regarded the content, not the scope of concepts, as fundamental, and in so doing emphasised the distinction between pure logic and pure mathematics. He also applied the principle of identity (as Hamilton, in his doctrine of the quantification of the predicate had already begun to do) in explaining the formulation of judgments much farther than had previously been done in logic, if we except a few treatises of Leibniz, long out of print. In his logical works Jevons's discussion of the methods of investigation is much more technical than Mill's. It is of great epistemological interest, however, on account of the clearness with which he shows that a deductive inference underlies every induction,— the proof of the correctness of an induction always consists in showing that deductions from the proposition to be proved lead to precisely those results which experience shows us actually taking place, and neither to more nor to less. Since deduction, in its turn, presupposes the validity of logical principles, the invalidity of pure empiricism is exposed. In· the latter years of his life Jevons published (*Contemporary Review*, 1877-79), a very severe criticism of Stuart Mill's philosophy, in which he placed pure empiricism in sharp contrast to evolution, and emphatically declared himself an adherent of Spencer's philosophy.

DR. HENRY SIDGWICK'S *Methods of Ethics* (1877) has given new life and new clearness to ethical discussion. He has drawn attention in particular to the fact that the term "utilitarianism" covers two different ethical systems, one of which is based on egoism, and the other on altruism, while both adopt the principle of utility as the ethical standard of measurement. He inquires carefully how far each system alone can carry us. He also attempts to show that utilitarianism underlies all the judgments of common-sense morality, and that the gaps or contradictions which such morality exhibits would disappear if this latent utilitarianism were recognised and adopted.[112]

The influence of the German school—especially of Kant and Hegel—on recent philosophical discussion in England and France is very remarkable. We may also notice in these countries, as in Germany, a phenomenon which is specially characteristic of the philosophical situation in the year 1880, beyond which this exposition of the history of modern philosophy does not extend. This phenomenon is the increasing division of labour within the sphere of philosophy, so that special logical, psychological, and ethical questions are discussed altogether apart from general philosophical problems.

The influence of the various philosophical tendencies upon one another and the specialisation of inquiry are the distinctive features of the last fifteen years, of which it is still too early to give an historical exposition.

All that remains for us to do, therefore, is to describe the course of philosophical discussion in Germany after the middle of the century.

BOOK X

PHILOSOPHY IN GERMANY 1850-1880

PHILOSOPHY IN GERMANY, 1850-1880

Of the two main philosophical currents of the nineteenth century positivism alone presents a continuous development of the lines of thought contained in the philosophy of the eighteenth century and in empirical science. Romanticism, indeed, is a decided and conscious reaction against both these tendencies—it is, in fact, nothing short of an attempt at a complete transformation of all that had been established in the seventeenth century with the birth of natural science. In Germany, the home of romanticism and of the romantic philosophy, this tendency predominated in the middle of the century. The representatives of the critical undercurrent were the only thinkers who were interested in asserting the continuity of philosophy with the other sciences—if we except Schopenhauer and Feuerbach, who, at that time, were still in the position of isolated thinkers, for whom the hour of recognition had not yet struck.

It would be as incorrect to explain the philosophical movement which took place in Germany in the latter part of the century as a continuation of the Franco-English positivism, as to explain positivism itself as a reaction against romanticism. The new movement had not to seek its premises in foreign countries. Its problems for the most part arose from the revival of natural science towards the middle of the century. Not only had scientific studies and the results to which they led become a subject of more general interest than during the first part of the century, when the air was full of poetry, religion and speculative philosophy, but science itself had returned with clearer consciousness to the great principles which its founders had enunciated.

The demand for an explanation of Nature as a series of demonstrable causes and effects, in other words, the demand for a mechanical explanation of Nature, now again, as in the seventeenth century, made itself heard. And contemporaneously with this, a great and comprehensive natural law was discovered and proved, *i.e.* the law that in physical nature no energy arises or perishes. Whenever such appears to be the case, there is a transformation of energy only, and these transformations take place in such a manner that the different forms of energy stand in definite quantitative relations to one another. This law—which with Darwin's doctrine of the origin of species in the struggle for existence is the most important result of the scientific investigation of our century—could not fail to set philosophical thought in motion, just as the Copernican theory and the founding of mechanics by Galilei opened new paths for philosophy. German philosophy, especially, had to face the question—How far can we retain the ideas developed by the philosophy of romanticism if we concur in the new scientific way of looking at things? This question received a threefold answer. Modern materialism rejected these ideas as altogether illusory, on the ground that the results attained by natural science force upon us the conclusion that matter is the sole existent. Lotze and Fechner, on the other hand, attempted to show that the fundamental assumption of the speculative philosophy of religion is also the ultimate and definitive assumption of the world-picture which scientific methods enable us to construct. Lastly, Albert Lange and Eugen Dühring, approximating more nearly to the position taken up by critical philosophy and positivism, emphasised the importance of the problem of knowledge, and asserted the independence of practical idealism over against empirical science ; while at the same time they accentuated the right of experience to determine the actual content of our conception of the world.

CHAPTER I

ROBERT MAYER AND THE PRINCIPLE OF THE CONSERVATION
OF ENERGY

KNOWLEDGE advances rhythmically, by means of action and
reaction, not only in philosophy but also in other sciences. Towards the end of the eighteenth century Natural Science passed
through a great and fruitful period, in which some of the most
important truths within the spheres of chemistry and physiology
were discovered. LAVOISIER introduced the quantitative method
into chemistry, and was thus enabled to establish the truth of the
old idea that no matter arises or perishes, but that the same
amount of it remains in existence throughout all changes,
though under different forms. Chemistry was thus converted
into an exact science. PRIESTLEY, INGENHOUSS, SENEBIER and
SAUSSURE discovered the principal laws of the transformation of
matter in plants and animals, and thereby established the great
doctrine of the circulation of matter in Nature, which shows us
the organic and inorganic world in close reciprocal connection.
They discovered that, under the action of sunlight, green plant-
cells elaborate organic matter, by taking up and giving off
again the carbonic acid contained in the air. The carbon
collected in the plant-cells serves as nourishment for animals ;
the animal functions cause combustion, and the carbonic acid
thus formed is breathed out into the air and the circular
process is repeated. A great cosmical interconnection [113] was
thus laid bare. The conception of the world sketched by
Copernicus, Bruno, Kepler and Galilei, and enriched by
Newton's discovery in attraction of the bond by which
phenomena are united and ordered, now received a further and
important enrichment.

The age, however, was far too much occupied with revolu-

tion and war, with romanticism and speculation, and a little
while after, with orthodoxy and mysticism to permit these
great ideas to exert their proper influence on general opinion.
Even in natural science itself their victory was delayed by
other tendencies. In the science of organic life more particularly, the new points of view encountered resistance ; for the
reaction against the Cartesian doctrine of the organism as a
machine was still in full force. The characteristics peculiar to
the organism were attributed to a special vital force which was
said to be quite different from all other natural forces. This
method of explanation, known as vitalism, necessarily led to
the rejection of all attempts to include organic phenomena in
the universal circulation of matter.[114] Moreover, the attention
of zoologists and botanists was entirely absorbed in describing
and systematising the different organic forms ; they did not
care to trace the process of development, in the course of
which these forms had arisen, nor to discover the causes which
determined this process of evolution. The natural philosophy
of romanticism favoured this æsthetic and formal conception
—of which indeed it was itself the outcome. The point of view
of the latter part of the eighteenth century took a long time
to establish itself within the spheres of botany and zoology ;
" natural philosophy" is frequently regarded as responsible
for this delay, but we must not forget that the latter was the
effect, rather than the cause, of the condition of the sciences.

A change set in after 1840. Men began to conceive life
as something more than a play of forms and a revelation of
ideas. DUMAS and LIEBIG brought out the significance of
chemical events in the plant- and animal-world. On the
medical side, too, a demand arose for a strictly mechanical
explanation of organic processes. HERMANN LOTZE gave
expression to this demand in some of his earlier writings,
more particularly in his *Allgemeinen Pathologie und Therapie als
mechanischen Naturwissenschaften* (1842), and in the section
on *Leben, Lebenskraft* (1843), which he wrote for R.
Wagner's *Dictionary of Physiology*. Physiologists were urged
to transform physiology into a strictly mechanical science. But
the chief influence in moulding thought at this time must be
attributed to a fundamental axiom formulated by ROBERT
MAYER (b. 1814, d. 1874), physician and physicist, in his
work entitled *Die organische Bewegung in ihrem Zusammenhange*

mit dem Stoffwechsel (1845), *i.e.* that in the course of the vital process there is a transformation only, never a creation, of force ; for force, like matter, is never created. Mayer bases his argument in proof of this axiom on the great law which he had discovered a few years previously, and which enabled him to place the law of the conservation of energy side by side with Lavoisier's law of the conservation of matter.

Robert Mayer's investigations are all based on an idea which occurred to him in early youth ; his inability to prove the truth of this idea by way of experiment was the tragedy of his life. As a child he had tried to construct a *perpetuum mobile*, and his want of success left a lasting impression on his mind. From that time forward he was continually ruminating on the relation between cause and effect, first of all as exhibited in physiology, which, as a medical man, lay nearest to his hand, but afterwards in chemistry and physics also. During a voyage to the East Indies, in the capacity of ship's doctor, the new idea flashed across him of the imperishability of force in nature ; this idea was suggested to him partly by his investigations into the genesis of organic heat, partly by the fact that the motion of the waves of the sea produces heat. He regarded it as a self-evident proposition that the effect cannot contain more than the cause, *causa aequat effectum.* This follows from the law of logical ground. Thus Mayer, like the dogmatic philosophers, makes no distinction between ground and cause ; hence, with Hamilton and Herbert Spencer, he had to assume as equally self-evident that the cause does not pass out of existence when the effect arises, but that the latter contains an equivalent to that which seems to disappear with the cause. Hitherto men had been content to think that motion ceased when it encountered a sufficiently stubborn resistance, and that heat was produced by friction. But, asked Mayer, does the motion pass out of existence ? and does heat arise out of nothing ? If that be so, the " red thread of science " is severed as completely as if chemists were to assume that oxygen and hydrogen pass out of existence when combined, and that water arises out of nothing. As we assume that oxygen and hydrogen are converted into water, so too we must assume that motion does not pass out of existence but is transformed into heat.[115] By the expression " transformed " Mayer merely meant to indicate that there is a constant

quantitative relation between the vanishing cause and the
effect which takes its place.   If the argument here brought
forward be correct, experience must exhibit a similar relation
of equivalence between the forms of energy which replace one
another.   Relying on previous experiments, Mayer attempted,
as far back as his first treatise (" Bemerkungen über die Kräfte
der unbelebten Natur," printed in Liebig's *Annalen der Chemie
und Pharmacie*, 1842), to determine the quantitative relation
between heat and motion.   He regarded the idea of a constant relation between quantities as of fundamental importance;
and indeed it is to this idea that the advance made by science
in the following years is largely due.   It is an important extension of the law of the preservation of energy already formulated
by Huyghens and Leibniz (see vol. i. p. 346), for it shows that
this law is also valid of the relation between the different
natural forces.   Mayer deduced from it the further inference
that there is but one force which occurs under different forms,
standing in definite quantitative relations to one another.

Although he did not succeed in his attempt to bring
forward a philosophical proof of the law of the conservation of
force, yet his line of thought is not devoid of epistemological
interest.   For the question whether between the event which
we call the cause and that which we call its effect there may
not exist a relation similar to that between logical ground and
its consequent is a perfectly justifiable one, and Mayer's line
of thought led straight up to it.   Experience must provide the
answer.—It is interesting to note that COLDING, a Danish
physicist, who, a year later, after Mayer's first treatise had been
printed, brought forward an independent proof of the axiom of
the conservation of energy and confirmed it experimentally, also
assumed it to be a law of reason.   HELMHOLTZ, too, in his
treatise, *Über die Erhaltung der Kraft* (1847) started from
an epistemological postulate.   The English JOULE who, like
Colding and Helmholtz, had arrived by a path of his own
at the same result as Mayer—a remarkable example of the
way in which several investigators may simultaneously be on
the track of one and the same discovery — adopted a more
purely experimental procedure ; nevertheless he intimates that
it is *a priori* improbable that there could be a destruction of
force without any equivalent effect.[116]

The new law had to fight its way to recognition ;

in the course of eighteen years (1842-60), however, it succeeded in gradually establishing itself; especially when it was found that it could be used as an instrument in making new investigations and discoveries. Its great importance consists in the fact that it enables the inquirer to raise certain definite questions whenever any peculiar expression of force appears or disappears. Just as the significance of the causal axiom is that whenever a change occurs it challenges us to look round for a preceding change, of which the new change might be the effect, so the significance of the axiom of the conservation of force (or as it is now called, following the proposal of an English investigator, of energy) is that it immediately sets us inquiring as to the relation between the forces which give place to one another.

From the point of view of philosophy the most important question is : What is the bearing of the new law on mental phenomena ? In this respect it is noteworthy that nearly all its discoverers started from distinctly spiritualistic and teleological conceptions. Mayer several times pronounced himself opposed to materialism, and expressed his conviction that scientific truths are related to the Christian religion as streams and rivers to the ocean. He gave utterance to these views at the Natural Science Congress at Innsbruck in 1869, and in so doing gave great offence to Karl Vogt and his friends. Colding's standpoint may be gathered from the following passage :—" The thought that natural forces are imperishable first occurred to me in connection with the view that the forces of Nature are akin to the spiritual element in Nature, to the eternal reason as well as to the human mind. In other words, I was led to the idea of the constancy of natural forces by the religious conception of life." According to Colding and Joule, when God created the world He deposited a certain total sum of force in Nature ; this total amount can neither be increased nor diminished ; it can only be distributed in different ways. This was what Descartes, in his time, had believed of motion (see vol. i. p. 229). Both Colding and Joule held that with the conservation of energy the conservation of all that was valuable in the world was secured ; for, like Leibniz, they made no distinction between energy itself and its use in the furtherance of life and of development (see vol. i. pp. 346-7).[117]

These inquirers, however, never attempted any closer

investigation or proof of their premisses ; like the philosophers
of the seventeenth century they started from certain ready-
made religious notions.   Hence it was but natural that a closer
inquiry should be made into the relation in which this newly
discovered law stood to the knowledge of Nature already acquired on the one hand, and the phenomena of mental life on
the other.   Nor need we be astonished that the result of this
inquiry was a parting of ways and the adoption of antagonistic
positions.   All that the law asserted was that when one kind
of physical energy ceases, a certain quantum of another kind of
physical energy takes its place.   The question at issue was :
How far and in what direction does the knowledge of this law
oblige us to modify our conception of the world ?

CHAPTER II

MATERIALISM

THE most violent reaction against the romantic philosophy —apart from that of the crassest orthodoxy—is expressed in the materialistic literature which flourished in Germany in the middle of the century. In romanticism the idea was everything ; here matter is declared to be the only thing in existence. The enthusiasm for science and for the commanding points of view which it had acquired by the help of the doctrine of the conservation of matter and of energy, was well calculated to cause this doctrine itself to be received as an all-sufficient philosophy, a key to all sides of existence. Undoubtedly the simplest way of answering the question, What is the significance of the doctrine of the conservation of matter and of force for our conception of the world ? was to say that this doctrine consti- tutes a complete world-conception. The philosophy of modern materialism claims to be nothing more than a systematisation of the logical consequences following from science. Here, at last, we seem to have found a firm foundation on which to base ideas and the conduct of life ! We need no longer have recourse to a mystical or spiritualistic foundation, for here we have something real and palpable on which to base both theory and practice ! Such a doctrine lends itself readily to popularisation. It is child- like, intuitive, easily accessible, and its exposition affords a good opportunity for adducing a number of scientific facts of general interest. Several of the champions of German materialism, *e.g*. KARL VOGT and JAKOB MOLESCHOTT, made valuable and original contributions to science. Others, such as LOUIS BÜCHNER, served the cause by their clear, pleasing, and enthu- siastic descriptions. It is the special merit of this literature that it was able to popularise knowledge. By its means a mass of information was disseminated in wide circles.

Büchner's *Kraft und Stoff* is one of the most widely read popular scientific books of our century. Sixteen editions appeared between 1855 and 1889 in Germany, and it has also been translated into several other languages. Even if materialism is not without a dogmatism of its own, yet it has done good service by opposing its dogmatism to the dogmatism of orthodoxy, and thereby conducing to a reconsideration of problems which had fallen into neglect after the romantic philosophy had professed to solve them. Moreover, the entire materialistic movement in Germany was supported by an idealistic interest in humanity and progress, and Büchner was quite right when he protested against confusing materialism as a method and theory with materialism in the sense of a practical direction of life. Materialism can afford to acknowledge the value of the highest and noblest ideas and feelings, although it believes that these, like all mental phenomena, are only products or forms of material happenings.

In view of the fact that materialism declares itself to be nothing more than the logical consequence of the results attained by natural science, it is interesting to observe not only that the discoverers of the law of the conservation of energy started from entirely spiritualistic premises, but also that the most important battles in the materialistic campaign took place between inquirers, all of whom took their stand on science. This does not necessarily prove that materialism is wrong, but it shows how difficult it is to draw correct conclusions, and how many different *motifs* help to determine each individual's conception of the world. Moleschott's famous work, *Der Kreislauf des Lebens* (1852), is directed against LIEBIG'S theologising expressions in his *Chemischen Briefen*, in which he had especially attacked a previous saying of Moleschott's : " Ohne Phosphor kein Gedanke " (No phosphorus, no thought). Contemporaneously with this polemic, a quarrel broke out between RUDOLF WAGNER in Göttingen and the zoologist KARL VOGT in Geneva. This quarrel reached its height in 1854, when, at a Natural Science Congress in Göttingen, Wagner defended the assumption of an ethereal soul-substance which moves the fibres of the brain as a musician moves the strings of a piano, and which is propagated from parents to offspring by partition [!].

Wagner based this assumption on the teaching of the Bible, although he is obliged to admit that it can only be maintained by drawing a sharp distinction between faith and knowledge. If once we quit the sphere of exact science our only trust must be in an undemonstrable faith, and Wagner adds : " In matters of religion I like best a simple implicit faith." To which Vogt replied with a bitter polemic entitled *Köhlerglaube und Wissenschaft* (Implicit Faith and Science) (1855). In a later work, *Vorlesungen über den Menschen* (1863), Vogt gives a more scientific exposition of his standpoint. He emphatically maintains that the brain is the organ of consciousness, and that consciousness stands in the same relation to the brain as every function to its corresponding organ. Although he admits that it is impossible to explain *how* consciousness arises in the cells of the brain, yet he is firmly convinced that they are inseparably connected. He is not prepared to recant the proposition he had laid down earlier, and which had created such a sensation, viz. that thought stands in the same relation to the brain as gall to the liver or urine to the kidneys—although, after all, a function does not stand in the same relation to the organ as a product to the place at which it is produced.

Moleschott, as we may gather from the title of his book, prefers to build on the doctrine of the conservation of matter. This great thought, he says, was brought to light by the encyclopædists of the eighteenth century. Recent scientific investigations have confirmed it ; the belief of the future must build upon it. The great circular process of Nature fills him with awe. The miner digs phosphate of lime out of the earth in the sweat of his face, and perhaps in so doing the material of the best brain and highest thoughts passes through his hands ; the peasant manures his field with the phosphate of lime, which thus becomes a constituent part of the wheat which nourishes the body and brain of man. In company with matter, life circulates through all parts of the world, with life thought, and from thought again springs the will to make life better and happier. If then we can supply organism and brain with the best possible matter, thought and will also will attain their highest development. The scientific inquirer is the Prometheus of our age, and chemistry is the highest science. The social question will find its solution if only [*sic*] we can discover the right way to distribute the matter with which the life of thought and of the will is bound up. We have here only quoted from the first edition of Moleschott's work; later issues contain many changes and additions. Moleschott, who was born in Holland in 1822, was working as a *docent* at Heidelberg when his book appeared; as, however, his liberty of teaching was interfered with he went to Zürich; later still he was Professor of Physiology at Turin and at Rome, at which latter place he died in 1893. His autobiography (*Für meine Freunde: Lebenserinnerungen von Jacob Moleschott*, Giessen, 1895) was published after his death. It gives us an interesting picture of this idealistically-minded physical inquirer, who could not rest satisfied with any one-sided culture. The following passage, which occurs at the conclusion of his *Kreislauf des Lebens*, is of importance for a right understanding of his standpoint: "It was one-sidedly materialistic only for those who can conceive matter without force, or force without any supporting substance. *I myself was well aware that the whole conception might be converted, for since all matter is a bearer of force, endowed with force or penetrated with spirit, it would be just as correct to call it a spiritualistic conception*" (p. 221). Moleschott's standpoint should be described as monism rather than materialism. "It deals with a true, indivisible two-in-one, and the opposition it sets up is not that between a materialistic and a spiritualistic point of view, but that between a two-in-one and a two hopelessly sundered, between the real and the imaginary" (p. 222). Only in contradistinction to the spiritualistic view does Moleschott call himself a materialist.

LOUIS BÜCHNER (born 1824) says, it is true, that he does not profess to explain the relation between mind and matter, between force and stuff; he is content to assert that they stand in necessary and inseparable connection. But even this is more than can be scientifically demonstrated; moreover, Büchner does not doubt for a moment that mind is only a property of matter, force a property of stuff. He was led to write his famous work *Kraft und Stoff* under the influence of Moleschott's *Kreislauf des Lebens;* for him too the imperishability of matter is the ultimate ground. In his opinion the conservation of energy is nothing more than a self-evident corollary from the conservation of matter, and might therefore have been deduced from Lavoisier's chemical

theory. In the fifth edition of his book, however, he interpolates a special chapter on the "immortality of energy," in
which the circulation of force is placed side by side with the
circulation of matter as its necessary correlate, so that both
together, from eternity to eternity, they form the sum of
phenomena which we call the world. Nevertheless he holds
fast to his belief that "all natural and spiritual forces are
indwelling in matter, so that matter is the ultimate basis
of all being." He declares mind to be a mere product
(although he had professed total ignorance as to its relation
to matter). "Just as a steam-engine produces motion, so the
intricate organic complex of force-bearing substance in an
animal organism produces a total sum of certain effects,
which, when bound together into a unity, are called by us
mind, soul, thought" (*Kraft und Stoff*, 7th ed. p. 130). Büchner
has gone still farther—without apparently being aware of it
—in later utterances. Thus, for example, in a polemic
directed against the present writer, he says : "The antithesis
between physical and psychical energy is only tenable if we
conceive body and mind, or, speaking more generally, force
and matter, dualistically from the beginning ; as conceived by
a materialistic monism they coincide, and *may perhaps be
regarded as two different aspects or modes of that which
underlies all things.* The law of the conservation of energy
necessarily leads to materialistic consequences in psychology.
In several of my writings, and quite recently in my fifth
letter on *Das künftige Leben und die moderne Wissenschaft*
(Leipzig, 1889), I have proved this statement by the help of
evidence supplied by psycho-physical facts and observations.
Hence I claim to have shown that psychical activity is, and can
be, nothing but a radiation through the cells of the grey substance of the brain of a motion set up by external stimuli "
(from an article in *Menschthum*, Gotha, 1889, No. 46).

It is clear from this passage that Büchner confuses two
different theories ; one, that mind and matter are phenomenal
forms of one and the same substance ; the other, that matter
is the underlying basis, so that psychical processes are *nothing
but* motion (or "radiation of motion"). He gives in his
adherence to both theories in the same breath. The incon-
sequence of so doing has escaped the notice of this indefatigable champion of the influence of scientific discoveries on our

conception of the world ; perhaps, as he was not mainly concerned to inculcate a definite philosophical theory, he hardly appreciated its full significance. His great zeal led him to believe that he had adduced evidence in proof of that which, unfortunately, is not susceptible of proof.

HEINRICH CZOLBE (1819-1873), like Büchner a medical man, but endowed with a keener critical sense, attempted to deduce the consequences which follow from the teaching of natural science. In his first work he is a consistent materialist. In his *Neue Darstellung des Sensualismus* (1855), and *Die Enstehung des Selbstbewusstseins* (1856), also in an article in the *Zeitschrift für Philosophie*, vol. xxvi., entitled "Die Elemente der Psychologie vom Standpunkte des Materialismus," he maintains that materialism runs counter to science as long as the latter retains the theory of specific energy of the sensory nerves, for, in so doing, it maintains a distinction between sensations and the external events corresponding to them. In opposition to this teaching Czolbe brings forward the view that it is essentially one and the same motion which, starting in the outer world, propagates itself to the brain by means of the sense-organs and nerves. There is no qualitative change at any point ; the difference between the different senses arises merely from the different intensities with which the motion is propagated by the different organs. The unity of consciousness is explained by the fact that when they reach the brain these motions are turned back upon themselves ; it is because the brain affords a theatre for these circular motions that it is the organ of consciousness. Thus we see that, without any further inquiry into the matter, Czolbe conceives both sensation and self-consciousness as motion in space. But he soon became aware—for he is a clear and logical thinker—that if sensation and self-consciousness are declared to be identical with motion the statement is convertible, and we are justified in saying, where there is motion of a certain intensity and in a certain form there is consciousness, which amounts to saying that Nature is animate throughout. Thus the most logical form of materialism leads out beyond itself.

Later, in his *Die Grenzen und der Ursprung der menschlichen Erkenntnis* (1865), and in a very interesting article entitled "Die Mathematik als Ideal für alle andere Erkenntnis und das Verhältnis der empirischen Wissenschaften zur Philosophie,"

Zeitschrift für exakte Philosophie (1866), Czolbe recognised the impossibility of explaining the world from a single principle, whether, with Büchner, we find this principle in matter, or, with the speculative philosophers, in mind, or, with the theologians, in God. We only arrive at an explanation if we start from several elements, taking element in the sense of that which is unanalysable. Such mutually irreducible elements are material atoms, the organic forces and the psychical elements (which, taken collectively, form the world-soul). Between these three kinds of elements there is harmonious inter-action, by which the purposive interconnection of Nature is effected. If not in origin, yet in direction and tendency, the world proves to be a unity. It is evident, therefore, that the problem of existence is far more complicated than materialism is inclined to believe. In his later inquiries, which have not yet all been printed, Czolbe comes very near Spinoza's fundamental ideas, which he attempted to develop empirically. For further particulars concerning the different stages of the philosophical development of this energetic thinker, readers are referred to Varhinger's article, " Die drei Phasen des Czolbeschen Naturalismus" (*Philosophische Monatshefte*, xii.).

From the beginning to the end of Czolbe's writings, the underlying demand is that all fundamental notions should be clear and comprehensible. His great wish was to exclude everything mystical and supersensuous, and to that end he tried, as far as possible, to think out every idea with geometrical clearness. It was out of respect for clearness, rather than for stringent proof, that he pronounced mathematics to be the ideal of science. As a youth he had read Hölderlin's poetry with the greatest enthusiasm, and had resolved to defend the Hellenic clearness and joy of life against all mysticism and all dualism. Clearness within the world of thought was, for him, closely bound up with joy in the natural world. Just as the application of the principle of clearness in thought may involve no small labour, so the practice of joy may involve no small resignation in real life ; but in the practical as in the theoretical sphere Czolbe was bent on fighting what he called " that idiotic transcendentalism." Even during his materialistic period he confesses that the underlying motive of his philosophy is the subjective need of comprehending and holding fast to the actual.

Materialism was, for him, nothing more than a postulate—a postulate, moreover, which had afterwards to yield to others.

ERNST HÄCKEL (born 1834, from 1865 professor of zoology at Jena) is often reckoned among the materialists. He himself, however, describes his standpoint as a monism which leads out beyond the antithesis between spiritualism and materialism, and takes as its basis the great pantheistic idea of the unity of Nature. For monism, there is no such thing either as mind or matter in the ordinary sense of the words, but only something which is both at once. His general philosophical opinions may be gathered more easily from his *Generelle Morphologie*, (1862-1866). The psychical is for him, as for Czolbe, one of the original elements of the universe, although it exists in very different degrees, from the soul of atoms and cells up to the soul of the highest organisms. This animation theory of Häckel's is open to the objection that it often appeals to the intervention of the soul in explanation of organic movements, instead of seeking for a purely scientific explanation ; while, on the other hand, he sometimes explains psychical phenomena as nothing more than the effects of the most complex and unstable carburets of the albuminous molecules of nervous tissue. He thinks he has got beyond both materialism and spiritualism, and yet we may find passages of his which have a spiritualistic ring, just as there are others which sound materialistic. He was not one of the thinkers who arrived at his first principles by steadfastly thinking out the laws of the conservation of matter and of force. It was Darwin's teaching which set him thinking, and the object of his search was a highest principle which could be combined with the great conception of the unity of Nature as shadowed forth in the new teaching. Monism, according to Häckel (*Gen. Morph.* ii. pp. 445-451), leads to the sublimest conception of God. In the great all-embracing causal law, the Deity is revealed as including the whole of Nature and as active in every natural phenomenon. The ordinary conception of God is really a belief in two Gods ; it is ambitheism, not monotheism, for it places God side by side with natural causes.

Häckel was one of the first German scientists to give in his adherence to Darwin. He was an ardent supporter of the Darwinian hypothesis, and attributed to it a certainty and a wideness of range in which its critical and careful originator could not always acquiesce. He was never tired of constructing the pedigrees of existing species, and he saw no difficulty in believing in a continuous evolution of organic matter. He had not the power of perceiving the limits of an hypothesis, nor did he grasp the necessity for verification ; otherwise he could never, as he did, have placed Darwin's hypothesis, just as it stood, side by side with that of Newton. Moreover, he reproached Darwin with taking the objections raised against his theory too seriously. The great discoverer shook his head over his young disciple's zeal : " Your boldness sometimes makes me tremble," he wrote (Nov. 19, 1868).

As we have already said, the doctrine of the persistence of matter and of force, and that of the development of species by means of natural selection, were the scientific results which were most calculated to stimulate thought during the latter half of the century. Now that we have glanced at the attempts made by men of science to erect a philosophy on these results, we must pass on to study the way in which they presented themselves to philosophers.

CHAPTER III

IDEALISTIC CONSTRUCTION ON A REALISTIC BASIS

(a) Rudolph Hermann Lotze

LOTZE is the most important representative of idealistic philosophy in the latter half of the century. His personality and intellectual development are exceedingly interesting, for we find in him the ideal *motifs* which formed the basis of the romantic philosophy, coupled with a faithful adherence to the strictly mechanical conception of Nature which had been adopted by science about the middle of the century. Lotze is a master in the art of developing concepts, in analysing a thought so that not one of its *nuances* escapes observation, in returning again and again to a problem and looking at it from different points of view. In the last instance, his ideal is the same as that which haunted the romantic philosophers, viz. to deduce all the development and all the interconnection of the world from one eternal idea, which contains within itself the ultimate basis of all that happens, as well as of the value of these happenings. But he was well aware that such a task transcends the power of human thought ; the romanticists were led astray here by the religious and poetical interests which, unnoticed by them, had penetrated into the domain of philosophy proper. Accordingly, Lotze is careful to keep his speculation free from the influence of the poetic and religious tendencies. He had too fine a poetic sense himself not to perceive that such a romantic blending would be anything but advantageous. And this poetic sense is closely allied with a sense for the individual *nuances* and relations which were too often èxplained away in the abstractions of speculative philosophy. • His appreciation of their importance led to the combination of realistic tendencies with speculative interest which characterises his philosophy.

He felt the paramount need of conceiving phenomena in their concrete nature and in their regular and definite interconnection ; it is the task of philosophic thought to discover the ultimate grounds on which this real interconnection rests. We see, then, that with Lotze the poetical, the scientific, and the philosophical elements are closely united ; and it is but rarely that any one thinker is equipped as Lotze was for the task he had set himself, and which the spiritual needs of his time laid upon him, viz. the attempt to reconstruct an idealistic philosophy on a realistic basis. He was convinced on the one hand that the philosophy of romanticism had overlooked the real conditions and the mechanical interconnection of Nature, without which the most significant ideas are helplessly ideal ; and on the other, that materialism takes for its alpha and omega that which is in reality only a form—although a necessary one,—a frame which embraces the content of existence in which all value is contained. The central point of his philosophy consists in an analysis of the concept of the mechanism of Nature, with the object of proving that this concept necessarily leads to the assumption of an ideal principle of existence, and that, in any case, it does not exclude the assumption that such a principle is the eternal spring of all good and all value. If we follow the course of Lotze's development we shall have no difficulty in detecting the different motives and interests by which he was animated. He was born, May 21, 1817, in Bautzen, the district from which Lessing and Fichte came. He studied philosophy, medicine, and physics at the University of Leipzig. He was here initiated into the two lines of thought, the union of which, after he had worked out each one on its own merits, was to be the work of his life. DR. HERMANN WEISSE, a writer on æsthetics and the philosophy of religion, was his teacher in philosophy. In later life Lotze used to say that he not only owed many single ideas to Weisse, but that he had been introduced by him into a circle of ideas which he had never afterwards seen cause to abandon. Weisse was the most important representative of philosophical theism. He forms the historical link between Lotze's conception of the philosophy of religion and that of Schelling, and, through the latter, with that of old

Jakob Böhme (cf. above, pp. 171 f., 267 f.). In a retrospect
of his own development (*Streitschriften*, 1857, p. 5) Lotze
emphatically asserts that when assimilating the ideas of speculative philosophy he never regarded them as forming a complete
system of thought, but merely as one particular form of intellectual culture. But he early adopted—and never afterwards
relinquished—the assumption that the ultimate ground of all
things must be conceived as spiritual. He studied medicine
and physics under E. H. Weber, Volkmann, and G. H. Fechner.
He thus made a first-hand acquaintance with scientific methods
and conceptions. He graduated as doctor of philosophy and
doctor of medicine in the same year, and he continued to be a
docent of both these branches even after he had been appointed
to a professorship of philosophy. After working for some
years at Leipzig he succeeded Herbart in his professorship at
Göttingen, where he wrote his chief works. The year before
his death he was called to Berlin, but succumbed soon after
to an illness from which he had long suffered (1881). His
life was a quiet one, dedicated to study, thought and academic
instruction. A rare combination of versatility and thoroughness enabled him to make himself acquainted with very
different spheres of thought, as may be seen, not only from
his medical and philosophical works, but also from a number of
smaller treatises and reviews, published, after his death, under
the title of *Kleine Schriften* (four vols.). When he wanted to
rest from his more arduous scientific work he occupied himself
with art and literature ; thus, for example, he rendered the
Antigone into Latin verse.

As a medical writer, Lotze, as we have already said, made
it his special task to maintain the character of physiology as a
mechanical science of Nature. He appeals in explanation of
the idiosyncrasy of organic phenomena not to a mystical vital
force, but to a demonstration of the definite and regular manner
in which the universal forces of Nature work in organisms.
Here, as everywhere in Nature, we must turn for an explanation to the reciprocal action of real elements. Organic life is
distinguished from the inorganic world not by being exalted
above the mechanical interconnection of Nature, but by the
particular manner in which the connected series of effects it
presents originated. The speculative philosophy of Nature had
taken the concept of organism as the type of the conception

of the universe ; any correction of this idea, therefore, must be of general philosophic significance. We may gather, therefore, that Lotze's labours in this direction were prompted not only by his medical but also by his philosophic interests (*Allgemeine Pathologie und Therapie als mechanische Naturwissenschaften,* 1842 ; *Allgemeine Physiologie des körperlichen Lebens,* 1851). These works even misled some materialists into welcoming Lotze as a brother in the faith, although he had distinctly stated that mechanism forms only a part of his conception of Nature, not the whole. This partitioning of the problem is characteristic of Lotze. He had worked out his general views on philosophy in his *Metaphysik* (1841) ; but when he began to teach he felt that he had left much unsaid, and used often to refer his hearers to future works, especially when touching on ultimate ideas. His *Medizinische Psychologie oder Physiologie der Seele* (1852) contains a full discussion of the relation between the spiritual and the material, and also enters into psychological inquiries which are of permanent interest. A plan which he had long entertained was carried out in the following years (1856-1864), with the publication of his *Mikrokosmus* in three volumes. This work was conceived as a pendant to Humboldt's *Kosmos* and Herder's *Ideen ;* it contains a psychology thought out in close connection with physiology and the history of culture, and ends with the development of the author's ideas on cosmology and the philosophy of religion. Lotze here found expression for all his interests, for all the different paths which his thought and feeling had travelled. The work was intended to be a popular exposition and has gained a considerable circle of readers. After the publication of his brilliant *Geschichte der Ästhetik in Deutschland* (1868), Lotze passed on to a concluding systematic exposition of his philosophy. He only succeeded, however, in completing two portions of it (*Drei Bücher der Logik,* 1874 ; *Drei Bücher der Metaphysik,* 1879). The third volume, which was to include æsthetics, ethics, and the philosophy of religion, was never written. Thus his philosophy remained uncompleted ; it was not granted to him to set the crown on his work and show how the many threads of thought which he had spun could be woven together into a unity. Short expositions of Lotze's teaching in the different spheres of philosophy are contained in the notes of his lectures (*Grundzüge*) which were published

after his death. Among these we may mention especially the
" Grundzüge der Logik und Encyklopädie der Philosophie,"
the second part of which gives a brief but clear summary of
his whole system. We now pass on to sketch the three most
important features of his philosophy.

(a) *The Mechanical Conception of Nature*

Lotze's thought has two starting-points : a lively feeling
of the value of spiritual life—a feeling that what is highest for
man is inseparably bound up with spiritual development and
its ideals—coupled with a firm conviction that a system of
mechanical causes and laws are necessary for the realisation of
these highest ideals. He can, as he says somewhere, believe
in ideas that work, but not in ideas that bewitch. These two
starting-points, however, never appear apart from one another.
When he sets out from one, he always attempts to demonstrate
the possibility of recognising the other. The most characteristic
as well as scientific feature of his philosophy is his attempt to
show, by means of an analysis of the concept of mechanism
itself, that the ultimate presupposition on which this concept is
based is that of a principle which, as soon as we gain a clear
conception of it, is seen to be the bearer and source of the
highest ideas. Lotze is determined to get at the bottom of
the matter ; by deducing the consequences of realism he
expects to find a basis for idealism. He is of opinion that
only such inquiries as are carried on in the spirit of realism are
able to bring us to the goal which idealism has set before
itself, *i.e.* knowledge of the world as the expression of an idea
which is itself of value. Romanticism had tried to deduce the
forms of reality from the highest idea. This proved an impossible task. We, on the contrary, starting from the given
must try to reason back to its ultimate presuppositions.
Not *deduction*, but *reduction* is possible. Thought must always
apply its forms to a given matter. General culture, like the
special sciences, operates with a mass of concepts, into the
origin, significance, and validity of which it never inquires.
Such concepts are cause and effect, matter and force, end and
means, freedom and necessity, matter and spirit. It is the
task of philosophy to introduce unity and interconnection
within the world of ideas by making the concepts which are

taken for granted in practical life and the special sciences the object of special investigation, and by determining the limits of their validity (*Grundzüge der Logik und Encyklopädie der Philosophie*, § 88).

The most important of these concepts is the one which is assumed in every investigation of reality, every time that we make an experiment or seek for an explanation ; *i.e.* the concept of an all-pervasive, all-embracing causal connection. This concept is not based on experience, but is presupposed in every experience. But since all the knowledge of Nature which we have acquired up to the present time is based on the reality of this concept it may be regarded as the expression of a fact. Philosophy has to think out this fact, *i.e.* that each particular element of our experience is bound together by means of an interconnection according to law with other elements,—or in other words, that there is a mechanical inter-connection—and deduce all the consequences which follow from it. Philosophy, it is true, cannot *deduce* this fact, but she may, perhaps, discover what is contained within it. *A plurality of real elements in reciprocal interaction* is the foundation on which the mechanical conception of Nature is constructed. We have already seen that Lotze was so firmly convinced of the necessity of this foundation that he did his best to procure it recognition within the sphere of physiology—where hitherto vitalism, with its appeal to a single prevailing and formative " vital force," had been in the ascendency.

But just because mechanical interconnection is a necessary feature of our conception of the world, it must not be the only or dominant feature. On the contrary, Lotze speaks of " the unlimited validity of mechanism together with its entirely sub-ordinate significance in the universe as a whole " (*Drei Bücher der Metaphysik*, p. 462). And a closer scrutiny of the concept in question will convince us that this is a true statement.

The mechanical conception of Nature, cannot, when presented as a complete conception of the world, take us beyond a manifold of elements (atoms) in reciprocal action. It proclaims a pluralism. But what is the relation between the elements and the interconnection in which they exist ? Could they, apart from this interconnection, exist independently, so that the latter may be regarded as inessential to their existence ? or must we not rather suppose that they are entirely determined by the connection in which they stand with the world as a whole ? Reciprocal action and interconnection cannot take place in the air, over or between the elements ; it presupposes their inner unity. For if I assume that the two elements A and B are independent, their reciprocal action is incomprehensible. An effect cannot be transferred ready-made from A to B. What happens in A can only have significance for what happens in B if A and B are at bottom *not* independent and absolutely separate beings, but their states the states of one and the same being which includes them both. A plurality of independent beings would render mechanical action and reaction incomprehensible ; understanding only comes with the belief in an infinite, all-embracing Being, of which the moments or points of action are the particular elements. The concept of a transition of force or of influence from one independent element to another is untenable. We can only understand an *immanent* (*causa immanens*), not a *transitive* (*causa transiens*) cause. States of one and the same being may be related as ground and consequent, but not states of two beings, absolutely independent of each other. — Among the many statements of this argument given by Lotze we may mention especially those given in the *Logik und Encyklopädie*, §§ 99-100 and *Drei Bücher der Metaphysik*, §§ 50-81.

Lotze's analysis of the concepts of causal relation and reciprocal action—which are the fundamental concepts of the mechanical conception of Nature—led him to the idea of an original substance, an all-embracing principle. His thought here follows the path which had led Spinoza to the concept of substance (see vol. i. pp. 301-307), and which Kant so often pursued in his early works. (See my treatise on the continuity of Kant's philosophical development in the *Archiv für Gesch. der Philos.* 1894, and above, pp. 41-49.)

The concept which romantic philosophy took *as its basis*, and from which it attempted to deduce everything else, was regarded by Lotze as the *ultimate postulate*, or as he also called it, the *ultimate fact of our thought*. It is impossible to determine more closely and clearly this universal principle which is presupposed in the simplest case of reciprocal action. We are dealing here with a limiting concept, which we can neither dispense with nor develop (*Drei Bücher der Metaphysik*, §§ 73 and 246). And yet this is the concept which

enabled Lotze to retain all that he regarded as essential in
the idealistic line of thought into which he had been initiated
by his teacher Weisse.   It enabled him to unite the two antagonistic currents in the world of thought.   He could not regard
either the absolute atoms of materialism, the monads of Leibniz,
or the " reals " of Herbart as final resting-places for thought ;
pluralism must be driven off the field by *monism*.   As regards
atoms, Lotze declares that the scientific interest is satisfied by
the assumption of such elements as are actually indivisible in
our experience.   But the assumption of a plurality of extended
elements—even if they are conceived as infinitely small—can
never be a final assumption for thought.   We must give up
either the unity of the atoms or their extension ; in an
extended atom every effect requires time, and is propagated
from part to part ; hence these parts would be more fundamental unities than the atoms themselves.   If the atomic
concept is to be a final one we must exclude all extension, and
conceive atoms as centres of force, each of which—in accordance
with the analysis of the concept of mechanism given above—
are starting-points for the working of the original substance
(*Drei Bücher der Metaphysik*, §§ 190-191 and 245.   Cf. the
interesting review of Fechner's " Atomenlehre" in the *Kleine
Schriften*, iii. pp. 215-238).

Lotze's reassertion of the mechanical conception of Nature
and the consequences he deduces therefrom form the most
important part of his philosophy, although it is not the side of
his thought which is generally dwelt upon by those who have
commended him.   His spiritualistic and theologising tendencies
are more often emphasised, both by admirers and opponents.
And yet his greatest contribution to thought is his analysis of
the fundamental concept of the scientific conception of Nature.
The fact that Spinoza and Kant preceded him in this task does
not diminish his merit—especially as he himself does not seem
to have been aware of the fact.   It is, however, a defect in his
treatment that he never entered on any epistemological examination of the limiting concept at which he had arrived ; he left
it in the form in which Romanticism and the older dogmatism
had conceived it.   Indeed Lotze never showed an adequate
appreciation of the significance of the theory of knowledge.

(β) *Metaphysical Idealism*

There is a certain indetermination about Lotze's line of thought as far as we have yet followed it. The question suggests itself, Is there no way open to us by which we can reach a more exact idea of the elements and of the original substance? In proceeding to study Lotze's answer to this question it is of the first importance to remember that he himself is quite aware that any answer must be based on analogy, and be determined by other than purely theoretical motives. The employment of the law of analogy and the need of finding our own spiritual nature in the universe, both of which we have detected in all the metaphysical idealists (especially in Leibniz, Herder, Schelling and Beneke) were clearly recognised and deliberately accepted by Lotze.

Lotze is an atomist, but he does not conceive the atoms themselves as material ; for extension, like all other sensuous qualities, is explained through the reciprocal action of atoms ; they themselves, therefore, cannot possess this quality. Like life and like all empirical qualities, the sensuous fact of extension is due to the co-operation of points of force, which, in their turn, must be conceived as starting-points of the inner working of the infinite primal Being. Lotze sees no reason why absolute beginnings may not have occurred in the course of the world's development in time ; such a supposition is not inconsistent with universal subjection to law, for a law only expresses the order in which the different states arise, not an external fate to which they are subject ; every new element, as it arises, finds its law, and this law is identical with " that nature of things which remains constant through all changes " (*Drei Bücher der Metaphysik*, § 33). And the particular elements themselves need not be perfectly homogeneous. A certain harmony or commensurability there must certainly be, otherwise they could not all be included in one world-order ; perfect similarity, however, is not necessary. It may be that elements of widely differing qualities, the general denominator of which we are unable to discover, are bound together under one natural law. In the last resort it is not a *logical* but an *æsthetic* necessity which makes the universe comprehensible to us (*Drei Bücher d. M.* § 59). It is not the formal consistency of the working of the primal Being, but the richness and fulness with which this working takes place that determines the nature of the particular elements. At this point it is evident that Lotze passes from purely theoretical motives to motives derived from feeling, but neither the one nor the other enable him to show more clearly how these great qualitative differences can be combined with the commensurability which the fact of reciprocal action presupposes.[118]

If we want to form a notion of the inner nature of the elements we must conceive them in analogy with our own spiritual nature. The mechanical conception of Nature only gives us information concerning the mutual relation of the elements ; it tells us nothing of their inner nature. It is concerned with external circumstances, and moves round and about things—it is a *cognitio circa rem*. Like the popular conception of Nature, it inclines to the opinion that it is altogether a matter of indifference for things whether we understand them or not. In opposition to such a view Lotze maintains (as early as his *Metaphysik* of 1841, p. 313) that subjectivity is just as much a part of reality as are external objects,—" Not only that which takes place between beings but also that which takes place within them is a true and real happening." In his later writings (first of all in his *Medizinische Psychologie*) he goes a step farther, for he asserts that our own subjective nature is the only case in which we know the inner nature of a thing, and have a *cognitio rei* as distinct from a *cognitio circa rem*. The only way, therefore, in which we can form an idea of the inner nature of other things is to conceive them in analogy with ourselves—as feeling beings (not as representing beings, for feeling is a more primitive form of consciousness than presentation). It is only by the help of this analogy that we can conceive things as real beings, existing for themselves and not as mere pictures. In so doing we are only employing the general method of reducing the unknown to the known (*Drei Bücher der M.* §§ 96-98). And " æsthetic necessity" also demands this analogy, for it cannot be reconciled with a universe of which a great, perhaps the greater, part is but the obscure foundation of a psychical life which only reaches consciousness in particular regions (see already *Allg. Physiologie*, § 129). We must assume, therefore, that the elements of the universe are animated in manifold degrees.

What is true of the elements of the universe is also true of

the all-embracing world-principle which renders their reciprocal
action comprehensible. If inner states are to be bound together into a unity and an interconnection, our own inner
spiritual life is the only example known to us in which the
possibility of such a preservation of unity in the midst of
fluctuating states is, at any rate, approximately realised.
Following his teacher, C. H. Weisse, Lotze conceives the
world-principle as absolute personality, and he defends the
transference of the concept of personality to the absolute Being
as follows :—the absolute Being must be personal because
personality alone possesses inner independence and originality,
while the concept of personality only finds imperfect realisation
in finite beings who are dependent on external conditions.
Lotze, it is true, admits that a personal life involves resistance
to be overcome and the faculty of suffering and receiving as
well as of working. But if it is asked, How can an absolute
Being, subject to no limitations, suffer? Lotze answers
(*Grundzüge der Religionsphilosophie*, § 34) that the feeling of
the Deity must be set in motion by the inner happenings
of its own creative imagination! But it is a great question
whether such a self-created opposition can have any serious
significance, especially since it can at any moment be destroyed at will. Personalities, as we know them at least,
have to fight against barriers which are neither self-created
nor easily set aside ; the analogy on which Lotze builds,
therefore, seems to break down at the critical point. Moreover, according to the most probable interpretation of his confused and hesitating utterances on the subject,[119] Lotze diverges
from Weisse in holding that the form of time is not applicable
to the absolute Being; a personal Being which does not
develop in time, a timeless life and a timeless suffering and
working,—these are concepts which make too great demands
on our power of drawing analogies! One thing more—
Lotze assumes that the opposition between matter and spirit
(and this applies both to the elements and to the world-principle)
is a contradictory opposition, so that they are the only conceivable alternatives, for only on this assumption are we forced
to conceive the elements and the world-principle as spiritual
beings, if we will not or cannot conceive them as material
beings. It is not a *logical* but an *actual* necessity, however,
which compels us to choose between spirit and matter in deter-

mining our ultimate conception. In real life we know these two forms of existence only ; but there is nothing inconceivable in the supposition that one or several other forms exist. Hence this is not a sufficient ground on which to base metaphysical idealism.[120]

Lotze is well aware that the coping stone of his whole world - conception is derived from feeling, not from strict thought. He maintains, on purely theoretical grounds, it is true, the necessity of ascending from the plurality of elements to the unity of the world - principle. " I can conceive no course of the world at all, either harmonious or unharmonious, unless we presuppose such a unity, for it alone makes the reciprocal action between particulars possible ; the disturbances of one thing by another are just as much a witness to the continual presence of this unity as is the co-operation of forces to an end " (*Drei Bücher der Metaphysik*, § 233). But though Lotze thus reduces everything to a single principle he is very well aware that this principle does not enable us to construct either the world as a whole or the elements out of which it is composed ; the second premise is lacking (*Drei Bücher der Met.* § 93). Hence it is only in practical conviction that we can hold fast to the thought that all beings and all events have their ultimate ground in that which is regarded as the highest end of the universe. What sort of an end this is we do not know, any more than we know how the struggle between the forces of Nature and the reality of evil in the moral world can be reconciled with the validity of the world-plan (*Mikrokosmus*, Book ix. chap. 5. *Drei Bücher der Met.* § 233). At the end as at the beginning of his career, Lotze's thought culminates in an ethical idea ; metaphysics, with him, has to yield to ethics ; in what *ought* to be we find the ultimate explanation of what *is*.

If by Pantheism we understand the doctrine that asserts an inner relation between God and the world, whether the Deity is conceived as a personal Being or not, Lotze's religio-philosophical standpoint may be described as ethical Pantheism. He claimed spiritual kinship with Fichte, but did not care to acknowledge any relationship with Spinoza. In the use of theological terms and expressions (especially in *Mikrokosmus* and in the *Grundzüge der Religionsphilosophie und der Moralphilosophie*, published after his death), he went farther than was either fit or right. Owing to this habit of speech (for it is really nothing more) he appeared to be in much closer accord with the popular theory of religion than was really the case. Yet every now and then (see especially *Mikrokosmus*, Bk. viii. chap. 4) he lays special emphasis on the difference between free and positive religion.

(γ) *Spiritualistic Psychology*

According to Lotze, as we have seen, there is no necessity to assume that the elements, reciprocal action between which produces the phenomena presented in experience, are perfectly homogeneous. We need assume no further measure of uniformity than is pre-supposed in reciprocal action. By means of this very vague canon, Lotze is enabled to retain the popular assumption of reciprocal action between soul and body. The elements pre-supposed in the concept of mechanism are assumed by Lotze to be partly physical and partly psychical. He attacks the assumption of a continuous series of physical phenomena. At certain points physical motion is interrupted in order that it may be "absorbed," that is to say, transformed into psychical energy. It is very doubtful whether Lotze had any clear idea of the significance of the newly discovered law of the conservation of energy when (in the year 1851) he made this assertion for the first time (*Allg. Physiol.* § 424); although, it is true, subsequent enlightenment on this point did not cause him to abandon the standpoint here adopted. He had urgent reasons for assuming a special soul-substance. He recognised two alternatives only : psychical phenomena must either be derived from a soul which is a principle peculiar to them, or they must be explained through the co-operation of physical forces (see " Selbstanzeige der medizinischen Psychologie," *Kleine Schriften*, iii. p. 4). Since the latter alternative is impossible, for the reciprocal action of physical forces can never explain the unity which characterises even the simplest expression of psychical life, Lotze is obliged to accept the former. Hence the greater part of Lotze's psychological investigations were undertaken with a view to discovering the way in which the psychical and physical elements interact. His psychology here reminds us of that of Descartes (see vol. i. pp. 235-239). According to his conception, there are certain spheres within which the soul is influenced by the physical elements ; outside these, psychical events take place exclusively according to their own laws, and in turn release a mechanical force which produces new physical changes (*Kleine Schriften*, iii. p. 7). Although in the present state of nerve-physiology and psychology it seems hopeless to attempt to mark off these different stages, Lotze (especially in his *Medizin. Psychol.* and *Mikrokosmus*) confidently proceeds to a closer investigation of the matter. The significance of material events for psychical life cannot, according to Lotze's conception of the nature of reciprocal action, consist in bringing to the soul ready-made sensations or ideas ; such events can only give signals which the soul must translate into its own language ; while conversely, the inner states of the soul as such cannot be transferred to material organs ; they are only the occasion for the activity of the latter. The material organs work in the service of the higher spiritual activities by supplying and preparing the material on which the soul exercises its force ; this constitutes their entire significance. The material being given, the higher spiritual activities (memory, thought, æsthetic and moral feeling) come into play within the soul itself ; hence it is not necessary to assume special material events corresponding to them. Lotze would certainly prefer to explain such material events, not as the causes, but as the effects of psychical states, produced by the propagation of the reverberations of the latter from the soul to the brain. We have an example of this in the persistence of a state of feeling long after the original stimulus which occasioned it has ceased.

We must not stop here to discuss any special points in Lotze's psychological theories, but we may mention in passing his brilliant and original doctrine of local signs, which throws light on the development of the perception of space[121] and his assertion of the significance of feeling as a fundamental element of psychical life, in opposition to the Hegelian and Herbartian psychology. Lotze has shed new light on a great many isolated points by his subtle and brilliant conceptions, and the felicitous language in which he frequently clothes them. On the other hand, his procedure is in defiance of all sound psychological method ; for, instead of seeking for the laws according to which psychical phenomena are connected together, he assumes that when the different psychical phenomena arise, presentations (or ideas) react on the soul itself, setting feeling free, and that this latter must, in its turn, react on the soul in order to set free expressions of the will. The same may be said of his assumption of a special faculty of thought in opposition to the doctrine of the association of ideas. His spiritualistic metaphysic has here forced upon his psychology far too artificial and scholastic a method of explanation. The result is that Lotze cannot recognise psychology as an independent empirical science, but regards it as applied metaphysic (*Logik und Encyklopädie*, § 93).

If Lotze's psychology reminds us in essential points of that of Descartes, yet we must remember that this similarity only exists so long as Lotze persists in employing the popular expressions which occur so frequently in his psychology as in his philosophy of religion. The soul a thing-in-itself and the body a thing- (or group of things) in-itself—there are many utterances of Lotze which might lead one to suppose this was his teaching as it was that of Descartes, and as it still is that of popular metaphysics. But in reality Lotze regarded this doctrine as nothing more than a provisional assumption. He differs from Descartes chiefly by his doctrine of the subjectivity of extension and by his analysis of the concept of matter, which led him to the assumption that matter is nothing more than a phenomenal form of the reciprocal action between psychical elements. Thus the dualistic conception of the relation between body and soul is destroyed. The qualitative difference between the interacting elements is hereby considerably reduced : instead of reciprocal action between psychical and physical elements we now have reciprocal action between psychical elements. Moreover, it is worth noticing that Lotze does not set about this reduction because he finds any difficulty in the Cartesian or popular metaphysic. The problem of the relation between soul and body did not, properly speaking, exist for him at all ; their reciprocal action did not present any more difficulty to him than the reciprocal action between two colliding bodies.[122] On the contrary, he is guided by general philosophical considerations which would have remained valid had he constructed his psychology on the basis of Spinoza's identity-hypothesis instead of on the Cartesian dualism. Metaphysical idealism is independent of any special psychological hypothesis. But since Lotze began as a Cartesian, these considerations led him to a conception which may be described as a *monistic spiritualism*, for soul and body are regarded as two *different substances*, which are yet *alike in kind.* Herbart's theory (see above, p. 254) and one which made its appearance in the Wolffian school (see note 1 of this volume) may be regarded as the predecessors of this particular theory.

There is another, and for his philosophy a very essential point, on which Lotze parts company with Descartes (and at the same time with Leibniz and Herbart). We have seen that he regarded the particular elements of the world as moments or expressions (actions) of the original substance, which is the only reality. But, in that case, the soul can no more be substance in the stricter sense of the word than can the physical atom. The independence of finite things is only apparent. "Our monistic conception," says Lotze, "has placed the ordering of the world, the existence and capacity of every thing for doing work, *absolutely and without reserve* in the hand of the one immortal being, on whom alone the possibility of reciprocal action depends" (*Drei Bücher der Met.* § 25, cf. §§ 72-73). The terms "substance" and "being," then, when applied to the soul mean nothing more than that which possesses the faculty of working and suffering (*ib.* § 243) ; and in the end he confesses (*ib.* § 307) that it is perhaps better to avoid the use of these terms altogether, since they are apt to lead to invalid inferences. As far back as his article, "Seele und Seelenleben" (in Wagner's *Physiologischen Handwörterbuch*, 1846 ; *Kleine Schriften*, ii. p. 198), Lotze had said that the reality of every soul is constituted entirely by its significance in the world as a whole ; its immortality does not depend on its nature, but on its place in the ethical world-order. In his *Mikrokosmus* and in his chief work, *Drei Bücher der Metaphysik*, he returns to the same thought. It was no false hope of finding a scientific justification of the doctrine of the immortality of the soul which led him to develop a spiritualistic psychology ; and here again he expects no scientific answer to this question. "No principle can serve us here except the general idealistic conviction that every created thing, whose continued existence is and remains a part of the sense of the world, will continue to exist ; and that everything will pass, the reality of which can only find a place in a transitory phase of the world's history. That this principle cannot be applied by men goes without saying ; we certainly can never know by what merits one being may lay claim to everlasting existence or for what shortcomings another is denied it " (*Drei Bücher der Met.* § 245).

If we notice the harmony between Lotze's earlier (1846 and 1864) and later (1879) utterances on this point, we shall hardly be inclined to agree with some of his more recent critics [123] that in later life he modified his doctrine of the substantiality of the soul in essential points, bringing it nearer Spinozism. But it would certainly have conduced to clearness if this distinguished thinker—to whose character any unworthy compromise would have been entirely alien—had asserted his divergence from current opinions in his early writings as decidedly as he did in his later ones. The leading representative of idealistic philosophy in the latter half of our century must have influenced his age by the weight of his thought, by his wide scientific knowledge, and by his spiritual conception of life, even if his ideas had not so frequently been clothed in a pictorial form, the best justification for which is that they are symbols.

(b) *Gustav Theodor Fechner*

Fechner and Lotze may be called the Dioscuri of German philosophy in the latter half of our century. They are alike in idealistic tendency, in wide scientific knowledge, in poetic sense, and in desire for a unified conception of the world. They pursued kindred ends, although to a certain extent along different paths. Hence it is of considerable interest to compare them, and all the more because, at certain crucial points, we must choose between them. The choice will depend—since their fundamental principle is the same, *i.e.* the construction of an idealistic world-conception on a realistic basis—upon which of them does most justice to the said realistic basis. Lotze evidently recognised this as a criterion, for he says in one place that idealism can only be maintained by means of investigations instituted in the spirit of realism. If, perhaps, to Lotze must be assigned the first place for skill in working out general philosophical principles, Fechner ranks before him in logical and emphatic assertion of their scientific basis. This is all the more remarkable as, in the first instance, imagination exercised a much greater influence on Fechner's thought than was possible in the case of his critical and sober companion. Fechner—like Kepler, whom he strikingly resembles—is an interesting example of how bold and imaginative speculations may lead to positive and exact results, provided that the thinker never loses sight of his fundamental thought, and is able to divest it of its mystical swaddling bands. Just as Kepler was gradually led from mystical speculations to the discovery of the famous laws which satisfied his longing to find definite mathematical relations obtaining in the real world, so Fechner's bold analogies led him to the conviction that there is a definite quantitative relation between the mental and the material. By working out this thought more exactly he became the founder of psycho-physics or experimental psychology.

Fechner was born at Lauwitz in 1801, and, in his youth, studied medicine and physics. In 1835 he was appointed professor of physics in Leipzig where he made a name for himself by the excellent work he did in this branch of science. C. H. Weisse, the philosopher of religion, was one of his most intimate friends, and exercised great influence on his—as he had on Lotze's—conception of religion. It is doubtful, however, whether Fechner would have won such an important place in the history of philosophy were it not that in the winter of 1839-40 he contracted a disease of the eye while studying subjective light and colour-phenomena, so that after many years of suffering he had to abandon his professorship. In philosophic thought, in the free exercise of his imagination, above all in absorption in the subjective world of mind he sought consolation for the loss of the bright and multi-coloured world which he could never forget, although, owing to his weakened sight, he could only enter it occasionally.

It became the work of his life to collate the two worlds and to discover the laws of their interconnection. In contrast to the philosophy of Romanticism he started from below and proposed to work upwards, instead of working from above down. And when empirical inquiry failed him he preferred to give the rein to his imagination in bold analogies rather than spin the slender webs of abstract thought. He gave vent to his turn for paradoxes in a series of humorous

writings published under the pseudonym of Dr. Mises. His
other works fall naturally into two groups.   In one of them—
which includes *Zendavesta* (1851), *Über die Seelenfrage* (1861),
Die Drei Motive des Glaubens (1863)—he developed his semi-
poetical, semi-speculative conception of the world ; the other
comprises his epoch-making works in the sphere of natural
philosophy and psychology, *Über die physikalische und die
philosophische Atomenlehre* (1855), *Elemente der Psychophysik*
(1860), and *Vorschule der Ästhetik* (1876).   Fechner's mental
powers continued unabated up to a great age, as may be seen
from his writings.   In his eighty-sixth year he sent an interesting contribution to a discussion on his psycho-physical
theory ("Über die psychischen Massprinzipien und das
Webersche Gesetz," Wundt's *Philosophische Studien*, iv.).   He
died shortly afterwards (1887).[124]

(a) *Poetical and speculative world-conception*

In his attempts to determine a conception of the world
Fechner opposes every conception which assumes that the rich
and variegated world of consciousness can be borne by or
derived from dark, obscure things or beings.   The "matter"
of materialism, the "soul substance" of spiritualism, and Kant's
"thing-in-itself" are constant objects of his polemic.   No less
zealously does he oppose those who separate God from the
world, spirit from Nature.   He rejects the belief in a non-
natural God as energetically as the belief in a non-spiritual
matter — orthodoxy, that is to say, as well as materialism.
He criticises the current conception-of-the-world because it
involves a dualism—a separation between the infinite and the
finite.   "The infinite is related to the finite as opposed, above,
beyond, outside of,—in fact an impassable barrier is placed
between them, as though they could never approach one
another ; but they do not lie outside one another ; on the
contrary, the finite is the content of the infinite, indeed
no other relation between them can rationally be conceived
except this — that the finite is the content of the infinite.
The infinite then is not beyond our reach—we should rather
say that it can be grasped at innumerable points of the finite ;
but it can never be comprehended" (*Über die Seelenfrage*,
p. 111).

This mistaken way of looking at things, Fechner thinks, is largely responsible for another prevalent misconception, viz. that only men and brutes are animated, at least on this earth. It is thought that experience prohibits us from holding any more extended theory of animation. But I only have immediate experience of my own soul ; I can only infer the existence of other souls by way of analogy. What is to hinder me then from extending the analogy from men and animals to plants and heavenly bodies, if there are cogent reasons for so doing ? The absence of a nervous system in plants is no proof to the contrary, for the lowest species of animals have no nerves. If it be objected that the plant is not an absolute individual, we may answer that individuality is always relative, for no living thing whatever can exist in absolute isolation from its environment. The transition from the animal to the plant world is so continuous that there is no justification for assuming so great an opposition between the two kingdoms as is connoted by animate and inanimate. The consciousness of plants may be as far below that of animals as the latter is below that of men. And why should not the heavenly bodies be animated ? Men and animals are bound up with the earth, and the earth-soul may be related to the individual souls of men and animals as the earth-body is to their bodies. It is an artificial abstraction to oppose human and animal life, on the ground that they are conscious, to the life of the whole earth. Perhaps lower souls are related to higher ones as are ideas and motives to particular souls. Lastly, all souls are part of the highest, all-embracing soul, whose life and reality is manifested in the causal law ; and the causal law is the principle of all particular natural laws, of all interconnection and all order in the universe.

Like Lotze, Fechner saw in the interconnection of the world according to law the basis for a philosophy of religion. This fact, which renders the idea of God impossible or superfluous for so many, was precisely what caused Fechner and Lotze to regard it as necessary. In this universal law they found the expression of the highest unity, the Eternal and Immutable, which embraces all things. The concept of law is the ultimate concept of all our knowledge ; hence on it, according to Fechner, our highest idea must be based. (See especially his treatise, " Über das Causalgesetz," in the *Berichten der sächs. Societät der Wissenschaften,* 1849 ; cf. *Seelenfrage,* pp. 205 and f. ; *Atomenlehre,* 2nd ed. p. 125.)

The concept of the world for Fechner, then, as for Lotze, is reducible to the concept of God, and that concept of God which embraces the fullest content approaches most nearly to reality, for a narrower one can only be the result of abstraction. Further, since the life of the world is the life of God, this life cannot be contained within itself, but develops and unfolds itself with and by means of the development of the world. God's perfection does not consist in a ready-made completeness, but in unlimited progress. This doctrine (in which Fechner follows his friend Weisse, while Lotze differs in thinking that we cannot suppose time to be valid of the Deity), in Fechner's view, is a realisation of the utterances of Christianity that God, Who is a Spirit, must be worshipped in spirit and in truth, and that in Him we live and move and have our being—utterances which are generally regarded as empty words. He admits that his doctrine is certainly not Christian if we regard as essential to Christianity, "the belief in the bite of the apple in Paradise with its mystical consequences, the irretrievable condemnation of the non-elect, miracles which contradict the laws of Nature, the apartness of God from His world, all the unedifying scaffolding which theologians generally build about Christianity,—out of which, indeed, they construct it" (*Über die Seelenfrage,* 194).

(β) *Psycho-physics*

Fechner's fundamental conception early led him to the conviction that the difference between the mental and the material cannot be a difference between two beings, the one non-material, the other non-spiritual. The material world is the outer, the spiritual world the inner side of the Deity. The difference between them is phenomenal, and depends on the difference of standpoint taken by the spectator, not on difference of substance (*Zendavesta,* ii. p. 341) ; or, as he expresses it later (*Elemente der Psychophysik,* i. p. 2), the difference between the spiritual and the material is the difference between the concave and convex side of one and the same circle ; he who stands within the circle sees the concave, he who stands outside, the convex side only, while he who is able to change his standpoint perhaps thinks that he has two different things before him.   Fechner here arrives at Spinoza's identity - hypothesis, for his interest as a physician led him to assert the continuity of physical events, while his interest as a philosopher of religion caused him to conceive the Godhead, the all-embracing spiritual principle, as expressing itself at every point in material phenomena, so that the latter cannot be separated from it nor exist outside it.   Fechner had arrived, we might almost say, at a theo-physic before he began to develop his psycho-physic.

He found a confirmation of his fundamental conception in the law of the conservation of energy, and he was the first thinker to make this application of the then newly discovered law (*Elemente der Psychophysik*, i. pp. 21-45).   He admits that no proof has as yet been brought forward to show that this law holds good of those material events which are bound up with spiritual activities ; but he thinks that all experiences point in this direction, and that, until there is any evidence to the contrary, we must assume it to be valid.   Experience teaches us that the material events with which the life of consciousness is bound up stand in reciprocal connection with other material events, both within and without the body, so that the total sum of physical energy which is at our disposal is used sometimes by the former and sometimes by the latter.   Physical energy is just as much consumed when we think as when we hew wood,—this is why we cannot do both at once so well as one at a time.

The only difference between Fechner and Spinoza here is that Fechner is eager to discover a mathematical functional relation between the two sides of existence.[125]   He at first assumed that they stand in direct proportional relation to one another.   Afterwards (he has noted the date and exact circumstances of the case : " Oct. 22, 1850, in bed before getting up ") it occurred to him that the mental does not rise and sink in simple proportion to the material, but that changes in the former correspond to proportional changes in the latter, so that the change ($\delta\gamma$) in intensity of a mental state is determined by the relation between the change ($\delta\beta$) of energy in the corresponding material state and the previously existing energy (β),

(*i.e.* $\delta\gamma = K\dfrac{\delta\beta}{\beta}$).   He thus passed from the region of indefinite speculations to an assumption which could be controlled by experiment. He found this view supported by the fact that the intensity of a sensation of light does not increase as quickly as the intensity of the physical stimulus. His own experiments as well as reading provided him with the material from which he generalised the law that the increase of a sensation does not correspond directly to the increase of the physical stimulus, but to the relation between this increase and the whole previous stimulus, so that, with an equal increase of stimulus, the stronger the previous stimulus, the less the increase of sensation. Fechner called this law " Weber's law " in honour of his teacher, E. H. Weber, the physiologist to whom he was indebted for some of the most important experiments on which it is based. It is not for us to discuss the validity, limitations or interpretations of this law ; our readers must consult recent works on psychology for that. We can only observe here that the step which Fechner thus took made exact experimentation possible within the sphere of psychology ;—to use an expression of Galilei's, he made something measurable which had not been so before. By means of its relation to the external stimulus, sensation, which, in and for itself as a purely subjective element, is not measurable, becomes quantitatively determinable. The road was now opened for *experimental psychology ;* its task was to seek for points of contact between psychical events and such events as can be directly counted, weighed and measured.

The point which Fechner set out to investigate, however, is not one with which the new science can occupy itself. He attempted to discover the relation between the activities of the mind and the corresponding events in the brain. But this relation is inaccessible to us. All that we can immediately perceive is on the subjective side, the psychical state, and on the objective side the physical stimulus. Fechner's law is valid (within certain limits) of the relation between these, and it is most probable that the brain process and the psychical process are in direct proportion to one another ; this view, moreover, is most in accordance with the identity-hypothesis supported by Fechner. Psycho-physics has, to a certain extent, become rather different from Fechner's original conception of it. But this by no means diminishes the importance of his great work, *Elemente der Psychophysik.* Between mental science and natural science—in accordance with the great law of the division of labour—a new discipline has been intercalated. The seed had been sown in fruitful ground in Fechner's mind, free as it was from prejudices and rich in possibilities and ideas. The inquirer who, after Fechner, has done most within the sphere of the new science, said at Fechner's grave : " The psycho-physics which he founded was only the first conquest on a field in gaining full possession of which there can be no more insurmountable obstacles now that such a beginning has been made " (W. Wundt, " Zur Erinnerung an Gustav Theodor Fechner " ; *Philosophische Studien*, iv. p. 477). Fechner him-self wrote a number of works in defence of the psycho-physical law he had established ; they are models of truth-loving and careful discussion and of courteous polemic ; they also witness to their author's originality and humour.

Closely connected with Fechner's endeavours to found an experimental psychology is his attempt to establish a theory of æsthetic, grounded in experience. His *Vorschule der Ästhetik* (1876) is an epoch-making work, the contents of which, however, do not fall within the scope of our discussion.

(γ) *Natural Philosophy*

Fechner's antagonism to the romantic philosophy appears most clearly in his *Atomenlehre*. Speculation, he says, pounces down on Nature like a bear on a bee-hive. It enjoys the honey which it finds collected there and does not consider that it was brought together by the combined activity of a crowd of tiny creatures. Natural science and physics, as well as chemistry, teach us that material events can only be under-stood when they are conceived as the results of interaction between minute and, for us, indivisible particles. Every part of the world, however small, is conceived by natural science as a little world, having heavenly bodies and systems of heavenly bodies. What appears to us as a continuous mass is, like so many of the cloud-masses in the sky, a group of different parts. Science does not believe in absolute atoms, but holds that divisibility extends beyond the reach of eye or microscope. Its atoms are assumed to be relative only, *i.e.* indivisible by us or by the forces of Nature with which we are acquainted, for science is governed by the need of tracing every effect to a definite position in space as its starting-point. Philosophical atomism completes that which physical atomism was only called upon to work out partially. We get such a philosophical rounding-off of the scientific conception when we assume that the smaller we conceive the atoms to be, the more exact will be the results we can deduce, if we conceive matter as made up of atoms. Science adopted the conception of atoms in order to have starting-points for energy. The share which every such starting-point takes in conforming to a law of nature we call the force proceeding from this point. All that we know of atoms is that they make these contributions ; it is on this account that philosophical atomism calls them "centres of force." There is, therefore, no reason for attributing extension to atoms (to the absolute, philosophical atoms), and the concept of matter is no longer materialistic. Fechner here seems to regard philosophy as an hypothesis in which we conceive as absolute that which, as a matter of fact, is always given as relative.

The groundwork of all our knowledge of existence is the law of the interconnection of phenomena ; we must determine the forces of the co-operating elements in accordance with this law. Fechner cannot, with Leibniz, Herbart and Lotze, regard atoms as psychical elements. They are for him the ultimate points at which spiritual beings arrive when they analyse the content of their consciousness.

Fechner regarded any further explanation as superfluous. The atom is the lower limit of our knowledge as the universal world-law which witnesses to the reality of an all-embracing Being is its upper limit. All our knowing moves between these two limiting concepts (*Seelenfrage*, pp. 215, 216).

(c) *Eduard von Hartmann*

In the year 1869 appeared a book which excited great astonishment, and attained a circulation such as rarely falls to the lot of a comprehensive philosophical work. This book was Eduard von Hartmann's *Philosophie des Unbewussten* ("Philosophy of the Unconscious"). The sub-title, " Speculative results reached by the inductive method of science," shows that the author aimed at establishing and developing philosophical ideas along the lines pursued by Lotze and Fechner. Hartmann found a wide circle of readers. They were attracted not only by the clearness and breadth of his exposition, by his extensive use of scientific examples, by his combination of a realistic foreground with a romantic and mystical background, but also by the fact that his system assigned a definite place to pessimism. Owing partly to the influence of Schopenhauer's works, which were then much in vogue, partly to the predominant tendencies of the time, a strong current of pessimism had set in. How much attention Hartmann excited may be gauged by the fact that, in the course of twenty years, no less than ten editions of his chief work were published, and that between the years 1870-75 fifty-eight works dealing with his philosophy were written !

EDUARD VON HARTMANN was born at Berlin in 1842. His father was a general, and he himself entered upon a military career. His leisure time was devoted to music, painting and philosophy. An affection of the knee obliged him to quit the service in 1865 ; and after he had realised that art was not his vocation he betook himself—"bankrupt in everything except in thought "—to philosophy. He had already occupied himself in philosophising and writing essays on philosophical subjects. Now he passed on to the composition of his *Philosophie des Unbewussten*, which is still regarded as his chief work, although it was followed by nearly thirty others—some small, some large. The most important of these is, without doubt, his *Phänomenologie des sittlichen Bewusstseins* (1879), which perhaps we should not be wrong in describing as the most important of all his writings. In our description of his philosophical standpoint we must only dwell on two main features.

(a) *Natural Philosophy and Psychology*

While Lotze and Fechner had made it a principle to take as their ground-work the scientific mode of explanation, and to establish their philosophy by deducing the consequences of its assumptions and results, Hartmann's philosophy bears the stamp of a neo-romantic reaction against the realism of science. His aim is to show that the scientific mode of explanation is not sufficient, that, on the contrary, side by side with the causes assumed by the mechanical conception of Nature, we must assume a spiritual principle to be at work ; to avoid anthropomorphism he calls this principle " the

Unconscious." He appeals to it whenever the causes which empirical science is able to assign are, in his opinion, insufficient. This is what he means by " arriving at speculative results by inductive methods."

Hartmann agrees with Fechner that matter must be conceived as a system of atomic forces. It would be as absurd to talk of a single atom possessing mass as of a unit possessing magnitude. If we regard atomic force as the ultimate element which the analysis of material reality reveals to us, Hartmann says, we can only arrive at definitive interconnection and coherency by conceiving the striving of the atomic force as that of a will, where there is only an unconscious idea of the end. We can never understand force until we conceive it as a will. Matter itself, then, is idea and will — and the distinction between matter and mind disappears. In organic growth again, we find a similar expression of unconscious will and idea, for the appearance of the organism as such realises an end, with reference to which the particular materials and processes must be regarded as means only ; their nature and conjunction are only comprehensible through the end, even though this end is not an object of consciousness. Between the formation of the organism and instinctive action there is only a difference of quantity. Instinct, according to Hartmann's assertion, cannot be explained by the material organisation, nor can it depend on a nervous mechanism, implanted once and for all, for in that case it could not vary in its expressions as it does even in the same organisation. Nor is it conscious reasoning. Hence the only thing left is to conceive it as unconscious will or idea. In the human mind the Unconscious expresses itself in sensuous perception, for the intuiting of external objects takes place through the unconscious co-operation of sensations. Association between ideas could not take place were it not that without conscious search ideas are produced which are connected with the ideas before the mind. Feelings and motives are produced by unconscious happenings, and are therefore frequently incomprehensible even to ourselves. Even when will is united with consciousness, the movement willed can only be executed with the assistance of an unconscious will ; for consciousness does not know which nervous centres in the brain must be stimulated before the movement can be executed. History shows us the Unconscious causing individuals to labour in the service of great cosmic ends, while all the time they think they are only furthering their own limited ends.   What is fate or Providence but the mastery of the Unconscious over the actions of men until conscious understanding is sufficiently matured to lead the latter to adopt as their own the ends of the world-history?   It is always the Unconscious which makes the co-operation of individual beings possible.   There are individuals of every possible grade—from atoms up to the whole of Nature, and in all of them the same Unconscious is at work.   The manifold has phenomenal significance only, not metaphysical.   Hartmann declares himself agreed in principle with speculative theism (as expounded by Schelling, Weisse, Lotze and Fechner), for his "Unconscious" ought really to be called "Overconscious."   He prefers the negative form, however, in order to keep clear of anthropomorphic ideas.   Here he overlooks the fact that even if the name selected by him could exclude such ideas they receive every encouragement from his description of the manner in which the "Unconscious" works.

Hartmann's method of procedure, *i.e.* to intercalate his "Unconscious" as a magical means which works everywhere equally well whenever he thinks he detects a hiatus in the explanation given by science, can hardly itself be called scientific. We may say of it, as Galilei said of the appeal to an almighty will, it explains nothing because it explains everything.   The interest which really prompted Hartmann to this concept of the Unconscious can hardly have been the desire to understand phenomena.   It was more probably due to the need of rest and faith in the value of the spontaneous and unprepared which supervened on his reflection, analysis and criticism. Thus we find him in one place (*Philosophy of the Unconscious*, 3rd ed.) saying: "Conscious reasoning is only denying, criticising, controlling, correcting, measuring, comparing, combining, classifying, inducing the general from the particular, ordering the particular case according to the general rule, but it is never creatively productive, never inventive.   Here man is entirely dependent on the Unconscious, and were he to lose the faculty by which he receives inspiration from the Unconscious he would lose the spring of his life, without which he would drag out a monotonous existence entangled in the dry schematism of the general and particular.   Hence the Unconscious is *indispensable* to him, and woe to the age which, in one-sided overestimate of the consciously reasoned, listens to the latter only, and violently suppresses the Unconscious." Consciousness cannot be the goal of development; it can only be a necessary means at a certain stage of development (*Phil. d. Unbew.* 3rd ed. p. 739). The experience, drawn partly from psychology, partly from history, of the significance of unconscious life provides Hartmann's thought with an adequate foundation. But he soon turns the Unconscious into a mythological being, a dæmon who interferes at all points with the interconnection of Nature, directing the atoms, disposing the molecules of the brain, and adjusting relations. Hartmann's philosophy takes on a mythological and dualistic character; this, it is true, comes out most strongly in the first editions of his *Philosophie des Unbewussten*, but it is too closely bound up with his leading principles to admit of being corrected away. His attitude towards Darwinism is specially characteristic, for he attempts to show that natural selection does not explain the origin of new forms, but is only a mechanical means which "the Unconscious" employs when it wishes to prepare the way for such forms! Darwin, Hartmann thinks, got no farther than the conditions, and overlooked the true productive power.

We need not be surprised, then, that Hartmann was often exposed to attacks from scientific men. In order, therefore, to prove that he was quite capable of entering into the scientific point of view he wrote an anonymous criticism of himself, *Das Unbewusste vom Standpunkt der Physiologie und der Deszendenzlehre* (1872). This anonymous criticism was so excellent and appropriate that it called forth the praise of his opponents, and was even quoted against himself. In the second edition Hartmann revealed his identity, and added notes in which he attempted to meet the objections he had raised against himself. How far he succeeded in so doing is open to question; he had evoked spirits which were not easy to lay. He admits that he had underrated mechanical causes and had overlooked many intermediate links. But he still employs the method of seeking for the gaps left by scientific discovery and filling them up by the help of his mystical *deus ex machina*. Since there is always a possibility that these gaps themselves will some day be filled up the application of this method is excessively precarious. Lotze had applied it in his spiritualistic psychology ; Hartmann extends it to his whole philosophy, quite for- getting that Lotze had clearly and energetically asserted the significance of mechanism. Hartmann's "speculative results" were *not* obtained by "inductive methods." Indeed he admits the inadequacy of induction (*Das Unbewusste*, etc. 2nd ed. pp. 359 and f.), and limits its significance to the confirmation of that which speculation has discovered by other means.

(β) *Pessimism and Ethics*

Hartmann assures us it would be a great mistake to suppose that he is a pessimist by temperament ; he teaches pessimism merely as a theoretical point of view, although, it is true, he had been led to adopt it by the disappointments and sufferings of his youth. He tells us elsewhere ("Mein Entwicke- lungsgang," *Ges. Studien und Aufsätze*, p. 35) that he wrote himself free of his *Weltschmerz* in his chapter on pessimism in the " Philosophy of the Unconscious," when it became refined to an objective, quiet *knowledge* of the misery of existence, and he himself won back the undisturbed serenity which the philosopher enjoys who moves in an atmosphere of pure thought, from which he can regard the world and his own pain merely as an object of investigation. He also points out that pessimism does not even theoretically make up the whole of his philosophy, it does not even give it its predominant colour (" Die Stellung des Pessimismus in meinem philosophischen System," *Zur Geschichte und Begründung des Pessimismus*, 2nd edition, pp. 18-28). He considered it his work in life to combine the evolutionary philosophy with pessimism, which latter is the result at which we arrive when we take happiness as our criterion in estimating the value of the world. He undertakes, that is to say, to reconcile the philosophy of Hegel with that of Schopenhauer, just as he had already attempted, in his fundamental concept of "the Unconscious," to combine Hegel's absolute idea with Schopenhauer's absolute will. Curiously enough, Hartmann here finds a point of union with Kant. Logical consistency obliged Kant to pronounce the problem of evil insoluble, for he proceeded from the Christian concept of God, with which the reality of evil stands in irreconcilable contradiction. The question, however, should be raised as follows : how must we conceive the absolute ground of the world, which, without doing violence to itself, could posit a world such as this ? And when the question is put in this form we find that Kant has cleared the way for its discussion by intimations in a pessimistic and in an evolutionary direction. Schopenhauer followed up the former, Hegel the latter. The time has now come to unite the results arrived at by each (" Kant als Vater des modernen Pessimismus," *Zur Gesch. und Begr. des Pess.* 2nd edition, pp. 136 and f.). (Cf. above, pp. 76 and f. and note 17 of this volume.)

Since an impartial scrutiny, Hartmann argues, cannot but convince us that there is a great deal more unhappiness than happiness in the world, the existence of the world cannot be deduced from reason. It owes its existence not to a rational but to an irrational principle. The explanation of this is that the volitional element of the Unconscious sundered itself from the ideational element. Hartmann revives Böhme's and Schelling's mystical doctrine of a dark element within the Deity, the breaking loose of which led to the development of the world. In some inexplicable manner the will, which in and for itself is blind, dissevered itself from all connection with representation or idea. Nevertheless this seeing element of the Unconscious has always played a part in the development of the world, striving to reconcile and reduce to harmony the blind and refractory element. Hence the two-sided impression produced on us by the world. Pessimism and evolution are equally right. There are two principles active in the world. Hartmann's philosophy of religion reminds us, at this point, of the teaching of Voltaire, Rousseau and Stuart Mill ; only that, according to Hartmann, development is the progressive deliverance of the suffering Deity, for through the dissolution of the will it undoes that which happened when the world became a reality. Hence it is of great importance that the knowledge of the misery of life should be aroused ; for this reason Hartmann thinks that Schopenhauer may be said to have initiated a new world-period (*Phänomenologie des sittlichen Bewusstseins*, p. 782). But this knowledge springs up very slowly in the human mind and only by means of the destruction of one illusion after another. At first men expect happiness in this life. When they discover that the goods which confer happiness are only apparent, this hope is transferred to a future life. This is the second stage of illusion. But the belief in the "beyond" cannot maintain itself; confidence in the life on earth revives, but now, taught by experience, men no longer expect the immediate enjoyment of happiness, but look for a state of general blessedness for the human race in some distant future and exert all their energies to prepare the way for this future. This is the third and last stage of illusion, in which men will probably remain for a long while. But the fact that a small minority have seen through this illusion in all its forms is, for Hartmann, sufficient justification of the pessimistic theory; its validity cannot be decided by a majority-vote (*Zur Gesch. u. Begr. des Pessimismus*, pp. 174, 254).

Hartmann's ethic is closely connected with his pessimistic theory. In his opinion there is an irreconcilable conflict between civilisation and happiness. Every advance in civilisation involves a retrogression in happiness. The more complicated the machinery of life, the more room there is for unhappiness. Sensibility to pain becomes keener, and developing reflection is quicker to see through illusions. Civilisation develops wants more quickly than the means to satisfy them. Hence we must choose between culture and happiness; between the theory of evolution and the theory of happiness. Happiness presupposes rest and peace, hence it must bring with it stagnation and dissolution. Development goes on and on until all possibilities are exhausted.[126] By means of development discontent is heightened and illusions destroyed, until at length life ceases. Deliverance is then consummated, and the independence of the blind will is annulled. The highest form of ethics, according to Hartmann, is that which is not merely based on humanitarianism and the impulse towards development, but which makes sympathy with God, the desire to deliver the bound and suffering world-principle, the foundation of morality. For then the end of "the Unconscious" is adopted as our own (*Phän. des sittl. Bew.* pp. 758 and f. 860-868. *Philos. d. Unbew.* 3rd edition, p. 748).

Hartmann's philosophy is inverted theology. He makes free use of the notion of an absolute cosmic end without ever seriously facing the difficulties involved in this idea. In spite of this, however, his ethical work (*Phän. d. sittl. Bew.*)

contains many excellent discussions of particular points, *e.g.*, the characterisation and criticism of the different standpoints. And on such particular points his thought is independent of the metaphysics of pessimism. His conquest of pessimism was more complete than he has described it. In practice he is an evolutionist and an optimist.

The only right course in this present time is to ratify the will to live, for only by complete surrender to life and its pain, not through cowardly renunciation and withdrawal, can we play our part in the cosmic process (*Philos. d. Unbew.* 3rd edition, p. 748). The age of pessimism is many years hence—so many that we are doubly astonished that Hartmann can be so well informed as to what is going to happen at their expiration. Owing to this postponement to a distant future pessimism loses the personal, practical significance it had with Schopenhauer. Hartmann's position relatively to Schopenhauer's may be compared with that of modern Christians, who believe the last day to be relegated to a dim future, relatively to the belief of the early Christians, whose whole life was governed by the constant expectation of its advent. Far-off possibilities cannot determine the conduct of life, nor can they destroy its value. It is only the life we know and live of which we can estimate the worth, and it is in this life that we must discover what we are to reverence as the highest.

CHAPTER IV

CRITICISM AND POSITIVISM

(a) Friedrich Albert Lange

IT was only natural that the decay of Romanticism, the rise of natural science and the claim of materialism to be the last word of science should heighten the influence of the tendency which, during the first half of the century, had appeared only as an undercurrent. The great attention and encouragement meted out at this time to Schopenhauer's and Herbart's theories are in themselves an indication of the new state of things. It was felt that a critical revision of the foundation of human knowledge was necessary in order to determine the attitude to be adopted towards the new stores accumulated by knowledge. In Lotze and Fechner, and to a certain extent in Hartmann too, we have, it is true, attempts in this direction, but they none of them really attacked the problem of knowledge itself. All these thinkers take realism as given, and proceed, more or less consistently, to seek for a basis for their idealistic constructions either in its assumptions or in its lacunæ. Interesting though Lotze's attempt, in particular, is, yet it is a discussion of the problem of existence rather than of the problem of knowledge. One of the first to call attention to the necessity of carrying on Kant's investigation of the problem of knowledge was EDUARD ZELLER, well known for his " History of Philosophy." He wrote a short treatise, entitled *Ueber die Bedeutung und Aufgabe des Erkenntnistheorie* (1862), which excited all the more notice as its author was known to belong to the Hegelian school. A few years later, FRIEDRICH ALBERT LANGE, in his valuable work on the history of philosophy : *Geschichte des Materialismus* (" History of Materialism ") refers to the theory of knowledge as a subject which had been neglected alike by romanticists and materialists. It was from an epistemological basis that he proposed to carry on the struggle for an idealistic conception of the world.

Lange is one of the most attractive figures in the history of modern German philosophy. Enthusiasm for ideals, keen critical power, great knowledge, and a strong grasp of realism were combined in him in rare proportions. Moreover, he displayed considerable literary ability. Unfortunately his life was destined to be a short one. He was born near Solingen in 1828, but spent his early youth at Zurich, to which his father, the celebrated theologian, J. P. Lange, had received a call as professor of theology in 1846. Thus the ground-work of his intellectual development was laid in the free air of Switzerland, and the effect of this may be traced throughout his life and work. He studied at Bonn University. His chief object was to prepare himself to enter the teaching profession ; to this end he studied philology, without, however, neglecting his scientific and philosophical education. His philosophical leanings soon defined themselves. In a letter of the year 1851 (see ELLISSEN'S *Friedrich Albert Lange. Ein Lebensbeschreibung.* Leipzig, 1891. Pp. 69-73) he maintains that all the ideas we can conceive of existence (of God and the world, of good and evil, etc.) must be framed in accordance with the laws of the human mind : these laws, therefore, are the ultimate basis of all our knowledge ; farther than these we can never pass. Lange regards psychology and theory of knowledge from the same standpoint as that to which Ludwig Feuerbach had been led by his critical study of religious and speculative ideas. Lange, however, does not appear to have been influenced by Feuerbach. The philosophical works which impressed him most strongly as a youth were Hegel's *Phänomenologie*, Herbart's *Psychology*, and the works of Schleiermacher. He speaks with enthusiasm of Schleiermacher in a letter written in 1849 (Ellissen, p. 244).

After spending some years as *docent* and teacher in a *Gymnasium* Lange became an editor and social agitator. He took part in the movement against Bismarck's domestic policy ; also in the struggles of the Working Men's Association for a fixed organisation. His work entitled *Die Arbeiterfrage* dates from this time. Like Mill's *Political Economy* this is one of the first books in which the social question is treated impartially and from a general point of view. Lange's view of the matter is that there must be a struggle with the struggle for existence, and that to carry on this first struggle is the peculiar duty of man (as at this time the *Origin of Species* only had appeared, not the *Descent of Man*, Lange could not avail himself of the point of view developed by Darwin in the latter, according to which ethical endeavour itself is regarded as a struggle for existence. See above, pp. 448, 449). He considered the political significance of the labour question to lie in the fact that it exercises a continual pressure on conservative institutions, the banks of which will give way if canals are not soon dug. Free-thinking men of the upper classes now have to choose whether they will strengthen banks or assist in digging canals. Lange had no difficulty in making his own choice. In Germany, however, people occupy themselves for the most part in strengthening banks, hence Lange soon found his way back to Switzerland. In the middle of all his labours as journalist and agitator he had found time to put the last touches to his chief work : *Geschichte des Materialismus* (" History of Materialism ") which, according to Ellissen (p. 145), appeared in the autumn of 1865, although the title-page gives 1866. It is no merely historical work. By a spirited description of the chief forms of materialism and the development of the natural sciences Lange hoped to be able to shed some light on the relation between the ideal and spiritual and the material ; and he unites this theoretical question with the practical social question. Although many portions of his work are now, of course, out of date, no one can read it without being informed and stimulated. Not long afterwards Lange brought out a new work on social philosophy, entitled : *Mill's Ansichten über die soziale Frage* (1866).

While in Switzerland Lange displayed an astonishing and many-sided activity, working in Winterthur as a bookseller, a teacher, and an editor. He took part eagerly in the agitation for a reform of the constitution of the canton of Zurich. He afterwards became professor at Zurich, and was then once more able to devote himself to his studies. But he soon began to attract attention in the fatherland whither he himself longed to return. In the year 1872 he was appointed professor at Marburg. He had been suffering for some years from an internal cancer, and his last years were full of pain. His sense of the ideal and his great enthusiasm for inquiry and freedom supported him ; he drew his spiritual nourishment chiefly from Schiller's philosophical poems. He died in 1875. An un-finished but interesting work on logic (*Logische Studien*, 1877) was published after his death.

As may be gathered from the title of Lange's chief work, the problem to which he addresses himself is : What should be our attitude towards materialism ? His standpoint here is the same as that of Fechner. His idea is to conquer material-ism by pushing it to its extremest consequences. The merit of materialism, and that which, in his eyes, invests it with its greatest historical significance, is the consistency with which it demands that all natural phenomena be traced back to material causes. Idealism, on the other hand, as Lange points out, imports a great danger into the theoretical sphere, for it tends to relax the demand for a strict mechanical explanation, and interpolates subjectively constructed links in the chain of objective causes. The functions of the nervous system as well as those of the brain must be explained according to general physical and chemical laws. According to Lange, who bases his argument on the law of the conservation of matter and energy, external influences operate by means of the sense-organs, the centripetal nerves, the brain, the centrifugal nerves and the muscles ; and the entire process must constitute a self-dependent and unbroken interconnection. It is unreasonable to assume that this interconnection is interrupted at any point. Consciousness itself is not a member of this interconnection ; it is the subjective state of the individual in which the process takes place,—it is another *side* of the process, not a *part* of it. Here, then, we reach the limits of materialism. Precisely because states of consciousness are not members or parts of the material process, are not explicable by the law of the con-servation of matter and of energy, they must lie outside the sphere of materialism, and materialism only falls into contradic-tion with itself when it claims to explain everything. It can at most explain the objective, material process which is the way in which the subjective state of the conscious individual appears to external observation. Lange thinks it not im-possible that some day we shall be able to determine those parts of the material process which correspond in time to a

certain state of consciousness in the individual ; but he entertains no hope of our ever being able to arrive at a nearer determination of the relation between the subjective state of consciousness and the objective nervous process (*Gesch. d. Met.* 1st
edition, p. 456 ; 2nd edition, ii. pp. 374 and f.). It is a justifiable assumption that behind the two corresponding worlds—the
world of matter and the world of consciousness—there is an
unknown third, which is their common cause (2nd edition, ii.
p. 166).

It is interesting to note how, after the victorious advance
of science, the great hypotheses of the seventeenth century
reappear in the middle of the nineteenth.   As Vogt, Moleschott and Büchner had revived the standpoint of Hobbes,
so Lotze revived that of Descartes, and Fechner and Lange
that of Spinoza.   This testifies to the fact that these hypotheses present the alternatives between which our thought
under present conditions has to choose.   A closer scrutiny will
show us that it is no mere resumption but rather a renewal of
the older hypotheses which we have here before us.   Not only
the scientific ground-work, but also the philosophical form is
other than with the great dogmatists of the seventeenth century.
We find greater critical acumen, and a clearer consciousness of
the fact that in a discussion which is hardly capable of resolution the task of the philosopher is to discover the best and
most logical points of view, rather than to construct definitive
systems.   Critical philosophy, which blossomed between these
two epochs, had not done its work in vain.

Lange's standpoint, while on one side it takes us back to
Spinoza, on the other looks back to Kant.   For he does not
regard the double form of existence—motion and consciousness
—as ultimate, but points out that the external world as well
as our own organism, including under the latter the brain and
sense organs, only exist for our consciousness ; they are, in
fact, a product of consciousness.   It is owing to the nature of
our organisation that we conceive the world as we do conceive
it.   Kant pointed this out, and the physiology of the senses
has since confirmed it.   Here again, then, to carry out materialism consistently is to pass beyond it.   For even if we concede
to it that our whole world-conception is a product of our
material organisation, this material organisation itself is only
an object of consciousness ; it exists immediately only in and

for consciousness.　Matter and organisation are ideas, even if
they are ideas which we construct necessarily and according to
definite laws.　The struggle between matter and spirit, then,
ends in favour of the latter.　The naïve belief in matter must disappear before a more exact investigation ; and its disappearance
does not in the least affect the triumphal progress of scientific
inquiry (1st edition, pp. 496-499 ; 2nd edition, ii. pp. 175, 411).

In the manner in which Lange here envisages materialism
he is preceded by Schopenhauer (see above, p. 246).　Almost
contemporaneously with Lange, ROKITANSKY, the famous
Viennese pathologist, brought forward a similar theory.[127]

In Lange's exposition of the history of materialism there is
a certain indecision with regard to the question as to how far subjectivism is to be extended.[128]　Sometimes he speaks as though
the opposition between the thing-in-itself and the phenomenon
were a product of our organisation, hence we cannot know if this
opposition has any significance beyond the sphere of our
experience.　In other places (especially in the 2nd edition) he
speaks of an order of things corresponding to our knowledge.
In a letter to Dohrn, the scientist (see Ellissen, pp. 258-262)
Lange explains that there are four different stages to be taken
into consideration here : (1) naïve faith in sensuous appearance ;
(2) the knowledge that the senses do not give us things as they
exist in and for themselves, but vibrations of air for sounds,
vibrations of ether for colours, etc.—this is the standpoint of
natural science ; (3) the knowledge that our understanding no
less than our senses is part of our organisation, and that consequently not even sensuous perception, as corrected by science,
can show us the thing-in-itself—this is Kant's standpoint ;
(4) the knowledge that the opposition between the thing-in-
itself and phenomenon is itself a product of our organisation,
hence its validity is open to question.　This fundamental doubt,
however, Lange thinks, cannot be urged against knowledge
itself.　It indicates the limits of science beyond which imagination only, not thought, can pass.　Lange blames Kant for
having remained in the third stage ; he blames Kant's romantic
successors because " they have for the most part passed beyond
the fourth stage and plunged into the realm of imagination ;
hence their systems present a blending of criticism and poetry,
while these ought to have been ranged side by side, within
clearly defined limits."

In this exposition Lange overlooks the fact that if our knowledge applies the same principles at its limits as those which it employs within its borders, it must necessarily retain the opposition between subject and object, knowledge and thing ; for if not we shall be obliged to assume, under one form or another, a creation out of nothing. For all our knowledge is subject to the law that everything which we understand can only be understood by the help of *several* premisses or conditions.[129] If this law is not recognised we become involved in the difficulties which, from the days of Nicolaus Cusanus (see vol. i. pp. 85 and f.) onward have constantly recurred in the history of thought.

Like Schopenhauer, Lange hopes to unseat materialism by means of idealism (in the sense of subjectivism). But he also champions idealism in the practical sense of the word. He is not content with asserting the subjective character of reality ; for by so doing reality remains what it is, bad or good. He maintains that the need of explaining and conceiving reality in accordance with scientific law is not more deeply rooted in human nature than the need of constructing ideal pictures and regarding them as expressions of the highest reality. The productive force which expresses itself in sensation and thinking is not content with the given but reaches out beyond it to form an ideal world. Man yearns for a completion of reality. All religions and all speculative systems are products of this need. They differ from the scientific picture of reality in that they are not constructed by the organisation which is common to all men, but by individual and personal tendencies and needs, and they do not admit of a complete empirical confirmation. It is very important to recognise this distinction, so that we may not take for literal truth what in reality is only a symbol.

The religious and speculative ideas must not be supposed to have significance for the knowledge of reality. On the other hand, they must be distinguished from mere fancies. Although in some places Lange makes poetry begin where knowledge ends, in other passages (see 1st edition, pp. 539, 541 ; 2nd edition, ii. p. 540) speculation is assigned a place between empirical science and poetry ; in the former matter, in the latter form predominates ; speculation seeks to combine the two. He draws a clearer distinction when he says the worth of an idea must be estimated according to its value for the development of our spiritual life, not according to its origin or the basis on which it rests (1st edition, pp. 346 and f. ; 2nd edition, ii. p. 595). Cologne Cathedral is something very different from and vastly more than a heap of stones! Lange even says that practical idealism may be united with the unknown truth, though not of course in the way in which materialism unites them : the idea is the picture and symbol of an unknowable absolute! (1st edition, pp. 346, 539, 541, 545 ; 2nd edition, ii. pp. 594 and f.).

We see here once more how difficult it is to abide by the notion of an absolute limit. Lange here becomes a Platonist in spite of himself. How does he know that the ideas which express that which is the most valuable for us are pictures or symbols? And on the other hand, if his sharp distinction between ideas and scientific knowledge is maintained, who will care to work at the development of ideas which have no sort of real significance. The significance of speculative ideas can only be maintained when they are regarded as hypotheses, in which human thought sums up the ultimate consequences of that which at any given time is regarded as certain. A closer scrutiny must then decide what theoretical and practical significance they may possess ; but we shall scarcely find practical significance when all theoretical significance is lacking. As regards this practical significance itself, Lange gives us no definite criterion, no measure. In his sketch of his conception of ethics (1st edition, p. 536) he says natural sympathy, which Auguste Comte takes as the basis of his ethics, does not suffice for an idealistic system ; he regards the idea of a totality of which we form a part as the *a priori* ground-work of ethics ; it is only through it that we can understand the inexorable stringency of the moral law. But directly after saying this he becomes doubtful : does not the idea often lead to error? and are we not driven, especially when we look at the systems of positive religion, to ask if it would not be better to rely simply on the ennobling effects of natural sympathy rather than to listen to prophetic voices, which have only too often incited men to terrible fanaticism?

Lange has not entered upon any closer investigation into the relation between formalism and realism in ethics. In his ethical ideas he was a pupil of Kant, or rather of Schiller, although he perceived the limitations of their conception.

Lange applies his doctrine of the symbolic character and practical value of the religious ideas not only to philosophical speculation but also to positive religions.   When materialism attacks Christianity for its implicit faith it overlooks, according to Lange, the possibility of a freer ideal conception of the content of orthodox tradition.   We must look at the value rather than at the literal form of ideas.   In a certain sense the ideas of religion are eternal.   Who can refute a mass of Palestrina's ? or demonstrate that Raphael's " Madonna " is an error ?   In the hidden spiritual life of the really pious soul there stirs something which the idealistic freethinker understands and with which he cannot but sympathise.   Lange wanted an interpretation of religious teaching in the spirit of Kant, Fichte and Schleiermacher, in which the ethico-ideal kernel of Christianity would be shelled from the husk of literalism ; Hegel's philosophy of religion, on the other hand, was too conservative for him.   He refrained from making any direct attack on positive religion lest he should thereby impair the unity of the nation and the power of the spiritual life.   If he must choose between the two, he would prefer a temporary sacrifice of enlightenment —as long as freedom of teaching is secured and the dominion of the priests arrested—to an impairing of this power.   His mind was open to the great oppositions presented by our age, and he expected philosophy to contribute towards the mitigation of the struggle a more penetrative understanding of Nature and of the laws of human development.   He closes his work with the expression of a hope that honest labour in this direction will not be without result.

The great interest in Kant's philosophy which Lange's work partly witnessed to, partly excited, stimulated the diligent study of the great philosopher whom the Romanticists believed themselves to have conquered.   A divergence of opinion arose on several points as to how Kant was to be interpreted.   This gave rise to a Kant literature, the outcome of which has been that his work, methods and place in the history of philosophy are in many respects more clearly understood than was previously the case.   Even though these investigations often turned on philological rather than philosophical considerations, yet this better understanding is of great importance.   We owe it chiefly to the labours of COHEN, FR. PAULSEN, LAAS and VAIHINGER.   B. ERDMANN'S and

R. REICKE'S researches among Kant's unpublished notes and letters have also thrown much light on the course of his development.

In a brilliant treatise entitled "Was uns Kant sein kann" (*Vierteljahrsschr. für wissensch. Philos.* 1881) Friedrich Paulsen has sought to determine the significance of Kant for our time. It consists not so much in the revival of his doctrines as in the spirit in which problems are treated. The so-called *Neo-Kantism*, then, does not denote a particular school, but the attempt to subject the concepts with which we operate to an epistemological examination. The sharp opposition to the romantic philosophy which the study of Kant induced made many converts to positivism.

(*b*) *Eugen Dühring*

The year after the publication of Lange's *History of Materialism*, appeared one of the most admirable epistemological works of the last half of the century, namely EUGEN DÜHRING'S *Natürliche Dialektik*. It adopts the standpoint of the critical philosophy, inasmuch as it proposes to subject to a still closer scrutiny the Kantian problem which had been submerged in the "deluge" of romanticism. Among recent German works Trendelenburg's *Logische Untersuchungen* is the only one dealing with the subject which is mentioned with warm approval; amongst foreign thinkers Comte and Stuart Mill are cited, although they did not specially investigate this subject. The book is already a literary rarity, for the author never published a second edition, perhaps because he afterwards modified his standpoint in a positive direction. And yet it is without doubt the best of all Dühring's works, both in form and matter. It is very interesting, too, for the light that it sheds on the relation between critical philosophy and positivism: two tendencies which struggle with one another not only in Dühring but also in all the philosophy of recent times. As far back as this Dühring approaches positivism very closely in two of his fundamental thoughts. He asserts, even more emphatically than Kant and Schopenhauer had done, that the law of ground (the principle of sufficient reason) is a law of our thought only, not a law of reality, which includes more than our thought. His second principle is that of *insufficient* ground ; according to which the burden of proof lies with him who brings forward a new statement ; for that which is already given must be regarded as established so long as no reason can be adduced why it should be abandoned. With the first of these principles Dühring turns his back on rationalistic dogmatism, with the second on idealism and dualism ; by means of both together he gets so far as to be able to build on the soil of reality without any intermixture of ideas derived from other sources. He continued Ludwig Feuerbach's work, and is the most celebrated representative of positivism in Germany. He himself calls his philosophy the philosophy of reality. The great fundamental features of reality which we learn to know in experience must form the basis both of our conception and our conduct of life. Philosophy is for Dühring no mere theory, but an expression of personal conviction.

According to Dühring, our century is reactionary in its tendencies—except within the technical sphere. He looks back to the seventeenth century as the Augustan age of science. It was in this century that true science had its birth, and no achievement of the present century can compare with this. Dühring is here thinking particularly of Galilei, Huyghens and Newton in natural science ; and Bruno, Hobbes and Spinoza in philosophy. We are still living on the great ideas they gave us. It is characteristic of Dühring to regard these great, powerful and fertilising fundamental notions as of far more significance than their special elaboration or empirical confirmation. This follows naturally, perhaps, from his historical outlook and his appreciation of genius ; but it blinded his eyes to the significance of the confirmation of these great ideas by particular experiences, a significance which a positivist should be the last to misunderstand. This tendency of Dühring's which was no doubt fostered by his blindness, and the consequent inability to keep himself in touch with what was going on, grew stronger as he developed, and had unhappy effects not only on his philosophy but also on his external circumstances.

While he eulogises the seventeenth century as the age of great thoughts, he praises the eighteenth century for having applied these thoughts in working out reforms. Since his own age appeared to him so miserable he turned with all the greater hope to the future. He felt himself called to foretell a movement in thought and life which could only find acceptance in the far future. The great energy and fulness of his thought is combined with the self-assurance of a reformer—but unfortunately also with a bitterness and a suspicion which his circumstances conspired to promote but which make a great part of his later writings, containing harsh attacks on those whom he calls his " enemies," very unedifying reading. His writings bear a strongly-marked personal stamp, both in the good and bad senses of the word. He has himself described his life and personality in a remarkable book, entitled, *Sache, Leben, und Feinde. Als Hauptwerk und Schlüssel zu seinen sämmtlichen Schriften* (Karlsruhe und Leipzig, 1882) (" My Cause, my Life, and my Enemies, being my Chief Work and the Key to all the Rest "). He is right in thus closely associating his cause and his life ; he was less right, perhaps, in thinking that his enemies were as intimately bound up with these as his title suggests.

EUGEN DÜHRING was born at Berlin in 1833. His family was of Swedish extraction, of which he was very proud. His father, who was imbued with the spirit of Rousseau, brought him up in an atmosphere of free religious thought. This education fostered independence and steadfastness of thought. Early in life he became greatly interested in mathematics and astronomy. After the death of his father he entered a *Gymnasium* (high school) which was also a boarding-school, but neither the intellectual nor bodily food there provided was suited to his needs. Afterwards he studied law and practised for some time as a lawyer. A disease of the eyes, terminating in blindness, cut him off from this sphere of work and was the occasion of his resolve to employ his stores of knowledge and ideas as a writer on scientific subjects. First his wife, afterwards his son, acted as his secretary. A number of works on philosophy, political economy, and the history of science prove that it was not in vain that this energetic inquirer put his trust in his inner resources when he was denied access to outer ones. Among his philosophical works, besides those already quoted, we may mention *Der Wert des Lebens* (1865), *Kursus der Philosophie* (1875, new edition 1895, under the title, *Wirklichheitsphilosophie*), *Logik und Wissenschaftstheorie* (1878), *Der Ersatz der Religion durch Vollkommneres* (1883), He worked with great success as a *privat-docent* at Berlin

University, his lectures being among the best attended there. His anger was great when, owing to the creation of professorships, he was placed in the background, and his criticism of the conduct of University affairs brought him into sharp conflict with influential circles. His indignation found vent chiefly in a series of violent attacks on Helmholtz. He charged this celebrated physicist with having taken to himself the honour of the discovery of the law of the conservation of energy which belonged by right to Robert Mayer. Dühring regarded Mayer as the Galilei of the nineteenth century. At the request of the philosophical faculty the authorities punished Dühring by depriving him of the right to lecture. There seems no doubt, from all the evidence available, that this was an unfair and harsh treatment of the blind philosopher, although his polemic was certainly unjustifiable both in manner and substance. That Dühring should have brought such an accusation against Helmholtz can only be explained by the fact that his blindness rendered current literature inaccessible to him ; for, as a matter of fact, directly Helmholtz discovered that Mayer had preceded him he lost no opportunity of attributing to him the honour which was his due. But Dühring was also influenced by his tendency, on which we have already commented, to overestimate the value of ideas in the form in which they first appear in comparison with that of their exact determination. The same spirit which caused him to rank the seventeenth century so far above the nineteenth caused him to place Robert Mayer so far above his rivals. A third co-operating element was his suspicious habit of mind, which was no doubt increased by the isolation which his blindness brought upon him and which led him to find "enemies" everywhere. After the professors, the social democrats and the Jews were his "enemies," —"opponents" in the cause of truth and apart from personal motives he declared himself to have never encountered (*Sache, Leben, und Feinde*, chap. 14). He is so firmly convinced that the powers of good are ranged on his side that he says at the conclusion of his autobiography, " At any rate my enemies have always been among those who are enemies of all that is best in human nature ! "

After devoting several years to free lectures, Dühring retired to a small town, not far from Berlin, where he occupies himself in writing on natural science and the history of

literature.   A great and noble power is thus, through misfortune
and through his own and other's faults, if not broken, at any
rate very seriously crippled.

(a) *Theory of Knowledge*

Dühring's inquiry into the nature of knowledge (*i.e.* in the
" Natural Dialectic) is conducted entirely in the spirit of the
critical philosophy.   He seeks to determine the characteristic,
both in form and method of procedure, which is peculiar to our
knowledge, in order that he may be able to decide how far we
may regard the forms and results of knowledge as expressions
of actual existence.   He sets out, that is to say, on a critical
examination of the relation between thought and reality.

It is a chief point with him that thought always seeks for
continuous interconnection, and always strives to advance.
Thus in mathematics we get the idea of infinity, since no limit
can be set to the increase or decrease of a magnitude.   In
logic, in virtue of the principle of sufficient ground, we come
upon an infinite series in which one *why?* does but give
place to another.   Dühring contrasts this law of continuous
interconnection and uninterrupted continuance with the principle
which he calls *the law of definite number*.   Every *real* datum,
every *actual* result is limited, and exhibits a definite number of
temporal and spatial facts.   Infinity and illimitability only
indicate the *possibility* of further advance—a possibility which
is certainly not always justified in reality.   Moreover, when
continuance is *really* present, it takes place by means of the
gradual addition of particular and definite elements.   Here
then, we have discovered, according to Dühring, a characteristic
difference between thought and reality.

Thought must be supple and untiring if it is to follow
reality in all its oscillations, if it is to rise and sink with
phenomena and discover all their interdependent relations.
But the law which it must obey in order to perform its
task adequately must not, as Dühring repeatedly asserts, be
supposed to hold good of Nature, of real existence.   A comparison between the real and formal sciences will show this
most clearly.   In astronomy we find definite given magnitudes
in antithesis to the unlimited generative power of pure mathematics.   In chemistry atomic numbers are examples of the law

of definite number. But all really given numbers and magnitudes are finite ; there is a definite number of heavenly bodies in the firmament, a definite number of atoms in matter ; in every moment a perfectly definite number of time-particles passes ; the earth has moved round the sun a certain definite number of times ; the causal series consists of a definite number of links.

Dühring is very resolute in deducing from the law of definite number the inference that the process of Nature, the sum - total of all the changes of Nature, must have had a beginning. An infinite regress is unthinkable. Hence the time which is filled with change must have been preceded by an eternal being, in which the distinctions, the inner differences, the series of which constitutes succession and change, had not arisen. Existence was then absolutely identical with itself. Time and the causal series had their origin at the transition from this uniform and unchanging state to the development of differentiation and change. This far-distant close of the causal series in an unchangeable state satisfied Dühring not only from the standpoint of thought, but also from that of feeling.

But Dühring has emphasised the antithesis between the ideal continuity of thought and the divisions and fragmentariness which characterise given empirical reality so strongly that he ends with an insoluble riddle. For how is a transition from absolute identity and homogeneity to difference and change possible ? His positivistic thought has brought him face to face with the very problem which Böhme and Schelling had raised in a mythological and speculative form (see vol. i. pp. 73-77, vol. ii. pp. 169-173). He tries to soften the paradox by pointing out that every time our experience shows us a new phenomenon or a new quality, we have an absolute beginning (*Kursus*, p. 79 ; *Logik*, p. 191). But there is a great difference here : for the new and that which has a beginning in experience arouses astonishment and presents a problem to thought which sets it in motion, while Dühring's sharp distinction between absolute identity and change makes the work of thought altogether hopeless. What Dühring really affirms here is no mere *difference* but a *conflict* between thought and reality. If we have the choice between the assumption of such a conflict and the assumption that existence, like thought, can never find a close, the latter alternative seems to deserve our preference.

There is a constant interplay of thought and reality. In the onward march of inquiry new continuity is discovered underlying seeming discontinuity ; to that extent, therefore, reality confirms the ideal of thought. On the other hand, however, fresh discontinuity is often discovered when the given had been thought to exhibit continuity and the problem as to how far reality is comprehensible lifts its head once more. Dühring's great eagerness in championing the rights of reality led the dogmatist in him to overpower the critical philosopher.

On the other hand, Dühring lays great weight on the inner connection between thought and reality. Existence continues itself in our thought when the latter unfolds according to its true nature. The relation between cause and effect in real events corresponds to the relation between premisses and conclusion (reason and consequent). Corresponding to the logical principle of identity is the identity of each particular thing with itself, although occurring in different contexts ; while the unity of Nature and the interplay of forces at the inception of phenomena correspond to the combinations and deductions of our thought. We are not here conceiving Nature in analogy with human consciousness, but as active in such a manner that human knowledge finds on investigation that it has to deal with a material of like nature with itself. And even if our analysis can never exhaust the great interconnection of Nature we are none the less constrained to assert the kinship between that which works in things and that which works in understanding.

That which we formulate in our scientific principles has been produced, according to Dühring, by forces working for a long time in a definite direction before they arrived at clear consciousness. Consciousness and thought rest on a something which is no more consciousness and thought than moving mechanical force is a phenomenon of motion. Hence we are justified in supposing that the underlying ground of consciousness, which does not appear in thought, agrees with the ground which makes the interconnection of Nature appear as though ordered according to the understanding (*Nat. Dial.* pp. 155, 225 ; *Logic*, p. 173 ; *Cause, Life, etc.* p. 303). That which moves us to think, then, is the same as that which moves Nature to work.

This line of thought gradually acquired such ascendency with Dühring that his later writings contain a violent polemic against the critical philosophy for asserting that we do not know the thing-in-itself because our knowledge is determined not only by the nature of things but also by our own nature. He attacks this conception as a stultification of science, as a hypocritical adaptation of the results arrived at by thought to the demands made in the interest of " another world." Here again, Dühring says, the law of definite number is the underlying principle. The concept of number is itself an example that we have at our command concepts which express the existing in such wise that there is no room for any interpolation conditioned by the nature of the ego between reality and the concept (*Logic*, p. 165).

Dühring, who elsewhere emphatically asserts the opposition between thought and being here, no less emphatically asserts the possibility of their perfect congruity. In the first case he is thinking of formal, in the second of real knowledge. It is not possible, however, we may here take occasion to remark, to maintain a complete separation between the two ; this may be learnt from the law of definite number itself which stimulates to fresh inquiries ; as for instance, how it comes about that changes occur precisely when these definite numbers are reached.

Nevertheless Dühring deserves the gratitude of the modern theory of knowledge for having shed so much light on the problem of the relation between quality and continuity, between definite turning-points and interconnected events. His whole standpoint is determined by the struggle between criticism and positivism, and challenges to a closer investigation of the relation between these two tendencies.

(β) *World-conception*

Dühring lays great weight on the importance of developing a *world-schematism*, which shall give a complete picture of the general features of real existence. To do this is the task of the philosophy of reality. This philosophy will systematise experience ; while previous metaphysic has been a kind of alchemy, which attempted to supply a mystical determination of the nature of existence.—At this point Dühring reminds us of Comte and Spencer. In his schematism, however, he shows himself more abstract than Spencer and less original than Comte.

His system, he says, recognises, not two realities, but one only, *i.e.* Nature and its parts. He comes very near materialism when he maintains that everything in the world has a material side, and that by tracing material phenomena in their perceptible interconnection we shall find all that possesses reality. But he goes further than mere phenomena, and in so doing he diverges from " the ordinary, truly crude materialism." It is true that he often uses the word *matter* in the sense of *being, world-medium, the bearer of all reality.* But he expressly affirms that the concept of matter must be so widened and deepened as to make it clear how the occasions for phenomena of consciousness as well as the possibility of all other natural phenomena arises. *The philosophical concept of matter* contains more than the concept of matter entertained by physicists and chemists, for it is no less than the concept of that which underlies all bodily and mental states, and which embraces the whole and complete reality (*Kursus*, pp. 62, 75; "Life, Subject," etc., pp. 302 and f.) Materialism is for Dühring nothing but a " pedestal," an exact foundation, an external mechanical frame for the conception of the world and of life ; not an exhaustive and full explanation of existence itself.

A doctrine which one would hardly expect to find in Dühring is that of the assumption of *ends* in Nature. If we are to understand him rightly on this point, we must remember that he distinguishes between "end" and "intention." If he attributes validity to the concept of end in our conception of Nature, he does so because the forms and dispositions active in Nature always exhibit certain tendencies, always work in certain directions, and above all things, because they work together and thus exhibit Nature to us as a systematic unity. These tendencies do not always lead to finished results, either in external Nature or in the life of human consciousness. But whether the end be attained or not the *combined working of manifold elements* is the chief characteristic of all events. In forming our conception of Nature, Dühring says, we must take into consideration not only general laws but also the directions and tendencies exhibited in actual events as well as the types and forms in which the activity of Nature exhibits itself. Nature consists of a graduated series, for the lower forms of existence are the foundation of the higher. The criterion by means of which we can distinguish between lower and higher forms can only be found in the results of the different tendencies, in the degree to which they are capable of attaining their natural end.   And the ultimate end must be the production of beings who not only exist and work but who are conscious that they exist and work ; only as the basis of the history of conscious beings has the history of mechanical Nature significance.   A world devoid of all consciousness would be a foolish incompleteness, a theatre without players or audience (*Kursus*, p. 104).   On the other hand, that conscious phenomena must be regarded essentially as the end is, according to Dühring, apparent from the fact that conscious and unconscious working can perform one and the same thing : it would be a mere luxury for men and animals to be conscious of their impulses and motives if it was merely a question of the attainment of external aims, and if we did not here find ourselves confronted with a something which in and for itself is an end (*Kursus*, pp. 158 and f.).

If in answer to this it be objected that conscious life is not always bound up with pleasure and that pain fills so large a place that it seems as though consciousness could not really be the end, Dühring would quote in answer a law which he calls *the law of difference*, which, under different forms and titles, plays a great part in modern psychology.   For Dühring it is not only a law of consciousness but a law of the universe. The antagonism between forces is one of the leading features of his world-schematism.   All expression of force, all motion and all development is conditioned by contrast, difference, opposition.   Moreover, all consciousness presupposes difference. Without difference no sensation.   In thought the same holds good.   The game of life would lose all its charm were there no resistance and no hindrances to overcome, and did not desire and satisfaction alternate with one another.   It is the rhythms and differences of existence which make it valuable to us ; our vital feeling is set in motion by the transition between opposite conditions.   Without harshness, bitterness and painfulness, we should never experience deep satisfaction in life. The emphasising of the circumstance that feeling is determined by opposites which made Schopenhauer a pessimist makes Dühring an optimist.   Schopenhauer is more consistent than Dühring in his treatment of the law of difference, for he assumes that unrest and motion lie in the nature of the world-ground, as a natural tendency ; while Dühring's philosophy can never hope to show how it was possible that successive differences and rhythmically changing states could supervene on that condition of perfect rest which he assumes in virtue of the law of definite number.

It is only by *combination* of the different forces that development becomes possible. Whether this combination result in a state of equilibrium or a new motion the tendencies of each particular force are preserved in the result developed. An unceasing conflict of forces would be an absurdity—and Nature shows us no such conflict. To avoid the absurd is a principle at once natural and logical. Only very exceptionally does this principle lead to the destruction and disappearance of untenable forms. Generally speaking Nature takes the positive route. Hence in Dühring's view the conception of the struggle for existence is a false one ; it brings forward the negative point of view only, and emphasises antagonism instead of combination. Dühring prefers Lamarck's theory to Darwin's.

(γ) *Ethics*

The ethical, according to Dühring, has its sole foundation in human impulses. But only its foundation—for Nature can err, and therefore a further development and correction is necessary. The higher the being, the greater the possibility that it will err. Moreover, it is for ethics to combine such elements as are not yet combined by the hand of Nature, or which even conflict with one another.

Like Comte, Dühring finds the foundations of the good in the sympathetic instincts. Nature herself has taken care that the suffering of others should affect our own feeling painfully, and perhaps no other feeling has developed so conspicuously as sympathy with the progress of culture. It does not lead to the subjection or annulling of our own individuality. On the contrary, ethical development consists in an individualisation as well as a socialisation : the two are necessarily combined, for the perfect development of the particular individual is only possible in a highly developed society. Under imperfect social conditions the free and characteristic development of individuals is impeded. Since existing States are essentially the product of force they are a constant check to this development. Only in a free society, originating in the free union of already formed organisations, can individualism and collectivism both flourish. In such a society the conditions of production and consumption will be under the guidance of the State, so that the whole interest of individuals can be concentrated on their work instead of on what it brings in. By this means alone can the whole of life be ennobled. Dühring's conception differs from socialism, for he does not consider it necessary to interrupt development by an historical miracle : the structures of the future will not arise, as Karl Marx thinks, through the increase of evil but through the hidden growth of the good. On this point, too, Dühring is distinctly optimistic, in spite of the fact that he believes himself to have discovered so much baseness in the world. He is a steadfast opponent of pessimism. He only countenances the *Entrüstungspessimismus* (pessimism of indignation), as represented by Byron and evoked by certain social conditions ; he despises the romantic *Jenseitigkeits-pessimismus* (other-world pessimism), while for the *Fäulniss-pessimismus* (pessimism of degeneration) so common amongst the upper classes he has nothing but contempt.

The consciousness of the good forces, which are gradually gaining the ascendency in human nature, develops into a *universal affect ;*—then we catch sight of the great unity of which the human world is but a single branch, then the thinker feels himself a part of this unity and moved by its forces, then the thought of our own fate is lost in the thought of the great order of things in which so many dispositions for good have found room to develop.

Dühring's philosophy may be described as one of the most interesting speculative attempts of our day, not only because of the problems it raises but also of the noble antique style in which it is written, and of the close connection between the thought and the personality of the thinker.

In planning this exposition of the history of philosophy, the year 1880 was taken as the ultimate limit of time. Only what was already complete and open to investigation before this date falls within the scope of the present work. Moreover, this year marks a distinct turning-point. Lotze and Fechner have practically concluded their labours, Darwin and Spencer likewise. The philosophical world begins to assume a new aspect. Firstly, intercourse between the different countries of Europe is very much on the increase. Philosophical journals appear in the capitals of Europe and the United States of America which serve as centres and intermediaries of reciprocal influences. Separate schools and tendencies are merging into one another, and we have, in their stead, a general discussion of philosophical questions. Secondly, the principle of the division of labour has been carried much farther than ever before in the history of philosophy. The experimental psychology founded by Fechner is attracting a great many of the best men and is fast becoming a separate science. Ethics and the theory of knowledge display a tendency to develop apart from that intimate connection with other philosophical disciplines which was universal in previous ages. These two features combined —*i.e.* the co-operation of different tendencies and the isolation of different branches—invest the period which has elapsed since 1880 with a character peculiar to itself. They also make it exceedingly difficult to give an historical exposition of the work achieved by thought during these years, while the fact that we are still in the middle of the discussion would, of course, render any such attempt altogether premature.

Although, as we have said, the year 1880 forms a natural halting-place, yet it is often difficult to decide whether the centre of gravity of an author's activity lies before or after this point. Thus, for example, in the preceding exposition no account has been given of Wundt's works, influential as they have been both with regard to particular disciplines and to systematic philosophy. This may excite surprise, since his *Physiologische Psychologie*, which may safely be quoted as his *magnum opus*, appeared in 1874. Wundt's works, however— both in virtue of their attempt to unite the results of English and German inquiry and of their tendency to specialism— present the leading characteristics of the coming period, to which they form an introduction ; the work of analysing and characterising them, therefore, must be left to the historians of that period. And the same holds good of many other works in the philosophical literature of different countries. With such recent works the historian is deprived of the help which he obtains when dealing with earlier periods, where the biography and course of development of the thinker lies open and complete before him. Only when this help is obtainable can the historian of philosophy impart real information with regard either to the history of civilisation or of science. Whatever fate may be in store for philosophy, her history can hardly fail to present a twofold interest ; for philosophical ideas are symptoms of the direction in which the spiritual development of the age is tending, and they are attempts to solve the great problems which have their root in the theoretical and practical relations in which man stands to the Universe of which he is a part. To this twofold interest the present work has endeavoured to do justice.

NOTES

NOTES

NOTES

1. p. 6. We will touch on one point here for which there is no appropriate place in the text. Wolff had transformed the Spinoza-Leibnizian identity-hypothesis into an external theory of parallelism to which the term "Duplizismus" might very appropriately be applied. This theory was particularly offensive to his theological opponents ; but it could not fail to raise difficulties on other grounds also, and it was therefore very adversely criticised, and finally abandoned by several of the Wolffians themselves. Kant's teacher, MARTIN KNUTZEN of Königsberg, an acute and independent thinker, who was no more satisfied with the ordinary theory of reciprocal action than with Wolff's external parallelism, attempted a solution of the question in which he revived the Leibnizian idea of the final elements of matter as "representing" (*i.e.* psychical) beings. This does away with the heterogeneity of the elements which, according to the reciprocal action theory, are said to act and react upon one another as body and soul. It is here assumed that the soul-monads differ from the body-monads in quantity only, not quality. Thus the Cartesian dualism to which Wolff had given a new form, vanished, and the problem of the relation between body and soul was extended so that it became the problem of the reciprocal action of things in general. Knutzen brought forward a theory which was afterwards developed by Herbart and, in a particularly characteristic manner, by Lotze. Cf. BENNO ERDMANN, *Martin Knutzen und seine Zeit*, Leipzig, 1876, pp. 64-97. A similar theory, moreover, was brought forward by PRÉMONTVAL, the most eclectic of the Berlin Academicians. See DESSOIR, *Geschichte der neueren deutschen Psychologie*, i. p. 45.

2. p. 7. "It is customary to divide psychical faculties into faculties of knowledge and faculties of desire, and to reckon the feeling of pleasure and pain among the latter. But it seems to me that between knowledge and desire lies the approval, the applause, the satisfaction of the soul, and that this is in reality very far removed from desire. We contemplate the beauty of Nature and of art with pleasure and satisfaction, but without the smallest stirring of desire. It appears to me desirable to assign a particular name to this satisfaction or dissatisfaction of the soul, which though it is indeed a germ of desire, is not yet desire itself. . . . I shall call it the faculty of approval, in order to distinguish it both from the knowledge of the truth and the desire of the good." MENDELSSOHN, *Morgenstunden*, Berlin, 1786, pp. 118, 119.

3. p. 22. That Lessing uses the concepts education and revelation

in a figurative sense cannot be doubted after the explanation he gives
in the preface that positive religions represent the course of development
of the human mind. To be popular he had to be anthropomorphic. His
standpoint comes out more clearly in some philosophical fragments written
in his younger days (e.g. in the treatise, *Das Christenthum der Vernunft*)
and in the conversations with Jacobi. The exposition of Lessing's standpoint given in the text has already appeared with a few inconsiderable
changes, as part of my treatise, "Apologi for Lessing" (Lessings Apologie)
in the *Nordisk Tidsskrift*, published by the Letterstedtschen Verein,
1889.

4. p. 26. Jacobi had sent a copy of his report of his conversation
with Lessing to Herder. In his answer, Herder (at that time superintendent at Weimar) says that, thanks to it, he has discovered in Lessing
an unexpected brother in the faith, and has been fortified in his adherence
to the divine Spinoza, whose philosophy, however, he does not accept on
all points. Moreover, he draws the attention of his "dear extramundane
personalist" to the fact that his *salto mortale* is impossible, "for we are
on level ground in Creation" (R. HAYM, *Herder nach seinem Leben und
seinen Werken*, ii. Berlin, 1885, p. 275 f.). Goethe agreed with Herder,
although his artistic standpoint led him to attribute greater importance
to the incomprehensibility of everything which cannot assume a definite
and individual form. In the winter of 1784-85 Spinoza was eagerly
studied in Weimar. We have an interesting document of this time in
the shape of a small treatise, written by the hand of Frau von Stein, probably at Goethe's dictation. This shows us clearly how Goethe proposed
to rectify Spinoza's views. Cf. on this point, DILTHEY'S treatise,
"Aus der Zeit der Spinoza-Studien Goethes" (*Archiv für Geschichte der
Philosophie*, vii.). Jacobi was amazed to find that Herder agreed with
Lessing, and showed Herder's letter to WIZENMANN (whose relation to
Jacobi is indicated by the following words : "I love his spirit and am
astonished at his unbelief"), when he must have received a second shock ;
for, in reply to the question of what he thought of Herder's confession of
faith, this young man, who was a believer in positive religion, answered,
"His Credo is mine also." What attracted Wizenmann to Spinoza was the
deep and close relation in which, according to his doctrine, God stands to
Nature (GOLTZ, *Thomas Wizenmann*, Gotha, 1859, i. p. 342 f.). On
the other hand, Wizenmann agreed with Jacobi in pronouncing Goethe's
"Prometheus" to be blasphemous (*ib.* p. 311).

5. p. 36. For a fuller exposition of my conception of Kant's
development see my monograph "Die Kontinuität im philosophischen
Entwickelungsgange Kants (published in German in the *Archiv für
Geschichte der Philosophie*, vol. vii.) where I quote sources. As Kant
(see the said monograph, p. 174 f.) says in several passages in his letters
that the "Critique of Pure Reason" is the product of twelve years' labour,
EMIL ARNOLDT (*Kritische Exkurse auf dem Gebiete der Kant-Forschung*,
Königsberg, 1894, p. 182) reckons these twelve years back from the time
when Kant put his work upon paper, which he believes to have taken
place in 1778. In and for itself there is nothing improbable in this
suggestion ; but when we take other passages also into consideration (I
have quoted them in the monograph side by side) which allude directly to
the year 1769 as the decisive turning-point, it is more natural to reckon

the twelve years from the publication of the "Critique." It is in favour of the 1766 date that Kant applies the expression "Critique of Reason" to the epistemological task he had set himself for the first time in his invitation (*Nachschrift*, etc.) to his lectures, 1765-66. But we must distinguish between the beginning of his study of the question and its first result. The latter, and with it the "decisive turning-point" must in any case be assigned to the year 1769. I take this opportunity to remark that when I was working at the fourth chapter of the monograph—in which I show that Kant's theory of the conception of space grew out of a subjectivisation of Newton's world-space, in a change from a *sensorium dei* to a *sensorium hominis* — the second part of VAIHINGER'S *Kommentar zu Kants Kritik der reinen Vernunft*, in which a similar explanation is given, had not yet been brought to my knowledge. My treatise was written in the summer of 1892, the same year in which Vaihinger's work appeared. I may here also be allowed to say a few words on the words quoted on p. 41, l. 23 "die Erinnerung des Hume." Kant makes use of this expression in the Introduction to the *Prolegomena*. I took the genitive as objective each time that I read the passage. According to Vaihinger (*Archiv für Geschichte der Philosophie*, viii. p. 439) the genitive is subjective, and *Erinnerung* means here "admonitio" *Ermahnung*, not "recordatio" *Andenken*. If he is right some of my remarks in my monograph (p. 385 of the *Archiv*) are no longer apposite, since, in that case, we cannot infer that Kant had studied Hume's "Critique" before the time at which it aroused him. I see, however, that ADICKES (who, at any rate, is not a "foreigner") has taken the words in the same sense as I did (see his *Kantstudien*, p. 95).

6. p. 39. The book has a previous history which is not without interest, and which has only quite recently been fully explained by DILTHEY ("Der Streit Kants mit der Zensur über das Recht freier Religionsforschung," *Archiv für Geschichte der Philosophie*, iii. p. 418 f.) and EMIL FROMM (*Immanuel Kant und die preussische Zensur*. Hamburg and Leipzig, 1894). It consists of several treatises, the first of which appeared in the *Berliner Monatsschrift*. The College of Censors prohibited the printing of the second treatise. The editor of the paper addressed a complaint to the King, and the matter came before the Cabinet. At this juncture, however, the ministers received a very ungracious royal letter, complaining that they had shown themselves disinclined to take severe measures against the press. They were reproached with having "spoken on behalf of the so-called Enlighteners" and were informed that the King expected them to protect positive religion, on which the order of the State depends, by keeping a careful watch over literature (a characteristic causal series!) Under these circumstances, ministers decided that they would leave the decision of the College of Censors unquestioned. Kant now published the collected treatises in book form. The expressions which I have used of Wöllner in the text are far too mild if Frederick the Great was right in dismissing a petition that Wöllner should be ennobled, with the following comment: "Wöllner is nothing but a deceitful, intriguing parson" (E. Fromm, p. 19).

7. p. 53. S. MAIMON and HERBART criticised Kant's classification of judgments, and the use which he makes of this classification in his theory of knowledge. On Kant's classification as compared with the ordinary

classifications of his day, see Adicke's *Kants Systematik als systembildender Faktor*, Berlin, 1887, pp. 30-41.

8. p. 54. Kant, who is altogether very uncertain in his use of terminology, often lets the wider and narrower senses of the word "Vernunft" run into one another. This applies, *e.g.* to the sense in which he takes it in the title of his great work, for under the pure reason which he proposes to investigate he understands at one time the faculty of *acquiring knowledge independently of experience;* at other times the special faculty of *knowing something which cannot be an object in experience.* Cf. on this point, H. VAIHINGER, *Kommentar zu Kants Kritik der reinen Vernunft,* i. p. 453 f., Stuttgart, 1881.

9. p. 54. Cf. on this point SCHOPENHAUER in his *Kritik der Kantischen Philosophie,* which forms the Appendix to the first part of his work, *Die Welt als Wille und Vorstellung* (6th edition, Leipzig, 1887, i. pp. 572-577).—A. RIEHL, *Der philosophische Kritizismus,* i. pp. 441, 446, Leipzig, 1876.

10. p. 56. *Kritik der reinen Vernunft,* 1st edition, p. 229. Cf. my treatise, "Die Kontinuität im philosophischen Entwickelungsgange Kants," p. 190 (*Archiv,* vii.).

11. p. 59. Kant's criticism of Leibniz's "Monadology" occurs in the *Kritik der reinen Vernunft,* 1st edition, p. 265 f. It appears from Kant's notes that in his lectures he did not, even in theory, insist as sharply and decidedly on the unknowability of the thing-in-itself as strict consistency with the results of his epistemological investigation demanded. Cf. *Reflexionen Kants zur kritischen Philosophie.* Kant's autograph notes, published by BENNO ERDMANN, ii. No. 1151, 1156-1158, Leipzig, 1884. *Lose Blätter aus Kants Nachlass,* edited by R. REICKE, i., Königsberg, 1889. Cf. in reference to Kant's pedagogic and didactic compromises when *docent,* EMIL ARNOLDT'S interesting observations in his *Kritische Exkurse auf dem Gebiete der Kant-Forschung,* pp. 387-399, 402-403, 454. MAX HEINZE ("Vorlesungen Kants über Metaphysik aus drei Semestern," —*Abhandlungen der phil.-hist. Klasse der kgl. sächs. Gesellsch. der Wissensch.* 1894, p. 658), admits to Arnoldt that existing evidence seems to show that Kant must have expressed himself more cautiously in his lectures than in his works, but adds : "There is much, indeed, which has the true dogmatic ring, since he does not always state the critical restrictions ; but then in his *heart he leaned towards these dogmatic propositions.*" This utterance strikingly expresses the result which may be deduced from a perusal of Kant's MS. lectures (written partly by himself, partly by his hearers), which have recently been brought to light by B. Erdmann, Reicke, Arnoldt and Heinze. We will borrow one more remark from Heinze's treatise (*ibid.* p. 518). While Kant used formerly to begin his philosophical course with empirical psychology—as may be seen from his "Nachricht" of 1766—afterwards, as we learn from his lecture-notes, he returned to the order followed by the Wolffians, in which psychology followed ontology and cosmology.—BENNO ERDMANN (*Einleitung zu Kants Prolegomena,* Leipzig, 1878, p. lxv.) and O. RIEDEL (Die monadologischen Bestimmungen in Kants Lehre vom Ding-an-sich : Hamburg and Leipzig, 1884), have shown that the doctrine of monads haunted the background of Kant's consciousness.

12. p. 60. The first ground : *Kritik der reinen Vernunft,* 1st edition,

pp. 26 f., 34 f., 286. *Prolegomena*, p. 163 f., Riga, 1783. The second ground : *Kritik der reinen Vernunft*, 1st edition, pp. 19, 288, 494, 637 ; *Prolegomena*, p. 104 f. ; *Grundlegung zur Metaphysik der Sitten*, 3rd edition, p. 106. " On a discovery, according to which all modern criticism of pure reason is rendered *de trop* by an older criticism : " p. 56, Königsberg, 1790.

13. p. 61. It is of no use to distinguish with A. RIEHL (*Der philosophische Kritizismus*, i. p. 434), between ground and cause. For matter is only *given* when the ideational faculty is *affected;* the temporal relation cannot be left out of account. The contradiction with Kant consists rather in the fact that though he predicates the causal concept of the thing-in-itself he does not venture to predicate the temporal relation of it also. Kant himself sought to disarm this objection by distinguishing between thought and knowledge (*Kritik der praktischen Vernunft*, 1st edition, p. 94 f. and in the preface to the *Kritik der reinen Vernunft*, 2nd edition) ; in empty thought we operate with the pure category; but for real knowledge sensuous perception is necessary. But even the merely " thinking " application of the causal concept becomes senseless if the temporal relation cannot also be predicated. This whole problem takes on a different complexion when Kant's temporal concept is subjected to revision, and when his proof of the validity of the causal axiom is limited to the sphere in which alone it has real significance. The doctrine of the thing-in-itself bears altogether a more realistic stamp in the 2nd edition than it did in the 1st, a fact to which JACOBI and SCHOPENHAUER have already drawn attention. On the main point, however, which is the main difficulty, the two editions agree with one another ; and the most important difference between them lies in another point (as already pointed out in my treatise on the Continuity of Kant's Development, pp. 392, 480 f. in *Archiv* vii.), viz. that in the 2nd edition, as also in the *Prolegomena*, the psychological analysis, the subjective deduction, retires into the background and the whole emphasis is laid on the objective and transcendental deduction.

14. p. 61. To the quotations given in the monograph a letter to Reinhold of May 12, 1789, may be added :—" The real nature of space and time and the ultimate ground why the former appears in three and the latter only in one dimension is and must remain an inscrutable mystery." Also *Reflexionen*, ii. Nos. 1187-88 where Kant distinguishes between succession and the ground of succession.

15. p. 63. Kant's utterances are not very clear, but they seem to lean in the direction of the identity-hypothesis. BENNO ERDMANN (*Einleitung in die Prolegomena*, p. lxv.) and O. RIEDEL (" Die monadol. Bestimmungen," pp. 7, 27 f.), interpret them as hinting at a theory similar to the monistic-spiritualistic hypothesis brought forward by Martin Knutzen (see Note 1), and afterwards by Herbart and Lotze. Against this, however, the following considerations may be urged :—(1) Kant expressly rejects the assumption of a soul - substance, while Knutzen, Herbart and Lotze all support it ; (2) the possibility on which he dwells is as follows : " Precisely the *same thing* which, in one connection, is called corporeal would in an another *at the same time* be a thinking being," (*Kritik*, 1st edition, p. 359) ; (3) Kant rejects three hypotheses : *i.e.* dualism, materialism, and pneumatism (*Kritik*, 1st edition, p. 379), which latter is, of course, a " monistic

spiritualism " ; (4) in any case, Kant differs from the monistic spiritualists by disputing the possibility of reciprocal action between matter (as phenomenon) and soul (as phenomenon) : " Commerce between the soul and phenomenal matter is quite inconceivable, for it could only take place in space. But the soul is not an object of perception," *Reflexionen*, ii. No. 1197 (cf. No. 1131). Cf. also *Lose Blätter*, i. p. 160 ; *Tugendlehre*, 2nd ed. p. 66. In a recently discovered (by Emil Arnoldt, *Kritische Exkurse*, p. 502) college notebook on Kant's lectures, 1793-94, we find also : " Bodies as bodies cannot affect the soul and the converse, because bodies can have no relations with a thinking being. The external relation in which a body stands to a substance can only be a spatial relation, hence this substance must also be in space, *i.e.* a body.

16. p. 65. *Kritik der reinen Vernunft*, 1st ed. p. 549 ; in the note Kant certainly tries to force on the antitheses a dogmatic line of thought —but in this he is not successful. Moreover, it is clear that the contradictory opposite of the absolute conclusion is not an absolute (given) infinity, but non-conclusion (*i.e.* continuous process).

17. p. 77. In his treatise on *Kant als Vater des modernen Pessimismus*, EDUARD VON HARTMANN (*Zur Geschichte und Begrundung des Pessimismus*, 2nd ed. : Leipzig, 1891), has exaggerated the pessimistic side of Kant's view to suit his theory. Thus he puts much stronger expressions in Kant's mouth concerning the incongruity between civilisation and individual felicity than he really used. While Kant (*Anthropologie*, 2nd ed. p. 314) speaks of the "perfecting of man through progressive civilisation, although often at a sacrifice of their joy in life " Hartmann (p. 104) quotes the last phrase as : " at the cost of their life-joy," which sounds much stronger. Again, when Kant (*Kritik der Urtheilskraft*, 2nd ed. p. 392) says that civilisation increases inequality and misery, Hartmann (p. 104) alludes to this passage as though it were Kant's last word on the subject which, as the context shows, is not the case.

18. p. 78. In his *Zum ewigen Frieden* (1795), Kant develops the thought of the "idea" and the "presumptive beginning," with special regard to the possibility that war might be driven out of existence through the formation of a union embracing the whole world. As in his two earlier treatises, so here, Kant abstracts entirely from moral motives and sympathetic feelings, and only inquires which egoistic interests would presumably make towards the ideal end ; *i.e.* a constitution based on right and including all men. He says, however, that it is a *duty* to make use, in this constitution, of the mechanism of interests. Kant gave a deeper, more penetrating psychological basis to Lessing's idea of the education of the human race. He expressly defends this idea against Mendelssohn, who thought (see his *Jerusalem*) that we could only speak of education and progress with reference to single individuals, not to the species (see the treatise, *Über den Gemeinspruch : Das mag in der Theorie richtig sein, taugt aber nicht für die Praxis*, 1793. As I have shown in my book, *J.-J. Rousseau und seine Philosophie* (Frommann's *Klassiker der Philosophie*) and in my treatise, " Rousseaus Einfluss auf die definitive Form der Kantischen Ethik " (*Überrichten der Verhandlungen der kgl. dän. Akad. d. Wiss.* 1896), Kant fell under Rousseau's influence once again (as he had twenty years earlier) at the time when his ethic was assuming its definite shape. I differ from F. W. FOERSTER, however, as to the point at

which this influence made itself felt, though in his interesting work, *Der Entwickelungsgang der Kantischen Ethik bis zur Kritik der reinen Vernunft* (Berlin, 1894) Foerster takes the same view as I do of the earlier stages of the Kantian ethics.

19. p. 79. Cf. what I have already said in this connection on Kant's ethics in my work *Die Grundlage der humanen Ethik* (German translation, 1880), p. 35.

20. p. 82. It was Kant's formalism which brought him so near mysticism. Hamann rightly speaks of a mystical love of form and an agnostic hatred of matter as characteristic traits of Kant's philosophy (*Metakritik. Schriften.* edited by Rothenstein, vii. p. 9, cf. his verbal utterances to Kant, vi. p. 227, see also pp. 212, 213). C. A. WILLMANS, a pupil of Kant's, wrote a treatise entitled *De similitudine inter Mysticismum purum et Kantianam religionis doctrinam* (Halis Sax. 1797), a portion of which Kant printed, with some qualifications, as an appendix to his *Streit der Fakultäten.* Afterwards Kant felt compelled to make a still more decided protest against his doctrine being confounded with a doctrine of possible supersensuous experiences, a possibility which he entirely denied. See the passage quoted by R. REICKE in his *Kantiana,* Königsberg, 1860, p. 81 f. Also JACHMANN'S *Immanuel Kant geschildert in Briefen an einen Freund,* p. 116 f., Königsberg, 1804.

21. p. 84. For examples of cases of conflict (the method of reaction) see *Kritik der praktischen Vernunft* (Kehrbach's Ausgabe), pp. 36, 112, 186 f.; *Anthropologie,* 2nd ed. p. 243; *Tugendlehre,* Introduction, § ix. (In this latter passage Kant shows at length that virtue is strength and that strength can only make itself known through resistance). See also the first chapter of the treatise : *Über der Gemeinspruch : Das mag in der Theorie richtig sein, taugt aber nicht für die Praxis* (1793). The passage in the text immediately following is taken from this treatise.

22. p. 87. Cf. *Reflexionen Kants,* ii. No. 1534 : "The faculty of producing the motives of the will simply from ourselves is freedom. This act does not itself depend upon the will, but is the spontaneity of the causality of the will." Freedom in this sense is not the faculty of choice : "Freedom is a positive faculty, not of choosing something, for there is no choice here, but of determining the subject" (*Lose Blätter,* i. p. 570).

23. p. 88. HERBART has already shown (*Gespräche über das Böse,* pp. 145-147, Königsberg, 1817) that Kant used the word "freedom" in a double sense. I agree with JODL (*Geschichte der Ethik in der neueren Philosophie,* ii. pp. 30-37, Stuttgart, 1889) that we must distinguish three different meanings of this word as used by Kant. As early as the *Kritik der reinen Vernunft,* p. 534 (1st ed.), Kant teaches the inadequacy of empirical causality as an explanation of voluntary actions : "Practical freedom presupposes that although something has not happened yet it ought to have happened, and thus its phenomenal cause was not sufficiently determinative to," etc. Cf. also pp. 536, 551 (note). As I have shown in my *Ethik* (chap. v.) the meanings of this vague word are by no means exhausted in these three.

24. p. 98. *Kritik der reinen Vernunft,* 1st ed. p. 695 f. *Prolegomena,* 1st ed. pp. 174, 179. "Critique of Judgment," §§ 59, 88, 91 (note).

25. p. 99. Much light has been thrown on this point by the explana-

tions of Kant's lectures recently given by EMIL ARNOLDT in his *Kritischen Exkursen auf dem Gebiete der Kant-Forschung*. See (in addition to what is quoted in note 11) *ib*. p. 465 f., where Arnoldt is speaking particularly of Kant's lectures on the philosophy of religion, in which he employs the ordinary theological way of speaking, without calling attention to the modifications in the meaning of the concepts required by symbolism and the critical philosophy.

26. p. 106. Very significant for the history of the development of taste is it that while in his *Beobachtungen über das Gefühl des Schönen und Erhabenen* (1763) Kant mentions "trees cut into shapes" (p. 4) as examples of beautiful objects, in the *Kritik der Urtheilskraft* (1790) he says that "the English taste in gardens," with its approximation to grotesques and its freedom from all constraint affords an opportunity to taste to exhibit its greatest perfection "in designs in which free play is given to the imagination" (§ 22, note).

27. p. 107. During the immediately preceding period (the period of *Sturm und Drang*) the word "genius" had been in great vogue. It expressed a striving after the boundless, a wish to get free from all rules and laws. Every obscurity and every unruliness were glad enough to deck themselves out with this word. "The word genius," says Goethe (*Aus meinem Leben*, 19th book) "was so misapplied that it was at last suggested that it should be banished from the German language entirely. And so the Germans would perhaps have deprived themselves of this word, which is only apparently foreign, while in reality it is common to all nations, had it not been that the sense for the highest and best, revived by a deeper philosophy, had happily re-established itself." That Goethe had Kant's definition of genius, given in the *Kritik der Urtheilskraft*, in his mind may be seen from the preceding passage, where he says of the misuse of the word genius, "It was long ere the time came when it could be declared that genius is that human power which gives laws and rules through acts and performances." There is a certain connection between Kant's concept of genius and his conception of consciousness as a synthesis. In every act of consciousness a hidden art is exercised in the combining activity which is the essence of all consciousness, although it need not itself be an object of consciousness. And the laws and rules of thought and action which can be *consciously* formulated are ultimately deduced from this hidden art. The *genial* then denotes only the culminating point of a form of activity which is present in *all* mental life.

28. p. 120. In "Edouard Allwills Papieren" (*Vermischte Schriften*, 1780) Jacobi has described a "beautiful soul," which, appealing to the rights of the exceptional, pushes them to extremes. Although Jacobi evidently disapproved of Allwill's conduct, yet he afterwards (*Jacobi an Fichte*, 1799, p. 32) uses in his own name the example of Desdemona quoted by the hero of the "Papers" (p. 236) in defence of the right of individual feeling to make exceptions. The expression "beautiful soul" may, perhaps, have been taken by Schiller and Goethe from the Allwill Papers, though Rousseau had already employed it. As I have called Jacobi a modern Herbert of Cherbury, I may add here that the similarity between them extends to the fact that Jacobi, like Herbert, wished for a sign—which, however, was never given. WIZENMANN relates in a letter, written from Jacobi's castle Pempelfort, near Düsseldorf, that one evening, as they

were sitting in the garden, Jacobi had said to him : " I often sit here watching the setting sun, and think with what rapture I should be filled if a miracle of His grace were to assure me of His existence. Then I stand up, on fire with the thought—God ! and feel as if I should like to call together the whole world to preach God to it." His enthusiasm was not quenched by the non-appearance of a sign. When he heard the evening breeze murmuring in the trees of the garden and was stirred by the depth and majesty of Nature he was filled with the conviction : " No chaos could possess the power of moving me thus " (GOLTZ, *Thomas Wizenmann*, i. p. 310 f.).

29. p. 128. There is a certain vacillation in Maimon's treatment of the concept of the thing-in-itself. The comparison with an imaginary number ($\sqrt{\div a}$) occurs in the *Kritischen Untersuchungen* (Leipzig, 1797) pp. 158-191. But in other passages the thing-in-itself (like matter and form) is spoken of as an idea which can only be approximately represented, like the irrational number $\sqrt{2}$. Maimon expresses himself in this way when he wishes to leave it uncertain whether the thing-in-itself is to be sought in an absolute object, or in an absolute subject (e.g. *Versuch einer neuen Logik*, p. 142, Berlin, 1794). The explanation is probably as follows : when Maimon altogether rejects the thing-in-itself he is most likely thinking of Kant's conception of it, while he himself had another conception of it in which the contradictions disappeared. In the *Philosophischen Wörterbuch* (Berlin, 1791), Maimon's best work in point of form and lucidity, he says : " I differ from Herr Kant only in this : According to him, things-in-themselves are the substrata without us of their phenomena within us. . . . While, in my view, the knowledge of the thing-in-itself is nothing but the *complete knowledge of phenomena*. . . . We approach to a knowledge of noümena in proportion to the completeness of our knowledge of phenomena " (p. 176 f.). In agreement with this is an observation contained in his autobiography (*Salomon Maimons Lebensgeschichte von ihm selbst geschrieben*, Berlin, 1792, ii. p. 43) which runs as follows : " The nature of *irrational numbers* shows us that we may have no concept of a thing as object, and yet we may be able to determine its *relation* to other things."

30. p. 129. A few years after the publication of Maimon's first works, JACOB SIGISMUND BECK'S epitome of Kant's works appeared, in which he comes to the same conclusion as Maimon, viz., that the theory of knowledge cannot recognise the thing-in-itself. He attempts to prove that the forms of perception and the categories denote different stages of development of the same activity of the understanding by means of which alone things exist for us. It is interesting to observe how different thinkers come to take the same path, but it is not necessary for us here to enter in detail into Beck's arguments. Beck's letters to Kant, published by R. REICKE (*Aus Kants Briefwechsel*, Königsberg, 1885) and Kant's letters to Beck, published by DILTHEY (*Archiv für die Geschichte der Philosophie*, ii.) gives much interesting information as to the personal relation which existed between them.

31. p. 134 With regard to the relation between the two treatises, cf. F. UEBERWEG : *Schiller als Historiker und Philosoph*, Leipzig, 1884, pp. 242-248, and F. JODL : *Geschichte der Ethik in der neuren Philosophie*, ii. p. 56 f.; cf. p. 507 f., Stuttgart, 1889. I am unable, however, to agree

with the result arrived at by both these writers, viz. that Schiller held consistently to the relation between grace and dignity as determined in the earlier treatise. He intimates, even in this treatise, that grace or harmony is the more valuable, and he says so more decidedly in the *Briefen über ästhetische Erziehung.* Thus he writes in the 27th letter : " In the midst of the formidable realm of forces and of the sacred realm of laws, the æsthetic impulse of form creates unnoticed a third and a joyous realm, that of play and appearance, where she emancipates man from the fetters of all relations and from all that is named constraint, whether physical or moral." And Schiller finds this third realm realised, " wherever man passes through all sorts of complications with bold simplicity and quiet innocence, neither forced to trench on another's freedom to preserve his own, nor to show grace at the cost of dignity." We have, then, a union of grace and dignity (which were before exhibited as opposites) in the æsthetic state, in which, too, the opposition between the physical and the moral has also disappeared.

32. p. 140. This comparison appears in an interesting form in a fragment by Friedrich Schlegel in the *Athenäum* ; " The French Revolution, Fichte's *Wissenschaftslehre*, and Goethe's *Meister* are the greatest tendencies of the age. The man who takes offence at this juxtaposition, to whom no Revolution can appear great which is not noisy and material, has not yet risen to the high and wide standpoint of the history of man " (*Athen.* i. 2, p. 56). BAGGESEN, however, had often drawn a similar comparison, at first with admiration, afterwards with disgust. Cf. for the latter, a passage in his letter to Erhard, May 17, 1797, on "the newest *Ichtish* and *Fichtisch* a priori *sansculotterie*, which has now followed in Germany on the a posteriori *sansculotterie* in France."

33. p. 153. I have made some remarks in my sketch of philosophy in Denmark in the nineteenth century (*Archiv für die Geschichte der Philosophie*, vol. ii.) on the influence which Fichte's later writings exercised on intellectual development in Denmark, owing to the fact that GRUNDTVIG was so strongly influenced by him in his youth.

34. p. 154. Fichte conceives the relation between the ego and the body as follows :—The body is the external material from under which the ego must appear in order to be able to struggle with material limitations. Since the non-ego occurs in the form of space the ego must do so also. " Matter can only be forced out of the space it occupies by other matter ; hence the ego, as working force in a material world must itself be matter, *i.e.* an immediately given, definite and spatially limited body. . . . Resistance takes the form of matter and so force must be taken up into this same medium of matter. *Die Thatsachen des Bewusstseins,* 1817, pp. 81, 83. Cf. *Naturrecht,* § 5. Compare this conception of Fichte's with that of Kant, see note 15.

35. p. 156. Fichte has repeatedly declared that the special content of experience and of life cannot be deduced from general principles, but nowhere more clearly and beautifully than in his lectures *Über das Wesen des Gelehrten* (On the Nature of a Scholar), p. 33 and f., Berlin, 1806.

" Temporal life can only be understood in its general nature, as the manifestation of the one primary and divine life ; but its special and peculiar nature can only be known by being lived and experienced ; and only in and by means of this experience can it be imitated in idea and in consciousness. In every single part of human life there is always something which cannot be taken up into the concept and which no concept, therefore, can ever anticipate or replace. It must be immediately experienced if it is ever to enter consciousness ; this is what is meant by the sphere of pure empiricism or experience." If we forget this "in our endeavour to explain the whole of life, we shall lose life itself." Under that which is to be taken as given Fichte includes the definite individual idiosyncracy of each particular ego : " The point at which we find ourselves when we first become masters of our freedom does not depend on ourselves ; the line which we shall describe from this point onwards throughout eternity is, in its whole extent, entirely dependent on ourselves " (*Wissenschaftslehre*, 2nd ed. p. 267). Even if an ethical explanation could be given of the manner in which the pure ego limits itself in the finite ego, it would afford no explanation of the definite individual peculiarity of each particular ego. In his later presentations of his theory, Fichte calls this splitting up into particular individuals a *projectio irrationalis*.

36. p. 159.   Cf. on this point my *Ethik*, viii. 4, p. 118 and f. (German ed.).   J. H. Löwe, *Die Philosophie Fichtes*, pp. 155-158, Stuttgart, 1862, has brought out very clearly the opposition in which Fichte's doctrine of individuality stands to other elements of his system.

37. p. 160.   In his youthful work, *Kritik aller Offenbarung* (Königsberg, 1793), p. 225, Fichte actually says that a strong wish to exercise spiritual influence and the firm conviction that this can only be done by means of the idea of a revelation may, through the effect of enthusiasm on the imagination, produce a belief, even if only for the moment.

A wish that revelation might be true may be justifiable if this wish itself is prompted by ethical motives (*Ibid.* p. 216).

38. p. 163.   The letters from Fr. Schlegel and his wife to Schleiermacher are given in *Aus Schleiermachers Leben*, Letters, vol. iii. pp. 129, 132-134, Berlin, 1861. For the peculiar manner in which Fr. Schlegel translated Fichte's *Wissenschaftslehre* into romantic "irony," see S. KIERKEGAARD, *Om Begrebet Ironie* (The Concept of Irony), Copenhagen, 1841, pp. 287-320. With regard to Kierkegaard's description of Schlegel's irony, however, we must remember that he confines himself entirely to his novel, *Lucinde*, which represents an extreme point in Schlegel's development. In the fragments in the *Athenäum* and elsewhere Schlegel has developed a much more important side of the concept ; he there treats it as the expression of the capacity of absorbing oneself in certain spheres or individuals as though they were everything, and of thus intuiting them in their idiosyncracy, which capacity presupposes an inner infinity in its possessor ; man must be a world himself if he can understand other men as peculiar parts of the world (cf. *Athenäum*, i. 2, p. 31 and f.). This concept expresses an essential aspect of the historical method, but it may be so turned and twisted as to pass over into pure caprice and sensuousness. The romantic school was in a state of constant oscillation. Romanticism oscillates between overweening self-pride (where the pure ego is made identical with the empirical ego) and mystical surrender of the self (where the empirical self disappears in the pure infinite ego). The interval between these two poles is filled up with a strongly-felt need to revel in all

forms of spiritual life (poetry, philosophy, religion)—if possible in all at
once. But no poetry and no science were found able to satisfy this need.
No wonder, therefore, that it finally landed many in the arms of the Catholic
Church, whose teaching and worship had up to that time remained unaffected
by the modern cleavage between the different spiritual spheres. Thus a
little later (1806 or 1807) we find Dorothea Schlegel writing to Schleiermacher ; " Consolation, sympathy, love, music, painting and beneficent
tears—I find them all in the Church" (*Aus Schleiermachers Leben*, iii. p.
416). With Schelling this transition corresponds to the transition to the
religious period of his speculation.

39. p. 165. When Schelling says, " Phenomenal sensibility is the
limit of all empirical phenomena and everything in Nature is bound up
with that which produces it " (*First Sketch*, p. 174), his words remind us
of the saying of Hobbes, that among all the phenomena of Nature the
most wonderful is that anything can be a phenomenon for us, so that if
phenomena are the principles by which we know everything else, sense in
its turn is the principle by which we know these principles, *De corpore*,
xxv. 1. (Cf. the sketch of Hobbes' philosophy in vol. i. of this work.)

40. p. 173. I have given a detailed account of Weisse's philosophy
of religion in my book, entitled *Filosofien i Tyshland efter Hegel*
(Philosophy in Germany after Hegel), pp. 181-219, Copenhagen, 1872.
I took the opportunity of making some observations on philosophical
theism in general in the conclusion of my treatise, " Lotze og den svenske
Filosofi" (Lotze and the Swedish philosophy), *Nordisk Tidsskrift*, ugd. af
den Letterstedtske Forening, 1890. (Translated in the *Philos. Monatsheften*, xxiv.).

41. p. 173. In my *Filosofien i Tyshland efter Hegel*, pp. 121-141,
I have given a résumé of Fichte's later teaching.

42. p. 196. Cf. Note 38. For Schleiermacher's conception of Fr.
Schlegel's character and personality, which he had to defend not only
against adversaries but also against his own friends, see *Aus Schleiermachers Leben*, Letters, vol. i. pp. 320, 349 f. The last-quoted passage
in particular illustrates Schleiermacher's power of entering into the personality of others (especially in cases when the chaff and corn are still
unseparated) as well as his loyalty and chivalrous feeling. It will be found
to be one of the most important documents we possess when the time
comes for a comparative ethic of friendship to be written.

43. p. 199. The lectures delivered by Steffens (1802) in Copenhagen,
and which proved to be of such great significance for intellectual life in
Denmark, owing to the influence they exercised on Dehlenschläger and
Grundtvig, were for the most part an exposition of the leading thoughts
contained in the *Beiträge*, with the addition, however, of reflections on
æsthetics and history in which the line of thought of the *Beiträge* was
extended from the sphere of natural to that of mental philosophy. Cf.
Indledning til filosofiske Foreläsninger (Introduction to Lectures on Philosophy), Copenhagen, 1883, pp. 91, 107 and f. where the individualising
and yet at the same time universalising tendency of Nature is brought out.
For further remarks on these lectures see my article in the *Archiv für
die Geschichte der Philosophie*, vol. i.

44. p. 199. DILTHEY (*Leben Schleiermachers*, p. 351), remarks that
it is the first sketch of Schleiermacher's Ethics more particularly, written

in 1804, which reminds us of the work of Steffens here quoted.—When the Berlin University was about to be opened Schleiermacher urged the advisability of giving an appointment to Steffens in order to avoid one-sidedness either in philosophy or natural science. He was personally anxious for the appointment since it would have ensured some acquaintance with general philosophy on the part of those attending his ethical lectures ; in order to secure it he offered to forgo a substantial part of his income for the first year (*Aus Schleiermachers Leben*, iv. p. 175). His attempts were not successful, however. Steffens went to Breslau instead and did not come to Berlin until several years after Schleiermacher's death.

45. p. 202. Cf. here Fichte's view, quoted in Note 37.

46. p. 206. It has been said that religion was for Schleiermacher merely one variety of æsthetic taste (see ALBRECHT RITSCHL, *Schleiermachers Reden über die Religion und ihre Nachwirkungen auf die evangelische Kirche Deutschlands*, p. 53, cf. 91 and f., Bonn, 1874). The converse would be more correct ; æsthetic taste is for Schleiermacher a species or variety of the religious need of expressing the relation between feeling and the content of life. Cf. W. BENDER, *Schleiermachers Theologie mit ihren philosophischen Grundlagen*, Nördlingen, 1876-78, i. p. 163. That Bender's view is correct may be seen more particularly in the *Philosophische Sittenlehre*, § 290.

47. p. 207. *Philosophische Sittenlehre*, § 343, "Where the morality of actions is produced by the individual acting, he alone can be the judge." Cf. *Die christliche Sitte*, p. 65, "So far as an action has its ground in the individuality of a man, so far it can be judged by no one but himself. Each man, however, is only his own judge in the matter, not his own teacher." It is perhaps characteristic that the latter remark occurs only in Schleiermacher's " Christian " and not in his " philosophical " ethics ; but it is correct from the philosophical point of view also, and finds its justification in his whole doctrine.

48. p. 209. J. E. ERDMANN, *Grundriss der Geschichte der Philosophie*, ii. pp. 465, 477, Berlin, 1866. Cf. also ALB. RITSCHL, *Schleiermachers Reden über die Religion*, etc. p. 59. A more correct view is taken by W. BENDER in *Schleiermachers Theologie*, i. pp. 173-175. DELBRÜCH thought the *Glaubenslehre* pantheistic and irreconcilable with the second edition of the *Addresses* (*Aus Schleiermachers Leben*, ii. p. 366 and f.), — a view altogether opposed to that of Erdmann and Ritschl. Schleiermacher has explained his reason for using "feeling " interchangeably with " immediate self-consciousness " in the *Glaubenslehre* as follows : — " The latter expression has advantages, certainly, since so many assign feeling to a lower region, but the term, 'self-consciousness' cannot be used without the addition of 'immediate' to distinguish it from reflective self-consciousness, hence, 'feeling' is to be preferred " (*Philos. Sittenlehre*, § 253). A difference between the conception of religion of the *Reden* and that of later works on which great weight has frequently been laid is that in the former religion is described as a purely passive feeling, while afterwards (and as DILTHEY shows, as far back as sermons of the same date as the *Reden*), more emphasis is laid on the practical character of religion. I am inclined to think, however, that the standpoint of the *Reden* is apt to be

expounded too one-sidedly. This seems to me to be the case in B. VON JODL'S otherwise excellent description of Schleiermacher's standpoint in his *History of Ethics*. For it is expressly taught in the *Reden* that "in order to take up the life of the world-spirit in himself and to have religion man must have found humanity, and he can only do this in love and through love ;—moreover, the development of humanity is not yet completed ; it is constantly renewing itself at manifold starting-points " (2. *Rede*). Now since religion is conceived as that which affords the highest point of view, or rather as the fundamental disposition governing our participation in human life and effecting the development of that life, the religious feeling can certainly not be purely passive. If Schleiermacher calls this feeling "the music of life," it is a music which not only charms the soul but also deepens its interest in its work, even though it itself no more imposes duties than it demands definite theoretical assumptions. Here again there is only a quantitative difference between the *Reden* (1st edition) and the later works. In the *Glaubenslehre* (§ 9) Schleiermacher draws a sharp distinction between æsthetic religiousness, the highest form of which is beauty of soul, and teleological religiousness, the highest state of which is not one of quiescence but of labour for the advancement of the "kingdom of God." This distinction (as also the distinction in the Dialectic between God and the world) is not recognised in the *Reden*, where the whole relation is left more undefined. In the *Dialektik*, too, there is a nearer determination of the relation between feeling and the other sides of consciousness than that given in the *Reden*. See especially Appendix C, § 51. "It (feeling) seems sometimes to appear alone, as though thought and will were submerged in it ; but this is only seeming, for there are always intermixed traces of the will and a germ of thought (or the converse) even though they are apparently vanishing."

49. p. 220. The considerations which induced Schopenhauer to call philosophy an art are very different from those which I have urged in my article on "Filosofi som Kunst" (Philosophy as Art) in the *Nyt norsk Tidsskrift* (New Norwegian Journal), 1893. (For a German translation of the same see the weekly paper *Ethische Kultur*, 1894.)

50. p. 224. Cf. also Helmholtz, *Handbuch der physiologischen Optik*, 2nd ed. p. 248 and f., where Fichte's *Thatsachen des Bewusstseins* is mentioned with praise, and where it is said that in the corresponding passages in Schopenhauer almost everything which is true may be traced back to this source.

51. p. 226. The difficulty here alluded to was brought forward by Herbart in his criticism of Schopenhauer's chief work on its first appearance (Herbart's *Sämtl. Werke*, xii.). It is not impossible that the objections raised by Herbart may have influenced Schopenhauer—in spite of his contempt for this and other critics—to give the further explanations which occur in the second volume ; it is at any rate remarkable that he returns to the subject there a second time. That these explanations do not meet the difficulty, however, is acknowledged by P. DEUSSEN (*Archiv für Gesch. d. Phil*. iii. p. 164) who attempts to defend them, but, as a matter of fact, goes back from Schopenhauer to Kant. In a conversation with Karl Bähr (1856) Schopenhauer stated that he had only read Herbart's "Critique" once in his life, *i.e.* when it appeared in 1820 (*Gespräche und Briefwechsel*

mit Arthur Schopenhauer, aus dem Nachlasse von Karl Bähr, Leipzig, 1894, p. 19). Nevertheless it may not have been without effect.

52. p. 232. For this psychological theory see my *Psychology*, vi.. E. 6. (English translation, pp. 284-287.)

53. p. 232. In his natural philosophy, as far as his conception of organic life is concerned, Schopenhauer is strongly influenced by the French inquirers, Cabanis, Bichat and Lamarck. Cf. an interesting article by PAUL JANET, "Schopenhauer et la physiologie française" (*Revue des deux Mondes*, 1888).

54. p. 236. Cf. LINDNER und FRAUENSTÄDT, *Arthur Schopenhauer von ihm, über ihn*, p. 592 and f., Berlin, 1863. Frauenstädt is no doubt right when he suggests (*Angef. Schr.* p. 434 and f.) that the first edition of Schopenhauer's chief work contains a more subjective conception than that afterwards unfolded. Schopenhauer was at first inclined to regard differences as purely phenomenal ; afterwards, however (in the *Parerga und Paralipomena*) he assumes that individual differences have their ground in the thing-in-itself.

55. p. 248. See *e.g.* W. WINDELBAND, *Geschichte der Philosophie*, p. 492, Freiburg, 1892.

56. p. 248. This expression (which occurs in the preface to his *Allgemeinen Metaphysik*) gave offence in strict Kantian quarters. Hence in a letter of March 26, 1833, Herbart explains that he called himself a Kantian because the charges which he hoped to effect in science by his criticism of metaphysical starting-points and his transformation of psychology are of subordinate importance in comparison with the determination by Kant of the great fundamental principles of philosophising. Moreover, Kant's enemies are his, *i.e.* speculative theology and the last remnant of scholasticism. (See *Ungedrückte Briefe von und an Herbart*, herausg. von R. Zimmermann, pp. 101-105, Vienna, 1877.)

57. p. 254. Herbart's theory of the relation between soul and body comes nearest to that of Martin Knutzen and PRÉMONTVAL (see note 1). This theory was developed in the Herbartian school, *e.g.* by LUDWIG STÜRMFELL, *Grundriss der Psychologie*, chaps. 15, 16, Leipzig, 1884.

58. p. 255. Cf. on this point my *Psychology*, v. B. vi. (English translation, pp. 141-144). Herbart's psychology and his metaphysic are here at odds with one another ; for if he has really succeeded in explaining the unity of consciousness by the reciprocal action of the elements, the metaphysical explanation of the unity and interconnection of consciousness by a soul-substance is superfluous ; while, if he starts with a soul-substance he cannot regard the unity merely as a product.

59. p. 257. Among Herbart's claims to recognition within the sphere of the critical philosophy his treatment of logic (*Hauptpunkten der Logik*, 1808, and the *Einleitung in die Philosophie*) ought not to be forgotten. Of special interest is his reduction of the theory of judgments, in which he reduces all previous classifications to one into affirmative and negative judgments ; also his anticipation of the doctrine of the quantification of the predicate. See especially *Einleitung*, § 53. We may notice that in the attempt to simplify the artificial classification of judgments which played so large and so unfortunate a part with Kant, Herbart was preceded by Maimon.

60. p. 259. Lotze remarks in his excellent exposition of the Herbartian

philosophy (*Geschichte der deutschen Philosophie seit Kant*, Leipzig, 1882) that Herbart is logically compelled to conceive God as a "Real" which could develop no activity out of relation to other Reals (§ 72). This criticism applies to Leibniz also—as well as to Lotze himself. On the question of immortality, too, Herbart's philosophy, as Lotze likewise remarks, finds itself in difficulties ; for in virtue of the doctrine of the everlasting "Reals" it is committed not only to personal immortality but also to the "uncomfortable assumption of their eternal pre-existence before this earthly life"!

61. p. 261. Beneke's place in the history of ethical thought has been interestingly described by FR. JODL (*Geschichte der Ethik in der neueren Philosophie*, ii. pp. 251-266) who brings out three main characteristics, (1) his opposition to Kant and to speculation, (2) the strong influence of the English school (especially of Bentham, one of whose books he had translated), (3), his position as Feuerbach's predecessor.

62. p. 264. Cf. the interesting remarks on Beneke's attitude towards the problem of the soul and body in Ueberweg's *Grundriss der Geschichte der Philosophie der Neuzeit*, 7th ed., Max Heinze, 1887, p. 408 (note).

63. p. 265. Beneke is also of interest as a logician, for he pointed out (as early as 1832 in his *Lehrbuch der Logik*) that the important aspect of thought for Logic is the content of a concept, not its extent (§§ 21, 57). He also traces back the doctrine of inference to the principle of substitution, according to which inference is merely the taking up of one judgment into another by means of the "partition" of concepts (or, as it was afterwards called, "quantification") (§ 170). Beneke and his disciples thought that Sir William Hamilton plagiarised his doctrine of the quantification of the predicate from Beneke. See DUSSLER, *Charakteristik der Werke Benekes* (Postscript to the 3rd edition of Beneke's *Text-Book of Psychology*, p. 299). Beneke's "Logic" excited attention in England. Stuart Mill writes, in a letter to Bain (1884): "I am reading a German professor's book on logic—Beneke is his name—which he has sent to me after reading mine, and which had previously been recommended to me by Austen and by Herschel as in accordance with the spirit of my doctrine. It is so in some degree, though far more psychological than entered into my own plans. Though I think much of his psychology unsound for want of his having properly grasped the principle of association (he comes very close to it now and then) there is much of it of a suggestive kind" (A. Bain, *John Stuart Mill, a Criticism*, London, 1882, p. 79).

64. p. 267. See with reference to the dispute on belief in immortality, PAUL MÖLLER: "Om Muligheden af Bevisen for Menneskets Udōdelighed" (On the Possibility of Demonstrating Human Immortality), *Posthumous Works*, v., and my work, *Die Philosophie in Deutschland seit Hegel*, pp. 17-29. To the short characterisation of Weisse's standpoint given in the text I may add (see also *Phil. in Deutsch.* p. 216 and f.) that Weisse is an adherent of the Lamarckian theory of development. Hence he is opposed to the purely logical evolutionary theory of the Romanticists. This explains, too, the importance which he attributes in his philosophy of religion to the reality of time. I cannot, unfortunately, devote more space to Krause's literary productivity, the results of which were, for the most part, published after his death by faithful pupils. The work referred to in

the text contains, in my judgment, the clearest and freshest statement of his general position.

65. p. 270. I have already given a detailed exposition of Trendelenburg's philosophical views in my *Phil. in Deutsch.* pp. 222-246.

66. p. 273. The characterisation of himself contained in the passages quoted from Feuerbach has only recently been made known by WILHELM BOLLIN in a work entitled *Ludwig Feuerbach, sein Wirken und seine Zeitgenossen.* Mit Benutzung ungedruckten Materials, Stuttgart, 1891.

67. p. 276. This line of thought of Feuerbach's is elucidated and confirmed by arguments given in my *Psychology*, v. B. iv., and vi. F. In his psychological theory Feuerbach was, to a certain extent, preceded by Hume. See vol. i. of this work, pp. 429 and f., 437 and f.

68. p. 284. For an account of philosophical development in Sweden see AXEL NYBLAÜ'S great work, *Den filosofiska forskningen i Sverige från slutet af ådertonde århundradet*, Lund, 1873. . Also a treatise by the same author entitled, *Om den Boströmska filosofien*, Lund, 1883. In my article " Filosofien i Sverig " ("Die Philosophie in Schweden," German translation in the *Philos. Monatsheften*, 1879) I have given a more detailed characterisation and criticism of Swedish philosophy.

69. p. 285. I have given a full account of Sibbern and his philosophy in *Tilskueren*, 1885. For an account of Danish philosophy in the nineteenth century cf. my article in the *Archiv für die Geschichte der Philosophie*, vol. ii.

70. p. 289. Kierkegaard's most important philosophical works are : *Begrebet Angst* (The Concept of Fear) 1844 ; *Stadier paa Livets Veg* (Stages in the Journey of Life), 1845 ; *Uvidenskabelig Eftersskrift* (Unscientific Postscript) 1846. I have given a full account of Kierkegaard in my book, *Sören Kierkegaard als Philosoph* (Danish, 1892, German (Frommann's *Klassiker der Philosophie*) 1896). There is much interesting information concerning Kierkegaard's dogmatic standpoint in CHR. SCHREMPF'S article : " Kierkegaards Stellung zu Bibel und Dogma," (*Zeitschr. für Theologie und Kirche*, Freiburg im Br., i. pp. 179-229).

71. p. 297. While de Maistre reminds us of Hobbes in his principle of authority and the weight he lays on war, his doctrine of causation calls to mind that of Malebranche, whom he also mentions with great admiration, and indeed follows in his mythico-pantheistism ; thus, *e.g.* he talks of the divine ocean in which at some future time all things and all men will be submerged. But he feels that he is here standing on the brink of heresy, for he adds at once : " Je me garde cependant de vouloir toucher à la personnalité, sans laquelle l'immortalité n'est rien " (*Les soirées de St-Pétersbourg*, 7 éd. ii. p. 203).

72. p. 304. Cf. on this question my *Psychologischen Untersuchungen* ("Über Wiedererkennen, u.s.w.," in the *Vierteljahrsschrift f. wiss. Philos.* xiv. 3, pp. 293-316). When Biran speaks of sensations existing outside the ego, he understands by the ego very much what I have called in my *Psychology* (v. B. v.) the real ego, *i.e.* the central and more active part of the content of consciousness. There can be no sensations outside the "formal ego" which expresses the unity and interconnection of consciousness.

73. p. 308. On phenomena of concretion, see *Philosophie des deux Ampère*, pp. 316 and f. *Essai sur la philosophie des sciences* (1834),

p. lviii. and f.   A. BERTRAND (*La psychol. de l'effort*) makes a wrong use of the term *concrétion* when he applies it to an association between two different ideas ; Ampère uses the term *commémoration* for such associations. When I recognise a tree it is a *concrétion* ; when I see the tree, and then think of the dog which was lying at its foot last time I saw it, it is a *commémoration*. I regret that Ampère's exposition was unknown to me when I wrote the chapter on immediate recognition in my *Psychologischen Untersuchungen*. But it is a great pleasure to me to find what an exact agreement there is between the views we have severally developed.

74. p. 309. Ampère exaggerates the difference between his theory and Kant's when he attributes to the latter the view that relations, forms of co-ordination, stand in no sort of connection with things-in-themselves. Against this see p. 61 of this volume.

75. p. 312. Jouffroy gives an interesting account of Cousin's first appearance as a teacher of philosophy in his *Nouveaux mélanges philosophiques* (2 éd. pp. 85-95). Renan (*Feuilles détachées*, 4 éd. 1892, p. 298 and f.) expresses himself as follows *à propos* of Cousin and what he owes to him : " A travers une foule de défauts, quel haut sentiment de l'infini ! quelle vue juste du spontané et de l'inconscient ! quel accent religieux, inouï depuis Malebranche, quand il parle de la raison ! Que l'on comprend bien les traces que gardèrent de ce premier enseignement des hommes tel que Jouffroy ! Je connus le cours de 1818 . . . sous les ombrages d'Issy vers 1842. L'impression fut sur moi on ne peut pas plus profonde. J'ai la conscience que plusieurs des cadres de mon esprit viennent de là . . . M. Cousin a été non un de mes pères, mais un des excitateurs de ma pensée."

76. p. 318. On the relation between Saint-Simon and his school, see PAUL JANET'S *Saint-Simon et le Saint-Simonisme*, Paris, 1878. In my characterisation of Saint-Simon I have been guided chiefly by GEORGE WEILL'S *Saint-Simon et son œuvre*, Paris, 1894, and CHR. ADAM'S *La philosophie en France* (Première moitié du 19ᵉ siècle), Paris, 1894. For the connection between the Polytechnic School and Saint-Simonism, cf. G. PINET, " L'Ecole polytechnique et le Saint-Simonisme" (*La Revue de Paris*, 15 Mai 1894). While Saint-Simon's works are not consecutive, and he is constantly breaking fresh ground, his disciples have produced a consecutive development of his doctrine in the *Doctrine de Saint-Simon* (1829) edited by HIPPOLYTE CARNOT, which reproduces in substance *Bayard's* lectures, and which is anterior in time to Comte's fantastically extravagant period which brought about the dissolution of the school. The further extension which the doctrine of critical and organic periods received in the *Doctrine de Saint-Simon* was due, we may safely say, to the influence of Auguste Comte's first important work (*Plan des travaux scientifiques nécessaires pour réorganiser la société*, 1822). Although Comte still called himself a pupil of Saint-Simon at this time, he was really quite emancipated. Stuart Mill, in his *Autobiography*, gives an interesting account of the way in which the Saint-Simonian doctrine of critical and organic periods affected him. The whole doctrine, as has been already shown, was first promulgated by Kant and Fichte ; they were the first thinkers to see that criticism and revolution had conquered ; but they also realised that history could not yet have said its last word. The same thought may be detected

in Rousseau and Lessing ; Lessing's *Education of the Human Race* was, indeed, a favourite book in Saint-Simonian circles.

77. p. 324. Comte's pupils go a step beyond their master, for they maintain that it was Saint-Simon who learnt from Comte rather than Comte from Saint-Simon. LITTRÉ, *Auguste Comte et la philosophie positive,* 2 éd. p. 90 and f. ROBINET, *Notice sur l'œuvre et sur la vie d'Auguste Comte,* 2 éd. pp. 139. Even if—as is only natural—Saint-Simon was influenced by the talented younger men who co-operated with him, yet there can be no doubt that he had developed his leading idea before he entered into relations with Comte. Priority in the idea of a positive philosophy which was to be the new spiritual power, so necessary after the critical and revolutionary periods, cannot be denied to Saint-Simon. As GEORGES WEILL (*Saint-Simon et son œuvre,* pp. 208-210), who has put this fact beyond question, rightly remarks it does not in the least detract from the very great significance of Comte.

78. p. 325. In place of the term "perfectioning" Comte afterwards (*Cours de philosophie positive,* 2 éd. iv. pp. 262-264) substitutes "development," because the word "perfectioning" might be taken to imply an ethical estimation.

79. p. 328. In a letter to Stuart Mill of June 27, 1845, he says : " Le trouble a consisté en insomnies opinionâtres, avec mélancolie douce, mais intense, et oppression profonde, longtemps mêlée d'une extrême faiblesse." He connects this attack with the fact that a few days before he had begun the composition of his new work, and adds : " *L'ensemble de ma composition aura beaucoup gagné à cette période exceptionnelle* où ma méditation était loin d'éprouver l'atonie de ma mobilité." The following year, after the death of Clotilde de Vaux, he confessed that his feeling for her had contributed to bring about the crisis (*Lettres d'Auguste Comte à Stuart Mill,* p. 413 and f.). The husband of Madame Clotilde de Vaux had been condemned to hard labour for life for a shameful crime ; his wife, however, regarded their marriage as indissoluble ; hence her relations with Comte never passed beyond those of an intimate friendship.

80. p. 330. Of the two most famous works on Comte, written by his pupils, that of Littré maintains that Comte's real significance terminated with the publication of his *Cours de Philosophie positive,* while in ROBINET'S work the *Politique Positive* is regarded as forming the real close, and Littré is attacked as an ungrateful and uncomprehending deserter.—It goes without saying that Stuart Mill only acknowledged Comte's first period. In his *Auguste Comte and Positivism* (1865) Mill gives an interesting appreciation of both stages of Comte's teaching. The split occasioned by Littré was afterwards reproduced within the circle of "orthodox" positivists. Some of them, with LAFITTE at their head, held that the positivistic priesthood must work through the intelligence on the heart, while others, with the English Congreve at their head, held that positivism, like Christianity in its time, must conquer by direct appeal to the proletariate and to women, *i.e.* that the heart can be immediately appealed to, without using the intelligence as an intermediary. See on this point CAIRD, *The Social Philosophy and Religion of Comte,* p. 171 and f., Glasgow, 1885.

81. p. 335. *Cours de philosophie positive,* 2 éd. vi. p. 612. "Kant a réellement mérité une éternelle admiration en tentant, le premier, d'échapper directement à l'absolu philosophique par sa célèbre conception

de la double réalité, à la fois objective et subjective, qui indique un si juste sentiment de la saine philosophie." Cf. *Discours sur l'Esprit positif*, p. 24. *Catéchisme positiviste*, 2 éd. pp. 8 and 150. Comte once confessed that he had never read Kant's chief work. But he had long ago learnt to know the ideas it contained at second hand. In a letter to Valat, written on November 3, 1824, he says that Kant's system contains "many very good things, together with a mass of extravagances," and he protests against the acceptance of Cousin's exposition of Kant's teaching. "Cousin est bien loin de comprendre la portée des idées-mères du philosophe de Koenigsberg." Nevertheless he reckons Kant here as belonging to the metaphysical stage, and draws a parallel between his own relation to Kant's philosophy and Galilei's relation to the peripatetic physics. The only work of Kant with which he was directly acquainted was the small treatise *Idee zu einen allgemeinen Weltgeschichte*, which his friend Gustave d'Eichthal translated for him (1824), and which he greatly admired. Had he become acquainted with it six or seven years earlier, he says, it would have saved him the trouble of writing his treatises of the years 1820 and 1822 (Letter to Eichthal, December 10, 1824).

82. p. 343. Comte touches on the question of the possibility of introspection for the first time in his *Lettres à Valat*, p. 89 (September 24, 1819). In his essay entitled "Examen du traité de Broussais sur l'invitation" (1828), (reprinted in the interesting collection, *Opuscules de philosophie sociale*, Paris, 1883, which contains all Comte's most important work previous to the publication of his *Cours de philosophie positive*) he commends Broussais for his polemic against introspection, and remarks : A man can observe his feelings, if they are not too violent, because they are not dependent on the same organ as observation ; but his own intellectual activity no man can observe for, if so, observer and object would be identical, and who, in that case, would conduct the observation ? The reason why subjective psychology has gained so many adherents in the last ten years (1818-28) is, he thinks, owing to Condillac's and Helvetius' apt criticism of ideology, which regards our knowledge as nothing but the product of external influences, and pays no attention whatever to the necessity of including inner dispositions in our consideration ; but this criticism was urged with more weight by Bonnet and Cabanis, and still more by Gall and Spurzheim (*Opuscules*, pp. 293-296). In the *Cours de philosophie positive* (i. p. 32, f., iii. p. 564, iv. p. 605, 2 éd.) he repeats his polemic against introspection, remarking at the same time that an elementary analysis is not applicable to the most complicated of all phenomena. He gives a practical proof of his assumption that feeling can be introspected in a letter to Valat, in which he analyses the motives which underlie his activities as an author (September 28, 1819). With reference to the whole question, see my *Psychology*, i. 8.

83. p. 345. In answer to Mill, when the latter had told him that he had decided to write a book on political economy, Comte says that although political economy is really a part of sociology yet it may sometimes be useful to treat it separately, especially when undertaken by any one with as good a head as Mill. *Lettres à Stuart Mill*, pp. 231 and f., 254 and f. Cf. on the other hand *Cours de la philosophie positive*, 2 éd. iv. p. 255. "Toute étude isolée des divers éléments sociaux est donc, par la nature

de la science, essentiellement stérile, à l'example de notre économie politique, fût-elle même mieux cultivée."

84. p. 346. Cf. *Cours de la philosophie positive*, 2 éd. iv. p. 392. Also *Lettres à Stuart Mill*, p. 121. "Cette noble école, qui . . . fut certainement la plus avancée de toutes celles du dernier siècle," p. 275 ; "C'est à l'école écossaise et non, comme beaucoup d'autres, à l'école germanique, que j'ai dû la première rectification des graves aberrations, à la fois morales et intellectuelles, propres à ce qu'on appelle l'école française; je n'oublierais jamais combien ma propre évolution a été d'abord redevable surtout à quelques lumineuses inspirations de Hume et d'Adam Smith." (By the "Scotch School" Comte evidently means the whole tendency initiated by Shaftesbury and Hutcheson, and not what is more generally called " the Scotch School," *i.e.* Reid and his followers.) Perhaps I may be allowed to remark here that the fundamental conception on which all my ethical writings are based grew up in my mind chiefly while I was engaged in a study of Comte, as my treatise, *Die Grundlage der humanen Ethik* (German translation, p. 56 and f.) testifies.

85. p. 354. Hence it is not correct to say with FIORENTINO *Manuale di storia della filosofia*, p. 581, 2 ed. Napoli, 1887, that Comte paid attention to the reciprocal relation between objects only, not to that between object and subject. It is indeed true that he has not drawn conclusions from the latter relation.

86. p. 356. See on this point *Politique Positive*, iv. pp. 187, 233 and f. ; *Catéchisme positiviste*, pp. 165 and f., 222. In his later period Comte set about another characteristic alteration in his classification. He sums up in a series of (15) propositions the most general principles of positive philosophy, and calls this " systematisation of positive dogma," *philosophie première*. He borrowed the name from Bacon. Following on this comes *Philosophie seconde*, *i.e.* the series of the seven fundamental sciences, which are again subdivided into two groups, *i.e. philosophie naturelle* (the first five sciences), and *philosophie morale* (the last two sciences), *Politique Positive*, iv. p. 226. In the *Catéch. Pos.* (p. 167 and f.) he speaks rather differently, classing Mathematics, Astronomy, Physics and Chemistry together as *Cosmology*, while Biology, Sociology (in the narrower sense) and Ethics together form *Sociology*.

87. p. 368. In his treatise on Bentham (*Dissertations and Discussions*, I.), where the expression quoted in the text occurs, Stuart Mill says : " Bentham's idea of the world is that of a collection of persons pursuing each his separate interest or pleasure, and the prevention of whom from jostling one another more than is unavoidable, may be attempted by hopes and fears derived from three sources—the law, religion, and public opinion " (p. 362).

88. p. 368. By distinguishing between the motive of the estimation and the motive of the action, I have attempted to avoid the difficulty which arises for Bentham when the question as to the foundation of the principle of utility has to be faced (cf. my *Ethik*, chap. iii. 1-2, 18.

89. p. 377. Cf. J. H. Newmann, *Apologia pro vita sua*, p. 10, London, 1879 ; see also L. E. FLÖYSTRUP, *Den Anglokatholske Bevägelse i det nittende Aarhundrede* (The Anglo-Catholic Movement in the Nineteenth Century), pp. 28, 30, Kopenhagen, 1891, and GEORGE WORLEY, *The Catholic Revival of the Nineteenth Century*, pp. 45-51, London, 1894.

The best place, perhaps, to get a bird's-eye view of Coleridge's philosophical ideas is his work entitled *Church and State*. Appendix B gives his doctrine of reason and the understanding, and Appendix E discusses his relation to older philosophers. In the *Biographia Litteraria*, i. chap. 12, he clothes his ideas in Schelling's terminology, and makes *very* extensive use of Schelling's own statements.

90. p. 378. Cf. the characterisation of Carlyle by Dilthey in the *Archiv für Gesch. der Philos.* iii. p. 263. Dilthey has collected from the Carlyle papers edited by Froude everything which sheds light on the course of his development.

91. p. 388. In my treatise on Recognition (" Über Wiedererkennen," etc., *Vierteljahrsschr. f. wissensch. Phil.* xiv. p. 189,) I have pointed out that Hamilton rendered valuable service to the doctrine of association by his "law of redintegration." Among older authors, in addition to Kant and Fries, Beneke (*Psychol. Skizzen,* i. p. 382 and f.), and Chr. Wolff (*Vernünftige Gedanken von Gott, der Welt und der Seele des Menschen*, § 238) deserve mention here. Hamilton may have been acquainted with both these works. Among Hamilton's pupils and critics there have been many discussions as to what was his exact conception of our knowledge of the so-called primary qualities of things (*i.e.* extension and form); is it determined by the nature of the subject? or are we here able to know things as they are in themselves? Stuart Mill (in his *Examination of Sir William Hamilton's Philosophy*) points out a contradiction between Hamilton's teaching on this point and his doctrine that all knowledge is relative, conditioned by the relation between subject and object. Mansel's (*Philosophy of the Conditioned*, London and New York, 1866, p. 84) and Veitch's (*Hamilton*, Edinburgh and London, 1882, p. 179) view of their master's teaching is that we have a *relative* knowledge of the primary qualities ; so that these qualities are only "primary" in comparison to the secondary, generally called sense-qualities. GEORGE GROTE (*Minor Works*, p. 293) opines that Hamilton changed his point of view with regard to this question, so that in the notes to his edition of Reid's works a knowledge of primary qualities-in-themselves is assumed, while formerly he had only assumed a relative knowledge. As Hamilton's edition of Reid's works is not in the Copenhagen Library I cannot express an opinion on this point.

92. p. 391. Cf. MASSON, *Recent British Philosophy*, 3rd ed., London, 1877, p. 252 and f. *Edinburgh Review*, July 1884, p. 218.

93. p. 365. Among them was one whose early development and early matured learning is at least equally remarkable. I refer to WILLIAM ROWAN HAMILTON (born 1805, died 1865) (not to be confused with the philosopher, William Hamilton) chiefly famous for his discoveries in optics and mathematics. At the age of three he could read and reckon ; at four he had a sound knowledge of geography ; a year later he was able to translate from the Latin, Greek and Hebrew, and was on intimate terms with Homer, Milton and Dryden ; at eight he read Italian and French, and improvised Latin poems ; before he had reached his tenth year he studied Arabic and Sanskrit, and in his thirteenth year he compiled a Syriac Grammar. And all this without any injury to his bodily or mental health. He assimilated everything without any trouble, and with perfect comprehension. He was endowed with a keen poetic sense, was a

friend of Wordsworth and himself wrote beautiful poems. From his ninth year he was an accomplished swimmer, so that his physical development was not neglected (*Nature*, May 3, 1883). When we compare his development with that of Mill's, and the education of these two with that of other children, we cannot help being struck with the great differences between the original groundwork on which education has to build.

94. p. 401. Cf. Stuart Mill's *Autobiography*. Bain's *John Stuart Mill* (pp. 163-174) contains an interesting study of the relation between Mill and his wife, based on the evidence of various witnesses, and on psychological investigation. THEODOR GOMPERZ (*John Stuart Mill: ein Nachruf*, p. 18, Wien, 1839) describes a visit to Stuart Mill in his home. Mill's wife took part in the conversation, interjecting sometimes "a few brilliantly witty words"; and even when the conversation passed into the purely philosophical sphere, her "almost devoutly listening husband turned to her for her opinion which she expressed in clear and well-chosen language."

95. p. 402. See *Memories of Old Friends from the Journals of Caroline Fox*, edited by Horace S. Pym (Tauchnitz edition, Leipzig, 1881), i. p. 150 and f.; ii. p. 218 and f. (cf. 77, 143). These journals give us a most interesting insight into the intellectual life of a number of the most distinguished English thinkers, poets, and men of science. Through a number of years Caroline Fox wrote down every evening all that she remembered of the sayings of the leading spirits who frequented her father's house.

96. p. 405. In my book, *Den engelske Filosofi i vor Tid.*, Kjöbenhavn, 1847, p. 47, my criticism of Mill—by which criticism I still abide—led me to speak of him in depreciatory terms, which I should now no longer use, and which are cut out in the German translation (*Einleitung in die englische Philosophie unserer Zeit*, translated by Dr. H. Kureller, Leipzig, 1889); moreover, they are refuted by Mill's posthumous essays on the philosophy of religion which had not then appeared. A renewed study of Mill and of his writings has still further increased my admiration for him.

97. p. 411. This circular reasoning was emphasised very strongly by STANLEY JEVONS in his unfinished work, *Examination of J. S. Mill's Philosophy*, which was interrupted by his death. See *Pure Logic and other Minor Works*, London, 1890, p. 254 and f. Jevons' criticism of Mill on this point is valid, but he proceeds to draw from it unwarranted generalisations as to Mill's significance as a thinker altogether. See also ARNE LÖCHEN's *Om Stuart-Mill's Logik* (On the Logic of Stuart-Mill), p. 165 and f., Kristiana and Kopenhagen, 1885. Jevons' criticism had already been published in the *Contemporary Review*, 1877-79, so that Löchen could make use of it. Löchen's work, however, is rich in interesting and instructive observations and investigations, and contains a valuable study of Mill's logic and theory of knowledge.

98. p. 412. I took this as the basis of my criticism of Mill's theory of knowledge in my earlier exposition. See *Einleitung in die engl. Phil. unserer Zeit* (German translation, Leipzig, 1893).

99. p. 416. In my *Psychologie in Umrissen auf Grundlage der Erfahrung* (second German edition, Leipzig, 1893) I have attempted to make the "uniting principle" my central point of view, and to show how the laws of association, as well as those of sensations, can be traced back to this

principle which, under the name of "synthesis," was already employed by Kant as the basis of his conception of consciousness. Hence I have been astonished to find myself frequently described, without any qualification, as an adherent of the English school. Thus *e.g.* PAUL CARUS (*Primer of Philosophy*, Chicago, 1893, p. 175) classes me among "those psychologists who believe that the doctrine of association offers a key to all the problems of mind." Wundt (*Physiologische Psychologie*, fourth edition, ii. p. 482 Leipzig, 1893) mentions me among the inquirers who hold "that all mental processes can be deduced from association." As early as my *Einleitung in die englische Philosophie* (1874) I criticised the association-psychology, *i.e.* the view which makes independent sensations and ideas the "Reals" of consciousness, and regards association as an external union, inessential to the sensations and ideas themselves. And throughout my whole psychology a criticism of this conception may be discovered, united, it is true, with an attempt to preserve the truths to the discovery of which it has contributed. At the same time I hold that we can only hope to correct the association-psychology by a careful inquiry into our own latent assumptions, and not by positing a special faculty of thought or an "apperception," which is to take the place of associations. Cf. my treatise "Über Wiedererkennen," etc. (*Vierteljahrsschrift f. wissenschaftl. Philosophie*, xiii. pp. 420-424 and *ib.* xiv. pp. 191-205).

100. p. 432. A general view of the attempts to construct a philosophy of religion both before and after Mill's time in England is given by O. PFLEIDERER, *Die Entwickelung der protestantischen Theologie in Deutschland seit Kant und in Grossbritannien seit 1825*, Freiburg, 1891. (But the exposition of Mill's views here given is not adequate. Pfleiderer makes a bad historical blunder on p. 407, where he speaks of Hamilton, who had died nine years before the publication of Mill's "Examination," *answering* Mill's attack!)

101. p. 440. I have given a more detailed biographical account and characterisation of Darwin in a popular work, *Charles Darwin*, Kjöbenhavn, 1889 (German translation, 1895). A few paragraphs from this little book have been incorporated in the text. The chief source is *The Life and Letters of Charles Darwin, including an autobiographical chapter*, edited by Francis Darwin, London, 1887.

102. p. 449. It is not impossible that this utterance was prompted by the memory of the well-known scene which took place between Huxley and the Bishop of Oxford (see *Life and Letters*, ii. pp. 320-322), only that Huxley preferred the monkey as ancestor not to a savage, but—to the Bishop of Oxford !

103. p. 449. Cf. my comments on the relation between Darwinism and ethics in my *Grundlage der humanen Ethik* (Deutsche Üb.), pp. 18-20, and in the *Etiske Undersögelsen*, pp. 17-23, Kopenhagen, 1891.

104. p. 452. In my account of Spencer's life and mental development, I have chosen my material from passages in his own writings (more especially from the interesting discussions in his essay on *The Classification of the Sciences, with reasons for dissenting from the Philosophy of M. Comte*, 3rd ed. pp. 31, 34, 36), from a short biography of Spencer, written with his assistance, by Prof. Youmans, published in an American journal (*The Popular Science Monthly*, March 1876), and from a speech of Youman's contained in the report of a dinner given in Spencer's honour at New

York in 1882. (*Herbert Spencer on the Americans and the Americans on Herbert Spencer*, New York, 1882, pp. 68-76.)

105. p. 458. This section of the *First Principles* should be compared with *Principles of Sociology*, part iii. (*Ecclesiastical Institutions*), chap. xvi. (Religious Retrospect and Prospect).

106. p. 461. I brought forward this objection in my *Einleitung in die englische Philosophie unseren Zeit* (of which the Danish original appeared in 1874), pp. 158 and f., 170, 188 and f.

107. p. 466. I drew Spencer's attention to these contradictions in a private letter of 1876, and in his answer he gave the explanation given in the text, and stated that they had hitherto escaped his attention.

108. p. 466. Cf. *First Principles*, 3rd ed. p. 318. "Though evolution of the various products of human activities cannot be said directly to exemplify the integration of matter and dissipation of motion [which Spencer believes to take place in every evolution, since the parts which form the whole lose their own motion in so doing] yet they exemplify it *indirectly*," (*ib.* 391). "The phenomena subjectively known as changes in consciousness are objectively known as nervous excitations and discharges, which science now interprets into modes of motion" (*Principles of Psychology*, 2nd ed. i. p. 508). "Though the development of mind itself cannot be explained by a series of deductions from the Persistence of Force, yet it remains possible that its obverse, the development of physical changes in a physical organ, may be so explained."

109. p. 476. I urged this objection against Spencer's theory of knowledge in my *Einleitung*, etc., pp. 222-224. In my *Psychology* (2nd ed.), pp. 485-487 I have discussed the subject again.

110. p. 481. An interesting critique of Spencer's sociology is given by ÉMILE DURKHEIM: *De la division du travail social*, pp. 218-247, Paris, 1868.

111. p. 483. See in relation to the difficulties attending a scientific ethic my *Etiske Undersögelsen* (chap. i.) and the first chapter of my *Ethik*.

112. p. 487. In the concluding section of my *Einleitung in die englische Philosophie unseren Zeit*, pp. 243-249, Leipzig, 1889, I have alluded to the work of Boole, Jevons, Sidgwick and several others whom I must here omit.

113. p. 493. On the "period of great discoveries" at the end of the preceding century see RASMUS PEDERSEN, *Planternes Näringsstoffer, Historisk Indledning* (Plant-food, Historical Introduction), p. 44 and f. Kjöbenhavn, 1883.

114. p. 494. For an account of vitalism in its different forms see LOUIS PEISSE, *La Médecine et les Médecins*, i. pp. 226-297, Paris, 1857. It must be clearly understood that what is meant by vitalism here is the tendency to *explain* vital phenomena by the assumption of a "vital force" —not the assertion that there is much in vital phenomena which, up to the present time, has not been explained either by physical or chemical causes.

115. p. 495. Cf. MAYER'S letter to Griesinger, July 20, 1844. "When I say heat is transformed into motion and the reverse, I do not mean that there is any *quantitative* relation between heat and motion when transformed into one another" (*Kleinen Schriften und Briefe* von ROBERT MAYER. Herausgegeb. von WEYRAND, p. 225, Stuttgart, 1893).

116. p. 496.   " If the resistance to electrolysis which is over and above that due to chemical change were not accounted for elsewhere, *it would prove the annihilation of a part of the power of the circuit, without any corresponding effect.* We shall see that this is not the case, but that in the evolution of heat, when the excess of existence takes place, an exact equivalent is restored " (JOULE, " On the Heat evolved during the Electrolysis of Water," 1843. *Scientific Papers,* i. p. 115, London, 1884.) " We *might reason,* a priori, *that absolute destruction of living force cannot possibly take place,* because it is manifestly absurd to suppose that the powers with which God has endowed Matter can be destroyed . . . . but we are not left with this argument alone, decisive as it must be to every unprejudiced mind " (Joule, " Matter, Living Force and Heat " 1847. *Scientific Papers* i. p. 269). Joule's standpoint does not differ in principle from that of Mayer's and Colding's. With regard to the latter cf. a sentence in his *Undersögelse om de almindelige Naturkräfter og deres gensidige Afhängighed* (An investigation into the universal forces of Nature and their reciprocal dependence.) *Videnskabernes Selskabs Skriften.* Femte Räkke. *Naturv. mathem.* Abth. ii. p. 129.) " The idea that a force could disappear into the corporeal without reappearing as an efficient cause seems to me *contrary to reason.*"

117. p. 497.   Mayer, *Kleinere Schriften und Briefe,* pp. 339 and f., 460. *Die Mechanik der Wärme,* 3. Ausg., p. 356 and f. Colding, *Naturvidenskabelige Betragtninger over Slägtskabet mellem det aandelige Livs Virksomheder og de almindelige Naturkräfter* (Scientific observations on the relation between the activities of conscious life and the universal forces of Nature) (Oversigt over det kgl. danske Videnskabernes Selskabs Forhandlinger, 1856), pp. 155-166. Joule, *Scientific Papers,* i. pp. 269, 273. As regards Mayer, it seems from his lecture at Innsbruck (*Die Mech. d. Wärme,* p. 357) that he did not believe in any interruption in the series of material phenomena, but that he assumed a parallelism between mental happenings and happenings in the brain.

118. p. 517.   On Lotze's hesitation on this point see MAX WENTSCHER, *Lotzes Gottesbegriff und dessen metaphysische Begründung,* pp. 19-29, Halle, 1893.

119. p. 518.   In a treatise entitled *Lotzes tankar om tid och timlighet i kritisk belysning* (Lotze's ideas on time and temporality in the light of criticism) REINHOLD GEIJER draws attention to the differing standpoints Lotze seems to have adopted with regard to the absolute validity of time. In my essay on " Lotze og den svenske Filosofi" ("Lotze und die schwedische Philosophie") (German translation in the *Philos. Monatsch.* 1890) I referred with approval to the explanation given by my Swedish colleague, although I myself entertained a different conception of the problem.   The matter, however, appears to be rather different from what Geijer, and I with him, thought there was reason to believe. According to the statements made by RICHARD FALCKENBERG in his article " Die Entwickelung der Lotzeschen Zeitlehre" (*Zeitschrift für Philosophie und philosophische Kritik,* Band 105), the *Grundzüge der Metaphysik* which appeared after Lotze's death was written in the year 1865 ; if this be so the chief reason for believing that it was only towards the end of his life that he disputed the reality of time disappears.   If in earlier writings he speaks of the time relation without qualification, as though it had absolute validity, this,

according to Falckenberg, is a justifiable use of popular ideas, where the context does not demand a more exact way of speaking. Lotze's definitive conception was unfolded in the *Drei Bücher der Metaphysik* (1879) and the *Grundzüge der Religionsphilosophie* (1875-79), according to which succession is valid of finite beings, while the Deity is exalted above all temporal differences. His earliest exposition (given in the *Metaphysik*, 1841) does not introduce this distinction, which certainly does not shed any light on the question (although the *psychological* distinction between succession and the abstract form of time is defensible). I am as unable as my Swedish colleague to read any meaning into the expression "a timeless happening and working" (*Grundzüge der Metaphysik*, § 58). My German colleague, on the other hand, thinks it expresses a significant idea.

120. p. 519. Cf. my *Psychology* (English translation, pp. 54-70) and my article on "Psychical and Physical Activity" (*Vierteljahrsschr. f. wissenschaftl. Philos.* xv. p. 249 and f.). It is interesting to remember that in his earlier period, Leibniz, the founder of metaphysical idealism, maintained as emphatically as Spinoza that the dualism, spirit-matter, is only actually and not logically necessary, *Philos. Schr.* ed. Gerhardt, i. pp. 237, 242, 268. Cf. LUDWIG STEIN, *Leibniz und Spinoza*, pp. 93 and f. S. MANDL (*Kritische Beiträge zur Metaphysik Lotzes*, p. 55, Bern, 1895), arrives at a result similar to my own to Lotze's standpoint in the philosophy of religion.

121. p. 521. See on this point Reinhold Geijer, "Hermann Lotzes lära on rummet" (H. Lotze's Doctrine of Space), (*Nyt svensk tidsskrift*, 1880) and "Darstellung und Kritik der Lotzeschen Lehre von den Lokalzeichen (*Philosophische Monatshefte*, 1885). Cf. my article "Lotze og den svenske Filosofi" (German translation in the *Philos. Monatsh.* 1890), and my *Psychology* (English translation, pp. 190-205).

122. p. 522. *Microcosm*, Bk. III. chap. i. (English trans.). "Why, then, should not an atom of the nervous system equally be able to exert impact and pressure on the soul, or the soul on it ; seeing that closer scrutiny discovers ordinary impact and pressure to be not a means to the effect, but only the perceptible form of a far more subtle process between the elements?"

123. p. 524. KRESTO KRESTOFF : *Lotzes metaphysischer Seelenbegriff*, Halle, 1890, pp. 46 and f. ; 73. MAX WENTSCHER, *Lotzes Gottesbegriff und dessen metaphysische Begründung*, pp. 11 and f. Halle, 1893. The relation of opposition in which, in spite of many points of contact, Lotze's conception had, from the beginning, stood to Herbart's conception likewise shows that Lotze's line of thought suffered no radical change with the course of years. Cf. on this point MAX NATH, *Die Psychologie Hermann Lotzes in ihrem Verhältniss zu Herbart*, Halle, 1892. Lotze's optimism is closely connected with his ethical monism. Although he himself often refers to the reality of physical and moral evil as a hindrance to the working out of his world-conception, yet an otherwise favourable critic has reproached him for lack of interest in "the fundamental dogma of all religions, the atonement," because he did not pay sufficient attention to evil. G. VORBRODT, *Prinzipien der Ethik und Religionsphilosophie Lotzes*, p. 97, Dessau und Leipzig, 1891.

124. p. 526. A. ELSAS : *Zum Andenken Gustav Theodor Fechners*,

(Grenzbote, 1888). J. E. KNUTZE, *G. Th. Fechner, ein deutsches Ge-
lehrtenleben*, Leipzig, 1892. Unfortunately I was not able to make use of
K. LASSWITZ'S book, *Gustav Theodor Fechner*, 1896 (Frommann's Klassiker
der Philosophie).

125. p. 529. In my earlier exposition ("Philosophy in Germany,"
1892) I was misled by some utterances in *Zendavesta* (ii. pp. 352 and f.)
into supposing that Fechner assumed reciprocal action between mind
and matter. Fechner, however, only intended to point out here how
important it is to change our standpoint and to discover the formula of the
reciprocal relation between the two sides. He here, no more than later,
assumes a transition from one side to another. In the *Elementen der
Psychophysik*, i. p. 8, he says : "We call the psychical a function of the
physical, *depending upon it*, and *vice versa*, in so far as a constant relation
according to law exists, such that from the existence and changes of the
one we may conclude to those of the other." Fechner often (*e.g. Elemente*,
i. p. 18, ii. p. 393) uses the expression simultaneous conditions, simultaneous or reciprocal dependence, of this kind of dependence. In his opinion,
changes in the brain, corresponding to psychical activities cannot (as Lotze
and the spiritualists think) be regarded as stimuli acting upon the soul
(*Elemente*, i. p. 18).

126. p. 539. On the relation between culture and happiness see my
Ethik, chap. vii., and my *Etiske Undersögelser*, chap. ii.

127. p. 546. KARL ROKITANSKY'S brilliant essay, "Der selbständige
Wert des Wissens" (*Sitzungsberichte der Wiener Akademie*, 1867) did
not, it is true, appear till a year after the *History of Materialism;* but as
early as 1862, he had pointed out in a speech, that Kant's idealism is the
true consequence of scientific thought. Cf. TH. MEYNERT, *Karl Rokitansky*, ein Nachruf (Collection of popular scientific lectures, Wien and
Leipzig, 1892, pp. 76 and f.) HELMHOLTZ, too (in his *Physiologischen
Optik*, 1867, pp. 443 and f.) maintains that, in the last instance, it is
unjustifiable to attribute to our ideas anything but a practical and symbolic
alidity. The physiologist, A. FICK (*Die Welt als Vorstellung*, Würzburg,
1870) arrives at a similar result.

128. p. 546. MAX HEINZE has drawn attention to this in his
interesting essay, "Der Idealismus Friedrich Albert Langes" (*Vierteljahrsschrift für wissensch. Phil.* i. pp. 185-185).

129. p. 547. Cf. my *Psvchology*, English translation, pp. 275 and f.

INDEX

Catalogue of Dover
SCIENCE BOOKS

DIFFERENTIAL EQUATIONS
(ORDINARY AND PARTIAL DIFFERENTIAL)

INTRODUCTION TO THE DIFFERENTIAL EQUATIONS OF PHYSICS, L. Hopf. Especially valuable to engineer with no math beyond elementary calculus. Emphasizes intuitive rather than formal aspects of concepts. Partial contents: Law of causality, energy theorem, damped oscillations, coupling by friction, cylindrical and spherical coordinates, heat source, etc. 48 figures. 160pp. 5⅜ x 8. S120 Paperbound **$1.25**

INTRODUCTION TO BESSEL FUNCTIONS, F. Bowman. Rigorous, provides all necessary material during development, includes practical applications. Bessel functions of zero order, of any real order, definite integrals, asymptotic expansion, circular membranes, Bessel's solution to Kepler's problem, much more. "Clear . . . useful not only to students of physics and engineering, but to mathematical students in general," Nature. 226 problems. Short tables of Bessel functions. 27 figures. x + 135pp. 5⅜ x 8. S462 Paperbound **$1.35**

DIFFERENTIAL EQUATIONS, F. R. Moulton. Detailed, rigorous exposition of all non-elementary processes of solving ordinary differential equations. Chapters on practical problems; more advanced than problems usually given as illustrations. Includes analytic differential equations; variations of a parameter; integrals of differential equations; analytic implicit functions; problems of elliptic motion; sine-amplitude functions; deviation of formal bodies; Cauchy-Lipshitz process; linear differential equations with periodic coefficients; much more. Historical notes. 10 figures. 222 problems. xv + 395pp. 5⅜ x 8. S451 Paperbound **$2.00**

PARTIAL DIFFERENTIAL EQUATIONS OF MATHEMATICAL PHYSICS, A. G. Webster. Valuable sections on elasticity, compression theory, potential theory, theory of sound, heat conduction, wave propagation, vibration theory. Contents include: deduction of differential equations, vibrations, normal functions, Fourier's series. Cauchy's method, boundary problems, method of Riemann-Volterra, spherical, cylindrical, ellipsoidal harmonics, applications, etc. 97 figures. vii + 440pp. 5⅜ x 8. S263 Paperbound **$2.00**

ORDINARY DIFFERENTIAL EQUATIONS, E. L. Ince. A most compendious analysis in real and complex domains. Existence and nature of solutions, continuous transformation groups, solutions in an infinite form, definite integrals, algebraic theory. Sturmian theory, boundary problems, existence theorems, 1st order, higher order, etc. "Deserves highest praise, a notable addition to mathematical literature," Bulletin, Amer. Math. Soc. Historical appendix. 18 figures. viii + 558pp. 5⅜ x 8. S349 Paperbound **$2.55**

ASYMPTOTIC EXPANSIONS, A. Erdélyi. Only modern work available in English; unabridged reproduction of monograph prepared for Office of Naval Research. Discusses various procedures for asymptotic evaluation of integrals containing a large parameter; solutions of ordinary linear differential equations. vi + 108pp. 5⅜ x 8. S318 Paperbound **$1.35**

LECTURES ON CAUCHY'S PROBLEM, J. Hadamard. Based on lectures given at Columbia, Rome, discusses work of Riemann, Kirchhoff, Volterra, and author's own research on hyperbolic case in linear partial differential equations. Extends spherical cylindrical waves to apply to all (normal) hyperbolic equations. Partial contents: Cauchy's problem, fundamental formula, equations with odd number, with even number of independent variables; method of descent. 32 figures. iii + 316pp. 5⅜ x 8. S105 Paperbound **$1.75**

NUMBER THEORY

INTRODUCTION TO THE THEORY OF NUMBERS, L. E. Dickson. Thorough, comprehensive, witn adequate coverage of classical literature. Not beyond beginners. Chapters on divisibility, congruences, quadratic residues and reciprocity, Diophantine equations, etc. Full treatment of binary quadratic forms without usual restriction to integral coefficients. Covers infinitude of primes, Fermat's theorem, Legendre's symbol, automorphs, Recent theorems of Thue, Siegal, much more. Much material not readily available elsewhere. 239 problems. 1 figure. viii + 183pp. 5⅜ x 8. S342 Paperbound **$1.65**

ELEMENTS OF NUMBER THEORY, I. M. Vinogradov. Detailed 1st course for persons without advanced mathematics; 95% of this book can be understood by readers who have gone no farther than high school algebra. Partial contents: divisibility theory, important number theoretical functions, congruences, primitive roots and indices, etc. Solutions to problems, exercises. Tables of primes, indices, etc. Covers almost every essential formula in elementary number theory! "Welcome addition . . . reads smoothly," Bull. of the Amer. Math. Soc. 233 problems. 104 exercises. viii + 227pp. 5⅜ x 8. S259 Paperbound **$1.60**

PROBABILITY THEORY AND INFORMATION THEORY

SELECTED PAPERS ON NOISE AND STOCHASTIC PROCESSES, edited by Prof. Nelson Wax, U. of Illinois. 6 basic papers for those whose work involves noise characteristics. Chandrasekhar, Uhlenback and Ornstein, Uhlenbeck and Ming, Rice, Doob. Included is Kac's Chauvenet-Prize winning "Random Walk." Extensive bibliography lists 200 articles, through 1953. 21 figures. 337pp. 6⅛ x 9¼. S262 Paperbound **$2.35**

A PHILOSOPHICAL ESSAY ON PROBABILITIES, Marquis de Laplace. This famous essay explains without recourse to mathematics the principle of probability, and the application of probabilty to games of chance, natural philosophy, astronomy, many other fields. Translated from 6th French edition by F. W. Truscott, F. L. Emory. Intro. by E. T. Bell. 204pp. 5⅜ x 8. S166 Paperbound **$1.25**

MATHEMATICAL FOUNDATIONS OF INFORMATION THEORY, A. I. Khinchin. For mathematicians, statisticians, physicists, cyberneticists, communications engineers, a complete, exact introduction to relatively new field. Entropy as a measure of a finite scheme, applications to coding theory, study of sources, channels and codes, detailed proofs of both Shannon theorems for any ergodic source and any stationary channel with finite memory, much more. "Presents for the first time rigorous proofs of certain fundamental theorems . . . quite complete . . . amazing expository ability," American Math. Monthly. vii + 120pp. 5⅜ x 8. S434 Paperbound **$1.35**

VECTOR AND TENSOR ANALYSIS AND MATRIX THEORY

VECTOR AND TENSOR ANALYSIS, G. E. Hay. One of clearest introductions to increasingly important subject. Start with simple definitions, finish with sure mastery of oriented Cartesian vectors, Christoffel symbols, solenoidal tensors. Complete breakdown of plane, solid, analytical, differential geometry. Separate chapters on application. All fundamental formulae listed, demonstrated. 195 problems. 66 figures. viii + 193pp. 5⅜ x 8. S109 Paperbound **$1.75**

APPLICATIONS OF TENSOR ANALYSIS, A. J. McConnell. Excellent text for applying tensor methods to such familiar subjects as dynamics, electricity, elasticity, hydrodynamics. Explains fundamental ideas and notation of tensor theory, geometrical treatment of tensor algebra, theory of differentiation of tensors, and a wealth of practical material. "The variety of fields treated and the presence of extremely numerous examples make this volume worth much more than its low price," Alluminio. Formerly titled "Applications of the Absolute Differential Calculus." 43 illustrations. 685 problems. xii + 381pp. S373 Paperbound **$1.85**

VECTOR AND TENSOR ANALYSIS, A. P. Wills. Covers entire field, from dyads to non-Euclidean manifolds (especially detailed), absolute differentiation, the Riemann-Christoffel and Ricci-Einstein tensors, calculation of Gaussian curvature of a surface. Illustrations from electrical engineering, relativity theory, astro-physics, quantum mechanics. Presupposes only working knowledge of calculus. Intended for physicists, engineers, mathematicians. 44 diagrams. 114 problems. xxxii + 285pp. 5⅜ x 8. S454 Paperbound **$1.75**

2

PHYSICS, ENGINEERING

MECHANICS, DYNAMICS, THERMODYNAMICS, ELASTICITY

MATHEMATICAL ANALYSIS OF ELECTRICAL AND OPTICAL WAVE-MOTION, H. Bateman. By one of century's most distinguished mathematical physicists, a practical introduction to developments of Maxwell's electromagnetic theory which directly concern the solution of partial differential equation of wave motion. Methods of solving wave-equation, polar-cylindrical coordinates, diffraction, transformation of coordinates, homogeneous solutions, electromagnetic fields with moving singularities, etc. 168pp. 5⅜ x 8. S14 Paperbound **$1.60**

THERMODYNAMICS, Enrico Fermi. Unabridged reproduction of 1937 edition. Remarkable for clarity, organization; requires no knowledge of advanced math beyond calculus, only familiarity with fundamentals of thermometry, calorimetry. Partial Contents: Thermodynamic systems, 1st and 2nd laws, potentials; Entropy, phase rule; Reversible electric cells; Gaseous reactions: Van't Hoff reaction box, principle of LeChatelier; Thermodynamics of dilute solutions: osmotic, vapor pressures; boiling, freezing point; Entropy constant. 25 problems. 24 illustrations. x + 160pp. 5⅜ x 8. S361 Paperbound **$1.75**

FOUNDATIONS OF POTENTIAL THEORY, O. D. Kellogg. Based on courses given at Harvard, suitable for both advanced and beginning mathematicians. Proofs rigorous, much material here not generally available elsewhere. Partial contents: gravity, fields of force, divergence theorem, properties of Newtonian potentials at points of free space, potentials as solutions of LaPlace's equation, harmonic functions, electrostatics, electric images, logarithmic potential, etc. ix + 384pp. 5⅜ x 8. S144 Paperbound **$1.98**

DIALOGUES CONCERNING TWO NEW SCIENCES, Galileo Galilei. Classic of experimental science, mechanics, engineering, as enjoyable as it is important. Characterized by author as "superior to everything else of mine." Offers a lively exposition of dynamics, elasticity, sound, ballistics, strength of materials, scientific method. Translated by H. Grew, A. de Salvio. 126 diagrams. xxi + 288pp. 5⅜ x 8. S99 Paperbound **$1.65**

THEORETICAL MECHANICS; AN INTRODUCTION TO MATHEMATICAL PHYSICS, J. S. Ames, F. D. Murnaghan. A mathematically rigorous development for advanced students, with constant practical applications. Used in hundreds of advanced courses. Unusually thorough coverage of gyroscopic baryscopic material, detailed analyses of Corilis acceleration, applications of Lagrange's equations, motion of double pendulum, Hamilton-Jacobi partial differential equations, group velocity, dispersion, etc. Special relativity included. 159 problems. 44 figures. ix + 462pp. 5⅜ x 8. S461 Paperbound **$2.00**

STATICS AND THE DYNAMICS OF A PARTICLE, W. D. MacMillan. This is Part One of "Theoretical Mechanics." For over 3 decades a self-contained, extremely comprehensive advanced undergraduate text in mathematical physics, physics, astronomy, deeper foundations of engineering. Early sections require only a knowledge of geometry; later, a working knowledge of calculus. Hundreds of basic problems including projectiles to moon, harmonic motion, ballistics, transmission of power, stress and strain, elasticity, astronomical problems. 340 practice problems, many fully worked out examples. 200 figures. xvii + 430pp. 5⅜ x 8. S467 Paperbound **$2.00**

THE THEORY OF THE POTENTIAL, W. D. MacMillan. This is Part Two of "Theoretical Mechanics." Comprehensive, well-balanced presentation, serving both as introduction and reference with regard to specific problems, for physicists and mathematicians. Assumes no prior knowledge of integral relations, all math is developed as needed. Includes: Attraction of Finite Bodies; Newtonian Potential Function; Vector Fields, Green and Gauss Theorems; Two-layer Surfaces; Spherical Harmonics; etc. "The great number of particular cases . . . should make the book valuable to geo-physicists and others actively engaged in practical applications of the potential theory," Review of Scientific Instruments. xii + 469pp. 5⅜ x 8. S486 Paperbound **$2.25**

DYNAMICS OF A SYSTEM OF RIGID BODIES (Advanced Section), E. J. Routh. Revised 6th edition of a classic reference aid. Partial contents: moving axes, relative motion, oscillations about equilibrium, motion. Motion of a body under no forces, any forces. Nature of motion given by linear equations and conditions of stability. Free, forced vibrations, constants of integration, calculus of finite differences, variations, procession and mutation, motion of the moon, motion of string, chain, membranes. 64 figures. 498pp. 5⅜ x 8. S229 Paperbound **$2.35**

THE DYNAMICS OF PARTICLES AND OF RIGID, ELASTIC, AND FLUID BODIES: BEING LECTURES ON MATHEMATICAL PHYSICS, A. G. Webster. Reissuing of classic fills need for comprehensive work on dynamics. Covers wide range in unusually great depth, applying ordinary, partial differential equations. Partial contents: laws of motion, methods applicable to systems of all sorts; oscillation, resonance, cyclic systems; dynamics of rigid bodies; potential theory; stress and strain; gyrostatics; wave, vortex motion; kinematics of a point; Lagrange's equations; Hamilton's principle; vectors; deformable bodies; much more not easily found together in one volume. Unabridged reprinting of 2nd edition. 20 pages on differential equations, higher analysis. 203 illustrations. xi + 588pp. 5⅜ x 8. S522 Paperbound **$2.35**

PRINCIPLES OF MECHANICS, Heinrich Hertz. A classic of great interest in logic of science. Last work by great 19th century physicist, created new system of mechanics based upon space, time, mass; returns to axiomatic analysis, understanding of formal, structural aspects of science, taking into account logic, observation, a priori elements. Of great historical importance to Poincaré, Carnap, Einstein, Milne. 20 page introduction by R. S. Cohen, Wesleyan U., analyzes implications of Hertz's thought and logic of science. 13 page introduction by Helmholtz. xlii + 274pp. 5⅜ x 8.　　　　　　　S316 Clothbound **$3.50**
　　　　　　　　　　　　　　　　　　　　　　　　　　　　　　　　　S317 Paperbound **$1.75**

MATHEMATICAL FOUNDATIONS OF STATISTICAL MECHANICS, A. I. Khinchin. A thoroughly up-to-date introduction, offering a precise and mathematically rigorous formulation of the problems of statistical mechanics. Provides analytical tools to replace many commonly used cumbersome concepts and devices. Partial contents: Geometry, kinematics of phase space; ergodic problem; theory of probability; central limit theorem; ideal monatomic gas; foundation of thermodynamics; dispersion, distribution of sum functions; etc. "Excellent introduction . . . clear, concise, rigorous," Quarterly of Applied Mathematics. viii + 179pp. 5⅜ x 8.　　　　　　　　　　　　　　　　　　　　　　　　S146 Clothbound **$2.95**
　　　　　　　　　　　　　　　　　　　　　　　　　　　　　　　　　S147 Paperbound **$1.35**

MECHANICS OF THE GYROSCOPE, THE DYNAMICS OF ROTATION, R. F. Deimel, Prof. of Mechanical Engineering, Stevens Inst. of Tech. Elementary, general treatment of dynamics of rotation, with special application of gyroscopic phenomena. No knowledge of vectors needed. Velocity of a moving curve, acceleration to a point, general equations of motion, gyroscopic horizon, free gyro, motion of discs, the damped gyro, 103 similar topics. Exercises. 75 figures. 208pp. 5⅜ x 8.　　　　　　　　　　　　　　　　S66 Paperbound **$1.65**

MECHANICS VIA THE CALCULUS, P. W. Norris, W. S. Legge. Wide coverage, from linear motion to vector analysis; equations determining motion, linear methods, compounding of simple harmonic motions, Newton's laws of motion, Hooke's law, the simple pendulum, motion of a particle in 1 plane, centers of gravity, virtual work, friction, kinetic energy of rotating bodies, equilibrium of strings, hydrostatics, sheering stresses, elasticity, etc. Many worked-out examples. 550 problems. 3rd revised edition. xii + 367pp.　　　S207 Clothbound **$3.95**

A TREATISE ON THE MATHEMATICAL THEORY OF ELASTICITY, A. E. H. Love. An indispensable reference work for engineers, mathematicians, physicists, the most complete, authoritative treatment of classical elasticity in one volume. Proceeds from elementary notions of extension to types of strain, cubical dilatation, general theory of strains. Covers relation between mathematical theory of elasticity and technical mechanics; equilibrium of isotropic elastic solids and aelotropic solid bodies; nature of force transmission, Volterra's theory of dislocations; theory of elastic spheres in relation to tidal, rotational, gravitational effects on earth; general theory of bending; deformation of curved plates; buckling effects; much more. "The standard treatise on elasticity," American Math. Monthly. 4th revised edition. 76 figures. xviii + 643pp. 6⅛ x 9¼.　　　　　　　　　　　S174 Paperbound **$2.95**

NUCLEAR PHYSICS, QUANTUM THEORY, RELATIVITY

MESON PHYSICS, R. E. Marshak. Presents basic theory, and results of experiments with emphasis on theoretical significance. Phenomena involving mesons as virtual transitions avoided, eliminating some of least satisfactory predictions of meson theory. Includes production study of π mesons at nonrelativistic nucleon energies contracts between π and μ mesons, phenomena associated with nuclear interaction of π mesons, etc. Presents early evidence for new classes of particles, indicates theoretical difficulties created by discovery of heavy mesons and hyperons. viii + 378pp. 5⅜ x 8.　　　　　　S500 Paperbound **$1.95**

THE FUNDAMENTAL PRINCIPLES OF QUANTUM MECHANICS, WITH ELEMENTARY APPLICATIONS, E. C. Kemble. Inductive presentation, for graduate student, specialists in other branches of physics. Apparatus necessary beyond differential equations and advanced calculus developed as needed. Though general exposition of principles, hundreds of individual problems fully treated. "Excellent book . . . of great value to every student . . . rigorous and detailed mathematical discussion . .. has succeeded in keeping his presentation clear and understandable," Dr. Linus Pauling, J. of American Chemical Society. Appendices: calculus of variations, math. notes, etc. 611pp. 5⅝ x 8⅜.　　　　　　T472 Paperbound **$2.95**

WAVE PROPAGATION IN PERIODIC STRUCTURES, L. Brillouin. General method, application to different problems: pure physics—scattering of X-rays in crystals, thermal vibration in crystal lattices, electronic motion in metals; problems in electrical engineering. Partial contents: elastic waves along 1-dimensional lattices of point masses. Propagation of waves along 1-dimensional lattices. Energy flow. 2, 3 dimensional lattices. Mathieu's equation. Matrices and propagation of waves along an electric line. Continuous electric lines. 131 illustrations. xii + 253pp. 5⅜ x 8.　　　　　　　　　S34 Paperbound **$1.85**

THEORY OF ELECTRONS AND ITS APPLICATION TO THE PHENOMENA OF LIGHT AND RADIANT HEAT, H. Lorentz. Lectures delivered at Columbia Univ., by Nobel laureate. Unabridged, form historical coverage of theory of free electrons, motion, absorption of heat, Zeeman effect, optical phenomena in moving bodies, etc. 109 pages notes explain more advanced sections. 9 figures. 352pp. 5⅜ x 8.   S173 Paperbound **$1.85**

SELECTED PAPERS ON QUANTUM ELECTRODYNAMICS, edited by J. Schwinger. Facsimiles of papers which established quantum electrodynamics; beginning to present position as part of larger theory. First book publication in any language of collected papers of Bethe, Bloch, Dirac, Dyson, Fermi, Feynman, Heisenberg, Kusch, Lamb, Oppenheimer, Pauli, Schwinger, Tomonoga, Weisskopf, Wigner, etc. 34 papers: 29 in English, 1 in French, 3 in German, 1 in Italian. Historical commentary by editor. xvii + 423pp. 6⅛ x 9¼.
S444 Paperbound **$2.45**

FOUNDATIONS OF NUCLEAR PHYSICS, edited by R. T. Beyer. 13 of the most important papers on nuclear physics reproduced in facsimile in the original languages; the papers most often cited in footnotes, bibliographies. Anderson, Curie, Joliot, Chadwick, Fermi, Lawrence, Cockroft, Hahn, Yukawa. Unparalleled bibliography: 122 double columned pages, over 4,000 articles, books, classified. 57 figures. 288pp. 6⅛ x 9¼.   S19 Paperbound **$1.75**

THE THEORY OF GROUPS AND QUANTUM MECHANICS, H. Weyl. Schroedinger's wave equation, de Broglie's waves of a particle, Jordon-Hoelder theorem, Lie's continuous groups of transformations, Pauli exclusion principle, quantization of Mawell-Dirac field equations, etc. Unitary geometry, quantum theory, groups, application of groups to quantum mechanics, symmetry permutation group, algebra of symmetric transformations, etc. 2nd revised edition. xxii + 422pp. 5⅜ x 8.   S268 Clothbound **$4.50**
S269 Paperbound **$1.95**

PHYSICAL PRINCIPLES OF THE QUANTUM THEORY, Werner Heisenberg. Nobel laureate discusses quantum theory; his own work, Compton, Schroedinger, Wilson, Einstein, many others. For physicists, chemists, not specialists in quantum theory. Only elementary formulae considered in text; mathematical appendix for specialists. Profound without sacrificing clarity. Translated by C. Eckart, F. Hoyt. 18 figures. 192pp. 5⅜ x 8.
S113 Paperbound **$1.25**

INVESTIGATIONS ON THE THEORY OF THE BROWNIAN MOVEMENT, Albert Einstein. Reprints from rare European journals, translated into English. 5 basic papers, including Elementary Theory of the Brownian Movement, written at request of Lorentz to provide a simple explanation. Translated by A. D. Cowper. Annotated, edited by R. Fürth. 33pp. of notes elucidate, give history of previous investigations. 62 footnotes. 124pp. 5⅜ x 8.
S304 Paperbound **$1.25**

THE PRINCIPLE OF RELATIVITY, E. Einstein, H. Lorentz, M. Minkowski, H. Weyl. The 11 basic papers that founded the general and special theories of relativity, translated into English. 2 papers by Lorentz on the Michelson experiment, electromagnetic phenomena. Minkowski's "Space and Time," and Weyl's "Gravitation and Electricity." 7 epoch-making papers by Einstein: "Electromagnetics of Moving Bodies," "Influence of Gravitation in Propagation of Light," "Cosmological Considerations," "General Theory," 3 others. 7 diagrams. Special notes by A. Sommerfeld. 224pp. 5⅜ x 8.   S93 Paperbound **$1.75**

STATISTICS

ELEMENTARY STATISTICS, WITH APPLICATIONS IN MEDICINE AND THE BIOLOGICAL SCIENCES, F. E. Croxton. Based primarily on biological sciences, but can be used by anyone desiring introduction to statistics. Assumes no prior acquaintance, requires only modest knowledge of math. All basic formulas carefully explained, illustrated; all necessary reference tables included. From basic terms and concepts, proceeds to frequency distribution, linear, non-linear, multiple correlation, etc. Contains concrete examples from medicine, biology. 101 charts. 57 tables. 14 appendices. lv + 376pp. 5⅜ x 8.   S506 Paperbound **$1.95**

ANALYSIS AND DESIGN OF EXPERIMENTS, H. B. Mann. Offers method for grasping analysis of variance, variance design quickly. Partial contents: Chi-square distribution, analysis of variance distribution, matrices, quadratic forms, likelihood ration tests, test of linear hypotheses, power of analysis, Galois fields, non-orthogonal data, interblock estimates, etc. 15pp. of useful tables. x + 195pp. 5 x 7⅜.   S180 Paperbound **$1.45**

FREQUENCY CURVES AND CORRELATION, W. P. Elderton. 4th revised edition of standard work on classical statistics. Practical, one of few books constantly referred to for clear presentation of basic material. Partial contents: Frequency Distributions; Pearsons Frequency Curves; Theoretical Distributions; Standard Errors; Correlation Ratio—Contingency; Corrections for Moments, Beta, Gamma Functions; etc. Key to terms, symbols. 25 examples. 40 tables. 16 figures. xi + 272pp. 5½ x 8½.   Clothbound **$1.49**

5

HYDRODYNAMICS, ETC.

HYDRODYNAMICS, Horace Lamb. Standard reference work on dynamics of liquids and gases. Fundamental theorems, equations, methods, solutions, background for classical hydrodynamics. Chapters: Equations of Motion, Integration of Equations in Special Gases, Vortex Motion, Tidal Waves, Rotating Masses of Liquids, etc. Excellently planned, arranged, Clear, lucid presentation. 6th enlarged, revised edition. Over 900 footnotes, mostly bibliographical. 119 figures. xv + 738pp. 6⅛ x 9¼.
S256 Paperbound **$2.95**

HYDRODYNAMICS, A STUDY OF LOGIC, FACT, AND SIMILITUDE, Garrett Birkhoff. A stimulating application of pure mathematics to an applied problem. Emphasis is on correlation of theory and deduction with experiment. Examines recently discovered paradoxes, theory of modelling and dimensional analysis, paradox and error in flows and free boundary theory. Classical theory of virtual mass derived from homogenous spaces; group theory applied to fluid mechanics. 20 figures, 3 plates. xiii + 186pp. 5⅜ x 8.
S22 Paperbound **$1.85**

HYDRODYNAMICS, H. Dryden, F. Murhaghan, H. Bateman. Published by National Research Council, 1932. Complete coverage of classical hydrodynamics, encyclopedic in quality. Partial contents: physics of fluids, motion, turbulent flow, compressible fluids, motion in 1, 2, 3 dimensions; laminar motion, resistance of motion through viscous fluid, eddy viscosity, discharge of gases, flow past obstacles, etc. Over 2900-item bibliography. 23 figures. 634pp. 5⅜ x 8.
S303 Paperbound **$2.75**

ACOUSTICS AND OPTICS

PRINCIPLES OF PHYSICAL OPTICS, Ernst Mach. Classical examination of propagation of light, color, polarization, etc. Historical, philosophical treatment unequalled for breadth and readability. Contents: Rectilinear propagation, reflection, refraction, dioptrics, composition of light, periodicity, theory of interference, polarization, mathematical representation of properties, etc. 279 illustrations. 10 portraits. 324pp. 5⅜ x 8.
S170 Paperbound **$1.75**

THE THEORY OF SOUND, Lord Rayleigh. Written by Nobel laureate, classical methods here will cover most vibrating systems likely to be encountered in practice. Complete coverage of experimental, mathematical aspects. Partial contents: Harmonic motions, lateral vibrations of bars, curved plates or shells, applications of Laplace's functions to acoustical problems, fluid friction, etc. First low-priced edition of this great reference-study work. Historical introduction by R. B. Lindsay. 1040pp. 97 figures. 5⅜ x 8.
S292, S293, Two volume set, paperbound **$4.00**

THEORY OF VIBRATIONS, N. W. McLachlan. Based on exceptionally successful graduate course, Brown University. Discusses linear systems having 1 degree of freedom, forced vibrations of simple linear systems, vibration of flexible strings, transverse vibrations of bars and tubes, of circular plate, sound waves of finite amplitude, etc. 99 diagrams. 160pp. 5⅜ x 8.
S190 Paperbound **$1.35**

APPLIED OPTICS AND OPTICAL DESIGN, A. E. Conrady. Thorough systematic presentation of physical and mathematical aspects, limited mostly to "real optics." Stresses practical problem of maximum aberration permissible without affecting performance. Ordinary ray tracing methods; complete theory ray tracing methods, primary aberrations; enough higher aberration to design telescopes, low powered microscopes, photographic equipment. Covers fundamental equations, extra-axial image points, transverse chromatic aberration, angular magnification, similar topics. Tables of functions of N. Over 150 diagrams. x + 518pp. 5⅜ x 8⅝.
S366 Paperbound **$2.98**

RAYLEIGH'S PRINCIPLE AND ITS APPLICATIONS TO ENGINEERING, G. Temple, W. Bickley. Rayleigh's principle developed to provide upper, lower estimates of true value of fundamental period of vibrating system, or condition of stability of elastic system. Examples, rigorous proofs. Partial contents: Energy method of discussing vibrations, stability. Perturbation theory, whirling of uniform shafts. Proof, accuracy, successive approximations, applications of Rayleigh's theory. Numerical, graphical methods. Ritz's method. 22 figures. ix + 156pp. 5⅜ x 8.
S307 Paperbound **$1.50**

OPTICKS, Sir Isaac Newton. In its discussion of light, reflection, color, refraction, theories of wave and corpuscular theories of light, this work is packed with scores of insights and discoveries. In its precise and practical discussions of construction of optical apparatus, contemporary understanding of phenomena, it is truly fascinating to modern scientists. Foreword by Albert Einstein. Preface by I. B. Cohen, Harvard. 7 pages of portraits, facsimile pages, letters, etc. cxvi + 414pp. 5⅜ x 8.
S205 Paperbound **$2.00**

DOVER SCIENCE BOOKS

ON THE SENSATIONS OF TONE, Hermann Helmholtz. Using acoustical physics, physiology, experiment, history of music, covers entire gamut of musical tone: relation of music science to acoustics, physical vs. physiological acoustics, vibration, resonance, tonality, progression of parts, etc. 33 appendixes on various aspects of sound, physics, acoustics, music, etc. Translated by A. J. Ellis. New introduction by H. Margenau, Yale. 68 figures. 43 musical passages analyzed. Over 100 tables. xix + 576pp. 6⅛ x 9¼.
S114 Clothbound **$4.95**

ELECTROMAGNETICS, ENGINEERING, TECHNOLOGY

INTRODUCTION TO RELAXATION METHODS, F. S. Shaw. Describes almost all manipulative resources of value in solution of differential equations. Treatment is mathematical rather than physical. Extends general computational process to include almost all branches of applied math and physics. Approximate numerical methods are demonstrated, although high accuracy is obtainable without undue expenditure of time. 48pp. of tables for computing irregular star first and second derivatives, irregular star coefficients for second order equations, for fourth order equations. "Useful. . . . exposition is clear, simple . . . no previous acquaintance with numerical methods is assumed," Science Progress. 253 diagrams. 72 tables. 400pp. 5⅜ x 8.
S244 Paperbound **$2.45**

THE ELECTROMAGNETIC FIELD, M. Mason, W. Weaver. Used constantly by graduate engineers. Vector methods exclusively; detailed treatment of electrostatics, expansion methods, with tables converting any quantity into absolute electromagnetic, absolute electrostatic, practical units. Discrete charges, ponderable bodies. Maxwell field equations, etc. 416pp. 5⅜ x 8.
S185 Paperbound **$2.00**

ELASTICITY, PLASTICITY AND STRUCTURE OF MATTER, R. Houwink. Standard treatise on rheological aspects of different technically important solids: crystals, resins, textiles, rubber, clay, etc. Investigates general laws for deformations; determines divergences. Covers general physical and mathematical aspects of plasticity, elasticity, viscosity. Detailed examination of deformations, internal structure of matter in relation to elastic, plastic behaviour, formation of solid matter from a fluid, etc. Treats glass, asphalt, balata, proteins, baker's dough, others. 2nd revised, enlarged edition. Extensive revised bibliography in over 500 footnotes. 214 figures. xvii + 368pp. 6 x 9¼.
S385 Paperbound **$2.45**

DESIGN AND USE OF INSTRUMENTS AND ACCURATE MECHANISM, T. N. Whitehead. For the instrument designer, engineer; how to combine necessary mathematical abstractions with independent observations of actual facts. Partial contents: instruments and their parts, theory of errors, systematic errors, probability, short period errors, erratic errors, design precision, kinematic, semikinematic design, stiffness, planning of an instrument, human factor, etc. 85 photos, diagrams. xii + 288pp. 5⅜ x 8.
S270 Paperbound **$1.95**

APPLIED HYDRO- AND AEROMECHANICS, L. Prandtl, O. G. Tietjens. Presents, for most part, methods valuable to engineers. Flow in pipes, boundary layers, airfoil theory, entry conditions, turbulent flow, boundary layer, determining drag from pressure and velocity, etc. "Will be welcomed by all students of aerodynamics," Nature. Unabridged, unaltered. An Engineering Society Monograph, 1934. Index. 226 figures. 28 photographic plates illustrating flow patterns. xvi + 311pp. 5⅜ x 8.
S375 Paperbound **$1.85**

FUNDAMENTALS OF HYDRO- AND AEROMECHANICS, L. Prandtl, O. G. Tietjens. Standard work, based on Prandtl's lectures at Goettingen. Wherever possible hydrodynamics theory is referred to practical considerations in hydraulics, unifying theory and experience. Presentation extremely clear. Though primarily physical, proofs are rigorous and use vector analysis to a great extent. An Engineering Society Monograph, 1934. "Still recommended as an excellent introduction to this area," Physikalische Blätter. 186 figures. xvi + 270pp. 5⅜ x 8.
S374 Paperbound **$1.85**

GASEOUS CONDUCTORS: THEORY AND ENGINEERING APPLICATIONS, J. D. Cobine. Indispensable text, reference, to gaseous conduction phenomena, with engineering viewpoint prevailing throughout. Studies kinetic theory of gases, ionization, emission phenomena; gas breakdown, spark characteristics, glow, discharges; engineering applications in circuit interrupters, rectifiers, etc. Detailed treatment of high pressure arcs (Suits); low pressure arcs (Langmuir, Tonks). Much more. "Well organized, clear, straightforward," Tonks, Review of Scientific Instruments. 83 practice problems. Over 600 figures. 58 tables. xx + 606pp. 5⅜ x 8.
S442 Paperbound **$2.75**

PHOTOELASTICITY: PRINCIPLES AND METHODS, H. T. Jessop, F. C. Harris. For engineer, specific problems of stress analysis. Latest time-saving methods of checking calculations in 2-dimensional design problems, new techniques for stresses in 3 dimensions, lucid description of optical systems used in practical photoelectricity. Useful suggestions, hints based on on-the-job experience included. Partial contents: strain, stress-strain relations, circular disc under thrust along diameter, rectangular block with square hold under vertical thrust, simply supported rectangular beam under central concentrated load, etc. Theory held to minimum, no advanced mathematical training needed. 164 illustrations. viii + 184pp. 6⅛ x 9¼.
S137 Clothbound **$3.75**

7

MICROWAVE TRANSMISSION DESIGN DATA, T. Moreno. Originally classified, now rewritten, enlarged (14 new chapters) under auspices of Sperry Corp. Of immediate value or reference use to radio engineers, systems designers, applied physicists, etc. Ordinary transmission line theory; attenuation; parameters of coaxial lines; flexible cables; tuneable wave guide impedance transformers; effects of temperature, humidity; much more. "Packed with information . . . theoretical discussions are directly related to practical questions," U. of Royal Naval Scientific Service. Tables of dielectrics, flexible cable, etc. ix + 248pp. 5⅜ x 8.
S549 Paperbound **$1.50**

THE THEORY OF THE PROPERTIES OF METALS AND ALLOYS, H. F. Mott, H. Jones. Quantum methods develop mathematical models showing interrelationship of fundamental chemical phenomena wtih crystal structure, electrical, optical properties, etc. Examines electron motion in applied field, cohesion, heat capacity, refraction, noble metals, transition and di-valent metals, etc. "Exposition is as clear . . . mathematical treatment as simple and reliable as we have become used to expect of . . . Prof. Mott," Nature. 138 figures. xiii + 320pp. 5⅜ x 8.
S456 Paperbound **$1.85**

THE MEASUREMENT OF POWER SPECTRA FROM THE POINT OF VIEW OF COMMUNICATIONS ENGINEERING, R. B. Blackman, J. W. Tukey. Pathfinding work reprinted from "Bell System Technical Journal." Various ways of getting practically useful answers in power spectra measurement, using results from both transmission and statistical estimation theory. Treats: Autocovariance, Functions and Power Spectra, Distortion, Heterodyne Filtering, Smoothing, Decimation Procedures, Transversal Filtering, much more. Appendix reviews fundamental Fourier techniques. Index of notation. Glossary of terms. 24 figures. 12 tables. 192pp. 5⅝ x 8⅝.
S507 Paperbound **$1.85**

TREATISE ON ELECTRICITY AND MAGNETISM, James Clerk Maxwell. For more than 80 years a seemingly inexhaustible source of leads for physicists, mathematicians, engineers. Total of 1082pp. on such topics as Measurement of Quantities, Electrostatics, Elementary Mathematical Theory of Electricity, Electrical Work and Energy in a System of Conductors, General Theorems, Theory of Electrical Images, Electrolysis, Conduction, Polarization, Dielectrics, Resistance, much more. "The greatest mathematical physicist since Newton," Sir James Jeans. 3rd edition. 107 figures, 21 plates. 1082pp. 5⅜ x 8.
S186 Clothbound **$4.95**

CHEMISTRY AND PHYSICAL CHEMISTRY

THE PHASE RULE AND ITS APPLICATIONS, Alexander Findlay. Covers chemical phenomena of 1 to 4 multiple component systems, the "standard work on the subject" (Nature). Completely revised, brought up to date by A. N. Campbell, N. O. Smith. New material on binary, tertiary liquid equilibria, solid solutions in ternary systems, quinary systems of salts, water, etc. Completely revised to triangular coordinates in ternary systems, clarified graphic representation, solid models, etc. 9th revised edition. 236 figures. 505 footnotes, mostly bibliographic. xii + 449pp. 5⅜ x 8.
S92 Paperbound **$2.45**

DYNAMICAL THEORY OF GASES, James Jeans. Divided into mathematical, physical chapters for convenience of those not expert in mathematics. Discusses mathematical theory of gas in steady state, thermodynamics, Bolzmann, Maxwell, kinetic theory, quantum theory, exponentials, etc. "One of the classics of scientific writing . . . as lucid and comprehensive an exposition of the kinetic theory as has ever been written," J. of Institute of Engineers. 4th enlarged edition, with new material on quantum theory, quantum dynamics, etc. 28 figures. 444pp. 6⅛ x 9¼.
S136 Paperbound **$2.45**

POLAR MOLECULES, Pieter Debye. Nobel laureate offers complete guide to fundamental electrostatic field relations, polarizability, molecular structure. Partial contents: electric intensity, displacement, force, polarization by orientation, molar polarization, molar refraction, halogen-hydrides, polar liquids, ionic saturation, dielectric constant, etc. Special chapter considers quantum theory. "Clear and concise . . . coordination of experimental results with theory will be readily appreciated," Electronics Industries. 172pp. 5⅜ x 8.
S63 Clothbound **$3.50**
S64 Paperbound **$1.50**

ATOMIC SPECTRA AND ATOMIC STRUCTURE, G. Herzberg. Excellent general survey for chemists, physicists specializing in other fields. Partial contents: simplest line spectra, elements of atomic theory; multiple structure of line spectra, electron spin; building-up principle, periodic system of elements; finer details of atomic spectra; hyperfine structure of spectral lines; some experimental results and applications. 80 figures. 20 tables. xiii + 257pp. 5⅜ x 8.
S115 Paperbound **$1.95**

TREATISE ON THERMODYNAMICS, Max Planck. Classic based on his original papers. Brilliant concepts of Nobel laureate make no assumptions regarding nature of heat, rejects earlier approaches of Helmholtz, Maxwell, to offer uniform point of view for entire field. Seminal work by founder of quantum theory, deducing new physical, chemical laws. A standard text, an excellent introduction to field for students with knowledge of elementary chemistry, physics, calculus. 3rd English edition. xvi + 297pp. 5⅜ x 8.
S219 Paperbound **$1.75**

8

DOVER SCIENCE BOOKS

KINETIC THEORY OF LIQUIDS, J. Frenkel. Regards kinetic theory of liquids as generalization, extension of theory of solid bodies, covers all types of arrangements of solids; thermal displacements of atoms; interstitial atoms, ions; orientational, rotational motion of molecules; transition between states of matter. Mathematical theory developed close to physical subject matter. "Discussed in a simple yet deeply penetrating fashion . . . will serve as seeds for a great many basic and applied developments in chemistry," J. of the Amer. Chemical Soc. 216 bibliographical footnotes. 55 figures. xi + 485pp. 5⅜ x 8.

S94 Clothbound **$3.95**

S95 Paperbound **$2.45**

ASTRONOMY

OUT OF THE SKY, H. H. Nininger. Non-technical, comprehensive introduction to "meteoritics" —science concerned with arrival of matter from outer space. By one of world's experts on meteorites, this book defines meteors and meteorites; studies fireball clusters and processions, meteorite composition, size, distribution, showers, explosions, origins, much more. viii + 336pp. 5⅜ x 8.

T519 Paperbound **$1.85**

AN INTRODUCTION TO THE STUDY OF STELLAR STRUCTURE, S. Chandrasekhar. Outstanding treatise on stellar dynamics by one of greatest astro-physicists. Examines relationship between loss of energy, mass, and radius of stars in steady state. Discusses thermodynamic laws from Caratheodory's axiomatic standpoint; adiabatic, polytropic laws; work of Ritter, Emden, Kelvin, etc.; Stroemgren envelopes as starter for theory of gaseous stars; Gibbs statistical mechanics (quantum); degenerate stellar configuration, theory of white dwarfs; etc. "Highest level of scientific merit," Bulletin. Amer. Math. Soc. 33 figures. 509pp. 5⅜ x 8.

S413 Paperbound **$2.75**

LES MÉTHODES NOVELLES DE LA MÉCANIQUE CÉLESTE, H. Poincaré. Complete French text of one of Poincaré's most important works. Revolutionized celestial mechanics: first use of integral invariants, first major application of linear differential equations, study of periodic orbits, lunar motion and Jupiter's satellites, three body problem, and many other important topics. "Started a new era . . . so extremely modern that even today few have mastered his weapons," E. T. Bell. 3 volumes. Total 1282pp. 6⅛ x 9¼.

Vol. 1 S401 Paperbound **$2.75**

Vol. 2 S402 Paperbound **$2.75**

Vol. 3 S403 Paperbound **$2.75**

The set **$7.50**

THE REALM OF THE NEBULAE, E. Hubble. One of the great astronomers of our time presents his concept of "island universes," and describes its effect on astronomy. Covers velocity-distance relation; classification, nature, distances, general field of nebulae; cosmological theories; nebulae in the neighborhood of the Milky way; etc. 39 photos, including velocity-distance relations shown by spectrum comparison. "One of the most progressive lines of astronomical research," The Times, London. New Introduction by A. Sandage. 55 illustrations. xxiv + 201pp. 5⅜ x 8.

S455 Paperbound **$1.50**

HOW TO MAKE A TELESCOPE, Jean Texereau. Design, build an f/6 or f/8 Newtonian type reflecting telescope, with altazimuth Couder mounting, suitable for planetary, lunar, and stellar observation. Covers every operation step-by-step, every piece of equipment. Discusses basic principles of geometric and physical optics (unnecessary to construction), comparative merits of reflectors, refractors. A thorough discussion of eyepieces, finders, grinding, installation, testing, etc. 241 figures, 38 photos, show almost every operation and tool. Potential errors are anticipated. Foreword by A. Couder. Sources of supply. xiii + 191pp. 6¼ x 10.

T464 Clothbound **$3.50**

BIOLOGICAL SCIENCES

THE BIOLOGY OF THE AMPHIBIA, G. K. Noble, Late Curator of Herpetology at Am. Mus. of Nat. Hist. Probably most used text on amphibia, most comprehensive, clear, detailed. 19 chapters, 85 page supplement: development; heredity; life history; speciation; adaptation; sex, integument, respiratory, circulatory, digestive, muscular, nervous systems; instinct, intelligence, habits, economic value classification, environment relationships, etc. "Nothing comparable to it," C. H. Pope, curator of Amphibia, Chicago Mus. of Nat. Hist. 1047 item bibliography. 174 illustrations. 600pp. 5⅜ x 8.

S206 Paperbound **$2.98**

THE ORIGIN OF LIFE, A. I. Oparin. A classic of biology. This is the first modern statement of theory of gradual evolution of life from nitrocarbon compounds. A brand-new evaluation of Oparin's theory in light of later research, by Dr. S. Margulis, University of Nebraska. xxv + 270pp. 5⅜ x 8.

S213 Paperbound **$1.75**

THE BIOLOGY OF THE LABORATORY MOUSE, edited by G. D. Snell. Prepared in 1941 by staff of Roscoe B. Jackson Memorial Laboratory, still the standard treatise on the mouse, assembling enormous amount of material for which otherwise you spend hours of research. Embryology, reproduction, histology, spontaneous neoplasms, gene and chromosomes mutations, genetics of spontaneous tumor formations, of tumor transplantation, endocrine secretion and tumor formation, milk influence and tumor formation, inbred, hybrid animals, parasites, infectious diseases, care and recording. "A wealth of information of vital concern. . . . recommended to all who could use a book on such a subject," Nature. Classified bibliography of 1122 items. 172 figures, includir.g 128 photos. ix + 497pp. 6⅛ x 9¼.
S248 Clothbound **$6.00**

THE TRAVELS OF WILLIAM BARTRAM, edited by Mark Van Doran. Famous source-book of American anthropology, natural history, geography, is record kept by Bartram in 1770's on travels through wilderness of Florida, Georgia, Carolinas. Containing accurate, beautiful descriptions of Indians, settlers, fauna, flora, it is one of finest pieces of Americana ever written. 13 original illustrations. 448pp. 5⅜ x 8.
T13 Paperbound **$2.00**

BEHAVIOUR AND SOCIAL LIFE OF THE HONEYBEE, Ronald Ribbands. Outstanding scientific study; a compendium of practically everything known of social life of honeybee. Stresses behaviour of individual bees in field, hive. Extends von Frisch's experiments on communication among bees. Covers perception of temperature, gravity, distance, vibration; sound production; glands; structural differences; wax production; temperature regulation; recognition, communication; drifting, mating behaviour, other highly interesting topics. "This valuable work is sure of a cordial reception by laymen, beekeepers and scientists," Prof. Karl von Frisch, Brit. J. of Animal Behaviour. Bibliography of 690 references. 127 diagrams, graphs, sections of bee anatomy, fine photographs. 352pp.
S410 Clothbound **$4.50**

ELEMENTS OF MATHEMATICAL BIOLOGY, A. J. Lotka. Pioneer classic, 1st major attempt to apply modern mathematical techniques on large scale to phenomena of biology, biochemistry, psychology, ecology, similar life sciences. Partial contents: Statistical meaning of irreversibility; Evolution as redistribution; Equations of kinetics of evolving systems; Chemical, inter-species equilibrium; parameters of state; Energy transformers of nature, etc. Can be read with profit by even those having no advanced math; unsurpassed as study-reference. Formerly titled "Elements of Physical Biology." 72 figures. xxx + 460pp. 5⅜ x 8.
S346 Paperbound **$2.45**

TREES OF THE EASTERN AND CENTRAL UNITED STATES AND CANADA, W. M. Harlow. Serious middle-level text covering more than 140 native trees, important escapes, with information on general appearance, growth habit, leaf forms, flowers, fruit, bark, commercial use, distribution, habitat, woodlore, etc. Keys within text enable you to locate various species easily, to know which have edible fruit, much more useful, interesting information. "Well illustrated to make identification very easy," Standard Cat. for Public Libraries. Over 600 photographs, figures. xiii + 288pp. 5⅝ x 6½.
T395 Paperbound **$1.35**

FRUIT KEY AND TWIG KEY TO TREES AND SHRUBS (Fruit key to Northeastern Trees, Twig key to Deciduous Woody Plants of Eastern North America), W. M. Harlow. Only guides with photographs of every twig, fruit described. Especially valuable to novice. Fruit key (both deciduous trees, evergreens) has introduction on seeding, organs involved, types, habits. Twig key introduction treats growth, morphology. In keys proper, identification is almost automatic. Exceptional work, widely used in university courses, especially useful for identification in winter, or from fruit or seed only. Over 350 photos, up to 3 times natural size. Index of common, scientific names, in each key. xvii + 125pp. 5⅝ x 8⅜.
T511 Paperbound **$1.25**

INSECT LIFE AND INSECT NATURAL HISTORY, S. W. Frost. Unusual for emphasizing habits, social life, ecological relations of insects rather than more academic aspects of classification, morphology. Prof. Frost's enthusiasm and knowledge are everywhere evident as he discusses insect associations, specialized habits like leaf-rolling, leaf mining, case-making, the gall insects, boring insects, etc. Examines matters not usually covered in general works: insects as human food; insect music, musicians; insect response to radio waves; use of insects in art, literature. "Distinctly different, possesses an individuality all its own," Journal of Forestry. Over 700 illustrations. Extensive bibliography. x + 524pp. 5⅜ x 8.
T519 Paperbound **$2.49**

A WAY OF LIFE, AND OTHER SELECTED WRITINGS, Sir William Osler. Physician, humanist, Osler discusses brilliantly Thomas Browne, Gui Patin, Robert Burton, Michael Servetus, William Beaumont, Laennec. Includes such favorite writing as title essay, "The Old Humanities and the New Science," "Books and Men," "The Student Life," 6 more of his best discussions of philosophy, literature, religion. "The sweep of his mind and interests embraced every phase of human activity," G. L. Keynes. 5 photographs. Introduction by G. L. Keynes, M.D., F.R.C.S. xx + 278pp. 5⅜ x 8.
T488 Paperbound **$1.50**

THE GENETICAL THEORY OF NATURAL SELECTION, R. A. Fisher. 2nd revised edition of vital reviewing of Darwin's Selection Theory in terms of particulate inheritance, by one of greatest authorities on experimental, theoretical genetics. Theory stated in mathematical form. Special features of particulate inheritance are examined: evolution of dominance, maintenance of specific variability, mimicry, sexual selection, etc. 5 chapters on man's special circumstances as a social animal. 16 photographs. x + 310pp. 5⅜ x 8.
S466 Paperbound **$1.85**

DOVER SCIENCE BOOKS

THE AUTOBIOGRAPHY OF CHARLES DARWIN, AND SELECTED LETTERS, edited by Francis Darwin. Darwin's own record of early life; historic voyage aboard "Beagle;" furore surrounding evolution, his replies; reminiscences of his son. Letters to Henslow, Lyell, Hooker, Huxley, Wallace, Kingsley, etc., and thoughts on religion, vivisection. We see how he revolutionized geology with concepts of ocean subsidence; how his great books on variation of plants and animals, primitive man, expression of emotion among primates, plant fertilization, carnivorous plants, protective coloration, etc., came into being. 365pp. 5⅜ x 8.
T479 Paperbound **$1.65**

ANIMALS IN MOTION, Eadweard Muybridge. Largest, most comprehensive selection of Muybridge's famous action photos of animals, from his "Animal Locomotion." 3919 high-speed shots of 34 different animals, birds, in 123 types of action; horses, mules, oxen, pigs, goats, camels, elephants, dogs, cats guanacos, sloths, lions, tigers, jaguars, raccoons, baboons, deer, elk, gnus, kangaroos, many others, walking, running, flying, leaping. Horse alone in over 40 ways. Photos taken against ruled backgrounds; most actions taken from 3 angles at once: 90°, 60°, rear. Most plates original size. Of considerable interest to scientists as biology classic, records of actual facts of natural history, physiology. "Really marvelous series of plates," Nature. "Monumental work," Waldemar Kaempffert. Edited by L. S. Brown, 74 page introduction on mechanics of motion. 340pp. of plates. 3919 photographs. 416pp. Deluxe binding, paper. (Weight: 4½ lbs.) 7⅛ x 10⅝.
T203 Clothbound **$10.00**

THE HUMAN FIGURE IN MOTION, Eadweard Muybridge. New edition of great classic in history of science and photography, largest selection ever made from original Muybridge photos of human action: 4789 photographs, illustrating 163 types of motion: walking, running, lifting, etc. in time-exposure sequence photos at speeds up to 1/6000th of a second. Men, women, children, mostly undraped, showing bone, muscle positions against ruled backgrounds, mostly taken at 3 angles at once. Not only was this a great work of photography, acclaimed by contemporary critics as work of genius, but it was also a great 19th century landmark in biological research. Historical introduction by Prof. Robert Taft, U. of Kansas. Plates original size, full of detail. Over 500 action strips. 407pp. 7¾ x 10⅝. Deluxe edition.
7204 Clothbound **$10.00**

AN INTRODUCTION TO THE STUDY OF EXPERIMENTAL MEDICINE, Claude Bernard. 90-year old classic of medical science, only major work of Bernard available in English, records his efforts to transform physiology into exact science. Principles of scientific research illustrated by specified case histories from his work; roles of chance, error, preliminary false conclusion, in leading eventually to scientific truth; use of hypothesis. Much of modern application of mathematics to biology rests on foundation set down here. "The presentation is polished . . . reading is easy," Revue des questions scientifiques. New foreword by Prof. I. B. Cohen, Harvard U. xxv + 266pp. 5⅜ x 8.
T400 Paperbound **$1.50**

STUDIES ON THE STRUCTURE AND DEVELOPMENT OF VERTEBRATES, E. S. Goodrich. Definitive study by greatest modern comparative anatomist. Exhaustive morphological, phylogenetic expositions of skeleton, fins, limbs, skeletal visceral arches, labial cartilages, visceral clefts, gills, vascular, respiratory, excretory, periphal nervous systems, etc., from fish to higher mammals. "For many a day this will certainly be the standard textbook on Vertebrate Morphology in the English language," Journal of Anatomy. 754 illustrations. 69 page biographical study by C. C. Hardy. Bibliography of 1186 references. Two volumes, total 906pp. 5⅜ x 8.
Two vol. set S449, 450 Paperbound **$5.00**

EARTH SCIENCES

THE EVOLUTION OF IGNEOUS BOOKS, N. L. Bowen. Invaluable serious introduction applies techniques of physics, chemistry to explain igneous rock diversity in terms of chemical composition, fractional crystallization. Discusses liquid immiscibility in silicate magmas, crystal sorting, liquid lines of descent, fractional resorption of complex minerals, petrogen, etc. Of prime importance to geologists, mining engineers; physicists, chemists working with high temperature, pressures. "Most important," Times, London. 263 bibliographic notes. 82 figures. xviii + 334pp. 5⅜ x 8.
S311 Paperbound **$1.85**

GEOGRAPHICAL ESSAYS, M. Davis. Modern geography, geomorphology rest on fundamental work of this scientist. 26 famous essays present most important theories, field researches. Partial contents: Geographical Cycle; Plains of Marine, Subaerial Denudation; The Peneplain; Rivers, Valleys of Pennsylvania; Outline of Cape Cod; Sculpture of Mountains by Glaciers; etc. "Long the leader and guide," Economic Geography. "Part of the very texture of geography . . . models of clear thought," Geographic Review. 130 figures. vi + 777pp. 5⅜ x 8.
S383 Paperbound **$2.95**

URANIUM PROSPECTING, H. L. Barnes. For immediate practical use, professional geologist considers uranium ores, geological occurrences, field conditions, all aspects of highly profitable occupation. "Helpful information . . . easy-to-use, easy-to-find style," Geotimes. x + 117pp. 5⅜ x 8.
T309 Paperbound **$1.00**

11

DE RE METALLICA, Georgius Agricola. 400 year old classic translated, annotated by former President Herbert Hoover. 1st scientific study of mineralogy, mining, for over 200 years after its appearance in 1556 the standard treatise. 12 books, exhaustively annotated, discuss history of mining, selection of sites, types of deposits, making pits, shafts, ventilating, pumps, crushing machinery; assaying, smelting, refining metals; also salt alum, nitre, glass making. Definitive edition, with all 289 16th century woodcuts of original. Biographical, historical introductions. Bibliography, survey of ancient authors. Indexes. A fascinating book for anyone interested in art, history of science, geology, etc. Deluxe Edition. 289 illustrations. 672pp. 6¾ x 10. Library cloth.
S6 Clothbound $10.00

INTERNAL CONSTITUTION OF THE EARTH, edited by Beno Gutenberg. Prepared for National Research Council, this is a complete, thorough coverage of earth origins, continent formation, nature and behaviour of earth's core, petrology of crust, cooling forces in core, seismic and earthquake material, gravity, elastic constants, strain characteristics, similar topics. "One is filled with admiration . . . a high standard . . . there is no reader who will not learn something from this book," London, Edinburgh, Dublin, Philosophic Magazine. Largest Bibliography in print: 1127 classified items. Table of constants. 43 diagrams. 439pp. 6⅛ x 9¼.
S414 Paperbound $2.45

THE BIRTH AND DEVELOPMENT OF THE GEOLOGICAL SCIENCES, F. D. Adams. Most thorough history of earth sciences ever written. Geological thought from earliest times to end of 19th century, covering over 300 early thinkers and systems; fossils and their explanation, vulcanists vs. neptunists, figured stones and paleontology, generation of stones, dozens of similar topics. 91 illustrations, including Medieval, Renaissance woodcuts, etc. 632 footnotes, mostly bibliographical. 511pp. 5⅜ x 8.
T5 Paperbound $2.00

HYDROLOGY, edited by O. E. Meinzer, prepared for the National Research Council. Detailed, complete reference library on precipitation, evaporation, snow, snow surveying, glaciers, lakes, infiltration, soil moisture, ground water, runoff, drought, physical changes produced by water hydrology of limestone terranes, etc. Practical in application, especially valuable for engineers. 24 experts have created "the most up-to-date, most complete treatment of the subject," Am. Assoc. of Petroleum Geologists. 165 illustrations. xi + 712pp. 6⅛ x 9¼.
S191 Paperbound $2.95

LANGUAGE AND TRAVEL AIDS FOR SCIENTISTS

SAY IT language phrase books

"SAY IT" in the foreign language of your choice! We have sold over ½ million copies of these popular, useful language books. They will not make you an expert linguist overnight, but they do cover most practical matters of everyday life abroad.

Over 1000 useful phrases, expressions, additional variants, substitutions.

Modern! Useful! Hundreds of phrases not available in other texts: "Nylon," "air-conditioned," etc.

The ONLY inexpensive phrase book **completely indexed.** Everything is available at a flip of your finger, ready to use.

Prepared by native linguists, travel experts.

Based on years of travel experience abroad.

May be used by itself, or to supplement any other text or course. Provides a living element. Used by many colleges, institutions: Hunter College; Barnard College; Army Ordinance School, Aberdeen; etc.

Available, 1 book per language:

Danish (T818) 75¢
Dutch (T817) 75¢
English (for German-speaking people) (T801) 60¢
English (for Italian-speaking people) (T816) 60¢
English (for Spanish-speaking people) (T802) 60¢
Esperanto (T820) 75¢
French (T803) 60¢
German (T804) 60¢
Modern Greek (T813) 75¢
Hebrew (T805) 60¢

Italian (T806) 60¢
Japanese (T807) 75¢
Norwegian (T814) 75¢
Russian (T810) 75¢
Spanish (T811) 60¢
Turkish (T821) 75¢
Yiddish (T815) 75¢
Swedish (T812) 75¢
Polish (T808) 75¢
Portuguese (T809) 75¢

DOVER SCIENCE BOOKS

MONEY CONVERTER AND TIPPING GUIDE FOR EUROPEAN TRAVEL, C. Vomacka. Purse-size handbook crammed with information on currency regulations, tipping for every European country, including Israel, Turkey, Czechoslovakia, Rumania, Egypt, Russia, Poland. Telephone, postal rates; duty-free imports, passports, visas, health certificates; foreign clothing sizes; weather tables. What, when to tip. 5th year of publication. 128pp. 3½ x 5¼.   T260 Paperbound 60¢

NEW RUSSIAN-ENGLISH AND ENGLISH-RUSSIAN DICTIONARY, M. A. O'Brien. Unusually comprehensive guide to reading, speaking, writing Russian, for both advanced, beginning students. Over 70,000 entries in new orthography, full information on accentuation, grammatical classifications. Shades of meaning, idiomatic uses, colloquialisms, tables of irregular verbs for both languages. Individual entries indicate stems, transitiveness, perfective, imperfective aspects, conjugation, sound changes, accent, etc. Includes pronunciation instruction. Used at Harvard, Yale, Cornell, etc. 738pp. 5⅜ x 8.   T208 Paperbound $ 2.00

PHRASE AND SENTENCE DICTIONARY OF SPOKEN RUSSIAN, English-Russian, Russian-English. Based on phrases, complete sentences, not isolated words—recognized as one of best methods of learning idiomatic speech. Over 11,500 entries, indexed by single words, over 32,000 English, Russian sentences, phrases, in immediately useable form. Shows accent changes in conjugation, declension; irregular forms listed both alphabetically, under main form of word. 15,000 word introduction covers Russian sounds, writing, grammar, syntax. 15 page appendix of geographical names, money, important signs, given names, foods, special Soviet terms, etc. Originally published as U.S. Gov't Manual TM 30-944. iv + 573pp. 5⅜ x 8.   T496 Paperbound $2.75

PHRASE AND SENTENCE DICTIONARY OF SPOKEN SPANISH, Spanish-English, English-Spanish. Compiled from spoken Spanish, based on phrases, complete sentences rather than isolated words—not an ordinary dictionary. Over 16,000 entries indexed under single words, both Castilian, Latin-American. Language in immediately useable form. 25 page introduction provides rapid survey of sounds, grammar, syntax, full consideration of irregular verbs. Especially apt in modern treatment of phrases, structure. 17 page glossary gives translations of geographical names, money values, numbers, national holidays, important street signs, useful expressions of high frequency, plus unique 7 page glossary of Spanish, Spanish-American foods. Originally published as U.S. Gov't Manual TM 30-900. iv + 513pp. 5⅝ x 8⅜.   T495 Paperbound $1.75

SAY IT CORRECTLY language record sets

The best inexpensive pronunciation aids on the market. Spoken by native linguists associated with major American universities, each record contains:

14 minutes of speech—12 minutes of normal, relatively slow speech, 2 minutes of normal conversational speed.

120 basic phrases, sentences, covering nearly every aspect of everyday life, travel—introducing yourself, travel in autos, buses, taxis, etc., walking, sightseeing, hotels, restaurants, money, shopping, etc.

32 page booklet containing everything on record plus English translations easy-to-follow phonetic guide.

Clear, high-fidelity recordings.

Unique bracketing systems, selection of basic sentences enabling you to expand use of SAY IT CORRECTLY records with a dictionary, to fit thousands of additional situations.

Use this record to supplement any course or text. All sounds in each language illustrated perfectly—imitate speaker in pause which follows each foreign phrase in slow section, and be amazed at increased ease, accuracy of pronounciation. Available, one language per record for

French	**Spanish**	**German**
Italian	**Dutch**	**Modern Greek**
Japanese	**Russian**	**Portuguese**
Polish	**Swedish**	**Hebrew**
English (for German-speaking people)		**English (for Spanish-speaking people)**

7″ (33 1/3 rpm) record, album, booklet. $1.00 each.

SPEAK MY LANGUAGE: SPANISH FOR YOUNG BEGINNERS, M. Ahlman, Z. Gilbert. Records provide one of the best, most entertaining methods of introducing a foreign language to children. Within framework of train trip from Portugal to Spain, an English-speaking child is introduced to Spanish by native companion. (Adapted from successful radio program of N.Y. State Educational Department.) A dozen different categories of expressions,. including greeting, numbers, time, weather, food, clothes, family members, etc. Drill is combined with poetry and contextual use. Authentic background music. Accompanying book enables a reader to follow records, includes vocabulary of over 350 recorded expressions. Two 10″ 33 1/3 records, total of 40 minutes. Book. 40 illustrations. 69pp. 5¼ x 10½.   T890 The set $4.95

13

LISTEN & LEARN language record sets

LISTEN & LEARN is the only extensive language record course designed especially to meet your travel and everyday needs. Separate sets for each language, each containing three 33 1/3 rpm long-playing records—1 1/2 hours of recorded speech by eminent native speakers who are professors at Columbia, New York U., Queens College.

Check the following features found only in LISTEN & LEARN:

Dual language recording. 812 selected phrases, sentences, over 3200 words, spoken first in English, then foreign equivalent. Pause after each foreign phrase allows time to repeat expression.

128-page manual (196 page for Russian)—everything on records, plus simple transcription. Indexed for convenience. Only set on the market completely indexed.

Practical. No time wasted on material you can find in any grammar. No dead words. Covers central core material with phrase approach. Ideal for person with limited time. Living, modern expressions, not found in other courses. Hygienic products, modern equipment, shopping, "air-conditioned," etc. Everything is immediately useable.

High-fidelity recording, equal in clarity to any costing up to $6 per record.

"Excellent . . . impress me as being among the very best on the market," Prof. Mario Pei, Dept. of Romance Languages, Columbia U. "Inexpensive and well done . . . ideal present," Chicago Sunday Tribune. "More genuinely helpful than anything of its kind," Sidney Clark, well-known author of "All the Best" travel books.

UNCONDITIONAL GUARANTEE. Try LISTEN & LEARN, then return it within 10 days for full refund, if you are not satisfied. It is guaranteed after you actually use it.

6 modern languages—FRENCH, SPANISH, GERMAN, ITALIAN, RUSSIAN, or JAPANESE *—one language to each set of 3 records (33 1/3 rpm). 128 page manual. Album.

Spanish	the set $4.95	**German**	the set $4.95	**Japanese***	the set $5.95
French	the set $4.95	**Italian**	the set $4.95	**Russian**	the set $5.95

* Available Oct. 1959.

TRÜBNER COLLOQUIAL SERIES

These unusual books are members of the famous Trübner series of colloquial manuals. They have been written to provide adults with a sound colloquial knowledge of a foreign language, and are suited for either class use or self-study. Each book is a complete course in itself, with progressive, easy to follow lessons. Phonetics, grammar, and syntax are covered, while hundreds of phrases and idioms, reading texts, exercises, and vocabulary are included. These books are unusual in being neither skimpy nor overdetailed in grammatical matters, and in presenting up-to-date, colloquial, and practical phrase material. Bilingual presentation is stressed, to make thorough self-study easier for the reader.

COLLOQUIAL HINDUSTANI, A. H. Harley, formerly Nizam's Reader in Urdu, U. of London. 30 pages on phonetics and scripts (devanagari & Arabic-Persian) are followed by 29 lessons, including material on English and Arabic-Persian influences. Key to all exercises. Vocabulary. 5 x 7½. 147pp. Clothbound **$1.75**

COLLOQUIAL ARABIC, DeLacy O'Leary. Foremost Islamic scholar covers language of Egypt, Syria, Palestine, & Northern Arabia. Extremely clear coverage of complex Arabic verbs & noun plurals; also cultural aspects of language. Vocabulary. xviii + 192pp. 5 x 7½. Clothbound **$1.75**

COLLOQUIAL GERMAN, P. F. Doring. Intensive thorough coverage of grammar in easily-followed form. Excellent for brush-up, with hundreds of colloquial phrases. 34 pages of bilingual texts. 224pp. 5 x 7½. Clothbound **$1.75**

COLLOQUIAL SPANISH, W. R. Patterson. Castilian grammar and colloquial language, loaded with bilingual phrases and colloquialisms. Excellent for review or self-study. 164pp. 5 x 7½. Clothbound **$1.75**

COLLOQUIAL FRENCH, W. R. Patterson. 16th revised edition of this extremely popular manual. Grammar explained with model clarity, and hundreds of useful expressions and phrases; exercises, reading texts, etc. Appendixes of new and useful words and phrases. 223pp. 5 x 7½. Clothbound **$1.75**

14

DOVER SCIENCE BOOKS

COLLOQUIAL PERSIAN, L. P. Elwell-Sutton. Best introduction to modern Persian, with 90 page grammatical section followed by conversations, 35 page vocabulary. 139pp. **Clothbound $1.75**

COLLOQUIAL CZECH, J. Schwarz, former headmaster of Lingua Institute, Prague. Full easily followed coverage of grammar, hundreds of immediately useable phrases, texts. Perhaps the best Czech grammar in print. "An absolutely successful textbook," JOURNAL OF CZECHO-SLOVAK FORCES IN GREAT BRITAIN. 252pp. 5 x 7½. **Clothbound $2.50**

COLLOQUIAL RUMANIAN, G. Nandris, Professor of University of London. Extremely thorough coverage of phonetics, grammar, syntax; also included 70 page reader, and 70 page vocabulary. Probably the best grammar for this increasingly important language. 340pp. 5 x 7½. **Clothbound $2.50**

COLLOQUIAL ITALIAN, A. L. Hayward. Excellent self-study course in grammar, vocabulary, idioms, and reading. Easy progressive lessons will give a good working knowledge of Italian in the shortest possible time. 5 x 7½. **Clothbound $1.75**

MISCELLANEOUS

TREASURY OF THE WORLD'S COINS, Fred Reinfeld. Finest general introduction to numismatics; non-technical, thorough, always fascinating. Coins of Greece, Rome, modern countries of every continent, primitive societies, such oddities as 200-lb stone money of Yap, nail coinage of New England; all mirror man's economy, customs, religion, politics, philosophy, art. Entertaining, absorbing study; novel view of history. Over 750 illustrations. Table of value of coins illustrated. List of U.S. coin clubs. 224pp. 6½ x 9¼. **T433 Paperbound $1.75**

ILLUSIONS AND DELUSIONS OF THE SUPERNATURAL AND THE OCCULT, D. H. Rawcliffe. Rationally examines hundreds of persistent delusions including witchcraft, trances, mental healing, peyotl, poltergeists, stigmata, lycanthropy, live burial, auras, Indian rope trick, spiritualism, dowsing, telepathy, ghosts, ESP, etc. Explains, exposes mental, physical deceptions involved, making this not only an exposé of supernatural phenomena, but a valuable exposition of characteristic types of abnormal psychology. Originally "The Psychology of the Occult." Introduction by Julian Huxley. 14 illustrations. 551pp. 5⅜ x 8. **T503 Paperbound $2.00**

HOAXES, C. D. MacDougall. Shows how art, science, history, journalism can be perverted for private purposes. Hours of delightful entertainment, a work of scholarly value, often shocking. Examines nonsense news, Cardiff giant, Shakespeare forgeries, Loch Ness monster, biblical frauds, political schemes, literary hoaxers like Chatterton, Ossian, disumbrationist school of painting, lady in black at Valentino's tomb, over 250 others. Will probably reveal truth about few things you've believed, will help you spot more easily the editorial "gander" or planted publicity release. "A stupendous collection . . . and shrewd analysis," New Yorker. New revised edition. 54 photographs. 320pp. 5⅜ x 8. **T465 Paperbound $1.75**

YOGA: A SCIENTIFIC EVALUATION, Kovoor T. Behanan. Book that for first time gave Western readers a sane, scientific explanation, analysis of yoga. Author draws on laboratory experiments, personal records of year as disciple of yoga, to investigate yoga psychology, physiology, "supernatural" phenomena, ability to plumb deepest human powers. In this study under auspices of Yale University Institute of Human Relations, strictest principles of physiological, psychological inquiry are followed. Foreword by W. A. Miles, Yale University. 17 photographs. xx + 270pp. 5⅜ x 8. **T505 Paperbound $1.65**

Write for free catalogs!

Indicate your field of interest. Dover publishes books on physics, earth sciences, mathematics, engineering, chemistry, astronomy, anthropology, biology, psychology, philosophy, religion, history, literature, mathematical recreations, languages, crafts, art, graphic arts, etc.

Write to Dept. catr
Dover Publications, Inc.
Science B   *180 Varick St., N. Y. 14, N. Y.*